THE LIFE OF MATTHEW HENRY

THE CONCISE COMMENTARY ON THE GOSPELS

THE LIFE OF MATTHEW HENRY

THE CONCISE COMMENTARY ON THE GOSPELS

Updated and revised from
The Life of the Reverend Matthew Henry
by J.B. Williams, F.S.A., Shrewsbury, England
and
The Concise Commentary on the Whole Bible
by Matthew Henry

Bridge-Logos

Gainesville, FL 32614 USA

The Life of Matthew Henry and
The Concise Commentary on the Gospels

Updated and revised from
The Life of the Reverend Matthew Henry
by J.B. Williams, F.S.A.
Shrewsbury, England, May 3, 1828
and
The Concise Commentary on the Whole Bible
by Matthew Henry

Copyright ©2004 by Bridge-Logos
Library of Congress Catalog Card Number pending
International Standard Book Number 0-88270-819-8

Unless otherwise noted, all Scripture is from the King James Version
of the Bible.

Published by:
Bridge-Logos
Gainesville, FL 32614 USA
bridgelogos.com

Contents

THE CONCISE COMMENTARY ON THE GOSPELS

FOREWORD

The Life of the
Reverend Matthew Henry
and
The Concise Commentary
on the Gospels

The Commentary on the Bible could have been created by no other than Matthew Henry, a pastor so devout and single-minded in his focus on God that his studies began in childhood and continued until the day he died. He lived as most men do—as a son, a husband, a son-in-law, a father, a hard worker, a good friend, and a provider—but Mr. Henry was destined to greatness, although he had no idea of the impact he would make on Christendom as he humbly went about his days. In fact, he began each new year on his knees, exhorting God to forgive him for his sloth of the past year and for wasting the gifts and time that God had given him. With the retrospect of history, we clearly know that which Mr. Henry, in his humility, could not acknowledge: that he was prolific, focused, and brilliant in his work. His legacy to those of us who follow him is the body of his work, breathtaking and brilliant.

The *Commentary* was first published as *An Exposition of the Old and New Testaments* (5 volumes published in London in 1708-10, and enlarged and reprinted in New York in 1896). Mr. Henry lived to complete the work only through Acts. After his death, selected non-conformist scholars prepared the Epistles and Revelation from Mr. Henry's copious and detailed notes.

THE LIFE OF THE REVEREND MATTHEW HENRY, A BIOGRAPHY

Although several biographies have been created to chronicle the miracle of Matthew Henry's work, only one captures the character of the man. It was written by J. B. Williams, F.S.A. in Shrewsbury, England and published in 1828. From his pen we are introduced to the inner life of Mr. Henry, revealed in his personal papers. We are brought into his family. We meet his friends. We follow him through his daily tasks. We rejoice when he falls in love. We share a father's agony when his children die. We smile at his self-effacing opinion of himself as being unworthy. We are inspired by his faith and enlightened by his insights. We weep as he officiates at the funerals of his brethren and colleagues, and feels the altogether human sorrow and exhaustion of losing so many dear to him. We are taught to walk with God through his daily practices and disciplines. In short, we are as enriched by his life as we are by his work.

Mr. Williams explains his intentions: *Throughout the volume an attempt has been made so to select and arrange the materials as to confirm the representations given of Mr. Henry in the most unobjectionable manner, in fact—to make him, as far as it was possible, his own biographer. Reflections are, in the main, left to the reader. And the nature of the evidence adduced is such (not being originally intended for the public eye) as will enable him to form a correct opinion. He will see a "Saint of the Lord," in the walks of life, incessantly discharging his active duties; he will behold him in solitude, contemplating himself and the busy world; he will continually hear him "speaking"—as from the tomb—in strains of wisdom, peculiarly solemn, devout, and impressive.*

The diary of Mr. Henry has been cited freely; and as a simple, unadulterated, and authentic memorial, its disclosures are invaluable.

The biography was written in style of Mr. Williams' time: oratorical and flourishing. The punctuation and sentence construction would horrify today's English teacher and mystify most readers, so we have modified it to read a little more easily, yet still retain the quality of antiquity and formality that allow the reader to "hear" the story told from the century in which it was written.

THE CONCISE COMMENTARY ON THE GOSPELS

The one who appreciates the treasure in this work finds himself in good company. The great preacher George Whitfield and hymn writer Charles Wesley were each deeply influenced by Henry, as have countless others over the past three centuries. To enjoy the maximum benefit one should understand Matthew Henry's purpose for writing. *"I am sure the work is designed, and hope it is calculated, to promote piety towards God and charity towards our brethren, and that there is not only something in it which may edify, but nothing which may justly offend any good Christian."*

This material is very logical and purposeful; and the mind alive to godliness will find hours and hours of rich stimulation. *"Those who allow themselves a true liberty of thinking, and will think seriously, cannot but embrace all Christ's sayings, as faithful, and well worthy of all acceptance. Let the corrupt bias of the carnal heart towards the world, the flesh, and self be taken away. Let the doctrine of Christ be proposed first in its true colors, as Christ and His apostles have given it to us and in its true light, with all its proper evidence, intrinsic and extrinsic. Then let the capable soul freely use its rational powers and faculties, and once it becomes free thought, freed from the bondage of sin and corruption, will, by a pleasing and happy power, be captivated, and brought into obedience to Christ; and, when he thus makes it free, it will be free indeed."*

It is interesting to note that although today some of Matthew Henry's thinking may seem at times a little archaic, when it was written, it was cutting-edge. John Ryland, Sr., an eighteenth century Baptist preacher and educator, wrote that he wished he could "be shut out from the whole world and read it without a moment's interruption." The apostolic Whitfield, whose labors and virtues inspired even the pen of Cowper, was trained as a Christian and a preacher by Mr. Henry's Commentary; he literally studied it on his knees, read it through four times, and to the close of life spoke of its author with profound veneration, ever calling him – the great Mr. Henry.

Biographer, Mr. Williams, notes, *His talent lay peculiarly in the improvement of a subject; and those portions of the inspired volume, which have been just adverted to gave him the fullest opportunity for its exercise. His method, unlike most other authors, but after the manner of inspiration, was, as he passed along, to dart into the reader's mind the truths he wished to convey, and in the form of concise sayings.*

The very defects and peculiarities of Mr. Henry, his profuse alliterations and "little fancies," are singularly adapted for edification. Even the "quaintness," which distinguishes such a multitude of his observations, and which is somewhat repulsive to the fastidious, has upon the fancy an effect positively enchanting; it holds it, not infrequently, as if spell-bound; and the "epigrammatic turns," notwithstanding their abundance, are so unconstrained and transparent, as to sparkle very often into brilliance.

In a single sentence, he often pours upon Scripture a flood light; and the palpableness he gives to the wonders contained in God's law occasions excitement, not unlike that which is produced by looking through a microscope. The feelings, too, which his subject had called forth in himself, he communicates admirably to others. In his whole manner—the same at nine years old as at fifty—there is freshness and vivacity, which instantly puts the spirits into free and agile motion: an effect somewhat similar to that play of intellectual sprightliness, which some minds (obviously the greatest only) have the indescribable faculty of creating, the moment other minds are brought into collision. But the crowning excellence remains; nothing is introduced in the shape of counteraction. There are no speeches, which make his sincerity questionable, no absurdities to force suspicion as to accuracy in theological knowledge or inattention to the analogy of faith, no staggering, and untoward, and unmanageable inconsistencies; nothing by which "the most sacred cause can be injured," or the highest interests of men placed in jeopardy, or which can render it imperative, exactly in proportion as the understanding is influenced, to repress or extinguish the sentiments, "in order to listen, with complacency, to the Lord Jesus and his apostles.

Why did we select *The Concise Commentary on the Gospels*?

Matthew Henry authored the *Commentary on the Whole Bible*, a masterwork. But we selected four little jewels. *The Gospels*—Matthew, Mark, Luke and John—are books of the Bible written by men who lived and walked with Christ for three years of His earthly life. Their firsthand experiences reflect parallel accounts of the expressed image and likeness of God, the Father. Matthew, Mark, and Luke reaffirm and reconfirm truths from sequential and slightly differing perspectives. John, close friend to Christ and the only disciple at the cross, paints a portrait of the character of Jesus as love and the Heart of God. Together, the four give us the *Gospels*, literally meaning, "Good News."

Mr. Williams tell us, *His statements correspond, with the loveliest uniformity, to the gospel system; all their bearings tend to promote the life of God in the soul; a "sweet savor of Christ" runs through them like a pervading principle of vitality; and so impregnates them, indeed as to communicate an impulse of devotion, perfectly sacred and sublime.*

The gospel of Christ (the language is Mr. Henry's in his "word of advice to the wanton and unclean") is a remedial law, and you hope to have a remedy by it. It is a charter of privilege and you hope to be privileged by it, but how can you expect either remedy or privilege by it, if you will not observe its precepts, nor come up to its conditions? **The gospel will never save you if it shall not rule you.**

Referring to the *Concise Commentary* maintaining the integrity of the full work: The abridgement was executed, to quote the opinion of the late Rev. S. Palmer, "with great judgment, so as to retain everything important and omit only what was redundant; and thus in fact to improve the work; as," he adds, "I can testify by a comparison of the original, and the abridgment in manuscript."

If you're studying the Bible and the life of Christ, there is no better place to begin than with the *Gospels*. And there is no better companion for understanding the deeper meanings than Matthew Henry and the *Concise Commentary on the Gospels*.

Every Christian is deepened by Matthew Henry's work. You will be, too.

Matthew Henry — 1662-1714

The Life
of the
Reverend
Matthew
Henry

THE LIFE OF THE REVEREND MATTHEW HENRY

By J. B. Williams, F.S.A.
Shrewsbury, England
May 3, 1828

lthough it is customary to value men according to their ancestry, their opulence, their literature, or other secular distinctions; and, although the memorials which record such particulars usually content the majority of readers, an attentive observer cannot fail to have remarked how little notice is taken in Scripture biography of circumstances so entirely adventitious. *Their* moral character is instructively placed in the utmost prominence, and measured by the highest standard. Not only is "the wisdom of this world" pronounced "foolishness with God;" but "the memory of the *just*," in distinction from all others, is declared "blessed;" and with "the righteous" exclusively is associated a promise of "everlasting remembrance."

It will not follow, however, that no records of the descendants of Adam are to be preserved, unless the parties, in a Scriptural sense, were "righteous." Nor yet, that lives should be compiled of *all* good men, because such was their genuine character. The absurdity of either inference is obvious.

Yet, can it be denied, that occurrences now and then warrant suspicion, that the latter sentiment, notwithstanding is repugnance to common sense, *is* indulged? Or that the danger occasionally

1

appears imminent, lest every good man, especially if "put into the ministry," how feeble soever his pretensions, should be exhibited, when gone to his reward in a distinct, if not a bulky memoir?

A late acute author advised that in attending to written lives, "those narratives should be selected which represent persons who were *distinguished* by unerring wisdom—for gifts, graces, and usefulness."

Nor is it easy to be impressed too deeply with a hint so discriminating, and judicious.

Only *as* that regard is bestowed, may "the administration" of biographical "service" be expected to supply "the wants of the saints;" and to "become abundant by many thanksgivings unto God."

Under such impressions the ensuing narrative was commenced, and prosecuted. And with whatever strength it might be objected, to any similar undertakings—that the mediocrity of the subject did not warrant them—the object cannot be anticipated in connection with Mr. Henry. For, without asserting that, like the Israelitish monarch, *he* stood higher than "*any* of the people," it may be affirmed confidently—that his claims to distinction and honor are well established; and that, let the numerical increase of similar records be as rapid, or as extensive as it may, there is no danger of unduly multiplying such lives as *his*.

Most readers are aware that, not long after Mr. Henry's death, a life of him appeared from the pen of Mr. Tong. And the volume, it is more than probable, will be regarded by some persons as a discharge in full of every obligation—whether due from immediate descendants, friendly admirers, or the public at large.

As the result of long and close intimacy, and of strict fidelity in the application, so far as they went of *facts*, its worth cannot be questioned. It is, the dissenting historians very justly observe, "highly valuable for laying open to us the soul of Mr. Henry himself."

But if the reader's attention be now drawn to the blemishes in a work thus estimated, and often admired, the motive will not, it is hoped, be misapprehended; especially as no wish is felt to diminish the weight of approving testimonies, or to create the slightest prejudice against Mr. Tong.

My sole object is to show, and every reader has a right to the information, *why*, instead of re-printing the former narrative, the present book has been written. Reasons for the course adopted *do* exist; and they may, notwithstanding many excellencies, in the glaring imperfections, which disfigure Mr. Tong's account; in its awkward, and somewhat repulsive arrangement, in its entire omission of some features of Mr. Henry's character, and its meager illustration of others.

The late Mrs. Sarah Brett of West Bromwich, one of Mr. Henry's daughters and a lady worth of her descent, sometimes adverted to this delicate subject. She stated that the widow offered her father's papers to Mr. Tong, as an old and particular friend, rather out of compliment, than from any serious expectation, or wish that he might attempt the "Life;" and that as the undertaking disappointed, so the performance dissatisfied the family.

The freest use has been made, however, in the following pages of the whole volume; and whenever even the phraseology suited, that also, without hesitation, has been adopted.

Those uninspired passages, which appear in quotes, are to be considered, unless the contrary is stated, as extracted from Mr. Tong's publication.

So far as it was practicable, a careful examination of the excerpts that good man introduced has been instituted; and the reference, in those instances, is made to the original manuscripts. Some corrections have been thus effected, but of so trivial a nature as to render any formal notice unnecessary, except only in a few places, for the better guidance of the reader's judgment respecting them.

The additions now first selected from unpublished documents are both varied and numerous. They are scattered throughout the volume, but with most profusion after the ninetieth page. On this difficult part of the work, corresponding attention has been bestowed, brevity diligently studied, and fidelity observed with unceasing assiduity. Occasional abridgements and transpositions have been made; and here and there, the completion of a sentence effected. Sometimes obsolete words or phrases have been changed, or expunged.

In the management and introduction of extracts, whether from Mr. Tong's memoir or the papers of Mr. Henry, I have attempted the union of chronology with that method of biography, which is sectional. Whenever the facts would consist best with the narrative, attention has been paid to the order of dates; but when the purposes of utility seemed most likely to be answered by classification according to the subjects treated or by putting "things of a sort together," *that* mode has been adopted.

Instead of throwing the whole into one general head, it is divided into chapters, as well in accordance with those lives which are most admired, as for the greater convenience of the reader.

The birthday and anniversary memorials used by Mr. Tong are not only, in one form or other, either substance or citation, preserved but increased. And, together with the records of relative and domestic trials, exhibited chronologically.

The former memoranda are well adapted to the circumstances of Christians in general; and, if perused at the same period of life, may answer the best possible purposes.

Where the originals are in Latin, as is the case with several of them, a translation has been thought sufficient.

Should the introduction of the other class of memoranda appear at first view too frequent, or too minute, the impression will not, it is thought, abide; especially if it be remembered that the subjection of the human race to the same occurrences—to affliction, and sickness, and death—is universal: that there is vast difficulty and importance in preparation for trials so inevitable and that the special utility of such records (next, perhaps, to the inspired promises) in aiding a work so necessary, and imparting in sorrow efficient consolation, is seldom, if ever, disputed.

The more miscellaneous citations employed for the development of Mr. Henry's character appear in a *collected* form, that they may be additionally impressive. To have introduced *them* according to their dates would have led, because unrelieved by incident, to dry and circumstantial detail. And not to have inserted them at all would have involved the omission of many such invaluable apothegms as were designated by Lord Bacon, with his accustomed point, "*mucrones verborum.*"

It is granted they might have been highly interesting, if classed together as unconnected remains, and in a separate chapter; but— whether *so* arranged their effect would have been equal to what it is conceived to be in their present illustrative form, seems at least questionable.

On this topic, however, (one purely of taste and fancy) there will be, no doubt, conflicting opinions. It shall, therefore, be only mentioned that the plan fixed upon, instead of being hasty, resulted from a careful examination of all the documents, both manuscript and printed, with a special regard to arrangement; and that it has the sanction of some of the best examples, ancient and modern; particularly the *Life of Dr. Doddridge* by Mr. Orton. The leading design not being a provision for mere light and transient perusal, but for repeated and devotional reading, the course pursued was followed with even less hesitation than would, otherwise, have been felt.

Throughout the volume an attempt has been made *so* to select and arrange the materials as to confirm the representations given of Mr. Henry in the most unobjectionable manner, in fact—to make him, as far as it was possible, his own biographer. Reflections are, in the main, left to the reader. And the nature of the evidence adduced is such (not being originally intended for the public eye) as will enable him to form a correct opinion. He will see a "Saint of the Lord" in the walks of life, incessantly discharging its active duties; he will behold him in solitude, contemplating himself and the busy world; he will continually hear him "speaking"—as from the tomb—in strains of wisdom, peculiarly solemn, devout, and impressive.

The diary of Mr. Henry has been cited freely; and as a simple, unadulterated, and authentic memorial, its disclosures are invaluable.

Some of the letters throw light upon the narrative, by illustration what otherwise would have been unknown; and explaining what, in their absence, could have been only conjectural. Very many epistles have been perused, though comparatively few are introduced. Some are referred to as original manuscripts and others appear at length, but the majority, being unsuitable to the object, was omitted.

The use in a biographical memoir of another class of manuscripts—sermons—will probably be condemned by the fastidious. But why, the question may be urged, should sermons, if applied with judgment, be regarded as less interesting in the history of a preacher, or be less useful than anecdotes or letters? In the exhibition of a divine (especially a nonconforming divine), they oftentimes furnish the most valuable illustrations both of habits and of character. Do they not, even in the hallowed narrative of the Redeemer's history, communicate an inexpressible charm? Who would blot from the Gospels the discourse upon the mount, because *it* was preached, and has been perpetuated as a sermon?

But an objection more serious may arise, possibly, from the introduction of so many things never intended by their author to be published. "Some may be ready to blame me," said Mr. Tong, "as having trespassed too much upon these religious privacies."

His answer must be mine —"Their apparent tendency, to excite and quicken us to greater spirituality, and diligence in duty, is a consideration which has over-ruled every thing else; and it ought, I think, so to do."

At this distance of time, that reply is even more appropriate than when originally given. And as the subject is considered, it will, perhaps, appear—that instead of blame attaching to a publication of such relics, responsibility has been incurred by their long, and monopolized concealment.

The papers of the Reverend and learned Francis Tallents, whose worth Mr. Henry perpetuated, have been sometimes resorted to—for the preservation, chiefly of a few instructive anecdotes, and weighty sayings, which, it is believed, were never before printed.

The diary of Mrs. Savage, Mr. Henry's eldest and favorite sister, has supplied occasional illustrations.

A like remark connects itself with the valuable remains of Mrs. Hunt of whom and her manuscripts, no account being known to exist, the following brief narrative may not be unacceptable.

She was the daughter of Sir Edward Ward, Lord Chief Baron of the Exchequer, by Miss Papillion, whose father fled from France to England after the repeal of the edict of Nantz. She was born January 5, 1677, and married May 22, 1701 at Hammersmith by Mr. Wade (the author of the "Redemption of Time") to Thomas Hunt of Boreatton in the county of Salop, Esquire; at which place she arrived on the 19th of the following July. She died January 21, 1716, leaving behind her three sons, four daughters, and the reputation of exalted piety and virtue. The Reverend John Reynolds of Shrewsbury, Mr. Henry's imitate friend, furnished her memorial in a characteristic epitaph.

After her death, many volumes of pious instruction, the result of enlarged spiritual communications, were found in her own handwriting. She bequeathed them to Mrs. Savage's daughter Mary, afterwards the wife of the Reverend Thomas Holland, a dissenting minister at Wem, in Shropshire.

Mrs. Holland presented them to Mrs. Hunt's youngest daughter, who married the Reverend William Adams of Shrewsbury, D.D.

Prior to that donation Mrs. Savage, her son Philip, her sisters, Mrs. Tylston, and Mrs. Radford, and other branches of the same indefatigable family made a transcript into four quarto volumes.

That transcript, kindly communicated by Mr. Stedman, is the one quoted in the ensuing memoir.

For Mr. Henry's diary acknowledgments are due, and are thus publicly presented to my worthy friend, Joseph Lee of Redbrook near Broad Oak, Esquire; whose urgency, together with that of his family, for a new life of their honored ancestor, considerably influenced the undertaking.

An inducement to the same service, several original letters written by Mr. Henry from Gray's Inn, as well as a copy of nearly all the Epistles, which passed between him and his father while there, together with a very considerable number of other curiosities, were offered by M. Stedman, and cordially accepted.

Of the Gray's Inn correspondence, however, scarcely any use has been made, because almost the entire must have been drawn subsequent to January 22, 1707-08.

While it is a gratification to me to meet an innocent and laudable curiosity by furnishing a more happy likeness of this eminent divine than any which has hitherto appeared; and to notice, also, sundry particulars connected with the history of his time, it cannot be too explicitly stated that my *chief* intention in the engagement now concluded is of another kind: namely, such a representation of the illustrious Commentator as shall answer the legitimate purposes of Christian biography. This has been attempted by a connected report of his history by an exhibition of the principle features of his character; by prominently displaying the principles upon which that character was formed; and by adding, in support of the whole, authentic illustrations. It is apprehended the effort has not been altogether unsuccessful.

At all events, the memoir delineates a genuine portrait—a picture of piety in its primitive beauty. Such full demonstration of the influence of true godliness is, indeed, given, as is adapted to increase veneration for Mr. Henry, if already cherished; and to produce it where, through lack of acquaintance, that feeling is unknown. The pleasures, which our author's numerous writings can scarcely fail to inspire, may thus be augmented. A contemporary existence with him, at least in imagination, is created. Many "lessons of virtue and sweet morality" are preserved; and the divine honor, in some humble degree, advanced.

Did mankind consider, with becoming attention, those who "sleep in Jesus," and who were remarkable for their religious attainments, how inconceivably happy and momentous would be the consequence. A vivifying influence, like that which penetrated the man who was let down into the prophet's sepulcher, might be experienced, even by those who are dead in sin. In connection with the operations of the Holy Ghost, such would necessarily *be* the result. And, if the sacred fervors with which many of the saints of the Most High were animated, and which yet glow in their words and memoirs, were only diffused among their brethren, yet journeying towards Heaven, how surely would be enkindled the fire of lawful and commanded emulation! The counsel is apostolic. Be not slothful, but followers of them who inherit the promises.

As a connecting link between the early Puritans and modern nonconformists, Mr. Henry possesses some claims to special notice from the successors of those eminent men: men who, as a body, were the mighty champions of religion and of liberty, and who, by an unequalled writer, have been styled with singular felicity, the "fathers of the modern church." Mr. Henry "*knew* their doctrine, their manner of life, their purpose, their faith, their long-suffering, their charity, their patience, their persecution, and their afflictions." With many of them he was intimate. Some he visited in bonds and influenced by the love of truth, as well as impelled by laudable imitation, he chose, in the face of all the scorn and contempt, with which then, as now, they were loaded, to walk in the same path.

If such conduct reproaches those who quit that good old way for the sake of being fashionable or to secure some object of temporal aggrandizement, or, in short, for any reason less cogent than intelligent conviction, it also furnishes Puritanism or nonconformity or dissent, be the designation what it may, with a testimony far more honorable, and more weighty, than the united malevolence of a whole legion of defamers can invalidate.

It is interesting, as a matter of speculation, to contemplate the benefits which Mr. Henry must have derived from his nonconforming predecessors. To ascertain the precise amount is of course, impossible. But it cannot be conceived that the observation bestowed by him upon such men, (not to mention his own father), as a Tallents, an Angier, a Newcome, a Lawrence, and a Baxter, with others who were like-minded could have occurred, without contributing to the production of that fine polish, which renders his own character as a Christian, superlatively brilliant and attractive.

Be the causes, however, which were concerned in an issue so splendid, what they may, who will not perceive that through infinite mercy, he attained "the stature of the fullness of Christ?" In common parlance he was "blameless, and without rebuke." "He had a good report of all men, and of the truth itself." Whether considered as a Christian, or a minister, in private life, or in public, he was an "example to believers—in word, in conversation, in charity, in spirit, in faith, in purity."

But it may be said, were there no shades? Was Mr. Henry *perfect*?

If an inclination existed to arrogate for him a state of "sinless perfection," the attempt would be in direct opposition to his own expressed sentiments. He regarded the notion of such an attainment upon earth as utterly visionary, and enthusiastic; and in his discourse, showing "how to close the day with God," he has exposed it with his usual plainness and energy! "There is no such thing," he would say, "in this life."

At the same time it must be confessed that the closest scrutiny has failed to discover *such* imperfections as could furnish matter for exposure. And, in the absence of anything distinctly tangible, there seems to be no virtue in subjecting an eminent saint and an admired author to ignorant or censorious animadversion. Particularly when a long period has elapsed since his course was finished with honor and with joy. If Plutarch's elegant remark on this subject, in reference to a luxurious Roman, be a lasting encomium upon the soundness of his judgment, it becomes, in application to a "man of God," who walked worthy of his high vocation, increasingly important and correct, also, beyond the possibility of confutation.

Nor is there danger of a Christian indulging in excessive veneration, because "good qualities are set in full light." Viewing all excellence as an emanation from the Redeemer's glory and aided, as well as cheered by the display, he rather joys in God through our Lord Jesus Christ. It was thus with the beloved disciple. The acknowledgment made by that holy man, when adverting to himself and other believers, is as devout as is instructive. "Of *his* [that is, Jesus the Incarnate Word] of *his* fullness have all we received, and grace for grace."

One point, however of dissimilarity between the case of Mr. Henry, and that of many of the ancient saints referred to may be noticed. *He* had enjoyed from infancy the unspeakable privilege of training "in the nurture and admonition of the Lord." *They* had not. But no other difference, be it observed, is thereby constituted than that of a mere *circumstance*—a circumstance, too, which can, in no instance, furnish a warrant for human glorying or self-complacent admiration. On the contrary, an additional reason and one of prodigious force is furnished by it, why the eye should be kept fixed with unchanging steadiness upon celestial operations. How, otherwise, can the divinely constituted connection between the means and the end be discerned— distinguishing mercies improved—pride abased—or God, from whom cometh every good gift, glorified?

Allowing to moral suasion, pious example, and other parental influence, as diligently applied, the very utmost efficiency; and attaching to them, as suitable, appointed, and invaluable means the highest warrantable estimate; it would be most injurious to confide in *them*, that efficacy which is the peculiar prerogative of the Holy Spirit. To a mind savingly illuminated, it seems impossible. Who that, on the one hand, contemplates unrenewed nature in its essential enmity to Jehovah's government; in the impetuosity of its evil affections and in its unrestrained submission to things "seen and temporal;" and—on the other, the humbling self-denying and holy requirements of Christianity—does not perceive the universality of our Lord's testimony—"Except a man be born again, he cannot see the kingdom of God?"

Whenever, therefore, we are presented with an instance of regeneration, or, in other words, a new birth unto righteousness, there ought to be ... and as correct thought is indulged, there will be, let instrumental causes have been what they may, an unfeigned admiring of Almighty power and the agency of unutterable love.

Thus it is that the peculiar beauty, because the entire spirituality of genuine religion will be seen, its exalted superiority to every counterfeit displayed, the need of a moral fitness of the mind to its existence made manifest, and the impossibility of its communication by merely human teaching—any more than by the use of violence, secular inducements, or any of the foul arts of intolerance—demonstrated. "Even the things which are in themselves glorious, will appear to have no glory, by reason of the glory that excelleth."

Such was, obviously, Mr. Henry's view of the subject. "I desire," said he, "while I live, and I hope to eternity, to be blessing God for my good parents and good education." But, as if dissatisfied with alluding to a privilege upon which he placed so high an estimate, without conducting the mind to the grace by which men are saved, he elsewhere emphatically reminds persons in his own favored circumstance—that the enlightening of their minds was their deliverance from a house of bondage, in which all mankind are placed by sin, a worse bondage than that of Egypt. "Let us," he adds, "be sensible of our obligations to God, and Jesus Christ. There is as much mercy, if not as much miracle, in our deliverance, as in that of Israel."

The attempt, under a consciousness of numberless imperfections, to delineate a character like Mr. Henry's might have induced an appeal in strong and importunate terms to the reader's indulgence. But, unwilling to be exposed to the charges or insinuations, usually and too often fairly incident to such apologies, it shall suffice to state for the consideration of mere critics, that, although the work is strictly that of an amateur, instead of having the benefit of studious retirement, it was commenced and has been prosecuted amidst the constant engagements of professional duty: engagements not only of a different nature, but absolutely preventive of either regular or continuous application.

It is hoped there is an absence in the whole volume of everything that can give offense to the candid and well informed among good people, whether within or without the pale of the Established Church of England. At the same time it is felt, not without emotions of grief, that there are, nevertheless, various descriptions of readers to whose taste it is ill adapted and from whom censure, rather than approbation, may be expected.

It contains, for instance, nothing to suit the devotees of romance and novelism. Such persons, and they are a numerous class, pay little, if any attention to the unrivalled narrative of the Bible. Enamored of the merest trash, they have no taste for sublime beauties. The glorious achievements of primitive believers, and the unparalleled life of Jesus Christ fail to attract them. Can it, therefore, be expected that the exhibition of a comparatively modern disciple should be more successful? Besides—with true history and especially biography, death stands inseparably connected. This produces unwelcome thoughts of mortality, and, in the cases referred to, every conscious approach to a *dying* hour is intolerable. The evolutions in a dance of dervishes are not more consentaneous and exact, that the uniformity of such persons in *banishing* the consideration of futurity.

"O that men were wise, that they would consider their later end!"

Ill-tempered bigots, the narrow-minded and self-righteous, will find as little to attract *their* good will. They will, indeed, discern the outgoings of Christian love and the expansiveness of humility and faith, and the sight, how momentary soever, will operate like dazzling sunbeams upon tender and diseased vision.

It will be far, also, from pleasing the advocates of a spurious, but prevailing candor—a candor, which though denominated charity, is the bane of principle and the murderer of truth. It is certain that Mr. Henry united the boldness indispensable to an earnest contention of the faith with charity, but it was *that* charity which, resting upon the basis of inspiration, discovers itself only in connection with the heart-searching and unerring dictates of the Bible. This will offend, if it does not irritate, the lukewarm, the skeptical, and the careless. By the severity of silent censure it may even provoke malignity.

Nor will this Memoir obtain any better reception among doctrinal and practical Antinomians. They will find such ease in selecting statements opposed to their favorite and pestilential dogmas, as, probably to provoke their pity for Mr. Henry as a legalist. They will hardly refrain from despising him for the scantiness of his knowledge; his intense opposition to moral evil will amaze them. It will be well if, in self-defense, they are not driven to bring his very Christianity into question.

But "wisdom," after all, "is justified of her children;" and thus much having been said, it shall only be added, in conclusion— that while upon ministers the volume has some *peculiar* claims, no individuals can be imagined who may not find in it much that is adapted for their instruction and encouragement. In the display of piety, indeed, all persons, especially Christians, are interested. And all Christians are or ought to be preachers, not officially as Mr. Henry, but by well doing, by the influence of a conversation becoming the Gospel, by the energy and contrivances of a godly zeal. It is the transcendent praise of the Church of the Thessalonians that they were not only followers of the apostle, but heralds of the work of the Lord.

CHAPTER 1

A.D. 1662 to A.D. 1680
*Mr. Henry's Birth, Education, Alarming Illness, Memorial of
Mercies, Self-examination and Evidences of True Grace,
Inclination to the Ministry, and Habits*

atthew, the second son of Philip Henry, M.A. and
Katherine his wife was born, October 18, 1662, at
Broad Oak, a farmhouse situated in the township
of Iscoyd in Flintshire, and about three miles from
Whitchurch in the county of Salop.

The learning and piety of Phillip Henry have been recorded in
a memorial so singularly beautiful as to have shed around the
name a luster peculiarly brilliant and sacred, if not unrivaled. Mrs.
Henry also, though not equally honored, no memoir having been
written concerning her, was a woman of uncommon excellence.
She united a cheerful and tranquil mind with intellectual
endowments of superior order; and, in full exemplification of an
inspired portraiture, habitually walked in all the "commandments,
and ordinances of the Lord blameless." Her celebrated son
remarked that, "in her sphere and capacity, she was not inferior
to what his father was in his."

It will not escape notice that the year Matthew Henry was
born was that in which, by the well known Act of Uniformity, his
apostolical father and about two thousand other invaluable

ministers were separated from their flocks, prohibited from exercising their high vocation, and, as far as human intent could go, consigned to oblivion.

The circumstance did not pass unobserved; and he records it in his diary as a thing, which "affected" him, that it pertained not to himself only, but to some of his particular friends. He instances Mr. Matthews of Leichestershire and Mr. Tong, who were respectively born in 1662. If the observance of divine dispensations were the way to "understand the loving-kindness of the Lord," surely that attribute may be seen in birth at such a juncture of a "holy seed." The constancy of God's injured servants was thus rewarded and provision was made in the ministry for another generation, for whom, in providential mercy, fairer and more peaceful days were appointed.

It is said that Mr. Henry's birth was premature. Recently ejected from Worthenbury, his persecuted parents had moved to Broad Oak only about a fortnight before the event. His appearance, therefore, under circumstances so unsettled, created inconvenience, and, being unexpected, surprise. The following day, which was the Sabbath, Mr. Holland, the excellent Rector of Malpas, administered the ordinances of baptism. Mr. Philip Henry desired him to omit the sign of the cross, but its indispensableness being urged, the good man replied, "Then, Sir, let it lie at your door." There were, however, no sponsors.

During infancy Matthew's health was delicate, and the malady, which removed his brother John to heaven, threatened his life, also. But God, who had a great work for him to do, spared the tender grape for the blessing that was in it, a great blessing to his family, his friends, and the church.

At a very early period his mind displayed the vigor and acuteness for which, through life, it was remarkable. It is credibly stated that at the early age of three years, he could read in the Bible with distinctness and observation.

The honour of initiating the young nonconformist to grammatical studies devolved upon Mr. Turner, a gentleman who, for a season, resided at Broad Oak, preparatory to an abode at the University. He was a man of integrity and worth, and became afterwards Vicar of Walburton in Sussex. He is chiefly known to the world as the author of a curious, "History of Remarkable Providences." The efforts of the scholar kept pace with his privileges, and childish things being put away early, the usual temptations to sloth, negligence, and frivolity were voluntarily escaped. His tender mother was often afraid lest he should apply too closely. She was forced, when he was very young, to call him out of his closet; and that his health might not suffer by inordinate confinement and application, to advise him also to take a walk in the fields.

If at Broad Oak the facilities for the attainment of literature were appropriate and valuable, a fact, which cannot be doubted, those for acquiring the far more important knowledge of religions truth, were no less so. There were the morning and evening expositions of Holy Scripture, the unceasing prayers of eminently devout parents, and in extraordinary abundance, the instruction, which associated with a consistent and holy example.

Some extracts from a letter written in 1671, when Matthew was only nine years old, to his father, then in London, will illustrate this period. Whether viewed as a development of progress in learning or as evincing the effects of godly education or as being probably the first specimen of his epistolary style, the selections will be alike interesting. "Every day since you went, I have done my lesson, a side of Latin or Latin verses and two verses in the Greek Testament. I hope I have done all well, and so I will continue till you come." He adds, in reference to tidings, which had been communicated respecting one of his relatives, and the resemblance to his subsequent style of writing will not pass unnoticed: "By this providence we may see that sin is the worst of evils, for sickness came with sin. Christ is the chief good; therefore, let us love him. Sin is the worst of evils, therefore, let us hate that with a perfect hatred."

The expectations indulged were, however, soon afterwards checked. A lingering fever attacked the interesting youth, then about ten years of age, with such extreme violence, as for some time, to induce daily apprehension of his death. In this trial, the faith of his parents triumphed over the agitations of natural tenderness. They trusted the Lord and invoked his holy name. The afflicted father, acting upon the counsel he gave to others—that weeping must not hinder sowing—fulfilled, as usual, the duties of his ministry. And when hope was almost extinct, he left home to preach at a distance; nor was his return cheered by more favorable appearances. The widow of the Rev. Zechariah Thomas was at the time on a visit at Broad Oak, and proved a comforter in sorrow. To her Mr. Philip Henry remarked that while absent, he had most solemnly and deliberately resigned his dear child to the will of God. The "good old gentlewoman" replied, "And I believe, Sir, in that place and time, God gave him back to you again." So it turned out. Recovery speedily followed, and Mrs. Savage, who heard the conversation, remarked many years afterwards that although at the time she was only eight years old, and could think but "as a child," she was much impressed; and believing that the brother's life was marvelously prolonged, he became additionally endeared to hear.

To detail the state of the sufferer's own mind during the progress of the disease is rendered impossible by the absence of materials. But it is not too much to infer, in connection with what remains to be stated, that the affliction contributed to produce susceptibility of impression, and resembled, in its influence, to borrow the appropriate imagery of Scripture, the breaking up of fallow ground.

In this important part of Mr. Henry's history—his translation from the kingdom of darkness to that of God's dear son—it will be best to adopt his own account. A manuscript dated October 18, 1675 satisfactorily furnished it. In the form of a "Catalogue of Mercies," it details at some length the progress of religion in his soul, together with his evidences upon which he formed a belief of its genuineness. He commences with praise for such mercies as were "*spiritual*," "for the Lord Jesus Christ, his incarnation, life, death, resurrection, ascension, and intercession for grace, pardon, peace for the world; the means of grace, for prayer; for good instructions; for good received at any time under the word; for any succor and help from God under temptation; for brokenness of hear; for any enlightening." And then adds, "Lord Jesus, I bless thee for they word, for good parents, for good education, that I was taken into covenant betimes in baptism; and Lord, I give thee thanks, that I am thine, and will be thine."

He then proceeds. *I think it was three years ago that I began to be convinced, hearing a sermon by my father on Psalm 51:17. "The sacrifices of God are a broken spirit; a broken spirit and a contrite heart, O God, thou will not despise." I think it was that that melted me; afterwards I began to enquire after Christ.*

December 7th, 1673. On a Sabbath-day morning, I heard a sermon that had in it the marks of true grace. I tried myself by them and told my father my evidences; he liked them and said, if those evidences were true (as I think they were), I had true grace. Yet, after this, for two or three days I was under great fear of hell, till the Lord comforted me. I having been engaged in serious examination—What hope I have that when I die and leave this earthly tabernacle, I shall be received into heaven—I have found several marks that I am a child of God, His ministers say:

1. There is true conversion when there have been covenant transactions between God and the soul. And I found that there have been such between God and my soul, and I hope in truth and righteousness. If I never did this before, I do it now, for I take God in Christ to be mine. I give up myself to be his in the bond of an everlasting covenant never-to-be forgotten. But hath it been in truth? As far as I know my own heart, I do it in truth and sincerity. I did it December 7, and September 5, and October 13, and many other times. I do it every day.

2. Where there hath been true repentance for sin, and grief, and shame, and sorrow, for it, as to what is past, with all the ingredients of it, as confession, aggravation, self-judging, self-condemning, etc. And I have found this in me, though not in that measure that I could desire. I have been heartily sorry for what is past. I judge myself before the Lord, blushing for shame that I should ever affront him as I have done; and ministers have assured me, that having repented of sin and believed on Christ, I am to believe that I am pardoned. Now I have done this and I do really believe I am forgiven for Christ's sake. This is grounded on several Scriptures, Proverbs 28:13; Isaiah 1:18; Isaiah 55:7; Matthew 5:4; Acts 2:37, 38; Acts 3:19; I John 1:9. And many other Scriptures there are where God doth expressly call people to return and repent. But hath this sorry been true? As far as I know my own heart, it has, it hath been true. "But I sin often. I lament and bewail it before the Lord, and I endeavour, by the grace of God, to do so no more.

3. Where there is true love of God. For to love the Lord our God with all our soul and with all our strength, is better than

whole burnt offerings and sacrifices. Now, as far as I know my own heart, I love God in sincerity. But is that love indeed sincere? As far as I can judge it is so; for,

(1.) I love the people of God; all the Lord's people shall be my people.

(2.) I love the word of God. I esteem it above all. I find my heart so inclined. I desire it as the food of my soul. I greatly delight in it, both in reading and hearing of it; and my soul can witness subjection to it in some measure. I think I love the Word of God for the purity of it. I love the ministers and messengers of the Word. I am often reading it. I rejoice in the good success of it. All which were given as marks of true love to the word, in a sermon I lately heard on Psalm 119:140: "Thy word is very pure, therefore thy servant loveth it."

From this interesting document it is obvious that Mr. Henry, before he attained his eleventh year, was led into that vital and essential part of true wisdom – the knowledge of himself and the state of his own soul: the "*great* soul of man," as he loved to call it. "For," said he, "it bears God's image." "There begins to be some hope of people," he used in afterlife to remark, "when they are *concerned* about their souls; about spiritual provision, spiritual health, spiritual trading and husbandry; about sowing to the Spirit."

On his father's ministry Mr. Henry waited with uncommon diligence, and he was often so moved by it, as to hasten, when the exercise was over, to his closet, weeping and making supplication that the things he had heard might not escape. Sometimes, his fears, lest good impressions should be effaced, rose so high as to render it difficult to prevail upon him to appear at dinner.

Once, especially, after a sermon illustrating the nature and growth of true grace, as compared in Scripture to a grain of mustard-seed (which, though insignificant in appearance, would in time produce great things) his concern to possess a principle so efficient and precious was intense. And in a walk with his father, being "unable any longer to contain," he communicated his anxieties. Nothing remains of the conversation, but the "young disciple" afterwards told one of his sisters, with delightful exultation, that he hoped he had *received* the blessed grain of true grace, and though, at present, it was very small, yet that it would come to something in time.

What greater joy could such a man as Philip Henry have had than to hear his only son, thus early enquiring for the way to Zion! And how unspeakable was the privilege to the son to possess in his father a scribe well instructed in doctrine of the kingdom of heaven; signally "apt to teach;" and ready at all times to encourage the timid, but sincere enquirer "in the ways of Jehovah." It is to be lamented that diffidence or shame so often hinder young converts from communicating their exercises. Little do they consider the temptations and sorrows to which, by such backwardness, they are exposed, or how exquisite is the pleasure of which those who are filled with zeal for the Lord God of Hosts are thus unnecessarily deprived. There is joy in heaven, and when it is known on earth, too, over one sinner that repenteth. This was strikingly manifested in the conduct of Paul and Silas. Although the jailer thrust those "companions in tribulation" into the "inner prison," and made their "feet fast in the stock," yet no sooner did he implore, through midnight spiritual counsel than, without and upbraiding word or even the slightest allusion to inflicted severities, they gladly seized the opportunity to exhibit the one great Sacrifice. "Believe," said they, "on the Lord Jesus Christ, and thou shalt be saved."

Philip Henry, like most of the puritans and nonconformists, was distinguished for a reverential observance of the Lord's Day. He had formed that holy habit in early life. It was strengthened by subsequent convictions and experience imparted to it confirmation and maturity. "It is comfortable," he once remarked, on recovering from an illness, "to reflect upon an affliction borne patiently and enemy forgiven heartily and a Sabbath sanctified uprightly."

That his children might be impressed the more deeply with like sentiments, and especially in order to the better sanctification of the holy rest, they were expected to spend an hour together every Saturday afternoon in devotional exercises. On these occasions Matthew presided and gave intimations of his subsequent delight in God's service too distinct and too impressive to be either overlooked or forgotten. If, at such times, he thought his sisters improperly curtailed their prayers, he would gently expostulate, telling them that "it was impossible, in so short a time, to include all the cases and persons they had to recommend to God." Nor were his admonitions otherwise than kindly received. Those holy women acknowledged in proper years, to the divine glory, how much they were influenced and encouraged by their brother's example and remarks.

It is believed that from his childhood, Mr. Henry had an inclination to the ministry. He discovered it by the remarkable eagerness with which he read the Bible, by a peculiar attachment to ministers, and by a pleasure in writing and repeating sermons, which were so predominate as to be almost prophetic. He loved also to imitate preaching, (a circumstance mentioned only as a fact, not as any thing uncommon), which he managed, considering his years, with great propriety, gravity, and judgment.

When very young he coveted the society of those who "feared the Lord and thought upon his name." He frequently met them in their assemblies for conference and prayer. He prayed with them and repeated sermons. Occasionally, likewise, he explained the chapters read, enlarging upon them very much to the benefit and comfort of his auditors. Surprise was naturally excited, and in one of the number, it should seem, alarm also, lest he should be too forward and fall a victim to pride. The apprehension was expressed to his judicious father. "Let him go on," was the answer; "He fears God and designs well, and I hope God will keep him and bless him."

The practice of copying sermons, which Philip Henry recommended to young people and which he himself diligently observed, was early adopted by his son, who continued it through life. Very many volumes yet remain in proof of his indefatigable industry, his excellent memory, and discriminating attention. He fully exemplified the advice given by this father's friend, and an excellent minister, Mr. Porter, "Remember and carry away what is bread in a sermon." The same good man complained perhaps with a mixture of sarcasm, "If there *be* any chaff *that* usually is carried away."

CHAPTER 2

A.D. 1680 to A.D. 1685
Removal to Mr. Doolittle's Academy, Account of Mr. Boiser,
Characters of Mr. Henry by His Contemporaries at the
Academy, His Return to Broad Oak, Catalogue of Mercies,
Acquaintances

he privileges enjoyed at Broad Oak were peculiarly fitted to prepare our author for a sacred office. His father, in addition to being an admired preacher, had amassed rich treasures of polite and useful learning. From this store he was always willing to communicate, and so felicitous was he in the work of instruction, as to be seldom equaled and perhaps never surpassed.

It is considered no disparagement to the persons who, for a short season, had the subsequent direction of Mr. Henry's studies to affirm, that the helps he enjoyed at *home* for the acquisition of knowledge, both civil and sacred, contributed above all others to his fitness for the Christian Ministry.

Mr. Philip Henry, having derived much advantage from being a student of Christ Church, Oxford, which he well knew how to appreciate, was led during many years to entertain a "kindness" for the universities and to recommend his friends who intended their sons for scholars to send them thither. But long experience altered his mind, and when, because of his abundant engagements, he determined to remove his son from home, instead of introducing him to either to the national seats of learning, where so many temptations were presented, he placed him in the family and under the tuition of that "holy, faithful minister, Mr. Thomas Doolittle, who then lived at Islington." This was the year 1680.

The following letter fixes the date of the journey thither and discloses some particulars, which, at this distance of time, are both curious and entertaining:

Dear Sisters,

I came safe, through the good Providence of God, upon Friday last into London and have reason to say, "It is of the Lord's mercies that I am not consumed for he holdeth my soul in life and keepeth all my bones. On Monday we (Philip Henry, himself, and his cousin Boiser) baited at Newport; went to see Mr. Edwards; and came, through Tong, to Wolverhampton that night about sunset. From thence we set out next morning about six or seven o'clock, and came through Birmingham to Henley, twenty miles from Wolverhampton; and there we baited and lay at Stratford-upon-Avon, five miles from Henley. On Wednesday morning we came from Stratford to Shipston, thence to Longcompton, thence to Enston, where we baited, and then came to Oxford between five and six. At Oxford I saw the Judges come in, Sir Job for one, and next morning heard the Assize sermon at St. Mary's. It was preached by one Mr. Lessy, a young man. The text was Hos. 4:1-3.

On Thursday at about three o'clock, we set out from Oxford, and came twenty miles that night, viz., to Wickham; and next day baited at Uxbridge; about three o'clock we came to Chelsea. We found my Aunt Dryer not well, and my aunt Sarah come to see her. We stayed there about an hour, and then came for London, where we arrived about six. I never saw so many coaches. If I should say we met above a hundred after we came into the town before we came into our inn, I should speak within compass.

On Saturday my father went to Islington, and I went to cousin Hotchkiss', and Mr. Church's – Mr. Church came with us to see, first Bedlam, and then the monument. The monument is almost like the spire steeple, set up in the place where the great fire began. It is 345 steps high, and thence we had a sigh of the whole city. Yesterday we went to Mr. Doolittle's meeting place; his church, I may call it; for I believe there is many a church that will not hold so many people. There are several galleries; it is all pewed, and a brave pulpit, a great height above the people. They began between nine and ten in the morning, and after the singing of a Psalm, Mr. Doolittle first prayed, and then he preached and that was all. His text was Jer. 17:9. In the afternoon my father preached on Lam. 3:22, at the same place. Indeed, Mr. Lawrence told him at first he must not come to London to be idle; and they are resolved he shall not; for he is to preach the two next Sabbaths I believe at Mr. Steel's and Mr. Lawrence's. On Sabbath day night, above five o'clock, cousin Robert and I went to another place and heard, I cannot say another sermon, but a piece of another by a very young man, one Mr. Shower; and a most excellent sermon it was on the evil of sin. The truth was, we could scarce get any room, it was so crowded.

This morning we went to Islington, when I saw the place we are like to abide in, and do perceive our rooms are likely to be very straight and little –that Mr. Doolittle is very studious, and diligent – and that Mrs. Doolittle and her daughter are very fine and gallant.

Dear sisters, I am almost ever thinking of you, and home, but dare scarce entertain a thought of returning lest it discompose me. I found it a great change.

Pray do not forget me in your thoughts, nor in your prayers; but remember me in both. So, commending you all to the care and protection of Almighty God, whose kingdom ruleth over all.

I rest,
Your ever-loving and affectionate Brother
Matthew Henry

London at the Castle, near Aldersgate,
July 18, Monday Afternoon 1680

Mr. Robert Bosier, who is referred to in the foregoing letter and accompanied the young theologian to London, was a person of great respectability and promise. He was related to Mr. Henry. After quitting Edmound's Hall in Oxford of which he was a commoner, he had resided for a season at Broad Oak, that he might be the better fitted for "holy orders." He was some years older than Mr. Henry, but their intercourse grew into esteem, which soon ripened into friendship—a friendship well rounded, reciprocally ardent, and interrupted only by death. Mr. Tong observed of Mr. Henry that he never heard him mention his cousin Bosier without some distinguishing mark of affection.

Both the happiness Mr. Henry had promised himself at Islington in the society of his friend, and the satisfaction, which his near relatives on their separation must have felt in superintendence so conscientious and faithful as Mr. Bosier's, was soon blighted. Only a few weeks elapsed before that valuable young man was seized with a fever from which, to the grief of all who knew him, he died. Mr. Doolittle noticed the event in a sermon on Sabbath afternoon, September 19, 1680, from Job 30:23. "I know that thou wilt bring me to death." Although little appears to have been said of the deceased, the instructions offered to the living were admirably devout, impressive and seasonable. "See," said the preacher, "the necessity of regeneration. Let the thought that you will be brought to death call off your affections from things below. Redeem the time. Make your peace with God, and be reconciled to him. You should not go to bed in wrath against others; and will you go to your graves in enmity against God? Be content with what you have. Be frequent in *thinking* of your removal. If you do but remove on earth you take care. Be as useful and profitable as you can, for when you are brought to death your work will be over. Be careful to be making preparations for it. We live to learn to die. Our business is *not* to get riches, honors, or pleasures, but that we may depart in peace with God. Every corpse is a sermon; every tomb a teacher; every funeral an oration – to persuade you to learn to die."

At Islington, as might be expected, Mr. Henry found other associates, who became much endeared to him. One of them was Mr. Samuel Bury, the son of an eminent nonconformist, who was ejected from Great Bolas in Shropshire. This youth subsequently settled as a dissenting minister in Bristol, and became the husband of that excellent lady whose life and remains, published by himself, have been so justly celebrated. The friendship, which thus commenced at the Academy between Mr. Henry and Mr. Bury, derived strength from many tender and virtuous considerations, it continued through life. And years afterwards, when earthly intercourse had terminated, it warranted Mr. Bury in furnishing the following minute and graphic delineation:

"I was never better pleased when I was at Mr. Doolittle's, than when in young Mr. Henry's company; he had such a savor of religion always upon his spirit, was of such a cheerful temper, so diffusive of all knowledge, so ready in the Scriptures, so pertinent in all his petitions, in every emergency, so full and clear in all his performances (abating that at first he had almost an unimaginable quickness of speech, which afterwards he corrected, as well for his own sake, as for the benefit of others), that he was to me a most desirable friend, and I love heaven the better since he went thither."

Before the narrative proceeds, it seems proper to introduce another testimony relative to this period of the history, though, like the preceding one, was penned after Mr. Henry's death. The author of it, Mr. Henry Chandler, was an eminent minister at Bath and the father of the learned Dr. Samuel Chandler of London. "It is now thirty-five years," he says in a letter to Mr. Tong, "since I had the happiness of being in the same house with Mr. Henry, so that it is impossible I should recollect the several passages that fixed in me such an honorable idea of him, that nothing can efface while life and reason last; this I perfectly well remember, that for serious piety, and the most obliging behavior, he was universally beloved by all the house. We were, I remember, near thirty pupils when Mr. Henry graced and entertained the family; and I remembered not that ever I heard one of the number speak a word to his disparagement. I am sure it was the common opinion, that he was a sweet tempered, courteous, and obliging a gentleman as could come into a house; his going from us was universally lamented."

How long Mr. Henry continued at this seminary is not easily discoverable. Persecution soon drove Mr. Doolittle from Islington; he removed to Battersea, and his pupils were scattered among private families at Clapham. But Mr. Henry, instead of accompanying them, returned, it is believed, to Broad Oak. Be this, however, as it may, it is certain that his studies, *when* resumed at home, we pursued, as at Islington, with unwearied diligence; and the following memorial, supposed to be one of his earliest performances after his arrival, will furnish evidence of his creditable proficiency in human learning, as well as of his growth in that "wisdom which is from above." It is entitled "Mercies Received."

1. That I am endured with a rational, immortal soul, capable of serving God here, and enjoying him hereafter, and was not made as the beasts that perish.

2. That having powers and faculties, the exercise of them has been no wise obstructed by frenzies, lunacy, etc., but happily continued in their primitive (nay happily advanced to greater) vigour, and activity.

3. That I have all my senses; that I was neither born, nor by accident made, blind, or deaf, or dumb, either in whole, or in part.

4. That I have a complete body in all its parts; that I am not lame or crooked, either through original, or providential want, or a defect, or the dislocation of any part, or member.

5. That I was formed, and curiously fashioned by an All-wise hand in the womb, and there kept, nourished, and preserved, by the same gracious hand, till the appointed time.

6. That, at the appointed time, I was brought into the world, the living child of a living mother; and that, though means were wanting, yet He that can work without means, was not.

7. That I have been ever since comfortably provided for with bread to eat, and raiment to put on, not for necessity only, but for ornament, and delight; and that without my pains and care.

8. That I have had a very great measure of health (the sweetness of all temporal mercies), and that when infectious diseases have been abroad, I have hitherto been preserved from them.

9. That when I have been visited with sickness, it hath been in measure, and health hath been restored to me, when a brother dear, and companion as dear, hath been taken away at the same time, and by the same sickness.

10. That I have been kept and protected from many dangers that I have been exposed to by night and by day, at home and abroad, especially in journeys.

11. That I have had comfortable accommodation as to house, lodging, fuel, etc, and have been a stranger to the wants of many thousands in that kind.

12. That I was born to a competency of estate in the world, so that, as long as God pleases to continue it, I am likely to be on the giving, and not on the receiving hand.

13. That I have had, and still have comfort, more than ordinary, in relations; that I am blessed with such parents as few have, and sisters also that I have reason to rejoice in.

14. That I have had a liberal education, having a capacity for, and being brought up to, the knowledge of the languages, arts, and sciences; and that, through God's blessing on my studies, I have made some progress therein

15. That I have been born in a place and time of Gospel light; that I have had the Scriptures, and means for understanding them, by daily expositions, and many good books; that I have had a heart to give myself to, and delight in the study of them.

16. That I have been hitherto enabled so to demean myself, as to gain a share in the love, and prayers of God's people.

17. *That I was in infancy brought within the pale of the visible church in my baptism.*

18. *That I had a religious education, the principles of religion, instilled into me with my very milk, and from a child have been taught the knowledge of God.*

19. *That I have been endured with a good measure of praying gifts, being enabled to express my mind to God in prayer, in words of my own, not only alone, but as the mouth of others.*

20. *That God hath inclined my heart to devote and dedicate myself to him, and to his service, and the service of his church in the work of the ministry, if ever he shall please to use me.*

21. *That I have had so many sweet, and precious opportunities, and means of grace, Sabbaths, sermons, sacraments, and have enjoyed, not only the ordinances, themselves, but communion with God.*

22. *That I have a good hope, through grace, that, being chosen of God from eternity, I was, in the fullness of time called, and that good work begun in me, which I trust God will perform.*

23. *That I have had some sign of the majesty of God, the sweetness of Christ, the evil of sin, the worth and weight of invisible things.*

24. *That when I have been in doubt I have been guided; in danger I have been guarded; in temptation I have been succored; under guilt I have been pardoned; when I have prayed, I have been heard and have been sanctified; and all by divine grace*

25. *That I am not without hope, that all these mercies are but the earnest of more, and pledges of better in the kingdom of glory; and that I shall rest in Abraham's bosom, world without end.*

26. Lastly, thanks be to God for Jesus Christ, the fountain and foundations of all my mercies. Amen, Hallelujah.

MatthewHenry
October 18,1682
Die Natali.

At Broad Oak, "that house of God and prayer," to which so many good people often used to resort, such exemplary piety attracted notice; and Mr. Henry, like the son of Elkanah, "was in favor both with the Lord, and also with men." Those who knew him, Mr. Tong remarks "coveted his company and were delighted with it."

CHAPTER 3

A.D. 1685 to A.D. 1686
Study of the Law at Gray's Inn, Habits, Correspondence,
Trial of the Rev. R. Baxter, His Visit to Mr. Baxter in Prison,
His Reading, His Study of the French Language,
His Correspondence at Home, His Sabbaths,
Letter to Mr. Illidge

difference of opinion has long existed as to the length of time, which ought to be devoted to preparatory studies by a candidate for the Christian ministry, prior to his commencement of public labor. Urgent reasons offer themselves in favor of a *protracted* course of initiation: such as (reasoning by analogy from acquisition of arts or trades, and connecting the superior importance of ministerial engagements) the nature of things – the value of extensive, and accurate knowledge, when accompanied by matured experience—the advantages arising from lengthened superintendence and trial—the example of the incarnate Redeemer, and ancient custom in the churches, etc. While the utility to the candidate of early, and frequent preaching—the brevity of human life—the necessities of souls—and the preservation of personal spirituality, furnish arguments for the opposite conclusion. The reasons thus adversely to, might probably have influenced Mr. Philip Henry's mind as to his son. If they did, the former class, in addition to their intrinsic force, being most in unison with early associations and established habits, naturally preponderated.

Mr. Henry, after he left Islington, was a frequent and welcome visitor at Boreatton. Mr. Hunt was no stranger, therefore, to his attainments, or to his designs in reference to the ministry. That "learned, and religious gentleman," however, advised his return to London, that the study of the law might be added to his other accomplishments; a practice which in the sixteenth century had much prevailed, both in this country, and on the continent. It does not appear whether Mr. Hunt was governed in the recommendation by any of the considerations just notices; or whether he had observed an ardor and impetuosity of mind to which further training would be beneficial; or whether he was influenced by more general reasons, such as the darkness of the times, the youth of the party, the convenience of legal knowledge to one whose worldly expectations were considerable; or whether he had in view the admitted advantages incident to the acquaintance with forensic literature as judiciously applied advice was "approved of both by the father and the son," and towards the end of April, 1685, Mr. Henry, then in the twenty-third year of his age, journeyed a second time to London; and in Holborn Court, Gray's Inn, Commenced a new, and apparently opposite course of studies.

There he became acquainted with several gentlemen, members of the same inn, who were exemplary for industry, religion, and virtue. He often mentioned the names of Mr. Turner of Canterbury, Mr. Edward Harley, Mr. Dunch, Mr. Birch, and Mr. Edward and Mr. Gilbert Horsman with respect and honour. Many years afterwards, when he had an opportunity of renewing his acquaintance with his old friend "Mr. Sergeant Birch," his diary does not fail to express the gratification.

In the "house of the law" Mr. Henry's diligence was constant and exemplary; and, had he addicted himself exclusively to the "manly study," he would have risen, probably, to distinction as a lawyer. Although not *fully* enamored of the "noble science." His application to it was such as to rouse the fears of several friends, and very near relatives, lest the result should be unfavorable to his early resolutions. The alarm, however, was needless: he remained true to his original purpose; and the "office of bishop," that excellent work, was still earnestly desired, and ever kept in view; though, occasionally, the discouragements of the times made him a little doubtful. The better to effectuate his ruling design he judiciously varied his pursuits, consecrating a portion of time to theological reading: promoting among his particular friends, social prayer, and religions conference: and occasionally expounding to them in Scriptures. If with Cardinal Ximenes he did not *say* to his friends that he would willingly exchange all legal learning for the explanation of a single passage of holy writ, he *acted* as if such was his judgment.

While resident at Gray's Inn, an affectionate and frequent correspondence was maintained with his father, and occasionally with his sisters; the whole series presents a collection of facts, alike curious and interesting.

Before, however, any further allusion is made to that collection, the reader may advantageously peruse one entire letter, addressed to Mr. Henry, soon after he left home, by his father. While it exhibits a beautiful specimen of wise and apostolic counsel, it excellently confirms several of the foregoing statements.

May 30, 1685
Son Matthew,
    We are glad to hear of your health and cheerfulness, which God in mercy continued! If you take meals in a

house daily, you must double your watch lest it put you upon inconvenience. My caution not to over-study yourself was occasioned by what you wrote, that you had read Littleton so often over, and had begun Cook upon him, which I thought could not well be, especially during the first month, which afterwards most diversions, without overtasking yourself; my meaning was that you should apportion your time wisely, according to present circumstances: part to reading, the morning especially; and part to acquaint yourself with persons, and places, and affairs; and which you have hitherto much wanted opportunity to acquaint yourself with; having some ground of hope that will improve by it, letting go the chaff and refuse, and retaining that which may you do good hereafter; for this present time you are to look upon as your gathering time, and to be as busy as the ant in summer, the factor in the fair market, the industrious merchant, when in the Indies. You purposed to lay hold on opportunities for hearing sermons not Latin ones only; I hope you perform, and also reflect after, and pen the heads at home, which both engages present attention, and lays up for time to come. It is the talk and wonder of many of our friends what we mean by this sudden change in your course and way; but I hope, through God's goodness and mercy, they will shortly see it was for good.

With yours I received one from dear Mr. St(eel), who would be glad to see you often, as I know my worthy friend Mr. Lawr(ence) would also; but their circumstances prohibit their coming to you, therefore you must go to them, not to be burdensome, but like a bee to the flowers, to gather from them.

Just now, this morning, your sisters, Katharine and Ann, are gone towards Salop to be there awhile. It is a change with us to want three of you at once, but hoping it will be for your improvement and theirs, we are well satisfied in the will of God ordering it so. Ere long there will be greater partings: how soon we know not; but if we may be with you together for ever, and with the Lord, that will be happiness indeed.

Be careful, my dear child, in the main matter. Keep yourself always in the love of God, let nothing come, however not abide, as a cloud between you and his favor, for in that is life. Rejoice in the great auction, and make the Pearl of Price sure, and the field too in which it is. Farewell. Much love is to you from all here and particularly from

Your Loving Father
P.H.

While Mr. Henry, notwithstanding the absence of that entire devotion to legal learning which has distinguished some of its pursuers, was so ardent as to need the hints of restraint suggested in the preceding letter, it must have been singularly gratifying to their author to find ample evidence in the communications he received, that "in the main matter," his son was "careful;" and that he cultivated with enviable diligence, that spirituality of the mind which is, whenever possessed, both "life and peace." "The more I see of the world," he writes, "and the various affairs of the children of men in it, the more I see of the vanity of it, and the more I would fain have my heart taken off from it, and fixed upon the invisible realities of the other world."

Can any thing be conceived of more characteristic of the writer than the following beautiful improvement of one of the most ordinary occurrences of life? The familiarity of the subject would, in almost any other case, have prevented a like impression. The turn given to it perhaps rarely occurs to the mind even now, when the facilities of the post-office, being so much increased, both in expedition and certainty, might, if ever, be likely to produce it; and yet more seldom is the thought so well improve.

July 5, 1685

It pleaseth me sometimes to think what a ready, speedy way of intercourse there is between me and home, though at such a distance; that a letter can come from your hands to mine, through the hands of so many who are strangers to both, in the space of sixty hours. But as ready as this way is, blessed be God, we have a readier way to send to Heaven at all hours; and can convey our letters thither, and receive gracious answers thence in less time than so. That the throne of grace is always open to which we have (how sweet a word it is) **ten parresiae** *– "liberty of speech," when we are with him and more than so,* **tenprosagogen en pepoithesei** *Eph. 3:2. We have access with confidence; we are introduced by the Spirit, as ambassadors conducted to the Prince by the master of the ceremonies. Esther had access to Ahasuerus, but not access with confidence: far from it, when she said I will go in, and if I perish, I perish. But we have waylaid open for us to the Father, by the blood of his Son, who ever lives to make intercession, in the virtue and value of his satisfaction. And if this were not a sufficient ground for the confidence, what is?*

In may that same year, 1685, it was that the infamous trial of Mr. Baxter was acted before the contemptible and scurrilous Jefferys at Guildhall; and in daring violation of law and reason, the venerable nonconformist was sentenced by that "unjust judge," to pay five hundred marks, to lie in prison till they were paid, and to be bound to his good behavior for seven years. Whether Mr. Henry witnessed the public obloquy of his father's ancient and beloved friend does not appear; but the following letter, which will not be read without interest, details a visit to the imprisoned saint. It is one of those pictures of days which are past, which, if rightly viewed, may produce lasting and beneficial effects: emotions of sacred sorrow for the iniquity of persecution: and animating praise that the demon in these happy days of tranquility is restrained, though not destroyed. Holiness, how much soever it may annoy, or even irritate, by its splendor, has, through the favor of the Most High, the fullest liberty to shine.

17th November 1685
Honored Sir,

On Saturday last I was with you good Mr. Laurence, who sends affectionate respect to you. He and some others of them, walk the street with freedom.

I went into Southwark to Mr. Baxter. I was to wait upon him once before, and then he was busy. I found him in pretty comfortable circumstances, though a prisoner, in a private house near the prison, attended on S(amuel) L(awrence) went with me. He is in as good health as one can expect; and, methinks looks better, and speaks heartier, than when I saw him last. The token you sent he would by no means be persuaded to accept of, and was almost angry when I pressed it, from one outed as well as himself. He said he did not use to receive; and I understand wince, his need is not great.

We sat with him about an hour. I was very glad to find that he so much approved of my present circumstances. He said he knew not why young men might not improve as well as by traveling abroad. He enquired for his Shropshire friends, and observed that of those gentlemen who were with him at Wem, he hears of none whose sons tread in their fathers' steps but Colonel Hunt's. He enquired about Mr. Macworth's and Mr. Lloyd of Aston's children. He gave us some good counsel to prepare for trials, and said the best preparation for them was a life of faith, and a constant course of self-denial. He thought it harder constantly to deny temptations to sensual lusts and pleasures, than to resist one single temptation to deny Christ for fear of suffering: the former requiring such constant watchfulness; however, after the former, the latter will be the easier. He said we who are young are apt to count upon Great things, but we must not look for it; and much more to this purpose. He said he thought dying by sickness usually much more painful and dreadful then dying a violent death; especially considering the extraordinary supports which those have who suffer for righteousness sake. He sends you his respects. Good Mr. Tallents also I saw that night, and sat with him awhile.

> *Your most dutiful son,*
> *Matt. Henry.*

In the correspondence carried on at Gray's Inn is exhibited, pretty fully both Mr. Henry's studies and engagements. It shows, notwithstanding the progress he made, and the application which would now be called hard study, that he followed the law, in his own apprehension only indifferently well, and that he was not very fond of it. He expresses the great discouragement he felt at the different opinions of lawyers, even the best, in almost every case of any difficulty. He nevertheless, went on with it, thought "not over fast;" usually laying it by towards evening that he might "read something more easy." He notices particularly Lambard's perambulation of Kent, which seems to have greatly interested him.

In one letter he expresses a fear lest he should scarce study so much in the summer time as in the winder, but, he adds, "We were not made to be Monks. There are necessary avocations which must be yielded to when they cannot be avoided.."

With a view to increase his knowledge, and his capacity also of improvement, he enlisted himself a scholar to Dr. Du Viel in the French language. Mr. Harley and the Messrs. Horsman were his fellow students. He considered it "some hindrance to the study of the law, and but little; for," said he, "it toucheth not the morning, which is Legibus as well as Musis Amica" – A friend to the law as well as to the Muses. In one quarter of a year, attended by the Doctor three days a week, on Monday, Wednesday, and Friday, at two o'clock in the afternoon, and for about two hours, he obtained so much "insight into the French as, with a little help of a Dictionary, to read with understanding any thing ordinary in the language." The Doctor was then discharged.

In one of the letters he received from his father, and which was literally a family vehicle of affectionate good will, his sister Katharine, afterwards Mrs. Tylston, indulged, as the representative of her sisters, her lively disposition, by thus humorously adverting to the employment which has been mentioned.

"We shall be very ambitious to be your scholars to learn French; but I think they say one tongue is enough for a women."

And his excellent mother, in the same epistle, left, it should seem, to be filled up by others, communicated (and with that enviable union of tenderness and wisdom for which she was distinguished) her parental anxiety and holy counsel.

Dear Child,

It is much my comfort and rejoicing to hear so often from you, and, although I have little to sent you but love,

45

and my blessing, your father being absent, I write a line or two to you to mind you to keep in with God, as I hope you do, by solemn, secret, daily prayer; watching therein with perseverance; not forgetting what you have been taught, and the covenant engagement, renewed again and again, that you lie under, to walk circumspectly, in your whole conversation; watching against youthful lusts, evil company, sins, and snares from the world, and the devil.

Your affectionate Mother, K.H.

Far removed from every thing ascetic, and exclusive, Mr. Henry delighted in select and suitable company, and notices, in one of his communications, the great advantage he found in his studies while at Gray's Inn, "by the society to which he was linked." He mentions also, his attendance upon a divinity disputation kept up weekly in an afternoon, by Mr. Morton's young men, about six or eight of them, when scattered from him; at which Mr. Glascock, a very worthy, ingenious young minister, presided. It was, he says, well managed, and the question he mentions to have heard discussed – *An fide sola justificemur?* – was affirmed much against the Baxterian way: namely, *"faith justifies, not as a condition, but an instrument."*

In subjects of that nature, connected as they were, and ever ought to be, with practical godliness, Mr. Henry found his chief delight. Nor were any pursuits of a miscellaneous, or literary, or legal description, allowed to diminish supreme attention to the great things of God's law. One further instance of his excellent spirit at this early age must suffice.

None (the reference is to his father's letters) hath been a messenger of evil tiding, for which let the name of God have all the glory; and let us still be prepared for evil tidings, not knowing what a day may bring forth. If we can make sure uninterrupted peace and tranquility in the other world, we have no great reason to complain of the interruptions of this world. It is the lower region of the air that is liable to variety of weathers, while the upper region enjoys a constant calm. And are we moving thitherward? And do we hope to be there shortly, where all tears are wiped away from the eyes, and all sorrow eternally banished from the heart? And shall we perplex ourselves about the little, little trifles of this vain empty world, the things whereof are vanity in the having, and vexation of spirit in the losing, nor ever will, or can, afford that content and satisfaction which men expect, and count upon, in the enjoyment of them; and which too few seek where it is to be had?

All his letters from Gray's Inn discover to great advantage his filial attentions; they convey a pleasant impression of his observation and prudence; they demonstrate his zeal for the acquisition of useful knowledge; and they exhibit, in the most unexceptional manner, his mental acuteness, his personal piety, and the consecration of every successive acquirement to the Redeemer's honour. They were worthy of Phillip Henry's son, and must have oftentimes proved an occasion of rejoicing, and praise before the heavenly throne. It is easy, in imagination, to behold the venerable parents perusing, week after week, those epistles of grace, and mingling with overflowing tenderness their mutual gratulations that their beloved child, though at so great a distance from them, was walking in the truth. And if fears as to the abandonment of the ministry continued to haunt the mind of his anxious mother, or any other friend, (which is said to have been the case), it is difficult to conceive of any device more judicious, or better adapted for their removal, than a succession of such letter.

In communications made by Mr. Henry from the great city, no reference is made to any other preachers than those of the established church: and as a reason for this it may not be irrelevant to state, that during his abode at Gray's Inn, such was the perplexity of the times – churches in connection with the ecclesiastical establishment were the exclusively authorized places of Christian concourse. But ever mindful of his father's counsels, (the more explicitly given, probably on this very account), to say nothing of his own inclinations, he repaired thither, not only on the day, but as opportunity served, during the week also. It was his complaint that he could not conveniently go so often as he would "to hear week-day sermons." And he adds, "There are not many desirable. Dr. Kiloton's are the best; but others often preach from him; and, which is most discouraging, he speaks so low that it is very difficult to hear him with understanding. I must keep the secret trade ageing, for there is not much to be going abroad."

Alluding to the services he attended on the Lord's Day he expressed himself most pleased with the discourses of Dr. Stillingfleet, at St. Andrew, Holborn, and Dr. Tillotson's at Lawrence Jury. None of these helps, however excellent in their kind, as they undoubtedly were, compensated for the loss of the heavenly manna enjoyed in his father's house; or as he often styled it, his "Broad Oak Sabbaths." Those who are enamored of that preaching which unfolds the glorious and sublime doctrines and precepts of revelation, in unceasing connection with the scenes of Calvary: (a mode of address which give to the pulpit exercises of the reformers, and of Philip Henry, and a host of other imitators, such as "rich and unequalled unction,") will understand the distinction; and, instead of accusing Mr. Henry of invidious comparisons, or even blaming him, he had, under such circumstances, indulged them, will compassionate his situation; nor will they fail to rejoice that the lines are now fallen to God's heritage in pleasanter places; and that within the pale of the established church, as well as without it, the number is not few of those who, having received the ministry of reconciliation, are "determined" to know nothing among men, "save Jesus Christ, and him crucified."

It would be anticipating a future division of the present work to delineate, in this early stage of it, Mr. Henry's character and conduct as a friend. At the same time in order that has been adopted requires, before proceeding further, the introduction of a letter addressed by him to one whom he regarded in that sacred character. The person referred to is Mr. George Illidge of Nantwich, whose "heart the Lord" having "opened" when very young, and who enjoying few religious advantages at home, attended the ministry at Broad Oak: his seriousness and zeal secured him a welcome, and his excellent conduct unfeigned respect. It is not known when the acquaintance between the two youths commenced, but it was turned to a good account; and became the means of eliciting dispositions the most strictly virtuous and useful. Were not the reader informed that the writer of the letter was only in his twenty-fourth year, he would almost fancy himself listening to the grave, and matured counsels of hoary and devout intelligence:

Gray's Inn, March 1, 1686
Dear Friend,

I think I remember, when I last saw you, I partly promised to write to you from hence, which I doubt I should either have forgotten, or have deferred the performance of, had I not been lately reminded of it in a letter from one of my sisters. And now I have put my pen to paper to perform my promise, what shall I write? News we have little, or not considerable; and you know I was never a good newsmonger; and to fill a letter with idle, impertinent compliments is very useless, and will pass but ill in the account another day; for sure; if idle words must be accounted for, idle letters will not be left out of the reckoning. What if I should, therefore (having no other business at present), give you a few serious lines, which may perhaps be of some spiritual advantage to your soul? I have been lately thinking of some great Scripture truths or principles; the firm practical belief of which would be of great use to a Christian, and have a mighty influence upon the right ordering of his conversation; and they are some such as these:

1) That "all things are naked and open to him with whom we have to do," Hebrews 4:13; a firm belief of God's all-seeing eye always upon us, wherever we are, and whatever we are doing, would be a mighty aweband upon the spirit, to keep it serious and watchful. Dare I omit such a known duty, or commit such a known sin while I am under the eye of a just and holy God, who hates sin, and cannot endure to look on iniquity? It was a significant name which Hagar gave to the well where God appeared unto her, Gen 16:14. "Beer-lahai-roi." The well of him that lives and sees me; for she said, 5:13. "Thou God seest me." This would be a very seasonable thought, when we are entering either into duty or into temptation, to lift up our heart in these words, "Thou God seest me," and, therefore, let duty be carefully done, and sin carefully avoided, considering that he who sees all now, will tell all shortly before angels and men, in the say "when the secrets of all hearts shall be made manifest," Luke 12:2.

2) That our adversary, the devil, "as a roaring lion goes about continually, seeking whom he may devour," 1 Peter 5:8. We do not see him , and therefore we are apt to be secure; but certainly it is so, and therefore we should never be off our watch. What folly is it for us to be slumbering and sleeping, while such a cruel crafty enemy is walking and watching, and ready to do us mischief? You know when Saul slept, he lost his spear and his cruse of water. Many a Christian has lost his strength and comfort by sleeping.

3) That "the grace of God, which bringeth salvation, teacheth us to deny ungodliness and worldly lusts, and to live soberly, righteously, and godly, " Titus 2:11–12. That the Gospel, as it is a Gospel of grace, requires a holy conversation, Christ died to save his people from their sins, not in their sins. The Gospel hath its commands as well as its promises and privileges, and, therefore there is such a thing as a Gospel becoming conversation, Phil. 1:27; living up to the Gospel love, as well as Gospel light.

4) That "Jesus Christ died to deliver us from this present evil world," Gal 1:4. We are apt to think Christ died to deliver us only from hell, and if that were done we are well enough. No, Christ died to deliver us from this world. So if our hearts are glued to present things, and our affections fixed upon them, we do directly thwart the great design of our Lord Jesus Christ in coming to save us.

5) That "we are not under the law, but under grace," Rom 6:14. This is a mighty encouragement to us to abound in all manner of Gospel obedience, to consider that we are not under the law that required personal perfect obedience, and pronounced a curse for the least failure, but under the covenant of grace, which accepts the willing mind, and makes sincerity our perfection. What a sweet word is grace! What a savor doth it leave upon the lips! And to be under grace, under the sweet and easy rule of grace how comfortable it is!

6) That the soul is the man, and that the soul is the man, and that condition of life is best for us that is best for our souls. It fares with the man as it fares with his soul.

He is the truly healthful man whose soul prospers and is in health. He is the truly rich man, not who is rich in houses, land and money, but who is rich in faith, and an heir of the kingdom. Those are our best friends that are friends to our souls, and those are worst enemies that are enemies to our souls; for the soul is the man, and if the soul be lost, all is lost.

7) That "we have here no continuing city," Heb. 13:14. That we are in this world as in an inn, and must be gone shortly. Why should we then conform ourselves to this world, or cumber ourselves with it. Should we not then sit loose to it, as we do to an inn? And what if we have but ill accommodation. It is but an inn; it will be better at home. If our lodging here were hard and cold, it is no great matter, or lodging in our Father's house will be soft and warm enough.

8) That "every man at his best estate is altogether vanity," Psalm 39:5. We ourselves are so, and, therefore, we must not dote on any temporal enjoyments. We carry our lives as well as our other comforts in our hands, and know not how soon they may slip through our fingers. Every one is vanity, therefore cease from man, from fearing him and from trusting him.

9) That "God shall bring every work into judgment, with every secret thing, whether it be good or evil," Eccl. 12:14. That every man must shortly give an account to God. The serious thoughts of this would engage us to do nothing now, which will not pass well in our accounts then.

10) That "the wages of sin is death; but the gift of God is eternal life, through Jesus Christ our Lord," Rom. 6:23. Heaven and hell are great things indeed, and should be much upon our hearts, and improved by us as a spur of constraint to put us upon duty, and a bridle of restraint to keep us from sin. We should labor to see reality and weight in invisible things, and live as those that must be somewhere forever. See hell the wages and due desert of sin, and heaven the free gift of God through Jesus Christ.

Many other such truths might be mentioned, which those are acquainted with the Scriptures, and with their own hearts, need not be directed to. It would be of use to a Christian to take some one such truth into his mind in the morning, and upon occasion in the day, to be thinking frequently of it, and to say, "This is the truth of the day; this is to be a spur to this day's duties; and this is to be the subject of this day's meditation, and of this day's discourse, as we have opportunity." I am apt to think such a course would be very beneficial. Hereby a good stock of truths might be treasured up against a time of need, and we might be able to bring forth new and old for the benefit of others. For certainly it is our duty, as we have ability and opportunity, to help our friends and neighbors in their spiritual necessities, to strengthen the weak, confirm the wavering, direct the doubting, and comfort the feeble-minded, to say to them that are of a fearful heart, be strong.

Discourse to this purpose, how profitable would it be both to ourselves and others, and how much better would it pass in our account another day, than a great deal of that vain impertinent talk which fills up the time of too many professors when they come together. And I fear it is a fault more acknowledged than amended.

I remember to have read, that when the famous Bishop Usher and Dr. Preston, who were intimate friends, were talking together; after much discourse of learning and other things, the bishop would say – Come, Doctor, one word of Christ now before we part. Christians who owe their all to Christ, should be often talking of him. And surely those that know the worth of souls cannot but be concerned for their ignorant careless neighbors, which concernedness should put us upon doing all we can to help them out that condition. And if there be any that are asking the way to Zion, with their faces thitherward, pray tell them the way. Tell them,

1) There is but one gate into this way, and that is the straight gate of sound conversion.

2) Tell them that the way is narrow, that there is not elbowroom for their lusts. Let them know the worst of it. And that those who would be good soldiers of Christ must endure hardness.

3) Tell them, notwithstanding this, it is a way of pleasantness; it gives spiritual, though It prohibits sensual pleasures.

4) Tell them there is life eternal at the end, and let them be assured that one hour of joy in heaven, will make them amends for an age of trouble upon earth.

They that saw in tears shall reap in joy. He that goeth forth and weepeth, bearing precious seed, shall doubtless come again with rejoicing, bringing his sheaves with him. Psalm 126:5-6.

I am at present somewhat indisposed, and have written confusedly, and, therefore, I would have you keep it to yourself. I hope you will not forget me at the throne of grace, for I have need of your prayers. Give my affectionate respects to your wife and mother and sister; to Mrs. Elizabeth Wilson, who I take for granted, is with you; to Mr. Hopkins, my Aunt Burroughs and Richard Gill, and all the rest of my very good friends, if with you, as if particularly named. I have nothing more to add, but to commend you all to God and to the word of his grace, which is able to build you up, and to give you an inheritance among all them that are sanctified. I am,

Your Real Friend
Matthew Henry

P.S. I wrote to Mr. Wilson a fortnight ago, but have heard nothing from him.

CHAPTER 4

A.D. 1686 to A.D. 1687
His Return to Broad Oak, His Preaching, Visits Chester,
Invitations to the Ministerial Office There, Returns to London,
Licenses to Preach Granted, Urged to Settle in London, Quits
Gray's Inn, Self-Examination Before Ordination, Episcopal
Ordination Considered, His Decision in Favor of
Nonconformity, Confession of Faith, His Ordination,
Return to Broad Oak

n the month of June 1686, Mr. Henry returned to Broad
Oak. It was quickly apparent that his law pursuits had in
no wise diverted him from his original design; the study of
the Scriptures was an interesting to him as ever; and his
desire to "make known the mystery of the gospel," instead of
being weakened, had increased; it was more intense, and more
enlightened.

Being invited by his friend, Mr. George Illidge, to Nantwich,
he preached there several evenings to a considerable audience and
with encouraging success. On the last of those occasions his subject
was Job 37:22, "With God is terrible Majesty." Mr. Illidge
observed a notoriously wicked man present. With a view to
ascertain the effects of his attendance, he called upon him the
next morning. The man and his wife were in tears. *His* convictions

of sin and sense of danger seemed to be pungent and salutary; and his apprehensions of the majesty and wrath of God awfully vivid; the woman wept from sympathy. Mr. Illidge offered up "supplications." Communicated suitable encouragement; and pressed an earnest warning against wicked company. The man taught his wife to read, practiced family worship, often accompanied Mr. Illidge to Broad Oak; and after a prudent lapse of time, was admitted to the Lord's Table. In appearance the change was universal and entire; religious joy was sometimes avowed; and for several years, he seemed to "run well." His wife, in judgment of charity, died "in the faith," but, he, Alas! after time, being "hindered," was guilty of very sad defection, and quitted the narrow way; it is feared – forever.

In such connection as this, how consummate appears the wisdom of apostolic counsel – " Let him that thinketh he standeth take heed lest he fall!" And how necessarily are self-examination, holy watchfulness, and unceasing prayer enforced.

It is natural to suppose that the encouragement, which thus attended Mr. Henry's first efforts, increased his satisfaction in the decision he has made for the ministry. Nor is it improbable that the issue, as narrated, may account, in some measure, for the uncommon seriousness, discernment, and caution, which especially in his later papers, everywhere displayed itself in relation to the nature and evidences of personal religion. "A hypocrite," he sometimes remarked, "is one who goes creditable to hell – unsuspected, one who *seems* religious, and that is all." And to the enquiry, "What is the reason of the apostasy of so many who began well?" He would answer, "They never had the law in their hearts; they never acted from a *principle*. A man may not only have the shape of a Christian, but he may have it drawn so much to the life as that it may pass for a living Christian; there may be some kind of breath, a motion, and sense; and yet he that knows our works may say, 'Thou art dead.' The scale in such a case hangs in a manner even, but sin and lust at last preponderate. Hypocrisy is the way to apostasy, and apostasy is the great proof of hypocrisy." But "those," said he, "who are sincere are willing and desirous to be tired; *they* desire the day of judgment, because everything will then be manifested; *they* are frequent and inward in secret duty; *they* have a low and mean opinion of themselves and their own performances; *they* bewail and mourn over the remains of hypocrisy; *they* make the Word of God their counselor in all doubtful cases; *they* ascribe the glory of all to Christ, and take none to themselves; *they* keep themselves from their own iniquity."

Mr. Henry's determination for the ministry was now fixed; and having been on a visit at Chester, and being invited by some friends there to preach to them in and evening, "the liberty not being granted," he complied; and two or three successive evenings, at the house of Mr. Henthorne, a sugar-baker, and at other houses, "he received all that came, preaching the kingdoms of God, and teaching the things which concern the Lord Jesus Christ with all confidence, no man forbidding him."

These services tended to produce a most favorable impression upon the minds of the hearers in reference to Mr. Henry's ministerial qualifications, and to the present circumstances of the dissenters in that city occasioned earnest desire that he might become their pastor.

By the death of two valuable ministers, Mr. Cook and Mr. Hall, a loss had been sustained, which their survivor, Mr. Harvey, an aged divine, was unable to repair. On account of the legislative restrictions, he had indeed preached very privately, and some of those who were connected with the former minister were not in regular communion with him.

About the latter end of the year 1686, a rumor of disposition in the government to grant indulgence became very current. This encouraged several of the persons last referred to, to wait upon Mr. Henry at Broad Oak and to urge upon him that, in the event of the expected liberty, he would "take the oversight of them in the Lord."

After advising with his father, he gave them encouragement, provided Mr. Harvey would give *his* consent to it. He informed them, at the same time, that he was speedily to return to the metropolis, and that he should reside there for some months. To all his terms, so that their request was compiled with, they assented.

Under such circumstances he once more, January 25, 1686-87, set out towards London, accompanied by the only son of his friend Mr. Hunt.

The first important news, which reached him in the great city, was that the king had empowered certain individuals to grant licenses exempting the several persons, named in a schedule annex, from prosecution or molestation. 1. For not taking oaths of allegiance and supremacy; or 2. Upon the prerogative writ for 20 pounds sterling a month, or upon outlawries, or excom Capiened. For the said causes; 3. For not coming to church; or 4. For not receiving the sacrament; or 5. By reason of their conviction for recusancey or exercise of their religion, a command to stay proceedings already had begun for any of the caused aforesaid. The price of one license was 10 pounds sterling. For a single person, but if several joined, the price was 16 pounds sterling, and eight might join in taking out one license.

Few dissenters applied, but the disposition of the court being sufficiently understood, many of them began to assemble. In the latter end of February, Mr. Henry wrote to his father, "That Mr. Faldo, a worthy minister of the congregational persuasion, had preached publicly in Mr. Sclater's meeting-house in Moorfields, both morning and afternoon, to many hundreds of people, who were much pleased at the reviving at the work."

When Mr. Henry's resolutions for the ministry were generally known in the metropolis, the reverenced and learned Mr. Woodcock applied to him, in favor of a lecture then instituting, chiefly for young persons. But he modestly declined the offer; he thought his services might be most wanted in the country, and might be more suitable there than in or about the city.

Followed by the congregation at Chester with importunate letters, as well as the personal communication of Mr. Henthourn, expressive of their desires for his settlement among them with the least possible delay, he soon returned from Gray's Inn in order to give himself the more entirely unto "the Gospel of God." His departure from that honorable society, like his entering and continuance among them, was worth of his high vocation. He took farewell of his legal associates in an excellent discourse from 2 Thes. 2:1, latter part. "And your gathering together unto him."

The business of ordination was next attended to with exemplary deliberation and seriousness. Not only did he avail himself of the counsel of his friends, particularly the Reverends F. Tallents and James Owen, but for more permanent advantage, he sketched a discourse on 1 Timothy 4:15, "give thyself wholly to them" – in which he stated the nature, and several parts of the ministerial work, and with it is for a man to give himself *wholly* to them *en toutois isthi*, to be wholly *in* them; he likewise composed a paper which he designated "Serious Self Examination Before Ordination."

That "paper" is so general in its nature and presents a combination of vigilance and wisdom so unusual and complete, as, notwithstanding the length of it, to render its insertion imperative.

It will reprove, if not convince, of awful presumption, all such as have inconsiderately rushed into the most responsible of all offices. To those who are contemplating the ministry, or who are about to enter upon its active and arduous duties, it will prove a friendly monitor, a useful test, and all-important directory. While, as a full exposition of Mr. Henry's own motives and principles, in reference to the same great "work," upon which he was entering, it is invaluable. It shows a temper of mind so conscientious, so humble, and so enlightened as to be perfectly apostolic, he magnified the office, but abased himself. And being unstained, visibly at least, with even common follies of youth, the severity of his self-judgment becomes additionally observable and impressive. The sins of the heart were, in his apprehension, more humiliating than gross acts of wickedness appear to be in the eyes of many.

As the reader proceeds through the volume, he will probably think it worthwhile to keep this interesting document in view, and to compare the prayers, and purposes, and resolutions it exhibits, with Mr. Henry's subsequent history, deportment, and success.

> *That is very requisite (he writes) for a man to examine himself seriously at such a time, will readily be granted by those who consider the nature of the ordinance, and of that work into which it is a solemn entrance.*
>
> *Search me, O God, and know my heart, try me and know my thoughts, and see if there be any wicked way in me, and lead me in the way everlasting.*

It is worthwhile for a man at such a time deliberately to ask himself, and, having asked, conscientiously to answer the six following questions:

Q. I. What am I?

This is a needful question, because in ordination I give up myself to God in a peculiar manner; and will God accept the torn, and the blind, and the lame? Surely no. The sacrifice must be searched before it is offered, that it might be sure to fit its end. Now, though the truth of grace is not perhaps necessary to the esse of a minister (for Judas himself was an apostle), yet it is necessary to the bene esse. A man cannot be a good minister without it. And therefore come, my soul, let us enquire, what am I? And let the inquiry be strict and serious, for a mistake here is fatal.

1. Have I ever been inwardly convinced of the lost and undone condition in which I was born, that I was by nature a child of wrath, even as others? Did I ever see myself wallowing in my blood, in a forlorn, out-cast, helpless state, lost and ruined forever without Christ?

2. Was I ever deeply humbled before the Lord for the original sin that I was born in, and the numberless actual transgressions in heart and life that I have been guilty of? Hath sin been bitter to my soul, hath my heart been broken for it, and hath my sorrow been of the right kind; hath the sight of a broken Savior broken my heart?

3. Have I sincerely closed with the Lord Jesus Christ, by a true and lively faith, taken him to be mine, and resigned up myself to him to be his? Have I accepted of Christ upon gospel terms, to be my Prince to rule, and

Savior to save me? Have I renounced all others, and resolved to cleave to the Lord Jesus Christ, let what will come? Is Christ precious to me; is he dearer to me than anything in the world besides? Could I be freely willing to part with all for Christ, and count everything but loss that I may win in Christ?

4. Have I a real hatred of every sin in myself, as well as in others? Have I not beloved lust, which I would have spared, or corruption, which I would have to remain unmortified? Doth sin appear sin in my eyes, and can I say with David that, "I hate every false way?" Are the remainders of indwelling corruption a burden to me? Do I long to be rid of sin? Are my resolutions sincere and my endeavors serious against sin, and all appearances of it and that because it is against God?

5. Have I a real love for holiness? Do I press after it, and earnestly desire to be more holy, using holy ordinances for this end, that I may be made thereby more and more holy? Am I fond of holy ordinances and holy people, and that because they are holy? Have I a real value for holiness wherever I see it? Do I delight in God's holy Word and that because it is holy? Do I call the holy Sabbath a delight and that because it is holy? Do I love the brethren because they are holy, and love them the better the more holy they are? Do I long to be made perfect in holiness in that other world?

To these weighty questions, my poor soul (though compassed about with manifold weakness, wants, and corruptions) doth, as in the presence of God, the Searcher of the hearts, give a comfortable answer, and if these be the signs and characters of true grace, I trust my heart doth not deceive me when it tells me, I have some sparks of it, though swimming in a sea of corruption. "But who am I, O Lord God, and what is my house, that thou has brought me hitherto? And yet as if this had been but a small thing, thou hast spoken concerning thy servant for a great while yet to come. And in this manner of man, O Lord God!"

Q. II. What have I done?

This is also a needful question, that searching and examining what hath been amiss, I may repent of it, and make even reckonings in the blood of Christ, that I may not come loaded with old guilt to put on a new character, especially such a character as this. Aaron and his sons must offer a sin-offering to make atonement before they were consecrated, Lev. 8:34. For he that comes near to God under guilt of sin unrepented of, comes to his peril, and the nearer, the more dangerous.

And therefore, O my soul, what have I done? My soul cannot but answer, I have sinned, I have perverted that which is right, and it hath not profited me. And in a serious reflection I cannot but observe.

1. What a great deal of precious time I have trifled away and misspent in folly and vanity, and things that do not profit. Time is a precious talent, which my Master hath entrusted me with and yet how long hath it been buried, and how much hath it run waste?

2. How many precious opportunities (which are the cream of time) have I lost and not improved through my own carelessness? Golden seasons of grace which I have enjoyed, but have let them slip, and been little bettered by

them; Sabbaths, sermons, sacraments that have come and gone, and left me as they found me? My fruit hath not been answerable to the soil I have been planted in. How often have I been ignorant under enlightening means; hard and cold under softening and warming ordinances; trifling and careless when I have been dealing with God about the concerns of my soul and eternity?

3. How often have I broken my covenants with God, my engagements, promises, and resolutions of new and better obedience, resolved against this and that since and yet fallen into again; many a time returning to folly, after God hath spoken peace to me, and after I have spoken promises to God? Presently after a sacrament, how have I returned to former vanity, folly, sensuality, and frothiness, to former pride, passion, and worldliness; so soon have I forgot the vows of God?

4. How unprofitable have I been in my converse with others; how few have been the better for me; how many the worse for me; how little good have I done; how little light have I cast in a sphere wherein God hath placed me; how little have I been concerned for the souls of others; and how little useful have I been to them? How vain and light have I been many times in my words and carriage, going down the stream of folly with others, when my seriousness might have stemmed the tide? How seldom hath my speech been with grace, and how often with corruption, not seasoned with salt?

5. In the general, how forgetful have I been of God and his Word, and of myself and my duty, and of the great concernments for my soul and eternity, living too much, as if I had no God to serve, and never a soul to save!

I might mention many particular miscarriages, which I have been guilty of in my heart and life, and which are known to God and my own heart; and yet after all, "Who can understand his errors? Cleanse thou me, O God, from my secret sins; have mercy upon me, O God, according to thy loving-kindness, and according to the multitude of thy tender mercies, blot out all my transgressions, for the sake of the Lord, my righteousness."

Q. III. From what principles do I act in this undertaking?

This is also a very material enquiry in every action, to ask whence it comes, especially in so great a turn of life as this.

1. I hope I can say that it is of faith; and I am concerned it should be so, for "whatever is not of faith is sin." It is good for every man that he be fully persuaded in his own mind. Now,

(1.) I am fully persuaded that Jesus Christ, as King of the Church, hath appointed and established the office of the ministry, to continue in a constant succession to the end of time, for the edification of the Church, and has promised to be with them always to the end of the world. So that the office of the ministry is no human invention, but a divine institution.

(2.) I am fully persuaded that no man ought to thrust himself upon the work of the ministry, without a clear call from God to it. Not that we are to expect such extraordinary calls as the apostles had, but with the ordinary call, by the meditation of ministers, who, as such, are authorized by Christ to try the abilities of those who offer themselves to the ministry. And if they find them fit, then to set them apart to that work, in a solemn manner, by the imposition of hands with fasting and prayer – and that the laying on of the hands of the presbytery is the most regular way of ordination, and most agreeable to Scripture.

(3.) I bless God that I am pretty well satisfied with the clearness of my call to the work, though I cannot but be sensible of great weakness and insufficiency for these things; yet I find that what abilities God has been pleased to give me (and let him have all the glory), do evidently look towards this work, so that if I be in any measure qualified for any service, it is for this. I find also mine own inclination strongly bent towards it, and that it hath been so ever since I knew anything, and especially I consider that I have been much excited and encouraged to it by divers (both ministers and others) able, skillful, and faithful, fit to judge, by whom my purposes have been much confirmed. All which goes a great way towards the clearing of my call, and the earnest invitation I have lately had to stated work in a particular place, doth much help to clear my call to the work in general.

2. I hope I can say, I act herein from a principle of true zeal for the glory of God; that this great thing I do, as I should do everything to the glory of God, that my light may shine, that Christ's kingdom may be advanced, the power of godliness kept up, the Word of life held forth; by all which God is glorified. The desire of my soul is, that "whether I live I may live to the Lord, or whether I die I may die to the Lord and that living and dying I may be the Lord's"

3. I hope I can say that I act herein from a principle of real love to precious souls, for the good of which I would

gladly spend and be spent. Methinks I love the precious souls of men so well, that I would fain be an instrument of convincing the unconvinced, converting the unconverted, and building up saints in holiness and comfort. I hope I know so much of the worth of souls, that I should think it a greater happiness to gain one soul to the Lord Jesus Christ, than to gain mountains of silver and gold to myself.

Q. IV. What are the ends that I aim at in this great undertaking?

It is a common saying, that the end specifies the action; and, therefore, it is of great consequence to fix that right, that the eye may be single, for otherwise it is an evil eye. A bye and base end will certainly spoil the acceptableness of the best actions that can be performed.

Now what is the mark I aim at in this great turn of my life? Let conscience be faithful herein, and let the Searcher of hearts make me known to myself.

1. I think I can say with confidence that I do not design to take up the ministry as a trade to live by or to enrich myself by, out of the greediness of filthy lucre. No! I hope I aim at nothing but souls; and if I gain those, through I should lose all my worldly comforts by it, I shall reckon myself to have made a good bargain.

2. I think I can say with as much assurance, that my design is not to get myself a name amongst men, or to be talked of in the world, as one that makes somewhat of a figure. No, that is poor business. If I have but a good name with God, I think I have enough, though among men I be reviled and have my name trampled upon as mire in the streets. I prefer the good Word of my Master far before the good word of my fellow servants.

3. I can appeal to God, that I have no design in the least to maintain a party or to keep up any schismatic faction; my heart rises against the thoughts of it. I hate dividing principles and practices, and whatever others are, I am for peace and healing; and if my blood would be sufficient balsam, I would gladly part with the last drop of it, for the closing up of the bleeding wounds of differences that are amongst true Christians. Peace is such a precious jewel, that I would give anything for it by truth. Those who are not bitter in their contendings for or against little things, and zealous in keeping up names of division and maintaining parties, are of a spirit which I understand not. Let not my soul come into their secret.

My ends then are according to my principles, and I humbly appeal to God concerning the integrity of my heart in them.

(1.) That I deliberately place the glory of God as my highest and ultimate end, and if I can be but any way instrumental to promote that, I shall gain my end and have my desire. I do not design to preach myself, but as a faithful friend of the bridegroom, to preach Christ Jesus my Lord, as the standard-bearer among ten thousands. And if I can but bring people better to know, and love, and honour Christ, I have what I design.

(2.) That in order to the glory of God, I do sincerely aim at the good precious souls. God is glorified when souls are benefited, and gladly would I be instrumental in that blessed work. I would not be a barren tree in a vineyard, cumbering the ground; but by God's help, I would do some good in the world, and I know no greater good I can be

capable of than doing good to souls. I desire to be an instrument in God's hand, softening hard hearts, quickening dead hearts, humbling proud hearts, conforming sorrowful hearts; and if I may be enabled to do this, I have what I would have. If God denies me this, and suffers me to labor in vain (though I should get hundreds a year by my labor) it would be the constant grief and trouble of my soul; and if I do not gain souls, I shall enjoy all my other gains with very little satisfaction. Though even in that case it would be some comfort that the reward is not according to the success, but according to the faithfulness. But I seriously profess it, if I could foresee that my ministry would be wholly unprofitable, and that I should be on instrument of good to souls, though in other respects I might get enough by it, I would rather beg my bread from door to door than undertake this great work.

Q. V. *What do I want?*

And what special things do I now desire of God, the God of all grace? When I know whither to go for supplies. I am concerned to enquire what my necessities are. The requests I have to put to God are such as these.

i. That he would fix and confirm and establish my heart in my dedication of myself to the work of the ministry. My carnal heart is sometimes ready to suggest to me that I had better take some other way of living that would be less toilsome and perilous, and more pleasant and gainful; and the devil joins issue with my heart, and sets before me the profits and preferments I might possibly have in another way, and the trouble and reproach I am like to meet with in this way. Now, O that my God would restrain the tempter, and satisfy me in my choice, and furnish me with suitable considerations with which to answer such suggestions; and in order thereunto, give me believing views of eternity, having deliberately devoted myself to the work of the Lord, keep it always in the imagination of the thoughts of my heart, and establish my way before him.

ii. That he would in a special manner be present with me in the ordinance of dedication, filling my heart with such an experimental sense of the excellency of Christ, and the comforts of the Holy Ghost, as that I may have cause to remember it by a good token as long as I live; that he would manifest himself to me, mark me for himself, and leave some sign behind him in my soul, that may make it evident God was there of a truth; that he would give me a comfortable earnest of the success of my ministry by a signal owning of me in my entrance upon it.

iii. That he would fit and qualify me for this great work to which he is calling me. When Saul was anointed king, "God gave him another heart, a heart fit for kingship." I would fain have another heart, a heart fit for ministerial work, filled with ministerial gifts and graces.

1. Ministerial gifts. Every good gift comes from above, and therefore I look upwards for gifts of knowledge in the mysteries of religion, gifts of utterance to explain and apply myself to others, and speak the Word with boldness. I have also need of prudence and discretion to order the affairs of my ministry.

2. Ministerial graces. Faith, love to go and souls. Zeal for God's glory and souls' good; patience to do, to suffer, and to wait; an inward sense of the weight of the things I speak of. Two graces I do more especially beg of God,

(1.) Sincerity. That I may be really as good as I seem to be; that inward impressions may always be answerable to outward expressions in all my ministrations; that my

eye may be single, my heart upright; and my ends fixed; that I may not cast the least glance at any low, bye, base end.

(2.) Humility. That God would hide pride from me and clothe me with humility, that I may see that I have nothing (except my sins) but what I have received; that I may never please myself with the praises of men, but hand up all the praise to God; that the least workings of pride and conceitedness may be checked in me.

iv. That God would open a door of opportunity to me, and make my way plain before me, that the call I have to my work may be clear and satisfying, and that God would bless and succeed my endeavors for the good of souls.

Q. VI. What are my purposes and resolutions for the future?

This is also a requisite enquiry, when I am to put on a new character, and one so honorable. What shall I do that I may "walk worthy of the vocation wherewith I am called?"

1. I purpose and resolve by the grace of God, that I will have no more to do with the unfruitful works of darkness, seeing it will not only be my duty as a Christian, but my office as a minister to reprove them rather. "Pride, passion, worldliness, wantonness, and vanity are things the man of God must flee" I Tim. 6:11. What have I to do any more with idols? What have I to do any more with sin? By the grace of God, it shall not have dominion over me. The ministerial character will add a great aggravation to every sin; and therefore, "O my soul! Stand in awe and sin not."

2. I purpose and resolve that, by the grace of God, I will abound more than ever in all manner of Gospel obedience; that I will strive to be more humble, serious, and watchful, and self-denying, and live more above the world and the things of it; that I will pray with more life, and read the Scriptures with more care, and not be slothful in business, but fervent in spirit, serving the Lord; that I will abound in good discourse, as I have ability and opportunity with prudence; endeavoring as much as I can "to adorn the doctrines of God my Savior in all things."

3. In particular, I resolve in the strength, spirit and grace of Jesus Christ my Lord, to consider well and perform my ordination vows; to hold fast the form of sound words, which I have heard and received in "faith and love which is in Christ Jesus;" and never to let go any truth, whatever it cost me; ever owning the Scriptures as "the only rule of faith and practice."

That I will wholly give up myself to the work, and employ all my talents in the service of God and the soul with seriousness and sedulity: that I will not only preach, but to the utmost of my power, defend the truths of God against all opposers, and do all I can to convince or silence gainsayers.

That I will endeavor to maintain not only truth, but peace and unity in the church of God; that I will patiently bear and thankfully accept of the admonitions of my brethren, and esteem such smitings as an excellent oil that shall not break my head.

That if ever God shall call me to the charge of a family, I will walk before my house in a perfect way, with an upright heart, not doubting but then God will come unto me; my house shall be a Bethel; wherever I have a tent, God shall have an altar; and Joshua's resolution shall be mine, "Whatever others do, I and my house will serve the Lord."

That if ever God calls me to the charge of a flock, I resolve, by his grace, with all possible diligence to lay out myself for a spiritual good of those over whom God shall set me; and in conversation I will endeavor to be an example to the flock going before them in the way to heaven, and will improve all the interest I have and all the authority I may have, for the honour of God and the good of souls and the edifying the mystical body of Christ.

Whatever opposition I may meet with in my work by the grace of God, I will not be terrified with it, nor frightened by the winds and clouds from sowing and reaping, but in the strength of my God, go in the midst of discouragements; and if God shall call me to sufferings, which I promise to expect and count upon, I will, by the grace of God, suffer cheerfully and courageously for the truths and ways of Christ, "Choosing rather, with Moses, to suffer afflictions with the people of God, than to enjoy the pleasures of sin, which are but for a season;" and I will esteem not only the crown of Christ, but reproach of Christ, greater riches than the treasures of Egypt, having respect to the recompense of reward.

This is the substance of what I promise in the strength of the Spirit in the grace of Christ, and having sworn by his strength, I will perform it, that I will keep his righteous judgments, and the Lord keep it always in the imagination of the thoughts of my heart, and establish my way before him.

Mr. Henry, by birth, by habit, and by conviction, was a non-conformist. But it having been suggested to him by a very worthy person with whom he had consulted, in reference to his intended ordination, that, possibly, it might be obtained episcopally, without those declarations, and oaths, to which so many of the wisest and best of men have objected, instead of even appearing to slight any peaceful overture, he willingly bestowed upon the subject the most deliberate and serious consideration.

His reasonings have been preserved. They show how far he was from being a mere-partisan, they demonstrate his title to the character of a judicious and impartial enquirer, and they furnish an example worthy of universal regard and limitation. No apology is thought necessary for preserving such a memorial; and it is so interwoven with the general narrative, and bears upon it so directly as scarcely to amount to a digression.

The question is – Whether it be advisable for one who hath devoted himself to the work of the ministry, but is by no means satisfied with the terms of conformity, to chose ordination by episcopal hands (if it may be had without any oaths or subscriptions according to the forms prescribed) rather than ordination by presbyters, as some time practiced by those of that persuasion?

The doubt is, not whether episcopal ordination be lawful, especially considering that the bishop may be looked upon therein as a presbyter, in conjunction with his com-presbyters, (and the validity of such ordination is sufficiently vindicated by the presbyterians in their Jus Divinium), but whether it be advisable or no?

1. *There is much to be said on one hand to prove it advisable; as,*

(1.) That episcopal ordination is established by the settled law of the land, and all other ordinations cessated, and made void by the same law

(2.) That the presbyterians do agree episcopal ordination to be valid, and have never urged any reordination in that case; but the episcopal party generally deny ordinations by presbyters, without a consecrated bishop, to be valid, and require reordination. And,

(3.) That the time may come, when the Act of Uniformity being abolished, and the unscriptural terms taken away, episcopal ordination may qualify a man for public service in the church of Christ, when presbyterian ordination will not qualify him, but altogether incapacitate him, rendering him unfit for public service without at least a tacit renunciation of former ordination; which will not easily go down with a tender conscience.

2. *That which may be said against it as not advisable, rebussic, stantibus, is this:*

(1.) It is the tacit owning of the prelatic power of ordination, which the bishops usurp and claim as the sacred prerogative of their mitres; and will by no means allow to every gospel presbyter. And doth not our submission there to implicitly justify that usurpation?

(2.) The pretended fasts and too formal prayers with which the bishops manage that solemn service, rendered it less comfortable to a serious, honest heart that knows the weight of that work upon which ordination is an entrance.

(3.) The making of two distinct orders of deacons and priests is certainly owned by submitting to two distinct ordinations; a Scripture deacon seems to be ordained to serve tables, and not to give himself to the Word and prayer, and it is very hard for one who is self-devoted to the ministry, to say that he thinks himself moved by the Holy Ghost to take upon him the office of a deacon.

May this be got over by saying that Diakonos is a Gospel minister, and one ordained to be so is a minister to all intents and purposes, without faith or ordination? But here are three things that stumble us.

(1.) The ordainer intends it to be not so, as appears by the form of ordination.

(2.) The bishops ordain the deacons without any presbyters joining with him, which methinks is unscriptural.

(3.) Ordination by presbyters seems to me more regular and conformable to Scripture, and more becoming one that disowns a prelatic power.

And though an Episcopus Proseses be willingly owned as conveniently necessary, especially in ordination, whether one professedly claiming to be Episcopus Princeps, and acting as such, challenging the sole power of ordination Jure divino, only in the ordination of priests, calling in the assistance of com-presbyters, who herein stand but for ciphers, only to grace the solemnity; I say, whether such an one can be conscientiously owned as a spiritual father and an ordainer in Christ's name, by one who knows no such principality established by Christ, the King of his Church?

And, perhaps, the three things, which were urged before for it, may be thus answered.

To the 1ˢᵗ. That episcopal ordination is established by the law of the land; a knowing Christian will soon answer, that sufficeth not to make it alone valid and to invalidate all others, especially considering the practice of the best reformed churches, and that though the church is in the world, yet it is not of the world.

Besides, the same law that established episcopal ordination establishes the dislike oaths and subscriptions, as the terms of it; and if those be disowned, notwithstanding that authority, why must the other be owned and submitted to for the sake of that authority? And by the imposed terms a just measure may be taken of the imposing power.

To the 2ⁿᵈ. That presbyterians allow episcopal ordination, but the episcopal party disown the validity of presbyterian ordination there is a reply ready; that this argument is of no more weight in this case, that that of the papists is a much greater; that the protestants grant a possibility of salvation in their churches, but the papists deny it in the protestant churches; the more uncharitable, unchristian, and antichristian they. And, besides other men's judgments are not the rule of my practice; but let every man be fully persuaded in his own mind and prove his own work; so shall he have rejoicing in himself alone, and not in another.

To the 3ʳᵈ. That episcopal ordination may open a door of opportunity, when presbyterian ordination may shut it (which has most strength in it to direct in point of prudence) this may be said – that duty is ours; events are God's. It is *easy to say that this may be; and it is as easy to say that twenty other things may be; but future events are hid from us, and we know not what a day may bring forth; many unexpected changes have been seen in a short time.*

Who knows but the day may come when God will vindicate the honor of the presbyterian ordination, and when such a submission to episcopal ordination (by one in other things otherwise minded, and when that which is purer and better, might be had) may be branded with the same name of cowardice, and called mean, if not sinful compliance?

And if we must look forward, supposing the worse should come to the worst, it is but being silenced with good company; and I am apt to think, a man might comfortably suffer for these two truths (though in all probability they will never stand alone to be suffered for).

1. That ordination by presbyters is (though not the only valid) yet the best, most Scripturally regular, and, therefore, the most eligible ordination.

2. That Jesus Christ never meant to make any of his ministers really priests, sacerdotes, otherwise than spiritual priests, as all believers are; nor that he ever meant to necessitate all his ministers to be deacons, that is, but overseers of the poor, or at best but half ministers at the first.

It may also be considered, how far the integrity and uprightness of the heart, in acting herein, according to light bestowed after serious consideration and prayer, may administer matter of comfort and satisfaction in a day of suffering, the sharpest of which surely is a day of silencing;

and if that should be the issue of it Abimelech's plea might be renewed. Surely in the innocency of my heart I did this; and it may be remembered that when Paul was called to preach the gospel, immediately he consulted not with his flesh and blood.

Mine eyes are ever towards the Lord. Show me thy way, O Lord, and lead me in the plain path because of my observers.

April 28th, 1687

It is impossible to state with accuracy how the apprehension entertained and expressed by Mr. Henry's friend, and which induced the foregoing deliberations, arose; or, what was the measure of attention, which it deserved. Mr. Tong throws out a conjecture in connection with the Petition of the seven Bishops wherein a due temper towards dissenter is declared, but that seems to have no foundation, inasmuch as the Petition so referred to was not framed until the next year: 1688. The probability is that it was ascribable to the sudden courteousness evinced by the clergy towards nonconformists, because of the King's declaration for liberty of conscience: a declaration regarded by both parties in proof of his Majesty's progress towards Rome, and by the priesthood, as endangering their ecclesiastical preferences, as well as their secular importance.

Had Bishop Wilkins been alive, whose abatements in church affairs were notorious, it would have admitted of doubt whether in him, a prelate, might not have been found who, in compassion to his scrupulous brethren, would have relaxed canonical rigors a little at least. But that assumption is forbidden as to Dr. Wilkins by his demise long before the year 1687; and there seems little ground to cherish it as to anyone else, since Mr. Tong, who was ordained the year in question, not only professes his ignorance of any such accommodating bishop, but states that although kindly and pressingly invited to conformity by Dr. Fog, the pious and learned Dean of Chester, and treated by him with all the candor and civility of a Christian, a gentleman, and a divine; yet, no hint was ever thrown out of any dispensation of the terms of conformity. But all the Dean's discourses with him proceeded upon the lawfulness of those terms.

Let it have originated how it may, Mr. Henry, as we have seen, well considered the subject. Nor did he fail, according to his usual custom, to consult his father. The answer did not arrive until the deliberations, which have been cited, were closed, but it is satisfactory to know that the conclusion of *both* the eminent men in question was the same.

The point being decided Mr. Henry applied, without delay, to those friends in London, leading presbyterian divines, to whom he was best known; and, on the 9th of May 1687, "after due examination, and exercise performed," and a "full confession of his faith," he was solemnly, but privately, ordained "by imposition of hands, with fasting and prayer."

His confession of faith was as follows:

1. I believe that there is a God, an incomprehensible, perfect Being; a Spirit, infinite, eternal, unchangeable in his being, wisdom, power, holiness, justice, and truth, having his being of himself, and giving being to all things.
I believe that the living and true God is but one.
And that in the unity of the Godhead there is a trinity of persons, Father, Son, and Holy Ghost, and that these Three are but One God, the same in substance, equal in

power and glory. This is a revealed mystery, which I do believe, but cannot comprehend.

2. I believe that this God, who was God from eternity, did in the beginning of time, create or make out of nothing, the world, the heaven, and earth, and all things visible and invisible, and this he did by the Word of his eternal power, in the space of six days, and all very good.

And that the same God doth by the same power uphold and maintain the creatures in that being which he at first gave them, by the constant concurrence of providence, for by all things subsist, from the highest angel to the meanest worm.

And that this God in the right of creation and preservation, is the supreme absolute sovereign and rector of the world, ruling and governing all his creatures and all their actions, according to the wise, holy, and eternal counsel of his own will, to the praise and glory of his own name.

3. I believe that God, as the governor of the world, hath given a law to his rational creatures, according to which they are to walk, in order to their glorifying and enjoying him.

And that to the present sons of men, the Scriptures of the Old and New Testament are given, as the only rule to direct them both in faith and practice.

That this book of Scripture was given by inspiration of God, holy men speaking and writing as they were moved by the Holy Ghost.

And that this is the foundation of all revealed religion, and a perfect sufficient rule of direction to the children of men.

4. *I believe that God made man upright in his own image, consisting of knowledge, righteousness and holiness, with dominion over the inferior creatures.*

And that he made a covenant of works with him, promising life upon condition of a perfect and perpetual obedience, threatening death upon disobedience; and giving him a command of trial, not to eat of the tree of knowledge of good and evil upon pain of death.

5. *I believe that man being left to the freedom of his own will, at the instigation of the devil, sinned against God in eating the forbidden fruit and so fell from his estate of holiness and happiness; and he being a common person, all his posterity fell with him into an estate of sin and misery.*

That all of the sons of men are born children of disobedience, wanting original righteousness, and under a corruption of the whole nature, slaves to the flesh, the world, and the devil. And consequently children of wrath, obnoxious to the justice of God and the condemnation of the law. And that no creature is able to deliver them out of this condition.

6. *That God having from all eternity of his mere good pleasure, elected a remnant of mankind to everlasting life, did in infinite wisdom, find out a way to save and deliver them out of this sinful and miserable estate, and to bring them into a state of salvation; and that was by giving his only begotten Son to be their Redeemer, who being God, and one with the Father, according to the determinate counsel of God, did, in the fullness of time, take upon him our nature, a true body, and reasonable soul, and became man, being conceived by the Holy Ghost, born of the Virgin Mary, and called Jesus.*

I believe that this Jesus was the true Messiah, promised to and expected by the patriarchs under the Old Testament.

That he lived a holy, sinless life, and fulfilled all righteousness, being made under the law; that he underwent the miseries of this life, the wrath of God for our sins, and as a sacrifice for sin, died a cursed death upon the cross, thereby satisfying divine justice for the sins of man, and so reconciling us to God, and bringing in an everlasting righteousness.

That he was buried, and that having conquered death, he rose again the third day, and having commissioned his apostles and ministers to preach the Gospel to all the world, he ascended into heaven, where he is and continues to be, God and man, our prevailing Intercessor with the Father, and the glorified Head over all things to the church. In all this gloriously executing the three great offices of Prophet, Priest, and King.

7. I believe that in Jesus Christ there is a new covenant of grace made and published in the Gospel, the tenor of which is that all those who in the sight and sense of their lost and undone condition by nature come to Jesus Christ, and truly repent of all their sins, and heartily renounce the devil, the world, and the flesh, and all their own righteousness in point of justification, and by a lively faith cordially resign themselves to Jesus Christ as their Prince and Savior, covenanting to be his humble servants, and serving him accordingly, (sincerely though not perfectly), in all manner of Gospel obedience, shall have all their sins pardoned, their peace made, their persons justified, their natures sanctified, and their souls and bodies eternally save.

8. I believe that the Holy Spirit doth effectually apply the redemption purchased by Christ to all the elect, by working in them that which is required of them, convincing them of sin, enlightening their minds with the knowledge of Christ, renewing their wills, and not only persuading them, but powerfully enabling them to embrace Jesus Christ, as he is freely offered in the Gospel.

And that the same Spirit continues to dwell in them, and to work all their works in them, weakening their corruptions, strengthening their graces, guiding their way, comforting their souls, witnessing their adoption, enabling them more and more to die unto sin, and to live unto righteousness, and keeping them faithful and steadfast unto the end.

9. I believe that all true believers make up one invisible sanctified church, which is the mystical body of Jesus Christ, receiving vital influence from him as from their Head, and having communion in the same spirit of faith and love.

And that all those who by baptism outwardly profess faith in Christ, as the true Messiah, make up the universal visible Church of Christ on earth of which Jesus Christ is the only ruling Head, and as such hath instituted ordinances for worship and discipline, which are to be observed and kept pure in particular churches, and hath appointed the standing office of a Gospel ministry, for the due administration of those ordinances, to the edification of the Church, and hath promised to be with them always to the end of the world.

10. I believe that God hath appointed a day in the which he will judge the world in righteousness by that Man whom he hath ordained, who will raise the bodies of all men from the grave, and judge them all according to their works, sending the wicked, impenitent, and

unbelievers into everlasting punishment, and receiving the righteous into life eternal, to be together for ever with the Lord.

And that then he shall deliver up the kingdom to God, even the Father, that God may be all in all to eternity.

The reasons, which induced privacy, prevented Mr. Henry from receiving the usual certificate. His ordainers signed only the following brief testimonial. Some of them, Mr. Tong remarks, were "very aged and very cautious."

We, whose names are subscribe, are well assured that Mr. Matthew Henry is an ordained minister of the Gospel.
Sic Testor.
W. Wickens.
Fran. Tallents.
Edw. Lawrence.
Nath. Vincent.
James Owen.
Rich. Steele.
May 9th, 1687.

Thus sanctioned, Mr. Henry returned to the country, determined, in dependence upon promised aid, to "serve God with his spirit in the Gospel of his Son." Under the date of 28th May, 1687 Mrs. Savage notices his arrival. She went to Broad Oak and found her "dear brother safe come home." "The next day, the Sabbath, we went," she writes, "to [Whitewell] Chapel. At night he preached concerning sparing mercy."

CHAPTER 5

A.D. 1687 to A.D. 1694
His Settlement at Chester, Religious Liberty, State of Society in
Chester, Mr. and Mrs. Hardware, Marriage to Miss Hardware,
Death of Mrs. Henry, Baptism of His Daughter,
Mr. and Mrs. Warburton, Marriage with Miss Warburton,
Commences a Diary, Birth of Another Daughter, Makes His
Will, Birth-day Memorial, 1691, Close of the Year 1691, Death
of His Youngest Daughter, Birth-day Memorial, 1692, Birth of
Another Daughter, Her Death, His Funeral Sermon on the
Occasion, Review of the Year 1693

deputation from Chester consisting, among others of
Mr. Greg, Mr. Coker, and Mr. Hall, soon waited upon
him. Mr. Greg was a gentleman of exemplary meekness,
humility, and serious godliness; one who had a good
report of all men, and who had been particularly instrumental in
bringing about his settlement. On the 1ˢᵗ of June Mr. Henry
accompanied them to his future dwelling-place; commencing the
following day, Thursday, a career of sacred usefulness, by preaching
the usual lecture. His text was, 1 Cor. 2:2, "I determined not to
know any thing among you save Jesus Christ and him crucified."
Mr. Tong was present, a witness of their joy and thankfulness. "It
may be truly said," he remarked, "that they received him as an
angel of God."

Chester had long been the residence of Mr. Harvey, the aged and worthy divine already mentioned. Mr. Harvey was "a good scholar and a judicious preacher," one who had not only labored in the word and doctrine, but who had also suffered for righteousness sake. He was now oppressed with increasing infirmities and unequal to much exertion. Many of the congregation who had listened to Mr. Cook and Mr. Hall had for some time assembled at Mr. Henthorne's house, where Mr. Tong ministered to them. At first they met only between the hours of public worship, most of them hearing Dr. Fog and Dr. Hancock, whose ministry they esteemed. At noon, however, and again in the evening they flocked to Mr. Henthorne's. Their numbers before Mr. Henry's arrival so increased as to render more spacious accommodations necessary. Mr. Henthorne, whose zeal abounded, supplied a large out-building, part of the Friary, which belonged to him, and it was immediately made ready. They set to work one Monday morning. The next Lord's Day it was opened.

Flattering as was Mr. Henry's reception and his prospects also, he would not promise to abide (and who does not admire his delicacy?) until he had received the consent of Mr. Harvey. Nor, indeed, did he preach the sermon, which has been noticed, until he had paid that venerable man a respectful visit. He assured Mr. Harvey that if he did not consent to his settlement he would return, and desired him to express himself freely. Mr. Harvey at once satisfied him of his goodwill and pleasantly added – there is work enough for us both.

It may be well to pause here for a moment in order to admire the altered state of things with respect to the affairs of religion in comparison with what it was only a few years before. The consideration deeply affected the mind of Philip Henry and furnished him an exordium to a sermon, which about this time he delivered at Weston near Hawkstone in Shropshire. An extract from it can scarcely fail to gratify and instruct the reader.

> *My brethren, beloved, upon this day six years ago we were met together in this place in a time of threatening drought to seek the Lord for rain. While I was preaching to you for your help and furtherance in the duty, it pleased the neighboring magistrates, without any provocation that we knew of, to give us disturbance in the work we were about; and not only so, but levy fines upon us as for evil doing.*
>
> *It hath now pleased our sovereign lord the king, by the good hand of our God upon us, to put an end, for the present, to those restraints, and to make the seventh year of release, according as the law was to the children of Israel by the hand of Moses.*
>
> *And here we are to take notice of it, not in any unbecoming way of peevish reflection upon those who were the instruments of our trouble; they are some of them gone to God, to give up their accounts about it, and we are going shortly to give up ours. And for those that yet survive, whatever their unkind thoughts are of us, our duty is to pray for them, and I hope we shall be found doing it accordingly.*

At Chester Mr. Henry found much agreeable society. Mr. Alderman Mainwaring and Mr. Vanbrugh (the father of Sir John Vanbrugh), though in communion with the Church of England, attended his weekday lectures. They ranked among his intimate acquaintance and uniformly treated him with great and sincere respect.

Others also of a like character, moderate and consistent dissenters and Mr. Henry's true friends, are entitled to honorable mention. George Booth, Esq., an eminent lawyer and near relative of the Earl of Warrington; Richard Kerick, Esq., a gentleman distinguished by his good sense, pleasant and instructive conversation, and genuine piety; and John Hunt, Esq., a faithful and prudent man, a younger brother of Mr. Hunt of Boreatton, and one who walked in the spirit and way of that excellent family. Nor must the name of Edward Gere, Esq., though already mentioned, be here omitted. Mr. Henry lived with him in friendship the most intimate and endearing, and usually styled his Fidus Achates. Beside these, Mr. Henry found among the principle tradesmen: particularly Mr. Henthorne, Mr. Samuel Kirk, Mr. Thomas Robinson, Mr. John Hulton, and several others valuable and steady associates.

In noticing the comforts of his settlement, the marriage not long afterwards of three of his sisters to Mr. Radford, Mr. Hulton, and Dr. Tylston, all excellent and pious men. And in so little time residents in the city, and his constant hearers must not be omitted.

But that which rendered Chester still more agreeable to him was an introduction to the Hardware family at Moldsworth. The son, Mr. John Hardware, had married a daughter of Mr. Hunt of Boreatton; and he had an only sister, dwelling with her parents of whose estimable qualities Mr. Henry, when in London, had heard enough to excite his curiosity and attention. His character also had been favorably represented at Boreatton in her hearing and she knew his sisters. So far, therefore, they were mutually prepossessed; nor had their personal acquaintance continued long before Mr. Henry disclosed his anxieties which, being known, were not ungraciously received. They were communicated through Miss Hardware's relatives.

Of her parents little is known, but that little is abundantly honorable to their memory. Her father was a serious Christian, very conscientious, remarkable for temperance and love to the duty of prayer. He was an old puritan. And her mother was eminent for wisdom and grace. She walked with God and looked well to the ways of her household.

Mr. Hardware and Mr. John Hardware, the father and brother, readily accepted Mr. Henry's offers, but Mrs. Hardware felt a good deal of hesitation. She viewed her daughter as her only one, and as the expectant of a considerable worldly portion, she contemplated her other recommendations, both personal and acquired. Several gentlemen of much larger estimate than Mr. Henry had tendered offers, which had been refused. On that account she feared the reproach of negligence of having made a sacrifice to the interests of a party. No one could esteem Mr. Henry more highly then she did; she valued him as a minister and a friend, but she thought it a duty to make better provision for her child. She knew that the ministry, especially of the nonconformists, was despised, and liberty very precarious. In the event of persecution, she was apprehensive lest her daughter, who had been tenderly brought up, and everywhere treated with respect and honour, might be deficient in the exercise of faith and patience. And, if she were not to stoop to the cross, a great addition would be made to Mr. Henry's troubles, at a time when comfort would be most needed.

All those scruples were at length happily removed; and, in August 1687, the felicity of both parties was consummated.

Mrs. Savage specially notices the beauty, as well as the piety of her new sister-in-law. The marriage brought to remembrance the fact that Mr. Hardware had once desired a like event in reference to Mr. Henry's mother; and the circumstance rendered the recent alliance additionally observable and interesting.

Mr. and Mrs. Hardware now removed to Chester; and Mr. and Mrs. Henry boarded with them. A favorable opportunity was thus furnished of judging how well their daughter had been bestowed. And when they thus additionally beheld Mr. Henry's pious and pleasant conversation, his excellent temper, great diligence, and prudence, they were far from repenting what had taken place. Mrs. Hardware, indeed, severely reflected upon herself for having opposed the marriage. She was now sensible of the advantages she and her husband enjoyed in their declining years by the expositions and sermons of their son-in-law, and by his prayers likewise, both in the family and in public. She admired the goodness of God in overruling her own inclinations, and choosing for her daughter and herself an inheritance, in all respects so superior to what, if her will had prevailed, she should have selected. She expressed her conviction that although, at the time not aware of it, the objections which have been narrated arose from covetousness and pride.

The union, propitious as in all respects it appeared, was, nevertheless like every sublunary joy of short duration. Near the time of her confinement, Mrs. Henry was attacked by the smallpox and had scarcely known the felicity of maternal affection when terrestrial mercies were exchanged for higher everlasting blessedness. She died on Thursday, February 14, 1689, aged twenty-five.

On the first communication of her sister's illness, which was the Saturday before the fatal event, Mrs. Savage, being unable "to content" herself, had happily repaired to Chester, where she remained for a season, comforting her brother in tribulation. Mr. Tong, then a resident at Knutsford, also visited the house of mourning. The united testimony of both those excellent persons is to the honour of the afflicted parties, and in them of God, who has in all generations been the refuge and strength of his people and their "very present help in trouble."

Mrs. Hardware, though overwhelmed with sorrow, seemed to bear the affliction with more composure than Mr. Henry. An eyewitness told Mr. Tong that when she saw her beloved child a corpse, she was enabled to check her grief and to say almost immediately with devout and patriarchal submission, "It is the Lord. I have done. I have done. I will not repine." She even attempted the consolation of others, and upbraiding herself for not having more freely consented to the nuptials, added, "God, who knew how long my child had to live, brought her into Mr. Henry's family to prepare her for heaven."

Between Mr. Tong and the bereaved husband the interview was peculiarly effecting. Mr. Henry's first words, so soon as tears would permit utterance, were, "I know nothing that could support me under such a loss as this, but the good hope that she is gone to heaven, and that in a little time, I shall follow her thither."

On Saturday evening, February 16, the funeral took place at Trinity Church in Chester, within the altar; and a sermon was afterwards preached in Mr. Henry's chapel by Mr. Lawrence, from Phil. 1:21 – "To die is gain."

It was no small alleviation of Mr. Henry's grief that the life of his "first born" was spared. A visit, too, from his excellent father augmented his comfort. The infant was publicly baptized by that holy man, and with peculiar solemnity. He called her, after her departed mother, Katharine. The dedication was accompanied by the confession of the sorrowing parent's faith, to which he added, with indescribable emotions, "Although my house be not now so with God, yet he hath made with me an everlasting covenant, ordered in all things and sure, and this is all my salvation, and all my desire, although he make me not to grow; and, according to the tenor of this covenant, I offer up this my child to the Great God, a plant out of a dry ground, desiring it may be implanted into Christ."

At this scene, which touched all the springs of nature and of grace, a large congregation, it is said, burst into tears.

Mr. Henry continued to reside with the parents of his lamented wife; and, notwithstanding the depth of his grief, was enabled to persevere in the entire discharge of his ministerial duties. At length, through the kind interference of his mother-in-law, his loss was repaired. Mrs. Hardware not only advised a second marriage, but recommended one of her own relatives, Mary, a daughter of Robert Warburton, Esquire of Grange in the county of Chester. Mr. Tong says, the youngest daughter—but that is questionable.

The testimony borne by that recommendation to Mr. Henry, in his conjugal character, is highly honorable; and it is due to the lady, who became his second wife, to notice that its value derives no small increase from the respectability and virtues of herself and her ancestors.

On this occasion, as on the former, the predilection for the "seed of the righteous," which Mr. Henry had been taught to cherish, was strongly marked. Miss Warburton's grandfather, Peter Warburton, Esquire, was Chief Justice of Chester, of honorable descent and distinguished learning and piety. Her father, Robert Warburton, Esquire, who, in consequence of the demise of two elder brothers in infancy, inherited the estate, possessed also the same "precious faith." Much attached to retirement, especially in his latter days, he spent the greater part of his time in reading and prayer. The Bible and the "Saint's Everlasting Rest" lay daily before him upon his parlor table. His house was a little sanctuary to the silenced ministers and those who adhered to them. The cause of nonconformity was fully approved by him, and he never deserted it. Miss Warburton's mother, Elizabeth, the daughter of Alderman Berkley of the City of London, was also a very strict and serious Christian.

The marriage was solemnized on the 8th of July 1690 at Grange. Mr. and Mrs. Philip Henry were present, rejoicing in their acquaintance with so worthy a family and their relation to it. After the lapse of a few days, they accompanied their son and daughter to Chester, and having left them there in comfort, returned to their habitation at Broad Oak, blessing God who had thus mercifully filled up the former breach and restored to their son the honour and comforts of matrimony. Mr. and Mrs. Hardware, having seen him again settled according to their desire, returned from Chester to their own estate at Bromborough Court in Wirral.

Hitherto Mr. Henry's memoranda, in the nature of diary, had been occasional only, general, rather than particular, and chiefly upon loose and detached papers. But now he felt it his duty to alter his plan. And he continued, almost to the close of life, a statement more regular and more minute. Mr. Tong says, from November 9, 1669. But that is obviously a mistake, probably a typographical error. Mr. Henry was then only seven years old. The true date is "November 9, 1690," and the record is as follows: "This day I concluded my subject of redeeming time from Eph. 5:16; and among other things, directed as very useful, to deep a short account every night how the day has been spent. This will discover what are the thieves of our time, and will show us what progress we make in holiness; and now, why should not I make the experiment?"

In due season, the second nuptials of Mr. Henry were crowned with fruit. The happy event occurred April 12, 1691, and it attracted

Philip Henry to Chester; where on the lecture day, he administered the baptismal ordinance, calling the infant Elizabeth, and preaching from Is. 43:10, "Ye are my witnesses, saith the Lord, and my servant whom I have chosen" – witnesses without Godfathers.

In consequence of the addition thus made to his family, Mr. Henry discovered, by the settlement of his worldly affairs, that consummate prudence which distinguished him through life; and which is lamentably not more frequent.

The memorandum he penned on the occasion referred to, is worthy of particular notice. It not only shows his own view of conjugal and parental duty, but it discovers, also, his extraordinary religious attainments at that early age: at a time, too, when there was nothing, either of vexation or disease, to produce weariness of life. On the contrary, the full and conscious enjoyment of those special mercies of God's good providence, which render an abode upon earth both pleasant and inviting, "I have now set my house in order; and, to the best of my apprehension, I have ordered it justly, as becomes my obligations of that kind. I have been deliberately weighing the case of a 'departure' hence; the things that invite my stay here are far from outweighing those that press my departure. Through grace, I can say, 'I desire to depart, and to be with Christ, which is far better.'"

The state of felicity in which Mr. Henry's family had been placed by the birth, which has been narrated, was now to undergo an affecting change. A cloud gathered around his tabernacle; and the infant, in whom he fondly delighted, became a source of corresponding anguish. Hooping-cough, dentition, and fever induced the following pathetic and devout memorial. It was written three days only before the fatal separation: "The child has had an ill night; she is very weak, and in all appearance worse; but I am much comforted from her baptism. I desire to leave her in the arms of him who gave her to me. The will of the Lord be done. I have said, if the Lord will spare her, I will endeavour to bring her up for him. I am now sitting by her, thinking of the mischievous nature of original sin, by which death reigns over poor infants."

The following passage, penned July 19, 1692, the day on which the little one expired, needs no comment to make it intelligible. Christian parents, especially if they have been bereaved, will fully understand it, and every reader may behold, as in a glass, the resource and duty of a believer, when bowed down with sorrow.

In the morning I had the child in my arms, endeavoring solemnly to give her up to God, and to bring my heart to his will; and presently there seemed some reviving. But while I was writing this I was suddenly called out of my closet. I went for the doctor and brought him with me, but as soon as we came in, the sweet babe quietly departed between the mother's arms and mine, without any struggle, for nature was spent by its long illness; and now my house is a house of mourning.

She was a pretty, forward child, and very apprehensive; she began to go and talk, and observe things very prettily. I had set my affection much upon her. I am afraid too much; God is wise, and righteous, and faithful. Even this also is not only consistent with, but flowing from covenant love. It is this day five years since I was first married. God has been teaching me to sing of mercy and of judgment. Lord, make me more perfect at my lesson, and show me wherefore thou contendest with me. Lord, wean me from this world by it. Blessed be God for the covenant of grace with me and mine. It is well ordered in all things and sure. O that I could learn to comfort others with the same comforts with which, I trust, I am comforted of God! This goes near, but O Lord, I submit. My dear wife is much distressed. The Lord sustain her. I would endeavour to comfort her. We are now preparing for a decent interment of my poor babe. Many friends come to see us. I am much refreshed with 2 Kings 4:26. "Is it well with thee, is it well with thy husband, is it well with thy child? And she said – It is well. " When I part with so dear a child, yet I have no reason to say otherwise, but that it is well with us and well with the child, for all is well that God doth. He performeth the thing that he appointed for me, and his appointment of this providence is in pursuance of his appointment of to glory, to make me meet for it.

One extract more will record the funeral.

I have been this day doing a work I have never done before, burying a child; a sad day's work; but my good friend Mr. Lawrence preached very seasonably and excellently, at the lecture in the afternoon, from Psalm 39:9. "I was dumb. I opened not my mouth, because thou didst it." My friends testified their kindness by their presence. There is now a pretty little garment laid up in the wardrobe for the grave to be worn again at the resurrection. Blessed be God for the hope of this.

In due time, it pleased the Father of Mercies to heal the breach by again making Mrs. Henry a joyful mother. The child, a daughter, was born April 3, 1693. On Thursday the 6th of the same month, she was baptized by her grandfather, Philip Henry, by the name of Mary; and, likewise, at the same time, another grandchild, the daughter of Mrs. Hulton, Katharine. The good man preached on the occasion in his accustomed edifying manner, from Gen. 35:5. "Esau asked, who are those with thee? And he said, the children which God has graciously given thy servant." He observed what a grave and religious, as well as respectful, answer Jacob gave to a common question, and insisted chiefly on two points – that children are the gifts of God – and that the children of the covenant are his gracious gifts.

In less than three weeks, however, Friday, April 21, this child also, after a day's illness, died. The stroke, so affecting and sudden, was received by Mr. Henry with primitive meekness and resignation. "The Lord is righteous: he takes and gives, and gives, and takes again. I desire to submit: but, O Lord, show me wherefore thou contendest with me."

On the following Sabbath, he endeavored publicly to improve his bereavement.

In the morning he expounded the 38th chapter of Job, where God so largely asserts his sovereignty and challenges all who presume to arraign the wisdom and equity of his proceedings. "Was it fit," Mr. Henry enquired, "that Job should quarrel with God as to his particular providences to him, when he was so unacquainted with the methods of his providence in general?" He preached from Rom. 5:14. "Nevertheless, death reigned from Adam to Moses, even over them that had not sinned after the similitude of Adam's transgression, who is the figure of him that was to come." After ably illustrating the dominion of death, especially in reference to infants who, though not guilty of actual sin, are the subjects of his kingdom, he thus addressed such as were, or had been, called to lose their little ones. "Resign, and give up your dying children to God. They cannot do it. You must do it for them. Father, into thy hands I commit my child's spirit. They are his by right, and his by your consent. You should restore them when he calls for them, and do it freely. I know it is hard, but it must be done. Let their deaths bring your sins to remembrance. Did you not sin in an inordinate desire of children? Perhaps in discontent or poverty, you have thought them too many.

It may be you were over fond of them or too indulgent. My pride, my passion, and my covetousness – these slew my child. Learn to bear it patiently. Do not murmur. If I were bereaved of my children, said the patriarch, I am bereaved; not I am undone. The Shunamite said, It is well, for all is well that God doth. If a sparrow doth not fall without the will of God, then a child doth not. Comfort yourselves at such a time in God's covenant with you and your seed. Fetch your comforts from the Lord Jesus who was dead and is alive and lives forevermore. Of the increase of his government there shall be no end. Consider what your children are taken from and what they are taken to. They are not born in vain, if they help to people the New Jerusalem."

The same evening "the infant was buried privately with a small company." "I have now," he writes, "laid my poor babe in the grave in Trinity Church, the fourth within this year buried there: two of my brother's children and two of mine. Yet the Lord is gracious. The Lord prepare me for that cold and silent grave."

In the review penned on the termination of the same year, 1693, Mr. Henry evidently had the bereavements already mentioned full in view. And it is worthy of notice how entire is the absence in relation to those events of either complaint or repining. There is, indeed, an expression of sorrow, but it arose from the tenderness of a contrite spirit. It stands associated with gratitude and was influenced, and rendered even sacred by the aspirations of evangelical hope. "I am now come to the close of another year, which has begun and ended with a Sabbath. I have received many mercies the year that is past. I have been brought low and helped. My dear wife is spared. I am yet in the land of the living, though many have been taken away. But how little have I done for God! What will become of me I know not. I find little growth. If any thing hath at any time affected me this year it hath been some sweet desires of the glory, which is to be revealed. I have often thought of it as that which would help in my present duty."

CHAPTER 6

A.D. 1694 to A.D. 1699
His Prosperity, The Death of Mr. Warburton, Death of Philip
Henry, Reflections on the Event, Birth-day Memorial 1696,
and Devout Close of the Year 1696, Death of His Sisters,
Mrs. Radford, and Mrs. Hulton, Letter to Mrs. Savage,
Birth-day Memorandum, 1697, Commencement of the Year
1698, Visit to London, Birth-day Memorial 1698, Death of His
Daughter Ann, Birth-day Memorial, 1699, Death of the Rev.
Mr. Harvey, Devout Close of the Year 1699, Attention to the
Orphan Children of His Brother and Sister Radford

After the death of Mrs. Hardware, which happened in December 1693, the candle of the Lord shone upon Mr. Henry for a few years, almost without interruption; and comparatively he enjoyed rest. But he had learned to remember in seasons of rejoicing, "the days of darkness." And there can be no question that the holy suavities, which, from his papers, he seems to have experienced, had a salutary influence upon the trials he was soon to pass through. Sometimes he expatiated upon the goodness of God in affording to his people, not infrequently, extraordinary consolations, that they may be the better fitted for trouble, observing that "those who were to be witnesses of Christ's agony, were the witnesses of his transfiguration."

The return of God's chastening hand upon him may be assigned to April 1696. On the 14th of that month, his father-in-law, Mr. Warburton, was taken, but in a good old age, to his reward. There was everything in the event to mitigate grief: long expectation and the pressure of complicated infirmities had prevented surprise; and death, beyond all doubt, was "gain." Still, notwithstanding every alleviation, the stroke was deeply felt.

But this was preparatory only. His own father, in the enjoyment of ordinary health and active usefulness, and far from being advanced in years, was shortly afterwards suddenly arrested by illness, and, in a few hours, carried to heaven. The day was indeed a day of grief and of desperate sorrow. No representation can equal his own account.

June 23, 1696.

This afternoon about three o'clock, my father's servant came for the doctor with the tidings that my dear father was taken suddenly ill. I had then some of my friends about me, and they were cheerful with me, but this struck a damp upon all. I had first thought not to go till the next day, it being somewhat late and very wet, and had written half a letter to my dear mother, but I could not help going. I am glad I did go, for I have often thought of 2 Kings 2:10. 'If thou see me when I am taken up from them ...' The doctor and I came to Broad Oak about eight o'clock and found him in great extremity of pain; nature (through his great and unwearied labors) unable to bear up and sinking under the load. As soon as he saw me he said, 'O son, you are welcome to a dying father; I am now ready to be offered up; and the time of my departure is at hand.' A little after midnight, my mother holding his hands as he sat in bed, and I holding the pillow to his back, he very quietly and without any struggling, groan or rattling, breathed out his dear soul into the hands of the Lord Jesus Christ, whom he had faithfully served.

And now, what is this that God hath done unto us? The thing itself and the suddenness of it are very affecting, but the wormwood and the gall in it is that it looks like a token of God's displeasure to us who survive. The Lord calls my sins to remembrance this day, that I have not profited by him while he was with us as I should have done. Our family worship this morning was very melancholy, the place was Allon Baccuth, the oak of weeping. The little children were greatly affected, and among the neighbors was heard nothing but lamentation and mourning. My dear mother cast down, but not in despair. I, for my part, am full of confusion and am like a man astonished.

On Friday following, the corpse being yet unburied, the time appointed for keeping a public fast arrived. Prevented by the solemn occurrence from observing it at Chester, Mr. Henry held it at Broad Oak. His own memorandum is as uncommon as it is instructive, and demonstrates not only an astonishing degree of self-command, but devotedness to God's glory perfectly enviable.

June 26, 1696.

This day is appointed a public fast. My place is now vacant. It did not use to be so, but God will have it so now. I had thought not to have done any things at Broad Oak, and had given notice accordingly, but I see the people come in and are greatly affected, that their minister should be taken away from them just before a fast which he had given notice of on the Lord's Day, both morning and evening; and had earnestly pressed them to the due observation of it. I remember I had often heard my father say "weeping must not hinder sowing," I therefore thought it my duty to spend two or three hours in the meeting place, putting the people in mind that we had kept too many fasts with dry eyes under melting ordinances, but God had caused us to keep this with wet eyes, under a melting providence. I preached from 2 Kings 12:20. "Elisha died, and the bands of the Moabites invaded the land." The removal of public useful instruments is a sad presage of public dreadful judgments.

Further extracts from the diary shall continue the affecting narrative. They sufficiently explain themselves. Any remarks would detract from their touching beauties.

June 27. The day of my father's funeral: melancholy work. O that by this providence I might contract an habitual gravity, seriousness, and thoughtfulness of death and eternity. Our friends most affectionately sympathize with us, and do him honour at his death. How has this providence made Broad Oak – like a wilderness – desolate, and solitary, and the poor people as sheep without a shepherd.

July 1. I returned late to Chester and found the children well. The next day I studied and preached the lecture from 2 Pet. 1:13-14. "Yea, I think it meet, as long as I am in this tabernacle, to stir you up, by putting you in remembrance; knowing that shortly I must put off this my tabernacle, even as our Lord Jesus hath showed me." O that it might be preached to my own heart, and written there; that in consideration of my being to depart hence shortly, I may double my diligence.

And now I have time to reflect on this sad providence. What shall I say to these things?

1. I bless God that I ever had such a father, whose temper was so very happy, and his gifts and graces so very bright, one that recommended religion and the power of godliness by a cheerful and endearing conversation that he had himself and taught others the art of obliging. I bless God that I had him so long, that he was not removed from me when I was a child; that I have not been left to myself to be a grief and heaviness to him. Nothing made me differ from the worst, but the free grace of God. To that grace be the glory of all the benefit that my father was to me, and the comfort I was to him.

2. I have a great deal of reason to be humbled, and ashamed that I have profited and improved no more by my relation to so good a man; that I have not so well transcribed that fair copy of humility, meekness, candor, and zealous piety. O that the remembrance of him may have a greater influence upon me, than the personal converse had!

3. Death comes nearer and nearer to me, "Lord, make me to know mine end, and teach me to number my days." In January last, death came into our classes and removed good Mr. Kinaston of Knutsford; in February death came into the Friary [the place where Mr. Henry's house stood] and took away Mrs. Cook; in March death came into my house and carried away my cousin Aldersey; in April it came into our family, in the death of my father Warburton; at the end of May I said with thankfulness, here is a month past in which I have not buried one friend. But June has brought it nearest of all and speaks very loud to me to get ready to go after. The Lord prepare me for a dying hour that will come certainly and may come suddenly, that when it comes I may have nothing to do but to die.

4. The great honour and respect paid to his memory, and the good name he has left behind him, should encourage me to faithfulness and usefulness. The Scripture is fulfilled, "Those that honour God he will honour," and "before honour is humility."

5. This should bring me nearer to God, and make me live more upon him, who is the fountain of living waters. My dear father was a counselor to me, but Christ is the wonderful Counselor. He was an intercessor for me, but Christ is an Intercessor that lives forever, and is therefore able to save to the uttermost. Nor are the prayers that he has put up for me and mine lost, but I trust we shall be reaping the fruit of them now he is gone. I have had much comfort in hearing God speak to me by this Scripture. Jer. 3: 4. "Wilt thou not from this time cry unto me, My Father, thou are the guide of my youth?" My dear father wrote to me lately upon the death of my father Warburton. "Your fathers, where are they? One gone, and the other going, but you have a good Father in heaven that lives forever. Abba, Father, the Lord teach me to cry so, and to come into the holiest as to my Father's house; and let these things be written upon my heart. Amen, Amen."

At the next sacrament he attempted, again, with great seriousness and deliberation, to improve the event; being desirous (as he expressed it) to bring the ordinance home to the providence; and to have a particular reference to *it* in the covenant he was then to renew with God at his table. A memorial so instructive, notwithstanding the length to which the narration has already been carried, could not with propriety be omitted.

1. I would in this ordinance of the Lord's Supper, very particularly eye God as a Father, as my Father. My father who is gone was to me a faithful reprover, teacher, and counselor. I desire, therefore, at this time more expressly than ever, to take the Spirit of God to be my reprover, teacher, and counselor. I was often refreshed in visiting my father, and conversing with him, I would by the grace of God have more fellowship with the Father, and with his Son Jesus Christ, whom I may be free with.

2. There are some things I would more particularly engage myself to upon this providence; the Lord direct, confirm, and ratify good resolutions. I will now labor and endeavour in the strength of the grace of Christ, (and the Lord give me a sufficiency of his grace.)

(1.) To be more grave and serious, partly as the fruit of this sad and solemn providence, which should not only affect me for the present, but alter me for the future, and make me habitually more serious; partly because my father being now removed, I have almost lost the epithet of a young man, which uses to pass for some excuse. It is time to lay aside vanity.

(2.) To be more meek and humble, courteous and candid, because these were the graces that my dear father was eminent for, and God owned him in them, and men honored him for them. I am sensible of too much hastiness of spirit. I would learn to be of a cool, mild spirit.

(3.) To be more diligent and industrious in improving my time, for I see it is hasting off apace; and I desire to have it filled up, because I see I must shortly put off this my tabernacle, and there is no working in the grave.

The work of the day being over, he goes on to remark. "I have been full of distractions, which have much discouraged me, yet I have had some communion with God in this day's work beyond what I expected, though not what I earnestly desired. I have solemnly renewed my covenants with the Lord at his table, and particularly those above written, The Lord give me his grace, that having made these vows I may make them good."

Honorable as the preceding extracts evidently are, to the memory of one of the most illustrious men whose name has been perpetuated in the churches, it is difficult to say whether they do not shed equal luster upon the bereaved, and heavenly-minded writer. Where are to be found the indications of a deeper, or more chastened sorrow; or the tokens of morel lowly resignation; or the aspirations of more sacred desires; or the evidences of piety, more elevated or more pure?

The following memoranda written at subsequent periods, and more remote from the bitter scene, discover a life spirit, and breathe a fragrance no less celestial.

October 18, 1696. This day compleats the thirty-fourth year of my age. I have endeavored this morning to get my heart affected with the sin in which I was born, and with the sins of my life hitherto; and with the mercy of my birth, and the mercies of my life hitherto. The Lord enable to live a life of repentance, and a life of thankfulness.

December 31, 1696. This year is at an end. ON the first day of it I preached from Prov 27:1. "Boast not thyself of to-morrow, for thou knowest not what a day may bring forth." My fathers, where are they? And where am I? Hasting after them I have lost much time this year; but if, thorough grace, I have got any good, it is a greater indifference to the things of this world. The Lord increase it.

In the month of August, 1697, three of Mr. Henry's sister were, successively, seized with alarming illness. Mrs. Tylston recovered; but two of them, Mrs. Radford, and Mrs. Hulton, both exemplary Christians, entered into rest. These were sore trials. "I find it, " he writes, "hard to submit. Let the grace of Christ be sufficient for me. I have said it, and I do not unsay it – Lord, thy will be done."

On the death of Mrs. Hulton, which occurred about three weeks later than Mrs. Radford's, he addressed to this sister, Mrs. Savage, the following admirable letter. The advice it contains to Christian mourners can never be out of season; and the train of thinking is an felicitous, as the testimony to the departed is honorable and exciting:

For Mrs. Savage, at Wrenbury Wood
Chester, September 8, 1697.

My dear Sister,

I find it very easy to say a great deal to aggravate our loss; and losers think they may have leave to speak. I can say that I have lost, not only a sister, but a true friend; one of my "helpers in Christ Jesus;" and one that was to me "as my own soul." To lose such a one in the midst of her days, at such a time as this, when so many decline, what shall I say to it? I endeavour to silence myself with this, that the Lord hath done it, who gives not account of any of his matters, and in whose hands we, and all our comforts are—"as the clay in the hand of the potter."

But there is something more for us to satisfy ourselves with. The cloud has a bright side as well as a dark one. If we look upon this providence as sent to fetch a dear friend home to heaven, and to help us forward in our way thither, the thing hath quiet another aspect. Are we not born from heaven, and bound to heaven? Is not that our home, our country? And are our relations any the less ours for being remove thither? And how long do we expect to stay behind? We knew no the other day that it was so little a while and we should not see her; alas! Now it is but a little while, and we shall see her, because we "go to the Father."

There is a matter for praise and thanksgiving, even in this sad providence: that we had such a relation: that we had her so long and had so much comfort in her, that she did shine so illustriously in gifts and graces, that she was enable to finish well; and had, as she said, "hope in her death." She blessed God for the Scriptures, which were her cordial, and did not seem to be under any cloud as to her comforts. That she hath left a good name behind her. She dies as much lamented as, I think, any woman in Chester since I knew it; for "her hands and lips fed many." That she hath left children behind her, who we hope may live to glorify God in this world, and that we do not "sorrow as those who no hope." I shall want her converse, and correspondence; but let us both converse, and correspond the more with Jesus Christ, and that will help to make up the want; nay, that will be "far better."

Mr. Lawrence hath helped us well to improve the providence. The Lord help us with grace sufficient. A letter from our Friend in heaven is better than one from the best friend we have on earth. The Lord perfect what concerns you. Let us learn to sing, both of mercy and judgment; and to sing unto God of both till we come to sing of mercy only in the world of everlasting mercy. Our dear love to you and the children.

I rest, Your affectionate Brother,
M.H.

Another anniversary of Mr. Henry's birthday having arrived, it was marked by reflections as appropriate and sensible as those, which have preceded. It is plain upon what subjects his eye had turned, and the improvement, though brief, is abundantly comprehensive.

October 18, 1697. Through the good hand of my God upon me, I have finished my thirty-fifth year – one half of the age of man; as if now in the zenith of akme; it is high noon with me; but my sun may "go down at noon." I was affected this morning, when alone, in thinking what I was born – a rational creature, a helpless creature, a sinful creature. Where I was born! In the church of God; in a land of light; in a house of prayer. What I was born for! To glorify God, my Maker, and prepare to get to heaven.

The next year was commenced with equal seriousness.

January 1, 1698. My family is now in peace and health through the goodness of God, but I know not what a day, much less a year, may bring forth. I have begged to be ready for the trials and afflictions of the year and for death, if it comes, thinking this day what a mercy it is to be born in a land where God is known, and not where he is an unknown God. I begin the year with a solemn renewed dedication of myself, my whole self, to God in Christ, as my God, and Father, and portion. Let this be the axis and centre of every year's revolution. Amen, O Lord so be it.

This year it was that Mr. Henry visited London for the first time since his settlement at Chester. The same regard to the glory of his Master, which has been so uniformly conspicuous, marked the commencement and prosecution of the journey. His friends were convened to implore a blessing; and his praise abounded, that he was not "forced from home, not going to follow a roving fancy, nor to seek his fortune."

He set out on Monday the 2nd of May, preaching at Nantwich, Newcastle, Lichfield, and Sutton Colefield on his way. The latter of these places he was the more willing to see, because it had been the residence of a minister so eminent as Mr. Anthony Burgesse.

In passing through St. Alban's, he paid a short visit to the Rev. Mr. Grew, nephew to Dr. Grew, a gravely serious man, who entertained him and his fellow traveler, Mr. Tong, with very good discourse, and showed them many mathematical curiosities.

During his stay in London he preached almost daily with great acceptance and favor. He was "followed from place to place." One sermon, which he delivered (at a fast kept at Mr. Howe's) from Acts 28:22. "A sect everywhere spoken against ..." and which was afterwards published, gave universal satisfaction.

He returned home laden with the praises and admiration of his fellowmen, and fellow Christians. But neither the attentions he received nor the popularity of his services produced any undue exaltation. They seem, on the contrary, to have increased his sense of unmerited goodness and to have filled him with penitence and astonishment. Under the date of October 18, 1698, he writes, "I have now weathered about thirty-six years. So long have I cumbered the ground; and yet I am spared. Others, much more useful, have never attained this age. I admire the patience of my God, and I wonder at my own folly, that being upon the brink of an awful eternal state, I am so little affected with it. The Lord teach me with a strong hand."

Soon afterwards another afflictive event occurred which made an impression both upon Mr. and Mrs. Henry unusually deep, and which, because of the ample scope it furnished and secured for the renewed exercise of those principles which have already been so prominently exhibited, deserves more than mere registration. Their little daughter Ann, being attacked by the measles, sunk almost immediately into the arms of death. The evening happened on Wednesday, November 16, 1698, and the surprise of her agitated parents was the greater, because, as Mr. Henry observed, though many children in Chester had the disease at the same time (his daughter Esther among the rest), yet *his* was the only one, to his knowledge, that died. "God in mercy," was the beautiful and appropriate supplication of Mrs. Savage, "Support and comfort the tender mother that she may be a pattern of patience and quiet submission; forasmuch as it is fit the Master of the garden would pluck off which flower he please." Nor were the sentiments of Mr. Henry less beautiful, less appropriate, or less instructive. "My desire is to be sensible of the affliction, and yet patient under it. It is a rod, a smarting rod. God calls my to remembrance—the coldness of my love in the hand of my *Father*. I desire in it to see a father's authority, who may do what he will, and a father's love who will do what is best. We resigned the soul of the child to him who gave it; and, if the little ones have their angels, doubted not of their ministration in death. We have hopes, through grace, that it *is* well with the child. Little children in heaven, we look upon as the Via Lactea, the individuals scarce discernable, but altogether beautifying the heavens. We spent the day in sorrow for our affliction, our friends sympathizing with us: one day committing the immortal soul to God, this day committing the dust to the dust of the earth as it was. I am "in deaths often." Lord teach me how to "did daily." I endeavored, when the child was put into the grave, to act faith upon the doctrine of the resurrection, believing in him who quickeneth the dead."

Besides the painful separations already mentioned, Mr. Henry, in the course of the year 1699, was bereaved of two endeared friends, whom he regarded as his own soul, and both nearly allied to him.

The one was Dr. Tylston, whose natural and acquired endowments, and, especially his elevated piety had excited in Mr.

117

Henry emotions of particular regard. He felt his death as "an unspeakable loss." Indeed, in a letter to his friend Mr. Thoresby, he expressly says, "So great a scholar, so good a man, so profitable a companion, and so true a friend I despair to meet with again in this world. He had just completed his thirty-fifth year, when his sun went down at noon."

Having completed his thirty-seventh year, Mr. Henry inserted in his diary the following remarks:

October 18 1699. I desire to be affected with God's goodness to me in my birth. Why did the knees prevent me? I bless God that I have no cause to curse the day wherein I was born, but having obtained help of God, I continue to this day. I desire to be thankful to God that he has not left me to live an idle life, but I have reason to lament my sins and my sinful thoughts, by which I have lost much time. I have reason to acknowledge God's goodness to me, in giving me so great a degree of bodily health and strength above many of my brethren. I find not any sensible decay or prejudice by my work; but I know that my soul is continually in thy hand, and I am not sure to live another year.

That wise consideration of his own circumstances and mortality, which, it will have been observed, connects itself more or less with all Mr. Henry's memorials, advantageously prepared him for those unexpected changes which, whether observed or not, overtake in a greater or less degree the whole of the human race. Till now he had enjoyed the fellowship of his ancient fellow-laborer in the Gospel, Mr. Harvey, whom, on his settlement he found at Chester and with whom he had lived, it is believed, in inviolable amity. But the time of separation was at length come; and the worn out pilgrim was suddenly called to perfect and endless rest. Such an event was likely to affect a mind so susceptible as Mr. Henry's. There were happily no circumstances to render reflection painful; and it seems due to both parties that his account of the closing scene should be preserved.

> *November 28, 1699. In the morning between seven and eight o'clock, I went to see Mr. Harvey. I found him newly departed out of this world. His passage was made easy and there were no bands in his death. When I had prayed with him the night before, I said, "I hope, Sir, you have now inward peace and comfort." He answered, "I trust I have," and said no more. He was taken ill but last Friday, and was so well that he baptized Mr. Cook's child the last Lord's Day in the meeting after Mr. Aynsworth had preached. O that I might hear the voice of this rod. I am called to prepare. It is a voice to me. I have this day been blessing God for the comfort we have had these twelve years past; and that I have endeavored to carry it aright towards him, bewailing it wherein I have been defective. As to the disposal of the congregation, I have solemnly and with the greatest indifference, referred it to God, resolving to be purely passive, and earnestly begging that it may be so ordered, as may redound most to his glory, and the furtherance of the Gospel in this place.*

On the lecture-day, Mr. Henry preached from Luke 14:21 concerning the "account which ministers are to give of themselves to God."

The recollection of the wormwood and the gall had upon Mr. Henry the happiest, because a sanctified effect, as is fully evinced by the following expressive memorial. It will show how, instead of fretting against the Lord or complaining of his dispensations, he humbled himself made special confession of sin and implored on his own behalf and the behalf of others all spiritual blessings in Christ Jesus.

> *December 31, 1699. I asked by earnest and importunate supplication,*
>
> 1. *For mercy and grace for my own soul, that while I preach to others, I myself am not be cast away; that my corruptions may be mortified; and the interest of Christ preserved and advanced within me. I would wrestle with God for his Spirit to cleanse and sanctify me.*
>
> 2. *For strength and success in my ministerial work, direction in the choice of subjects, and the guidance and assistance of the Spirit in studying sermons, to secure me from error and mistake, to lead me into all truth, and to furnish me with acceptable words, to be in me a Spirit of supplication.*
>
> *And that the blessing of God may accompany all my endeavors. O that I may be instrumental to win souls to Christ and to build them up, that I may not labor in vain, but that God would give the increase. It is still my heart's desire to be more ready, and more mighty in the Scriptures.*
>
> 3. *For the staying of God's controversies with me, and my family, that God would make no further breaches, but this with submission to his blessed will.*
>
> 4. *For the sanctifying of the breaches which have been made, that the impression of the providences of the year may not wear off, or be forgotten, but that I may see my soul to be in my hand continually.*
>
> 5. *For the beheaded families, the widows and fatherless, etc.*

Mr. Henry did not, however, satisfy himself with *praying* for the fatherless. He espoused the cause of his sister Radford's orphan children, three daughters and one son, who having lost both father and mother, were left quite unprovided for. The situation in which he was then placed was new to him, and it involved duties, which necessarily interfered with his ministerial work, but it gave occasion for a further display of his varied and eminent virtues.

On administering he writes, *I took the oath in the bishop's court with a resolution, by the grace of God, strictly to observe it, and I have earnestly prayed that he would give me renewed degrees of wisdom for this new care.*

Nor ought the mention to be omitted that Mrs. Henry, to her great honour, so far from obstructing his benevolent designs, heartily concurred in them, aided their advancement; and, amidst numerous and increasing avocations, treated the children with a kindness and assiduity truly maternal. Some of them remained in the family for several years. They all profited by instruction; they adorned Christianity; and acknowledged with gratitude, the tender and affectionate attention both of their uncle and aunt.

CHAPTER 7

A.D. 1700 to A.D. 1704
Devout Commencement of the Year, Self-Dedication at the Commencement of 1701, Birthday Memorial, 1701, Close of the Year 1701, Commencement of 1702, Birth-day Memorial, 1702, Close of 1702, Commencement of 1703, Birth-day, 1703, Close of 1703, Commencement of 1704

hether Mr. Henry commenced the eighteenth century with the following devotional exercise is not quite clear. It is conjectured that he did. At all events, it was excellently adapted for such a season; and, in the absence of certainty to *which* anniversary, between 1698 and 1702 it belonged, the present place cannot be very improperly assigned to it.

This new-year's day, I have solemnly renewed the resignation and surrender of my whole self to God, as my God, deliberately and upon good considerations. I have renounced the world and the flesh, as knowing they cannot make me happy, and have devoted my whole self to the blessed Spirit, to be enlightened and sanctified and so recommended to the Son as qualified for an interest in his mediation, according to the tenor of the Gospel. I, likewise, devote myself, through the Spirit, to the Lord Jesus Christ, as my Advocate with the Father, and my way to him; by him to be recommended to the grace and favor of God the Father, relying upon Christ's righteousness alone. Without him, I am less than nothing, worse than nothing. I, likewise, devote myself, through the Lord Jesus Christ to God the Father, as my chief good and highest end, as the author of my being to whom I am obliged in duty and the felicity of my being, to whom I am obliged in interest. O Lord, truly I am thy servant, I am thy servant. May I ever be free in thy service and never desire to be free from it. Nail my ear to thy doorposts and let me serve thee forever.

Such was the uniformity of Mr. Henry's earthly pilgrimage as to render it necessary in attempting a true impression of his history and character, to exhibit, perhaps somewhat more copiously than would otherwise have been eligible, the secluded operations of his devout and heavenly life. Not with a view to eke out the narrative, but to pursue it for the reader's edification—to throw upon it the best possible light and to illustrate, in its more minute details, as well as more general discoveries, the spirit of our holy religion.

The present chapter will, therefore, be appropriated to some continuous extracts of this description, and without comment, that the mind may have the better opportunity of catching the holy flame which pervades them throughout, and which, like the "soft fires" of Milton (ascending from things natural to things spiritual), is calculated not only to "enlighten," but "with kindly heat to foment and warm the soul."

Mr. Jay's excellent remarks upon the periodical reflections of Dr. Doddridge (who probably took the hint from the specimens Mr. Tong published of Mr. Henry's) so exactly characterize the patter of a diary now to be introduced, as well as the other specimens in the present volume, as to render an inclination to cite them irresistible.

"We see a man not only looking backward, but forward; not only complaining, but resolving; not only praying, but striving; attentive indeed to his pains and pleasures in the divine life, but always connecting with practice—you see him investigating his moral character as well as his spiritual state. You see what methods he took to conquer evil propensities and to strengthen religious habits. You see how he kept alive the zeal that carried him through so many difficulties, and acquired the patience that supported him under so many trials."

1701, January 1. I solemnly renew the dedication of myself unto God, thankfully acknowledging and admiring his patience and forbearance towards me, that he has continued such a dry and barren tree as I am in his vineyard for so many years, and continued to me the gifts of his bounty and grace; and particularly acknowledging the last year to have been a year of much mercy, especially in the encouragement given to my ministry.

Lamenting and bewailing my great unfruitfulness, and that I have governed my thoughts, appetites, passions, and words no better; that I have husbanded my time and opportunities no better; and improved so little in knowledge and grace; and done so little to the honor of my great Creator and Redeemer.

But being also more and more confirmed in my belief of the being and attributes of God of the mediation of the Lord Jesus Christ between God and man, and of the reality and weight of invisible things, and being more and more satisfied that this is the true grace of God wherein I stand, and am resolved, in the strength of God, to stand in it.

I do solemnly resign and give up my whole self to God in Jesus Christ. I commit my soul and all the concerns of my spiritual state to the grace of God, and to the word of his grace, subjecting myself to the conduct and government of the blessed Spirit, and to his influences and operations, which I earnestly desire and depend upon for the mortifying of my corruptions, the strengthening of my graces, the furnishing of me for every good word and work, and the ripening of me for heaven.

I commit my body and all the concerns of my outward condition to the providence of God to be ordered and disposed by the wisdom and will of my heavenly Father. Not knowing the things, which may befall me this year, I refer myself to God. Whether it shall be my dying year or not, I know not, but it is my earnest expectation and hope that the Lord Jesus Christ shall be magnified in my body, whether it be by life or death, by health or sickness, by plenty or poverty, by liberty or restraint, by preaching or silence, by comfort or sorrow. Welcome, welcome, the will of God, whatever it be. The Lord give me grace to stand complete in it.

October 18, 1701. This day, through the good hand of my God upon me, I have finished the 39th year of my pilgrimage, and having obtained help of God, I continue hitherto, knowing whom I have trusted and trusting whom I have known. The greatest comfort of my life has been that God has been pleased to use me for his service, and my greatest grief, that I have been so little serviceable to him. I have thought much this day what a great variety of cross events I am liable to while in the body, and how uncertain what may befall me in the next year of my life— pain or sickness, broken bones, loss in my estate, death of dear relations, reproach, divisions in the congregation, public restraints and troubles. My 40th year may be as Israel's was: the last of my sojourning in this wilderness. The worst of evils would be sin and scandal. The Lord keep me from that and fit me for any other.

December 31, 1701. Believing prayer to be an instituted way of communion with God, and fetching in mercy and grace from him, I have comfort in it daily. My daily prayers are the sweetest of my daily comforts. Having of late had my body feasted above the ordinary meals, I desire this day to have my soul fed more plentifully with the duty of prayer, and thus to close the year, which (Janus like) looks both ways. I have not had this year such remarkable afflictions as some other years. The greatest has been the death of my dear and honorable friend Madam Hunt of Boreatton. But my errands to the throne of grace today are:

1. By way of lamentation and humiliation.

I have reason to lament greatly the strength of my own corruptions and weakness of my graces. By reason of the former, I am as smoking flax. By reason of the latter, I am as a bruised reed. I am still full of vain thoughts and empty of good thoughts. Many of my secret prayers are wretchedly disfigured and spoiled by a multitude of distractions and diversions of mind: the flesh and the things of the flesh still minded, to the prejudice of the Spirit, and the neglect of the things of the Spirit.

I have lost a great deal of precious time and not filled it up, or else I might have gone forwarder in my notes on the Evangelist John. Sins easily beset me, and I do not the things that I would.

I have very much reason to bewail my manifold defects in my ministerial work, my coldness in prayer: that I speak not of the things of God with more clearness and concern. O, how many, how great are the iniquities of my holy things.

I bewail the little success of my ministry and the miscarriages of some this year, for hereby my God will humble me. Grief also, great grief for the sin of some of the young ones whom I have catechized and taken pains with are no comfort to me. Lord, show me wherefore thou contendest with me?

The low condition of the church of God ought to be greatly lamented; the protestant interest small, very small; a decay of piety; attempts for reformation ineffectual. Help, Lord!

By way of prayer and supplication, I have many errands at the throne of grace this day.

The pardon of sin, victory over my corruptions and temptations, mortifying of my lusts, which go not forth but by prayer and fasting. In reference to sin, I desire I may be enabled to act faith upon Rom. 6:14. "Sin shall not have dominion over you, for ye are not under the law, but under grace," and, Ezek. 36:25-27. "Then will I sprinkle clean water upon you, and ye shall be clean from all your filthiness, and from your idols will I cleanse you; a new heart also will I give you, and a new spirit will I put within you."

The increase of my ministerial gifts, a sound judgment, a clear expression, a door of utterance, and readiness in the Scriptures: in reference to which I desire I may be helped to act faith upon Exodus. 4:12, "Go, and I will be with they mouth, and teach thee what thou shalt say," and, John 14:26. "He shall teach you all things."

The success of my ministerial labors, that sinners may be converted, saints built up, and the congregation flourish: in reference to this, I desire to act faith on Matt. 28:20, "Lo, I am with you always;" and Isaiah 55:10-11, "As the rain cometh down ..."

The blessing of God upon my wife and children, that God will give his grace to my dear little ones, and drive out the foolishness bound up in their hearts: in reference to which I desire to act faith on Isaiah 44:3, "I will pour out my Spirit upon thy seed, and my blessing upon thine offspring."

My other dear relations I would recommend to God's protection, and blessing in prayer, my friends, acquaintance, brethren in the ministry in London, in Dublin, in Cheshire, and Lancashire particularly; and the congregation at Broad Oak, and their minister, some Members of Parliament, and other gentlemen of my acquaintance.

January 1, 1702. The covenant of grace being a new covenant, because ever new, and often to be renewed, I have, this new year's day, early in the morning, while it is yet dark, solemnly renewed it upon my knees, and be it a memorandum indeed, ever remembered, and never forgotten.

Humbly acknowledging my dependence upon God as my Creator and the Author of my being, my obligations in duty to him as my Sovereign Lord and Ruler, and my engagements in gratitude to him as my Protector and Benefactor, and mentioning with thankfulness, the many mercies of my life hitherto and particularly those of the year past, during which I have found myself the care of a very kind Providence, which has made the steps of my pilgrimage comfortable, which has preserved to me the use of my reason and understanding, limbs and senses, hath continued my liberty and opportunity to exercise my ministry, hath provided plentifully for me and my family, and loaded me daily with his benefits. For all which I praise his name, and for the mediation of Jesus Christ, to which I owe all.

Acknowledging also, and lamenting the remaining strength of my corruptions, and my bent to backslide from the living God, taking to myself the shame of my many defects and follies, notwithstanding my frequent renewing of my covenant with God and flying to Christ for righteousness, pardon, and peace.

I once more bind my soul with a bond to be the Lord's wholly and only and forever his. Into thy hands, O God, I commit my spirit to be ruled, cleansed, and sanctified throughout, qualified for thy service in this world and for the fruition of thee in the other. My body I present unto thee as a living sacrifice, holy and acceptable, for it is my reasonable service. My ministry I devote to thy honor, and the continuance and success of it I submit to thy will. All my worldly comforts I lay at thy feet to be disposed of as thou pleaseth. My life itself is thine, O God of my life, "my times are in thy hand." Whatever may be the events of this year, let divine grace be sufficient for me, to enable me to accommodate myself to the will of God in them; and then nothing can come amiss. If God will be with me and keep me in the way that I go throughout the remaining part of my pilgrimage, in the world where I am but a stranger, and will give me bread to eat and raiment to put on, and a heart to love him, and serve him, and live to him, so that I may come at last to my heavenly Father's house in peace, then shall the Lord by my God, my Lord, and my God for ever. Amen. Hallelujah.

Matthew Henry

October 18, 1702. This day I have completed the 40th year of my life. Of life did I say? Rather indeed of my inactivity and folly, but of the tender mercy, kindness, and forbearance of God towards me. To Christ my Mediator I joyfully acknowledge myself a debtor for the supports and aids and comforts of life; and to that same Christ I wholly *trust that I shall receive from my God wonderfully propitiated, the forgiveness of my sins, grace for help, and preservation even unto eternal life.*

December 31, 1702. 1. *As to myself and family, the days of another year are numbered and finished, a year not made particularly remarkable by any great change in my circumstance; no new thing created, but, as usual,*

(1.) The usual matter of complaint against myself. Folly is still found, bound up in my heart, though I hope, through grace, corruption is dying, yet not without some struggles and much opposition from a naughty heart, I desire to lament my unskillfulness and lack of preparation in Scripture, my dullness in holy duties, particularly in secret. I wish I had prayed more for the success of my ministry, but sometimes I have thought I should pray more for grace, to make me faithful myself, that I may be accepted of God, though not of men. But, perhaps, I should pray more for the prosperity of the work of God, even in my hand, though most unworthy; vain thoughts—crowds of them—are a matter of complaint daily. Never was corrupt soil more fruitful in weeds.

(2.) The usual matter of thanksgiving to God. I have had great measure of health, few of my brethren so much. I note it, because perhaps the ensuing year may bring sickness or death with it. I have not ailed anything considerable, and sometimes the highest degree of health is the next degree to sickness. I have not so many sensible memorandums of my frailty, as those have that are often ailing. The Lord grant I may, by the power of grace, be kept more mindful of it.

Ever since brother Radford died, which is now three year ago, death has made no breach among my relations. Since I set out in the world, I never was so long without the death of children or others near and dear to me. My children are very healthful and have had no ill accident. My dear wife, though often indisposed, yet blessed be God, under no languishing distemper, and my dear mother still continued in usefulness.

As to my ministry, that which has been most discouraging this year is that few young ones have come into communion. I think fewer than any other year.

As to my estate, I have lived comfortable upon it with what I have received here, but while in these circumstances, I cannot expect to lie by much. Perhaps troubles may come which may sweep away all. I have some comfort, that I hope I do some good with what I have and spend none of it ill.

2. As to the public, the death of the king this year has made a great change in the face of things, though not yet such a change as many feared. Our successes abroad, both by sea and land, have been very great, which magnifies the present government, and that we have reason to rejoice in. The discontented in the last reign are now pleased. I wish they may ever be so. The high-church is very high, both against the low and dissenters. Now Lord, behold their threatenings. We are alarmed to think of sufferings, and we need such alarms.

I have heartily wished that the bigotry of some violent conformists on the one side and of some dissenters on the other might drive the sober, moderate, and peaceable on both sides nearer together, and prepare things for a coalescence when God's time is come, which I earnestly pray for, and which, perhaps might be effected if they could disentangle themselves as much from the high-church as I think we are from the high-dissenters, or I wish we were.

January 1, 1703. "*Looking for the blessed hope.*" *This new year's day I have much weakness and compassed about with many infirmities, upon my knees, made a fresh surrender of myself, my whole self, all I am, all I have, all I can do, to God the Father, Son, and Holy Ghost, my Creator, owner, ruler, and benefactor; all my affections to be ruled by the divine grace, and all my affairs to be overruled by the divine providence, so that I may not come short of glorifying God in this world, and being glorified with him in a better.*

Confirming and ratifying all former resignations of myself to God, and lamenting all the disagreeableness of my heart and life therewith, and depending upon the merit of the Redeemer to make this and all my other services acceptable, and the grace of the Sanctifier to enable me to make good these engagements, I again bind my soul with a bond to the Lord, and commit myself entirely to him; particularly, as to the events of this year which I am now entering upon, not knowing the things that may abide me in it.

If this year should be a year of continued health and comfort, I commit myself to the grace of God to be preserved from carnal security, and to be enabled in a day of prosperity to serve God with joy.

If my opportunities as a minister should be this year continued, I commit my studies and ministerial labors at home and abroad to the blessing of God, having afresh consecrated them all to his service and honor, earnestly desiring mercy of the Lord to be faithful and successful.

If I should be this year at any time tried with doubts concerning my duty, I commit myself to the divine conduct with an unbiased desire, praying to know what God will have me to do, and with a fixed resolution by his grace to follow his direction in the integrity of my heart.

If I should this year be afflicted in my body, family, name, or estate, I commit my all to the Divine disposal. The will of the Lord be done, only begging that the grace of God may go along with the providence of God in all my afflictions, to enable my both to bear them well, and to use them well.

If this year I should be disturbed or molested in the exercise of my ministry, if I should be silenced or otherwise suffer for well doing, I commit the keeping of my soul to God as a faithful Creator, depending upon him to guide me in my call to suffer, and to make that clear, and to preserve me from perplexing snares; depending upon him to support and comfort me under my sufferings and to bring glory to himself out of them; and then, welcome his whole will.

If this year should be my dying year, as perhaps it may be, I commit my spirit into the hands of my Redeemer to be washed with his blood and presented in his arms with exceeding joy. My wife and children I commit to him to be owned, blessed, and preserved by him when I am gone. "In thee, O Lord, have I put my trust, let me never be ashamed..."

October 18, 1703. *To day is completed the forty-first year of my wandering in this wilderness. Very many of my days have slipped by fruitlessly and unprofitably. And, what ought to make me ashamed, all truly peaceful, and full of divine benignity, and ever to be recorded with gratitude to God. What remains I know not: a few days perhaps and full of trouble, but the will of my Lord be done. To me to live in Christ; so shall it always be, and eternally, and to die gain.*

December 31, 1703. (After reciting, as on some former occasions, his sins and mercies, and observing that, even under the Gospel, there must be a remembrance of sins every year, he proceeds.) Not such as speaks any deficiency in the sacrifice, as that under the law did, but such as speaks deficiency in my daily repentance, which ought, therefore, to be renewed, and the imperfection of the work of sanctification.

Unfixedness of thought, a wretched, desultoriness. Some speak of time well spent in thinking, but I find unless in speaking, reading, or writing, my thinking doth not turn to much account. Though I have had comfort in some broken good thoughts, yet I can seldom fix my heart to a chain of them. O that the thoughts of my heart may be forgiven.

I have oft bewailed my barrenness in good discourse and unskillfulness in beginning it, and coldness of concern for the souls of others. In reflection on this year, I find it has not been much better. I bless God I love good discourse and would promote it, but I want zeal. The Lord pity me.

I have great reason to be thankful for continued health, for comfort in my soul, not made a terror to myself. I have oft thought this year what a mercy it is to be kept out of the horrible pit and miry clay.

I have had much satisfaction this year in my nonconformity, especially by reading Mr. Hoadly's books, in which I see a manifest spirit of Christianity unhappily leavened by the spirit of conformity.

January 1, 1704. Acknowledging my continued dependence upon God as my Creator, Preserver, and chief good, and my continued obligations to him in duty as my Lord and Ruler, and in interest as my Benefactor and

Protector—believing that he is, and that he is the rewarder of them that diligently seek him.

Relying upon the merit, mediation, and everlasting righteousness of my dear Lord and Savior Jesus Christ, who loved me and gave himself for me, as my way to the Father, and the spotless robe wherein alone I can appear before him.

And submitting my soul to the operation and influences of the blessed Spirit of grace, without which I am nothing and can do nothing.

Thankfully owing God's goodness to me the last yea, in lengthening out my life, health, comfort in soul, peace, plenty, settlement, relations, liberty and opportunity; and admiring his patience, forbearance, longsuffering in sparing me in his vineyard, who deserved to have been cut down and cast into the fire as a barren tree.

Lamenting my foolishness, the foolishness which is still bound up in my heart, and that which still breaks forth in my life, and particularly that my improvements in grace and usefulness last year did not answer the covenants which began it.

Because of all this I make a sure covenant and write it.

In the strength of the grace of Jesus Christ, on which alone I depend to work all my works in me and for me, I covenant for this new year and for my whole life to walk closely with God in all holy conversation, to keep my heart with all diligence. To thee, O my God, I commit the keeping of it. To take heed of my ways, that I sin not with my tongue, and do thou stand watch, O Lord, before the door of my lips. I covenant to redeem my time, and to thee, O God, do I consecrate this year and all the hours of it. The Lord enable me to fill it up with good according as the duty of every day requires. I bind myself to follow the Spirit of God in all affections and the providence of God *in all my affairs, whatever God shall appoint me to this year: to health or sickness, to plenty or loss, to evil report or good report, to liberty or restraint, to the house of mourning or the house of rejoicing, to life or death. Behold, here I am, let him do with me as seemeth good in his eyes. Only whatever the providence of God allots for me, let the grace of God be sufficient for me, to enable me to accommodate myself to it; and then welcome the will of God.*

CHAPTER 8

n the early part of the year 1704, Mr. Henry, accompanied by Mrs. Henry, again visited the metropolis. The precise occasion of the journey does not fully appear; nor is it material. One remark, however, made by him on leaving Northampton, may be properly cited as indicative of the spirit in which he traveled—the same spirit indeed, which gave consistency and elevation to his whole character, both at home and abroad.

"It is easy to leave an inn; why should it not be easy to leave this world, which is but an inn, to go to our house, our Father's house? The troubles of traveling exercise our patience and submission to God's will. By submission in lesser things, we learn greater. But they also give us to experience the goodness of God in our preservation and encourage us to hope in that goodness in our journey for heaven."

The record of a sermon he heard preached on Sabbath-morning, the day after his arrival in London, by John Howe is not less worthy of attention. It is perfectly characteristic of both the parties. It is, moreover, pregnant with universal instruction; and embraced as such may be a balm of healing and refreshment to such especially as, under a prevailing sense of unworthiness, move heavily along the narrow way.

"The text," says Mr. Henry, "was Jude 21; and I must never forget what he said in the close of the sermon. 'I would deal for your souls, as for my own, and for myself I declare before you all, I depend purely upon the mercy of our Lord Jesus Christ for eternal life.'"

Till now, Mr. Henry's health, though delicate when a child, had continued good. Henceforward the inroads made upon his frame by disease were frequent and alarming.

On Lord's Day, August 27, the same year, 1704, while reading the chapter in the morning service, he suddenly fainted. Recovering speedily, he however proceeded in his beloved work. Had he taken rest, the subsequent effects would probably have been prevented. But unskilled in the art of self-sparing and impelled by holy zeal, instead of relaxing, as he ought to have done, the next day he fulfilled as appointment to preach at Nantwich, and the day following, another at Haslington. The latter was a funeral sermon for an aged and faithful minister, Mr. Cope, pursuant to his desire, and to a large congregation. These engagements, by the excitement they produced, added much to his exhaustion.

On his return home, the consequences were distinctly visible, and indisposition so much increased as to confine him altogether to the house. Not having for fifteen years been detained from public worship on the Sabbath, he naturally felt the imprisonment, but not so as to overlook existing mercies. The fever continued more than three weeks, but he was able, during the whole time, and he gratefully recorded it, both "to light the lamps and to burn the incense;" that is, daily, with only one exception, to expound and pray in his family, morning and evening.

It was during this visitation, when the physicians would not sanction his usual services in the sanctuary, that he assembled his family for worship, telling them with instructive emphasis that if he must not go to the house of God, he would go to the God of the house. And so as soon as health returned, he did not wait for the Sabbath, but selected the lecture-day for resuming his public appearance. "I was willing," said he, "to go thither first, where I most desire to be. I would take the first opportunity of paying my vows."

Here the order of the history requires that further extracts from the diary should be inserted; a circumstance, which it is presumed the judicious reader will not regret.

January 1, 1705. Not renouncing, but repeating and ratifying all my former covenants with God, and lamenting that I have not lived up more closely to them, I do, in the beginning of this new year, solemnly make a fresh surrender of myself, my whole self, body, soul, and spirit, to God the Father, Son, and Holy Ghost; my Creator, Redeemer, and Sanctifier; covenanting and promising not in any strength of my own, for I am very weak, but in the strength of the grace of Jesus Christ, that I will endeavour this year to stand complete in all the will of God.

I know that this is the will of God, even my sanctification. Lord grant that this year I may be more holy and walk more closely than ever in all holy conversation. I earnestly desire to be filled with holy thoughts, to be carried out in holy affection, determined by holy aims and intentions, and governed in all my words and actions by holy principles. O that a golden thread of holiness may run through the whole web of this year.

I know it is the will of God that I should be useful, and by his grace I will be so. Lord, thou knowest it is the top of my ambition in this world to do good, and to be serviceable to the honor of Christ and the welfare of precious souls. I would fain do good in the pulpit and good with my pen; and, which I earnestly desire to abound more in, to do good by my common converse. O that the door of my opportunities may be still open, and that my heart may be enlarge with holy zeal and activity for God this year, and that I may be thoroughly furnished with knowledge, wisdom, and grace, for every good word and work.

If it be the will of God that this should be a year of affliction to me, a year of sickness or reproach or loss, if my family should be visited, if my liberties should be cut short, if public troubles should arise, if any calamity should befall me, which I am least apprehensive of now, I earnestly desire to submit to the divine disposal. Welcome the holy will of God. Let me have God's favor, and the assurance of that, and by his grace nothing shall come amiss to me.

If it be the will of God that I should finish my course this year, let me be fonud of Christ in peace, and by the grace of God, death shall be welcome to me. My wife and children, relations, and my congregation, which is very dear to me, my ministry, myself—may I commit all to God, whose I am, and whom I desire to serve. Let me be the Lord's only, wholly, and forever. Amen. The Lord say Amen to it.

October 18,1705. I have this day completed the forty-third year of my useless live. By the grace of God I live; I hope in his mercy and I pant for his glory. May the small remnant of my time be a season of repentance for the sins and of gratitude for the mercies of the former part of my life. May God be my sun and shield, and may I be his servant, and a subject of his kingdom, even unto the end and for ever. Amen and Amen.

December 31, 1705. *We bring our year to an end, like a tale that is told. Lord teach us to number our days.*

In the review of the year I find,

1. That I have as much reason as ever to be thankful to God. It has been a year of much mercy. My life has been continued to the end of it, though many of my brethren in the ministry have been removed in the midst of their days, who, had they lived, would have done God more service that I can; particularly my dear brother, Mr. Chorlton. I have had a good measure of health for my ministry and study, no recurrences or remains of my last year's illness.

God has this year brought my children through the smallpox, and borne up my dear wife under great weakness.

My mother, also, though brought low, has been helped.

My door of opportunity continues open at home and abroad, and I am willing to hope some good is done.

That which is especially remarkable as the mercy of this year, is the happy posture of our public affairs, particularly at home. After a mighty struggle, moderate counsels have prevailed. God has wonderfully inclined the queen's heart to such counsels; and useth her as an instrument of great good to the land, that the excellency of the power may be of God. Patrons of our liberty have

*been strangely raised up among those who have no
kindness for us or our way. The intemperate acts of bigots
have proved to make mightily against themselves; there
are many adversaries, and yet the door continues to open.
Great endeavors have been used to render us contemptible,
odious, dangerous, and what not, and yet we live and go
on, and young ones are coming in, and some hopeful ones.
O that the power of godliness, holiness, seriousness, and
heavenly mindedness might prevail more among us, and
then we should have a very hopeful prospect. And who
can tell, but infinite wisdom may yet find out a way for
comprehending us though the present temper of our
neighbors rather than set it at a greater distance than ever.*

*2. I have reason to make the old complaints of dullness
and weakness, and coldness of affection to divine things.
The Lord strengthen the things, which remain!*

*Care about my children, providing something for them
has been often in my head; and perhaps more than it should
be. Lord, I cast the care upon thee, who hast provided
well for me; the Lord care for them and teach me my duty,
and then with him I will leave the event.*

*January 1, 1705-6. It is of the Lord's mercy that I am
not consumed. By night, on my bed, I endeavored to seek
him whom my soul loveth; and now I begin this new year.*

*1. Earnestly praying for the graces of the year with a
humble subjection of soul to the blessed Spirit of God,
that I may, some way or other, eminently honour and
glorify God this year, that I may live this year to some
purpose, to better purpose than I did the last. O that no
temptation may so overtake me this year as to overcome
me. To the conduct of divine grace, which is, I know,
sufficient for me. I here solemnly resign myself, my
thoughts, my affections, my will, and all the intents of my*

heart to be directed into the right way, and kept and quickened in it. Let me this year receive grace for grace.

2. Patiently waiting for the events of the year with a humble submission to the holy will of God. I know not what the year shall bring forth, but I know it shall bring forth nothing amiss to me if God be my God in covenant. If it bring forth death, that I hope shall quite finish sin and free me from it. Lord, let thy servant depart in peace, according to thy word. I commit my family to my heavenly Father, to God, even my own God, my Father's God, my children's God. O pour out thy Spirit upon my seed, thy blessing, that blessing, that blessing of blessings upon my offspring, that they may be praising God on earth when I am praising him in heaven. Amen, Amen.

January 1, 1707. My own act and deed, through the grace of God, I have made it many a time and now I make it the first act of this new year: to resign myself afresh unto the Lord, not only for the year ensuing, but for my whole life and forever.

1. To thee, O God, I give up myself to be used and employed for thee. I desire to live no longer than I may do thee some service. Make what use of me thou pleaseth, only let me obtain mercy of the Lord, to be found diligent, humble, and faithful. O that the work of this year may be better done than that of the last, and my time more filled up; and that I may never grow weary of well doing.

2. To thee, O God, I give up myself, to be disposed of by thee as thou pleaseth. I know not what the year may bring forth to me or to my family. But welcome the holy will of God; and God, by his grace, make me ready for it. If it be the last year of my life, my dying year, may I but finish my course with joy; and farewell this world.

Whatever afflictions may this year befall me, I desire none of them may move me from God and my duty.

It may be properly noticed here how greatly the afflictions which had befallen Mr. Henry, since the death of his father, had been mitigated by the preservation and general convalescence of his widowed mother. She had shared his trials, eased the burden by hearing a part of it, and by the brilliance of her Christian character, had eminently adorned the Gospel, and encouraged him in the "work of the Lord."

At length, however, the period of declining health and advanced years had intimated all that was approaching, and to which Mr. Henry alludes in one of the foregoing excerpts, arrived. On the morning of the Sabbath, May 25, 1707, he was visited by the melancholy tidings of her departure.

The necessity of doing more than barely noticing the event is superseded by the statements already in print and referred to at the foot of this page. There is, nevertheless, one fact recorded in the diary of her sorrowing son, which cannot with propriety be passed over. It is one of these episodes, which, by naturally connecting itself with the main subject, gives a charm, rather than an interruption to the narrative.

"I find with the profits and rents of this current year, that there will be little more than to discharge my dear mother's funeral and legacies, but no debts at all. She lived with comfort, bore her testimony to the goodness of God's providence that she had experienced all her days, did not increase what she had, nor coveted to lay up, but did good with it and left a blessing behind her."

To return to the anniversary reflections:

October 18, 1707. To borrow Caleb's words, Josh. 14:10, the Lord has kept me alive these forty-five years. So long I have lived under the divine protection, a wasting candle kept burning. But to how little purpose have I lived. Thus long I have cumbered the ground. O that I may yet bear fruit.

December 31, 1707. As to the year past, I have as much reason as ever to lament my barrenness and unfruitfulness that I have not made a better proficiency in knowledge and grace. I find myself growing into years, being now turned forty-five. I begin to feel my journey in my bones, and I desire to be thereby loosened from the world and from the body. The death of my dear and honored mother this year has been a sore breach upon my comfort, for she was my skillful, faithful counselor; and it is intimation to me that now, in the order of nature, that I must go next. My estate is somewhat increased. The Lord enlarge my heart to do good with it, but as goods are increased, they are increased that eat them. My children are growing up, and that reminds me that I am going down. As to my ministry here, Mr. Mainwaring's leaving me, and his wife has been very much my discouragement. But Providence so ordered it that Mr. Harvey's congregation are generally come in to us, or else we begin to dwindle, so that I should have gone on very heavily.

January 1, 1707-8, early. Christ is a Christian's all; and he is my all.

Unto thee, O blessed Jesus, my only Saviour and Redeemer, do I make a fresh surrender of my whole self this morning, body and soul, and spirit; to me to live in Christ, particularly this ensuing year.

All my time, strength, and service, I devote to the honour of the Lord Jesus: my studies and all my ministerial labors, and even my common actions. It is my earnest expectation and hope and desire, it may be my constant aim and endeavour, that Jesus Christ may be magnified in my body.

In everything wherein I have to do with God, my entire dependence is upon Jesus Christ for strength and righteousness; and whatever I do in word or deed, I desire to do all in his name, to make him my Alpha and Omega; the anointed of the Lord is the breath of my nostrils, through his hand I desire to receive all my comforts. I have all by him, and I would use all for him.

If this should prove a year of affliction, a sorrowful year upon my account, I will fetch all my supports and comforts from the Lord Jesus, and stay myself upon him, his everlasting consolations, and the good hope I have in him through grace.

And if it should be my dying year, my times are in the hand of the Lord Jesus; and with a humble reliance upon his mediation, I would venture into another world looking for the blessed hope. Dying as well as living, Jesus Christ will, I trust, be gain and advantage to me.

Good Lord, keep this always in the imagination of the thought of my heart, and establish my way before thee.

October 18, 1708. *Today I have finished the forty-sixth year of my life. My infancy, however, was useless. My childhood and youth were not directed to proper objects, and even in my maturer age, how many months and days have I spent to little purpose! So that I have lived scarcely one-tenth part of my time. Forgive, O Lord, my idleness and sloth. For me to live may it be Christ.*

CHAPTER 9

A.D. 1709 to A.D. 1712
Invitations to Mr. Henry from Distant Churches, Devout
Commencement of 1708-9, Letter from the Rev. Mr. Tong,
Mr. Henry's Perplexity, Consults Dr. Calamy, Letter from
Dr. Calamy, the Character of the Applications Which Have
Been Noticed, Birth-day Memorial, 1709, An Invitation from
Hackney Renewed, His Determination to Leave Chester,
His Reasons for it, Birth-day, 1711, His Perplexity and
Distress Continue

emorials like those, which have engaged the reader's
attention and completed Mr. Henry's history to the
present period, cannot fail to have prepared him
for the statements which are now to be making
respecting his extended and well-established popularity.

After his visit to London in 1698, he seems to have been an
object of desire by almost every church whose pastor, if at all
renowned, was either removed or laid aside. And some of the
efforts made to obtain his removal were uncommonly bold and
persevering.

The first known instance of the kind happened after the death
of the eloquent and learned Dr. Bates at Hackney; and, the better
to ensure success, the communication was made to Mr. Henry

to ensure success, the communication was made to Mr. Henry through his beloved friend, the Reverend John Shower. It failed, however, of success.

A like attempt followed the death of Reverend Nathaniel Taylor, one of the lecturers at Salter's Hall, and who, on account of his splendid talents, was styled by Dr. Doddridge as the "Dissenting South." The peremptory nature of the refusal given to the Hackney invitation had so far, in the first instance, discouraged the applicants, as to have induced them to seek Mr. Chorley of Norwich, but he, having declined compliance, though elected, it was resolved, at all events, to present an invitation. They judiciously accompanied it by persuasive letters from Mr. Howe, Mr. (afterwards Dr.) Williams, and Dr. Hamilton. Those excellent men urged some existing disputes in the congregation—pressing at the same time an assurance that Mr. Henry's acquiescence would at once hush the clamors of both parties. The only anxiety he felt seems to have been to know the divine will. "Had we an oracle to consult," he writes, "I could refer to the divine determination with so great an indifference, that if it were referred to me, I would refer it back to God again."

After many serious thoughts, and not a few uneasy ones, he replied to the invitation in the negative. Some time afterwards, the matter is thus referred to:

> *The invitation to the congregation at Salter's Hall was a surprise to me. I begged God to keep me from being lifted up with pride by it. I sought of him a right way. Had I consulted either my own fancy, which had always a kindness for London ever since I knew it, or the worldly advantage of my family, I had closed with it; and I was sometimes tempted to think it might open a door of greater usefulness. Though I think ministers married to their*

ministry, yet I cannot see any Scriptural ground to think that Mr. John Evans might have been had there, and might have been more acceptable to some, and more useful than I. But I had not courage to break through the opposition of affections of my friends here to me and mine own to them, nor to venture upon a new and unknown place and work, which I feared myself unfit for. It has been looked on as the honour of ministers to continue in the same place, notwithstanding temptations to remove. I bless God I am well satisfied in what I did in that matter, though it was once and again a sudden resolve. If ever it pleases Gods to call me from this place, I depend upon him to make my way clear. Lord lead me in a plain path.

The next effort proceeded from Manchester, almost immediately after Mr. Chorlton, a divine of singular eminence and attainments, was taken to his reward. It was made in person by a special deputation, but at once withstood. "I cannot think," he remarked on that occasion, "of leaving Chester till Chester leaves me."

In the year, 1708, he was again harassed by a solicitation from London to accept a joint pastorship with Mr. Shower at the Old Jewry. He merely replied in a letter to Mr. Shower himself that the reason of not accepting his invitation was that he loved the people at Chester too well to leave them.

The same year, 1708, the learned and Reverend John Spademan, Mr. Howe's successor at Silver Street, being removed to a better world, Mr. Henry was again assailed; and, the better to ensure success, the requisitionists employed the influence of Mr. Tong. That faithful man, knowing the steadfastness of his friend, and fearing, no doubt, lest by seeking too much, all would be lost, only urged him to allow an invitation. Mr. Henry replied in the negative. The congregation, however, without his knowledge, actually elected him to be their pastor jointly with Mr. Spademan's late colleague, the Reverend Samuel Rosewell. And the singular adventure was followed by numerous communications urging compliance—particularly from Mr. Burgess, Mr. Tong, Mr. (afterwards Dr.) J. Evans, Mr. (afterwards Dr.) D. Williams, Mr. Hunt and Sir Henry Ashurst and a "Letter subscribed by various Ministers."

It is not possible to state exactly the effect produced upon Mr. Henry by these measures, but judging from the way in which he not long afterwards expressed himself, it does not seem that he was, at the time, either much moved or perplexed.

> *January 1, 1708-9. The inscribing of a double year, eight and nine, puts me in mind to look back upon the year past, which I have reason to do with thankfulness for the many mercies with which God has crowned it, and with sorrow and shame for the many sins with which I have blotted it, and to look forward to the year now beginning which I have endeavored to begin with God.*
>
> *My outward concerns, as to my health and safety, the prosperity of my affairs, provision for my family, the continuance of my life, and the lives of my relations and friends, comfort in my children and congregation, I have committed, and do commit, to the conduct and disposal of God's gracious providence, which I depend upon to order everything for good to me. Here I am, let the Lord do with me and mine as seemeth good unto him. That Providence, I trust, will so order every event as that nothing shall be an invincible temptation to me to draw me from God and duty in any instance.*
>
> *The affairs of my soul and all the concerns of the spiritual and divine life, I commit to the special grace of*

*God, which I trust shall be sufficient for me, to enable me
to keep a good conscience, to do my duty well as a mater
of a family and as a minister, to persevere to the end, and
to finish well. Lord, neither leave me nor forsake me; I
will seek thy precepts. O, forsake me not utterly. The Lord
"preserves me to his heavenly kingdom." Amen. Amen!*

In a letter written to him by Mr. Tong early in the year 1709,
several of the facts, which have been stated, are touched much
more distinctly, and while the pleas and allusions excellently
illustrate Mr. Henry's character and show his extensive popularity,
the supposed annoyances, naturally incident to what had passed,
are plainly referred to, but with a tender delicacy, highly honorable
to the writer, whether viewed as a gentleman, a friend, or a
Christian.

To the Reverend Mr. Henry, at his House in Chester.
February 24, 1708-9.

Honored and Dear Sir,
    *I begin to think it long since I heard from you, but
shall reckon the pain of expectation abundantly
recompensed, if I may but, at length, enjoy the pleasure of
the desired answer. The gentlemen who have given you
such repeated and pressing invitations are daily with me,
and discover the greatest concern imaginable about the
issue of their addresses to you. They suggest a great many
things as what to them appear strong, and conclusive for
them; and the more difficulties they meet with in their way,
the more zealous and earnest are they to gain their end. I
must say, I think if ever any were animated in such an
affair by Christian and Catholic principles, they are the
people. They would fain please themselves with the thought
of having the Friday lecture revived, which has been*

discontinued since Mr. Spademans's death, and which they will allow 50 pounds sterling a-year [Editor's note: In today's exchange, roughly $100 USD.] *for (besides their other subscriptions): they cannot forbear to say how glad they would advance half a hundred guineas immediately towards the charge of your remove. I tell them these are not the arguments that will take with you, and they think so too and are very confident that the plea of greater service is clearly on their side.*

The whole city, from Westminster to Wapping, seems very heartily to wish and long for your coming. These things I cannot forbear mentioning; though at the same time, I consider, if they should meet with contrary sentiments and resolutions in you, I do but make myself thereby uneasy and vexatious to you; but I hope I do not displease God in it; because I really think his honor is concerned in it, and would be promoted by your compliance; but I ought to remember I speak to one of a discerning spirit, and that you have had already too much trouble from

Your most affectionate, W. T[ong].

Still unwilling to listen to the overtures, Mr. Henry wrote to desire Mr. Rosewell's congregation to acquiesce in his purpose to continue at Chester.

The requisitionists, however, continued their importunity, aided by not a few, both ministers and laymen, who deservedly raked among the judicious and excellent of the earth. The matter thus pressed became a snare. Mr. Henry was involved in continual perplexity and uneasiness. He was subjected also (and the Diary feelingly complains of it) to much hindrance in his business, to many harsh censures, and to the malignant cowardice of anonymous letter writers. An enemy scoffingly remarked that he would not have him go to London, for he would do there more mischief than at Chester.

In his distress, Mr. Henry, at length, applied to Dr. Calamy, and in order to receive the advice and directions of that justly celebrated man with increased advantage, a meeting took place at Holme's Chapel in Lancashire. The Doctor was then on his way from Scotland to London. The interview will be vest explained by the following excellent letter:

For the Reverend Mr. Matthew Henry,
at his house in Chester, Westminster,
June 18, 1709.

Dear Sir,
I thank you for your company at Holme's Chapel, which was very kind and exceedingly agreeable. At my return I was in a great hurry, and no other could be expected after such a long absence. But I have not forgotten my promise to you, which this comes to discharge.

No other can be supposed than that there should be a great variety of sentiments about such an affair as yours. But I find you are so happy, both in city and country, as to me with this favorable opinion, that you, in the issue, will do nothing but what, all things considered, appears to you to be most for the glory that this, instead of being any thing of hindrance to the closest consideration even to the last, will (as it certainly should) be an inducement to receive all the light that can be obtained. I cannot, for my part, pretend to give any light; but I will frankly give you my thought and remarks, and shall be glad if they may be of any use.

I observed, by your discourse, that you were not apprehensive of more usefulness at Chester than at London, nor fearful of breaking the Chester meeting upon your removal. But that affection to your people on the one hand and some fear of uneasiness in the post you were invited to, on the other hand, were the great things that stuck with you. As to affection, in this case methinks it should yield to judgment; and I cannot suppose but it will, though there way be a struggle. I thought I found your judgment for London (suppositis supponendis) when we were discoursing. And what your plenipotentiary dropped when with some of the people of Silver Street, intimated as much; for he told them that your heart was with them, which I suppose was by your order, or at least allowance. Now, certainly heart cannot mean less than affection, as well as judgment. It may still, indeed, grate on your tender spirit to part from so many dear friends; and yet, as you cannot but do it if duty calls; so, methinks, it should be no hard matter for a man to go where his heart is, though he meets with a pull in going.

But still I find fears as to the post you are invited to. And how came you by them? Are they not, in a great measure, owing to letters, which the writers are afraid or ashamed to set their names to? And are they not declared groundless by some whose friendship in our parts you value, who know the particulars of the case? And are these then fit to give the turn and determine a man for his future life?

But what are they? Will you allow me to scan them? You seem to fear inability for the expected service. But why may not God be safely trusted as to that, after his carrying you through so many years' acceptable and successful service already? You fear not answering expectations. Suppose you should not, where they are *raised too high. If yet you are more useful here than anywhere else, where is the damage? You fear uneasiness in Mr. R[osewell] and some of his friends, and that they may create uneasiness in you. Suppose this true; should it give the turn and determine? I think not, for the question is where you may be capable of the most useful services. Besides, should this turn the scale, should base ease determine, it is impossible but you may meet with as great uneasiness there as you fear here. Or, if ease is sacrificed, it may perhaps be as easily secured here as there, by prudential methinks. For poor Mr. R[osewell] has visibly weakened himself by an over-great fondness of sole pastorship. Whether you come or no, he cannot carry it. And, though for the present he might perhaps be rather better pleased to be alone, yet he would find the effects in a little time; and, if he must have a joint pastor (as he certainly must), there is none more agreeable than yourself, either to him or to his most particular friends. And this I think you may depend upon anything.*

Well then, let us suppose the worst. Is it reasonable for you for fear of disobliging two or three (the impression of which would soon wear off) to refuse to follow your heart, to refuse to go where duty seems to call, and at the same time have a hand in dispersing a flourishing congregation? You must allow me to insist on this latter consideration now, though I could not so fully do it at Holme's Chapel. For I am now satisfied that you will not only disoblige many more good friends by a refusal than can be imagined in the least disturbed by a compliance, but that there will be danger of our having a hand in dispersing the congregation.

It is true that Mr. Rosewell will not want an auditory. He will certainly fill the place. But, if the graver persons withdraw, it will be a public damage. This you may prevent.

It is dubious whether another man can. I have consulted some of the most discerning persons among them. They positively assure me that if you refuse them they can think of no man in whom they are likely to center with any unanimity. For you they all long. In you they will all heartily acquiesce. Has not this its weight? Mr. Rosewell in all probability would be as well pleased as any of them in a little time. Our joint agreement to guard against two interests in the congregation would prevent uneasiness, and I doubt not produce great harmony and friendship. I profess I verily believe if you accept this motion, you will have a respectful, loving, united flock. And as to your colleague, things may be so settled as to prevent all danger. You will be very useful here and perhaps not much less useful at Chester and in the neighboring parts by a yearly visit, that by constantly residing there.

I must add that, notwithstanding your last discouraging letter, the people still have expectations that, upon further thought, you will become theirs. Your plenipotentiary's telling them that your heart was with them, has much encouraged them. He promised them that they should hear from you (or at least from him) after he had represented matters as they appeared to him; and this has added to their encouragement. Nor were they a little pleased to hear from me of your thoughts of coming to town the next month. They firmly adhere to you and will not admit a thought of anyone else. Methinks this is a call to reconsider; and where can you consider better than here amongst them? You will here have that light by a little conversation that a hundred letters could never give you. May I then beg that you will hold your purpose of giving us a visit the next month? Our brethren will be glad to see you. You will find the foregoing representation I believe most exactly true; and be convinced that your accepting the invitation given is really necessary to the common interest.

But I would also move for a line or two to Mr. Gunston or some other person before you come a little softer than the last. Do but let them now that coming to town about your book, you will be ready to hear anything that they who profess so great a respect for you have got to say to you, and it will be enough. Excuse my freedom and impute it to real respect and it will be but just and kind. I pray God direct you and shall be thankful of you remembrance of

Sir, Your brother and Servant
Edm. Calamy.

Ingenious and persuasive as this epistle undoubtedly was, it failed to have the desired effect. Mr. Henry still retained his objections, not because he did not feel the force of Dr. Calamy's arguments not because he was of an obstinate or captious temper, but his kindness for the place and people of Chester prevailed above his judgment, interest, and inclination.

The applications, which have been noticed, discover greatly to his honor, the high station he occupied in public esteem. They impel admiration also of the good sense of their promoters by demonstrating that, with a laudable preference for distinguished talents, they entertained such a correct views of the ministry as to seek them, only in union with conspicuous and well-attested piety. But, allowing to this view of the subject the utmost latitude and conceding to ministers, also in mitigation of such interference, the delicacy oftentimes attendant upon making known their inclination to remove, granting likewise that such knowledge may be an incentive to discontent and ill treatment and division, and in the absence of a new pastoral charge of forced separation. Still, may it not be fairly questioned whether an application to a settled pastor, living happily among his own people and not known even to think of moving, be reconcilable with those principles which inculcate love to our neighbor as to ourselves and which condemn in every supposable instance the slightest emotion of covetousness? Is the robbing of churches limitable to sacramental utensils, official vestments, or mere paraphernalia, and books?

The state of Mr. Henry's own mind, amidst the flattering occurrences, which have been mentioned, is easily inferable from the following sensible memorandum. It was written at the time, but instead of manifesting any self-complacency, it furnishes as beautiful an instance of the union of humble sobriety with intelligent and devout elevation, as can well be imagined.

> *October 18, 1709. Today have I completed the forty-seventh year of my sojourning in this wilderness. Through the whole course of my life hitherto, I have found God merciful and propitious to my supplications; the world I have found empty and unfitted for happiness; and my own heart deceitful, and prone to iniquity. May I therefore, always honor God, despise the world and carefully examine my heart. Here I am, Lord what wilt thou have me to do?*

In May of 1710, on the demise of the Reverend Robert Billio, who, after Mr. Henry's refusal, had been chosen successor to Dr Bates at Hackney, the solicitations of the congregation were renewed with increased importunity. Two visits were subsequently paid and after long continued and serious thought, not to say the most distressing varieties of mental conflict, Mr. Henry determined to leave Chester. The circumstances already mentioned render it almost imperative that the history and reasons of a determination so opposite to every former decision be stated somewhat at length. Happily, they can be furnished in Mr. Henry's own words written while in London:

About Midsummer in 1710, I had a letter from the congregation at Hackney, signifying to me that they had unanimously chosen me to be their minister in the room of Mr. Billio, who was lately dead of the smallpox. They desired that I would accept their invitation. In prosecution of which they told me I should find them as the importunate widow that would have no nay. I several times denied them. At length they wrote to me that some of them would come down hither. To prevent them, I being not unwilling to take a London journey in the interval between my third and fourth volumes, I wrote them word I would come up to them, and did so in the middle of July, but was down again before the first Lord's Day in August. Then I laid myself open to the temptation by increasing my acquaintance in the city.

They followed me after I came down, with letters to me and to the congregation. In October I wrote to them that if they would stay for me till next spring (which I was in hopes they would not have done), I would come up and make a longer stay for mutual trial. They wrote to me that they would wait till then.

In May, 1711 I went to them and stayed till the end of July, and before I parted with them, signified to them my acceptance of their invitation and my purpose to come to them, God willing, the spring following. The ministers there had many of them given it under their hands that they thought it advisable and for greater good and a more extensive usefulness that I should remove to Hackney.

However, I was determined to deny them at Hackney and had denied them, but the Mr. Gunston, Mr. Smith and some others came to me from London, and begged of me for the sake of the public, that I would not deny them, which was the thing that turned the scales. I never had been till this journey as much as one first Lord's Day of the month out of Chester, since I came to it twenty-four years ago.

By this determination, I brought on myself more grief and care and concern than I could have imagined, and have many a time wished it undone again, but having opened my mouth, I could not go back. I did with the utmost impartiality (if I know anything of myself) beg of God to incline my heart that way which should be most for his glory, and I trust I have a good conscience willing to be found in the way of my duty. Wherein I have done amiss, the Lord forgive me for Jesus' sake and make this change concerning the congregation to work for good to it.

Having this morning (as often, very often before) begged of God to give me wisdom, sincerity and humility, and to direct my thoughts and counsels now, this important affair must at last be determined. I think it prudent, having before set down the reasons for my continuing at Chester, now to set down the reasons, which may induce me to accept of this invitation to Hackney, that it may be a satisfaction to me afterwards to review upon what grounds I went and be a testimony for me that I did not do it rashly.

1. I am abundantly satisfied that it is lawful for ministers to remove, and in many cases highly expedient and necessary to the edifying of the church; and this not only for the avoiding of evil, as in the case of persecution, which can be a reason no longer than while the persecution lasts or of the uncomfortable disposition of the people, but for the attaining of a greater good and the putting of a minister into a larger sphere of usefulness. This has always been my judgment according to the word of God and I have practiced this accordingly in being often active to remove other ministers, which I have afterwards had satisfaction in. And this has been the judgment of the congregation at Chester, between whom and their ministers there have never been those solemn mutual engagements that have been between some other ministers and their congregations nor any bond, but that of love.

2. *My invitation to Hackney is not only unanimous but very pressing, and importunate and the people here in waiting so long for my determination, and in the great affection and respect they have showed to my ministry since I came among them, have given the most satisfying proof of the sincerity and zeal of their invitation; and upon many weeks' trial, I do not perceive anything in the congregation that is discouraging, but everything that promiseth to make a minister's life both comfortable and useful.*

3. *There seems to be something of an intimation of Providence in the many calls I have had in this way before, and particularly to this place, upon the death of Dr. Bates, though I never either directly or indirectly sought them, but on the contrary, did what I could to prevent them and this particularly.*

4. *There is manifestly a much wider door of opportunity to do good opened to me here at London than is at Chester in respect to the frequency and variety of week-day occasions of preaching and the great numbers of the auditors. The prospect I have of improving these opportunities and of doing good to souls thereby is, I confess, the main inducement to me to think of removing hither, and what I have seen while I have been here now has very much encouraged my expectations of that kind.*

5. *In drawing up and publishing my Expositions and many other of my endeavors for the public service, I foresee it will be a great convenience to me to be near the press, and to have the inspection of it, and also to have books at hand that I may have occasion or in the prosecution of my*

studies, and learned men to converse with for my own improvement in knowledge and to consult with upon any difficulty that may occur.

6. I have followed Providence in this affair and to the conduct of that, I have (if I know my own heart) in sincerity referred myself, hoping and praying both myself and my friends for me that God would guide me with his eye and lead me in a plain path. When I was purposing to send a final denial, Providence so ordered it that the very post before I had a letter subscribed by divers of the London ministers persuading me to accept the call, whereupon I wrote to them that would come to them six months upon trial, thinking that they would not have consented to be kept so long in suspense, but it proved that they did; and so I have been drawn step by step to this resolution and though have industriously sought, I have not found anything in this side to break treaty.

7. I have asked the advice of ministers upon a fair representation of the case, which I drew up. Many, upon consideration of it, have given it under their hands. They think it advisable for me to remove and none of them has advised me to the contrary, but have told me I am myself the most proper judge of it. Many private Christians also in London and some that seem to me to be the most judicious and public-spirited have, by letters when I was in Chester and by word of mouth here, persuaded me to accept this call, as judging that by the blessing of God I might be useful here to that agree as to balance the inconveniency of my leaving Chester. Nay, that even here might in many respects be serviceable to the country.

8. I have some reason to hope that my poor endeavors in the ministry may, by the blessing of God, be more useful now to those to whom they are new than to those who have been so long used to them and so constantly; with

whom also I trust another hand may do more good, as mine did, by the grace of God in the first seven years of my being there. And I have known many congregations from whom ministers have removed and those to whom it has created the greatest uneasiness and discontent for the present, which yet have afterwards been so well settled beyond their own expectations under other ministers, that they have flourished even more than ever they had done before.

9. Though the people at Chester are a most loving people and many of them have had and have an exceeding value for me and my ministry, yet I have not been without my discouragements there, and those such as have tempted me to think that my work in the place has been in great measure done, many that have been catechized with us, many that have been long with us have left us, and very few have been added to us.

10. Whereas I have been thought to have been useful in the country by my preaching as God has enabled me in many places about, I have now reason to think that though I should continue at Chester, I should be quite taken off from that part of my work, having found, as I came up and once before, that riding long journeys and preaching brought an illness upon me which I was never till the last winter visited with so that my service would be wholly confined within the walls of Chester; whereas here by divine assistance I might do a great deal of work of that kind without that toil and peril.

11. The congregation at Chester, though it cannot be expected they should consent to part with minister they have so long had a satisfaction in, yet they have been pleased under their hands to leave it to my own conscience and affection; now as to my own conscience upon a long and serious consideration of the matter (and if I know my own heart, an impartial one) and after many prayers to God for direction, I am fully satisfied that I may lawfully remove and that there is a prospect of my being more useful if I do remove and therefore it is expedient that I should; and as to my affections, though they are very strong towards Chester, yet I think they ought to be overruled by my judgment.

Another anniversary of his birthday now arrived, but the record makes no allusion to the situation in which he had placed himself. His mind seems to have been absorbed by the flight of time, and the nearer approach of eternity.

October 18, 1711. I have now finished my seventh climacteric year in which I have first felt the pain of the gravel and the stone by which it is easy for me to discern that death has begun; perhaps in a little time it will be death itself. The will of the Lord be done. Only let patience have its perfect work. I enter now upon the jubilee of my life, my fiftieth year—the term of life approaches may I be fitter for eternal life.

It must, however, be remarked before quitting this part of the narrative that notwithstanding the testimony which was borne to the congregation at Chester that they were pleased under their hands to leave the affair to Mr. Henry's own conscience and affection – after his determination was known, the diary shows how much that was painful he had to endure, were he had expected different and better treatment. Indeed between the anger and incivility of some and the affectionate regards of others, his distress became singularly pungent and his aspirations for meekness and guidance uncommonly affecting.

At the same time, it is only just to observe that the vexations he suffered and to which at this time he so often and so feelingly refers may have been and probably were occasioned at least in part by the vacillating state of his own mind. He endeavored, it is true, to conceal his feelings, and he thought no doubt with success; but quick-sighted observers would naturally, under such circumstances, perceive some sure indications both of his own emotions and indecision, and such a discovery in proportion to its clearness would operate, in many cases, so as to excite and to strengthen the irritability and annoyance, which his expressed determination had awakened. But whether that were so or not, there is abundant evidence throughout his papers that notwithstanding his judicious efforts to arrive at a right conclusion and notwithstanding his deliberate, and as we have seen written, resolutions in favor of settling at Hackney, his hesitation was very considerable and his perplexity to the last, far greater than from so vigorous and energetic a mind might have been expected. "I have, upon my knees" are his words at the end of that year, 1711. "I have upon my knees in secret acknowledged to the Lord that I am in distress in a great strait. I cannot get clear from Chester or if I could cannot persuade myself cheerfully to go, I cannot get clear from Hackney or if I could, I cannot persuade *uxorem meam* cheerfully to stay."

And this is only a specimen of other and every numerous memorials. Even the day before his removal to Hackney, which was the Sabbath, he writes in reference to himself and his hearers – A very sad day. "O that by the sadness of their countenances and mine, our hearts may be made better. I expounded the last chapters of Joshua, and Matthew; and preached from 1 Thess. 4:18 'Comfort one another.'" I see he adds, "I have been very unkind to the congregation who love me too well." When he reached his new abode, he vented his anguish in such sighs as these: "Lord, am I in my way? I look back with sorrow for leaving Chester; I look forward with fear, but unto thee I look up."

CHAPTER 10

An Account of the Discharge of His Ministry at Chester Embracing the Whole Period of the Foregoing Narrative, Between the Year 1687 and the Year 1712

aving thus traced Mr. Henry's history to that important era in it when he left Chester, a distinct exhibition of his ministerial course during his abode in that city shall be attempted before we proceed further. Much instruction will thus be derived from his exemplary conduct. His very spirit and manners will be brought under review. And it will be sufficiently apparent why it was that so much earnest desire prevailed in other churches, and among not a few of his more distinguished brethren, to secure his services in sphere of labor, wider and more inviting than at Chester.

On the Lord's Day, Mr. Henry met his congregation at nine o'clock and commenced the services by singing the 100th Psalm. Praise was succeeded for a few minutes by prayer. He then read and expounded part of Old Testament, proceeding regularly from the book of Genesis. Having sung another Psalm, about half an hour was devoted to intercession. The sermon followed and usually occupied about an hour. He again prayed, and after singing commonly the 117th Psalm, the benediction was pronounced.

The same order was observed in the afternoon, only he then expounded with like regularity, a part of the New Testament, and at the close of the worship was sung either the 134th or some part of the 136th Psalm.

Such on the Sabbath was Mr. Henry's habitual employment. In singing, he used David's Psalms or sacred hymns of which (Dr. Watt's not being then published) he compiled a suitable and arranged collection. He preferred Scriptural Psalms and hymns to those, which are wholly of human composition, the latter being generally liable to this exception—that the fancy is too high and the matter too low, and sometimes such as a wise and good man may not be able, with entire satisfaction, to offer up as a sacrifice to God.

In the work of praise, he greatly delighted. It is congenial with devout sensibility, and was eminently suited to his lively and thankful temper. Having heard his excellent father say, "that our prying days should be praising days; and whatever the cup is, we should take notice of the mixtures," Mr. Henry never forgot it. And he sometimes devoutly observed "a life of praise and a life of usefulness is true angelical life."

In the exercise of public and social prayer, Mr. Henry was almost unrivalled. There was no pompous finery, no obtuse and complex elaboration, no disgusting familiarity, no personal reproofs or compliments, no vain repetitions, no preaching. He prayed and his style was reverent, humble, simple and devout. By impressive comprehensiveness, by the happiest adaptation of his petitions to circumstances, and, by peculiar fervency of manner, he successfully stimulated his fellow worshippers. His habits evinced the truth of his recorded experience, that "warm devotions contribute much to communion with God." And when, in the abundance of his zeal for "Gospel worship," he would say as he sometimes did, "We should be in it as the angels, who are seraphim-burners"—his own example beautified and confirmed the observation.

In supplication for mercy, Mr. Henry was very earnest and particular: pleading the name and sufferings and mediation of the Lord Jesus Christ for the pardon and peace. He was large and full in praying for grace, and used to mention the particular graces of the Holy Spirit—as faith, love, hope, patience, zeal, and delight in God, earnestly begging that these might be truly wrought in all, and might be preserved, exercised, increased, and evidenced to the divine glory.

Some have thought the use of the Lord's Prayer best avoided. They conceive it to have been taught the disciples as members of the Jewish church and adapted only to the time of waiting for Messiah's kingdom. And when it is considered that the disciples, before the Savior died, were instructed to pray in his name, and that the form in question does not occur either in the Acts of the Apostles or the Epistles, it must be admitted that the sentiment has considerable countenance. Others advocate its adoption in secret only and alone, resting the opinion upon the command. "When thou prayest, enter into the closet and pray." But Mr. Henry, like his venerable progenitor, approved and used it as a proper form as well in public and in private. But so doing, nevertheless he incurred censure and added to the instances, already numberless, that even men of sense and piety in zeal for a particular opinion may be lamentably deficient both in charity and expansion. "I wrote," he says, "to Mr. Farrington. Why he should not be offended at my using the Lord's Prayer."

The expounding of Holy Scripture, an ancient and invaluable custom, uniformly formed on the Sabbath a part of Mr. Henry's public services in the evening, as well as the morning. During his abode at Chester, he explained to his congregation, more than once, the whole of the sacred oracles. How impressively this duty was performed, the Commentary is a perpetual testimony; nor will any reader, who is happily enough to be acquainted with that matchless publication, wonder that those who first and gladly received those services were remarkable, like the noble Bereans, for their Scriptural knowledge.

It conduced to Mr. Henry's ministerial proficiency that the thoughts he cherished of the great work to which he was devoted, were just and elevated; and therefore, in some degree at least, proportioned to its magnitude. It was never through his instrumentality, degraded for a moment by any unhallowed associations, either in pursuit of worldly emolument or mere external respectability, still less of ease and sloth. Keeping the design of the institution continually in view, he magnified his office and seeking as a necessary consequence, with a steady and exclusive aim, the edification, and by sound conversion, the increase of the body of Christ, the best gifts were habitually, and with instructive and preserving earnestness, coveted. "I endeavored," are his words, "when reviewing a sacramental opportunity, to wrestle this day with God in secret and at his table for two things (and oh! that I might prevail) the heart of the upright and the tongue of the learned. I would excel in my work."

The sincerity of those aspirations was happily demonstrated by unremitting preparation for the pulpit. To the leading object every other was subordinate. All he read and all he saw, as well as the things he heard, were regarded by him with less or with more attention as they bore upon that. Nothing crude or indigested found its way through his agency into the some assembly.

Upon the Scriptures he bestowed his chief and profoundest attention: he studied his sermons with vast diligence and care, and wrote them, also, at considerable length: generally eight very crowded duodecimo pages. Some advices, yet extant, addressed to ministers well exemplify this part of his character; and, by the absence of any mention of writing, they show a laudable freedom from dogmatism and intrusiveness as to his own particular modes. He wisely judged that matters of mere convenience or taste are best left to the discretion and habits of mankind. So that sermons were well studied, it was not in his apprehension, material, whether the process was carried on with a pen or without one, in the closet in a garden in the fields or elsewhere.

> *"Take heed of growing remiss in your work. Take pains while you live. Think not that, after a while, you may relax and go over your old stock. The Scripture still affords new things, to those who search them. Continue searching. How can you expect God's blessing or your people's observance, if you are careless? Be studious not to offer that which costs nothing. Take pains that you may find out acceptable words. Let all your performances smell of the lamp. This will engage the attention of your people. Feed the flock of God, which is among you. Feed the ignorant with knowledge, the careless with admonition, the wandering with direction and the mourning with comfort."*

In the pulpit it was that Mr. Henry's talents shone with their fullest brilliance. Nor did any "odd or affected tones" or any violent and unseemly agitations cast over them, as is sometimes the case, the least shade. Like Bishop Earle's "Grave Divine," he beat upon his text, not the cushion. In addition to a fascinating manner, his imagination, at all times excursive and vigorous, furnished such a combination of ingenious biblical illustration as to place divine truth in a vivid and striking light; and himself also; as a preacher, upon the very pinnacle of popularity, he was often attended by persons of the highest respectability. Hence, we find him furnishing a copy of his sermon notes on Job 18:4 – "Shall the earth be forsaken? At the request of my Lord James Russell's Lady." He recorded elsewhere a time when he was in London that the Countess of Oxford was at the morning lecture.

In Mr. Henry's younger years, especially, the vehemence of his affections both in prayer and preaching were such as occasionally at least to transport not himself only, but his auditory also, into tears.

"You think," he said on one occasion, "we are too earnest with you to leave your sins and accept of Christ, but when you come to die, you will see the meaning of it. We see death at your backs."

Notwithstanding the masterly and striking specimens of Mr. Henry's discourses already in print, a single style in which he indulged shall be here adduced. It is taken from one of his ordinary sermons, and will remind many readers of the impassioned and fervid eloquence of Baxter, if not of the address and ardor of the Apostle Paul.

> *It is no time to daily and trifle and speak softly when precious souls lie at stake and their eternal condition is so nearly concerned. We cannot but speak the things, which we have seen and heard. Knowing the terrors of the Lord, we persuade men. The blood of your souls would lie at our door if we should not give you warning. What shall I say to startle you? That I am sure which is weighty enough, though neither new nor unheard of, nothing that is surprising, and therefore, the less likely to startling, shall I tell you.*
> *1. That the God with whom we have to do is a holy, righteous, all-seeing God. That which makes sinners secure*

is their mistake concerning this. They think of the Almighty as if he were easily imposed upon, altogether such as one as them. Thus they cheat themselves, but be not deceived. Know that God's eye is always upon you. He is acquainted with your secret sins. He hates every sin; and to all who are impenitent, he "is a consuming fire." He is too wise to be deceived. He is true to his threatenings.

2. That you have precious and immortal souls within you, which must shortly appear before God in judgment to be determined by a righteous doom to an unchangeable condition. You have a jewel in your hands of inestimable value. It is the soul of man, thy precious soul, that is concerned. It is not a trifle or a thing of naught, but thy own soul, which should be dear to thee. Thou hast but one, and once lost, it is irrecoverable lost. The gain of all the world cannot compensate it. This soul, at the best is in a very hazardous state. It lies at stake it is in great danger. Thou art on trial for thy life.

3. That if you live and die in graceless unsanctified state, as sure as God is in heaven you will be to eternity in the lowest hell. Though you make never so great a profession, though you attain never so high a reputation among men, though you prophesy in Christ's name, though you excel in gifts, though you abound in usefulness—yet all this, without a living principle of grace in your hearts, will never bring you to heaven. And believe it, Sirs, grace and holiness are quite other things than what the world takes them to be. Religion consists in humility and self-denial, and the reigning love of God and contempt of the world. He is the Christian who is one inwardly.

4. That there are thousands in hell who, when alive in the world, thought themselves as safe, and in as good a condition as you do. Multitudes have been deceived with counters for gold, have thought they were rich when they were not so. There is a generation of such. We have reason then to be jealous of a cheat in that in which so many have been cheated before us. This should startle us. Take heed lest, while you sleep as others did, you perish as they did. How secure was the rich man in the midst of his prosperity. But God called him a fool.

5. That the unsanctified heart may have a great deal of peace, while yet it is the devil's palace; and while he, as a strong man armed, keepeth it. It would startle you to think of belonging to the devil, of being under his power, of being led captive by him, of being set on by him, of having him to work in you. You would startle if the devil were to appear to you. Why, he is really working in the children of disobedience, as if he appeared to them. When you are going on in a sinful way, and yet say you shall have peace, it is the devil that tells you so; you are in the midst of enemies.

6. That while you are asleep in carnal security, your damnation slumbereth not. The Judge stands before the door. Death is at hand, perhaps within a few days, a few hours of you. You have no lease of your lives. You would startle at it, though you put far off the evil day, if I could assure you that you should live but one year. And will it not awaken you that I cannot assure you nor can you assure yourselves that you shall live a day? The veil of flesh is easily and quickly rent, and then appears the awful scene of eternity. Eternity. Do not you see many around you, as likely to live as yourselves, snatched away? How startling was the declaration: This night shall thy soul be required of thee! A criminal who is condemned to die tomorrow cannot forget it. It fills him eating, drinking, and sleeping. Can we forget the amazing doom, the amazing sight, the amazing gulf that we are just upon the brink of, just ready to step into?

7. *That as the tree falls so it lies, and so it is like to lie to eternity. As death leaves us, judgment finds us. The doom is irreversible, the sentence irrevocable, the condition on the other side death unchangeable. A gulf will be fixed. It is too late to repent in the grave. Up and bestir. You have only a little inch of time in which to be doing.*

But let me direct you. When a man asleep is roused a little, he is, in some measure, capable of advice. Know then generally what you must do. Sleep no longer. Be secure no longer.

1. Suspect yourselves as to your spiritual state. Self-suspicion is the first step towards awakening. What if, after all, my faith should be, but fancy my hope presumption? What reason have I to be so very confident? May I not be deceived? Many who eat bread with Christ, yet lift up the heel against him. The disciples, when our Lord intimated that one of them should betray him, began to say unto him one by one, "Is it I?" Do not, in a matter of such great importance, always take things upon trust.

2. See, and be convinced of the miserable state you are in while out of Christ. You are not the more safe for being secure. Look about you, Sirs, consider, as men do, who are newly awakened where you are. See yourselves wretched and miserable, children of wrath. Be sensible of the guilt of sin that lies upon you, of the power of sin that rules in you. You are under the power of Satan. You are exposed to the curse of God. There is but one life between thee and hell. And is this a condition fit for a man to sleep in?

3. Stir up yourselves to a due concern about your souls and your eternal welfare. "If you will enquire, enquire ye." Enquire as they did when awake, who are mentioned by the prophet Micah, "wherewith shall I come before the Lord?" Enquire as those new converts in the Acts of the Apostles, "Men and brethren what shall we do?" Enquire as the jailer did, "Sirs, what must I do to be saved?" There begins to be some hope of people when they look about them as men concerned. Here I am now, but where must I be to eternity, if I should die tonight and go to judgment, what would become of my precious soul? That is the holy fear, which is the beginning of wisdom. Seek unto Jesus Christ for life and light. Christ shall give thee light. We must go to him by an active faith and consent to the Gospel proposal of salvation by him. Say, 'Whither shall I go but to Christ?' Sense of danger should drive us to him with all speed. We are never truly awake and up, till by faith, we have put ourselves in the Lord Jesus Christ."

4. Set yourself with all diligence to do the work you were sent into the world about. Awake to righteousness. Up and be doing. Your work is great, your journey long, your enemies many, oppositions powerful, strength small, time short and uncertain. Son, go work today in the vineyard. Dost thou not see how it is grown over with thorns?

5. Strike while the iron is hot. Take heed of delays. Those have ruined thousands. "Yet a little sleep," said the ancient slumberous men. They are roused and disturbed a little, but they only turn and go to sleep again, and so become conviction-proof and can sleep in the midst of a thousand calls. Take heed of putting by conviction. It is a bad freezing again after a thaw. Let not his call be lost after all the rest. What effect it will have I know not, but I have delivered my soul.

When about twenty-six years of age, Mr. Henry's bodily health was considerably affected. Indisposition attributed entirely to inordinate excitement and exertion laid him indeed aside. A letter written to him at the season, this excellent father, yet remains to finish a curious relic of the times and to convey instruction, which may not, at this day, be without its use:

> *"Surely you should be careful of yourself, for prayers ought to be seconded with endeavors. I do not mean that you should spare yourself in the sense in which the Satan spoke in Peter, for I see our opportunities passing away; and I cannot say whatever others think: that you do too much and should abate but one thing, which I gave you a hint of when with you, and I again mind you of; and that is, in the loose you take in your earnestness, keep the reins upon it and let it neither run too far nor last too long; for I have myself, by experience, found some prejudice by it, especially in my sight. And another thing as to your health is that being subject to fears, and you are, I think you should not, when you are warmed with preaching, either drink small beer, which is an error on the one hand, or sack, which commonly offered on the other, but both together not full drought, but a little at a time—by degree and little warmed, not hot, which I find doth best, and I believe so will you."*

But if Mr. Henry became more temperate, he did not either chill or freeze. His feelings and earnestness did not either chill or freeze. His feelings and earnestness were, perhaps, better regulated, but they were not destroyed. In his diary for Sept 10, 1699, when he was in his 38th year, he thus writes, "I preached of God the chief good, from Psalm 73:25. Who have I in heaven but thee? And there is none upon earth that I desire besides thee. I had some enlargement of affections and I find some prejudice to my bodily strength by my over earnestness, but I cannot help it; for I believe the things I speak to be true and great, and I would be in my work as one in earnest."

This fervent manner of preaching he continued to the end of his life.

Mr. Henry was not more remarkable for his fervor than for variety, which he so admirably kept up to his ministrations. Loving to give Scripture (it is his own statement) its full latitude, he took a wide range in the choice of his subjects and studiously presented religious truth in its connections and its tendencies. He attained to large and comprehensive view, "listening to the voice which speaketh from heaven," whether addressed by the visible creation, the beauties of natural scenery, the discoveries of science, the thunders and the lightnings of Mount Sinai, or that overwhelming exhibition of mercy, which proclaims to apostate and perishing transgressors—the redemption that is in Christ Jesus.

With this regard to variety, Mr. Henry avoided the practice of many "ancient worthies," who having chosen a subject for the pulpit, pursued it week after week from the same text. He preferred employing different texts or the discussion of even the same general truth; and improvement well adapted to relieve both the preacher and hearers from the wearisome insipidity inseparable from continued iteration.

At the same time, it is only just to observe that in the discourses of the more remote puritans and nonconformists and not a few prelates, there was such a development of the economy of redemption and such a constant reference to the Savior, as to cast a veil over a multitude of defects, however palpable, and to give to their sermons, also as to those of the Apostles, an unparalleled, yea, by divine influence an irresistible, charm. No other theme can so powerfully, if at all, excite devotional ardor as a vivid impression of this one grand truth—that Christ was delivered for our offenses, and was raised again for our justification. No wonder then, that it was "most present to Mr. Henry as it was to the venerable men above referred to, to be preaching Christ. That then, to borrow his own phrase, he was most in his element. Well did he observe, when expatiating upon the subject, that although the Scriptures are the circumference of faith, the rounds of which it walks and every point of which compass it toucheth; yet the center of it is Christ. That is the polar star on which it resteth."

It is not improbable that, next to the pattern exhibited at Broad Oak, the intimacy of Mr. Henry with the Reverend Fancies Tallents served to increase his attachment to this style of preaching, as well as conduced to his distinction and usefulness in the church. The name of Mr. Tallents has been mentioned before. It is well known; and it is not too much to affirm that he was equally eminent for his learning, his wisdom, his moderation, and his piety. To the youthful prophets around him, he was a father. Though far advanced in years, he cultivated their friendship. He accurately observed their public performances. He discovered a lively interest in their respectability and success, and mingling with counsels and rebukes the most affectionate kindness, he secured their attention and esteem.

The nature and effects of that intercourse are well evinced in the two following letter. They were both addressed to Mr. Tallents by Mr. Henry; not is it easy to say upon which party they confer most honor:

July 21, 1694

Dear and honored Sir,
I am greatly obliged to you, not only for your very quickening words when I was with you, but for your very quickening lines, which you sent after me. I reckon when I come to Salop, it is as the old puritans went to Dedhan— to fetch fire. I desire to bless my God for any influences of

grace and comfort, which I have often experienced through you, and I am ashamed that the impressions thereof have been no more strong and lasting. I thank you for the hint you gave me to speak more of the doctrine of God's election and free grace, which I shall endeavor to observe. It refreshed me to think that there are many of those whom I am called to speak to in God's name, whom I trust the Lord hath loved with an everlasting love; and though there are so many who do not believe our report, yet there are some to whom the arm of the Lord shall be more and more revealed. By an effectual choice he hath wonderfully and graciously secured the glory of his Son, the happiness of a remnant of his creatures; and in subordination to these, the comfort of his poor ministers. In my Master's work, I am but a yesterday, yet I find that there is not now that encouraging success, which there was at the first opening of the present door of opportunity, which makes me ready to ask sometimes, "Is the Lord among us or is he not?" But surly he is and in more ways than one is doing his own work. I have received with satisfaction what you direct me to Turrentine, and return you many thanks for your hint in the matter. I beg your prayers for me that the Lord, when I preach, will lead me into the mystery of the riches of free grace for conviction and direction. I endeavor to do it as means by which free grace usually works its own work, but I desire to wind up all in the glory of God, "not unto us, O Lord, not unto us, but to thy name be that glory." I beg the continuance of your prayers and when you can spare a little time, a line or two from you will be much a refreshment to

Your most affectionate and obedient Son in the Lord, Matthew Henry

For Mr. Francis Tallents,
Minister of the Gospel at Salop, these.
Broad Oak, October 29, 1695

Dear and honored Sir,
    I desire to be thankful to God for your love to me, and
your kind letters. Yours which I met with here, at Broad
Oak, hath in it very quickening and refreshing
memorandums of our dear Lord Jesus Christ, whom we
should think more of and live more upon, did we remember
that he is the head of our religion. I have found comfort
and satisfaction in preaching some sermons lately, though
in much weakness, concerning the mediation of Jesus
Christ; and our coming to the Father, as a Father, in
everything we have to do with him by, Jesus Christ—"the
new and living way" through which "we enter into the
holiest" and heaven is made familiar to us. I desire you,
when you put up a petition for me, it may be this – that I
may be a true minister of Jesus Christ, not only appointed
by him, but affected with his love, acquainted with the
mystery of it, and an instrument to bring others acquainted
with it etc. etc. I rest your obedient son in the common
faith.

Mat. Henry.

Mr. Henry's aim in his ministry was not to conceal or palliate the guilt and extent of human depravity, nor to disprove or explain away the necessity of divine influence in saving sinners; but he labored to confirm those fundamental truths and to lay open the secrets of the heart in order that his hearers might be convinced of sin or righteousness and judgment. He then invariably conducted them to Calvary. There he delighted to linger, urging them individually to behold the Lamb of God. And so unanswerable, did he press the obligations of sinners to believe as to leave all who remained obstinate and impenitent, without excuses. "I do not stand here," he would say, "to mock you with an uncertainty or to trifle without about an indifferent thing; but in the name of Christ, my Master, to make a serious offer to you of life and salvation, upon the terms of faith and repentance."

Whatever their diversity of thought, or subject, or attainments, he urged upon his brethren, without exception, a like course. "Let Jesus Christ," said he, "be all in all. Study Christ. Preach Christ. Live Christ."

He recommended both by his advice and example, that uniform regard to simplicity and plainness of speech, which constitutes one of the main excellencies of a public instructor. It would be a mistake, nevertheless, to suppose that he encouraged vulgarity and coarseness or any destitution of that which is ornamental and attractive. The use he advised of the language of inspiration is conclusive against such a sentiment. With him, plainness stood in opposition to all that is unintelligible and ambiguous, or veiled or obscure.

> *Let all your performances (said he) be plain and Scriptural. Choose for your pulpit subjects of the plainest and most needful truths, and endeavor to make them plainer. Be serious in the delivery. Affect not fine words, but words, which the Holy Ghost teaches—that is, sound speech, which cannot be condemned. Enticing words of man's wisdom debases your matter. God needs not to be painted. Scripture expressions are what people are used to and will remember. Consider the lambs of the flock. You must take them along with you. Do not over-drive them by being overlong or over-fine.*

Unlike those divines who have been designated "fugitive," because, as cowards, they run away from their text, Mr. Henry adhered with admirable closeness to the passage he professed to explain—neither, on the one hand, pressing into its service foreign or irrelevant truths and still less far-fetched inventions nor, on the other hand, evading any topic to which he was naturally led. Although, after years of pulpit service, he could and did say to his assembled congregation, "That which I have mainly insisted upon is turning to God, and walking with God." Yet he could also affirm, in connection with that solemn appeal, that he had not shunned to declare the whole of God's counsel. Into what path soever his text directed him, there he walked unshackled by human authority and fearless of consequences.

When urging the performance of Christian duties, he endeavored to furnish the necessary "rules and directions in the express words of Scripture."

In like manner, he sometimes illustrated important truths by "Scripture allusions." One instance may suffice. After exposing the nature and evils of carnal security, he thus pointed out its danger: we are in danger by it of having our hair cut—that is of losing our strength as Sampson did when he slept upon Delilah's lap. Security is weakening; it weakens our resistance of temptation and our performance of duty. We are in danger by it having tares sown in our hearts, as they were in the cornfield while men slept. Corruptions prevail and get head while we are secure and off our watch. We are in danger by it of being robbed of our spear and cruse of water, as Saul was when he slept. When secure, we lose our defense and our comfort, and so lie exposed and disquieted. We are in danger by it of being nailed to the earth, as Sesera was when he slept in Jael's tent: of minding earthy things, of having head and heart fixed to the world. The rich fool was thus nailed to the earth, and he counted upon good laid up for many years.

We can never reach heaven while we are fastened to the earth. We are in danger by it of being given up to sleep, as the disciples were in the garden. "Sleep on now." It is a dismal thing to be let alone in carnal security. We are in danger of sinking into destruction. Jonah was when he slept in the storm. Security has slain its ten thousands who have gone sleeping to hell. And what is hell? But to lie forever under the power of that soul-sinking word. Depart from me with a gulf fixed to cut off all access.

The slightest attention to the subject will convince the reader how studiously Mr. Henry's sermons were adapted to the promotion of the true faith and knowledge and practice of the Gospel. Not, it is observable, by noisy declamation or elaborate argument, but by opening to men the Scriptures. He never started the erroneous opinions of others or the display of his own skill in refuting them.

It is worthy of notice that Mr. Henry carefully avoided useless criticisms and controversy. He uniformly discountenanced such preaching: to puzzle and amuse rather than to instruct, edify, and save.

"Take heed," was his counsel, "of affection novelties in religion lest you fall into vanities or worse. Ask for the old way; keep to the faith once delivered to the saints; keep to the proportion of faith. Take heed to your doctrine: that it jostle not our God's grace, nor man's duty; but take both together. Arminianism makes grace a servant to man's goodness. Antinomianism makes it a servant to man's badness."

To render his addresses to the more appropriate, he was frequent in his pastoral visits and took a lively interest in the circumstances of this flock. At an ordination, he thus commended the same habit. "Be familiar with your people, not high or strange.

Converse with them for their good. Acquaint yourselves with the state of their souls, their temptations, their infirmities. You will then know the better how to preach to them. Your flock being volunteers, you may be the more encouraged in dealing with them, and encourage them to ask you questions about their souls."

There appears to have been nothing in Mr. Henry's spiritual vision either diseased or distorted. While doctrines, instead of being asserted as with oracular authority, were proved by well-selected and convincing arguments, the duties of genuine Christians were unanswerably enforced, and their privileges and enjoyments illustrated with singular ingenuity and the most captivation eloquence. In the whole and every part of the system of revelation, he traced not only the operations of astonishing wisdom, but a tendency toward the most pure and holy. "Some truths," said he, "are plain and easy. Others are more deep and mysterious, but all are designed to fructify the holy land and to 'make glad the city of God.' It is but half Christianity that rests in the acts of devotion; it is not an entire Christianity that is not honest, as well as godly. Without this, the profession of religion will be looked upon as a pretence—a seeming religion, which is vain."

Hence his sermons, whatever was the subject, were uniformly practical; and the morals he taught were founded, like those of the New Testament, upon the doctrines, which are according to godliness, ever left at an immeasurable distance, the purest ethnics of heathenism and the most admired dissertations of a fashionable theology. "The very life and soul of religion consist," he would say, "in a conscientious regard to Jesus Christ that Christianizeth morality, and turns moral virtue into evangelical holiness."

Adverting in his diary to a course of sermons then in progress, he says, "I preached from 2 Cor. 1:20, and entered upon the subject of the divine promises, while the stated Sabbath-subject is the divine law, that we may press holiness and comfort together."

"Duty and comfort," he sometimes remarked, "go abreast. Neither is to be neglected. Many are willing to separate them. They love, with Ephraim, to tread out the corn, but not with Judah to plough, and with Jacob to break the clods. They love to hear of comforts; those are smooth things; but not to hear of duty. What, however, God has joined, let not us think to separate. Those who would reap in glory, must sow in duty. Justification is to be tried by sanctification. They are ever more concomitants."

The character of Mr. Henry's preaching, in short, was anything rather than what Dr. South styled "gilding the apprehension, and playing upon the surface of the heart." It was uniformly pointed, discriminating, and applicable.

Instead of dealing in useless generalization, his sermons were fashioned after inspired examples, and abounded, as we have seen, in close and pungent addresses directed at once, but with admirable prudence, tenderness, and skill to the understanding and the conscience of every hearer. Advising others, on the one occasion, to distinguish in their preaching, that they might neither strengthen the hands of the wicked nor make the hearts of the righteous sad, he remarked it was a "reigning sign of hypocrisy when the hear cannot endure a searching ministry, while the ministry of the prophets torments."

It was simply from an earnest desire to be useful in saving souls that Mr. Henry was induced at any time to adopt such a style of address as was calculated to alarm. Like his venerable father, he could look at his hearers and say, without the fear of contradiction, "I love to be the messenger of good tidings. My temper and spirit is to encourage poor sinners to come and repent."

He nevertheless felt it his duty, as a faithful watchman, to "warn" men of their danger. "We have no other way," said he, "of delivering our soul, but by telling 'the wicked man' that he shall surely die; that is, be eternally miserable in the world to come. Nor is this legal preaching, for Christ so preached very often. The Scriptures, which speak of hell, are to be mostly found in the New Testament. 'He that believes not shall be damned,' is part of the Gospel, which we are commissioned to preach."

Still, as has been already hinted, Mr. Henry was far from slighting the claims of believers; he delighted to minister to their comfort. To them, he unfolded the "precious promises," and exhibited the inconceivable recompense. He reminded them that "spiritual life is eternal life begun, that present light and love are the beginnings of eternal light and love, that the citizenship of the saints is now in heaven, that although as yet grace be like the smoking flax, yet that there is a spark, and it will shortly blow up into a flame."

Ample as was the classification before noticed, he did not invariably confine himself to that arrangement. He considered the improvement of providential occurrences both merciful and afflictive, and whether of a general or more local nature, essential to making "full proof of his ministry." He frequently, therefore, delivered sermons of a miscellaneous character and adapted especially to the young: the seasons of the year and the various exercises of mourning and joy, which to a vigilant pastor, present some of the finest opportunities of effective ministration. The command "be instant in season and out of season" is charged, he observed, "with great solemnity. And is it not in season when persons are in affliction? An interpreter will then be one of a thousand."

In addition to this ordinary engagement on the Lord's Day, Mr. Henry maintained a weekly lecture on Thursday. At those seasons, he preached a course of sermons on 1 Cor. 7:29-31; 1 Cor. 13; Heb. 11 and Hos. 14, and afterwards on Scripture questions, which latter series occupied no less than twenty years. On the lecture evening preceding his administration of the supper, he varied even this selection, and turned his meditations more directly towards the approaching solemnity. Among other themes, on which he them dwelt may be mentioned the addresses made to the incarnate Redeemer: as "Lord, if thou wilt thou canst make me clean," and the answers to those addresses, as, "I will: be thou clean."

It is not certainly known whether the services referred to were attended by many or by comparatively few. The probability, however, from the absence in Mr. Henry's diary of complaint, is that his stimulating counsels were observed; and that no inconsiderable part of his congregation manifested a due regard to pastoral encouragement and their won interests by their habitual presence. The redemption of time, especially for religious exercises, formed a distinguishing feature of ancient nonconformity. And there is reason to conclude that whenever a lecture between the Sabbaths was accessible, whether at Chester or in the vicinity, it was frequented by all within reach, who were pressing into the Kingdom of God, unless they were lawfully hindered.

The diary of Mrs. Savage sometimes, on such occasions, notices with visible pleasure that there was "a full meeting." And after one of her accustomed records, another lecture being appointed the next day elsewhere and at some distance, she memorialized the attendance of some of her neighbors and of her husband and herself, not withstanding their extensive and weighty employments. Was such ardor discovered because the word of the Lord was more "precious" in those days than now? Or, is the saying come to pass, which is written, "because iniquity shall abound, the love of many shall wax cold?"

"It is the will of God," said Mr. Henry, "that we should be diligent in our business all the days of the week, according as the duty of every day requires. But it is a corrupt and profane inference that, therefore, we are not on those days to pray in our families or hear sermons. In the six days, we must do all our work. And is not serving God and working out our salvation part of our business? Have we not souls to work for, as well as bodies? God must have his day out of every week, so he must have his hour out of every day. There is, as we may see in the 145th Psalm, a song not only for the Sabbath-day, but for every day. We should spend as much for our souls in the week-days, as for our bodies on the Sabbath."

Mr. Henry attended to the ordinance of the Lord's Supper with the members of the church in the public assembly on the first Sabbath in every month. He remarked that among the Jews, the beginning of the month was esteemed sacred; and, although he did not consider the Jewish law as to the new moons still in force, yet he thought, from general reasoning, the conclusion a safe one, that whatsoever may be our divisions of time, it is always good to begin such divisions with God—seeking first his kingdom, and its righteousness.

In the "breaking of bread," the emotions of love and praise, which actuated his soul, were commonly so predominant as to infuse into the whole service a character of sanctity and elevation, well adapted to beget corresponding affections in his fellow communicants. "The table of the Lord was often to them as the mount of transfiguration where they saw the King in his beauty, and beheld the land that was afar off." And although in his diary, he sometimes complains of dullness at such hallowed seasons, it was seldom or never apparent to others; and, "I think," said Mr.

Tong, "he had as little reason to complain as most men, but where there are ardent breathings after sinless perfection, every defect will be sensibly felt and lamented." On one occasion, whether sacramental or not, does not appear, Mr. Henry remarked, "We have now the pleasure of ordinances, drops of joy, but in heaven we shall bathe ourselves in the ocean of delights. The joy will be spiritual, pure, and unmixed. Present joys are fading and transitory like the crackling of thorns under a pot, but the joys of heaven will be still flourishing. The light of joy is an everlasting light, which is held too high to be blown out by any of the blasts of this lower region."

In the other New Testament appointment, that of baptism, Mr. Henry did not less excel; and he so preferred its public administration as seldom, unless the circumstances were extraordinary, to abandon that preference. He baptized several of his own children, an act which some of his friends thought improper, but he advocated the practice. He contended that it was no less fit that for a minister to share in the commemorative elements, which he dispensed to others. He availed himself of those occasions to evince the Scriptural authority of infant baptism. He felicitously explained the nature and advantages of the institution in reference to the children, and without substituting similitude for argument, expressed his pleasure in the familiar illustration of his excellent father. That eminent divine likened the observance to the taking of a beneficial lease for a child while in the cradle, and putting his like into it.

In the very valuable treatise, which has already been mentioned, Mr. Henry bears that ordinance as observed by paedobaptists, the following interesting testimony, "I cannot but take occasion to express my gratitude to God for my infant baptism, not only as it was an early admission into the visible body of Christ, but as it furnished my pious parents with a good argument (and, I trust, through grace a prevailing argument) for an early dedication of my own self to God in my childhood. If God has wrought any good work upon my soul, I desire, with humble thankfulness, to acknowledge the moral influence of my infant baptism upon it."

To the many who had not in infancy been partakers of the baptismal rite, he, according to the uniform practice of the paedobaptist ministers, administered it at an adult age. He embraced those opportunities especially to urge upon observers a practical improvement of the ordinance: a theme on which he greatly excelled.

The attention paid by Mr. Henry to the rising generation was exemplary, constant, and attractive. For his own excitement and the guidance of others also, he not infrequently observed that Peter was charged to feed the lambs, as well as the sheep.

It was ever a main object of his solicitude to promote, among his young friends, a spirit of seriousness while young. He thought no pains ill bestowed that conduced them to live a preference for "serious companions, serious books, and a serious ministry." "Nothing," said he, "fosters vanity, especially among the more refined part of mankind, more than vain books, idle plays and foolish romances. Read, therefore, serious books: the book of the Scriptures. It the most serious of all, and there are many others— such a Baxter's Call, Allein's Alarm, etc. Think of death and judgment and eternity. Some have said it would make any man serious to think awhile upon Matt. 16:26. "What is a man profited if he shall gain the whole world, and lose his own soul? Or, what shall a man give in exchange for his soul?"

For similar reasons he urgently pressed a habit of considerate thoughtfulness. That he described to be "the laying of the heart and mind close to the things we know. It is looking diligently. It is like a burning glass, which conveys the beams of divine truth to the soul in such a manner as to kindle in it a fire of devotion. Without it, we cannot, especially in a crowd of sensible objects, see Him who is invisible."

In addition to sermons often expressly preached to the young, some of which were printed, the work of catechizing was indefatigably performed every Saturday afternoon. The exercise commenced and ended with prayer. It usually occupied more than an hour and was attended not only by the catechumens, but by theirs also, who, fondly anticipated the "holy rest of the Sabbath of the morrow," and esteemed the service a suitable preparation. His sermon "concerning the catechizing of youth," presents a detailed statement of his views. It contains not only a variety of important reasons in support of the service against cavilers, but many remarks and instructions deserving of the most serious attention—some of them entitled to praise for their sagacity, and all of them distinguished by their comprehension, their unaffected goodwill, and their special adaptation for usefulness.

The formulary, which he commonly used on the occasions referred to, but without confining himself to it, was that of the Westminster Assembly. He divided the answers into several lesser propositions, explained them, supported them by suitable text of Scripture; and they deduced practical inferences. His Scripture Catechism, "in the method of the Assemblies," affords ample illustrations. The course he pursued with such as are unequal to the engagement is fully developed in a "Plain Catechism for Children," which was published by him at the desire of Mr. Chorlton of Manchester.

When any of those young persons, of whom he had entertained hope, grew vain and careless, he deeply lamented their state, and ceased not to pray to God that he would recover them out of the snare of the devil before their hearts were hardened through the deceitfulness of sin.

But in the labor of love, which has been noticed, it was Mr. Henry's happiness and honour to be remarkably successful, as well as persevering.

Like his admired father, he encouraged young people to renew their baptismal engagements by a public confession of the Savior. When, therefore, he perceived in any of his catechumens symptoms of thoughtfulness upon religious subjects, he specially noticed them; and as soon as there was "a competent number," conversed with them severally and apart upon their everlasting interest. Afterwards, in the solemn assembly, he catechized them concerning the Lord's Supper, by a form, which he printed. He next appointed a day in the week preceding the monthly sacrament, in which, before the congregation, he was their intercessor at the heavenly throne. He addressed a sermon especially to them. And the following Sabbath, they were welcomed to the Redeemer's table. Such, in his judgment, as in that of his father also, was the true confirmation or transition into a state of adult, and complete church membership.

It will not escape observation that the method pursued in admission to Christian fellowship was that which was recognized by presbyterians, rather than congregational churches. Mr. Henry, in the common with the majority of his brethren at that period, considered the ordinances of Christ strictly as mysteries of which his ministers are the exclusive stewards; and, therefore, that a trust, a dispensation was committed to them—including in it a power so distinct from the church, as to vest in themselves the sole authority, both of accepting and rejecting professed Christians. Thus, addressing some of his younger brethren at an ordination, Mr. Henry remarked, that, "In admission to special ordinances they were entrusted with the keys." And then added the following necessary and judicious advice, "Be very cautious to avoid extremes. Let not those who are grossly ignorant or scandalous be suffered to profane and holy things of the Lord. Yet, let not those be rejected who are weak in faith, and who, in small matters, differ from you."

Societies strictly congregational, however, regard the matter differently and are of opinion that the church, and not the pastor only, is to receive members into communion, and in like manner, to exclude such as walk disorderly. As all the saints in Rome were directed to "receive one another," so the faults of offenders are, after preparatory and prescribed measures, to be told to "the church," whose course in the case of continued obstinacy, is defined by holy Scripture with awful precision.

Mr. Henry's attention to discipline combined spiritual wisdom with holy zeal: from precipitation and supineness, he stood equally remote. He could adopt the apostle's spirit-stirring appeal, "Who is weak, and I am not weak? Who is offended, and I burn not?" without trespassing either upon faithfulness of tenderness. After hearing sermons by Mr. Newcome of Manchester, on 2 Tim. 2:19, "Let every one that nameth the name of Christ, depart of iniquity," he prayed, "The Lord do me good by these sermons. Professors have need of such cautions." And afterward adds, "I expounded such a day on Paul's farewell, Acts 20. O that I could follow his example, warning everyone night and day with tears."

In reference to that which perhaps may be called the most difficult part of pastoral duty, he could never lose the impression of his father's sentiment. "Every time you see a brother sin, and forbear reproving him, would you be contended," said that holy and conscientious man, "that God should write hatred in his debt book?"

When evil reports concerning any of his flock needed attention, he "enquired diligently into the facts; he weighed every complaint and every plea. And, if the statement was proved, reproof was fully administered, but with the utmost affection. His object was not to indulge any angry feeling, but to reclaim the offender, "Brethren." Said the chief of the apostles, "If a man be overtaken in a fault ye know is spiritual, restore such an one in spirit of meekness, considering thyself, lest thou also be tempted."

Notwithstanding signs of penitence, if the sin was open and scandalous, private rebuke was followed by suspension. That painful measure was resorted to on one occasion, in reference to three individuals. And, to increase the solemnity, Mr. Henry not only pronounced the sentence publicly, but accompanied it by a congregational fast.

When success crowned the means, he "thanked God, and took courage." But, when the discipline was unavailing; when the parties, through the pride of their hearts, outbraved censure and persisted in iniquity; when, instead of judging themselves and repenting of the evil, they indulged in the bitterness of malevolence and willingly submitted to satanic captivity; when, although nothing could be more remote from the face, they denounced him as rigorous, uncharitable, and severe, his soul was deeply penetrated and cast down.

Having mentioned the sin of one in whom he had promised himself comfort, he adds, "Then said I, have labored in vain and spent my strength for naught." And again, "These things are a temptation to me to lay aside the pastoral charge, but I dare not. I cannot do it. My God will humble me. Let him that thinketh he standeth, is thought by his friends to stand, take heed lest he fall. The Lord makes it a warning to me and to us all."

It was remarked concerning some of the unhappy persons who, hating reprehension, abandoned Mr. Henry's ministry, then they shared the fate of apostasy and withered temporally, as well as spiritually. They "stood like pillars of salt," says Mr. Tong, "monuments of God's anger, and warnings to others to hear and fear and not do so wickedly."

The sick and afflicted were special objects of Mr. Henry's attention: whether rich or poor, whether connected with the established church (and he was often sent for to visit such) or otherwise, or whether they were strangers merely passing through the city, nothing short of invincible necessity prevented his attendance when called for.

Nor, indeed, did he wait for applications. By enquiring among his friends, he "sought out" the afflicted. When his prayers in the congregation were anonymously desired, he would publicly request the writers to furnish their names, not only that he might remember them the more appropriately, but that he might know how to render them other service, also. In his diary, he is almost daily to be traced, when at home to the chambers of the sick and distressed, the Sabbath not accepted. Sometimes he visited four or five in a day. The names are commonly recorded, and brief mention is made both of their state and frame of mind. The event was not overlooked. And if they recovered, he not only blessed God, but by apt exhortations, reminded them of the vows and resolves which were past.

Nothing could more clearly evince his concern for and attention to the poor than his prevailing and earnest anxiety that they might attain religious knowledge and be themselves able to understand God's holy word. "It is sad," said he, "that to a Christian, the inside and outside of a Bible should be the same." "How gladly," are his words in an address to his congregation, "how gladly would

I help the meanest. I would undertake in one month's time and less to teach the most ignorant, all who will only give their minds to it, and without hindering you from your callings, fully to understand the principles of religion."

Mr. Henry was no encourager of an indiscriminate introduction of religious phraseology or experience. He nevertheless delighted in "holy conversation," and he thought Christians not only too careless of social intercourse, but deficient in its management. "Discourse together," he would say, "and discourse of the most quickening considerations. Christ often spoke of his death, even on the holy mount. Talk of sufferings and clouds and troubles. Make a bargain to rouse one another by reproofs and warnings. This was the way of the ancients, and it was a good way. It kindles and inflames gracious affections. It obliges people to study the Scriptures and good books, and especially their own hearts. I appeal to those who have been acquainted with it, whether it does not contribute very much to the growth of knowledge and grace. It is a duty much neglected. He adds, "There is need of a great deal of Christian prudence and wisdom in the management of the duty in question. Sometimes it is even perverted and made the fuel of pride and contention, etc. That, however, is not a reason that it should be neglected, but that it should be attended to with more care."

The other kind of conference was confined to persons more advanced in life. Those of Mr. Henry's congregation, who ranked as principals or who were distinguished by their moral worth or intellectual endowments, usually attended. They met more frequently than the juvenile party and at each other's houses, where they partook of refreshment at the family table and pursued conversation becoming the Gospel. Their meetings terminated, as in apostolic days, with prayer. In these social, but retired scenes, Mr. Henry greatly delighted. Feeling unrestrained, he gave full scope to his conversational powers; and uniting to unaffected piety and in an eminent degree, "the scholar's learning with the courtier's ease," every mind was captivated. It would be difficult to affirm which was predominant: the esteem or the admiration of his associates. One who knew him intimately remarked that no man was more serious in religion, no man more pleasant in conversation, no man more honest in everything. And Mr. Tong says, "He was the best companion in the world."

To the proof already adduced, how continually Mr. Henry gave himself to prayer and the ministry of word, may be added his devout observance with his congregation of quarterly fasts. They were then common. The state of the society on such occasions was noticed with moving earnestness; spiritual unprofitableness was lamented, pardon of sin implored, and the divine presence with a more plentiful effusion of the Holy Sprit sought with extraordinary importunity. Nor did he fail to intercede for the peace and prosperity of the city where he dwelt, the land of his birth, and the churches of God universally.

While at Chester, he saw the whole the Lord's work uniformly prospering in his hands. The congregation became indeed so numerous as to render necessary the erection of a new and much enlarged meeting house—one which he describes as "very commodious, capacious, and pleasant," and which yet remains. It is situated in Crook Lane. The foundation was laid in September 1699, a short time before the death of Mr. Harvey, and obviously from the narrative already given, uninfluenced by a spirit either of rivalry or opposition. It cost 5321 pounds sterling. 16 shillings. 1 pence. *[Editor's note: In today's exchange, roughly $1600 USD.]*

At the opening, August 7, 1700 Mr. Henry delivered an appropriate and excellent sermon on Joshua 22:22-23: "The Lord God of gods, the Lord God of gods he knoweth and Israel he shall know, if it be in rebellion or if in transgression against the Lord –

that we have built us an altar." He entitled it "Separation without Rebellion," but though it was fairly transcribed, he did not publish it, most probably, says Mr. Palmer, by reason of his great solicitude to avoid giving offence to any members of the established church." It was made public, however, in the year 1726 with a commendatory preface by Dr. Watts; and it has now a place in the Miscellaneous Words: a fair specimen it furnished by it of the writer's ability. Candor and moderation, and it is well calculated not only to instruct such as are unacquainted with English nonconformity, but to confound prejudice, whether it arise from education, ignorance, or pride.

After Mr. Harvey's death, his son, the Rev Jonathan Harvey, preached for a season to the remnant of the congregation, then rapidly declining, a circumstance which rendered Mr. Henry's situation not a little delicate and oftentimes difficult. But he pursued a straightforward, prudent and honorable course, and the issue was accordingly. "I have had many searching's of heart," he writes about Mr. Harvey's congregation, who came dropping into us. "As I have endeavored in the matter to approve myself to God and my own conscience; and my heart doth not reproach me. So blessed be God, I hear not of any person one or other that doth."

In consequence of that resignation, the difficulties, which had existed and have been alluded to, were in a great measure removed. The bulk of the remaining congregation uniting with that at Crook Lane, a gallery was erected for their better accommodation. The work commenced April 7, 1707 and cost 85 pounds sterling. 0 shillings. 5 pence. *[Editor's note: In today's exchange, roughly $170 USD.]* "We know," said Mr. Henry, "how to enlarge the straightness of the place. God by his grace enlarge the straightness of our hearts."

The number of communicants now rose to above three hundred and fifty; unanimity prevailed; and the comfort of our author abounded. Mr. Harvey did not long survive. He died of consumption on Tuesday April 6, 1708 in the thirty-first year of his age. Mr. Fog preached at his funeral (which Mr. Henry attended) from Job 14:14: "If a man die, shall he live again? All the days of my appointed time will I wait till my change come," and spoke to him very well.

The attendance of a large and increasing auditory as the fruit of Mr. Henry's labors came far short of the object he sought. He records it as his desire to be very earnest with God in prayer for the congregation, that their souls might prosper, and that the word of the Lord might prosper among them. And his request was granted. With adoring gratitude, he beheld many who, through his own instrumentality, renounced the service of the world and Satan. Such he welcomed as his children into the household of faith, and he witnessed their walk in the truth with unfeigned and paternal joy.

"All who sleep in the dust of the earth shall awake, but they that be wise shall shine as the brightness of the firmament; and they that turn many to righteousness as the stars forever and ever."

CHAPTER 11

*An Account of His Zealous Attempts While at Chester to do
Good Beyond the Limits of His Own Congregation, Still
Embracing the Whole Period of the Foregoing Narrative,
Between the Year 1687 and the Year 1712*

The late Rev. R. Cecil said, "The man who labors to please
his neighbor for his good to edification, has the mind that
was in Christ. It is a sinner trying to help a sinner. How
different would be the face of things if this spirit *prevailed*!
If churchmen were like Leighton, and dissenters like Watts and
Doddridge and *Henry*."

With the condition of the generality of mankind, Mr. Henry
was deeply affected, and there is earnestness in his representations
of it, which renders them peculiarly impressive and stimulating.
"People are lying," said he, "under divine wrath, and the curse of
the law. They are held in the devil's snare and held captive by him
at his will. They yet think their condition good. They are dead in
sin and so feel nothing. Their peace is like the sleep of a man in a
lethargy; it is *not* peace – but senselessness and stupidity. They
love darkness and sit in it. My heart bleeds for them. Men are
destroyed for lack of knowledge."

Nor did he contemplate the state of professed Christians with
less grief or less anxiety. "There are," he writes, "but few who are

truly religious, who *believe* the reports of the Gospel, and who are willing to take the pains, and run the hazards of religion. Many make a fair show in the flesh, but few only walk closely with God. Where is he that engageth his *heart*, or that stirs up himself to take hold of his Maker? It is our common complaint that there are so many poor, but who complains that there are so many *ignorant*, which a man may be, and yet be able, like a parrot, to *say* his creed and catechism. Those who knew not the way of the Lord, yet said, "the Lord liveth." Many are painting their own cabin though the ship sink. Most men are mindless of the public."

Thus excited his efforts for the illumination and benefit of his neighbors were unwearied. He had not long resided in Chester before he commenced a lecture to the prisoners under confinement in the castle.

The origin of this labor of love was assigned, indeed, to the jailer's wife. She being a religious person, cherished a tender concern for the wretched individuals who had sinned themselves into such circumstances; and observing the remissness and formality of those who challenged it as their province to communicate instruction, persuaded some of them to send for Mr. Henry.

But, however the visits originated, Mr. Tong conjectures, and with great apparent probability, that much encouragement was derived for their continuance from an occurrence connected with the imprisonment, under the five-mile act of the Rev. Ralph Hall, already mentioned, and one of the ejected worthies. The case was this, and at the time of Mr. Henry's settlement at Chester, it was fresh in the memory of many. During Mr. Hall's confinement in the Northgate prison, his unceasing instructions and prayers were instrumental, as upon pretty strong evidence it was charitably believed, to the conversion of a profligate soldier, who was condemned, and afterwards executed for murder.

For about twenty years Mr. Henry persevered in his attendance: until, in fact, it became so obnoxious, especially to the curate of St. Mary's, as to induce the governor to discourage and terminate it.

In Mr. Henry's zealous ministrations, the villages and towns around Chester also largely participated. At some of them, particularly Moldsworth, Grange, Bromborough, Elton, and Saighton, he preached a monthly lecture. At Beeston, Mickledale, and Peckferton, Wrexham, Stockbridge, Burton, and Darnal still more frequently. In short, a week seldom elapsed in which he is not traceable, by his diary, to one or more of those places, publishing to the people the Gospel of the kingdom.

Prior to *his* settlement at Chester, the state of the surrounding and adjacent villages, was, in a spiritual aspect, most deplorable; "gross darkness covered" them. A few only, and those scattered here and there, were found, who retained the savor of religion, who read the Scriptures and prayed in their families. Most of them were persons advanced in years, the relics of declining puritanism. To them he was like life from the dead.

Actuated by a spirit perfectly missionary, Mr. Henry did not *confine* himself even to the places, which have been named. He extended his exertions far and wide. Frequent were his journeys to Whitchurch, Wrenburywood, Wem, Boreatton, Prescot, and Shrewsbury; and, usually, he made Broad Oak in his way either going or returning. At all those places his labors met with great acceptance and success. At Boreatton and Prescot, he for many years, occasionally administered the Lord's Supper; though not, as it should seem, very cordially. He did not much like what was "*merely* occasional," though willing to encourage, as he could, "the keeping up of religion in a family of note, where it had been uppermost."

To Nantwich, Newcastle, and Stone, he paid *annual* visits; and sometimes to Market Drayton and Stafford, preaching wherever he came. Some time before his removal to Hackney, he journeyed, likewise, once a year, into Lancashire, testifying the Gospel of the grace of God at Manchester, Duckenfield, Stockport, Bolton, Chowbent, Hindley, Warrington, and Liverpool.

The union formed by the "Dissenting Ministers" in Cheshire for Christian edification, and the advancement of the Redeemer's kingdom, had, in Mr. Henry, a cordial friend, and an able and zealous advocate. That union arose out of the agreement published by the Presbyterian and congregational ministers of London, and was recommended by them for general adoption. The Cheshire Union was formed in 1691, and met twice a year, in May and August; for some time at Knutsford and Bucklow Hill alternately; but afterwards at Knutsford only.

At those meetings, after the work of prayer and preaching was over, the ministers consulted together about the affairs of their several congregations. Whatever difficulties presented themselves in connection with the admission of any to church membership or suspension from it; or the removal of ministers from one place to another, were here proposed; and advice was accordingly given. Affairs of the state or the established church were never meddled with.

On such occasions it was that the times and places for public ordinations were determined.

The first of these ordinations, which is mentioned by Mr. Henry, occurred on the 27th of September 1692, at Knutsford, where he met several ministers both of Cheshire and Lancashire. The candidates were Mr. Hartley, Dr. Adam Holland, Mr. Dearnly, Mr. Traverse, Mr. Edge, and Mr. Haly; the ordainers were Mr. Risley, Mr. Crompton, Mr. Angier, Mr. Bradshaw, Mr. Aspinwal, and Mr. Ainsworth. The candidates were examined in the languages the evening before, at the house of Mr. Kynaston, the resident minister; and they read and defended their Theses. The day after was kept as a fast, Mr. Bradshaw prayed; Mr. Aspinwal preached from Rom. 10:15. How shall they preach except they be sent? Mr. Crompton, as moderator, took their confessions and ordination vows; and Mr. Angier concluded with an excellent exhortation. Mr. Henry recorded it as a good day. The candidates, he notes, gave satisfaction, adding, "Blessed be God for the rising generation; the Lord double his Spirit upon them."

Mr. Hartley settled at Ashby de la Zouch; Dr. Holland at Macclesfield; Mr. Traverse at Lichfield; and Mr. Haly at Leominster; Mr. Dearnley died about the beginning of June 1701, at Ringay in Cheshire, greatly lamented by all who knew how judicious, how humble, how serious, and how acceptable a minister he was.

In that ordination it will be observed, Mr. Henry was not actually engaged. The fact is, that for many years, subsequent to the commencement of his ministerial labors, he *declined* officiating. Not because he disliked such services or neglected attendance upon them, but from a desire that the assistance of ministers more advanced in years might, on such solemn occasions, be employed. As, however, "the ancients" departed to the heavenly Zion, his scruples abated; and, by degrees, the churches received in this, as in other respects, the full benefit of his gifts.

His scruples, however, seem to have been first surmounted on a different ground. A successor to the pulpit of his venerated father being found in an intimate and beloved friend, Mr. (afterwards Dr.) Benyon, Mr. Henry's assistance was secured. Under the date of January 23, 1699, he thus writes

I went to Broad Oak, my brother Hulton with me, to join in ordaining Mr. Samuel Benyon; I have always declined joining in such work, judging it fittest to be done by aged ministers, but this I could not decline; worthy Mr. Tallents designed to be with us, but durst not venture, which was a great disappointment; Mr. Owen and Mr. Lawrence came in the evening. Mr. Benyon was examined in the languages, and philosophy, and made a Thesis – An Revelatio Divina fuerit necessaria ad salutem lapsi hominis – (whether a divine revelation were necessary for the salvation of fallen man) – and defended it. We rejoiced in his great abilities.

The 24th was kept as a fast-day in Broad-Oak meeting house, a competent number present; Mr. Latham prayed, Mr. Lawrence gave an account of the business we met about, prayed and sung a Psalm; Mr. Doughty prayed, I preached from Isaiah 6:8. Here am I, send me; and prayed. Mr. Owen, as moderator, demanded a confession of his faith and ordination vows, which he made abundantly to our satisfaction. We then proceeded to set him apart. Mr. Owen concluded with the exhortation. We have reason to say it was a good day, and the Lord was among us.

Subsequently, Mr. Henry was often occupied in the same useful and important work. A brief narration of the several instances falls properly within the scope of the present chapter, as constituting no inconsiderable part of his history beyond the limits of his own congregation. At the same time, it is illustrative of the state of the dissenting churches in Cheshire and elsewhere at that period; and the statement is even due to the memory of those of his brethren whose names are mentioned in association of his own.

June 17, 1700. – I went to Macclesfield to join with my brethren, the ministers of Cheshire and Lancashire in an ordination. I have formerly declined that work, but now I see it is a service that must be done. I am satisfied with the validity of ordinations by the laying on of the hands of the presbytery; and, though we want a national establishment, yet that cannot be essential. I went with a true desire to honour God and promote the interest of Christ's kingdom. The next day was the day appointed for that work. I engaged with fear and trembling. Mr. Scoles prayed and read a Psalm and chapter; Mr. Lawrence prayed; Mr. Chorlton preached, Ephes. 3:21, Unto him be glory in the church by Christ Jesus, throughout all ages, world without end. Amen. Mr. Jones prayed; then Mr. Angier, who was moderator, demanded of the candidates in order, a confession of their faith, and a distinct answer to the questions; which was done fully. The candidates were Mr. Samuel Eaton of Manchester, Mr. Stephen Hughes of Wrexham, Mr. Brooks of Blakely, Mr. John Bradley of Knighton, Mr. Richard Milnes of Stopford, Mr. Fletcher of Chorton, and Mr. Grimshaw of Manchester. The ordainers Mr. Angier, Mr. Chorlton, Mr. Lawrence, Mr. Jones, Mr. Scoles, Mr. Aldred, and myself. After the ordination, I gave the exhortation. I desire to give glory to God for any assistance therein. We had a very great assembly, and I trust God was in the midst of us of a truth. We gave them certificates. Mr. Billingsley of Hull was providentially with us. It was a very comfortable day; blessed be God.

In June 1702, an ordination was appointed at Warrington; Mr. Jonathan Harvey of Chester was one of the candidates. With him Mr. Henry spent some time at his house before they went out; and spoke something from Psalm 71:16, I will go in the strength of the Lord God; I will make mention of thy righteousness, even of thine only. After that, the same day, they went to Warrington. He writes:

> I have had much struggling with myself, being tempted to decline what might give offence, and yet in the integrity of my heart (I hope I can say) I do it (attend the ordination): when the wheel turns against us, the greatest caution and tenderness we can now use, will not be remembered in our favor; but diligence and courage in improving our day of liberty will be reflected upon by ourselves to our comfort. Welcome the will of God.
>
> The 16th day was a day of fasting and prayer, and imposition of hands in a very great congregation at Warrington, where, I trust, God was with us of a truth. The ordained were Mr. Rice Pruthero of Braggington in Montomeryshire, Mr. James Whittel of Lee in Lancashire, Mr. John Heywood of Blackley in Lancashire, Mr. Reynald Tetlaw of Tinsel in Cheshire, Mr. James Lawton of Liverpool, Mr. Nicholas Waterhouse of Ringhay in Cheshire, and Mr. William Pendlebury of Kendal in Westmoreland. The ordainers were Mr. Risley, Mr. John Crompton, Mr. Eaton, Mr. Ainsworth, Mr. Jones, Mr. Aldred, and myself. Mr. Charles Owen began with prayer and reading. I prayed, Mr. Jones preached from 2 Cor. 12:15. I will very gladly spend and be spent for you. I took the confession and vows, and Mr. Risley concluded with a serious exhortation. The work of the day was done to general satisfaction. There were many other ministers present.

August 17, 1702. I went in the evening, Mr. Bradley being with me, to Wrexham, and met Mr. James Owen, etc., there, for the ordaining of Mr. John Evans and Mr. Edward Kenrick. We spent some time in the evening in examining Mr. Evans, whom God has endowed with excellent parts. The 18th was a day of fasting and prayer, in a numerous congregation. Mr. Charles Owen, Mr. Jenkin Thomas, and Mr. Benyon prayed. Mr. J. Owen prayed and preached; then Mr. Evans and Mr. Kenrick made their confessions and vows, with much seriousness, and were solemnly set apart. I closed with the exhortation, and hope we had the presence of God with us. I returned to Chester that night, and though I had a fall from my horse, was preserved from hurt; praised be God.

August 5, 1706. – I went to Knutsford; took the candidates' Theses. An ordination fast at Knutsford. We ordained Mr. Leoline Edwards of Tinsel; Mr. Thomas Perrot of Newmarket [in Flintshire]; and Mr. Silas Sidebothom of Wheelock. I hope many were edified; Mr. Angier prayed; Mr. Lawrence preached 2 Tim. 2:2 – The same commit thou to faithful men. I took the Confession of Faith and gave the exhortation. We had much comfort together. We were about eighteen ministers.

The next year, 1707, another ordination was attended at Knutsford. Mr. Tong says May 7th; but that is a mistake; it was the 13th. The candidates were Mr. Twemlow and Mr. Garside. Mr. Garside was the son of that good, aged, humble, minister, who lived and died near Macclesfield several years before; greatly esteemed by all who knew him; and, especially, by the good people at Chester; to whom he used to preach very privately in the times of persecution. He was a person of uncommon learning and judgment; of considerable gifts in preaching and prayer; and of great simplicity and godly sincerity; he affected plainness in his garb and way of living, beneath what his friends thought was due to his station as a minister; but he was contented and best pleased with it. It was a great satisfaction to those of his friends who were then alive to see his son so well qualified for the ministry, and solemnly engaged in it. Mr. Henry writes:

Mr. Low, Dr. Holland, and Mr. Angier prayed. Mr. Lawrence preached Psalm 16:13. Show me the path of life. Mr. Twemlow and Mr. Garside were set apart by imposition of hands. We were minded of our ordination vows. O that the obligation of them may abide always upon me. We were refreshed with the society of our brethren, not without some allays. Mr. Birch has left his congregation and gone to Yarmouth. Heats and reflections upon it.

September 1, 1707. I went by appointment to Winslow, willing to become all things to all men, and to spend and be spent. O that I may obtain mercy of the Lord to be sincere! Dined at Grange; in the evening met Mr. Angier at Mr. Wimslops, and we were refreshed together.

September 2. A solemn fast in the congregation at Dean Row for the ordination of Mr. Hugh Worthington, whom they have chosen to be their pastor in the room of Mr. Birch. I preached on 2 Cor. 5:18, the ministry of reconciliation. Mr. Angier prayed over him. Mr. Jolly of Sheffield gave the exhortation from Mat. 28:20, I am with you always. He had many things very affecting. The Honorable Mr. Cecil Booth was with us in the evening.

September 3. I returned home in safety, and found my tabernacle in peace; dined in Grange. Mr. Jolly is of a healing, loving spirit.

October 20, 1707. I went by Wrenbury Wood to Nantwich to an ordination. The evening was spent in examining candidates at Mr. Lawrence's. Mr. Richard Lesingham of Grantham in Lincolnshire, who brought very good testimonials; Mr. William Brayn of Newcastle; Mr. John King of Stone; and Mr. John Kenrick of Wrexham.

October 21. An ordination fast. Mr. Lawrence began, Mr. Irlam prayed. Dr. Holland preached from Acts 26:17, 28, "Delivering thee from the people and from the Gentiles, unto whom now I send thee; to open their eyes, and to turn them from darkness to light, and from the power of Satan unto God, that they may receive forgiveness of sins, and inheritance among them which are sanctified by faith that is in me." I took the confession, and gave the exhortation. We were in all about twenty ministers. The candidates discovered much seriousness; and we hope they are all likely to serve our great Master. We were much refreshed, and there were none to make us afraid.

The next ordination service in which Mr. Henry engaged seems to have been attended to by him with more than common interest. It occurred at Whitchurch, a place respecting which his diary is full of expressions of kindness. "I cannot," he writes, "*but* have a love to *that* people in particular. I was of old a member of the congregation;" that is, when they worshipped at Broad Oak. For when Dr. Benyon, a name already mentioned, left Broad Oak at Midsummer, 1706, to succeed the Reverend James Owen at Shrewsbury, the society over which he had presided, and which had been collected by Philip Henry, removed to Whitchurch, where they, almost immediately, commenced building a meeting house. "There were many adversaries, but God can make it," said Mr. Henry, "an open and effectual door;" and so it proved. On the 13th of September, the following year, 1707, the building was opened by a sermon from Mr. Henry, on Mat. 18:20, "Where two or three are gathered together in my name, there am I in the midst of them." The next day he expounded 2 Sam. 6 and 1 Thess. 2; and again preached from Rom. 13:10, —Love is the fulfilling of the law—administering, also, the Lord's Supper, "To the congregation in their new place." His exhortation at the table was founded upon 1 Kings 8:22, "They went into their tents joyful and glad of heart for all the goodness that the Lord had done to David his servant, and for Israel his people."

After Dr. Benyon's resignation, the people had been supplied by a Mr. Bell, Mr. Henry frequently visiting them. Indeed, subsequently to the opening of the chapel, he spent one *Sabbath* among them. March 14, 1707-8; on which occasion they celebrated the Eucharistic feast. Mr. Benyon was then their helper, and the people exceedingly pleased with him; for which, says Mr. Henry, "I desire to bless God as an answer to prayer."

The ordination of that promising young minister shall be stated in Mr. Henry's own words.

> *April 12, 1708. – In the afternoon I went, brother Hulton with me, to Whitchurch, for to-morrow's work. Mr. Lawrence and I examined Mr. Benyon. Mr. Tallents had given him his Thesis – Justitia qua coram Deo Susistimus est Justitia Christi Mediatoris – "The righteousness by which we are justified before God is the righteousness of Christ the mediator."*
>
> *13. This day was spent in ordaining Mr. Benyon. Mr. Lawrence began Mr. David Jones of Salop, preached on 2 Tim. 2:15. Mr. Doughty prayed. I took his confession, prayed over him, and gave the exhortation.*
>
> *To you of this congregation let me (said Mr. Henry) address myself. How earnestly do I desire your welfare, to hear that your souls prosper, and that your conversation is and becomes the Gospel. I have reason to bear you much*

upon my heart. I have done so; and I hope I shall while I live. I often call to remembrance the days of old; the years I spent in communion with you. I remember my father, in 1673, saying, that there were three things for which he praised the people of Whitchurch. 1. That they were sound in their judgments; not carried about with the wind of opinions. 2. They were of one mind and way. 3. That they had none of those tippling, talking clubs and fellowships, that are in some other towns among professors; whereby a great deal of harm is done, both to themselves and to their profession. Is it so still? May it ever be so!

Mr. Benyon performed with great seriousness, and gave universal satisfaction.

A lapse of several years now occurred before Mr. Henry again appeared as a principal in the work of an ordination. The record is as follows:

May 7, 1712. Met at brother Hulton's, and spent the day in prayer, and ordained cousin Dan. Madocks, who has been a preacher several years, but has never been ordained. Mr. Murray, Mr. Bassnet, Mr. Benyon, and Mr. King prayed, and joined in imposition of hands. I preached, and gave the exhortation. Amos 2:11. I raised up of your sons for prophets.

The secrecy observed at the ordination of Mr. Henry, and the extreme wariness of the testimonial he then received, have already, though briefly, been noticed. And, in again adverting to it, in consequence of the observations, he made in reference to Mr. Jonathan Harvey's ordination, it may be remarked, that in our present altered circumstances, the state of things which induced such caution, can, perhaps, be scarcely conceived of aright. Cradled

219

and nurtured in liberty, as, through divine mercy, Britons, have long been, a faint impression only can be caught of the intolerant and anti-Christian measures, which harassed our religious progenitors. Between the passing of the Act of Uniformity and the revolution, no ordinations, such as were prelatic only excepted, could be *public* without hazard. And, until the near approach of that happy time, it was not possible for the rumor of such a service, among dissenters, to have circulated, without exciting jealousy and alarm. Even six years later than the passing of the Toleration Act, Mr. Howe and Dr. Bates declined the officiating at a service of this nature. Such reserve and prudence, and in such men, proclaim the dangers referred to, in language sadly audible and distinct.

It may not be amiss to observe, that although, for a long time, Mr. Henry, as we have seen, was backward to engage in the business of ordaining, and after he did engage was ever careful, in obedience to the inspired command, to "lay hands suddenly upon no man," he was, nevertheless, both in judgment and practice, in favor of such ordinations only as were exclusively *ministerial*. This was evidenced by his particularity in obtaining a second certificate as to his own; at a time too when he enjoyed universal acceptance and esteem; when he could number many seals to his ministry; and, therefore, when such a testimony could be of no other value than for his own satisfaction.

This is the rather mentioned, because of the practice which once prevailed among some independent or congregational churches of performing the work of ordination among themselves; the neighboring ministers, who were invited, being only spectators and witnesses of their faith and order. An instance of this occurred in the reference to Mr. Birch, whose name was before introduced, and on which Mr. Henry makes the following remark: "Mr. Birch, who was ordained by the *people*, and had been their pastor above twenty years, at his removal, being not satisfied with the want of ministerial ordination, procured three or four ministers privately to ordain him, with the imposition of hands; the moderate of that congregation [Dean Row] are contriving to gain that point from the other party."

In most of the cases which have been related, it will be remarked that several candidates were ordained together, and at places oftentimes, remote from the people to whom they were to minister. Such, commonly, was the English Presbyterian mode; and may be accounted for, not only by a reference to arguments connected with the practice of Episcopalians, and to which most of them had been accustomed, but from the fear of danger, then almost inseparable from such services; a fear which would necessarily increase and spread, in proportion to their number and publicity.

The first ordination in which Mr. Henry engaged, Dr. Benyon's, was of a different character, being performed in the midst of the congregation he was to serve.

On a subsequent occasion, Mr. Henry complied with the urgent wish of the congregation at Dean Row, to assist the reverend and worthy Timothy Jolly, in ordaining Mr. Hugh Worthington as Mr. Birch's successor; and the following reason is assigned for the compliance. I am "willing to become all things to men."

It was only by degrees that ordinations, among the nonconformists, came to be performed, as now they almost invariably are, in the presence of the congregation over whom the oversight is taken. This certainly is an improvement, as having in it a recognition of the union between the pastor and the flock; and as tending to excite the parties mutually to the discharge of their relative duties.

How excellently does the following brief address, delivered by Mr. Henry on an occasion similar to those, which have been detailed, explain the nature and design of the service, whether performed, according to the Presbyterian, or the congregational mode. Like the New Testament, it recognizes neither lordly preeminence, nor priestly prerogatives; it pretends to no mysterious communications, nor to any uninterrupted succession; but is throughout rational, and sober, and well-defined: -

The question, which God put to Elijah, we desire to put to ourselves. What do we here? And the question Christ put to the people concerning John, we would put to you. What came ye out for to see?

We who are ministers should be able to give a good account what *we* do here. We are not here to strive or cry, or to have our voice heard in the streets; not to affront the government or the public establishment. We desire to be found of the quiet in the land; not to contend with our brethren, or to condemn those we differ from; to the same Master they and we must stand or fall. We hope we take not too much upon us; but, as ministers, we are to give ourselves "to the word and prayer;" as in other things, so in this, by prayer to recommend to God, and by the word to recommend to you.

Some who are here are to give up themselves to the service of Christ in the work of the ministry. We pretend not to commission them; they have their commission from Christ; nor to consecrate them, they have their consecration from the Holy Ghost. We pretend not to give them the Holy Ghost: it is not in our power; but, solemnly to set them apart, or rather to recognize their setting of themselves apart, to this great work; and to bless them "in the name of the Lord." We hope the ordination of Timothy, with the laying on of the hands of the presbytery, will bear us out before

God in what we do; and there is a promise to two or three touching any thing they shall agree to ask.

You who are the candidates are concerned to consider what *you* do here. You are here to dedicate yourselves to Christ and his honour, and service. You have made some trial of his work, and you are now to be *bound*, as those that like it well and would not go from it. You are to have your ears bored to his door-posts. You have sat down and counted the cost, and are at a point. You are resolved to make the ministry your business, and give yourselves to it.

The people are to consider what they came hither to see. We are to give them a charge *in your sight*, that you may see what obligations your ministers are under to their work; that you may esteem them highly; that you may help them with your prayers; that you may value the privilege of a standing ministry; and that you may be thankful for the gifts, and powers given to men.

For your satisfaction we are to tell you what has been done concerning those who are now to be offered to God. They have been educated in learning, in the schools of the prophets; they have given proof of their abilities. Every scholar is not fit to make a minister. *They* have been tried, and found "apt to teach;" they have been tried by the people to whom they are to minister, and are found fit for them, and of a good conversation; not only blameless, but exemplary; they have showed themselves able, not only to preach the truth, but to defend it.

We are also to tell you what is *now* to be done. They are to make a confession of their faith. We leave them to do it in their own words, that ye may "understand their knowledge in the mystery of Christ;" and that ye may be satisfied of their soundness in the faith. They are to make their vows to the Lord, and they shall be their free-will offerings. Remember you are in the presence of God.

For several years the care of all the neighboring churches may be said "daily to have come upon" Mr. Henry, especially such as he could visit between the Sabbaths. The engagements thus fulfilled, included a circuit of about thirty miles, and embraced frequent lectures, public ordinations, and funeral sermons, both for ministers and others. A resolution which he early made never to refuse an invitation to preach when it was in his power to comply, being well known the applications were numerous.

In the prosecution of those zealous designs and labors, which have been noticed, it will not be supposed that Mr. Henry had to encounter no difficulties. In common with all who watch for souls he had *many*. They arose, mainly, from ignorance and worldliness, and indifference; a trial whose force is known only to such ardent and indefatigable laborers. But all were cheerfully surmounted; in full illustration of his own remark that, a "Christian ought to take his work," whatever it be, and however hindered in its prosecution, "and sing at it." After riding to preach at a distance from home, and in weather which furnished persons in the immediate neighborhood with an excuse for not attending, he merely said , "We must endure hardness, and be glad of opportunities to do good, though but to a few."

Mr. Henry, no doubt, contrasted his peaceful discharge of ministerial duty with the opposition and perils of his forefathers; and the consideration was well adapted to relieve the pressure of many annoyances, and even obstacles. But, although not actually exposed to bonds, his career was far from being unchecked. The uncertainty of public affairs was oftentimes very trying. Even in *his* day, the political horizon, over the heads of the non-conformists, occasionally gathered blackness; and voices were "heard in the air" which muttered oppression, and cruelty, and imprisonment. It is interesting, however, to know that the mantle of fortitude and conscientiousness, which dignified his father, and the noble army of the ejected, fell, when they ascended, upon him. As a preparation for anticipated suffering, he, on one occasion, calmly observed, that "the evil things of the world are not real and substantial evils; that they do not affect the soul. The spirit," said he, "may be safe and happy. *That* is the formidable prison which lays hold on spirits."

With another class of opponents—slanderers and busybodies—Mr. Henry took an effectual course. Keeping in view, in the efforts of his zeal, only legitimate objects, he adopted for their attainment those methods, alone which are divinely prescribed. Far removed from pusillanimous timidity on the one hand, and inconsiderate rashness on the other, he took care that no unhallowed policy, nor vain regrets, should sully his measures, or embitter his peace. And, by a steady adherence to the Scriptures of truth; by an earnest contention for the once-delivered faith; by uncompromising opposition to heresy in doctrine, and immorality in practice; and above all, by a prudent and holy example, he "put to silence the ignorance of the foolish."

His official engagements were so judiciously arranged, as that neither the extent, nor the multiplicity of occasional services was ever allowed to supercede, and, as little as possible, to encroach upon, the stated duties of home. In paying his annual visits even to the *distant* places, which have been mentioned, the journey was always performed within the week. He greatly preferred any toil to absence, from "his own people" on the Lord's Day.

The first time after his settlement at Chester he went to London, he noticed in his diary, that, until then, he had been in no pulpit on the Sabbath besides his own and his father's for ten years. And long afterwards, he observed, that he was absent from Chester on the first Sabbath in the month only once in twenty-four years.

In estimating Mr. Henry's pulpit exertions the *self-denial*, which they involved, must not be overlooked. Some ministers delight in publicity, and bustle and even show. But he courted privacy and quiet. The reference made by him in his "discourse on meekness" to the paraphrase written by Lord Chief Justice Hale upon a part of Seneca's Thyestes, furnishes an exact illustration of his own temper in this particular, as it did of the temper of that great, and immortal judge. But Mr. Henry's manuscripts, also, contain abundance of other evidence. It appears for them how, while engaged about the Exposition, he rejoiced, and even made it a matter of special thanksgiving, that, *that* part of his work, at least, was "cut out in retirement, and not in noise and hurry." Alluding to a renewed application to preach a funeral sermon for a deceased minister, and which involved a long journey, he says, "I promised to go. It is against the grain; but I would not do any thing that looks like breaking my word, taking state, or loving my ease." At another time he writes, "Private comfort must always give way to public service, in which I am willing to spend and be spent." "The Lord assist me, and accept of me." Again, "I went out with a desire to good and to honour God. Lord, thou knowest all things, thou knowest that I love thy work, and desire to know *where* I should be employed. I would not let my work at home stand still while I go abroad, but in hope of doing much more good. Lord, teach me "thy way." "I hope I can say, through grace, *therefore*, I am so much in my work, because the love of Christ constraineth me; because I find it "good for me to draw near to God."

Extracts like these show, sufficiently, that it was not to a love of fame or publicity, that the vigorous constancy, which has been recorded, must be attributed, but to *principle*, well founded, and well sustained. It was a love for souls and their Redeemer, and his blessed service, like that which animated the apostles, which induced such frequent preaching; which excited for twenty successive years, in short, till forbidden, the gratuitous setting forth of the way of salvation to imprisoned culprits; which secured the hearty relinquishment of the delights of the closet (and to Mr. Henry they *were* delights) for village lectures, and spiritual conference; and which led, so that men might be saved, to an equal and utter disregard of inclement seasons, malignant opposition, and irritating reproach.

He, as is affirmed of Moses, had respect to the "recompense of reward." *His* eye, like that of all those wise and holy men who, in their respective spheres, have been "burning and shining" lights, was fixed upon a "crown of rejoicing in the presence of Christ Jesus." If Hierom thought a voice was ever sounding in his ears, "Arise, ye dead, and come to judgment" – Mr. Henry seemed *as* constantly impressed with the Master's inviting assurance, "Where I am there also my *servant* be."

That compassionate desire for the good of mankind, which was, before noticed, derived incalculable energy from the contrast he delighted to draw between the past and existing dispensations of revealed mercy; from the contemplation of inspired promises; and from the steadfastness of unwavering faith. Supplied by these, as by so many invisible streams, his zeal flowed like a river, bearing down all opposition and gaining accessions of strength and impetuosity, even from the hindrances, and the dams, which were intended to impede, if not to prevent, its course.

"The grace of the New Testament," he writes, "is substituted in the room of that of the Old. Discoveries of grace are now more clear, and its distributions more plentiful. The *Spirit* is now more fully "poured" out. Then the house was filled with glory; but now the earth is filled with glory. The partition wall is broken down.

We live in a time of improvement and reformation. The promises are more spiritual. Life and immortality are brought to *light*. We are under the dispensation of the Spirit."

Mr. Henry's ardor in the best of all causes was strikingly manifested in reference to the manuscript treatise of his beloved friend Mr. Reynolds, entitled, "Zeal a Virtue, or a Discourse concerning Sacred Zeal." So fervent was his desire for that impressive and exciting work to be made known and circulated, that he actually sent it to the press without the author's knowledge. But for which circumstance it had, in all probability, never appeared.

Mr. Henry hailed every symptom of approach towards the latter day glory with ineffable pleasure. When rumors were afloat, in the year 1703, during the warfare of England with France and Spain, instead of being appalled, he cheerfully observed, that "perhaps, the wars of the nations may end in the peace of the church; and that the greatest perplexities of the children of men may introduce the joys of the people of God. We hope glorious times *are* reserved for the church."

But, he did not limit his believing exultation to such statements, any more than to seasons of public excitement. In secret, when no eye saw him but that of God, he discovered the same ardor, and the same elevation; a proof at once of the genuineness, as well as the vehemence of his zeal. The following instructive record stands connected with the devotions of the *closet*. "I hope I prayed in faith, and with some fervor for the sanctifying of God's name, the coming of Christ's kingdom, and the doing of his will. O that earth may be made more like heaven, and saints more like angels."

CHAPTER 12

The congregation to which Mr. Henry removed from Chester was the first of its kind formed at Hackney; and for many years, the only one. Nor does it appear to have received, either under Dr. Bates, its earliest minister, or his successor, Mr. Billio, any considerable increase; for, at the time of his settlement, and he immediately followed the excellent men just mentioned, the communicants were fewer in number than one hundred.

Mr. Palmer represents the meeting house in Mr. Henry's time as an old irregular building, originally formed out of dwelling-houses, and on the opposite side of the way to the one since erected.

Our author's pastoral engagements there, commenced on Lord's Day, May 18, 1712. In the morning he expounded Gen. 1 and in the afternoon, Mat. 1 beginning the world, as it were, anew. He preached to an encouraging auditory from Acts 16:9, "Come over into Macedonia and help us," but his mind was unhappy and depressed. "O that good may be done," is the aspiration written at the time, to which he adds, "I am sad in spirit, lamenting my departure from my friends at Chester; but if they are well provided for, and the work of God go on among them, I shall be easy, whatever discouragements I meet with."

The same course of zealous and active exertion that has been before described, was pursued here, both within, and beyond the bounds of his own congregation. Instead, however of commencing public worship with the 100th Psalm, at Hackney, he began with a short prayer.

More than once he delivered the Lord's Day morning lecture at Little St. Helen's, and then returned to Hackney, preaching and expounding, as usual, both parts of the day. Sometimes after his own morning and afternoon services, he went to Mr. Lloyd's meeting house in Wapping or to the Charity School at Shakespeare's walk, or to Rotherhithe, delivered the evening lecture, returned home, and attended, as if unfatigued, to the several parts of domestic worship.

Not long after his residence at Hackney, he took a part in the ordination at St. Albans of Mr., afterwards Dr., Samuel Clark, the successor of the Rev. Jonathan Grew, deceased. Dr. Williams, Mr. Smith, and Mr. Cotton accompanied him. On the 17th of September, 1712, the service was attended to. "Mr. Smith," they are Mr. Henry's words, "preached. Dr. Williams presided. I gave the exhortation; a numerous auditory—a comfortable day. We were six ministers from London. There met us Mr. Boid of Hampstead,

Mr. Walker of Brentford, Mr. Hughes of Ware, Mr. Guise of Hertford, and Mr. Wright of Hitchin. Mr. Clark performed his part exceedingly well."

18th. I visited Mrs. Grew; looked a sorrowful look towards Chester, returned with the same company."

This ordination, it will be observed, was strictly a congregational one.

Some further extracts will show that, notwithstanding the increased weight and number of Mr. Henry's engagements, those habits of personal piety and self-dedication which have been so fully noticed, were still continued in the same spirit of Scriptural and elevated devotion.

October 18, 1712. Today I have filled up, or rather the Lord has filled up unto me, the fiftieth year of my life, and I now enter on old age. With so many years has the divine forbearance indulged me, (who by reason of my sins am heir to death) nor has God only given life, but he has enriched it with all good things pertaining both to life and godliness. Forever blessed be his name. But what have I done more than others for the glory of God and the good of the church. I have, indeed, lived an idle, slothful, inactive, and useless life. Have mercy on me, O Lord, and let what remains of my life be entirely devoted to my Redeemer; and when no more shall remain, let this life be sweetly changed for the life everlasting.

January 1, 1713. Firmly believing that my times are in God's hand, I here submit myself, and all my affairs for the ensuing year to the wise and gracious disposal of the divine providence; whether God appoint for me health or sickness, peace or trouble, comforts or crosses, life or death, his holy will be done.

Believing that my heart is in God's hand, this precious soul of mine I commit to the conduct of the divine grace, and submit to the influences and operations of the blessed Spirit to be wrought up to a conformity to the will of God in everything. I depend upon God to give me a wise and understanding heart for all the services I may be called out unto, and from him I hope to obtain mercy to be found faithful.

The sphere of my usefulness is much enlarged. O that my heart may be proportionally enlarged; and as the day is, so let the wisdom, and strength, and grace be. Temptations to spiritual pride are many. O that the grace of God may be sufficient for me, to keep me humble, very humble; to keep up in me always a humble sense of my own unworthiness, weakness, and many follies and infirmities; and a humble dependence upon the Lord Jesus Christ, as all in all, both for righteousness and strength.

As at Chester, so in the metropolis, the *young* shared a large portion of Mr. Henry's attention. Catechizing had never been wholly omitted in and about London, but he was instrumental in a more general revival of it. Besides attending to that duty at Hackney on Saturdays (which he commenced performing almost immediately after his settlement there), he undertook a catechetical lecture in London at the meetinghouse, which once belonged to his honored tutor, Mr. Doolittle. And that lecture was not only well attended, but some young persons were known to Mr. Tong, who going only as spectators, ascribed their first religious impressions to the instructions then received.

His papers abound with proofs of the intense interest, which he took, both in their temporal and spiritual welfare: nor was this care confined to the families of opulent congregations; it extended equally to the children of the poor. "I went early," he writes, "January 1, 1712-13, to Gravel-lane, in Southwark, Mr. Marriot's meeting place, where there has been a charity school for twenty-five years; the only one among the dissenters; there I preached an anniversary sermon on Prov. 3:9. 'Honour the Lord with thy substance.' A collection was made amounting to about 35 pounds sterling. *[Editor's note: In today's exchange, roughly $70 USD.]*

His sentiments as to those institutions, having been preserved in Mr. Tong's Memoir, need not be here recited. It may be noticed, however, in corroboration, which having the disposal of a considerable sum entrusted to his care, he evinced his attachment by bestowing 20 pounds sterling of it to a charity school. *[Editor's note: In today's exchange, roughly $40 USD.]*

To instance, more at length, Mr. Henry's indefatigable labors in and around London, is unnecessary. It shall suffice to add, that often he was daily, and not infrequently twice and thrice the same day, employed in the arduous, but to him, delectable work of preaching. If any minister erred in *excess* of labors, he was the person. "His motion in holiness and service was the swifter as he came nearer to the centre of his rest."

He did not long survive his removal to Hackney, but his descent to the grave, though at last sudden, was gradual. His frame had been severely tried by the attacks heretofore noticed; and, during the last two years of his life, their frequency and violence increased. They visibly indicated a yielding constitution, and so attracted his own notice, as to occasion frequent allusion to the probable issue, but with enviable composure, if not delight.

Before he left Chester, he engaged, while able, to visit that city annually for a few Sabbaths. This arrangement, suggested by the congregation at Hackney, the better to secure his acceptance of their invitation, was most scrupulously observed. His own account will best furnish the detail, and it is too interesting to be omitted.

July 20, 1713. I am now set out in the coach for Chester to visit my friends in the country, as I purposed and promised when I came hither, aiming at God's glory and the edification of souls. In prospect of that the charge and trouble of the journey shall be as nothing to me.

On the 23rd we came to Whitchurch. Many of my friends met me there to my great reviving. In the afternoon I went and preached at Broad Oak, from Rom. 1:11. "For I long to see you that I may impart unto you some spiritual gift, to the end you may be established." The next day I went to Chester, where my friends received me with much affection and respect, so that I could not but say it was worth the while to come. On the Lord's Day I preached from 1 Tim. 6:12. "Lay hold on eternal life." It was very pleasant to me to preach in the old place, where I have often met with God and been owned by him. On the Wednesday we kept a congregational fast; the next Lord's Day I preached, and administered the Lord's Supper to my beloved flock, a great congregation. On Monday I went to Middlewich, preached a lecture there from Matt. 24:12. "Iniquity abounds." The next day to Knutsford, to a meeting of ministers. I preached from Col. 2:8. "Though absent in the flesh, yet present in the Spirit;" about the spiritual communion of saints.

On the Lord's Day, August 9, I preached at Chester, from Tit. 2:13. "Looking for the blessed hope." I took an affectionate farewell of many of my friends and prayed with many of them; the next day set out from Chester, with much ado, for Nantwich, where Mr. Mottershed is well settled. I preached from Josh. 1:5-6. "As I was with

Moses, I will be with thee; be strong and of a good courage." From thence that night to Wrenbury Wood, and preached there from John 1:48: and from thence to Danford, and preached at Whitchurch, from 1 Pet. 5:10, and took my leave of my dear friends there. I went into the coach alone; came to London the 15th, and found my tabernacle in peace."

Shortly after his return home, symptoms of diabetes manifested themselves, and he was laid aside for one Sabbath. "A melancholy day," he writes, "yet not without some sweet communion with God. It is just upon me for an inordinate desire to be at my study and work again." Still feeling the effects of the shock, he says soon after, "I cannot now rise so early, nor stick so close to my study as I could have done before my last illness. The Lord perfect strength in me."

The following month his system, already tottering, sustained another, and while it continued, violent nephritic attack. The seizure was on the Lord's Day, but he officiated as usual, and through the week toiled incessantly. On Tuesday he went to London to his catechizing. On Wednesday he delivered the lecture at Hackney, and attended the funeral of his neighbor, Mr. Ironmonger, who was buried at Stepney. On Thursday evening he preached at Spitalfields. On Friday he joined in a fast, and gave the sermon at Mr. Fleming's, at Founder's-hall. On Saturday he felt himself well.

Another birth-day anniversary having arrived, it was noticed in the following tender and expressive terms. "October 18, 1713. The fifty-first year of my life has this day closed. In the course of it, many of my friends have reached their goal. I am yet alive, but in the midst of death. May my soul be meetened for the heavenly life, and then, the will of the Lord be done."

The interval of convalescence was short. He very affectingly noticed the alteration of ease and pain. Under any circumstances the statement would be valuable, but the eventually sudden termination of his course has rendered it doubly so.

> *Lord's Day, December 13. This morning a little after midnight, I was seized with a fit of the stone; but blessed be God, the pain in about an hour went off; though fatigued with it, yet the poor body was fitted in some measure to serve the Lord. I went to London, and preached the morning lecture at Mr. Robinson's from John 20:1. "The first day of the week, early while it was yet dark." I preached at Hackney, from Romans 2:8-9.*

> *Thursday, December 17, I went to my study early in the morning; but, before seven o'clock, I was seized with a fit of the stone, which held me all day pained, and sick. I lay much on the bed. I had comfort in lifting my heart to God, and pleading his promises, and encouraged myself in him: about nine o'clock in the evening I had much ease, but weak.*

> *Friday, December 18. I am very well today, though very ill yesterday. How is this life counterchanged? Yet I am but girding on the harness. The Lord prepare me for the next fit; and for the last.*

It was an observation of Mr. Henry's that "the more we have of the foretastes of heaven, the less evil we shall see in death; which," said he, "is not a bar, but a bridge in our way to glory." And now, standing upon the threshold of a new year, and as if conscious that it *was* the last, he looked the king of terrors steadily in the face; and through faith in Him who hath "overcome," and who hath opened the kingdom of heaven to all believers, he triumphed.

> *January 1, 1714. Reflecting with thankfulness upon the many mercies of the year past, a good measure of health; health in my family; encouragement in my ministry, both in the congregation here, and at London; the comforts of my journey to Chester; the happy settlement of the congregation there; the continuance of the public tranquility; and, I trust, through grace, some sweet communion with God in his ordinances and some progress heavenwards, and my work pleasant to me.*
>
> *Reflecting with sorrow and shame upon my manifold defects and shortcomings in holy duties, and at other times inward impressions not always answering outward expressions, having begged for pardon in the blood of Christ.*
>
> *In this morning renewed the dedication of myself to God, my own self, my whole self, body, soul, and spirit. Father, I give thee my heart; use me for thy glory this year; employ me in thy service; fit me for thy will. If it should be a year of sickness and pain; if a year of family affliction; if a year of public trouble; if of silencing and suffering, bonds and banishment; if it be my dying year, **welcome the holy will of God**; if a year of continued health, peace and liberty, Lord, I desire to be busy in the improvement of it, both in study and preaching, in an entire dependence upon divine grace, without which I am nothing, and can do nothing.*

That day he preached a sermon to young people, from Proverbs 23:26. "My son give me thy heart." Adding to the mention of it in his diary the following affectionate and devout aspiration. "Lord take *my* heart, and make it such as it should be." "I received," he proceeds, "and read the life of Mr. Trosse of Exeter, a wonder of free grace."

It was on the 7th of April following that he attended the ordination of Mr. James Wood of Dublin, the successor of Mr. Burgess. He gave the exhortation; he expatiated upon the various characters given to ministers in holy Scripture – as stewards, builders, and husbandmen; and showed very particularly their duty under each. Mr. Mayo and Mr. Cotton prayed. Mr. Tong preached from Revelation 2:1. "Seven stars." Dr. Williams took the confession. Mr. Evans concluded.

After this he addressed himself to a renewed fulfillment of his promise, by again visiting Chester. But before that narration is introduced, the reader shall have the opportunity to peruse the concluding sentence of the diary.

> *May 30, 1714. Lord's day, I expounded Exod. 38 and Luke 7:5-11. I preached from Rev. 5:9. "For thou wast slain." I prayed with Mrs. Hutchins not well. Communion with the Lord at his table. Preparing for my journey.*

On Monday, May 31, Mr. Henry set out. During his stay in the country, his labors were abundant; he visited Wrexham, Knutsford, and Chowbent, testifying everywhere "the Gospel of the grace of God." A remark, which he made during this visit, shows more satisfaction than he had before felt, in his removal to Hackney. "I am here [at Chester] among my old friends, yet I find my new ones lie very near my heart among whom God has now cut out my work."

It deserves observation that the two last Lord's Days Mr. Henry spent upon the earth were employed in the immediate and public contemplation of that Sabbatism of rest, upon which he was so soon to enter. On one of those days, he preached from Heb. 4:9. "There remaineth, therefore, a rest for the people of God," and on the other, from the first verse of the same chapter. "Let us, therefore, fear lest a promise being left us of entering into his rest, any of you should seem to come short of it." Mr. Tong has preserved the outline of both the discourses.

The day after the last of them was delivered, viz. Monday, June 21, Mr. Henry commenced his return to Hackney. He was observed to be heavy and sleepy, but his uniform answer to enquiries was – well. A friend, Mr. Sudlow, an apothecary, remarked, however, before he left Chester that they should never see him again.

Passing by Dudden, he drank a glass of the mineral waters. Ere he reached Tarporley his horse threw him, but he denied that the fall occasioned him any inconvenience. All invitations to tarry there he resisted, and *would* proceed to Nantwich, where he had engaged to preach. His text was Jer. 31:18. "I have surely heard Ephraim bemoaning himself thus. Thou hast chastised me, and I was chastised as a bullock unaccustomed to the yoke; turn thou me and I shall be turned; for thou art the Lord my God." The absence of his usual liveliness was universally noticed.

His old and intimate friend Mr. Illidge, who was with him, had been desired by Sir Thomas Delves and his lady, to invite him to Doddington, a house famed for piety; he accepted the invitation; and the steward waited to conduct him thither. But he soon became unable to go on, and at the Reverend Joseph Mottershed's, went to bed. He requested his friends to pray for him: "for now," said he, "I cannot pray for myself." He spoke of the excellency of spiritual comforts in a time of need, and blessed God for the enjoyment of them. To Mr. Illidge, who was accustomed to notice the sayings of dying men, he had remarked in London the preceding

241

month, that this was his. "A life spent in the service of God and communion with him is the most comfortable life anyone can live in this world."

The next morning, Tuesday June 22, about five o'clock, he was seized with apoplexy, and, after laying three hours speechless, with his eyes fixed, "he fell asleep."

> In vain our fancy strives to paint
> The moment after death,
> The glories that surround the saint,
> When he resigns his breath.
>
> One gentle sigh his fetters breaks;
> We scarce can say, "He's gone,"
> Before the willing spirit takes
> His mansion near the throne.
>
> Faith strives, but all its efforts fail
> To trace her heavenward flight;
> No eye can pierce within the veil,
> Which hides that world of light.
>
> Thus much (and this is all) we know,
> They are supremely blest;
> Have done with sin, and care, and woe,
> And with their Saviour rest.
>
> On harps of gold his name they praise,
> His presence always view;
> And if we *here* their footsteps trace,
> There *we* shall praise him, too.

On Thursday, June 24, prior to removing the body from Nantwich, the Reverend Mr. Reynolds of Shrewsbury, preached the appropriate sermon, which has been cited. Mr. Acton, minister to the Baptist congregation, had the day before taken particular and respectful notice of the great loss which had been sustained. Mr. Withington, Mr. Gardner's (who succeeded Mr. Henry) assistant at Chester, improved the event, both on Thursday and on Lord's day morning; and Mr. Gardner in the afternoon, from 2 Kings 2:12. "My father, my father, the chariot of Israel, and the horsemen thereof."

The bearers at the funeral, which took place on Friday, June 25, were Mr. Doughty, Mr. Woods, Mr. Murrey, Mr. Gardner, Mr. Benyon, and Mr. Mottershed. When the procession reached Chester, eight of the clergy, ten coaches, and a large company of horses met it; many dissenting ministers followed the mourners; and persons of note and distinction paid universal respect.

The precious remains were lodged in Trinity church.

The news of Mr. Henry's death on reaching the metropolis, awakened inexpressible sorrow. The voice of lamentation was heard, especially from the dissenting pulpits, in every direction.

Two sermons were addressed to the Hackney congregation upon the event, and both were published. The one by Dr. D. Williams, June 27, the other by Mr. Tong, July 11. They were admirably calculated to perfume the name of the deceased, to console surviving mourners, to gratify descendants, and to instruct, and edify the church.

CHAPTER 13

His Private Character

both Mr. Henry's marriages have been narrated. It will be remembered how specially, in the second, Mrs. Hardware, the mother of his departed wife, aided him. And he had no reason to repent his attention to her advice. In Miss Warburton, as in Miss Hardware, he found "a good wife," and *he*, as a husband, by a uniform manifestation of prudence, fidelity, and affection, was "greatly beloved." His letters and diary are full of the most convincing tokens of his conjugal regards: and his widow's sorrows, when the separation took place, proclaimed loudly the deep sense she entertained of the magnitude of her loss.

They had nine children; Elizabeth, Mary, Esther, Ann, Philip, Elizabeth, Sarah, Theodosia, and Mary.

Mr. Henry, in every sense of the phrase, was a domestic man. He rejoiced "in the wife of his youth;" and studiously contributed to the happiness of his household; instead, like many, of going abroad for enjoyment, he sought and found it in his own home. Recording a journey to a distance to preach, he says—"In the evening I came to Chester late, and through much rain; but it was *home*."

His whole conduct to his offspring was marked by kindness. The advice he gave to others, he acted upon himself. "Do all you can to make your children love home." "Continual chiding and finding fault," he abhorred. "Remember," he would say, "that children are *but* children. If parents would not correct them except in a praying frame, when they can 'lift their hands without wrath,' it would neither provoke God, nor them."

His care and anxiety for their spiritual interests were uniformly conspicuous. He beheld them with deep and serious attention, observing, sometimes, how awful a consideration it is that when a child is born he will outlive all the ages of time.

The sermon in the miscellaneous works, entitled, "Christ's Favor to Children," develops Mr. Henry's sentiments with most instructive minuteness. He has there placed parental obligations in a strong and affecting light: directing with happy precision in the performance of essential duties, imparted instructions at all times suited to the young, and so ministered advice and encouragement to those who have their superintendence, as to indicate, with equal perspicuity, the soundness of his principles, the ardor of his piety, and his great insight into mankind.

Such remarks are not less applicable to the directions to parents contained in his Treatise on Baptism.

In the education of his own children, he copied the example, which had been exhibited at Broad Oak: an example in which it may be difficult to determine whether the wisdom of the discipline or the sanctity of the instruction, most predominated. "I have known those," says Mr. Tong, "who upon their first acquaintance there, were surprised to see so much 'beauty of holiness,' and were ready to say, 'Surely God is in this place. This is none other than the house of God, and the gate of heaven.'"

Mr. Henry, like his father, seems to have attempted everything in this difficult part of parental responsibility, which was calculated to restrain evil propensities, and to inspire the fear and love of God. "I know," the address was made to Christian parents, and himself also—"You cannot give them *grace*: that is God's gift, but duty is required. Children must be nursed for God, and our care should be that they may be pious."

He labored to counteract the first risings of evil tempers in his children. He often asked them, and he advised others to do the same, "Whom is it that God resists? What is the first of the seven things, which the Lord hates?" And he not only inculcated in the abstract, a strict regard to verity, but he enforced and adopted as his own, an impressive remark made to him in conversation by his friend, "Mr. Wynn of Coperlenny," that generally, those who make conscience of speaking truth, prosper in the world; and that none are more visibly blasted than those who make no conscience of a lie.

In attention to domestic *worship*, Mr. Henry reverently imitated the constancy and punctuality of his father. Like that illustrious saint so often mentioned, he assembled his family, whatever happened and whoever were under his roof, as early in the morning as circumstances would permit; and also, in like manner in the evening, "being ashamed," they are his own words, "to put God off with drowsy devotions."

He was comprehensive, but neither tedious nor hurried. The exercise commenced by invocation, in a few words, of the ineffable name, for aid and acceptance. He then read in the morning, a portion of the *Old* Testament Scripture, in regular course; and, in the evening, with like regularity, a portion of the *New*. Unless the chapter was short, he divided it into sections, confining himself generally to eight or ten verses, of which he gave a brief and edifying explanation.

After the exposition some part of a Psalm was sung: everyone had a book; and so neither the sense nor the melody suffered that interruption which is incident to reading line by line, "How the houses of the good old protestants were perfumed with this incense daily, especially on Lord's Days, we," says Mr. Henry, "have heard with our ears, and our fathers have told us."

Prayer succeeded singing. The whole was usually comprehended within the space of half an hour, or a little more.

When prayer was over, his children received his blessing, which he pronounced with great seriousness, solemnity, and affection.

The better to engage the attention of his family, he required from them, at the close of the exercise, an account.

On the Sabbath, the same order was observed: the household assembling about eight o'clock. Nor were his public engagements on that sacred day allowed to interfere, either with the observance itself or his own personal attention to it.

It is narrated of that eminently holy man, the Reverend R. Rogers of Wethersfield, that having been long "troubled," he set apart a day to seek of God why he so often hid his face from him. After three hours spent upon his knees he came down cheerful, saying he had "found it:" namely, that being busy for his sermon, instead of praying with his family on the morning of the Lord's Day, he had neglected that duty and left it to his wife. He afterwards altered his course in that particular.

The worship being concluded, Mr. Henry took his family to the solemn assembly. After dinner he sang a Psalm, offered up a short prayer, and so retired to his closet till the time returned for meeting the congregation. In the evening, he generally repeated in his own house both the sermons, on which occasion many neighbors attended. Singing and prayer followed the repetition; two verses more of a suitable hymn were then sung, the blessing pronounced, and the younger children catechized. After supper he sung the 136th Psalm; then catechized his elder children and servants; heard them repeat what they could remember of the sermons; and concluded the day with supplication.

Besides the *daily* oblations and Sabbath services, which have been noticed, Mr. Henry often kept family fasts—sometimes in unison with invited friends, at others with his own household. And frequently he fasted alone. On these occasions, like the believing patriarch, he wrestled for "spiritual blessings" and whatever were the cares, or fears, or trials of himself or his friends, they were committed, with filial simplicity and confidence to God.

A pious custom then happily prevailed of assembling friends in private for imploring the divine favor and commemorating with praise and thanksgiving deliverance from domestic or other afflictions. This custom also, Mr. Henry observed. On such occasions, he would remind his "brethren and companions," that "distinguishing mercy calls for distinguishing thankfulness and obedience."

His piety "at home," embraced the whole compass of relative religion; he was an "example to believers," not only as a husband, a father, and a master, but also as a son, a son-in-law, a brother, and a friend.

As a son and a son-in-law, he was respectful, attentive, and affectionate. In early life he often declared that no place was so good to him as his father's house; and, when he settled at Chester, he did not conceal the laudable satisfaction he felt in its nearness to Broad Oak. His diary shows the frequency of his journeys thither; and it evinces, likewise that natural affection was strengthened and even hallowed, by appointment periodically made between himself and his father, for he preached on weekdays at some intermediate place between Chester and Broad Oak: as Shockledge, Ridley, and Peckferton. Their affectionate visits to each other became thus subservient to the purposes of their sacred vocation. After the death of his father, Mr. Henry showed to his aged and widowed mother even "double honor."

In the fraternal character he shone. "I think," says Mr. Tong, who had the best opportunities for observation, "few came up to him, and none that I ever knew excelled him." The estimation in which he was held by his sisters had been before noticed, and was frequently manifested; not often, perhaps, more distinctly than in a letter yet remaining, and addressed to him when he was a student at Gray's Inn by his excellent father, "Yours came safe to hand, and is as welcome to us, as ours can possibly be to you. Your sisters flock about it as bees about a honeycomb, and are as much refreshed by it." Indeed, the harmony at Broad Oak was such that not the least angry or unkind word was ever known to pass between them. And after they had attained maturity, and were severally transplanted into their own families, instead, as is too commonly the case, of emulation or indifference, disturbing their attachment, or withering their comforts, they remained *one*—in interest and affection.

In the choice of his associates and, indeed, in all his intercourse with society, Mr. Henry manifested through life the caution, which had been instilled into him from infancy and which he habitually recommended to others.

> *Those who profess religion profess friendship to God; and is it not (he would say), a contradiction to that profession for us to make those our bosom friends whom he "beholds afar off." To the evildoers, we must say— Depart, not as if it were unlawful to have ordinary commerce with the worst of men. Then must we needs "go out of the world;" we cannot but have dealings with them; we must pay civil respects to them, but we must not choose and court them for our acquaintance. Especially take heed of choosing and courting such into near and standing relations. He that goes near the fire is in danger; but he who takes fire into his bosom and goes upon hot coals is a madman.*

His rule as to friendship and acquaintance was: "few and good." And the apothegms he had left among his papers, not only indicate his quick sightedness, and accuracy of observation in reference to professed Christians, but also show how difficult it must have been to have imposed up him. They thus furnish a valuable, through indirect, testimonial of the excellence of those valued persons who were his chosen friends.

Commonly (said he), such as are least loving and respectful to others, are most high in expecting love and respect from others, and most heinously resent the denial of it.

Sincere love is that which looks at God and not self in what it doth. It is "love unfeigned."

I often suspect those whose religion and love lie in their tongues—blessing "with a loud voice."

To be sincere is to be plain like Jacob, without complimenting. Everything he said and did was natural and not forced.

You reckon that plain, that is of one color. Now, a sincere Christian is of the same color within doors that he is without; on the weekdays the same that he is on Sabbath days. He makes no great show, no talk; all his glory is within. He is swift to hear and glad to learn: a fool in religion is full of words.

Mr. Henry was a steady, sympathizing, and active friend. He used to set apart some time to pray for his relations and friends by name. He paid them also frequent visits; he addressed them by kind letters; and he took pleasure, as opportunity served, in their company at his own house. There they were ever entertained with cheerfulness. It was under such circumstances that he observed, "God gives us leave to be cheerful; we have cause and command to be so."

He was an enemy, however, to trifling and levity. Nor did he, for a moment, confound happiness with those propensities,

True joy (said he) is seriousness, doth not become a man, much less a Christian. Christ appeared to dislike the joy of his disciples, even in the success of their ministry, when they seemed to be transported with it. In heaven there is joy, but no vain mirth.

In the afflictions of his friends, he was literally *afflicted*. Sympathy and kindness incessantly displayed themselves and when death rendered intercourse impossible, his unaffected sorrow and his readiness to serve needy survivors, gave to his sincerity the fullest demonstration.

Not only did his birth and passions and talents fit Mr. Henry, to associate with men of rank and fortune and intellectual eminence, but it pleased God to honor him with not a few valuable friends among persons so distinguished.

And the list, brief as it is, may well flush the cheeks of those descendants of ancient nonconformity, who, in modern days, affect to despise their progenitors, wither for mental imbecility, unnecessary freedom of thought, or a supposed want of external respectability.

Mr. Henry's diary particularly notices among his friendships, Lady Levit and Lady Ward and Mrs. Hunt, "wife of Mr. Hunt, merchant, London," there styled his "worthy good friend."

He was intimate with the Earl of Willoughby, and after preaching at Chowbent, it was not an uncommon thing to trace him direct from the conventicler "to Shaw Place, Lord Willoughby's house, near Rivington." He describes his lordship as the 21st peer of his family, as a very grave, serious gentleman, showing him great respect and speaking with savor of divine things. His lady and daughter were much for the church.

The names of Lord James Russell and Lord Paget are so mentioned by Mr. Henry as to indicate mutual respect and familiarity. He notices, having dined at Lord James Russell's, when in London in 1710.

At Sir Robert Duckenfield's, he was a frequent visitor; the family, he remarks, were numerous, fearing God, and, he adds, "The eldest son by this lady designs for the ministry and is with Mr. Cunningham."

Nor was he less frequently at Abbott's Bromley, the mansion of Sir Charles Wolseley, Baronet. On occasion of one of those visits, he records the satisfaction he felt in having had two or three hours' intimate conversation with Sir Charles, then above eighty years of age. "He speaks," is his account, "with much savor of another world. He said, he wished he had been a minister. Lord Say and Seal was his father-in-law. He spoke much of *his* great piety."

He was on terms of intimacy, likewise, with Sir Charles Houghton, Baronet; and, after preaching at Chowbent, often visited Hoghton Tower, as well as Shaw Place—sometimes both. This was the case, May 26, 1708, under that date he writes, "I had much edifying conversation with Sir Charles Houghton, only he express too great an esteem for my poor performances. I came back to my Lord Willoughby's."

Sir Henry Houghton's name must not be omitted, nor that of his sister, Madam Mary Houghton, who, being taken suddenly "very ill at chapel," in Chester, September 17, 1710, died two days afterwards at Mr. Henry's house.

To the preceding list may be added the Lord Chief Baron Ward, Sir Henry Ashurst, Sir John Chetwode of Oakley near Market Drayton in Shropshire, Captain Cromwell, Sir Robert Coffey, Sir Thomas Abney, Sir John Hartopp, Sir Richard Blackmore, Sir William Ashurst "at Highgate," Sir Walter Young, Sir Gabriel Roberts, and Sir Andrew Kennedy.

Among his lay friends may be instanced Edward Harley, Esquire, usually called Auditor Harley, and brother to the Right Honorable the Earl of Oxford, of whom, after an interview, August 4, 1712, Mr. Henry says, "He discourses of Christ and heaven with his ancient seriousness." Mr. Clive of Styche near Market

Drayton, Thomas Corbet of Stanwardine, Esquire, George Clive of Walford, Esquire, and Mr. Harris of Prescot, Mr. Benyon of Ash, his kinsman, Mr. Yates of Danford, Mr. Higginson and Mr. Eddowes of Whitchurch all in Shropshire. In Flintshire, Luke Lloyd, Esquire of Bryn, the ancestor of the Right Honorable the Lord Kenyon; Mr. Woods of Atherton in Lancashire; and Mr. Robert Mort of Warton Hall in the same county. The father of the last-mentioned gentleman was one who feared God above many; he was an illustrious example of humility, charity, and primitive Christianity, and was universally loved and honored, even the most profane of his neighbors were scarcely known to speak ill of him. He greatly honored God and his posterity was blessed. He was related to Mr. Tong's father, and after his decease was kind to his widow and children.

Mr. Henry's intimacy with his brethren in the ministry was, as might be expected, extensive. In addition to the worthies whose names have already occurred and others who will be mentioned hereafter, may be noticed Dr. Watts, "good Mr. Pomfret," the Reverend Peter Finch of Norwich, Mr. Brian of Grantham, afterwards of Stafford, the Reverend Mr. Knight: "a conformist minister in Cambridgeshire and Chaplain to the Earl of Oxford (a good man)," and the Reverend Mr. Mather of New England. He specially takes notice of the refreshment he found in the company of Mr. Reynolds of Shrewsbury, because of his learning and piety. The name also of the Reverend Samuel Angier, of whom an interest account may be seen in the Nonconformist's Memorial, though mentioned before, must not be omitted here. After a visit to him at Duckenfield, Mr. Henry says, "I preached in Mr. Angier's place. He has little sight and is solitary. He tells me that he entertains himself now that he cannot read with saying over chapters to himself. He is learning the 119th Psalm."

Such were some of Mr. Henry's acquaintances and intimate friends; and the amenity of his manners, his "mild demeanor and rare courtesy." attracted general esteem. He indulged in no eccentricities, not had he any taste for that coarse vulgarity, which confounds rudeness with sincerity. But as a gentleman upon Christian principles, he honored "all men," he loved "the brotherhood," he condescended to "men of low estate."

Honor (said he) magistrates. Give them civil respect; *that is due* to them and their place; to their dignity though they stain it; to their power though they abuse it. Honor learning and learned men, especially piety and pious men, though poor in the world. Honor true devotion wherever you meet with it. Think what a poor despised Christian, who fears God, will be shortly. But be not levelers. The wise God has not leveled the world, any more than the surface of the earth.

Among the honorable testimonies borne to Mr. Henry, one contained in the concluding words of a memorandum written by Mr. Reynolds of Shrewsbury, after he had seen Mr. Tong's memoir of his departed friend, cannot but be instanced. It is short, but beautiful, full of pathos, and full of simplicity. "Farewell, dear saint! Thy memory is fragrant upon earth. Thy works will perpetuate thy fame; thy spirit is retired to those that are perfect. I follow, though sinning, tired, and sighing. One motive more I have to quicken me in my way, that I may meet the loving, beloved, holy, happy Henry there."

It would be easy to compress into a single paragraph a comprehensive exhibition of the commentator's moral likeness. It *has* been done, indeed, by one of his contemporaries, and with characteristic peculiarity and force. The introduction of the sketch without comment, cannot, it is thought, give just occasion of offense to any.

Mr. Henry (the writer is the eccentric, but by no means contemptible John Dunton) is son to that famous Henry, whose life was lately printed in London. I am told he does patrizare; for all his actions appear to be perfectly devoted to God, strictly observing St. Paul's rule in the 4th of the Philippians: "Whatsoever things are true, whatsoever things are honest, whatsoever things are lovely, whatsoever things are of good report; if there be any virtue, if there be any praise, think on these things," which Mr. Henry does with that exactness and sincerity—the very churchmen love him; and even malice is angry that she can find no cause to be angry with him.

Assuming the correctness of the portrait thus drawn, and its fidelity is unquestionable, the biographical delineation might here have safety terminated. The ends proposed to be answered will be better accomplished, however, by somewhat greater minuteness, by illustration rather than eulogy, by diversifying the aspects of character, and by surveying more closely its component qualities— qualities which were too manifest and too instructive to be blamelessly overlooked, and which formed a constellation of virtue so brilliant as not to be adequately perceived by a casual or ordinary glance. Just as the grandeur of the heavens, though perceptible to every eye, is *unfolded*—only to gaze of an observant, and distinguishing astronomer.

SECTION 1

His Remarkable Diligence and Improvement of Time

From the specimens already furnished, it is obvious that the testimony borne to the Waldenses and Albigenses—that they are always working, learning, or teaching—was eminently applicable to Mr. Henry. But further evidence must be offered.

One year he preached two hundred and eleven times, besides his expoundings and family repetitions in some years probably many more. "How frequently," says Dr. Daniel Williams "did he preach seven times a week."

He caught, in fact, the very spirit of the illustrious confessors who have been just referred to and of their rivals, the early Puritans and nonconformists, *his* forefathers in the sacred office. He emulated not only their inflexible courage and unabating perseverance, but their early rising and their incessant toil. "Value your souls," was the remark he sometimes made, "and you *will* value your time. Whatever you do, take heed of idleness. That is the devil's anvil, on which he hammers out many temptations.

In advising others, he would say, "Do not lose the morning." And he practiced as well as taught. Like his divine Master, *he* often rose "a great while before day." He was commonly in his study at five, and sometimes at four o'clock. There he remained till seven or eight. After family worship and some slight refreshment, he returned till noon, and oftentimes, again after dinner, till four in the afternoon. He then visited the sick or his friends, and attended to other business. In the evening, after his family was dismissed, and before he yielded himself to sleep, he again retired to his study. Of sleep, he remarked—that it "is God's gift to those he loves; nature requires it; grace, gives thanks for it, but those who love it more than their business when they should love it only in *order* to their business, expose themselves to a great deal of sin. I desire to close the day—return to thy rest, O my soul; to begin the day with return to thy work, O my soul; rest in the arms of God's mercy; work in the strength of his grace."

Nothing created him more uneasiness than needless intrusions. Whether those inroads upon time arose out of mistaken politeness or the influence of inconsiderate friendship, they invariably extorted lamentations and self-reproach, both pungent and reiterated.

In his diary he often complains of the precious hours *lost* in the company of those he loved; he often laments that friends are the thieves of time; and, when noticing even gratifying intercourse with some of his brethren, and others who he highly esteemed, he says on one occasion, "I would not for anything live such a life for a few days together. I am always best when alone. No place is like my own study, no company like good books—especially the book of God." Again: "When I lose time at home, I wish I was abroad preaching. When time abroad is not filled up as it should be, I wish myself at home studying. God, by his grace, help me to *fill up* time—to be busy while working time lasts."

The reader will have observed in the birthday and other memorials, before introduced, the same instructive sentiments. As the sands of life diminished, Mr. Henry's parsimonious regard to the precious treasure increased; even the smallest loss was pathetically bewailed. Though far removed from an ungrateful temper, and still more so from any disposition to slight the kindness of his friends, he would, when invited to their houses and most plentifully accommodated, if too long detained, breathe the Psalmist's wish: "O that I had wings like a dove, then I would fly away, and be at rest." It was after undue occupation by company and to little advantage that the following memorandum was penned: "I look upon this as a lost day. Lord, forgive my trifling. I would rather preach twice every day in the week, than spend another day so unprofitably."

In estimating the industry of this excellent man, his correspondence must not be overlooked. Judging from the diary and existing specimens, though seldom adapted for biographical purposes, it was extensive. The selections introduced into the present volume suffice, nevertheless, to show how perfectly Mr. Tong was justified in the statement that "his letters were full of prudent advice, most pleasant and ingenious observations; diverting, and, at the same time, improving; and all breathing true Christian love and friendship." It is noticed by the same accurate observer that Mr. Henry was not only kind in writing "*to* his friends," but also "very speedy in *answering*" the communications he received.

From the whole of his history, the Scriptural injunction, "Whatever thy hand findeth to do, do it with thy might," derives an impressive illustration. But in nothing was it more strikingly evinced than in the preparation of the Exposition. While writing that great work, he not only made it his frequent traveling companion, but notwithstanding many interruptions and even frequent suspension by other engagements (as is apparent from the chronological list of his writings hereafter given), it was often prosecuted at mere intervals—literally by "little and little." What can be more perfectly surprising than the following instance? It occurred at the birth of his daughter Theodosia: "Between two and three o'clock this morning, while my wife was ill, I retired to my study to seek God for her and my children. Being willing to redeem time, I did a little at my Exposition [*The Commentary on the Bible*], and Ezra 3 the latter end was before me, of the mixture of joy and sorrow; showing that the remembrance of former troubles ought not to drown the thankful sense of present mercies."

Admirable as this example is, its complete *imitation* cannot be universally obligatory. There are many who have neither physical strength nor vigor of intellect, nor elasticity of natural spirits, adequate to such exertions; many who, how sincerely soever consecrated to the Savior, are as unequal to them, as a child would be to the toils and cares of mature age. Mr. Henry used to say, that—if God had given more to him, he expected more from him; but would accept of less from those to whom less was given.

Good stewardship is spiritual wisdom, and consists not in aiming at things too high, but in the faithful use and improvement of the talents with which we are entrusted. This was Mr. Henry's view of the subject. Hence, without defining proportions, either of time or exertion, he confined himself, when advising others, to points of universal application. "Be diligent in your particular callings. Bestow the bulk of your time upon them. Understand your employment; and mind it with all seriousness."

SECTION 2

His Christian Love—His Hatred of Censoriousness—His Opposition to Error—His Candor, Moderation, and Prudence

"Love," Mr. Henry remarked, "is the golden thread that runs through the whole Gospel. God's love to us, ours to him, and one to another." Wherever, therefore, he beheld the divine image, thither his affection was not only attracted, but manifested. His extensive charity towards *all* Christians under their relation to their common Lord, and common character as saints is specially noticed by Mr. Reynolds.

Mr. Henry accustomed himself to contemplate true believers, notwithstanding a difference of apprehension about lesser things, as having "access through Christ, by one Spirit, unto the Father." "*There*," he would say, "is the centre of the saints' unity—one in us, not one in the pope or a general council, but one in God and Christ."

Alluding to the prospect of an interview with his personally unknown friend, Mr. Thoresby, he thus beautifully expressed the habitual temper of his mind.

> *This is not the world we are to be together in; but there is such a world before us; where we "shall be together for ever and with the Lord." To the general assembly of the Church of the first-born, which are written in heaven, we are already come in faith and hope; by virtue of which we meet daily at the same throne of grace, and have comfort in a spiritual communion with "all that in every place call on the name of Jesus Christ our Lord; both theirs and ours." This is in earnest of that blissful state in which we shall be with all the saints, none but saints and saints "made perfect;" where Luther and Calvin are both of a mind. God keep us "looking for that blessed hope."*

Agreeably to the Scriptures, he regarded *all* believers as "saints;" and though in compliance with custom or in accommodation to current prejudice, he often prefixed in his publications the epithet—saint—before the name of an "Evangelist" or an "Apostle," yet from his manuscripts, not to mention his printed works, it is obvious that to avoid an approximation to popery, he preferred its disuse. A single instance does not occur to the writer, in which Mr. Henry, in any of the numerous papers, which have passed under review, used that term to distinguish any even of those who saw the Lord from their Christian *brethren*.

For the reputation of others, especially God's faithful servants, he uniformly observed a particular tenderness. Indeed he had been trained to this from his infancy. His excellent father was a famous for a steady opposition to "evil speaking," and seems to have taken pains to infuse into all around him the same spirit. *He* would tell his children of a gentleman whose custom it was, when he came among such of the ungodly as were likely to utter reproaches against the Puritans (so the people of God were then nicknamed), to inform them beforehand, "Sire, I desire you to take notice—I am one of those you call Puritans; and, therefore, if you like my company and mean I should stay with you, pray forbear talking evil of them, for I cannot away with it." And the good man noticed, with evident approbation, how much sin was thus prevented.

The son herein, as in other respects, did honor to his progenitor. He was few of his words in reference to character, candid towards his absent brethren, and as deaf as an adder to whisperers and tattlers. "How many are there," he would sometimes indignantly remark, "who go about as talebearers; in one place to pick up slanders or to dig for them and then scatter them in another. Look upon such," he added, "as incendiaries. Avoid them as you would those who should attempt to set fire to your clothes."

Unless he felt called to other duties, Mr. Henry uniformly contented himself with deducing from the misconduct of others and excitement to prayer and circumspection. After noticing, in reference to one of his brethren, a circumstance, which occasioned him grief and surprise, he merely says: "The Lord give us wisdom, and watchfulness, and resolution. It is dangerous to *begin* sinful familiarities."

Christian candor was a virtue, which contributed in no small degree to adorn Mr. Henry's character. He records it as an occasion of comfort to himself that he felt able truly to say, he was far from lessening any man's excellencies, either for intellectuals or morals, for the sake of his differing from him. "Delight," he nobly advised, "in the holy generosity of speaking *well* of those who differ from you."

But it must not be inferred that Mr. Henry was, therefore, unconcerned about error, or that the danger of such sentiments, as were obviously contrary to inspiration, was either unseen or unfeared. Although he shunned everything dictatorial, intolerant, and censorious, he was never indifferent to the interests of the Christian faith. He never even temporized nor did he confound things that differ, and still less did he mistake the tameness of cowardice or selfishness or a love of ease for commanded charity. He knew that divine virtue can have no legitimate operation apart from, any more than in opposition to, the essential truths of the Bible.

Noticing the release of the Rev. Thomas Emlyn (whose popularity was increased by persecution) from prison after two years' unjust confinement, Mr. Henry says, "He was with me today, September 1, 1705, and adheres to the Arian heresy. I had a deal of talk with him, endeavored to show him that even his own principles are nearer to the orthodox than the Socinian, which yet he was inclined to speak favorable of. The Lord keep *me* in the way of truth." At another time, April 26, 1707: "Mr. Emlyn called upon me—I perceive he not only retains his corrupt opinions, but seems to me to speak favorable of deism. He tells me there are *many* deists; and he finds, in conversation, that they triumph in this—that when they meet with such as condemn them, they cannot get them to enter into a fair argument."

In reference to certain schemes of miscalled rationality, Mr. Henry shrewdly remarked, that "pride is the cause of heresy;" and immediately added, "It was a pleasure to Socinus, that arch-heretic, that he had no master. We wish it had been his fate to have had no scholars."

Of popery, likewise, he entertained a great abhorrence. Regarding the whole system as an unhallowed encroachment on the Savior's prerogative, he aimed, by sound and Scriptural argument, to overthrow it. Few single discourses show the tremendous mischief more forcibly than the one he published, and in which the whole Romish hierarchy is designated "a spiritual tyranny."

Though Mr. Henry was as far removed as any man from undervaluing the judgment of the learned, especially if "they feared the Lord," yet he would call no man *master*, nor would he regard any body of men or Christians, how excellent soever, under that character. The right of private judgment in matters of faith he held to be strictly inalienable and sacred. He regarded implicit obedience to *human* dictates not only as not according with a man's duty to God, but as in direct hostility to the claims both of revelation and reason. He remembers that everyone "must give an account of himself to God. And we know," said he, "who followed like an ox to the slaughter."

When the occasion required it, he hesitated not to make an open avowal of his sentiments, avoiding bitterness, indeed, but speaking unequivocally and without fear. Having in his ordinary ministrations preached from Eph. 4:9 on the Redeemer's descent into the lower parts of the earth, he said "somewhat of Christ's descent into hell;" and alluded to the creed called the apostles'— "an article," he adds, "which gives too uncertain a sound to be of any use there. Blessed be God for a creed in the Bible."

It is true that in training enquirers, whether young or more advanced, he valued and preferred the *Assembly's Catechism*; but it is true, also, that the subjection of his understanding was reserved, free and unbiased for the inspired oracles. His counsel was unvarying: "Set yourselves at the feet of Christ—that is the learner's place."

The esteem Mr. Henry cherished for all pious conformists was very cordial and very exemplary; he loved them as brethren in Christ Jesus. "I hate," he would say, "to see religion and the church monopolized—as if Christ took his measurers from our little fancies and opinions. Those I call Christians not who are of this or that party, but who call upon the name of Jesus Christ our Lord: those, whatever dividing name they are known by, who live soberly, righteously, and godly in this world. The question bye and bye will not be—in what place or what posture we worshipped God, but, did we worship in the spirit?"

On Sir William Dawe's arrival at Chester, after his consecration to that see, Mr. Henry not only mentions the "great ceremony with which he was met," but adds," I have prayed that God will make him a great blessing to this place."

"I am much pleased," he writes, "to hear of a good man, who is now vicar of Ellesmere—Mr. Dean."

Referring to an evening spent with Dr. Oldfield, he remarks, with obvious gratification, "We talked of a better correspondence between the moderate churchmen and dissenters."

Mr. Henry evidently felt pleasure while recording another passage: "Mr. Bradbury told me that he was lately waiting on the Archbishop of Canterbury, and was well pleased with his truly Puritan spirit."

A dissenting minister having proclaimed his want of judgment, if not a more serious defect by dealing out invectives again the established liturgy, Mr. Henry joined with many of his brethren in Staffordshire in a protestation *against* Mr. Sparry's profane expressions concerning the *Common Prayer*.

Nor did he infrequently make known the aversion he felt towards the contracted spirit of a bigot; whether it existed among nonconformists or churchmen, the evil was unsparingly reprobated and exposed.

At the time of the public thanksgiving in September 1704, for the victory obtained by the Duke of Marlborough at Blenheim, he was laid aside by indisposition. His friend, Mr. (afterwards Dr.) John Evans, then of Wrexham, supplied his lack of service in an excellent sermon from Judges 5:12. But Mr. Henry mentioned it as grievous to him that on that day, when all good protestants and Englishman had such an opportunity of common joy, an eminent dignitary of the church, in his sermon at the abbey in Chester, was very severe in reflecting upon the dissenters and charging them with inexcusable forwardness. "Is there no peace then to be had," asks Mr. Henry with some emotion, "unless we will submit in everything to those who say to our souls—bow down that we may pass over?"

Referring to the treatise entitled the "Rights of the Christian Church," which appeared in the year 1706, he says, "It is a book which makes a great noise; it cuts the sinews of church tyranny and exposeth persecution, but is manifestly Socinian; it vindicates the dissenters from schism, and it maintains their liberty, though it much diminishes the ministry and ordination, and speaks slightly of divine institutions. Yet I hope it will be a check to the spirit of bigotry."

Mr. Henry deplored the proneness of mankind to make religion so much the matter of dispute; and to waste in argumentation the zeal, which ought to be employed in what is practical. "That wickedness," he writes, "commonly goes under a specious color, but God searches the heart; he knows upon what principle men act, who, in their contest about religion, seek their own glory and not his. Multitudes lose the power of godliness, and with it, not doubt, lose their own souls, while they are eagerly contesting about the forms; the form of words the form of worship, the form of government. Those who bestow the vigour of their spirits upon contention with their brethren, can never strive in prayer."

He remarked on one occasion that, "no fire of contention hath burned so hot as the ignis sacer,"—"When a town," said he, "hath been burned, the churches and steeples have flamed the highest."

With a view to lessen evils he could not cure and to prevent those inferences, which specious and infidel spirits often weave into a covering for ungodliness, he would say to all, and especially youthful and inexperienced observers, "Be not prejudiced against the ways of religion, by the divisions that are among its professors. It is too true there are strifes among Christians, but it is not because of their Christianity. That forbids it. In the great things wherein they are agreed are many more, and more material, than those things wherein they differ. Our Lord Jesus Christ has told us of such divisions before. It always was so. God has wise and holy ends in suffering it, and will at last bring glory to himself out of it."

The attachment cherished by Mr. Henry for the principles of nonconformity, resulting, as we have seen, from the most careful examination and decided conviction, invested his candor with charms which would otherwise have been impossible. Nor is it less honorable to his integrity than demonstrative of the soundness of his principles that neither his popularity, his intercourse with affluent churchmen, the ablest opposing statements, nor the railings of the proud could either shake his steadiness or render the restitute of his course as a dissenter doubtful. In the midst of all, experience and reflection seemed to establish him still more in the decision he had made. "I am pleased," he writes, "with Mr. Palmer's answer to Wesley, and I bless God who raised up men fit to be advocates for an injured cause."

Again, "I am much confirmed in my nonconformity from the consideration of the imposing of the sacramental test, by which the ordinance of Christ, far different from the discipline of the primitive times, is not only allowed, but forced upon, all the vicious officers of the army and navy (which are not a few), to the scandal of our holy religion."

After inspecting a specimen of Dr. Sacheverell's remarks, "I am confirmed by it."

Mr. Henry frequently styled the Bartholomew ejection, a fatal day—a day to be remembered with sorrow, on account of the silencing of so many ministers. On its anniversary, August 24, 1707, he says, "Lord lay not to the charge of the land the *guilt* of this day forty-five years. Open the eyes of those who justify what was then done."

The lively interest he took in all that related to the cause of nonconformity, his regard to the relics of its early representative, the desire he cherished for the maintenance of its honor, and the satisfaction he felt in its illustration and history are apparent in every part of his manuscripts and diary.

After noticing a letter received from the Rev. John Evans, the author of *the Sermons on the Christian Temper*, informing him of the smiles of the court upon the dissenters, he writes, "I wish they might as well bear them with humility, and modesty, as our fathers did its frowns: with meekness and patience." And alluding to the conversation of a friend with one of the judges on the circuit, who spoke of them respectfully, he adds, "God give them grace to carry it so as they may merit respect."

His friend, Mr. Tong, having visited him in the year 1708 and informed him of the good posture of the dissenting interest in London, he says in the diary, "I thank God, and take courage."

In a letter to Mr. Thoresby, dated Chester, April 29, 1709, he expresses himself still more distinctly.

> *You cannot think how it rejoiceth my heart to hear from one so well able to judge, of that excellent spirit, both of devotion and moderation, which you observed in London. Blessed be God for such promising tokens of the continuance of his presence with us, and such earnests of further mercy he has in store for us. I have been very much pleased to observe the growth of the spirit of moderation and charity among the dissenters, as far as my acquaintance has reached. I speak it with assurance, it prevails more and more; and with pleasure, that in my narrow sphere, I hope I have contributed something towards it. And I am now pleased to hear that there are those in other places who have the same spirit towards the dissenters; and that the spirit of Lesly and Sacheverell has not the ascendant every where so much as it has in these parts. God, by his grace increase holiness, and love among us; and then—the wilderness will be a fruitful field.*

No great while before his decrease, after a visit from Mr. Evans, he records it with visible pleasure that "that good man was undertaking to collect the history of nonconformity from the reformation to 1641: a work," he adds, "for which he is very fit."

The moderation so conspicuous in the character now delineating was not *limited*, it should be remarked to the points and occurrences, which have been mentioned. It extended itself equally to those daily habits of a different description, wherein not a few men, in other respects wise and eminent, have failed.

Mr. Henry noticed, "Moses received the law fasting." And speaking of intemperance, observed that it was by eating "we all fell." "Nothing," said he, "is more contrary to the profession of a Christian than the life of an epicure." And he advised all to "take heed of the beginnings of intemperance." "No certain rule," he would say, "can be prescribed, but quantum sufficit. When in danger, try whether you have learned the first lesson in Christ's school—to deny yourselves."

Advertising to the fact that there are those who are "mighty to drink wine," he remarked, "It is rather the commendation of a barrel than a man, to be able to contain much liquor." In short he preached and recommended, not on this subject only, but generally, a spirit of holy watchfulness.

"In the absence of *that* duty," said he, "a Christian is like a city without gates and bars." "Suspect a snare," was his counsel, "in every employment and in every enjoyment."

The same principle discovered itself fully as to worldly possessions and acquirements. Mr. Henry entered into the very spirit of a remark once made by an ancient and reverend preacher, Dr. Arrowsmith, and which, in a single sentence conveyed a volume of instruction—as "a man may touch pitch and not be defiled if he touch it with a cold hand; so in the pursuit of earthly things: if we are not *hot* we may avoid the contamination."

Though literally abounding, even lawful comforts were used by Mr. Henry with indifference, as one whose affections were "set upon things above." "We see present things," he observes, "but we must not *look* at them. Herein surely consists the very life and power of religion. Herein surely consists the very life and power of religion."

Sometimes, in pointing out "the *folly* of coveting to spread a large sail," he urged for consideration, "we are but thereby so much the more exposed."

And as to money, useful and valuable as in its due place, it undoubtedly is, he remarked, with a view to check the love of it, that it "has no currency in the other world. The great day," said he, "will burn up all those things upon which men now set their hearts."

It grieved him to see professed Christians living as if their happiness were bound up in the creature. "Many people think," said he, "that there is no harm in spending upon themselves, if they can afford it; little considering how greatly the precious soul is hereby wronged." All such he advised to "lay out no more in the repairs of their cottage than will be allowed in their accounts."

When he perceived any "angry at those who stood in their light;" in other words, envious and jealous. He thought it a sign that the things, which are "seen and temporal," were most looked at. And, "Will you," he asked, "who are hoping for treasure in heaven, pant after the dust of the earth?"

An occurrence happened after Mr. Henry's removal to Hackney, which places the view which has been given of this part of his character in a very interesting light, the statement being written by himself at the time prevents misconception: and renders doubt impossible.

March 8, 1713. Lord's Day. In the evening I went to London. I preached Mr. Rosewell's evening lecture, Psalm

89:16—the joyful sound. As I came home, I was robbed.
The thieves took from me about ten or eleven shillings.
My remarks upon it were,— 1. What reason have I to be
thankful to God, who have traveled so much, and yet was
never robbed before. 2. What a deal of evil the love of
money is the root of, that four men would venture their
lives and souls for about half a crown apiece. 3. See the
power of Satan in the children of disobedience. 4. See the
vanity of worldly wealth, how soon we may be stripped of
it. How loose, therefore, we should sit to it.

It would be erroneous, however, to infer from Mr. Henry's moderation of reference to the "life that now is," that he was *negligent* of his temporal affairs or that he encouraged others either in indolence or unconcern. His rule was this: not to be "idle or careless or prodigal, but graciously indifferent."

Having early embraced it as a maxim, that the "prudent Christian will be a prosperous Christian," he diligently applied himself to the cultivation of the habit of prudence, and always took care to "guide his affairs with discretion." It is true his caution often subjected him to reproach, but it kept him out of difficulties, and from the necessity also, of making humiliating concessions.

By these means, he attained to great steadfastness and reputation. At so vast a distance did he stand from selfishness, credulity, and incaution that every eye within his circle looked to him for direction and counsel. He was the Ulysses of his congregation.

When advised with, his discourse was familiar and minute, and, in addition to that sound instruction, to which his great sagacity and long experience contributed, he commonly cited some appropriate portion of Scripture to bear upon the subject. Far

273

from encouraging Christians, when perplexed or afflicted, in a *gloomy* apprehension of things, he studiously pointed out the evil of such a course and allured heir attention upwards. "Let not one affliction," he would say, "drown the sense of a thousand mercies. Our great duty is to trust in God, to commit our way to him; and when our fears take us off from that, so that we cannot find in our hearts to let him dispose of us, they are sinful. Prevailing fears are briars and thorns, which choke many a good duty."

He never failed to remind his friends that God had *promised* to direct the steps of those who in "all their way acknowledge him;" and, therefore, he uniformly and pressingly commended attendance at the throne of grace, especially in seasons of distress. Sometimes he expressed the pleasure those visits afforded him in which his friends requested him to pray with them. And how agreeable soever the company was which he met on such occasions, or how excellent soever the entertainment. If a separation took place *without* united prayer, he felt both uncomfortable and disappointed. On one occasion such an occurrence is recorded very mournfully. It is believed a necessity, for the complaint did not often occur. His friends at Chester (and no doubt at Hackney, too) *loved* prayer; they had been trained to the enriching practice. If any drew near to an hour of sorrow, if any journey was in prospect, if any affair of consequence was to be managed, if any child was to be apprenticed or otherwise disposed of, it was usual with them to commit all to God—not only in their closets and families, but with their ministers. In this "good old way," Mr. Henry found and encouraged them, nor did any circumstances of meanness or poverty prevent his personal concurrence. "How sweet a thing it is to pray," he would say, "*minding a particular errand.*"

Occasionally he was consulted in reference to projected publications; and sometimes the works themselves were submitted to his inspection. Thus he writes,—1705-6, April 16. I read a manuscript of Mr. Cheney's, against the Bishops' Courts. 1706, October 21. I read a manuscript of Sir Charles Wolseley's, concerning prayer, with much pleasure. May 24, 1714. I spent some time of late in perusing a manuscript of Mr. Galpin's, on 2 Sam. 23:5. "An everlasting covenant."

SECTION 3

His Benevolence—Public Spirit, and Loyalty

The estimate set upon the good things of this life by Mr. Henry; and his moderating also, in the enjoyment of them, have already been noticed. And it will not be forgotten how, without *loving* money, he gave thanks for his worldly possessions. He knew who hath said, "It is *more* blessed to give than to receive," and no process of arguing was necessary to convince *him* that "he is not a worldling who only has earthly things, but he who affects them."

The papers of Mr. Henry contain little to satisfy curiosity, either as to the amount of his annual income or the exact proportion of it devoted to charitable purposes; though enough is visible to evince a constant recognition of stewardship and a believing reference to the appointed account. "We honor God, with our substance," he remarked, "if we use our estates and the interest they give us for the promoting of religion in the places where we live, and the support and encouragement of the ministry, the education of youth, the disposing of Bibles, and other good books directly tend to that honor."

Upon himself and upon others, he enforced such sentiments as were calculated to *promote* a charitable disposition. "We lose," said he, "what we save. Withholding that which is meet tends to spiritual poverty: the worst of all husbandry. It is like grudging seed to the ground." As occasion served, he plainly pointed out the great evil of covetousness. Sometimes he urged upon all around him their exposure to that sin, and advised them to suspect themselves guilty of it. "We are born," said he, "with the world in our *hearts*." Noticing that many "think themselves not covetous because they are content with what they have," he added, in allusion to the parable, "so was that fool."

In the exercise of a benevolent temper, Mr. Henry remembered the example of him who "maketh his sun to rise on the evil, and on the good, and sendeth rain on the just, and on the unjust. Like the children of the highest, therefore, he was kind to the *un*thankful, and to the evil." After landing seven guineas to obtain a discharge for the son of a poor friend who had enlisted, he observed that many reasons offered themselves why he should have *abandoned* him. "But," he adds, and it is a fine development of genuine Christianity, "the mercy of God to me a provoking, backsliding sinner answered them all. God doth not cut men off, though. By their iniquity, they have sold themselves."

His benevolence was unlimited; while it visited unworthy neighbors and embraced in a peculiar manner the "household of faith," it extended to *all* men. When many of the "poor Palatines, driven from their country" by persecution, visited Chester in the year 1709, "to the discontent of the high church party, though only going for Ireland," he writes, "I have lent them my stable to sleep in. Into a stable it was that Christ was thrust."

The state of the reformed churches in general deeply interested him; and for those of France in particular, as dwindling and ruined, his supplications were numerous and fervent. He often applied to them that beautiful and encouraging passage, "The vision is yet for an appointed time, but at the end it will speak, and not lie.

Though it tarry, wait for it, for it will surely come. It will not tarry."

In prospect of a peace with France, he wrote a letter to the Bishop of Sarum, entreating him "to do his utmost that the French Protestants might not be neglected in the treaty," to, which the good prelate replied, "that the business of religion would not be neglected."

It was a regard to the business of religion, or in other words, the best interests of his fellow countrymen, which rendered Mr. Henry so eminently conscientious and diligent in the observation of national and appointed fasts. For a time, particularly in the years 1691 and 1692, those observances were appointed monthly. On such days, he always chose for the exposition and sermon some appropriate portion of Scripture, and stood before the people, not infrequently, five successive hours, maintaining to the last, even when unassisted by his brethren, his accustomed energy and liveliness. They were days of unutterable intercession. His prayers abounded with Scriptural arguments; and his prevailing sense of public necessity, combined with supreme longings for heavenly supplied, excited affections, at once ardent and devout. "It is not," he remarked, "the strength of our navy, the extent of our alliances, the prudence of our statesmen, or the valor of our generals, that we can depend upon—an arm of flesh is but broken reed."

To these facts may be added the corroboration of many of his manuscript sermons yet extant. Those valuable remains illustrate, also, with happy precision, the aspect of the country, both in a moral and religious point of view. One of them furnishes portraiture of the professedly Christian world, so affecting and so well adapted to promote caution and holy excitement, as to forbid its omission. Preaching in 1702, June 10, the day of "a public fast on the queen's declaring was with France and Spain," he thus addressed his hearers, "The evidences of our iniquities are too plain to be hid, too many and too gross to be hid under the mantle of charity itself. Three sorts of iniquities testify against us: the daringness of atheists and unbelievers, the debaucheries of the profane, the declinings and divisions and disagreeable walkings of those who profess religion. I mean not those of any particular party, but such as run not with the profane to an 'excess of riot.' Even they are wretchedly degenerated from the pious zeal and strictness of their predecessors. Their love waxeth cold and their differences are mismanaged; diversity of apprehensions causeth alienation of affections and we do not see that disposition to union and accommodation, which we could wish. The breach is yet "wide as the sea." How great is the worldliness and pride of professors—their private feuds and quarrels! And that which aggravates these sins is that the light of the gospel still shines so clearly, and we have great peace and liberty. And 'shall not God visit?' Shall not a camp be troubled in which there are so many Achans? I am not propagating fears, and jealousies, but—repentance."

Similar observations would apply to the appointments for public thanksgiving. Mr. Henry celebrated the victory of Ramillies in 1706, uniting with it the success of affairs in Catalonia by discoursing twice, the same day, from Gen. 14:19-20. "Melchisedek blessed him, and said, blessed be Abram of the most high God, possessor heaven and earth: and blessed be the most high God, which hath delivered thine enemies into thy hand." He thought that the occasion of rejoicing being doubled, praise ought to be so also. And when in 1708, a day of public praise to God for defeating the attempted invasion and for the victory gained near Oudenarede, was appointed, he preached twice from Gen. 49:9. He observed the same course diligently and faithfully, all through the war. It shall, however, only be added, as one of his remarks that in the reign of King William, days of humiliation were most frequent—and in the reign of Queen Anne, days of thanksgiving.

In illustrating this portion of Mr. Henry's character, the part he took in reference to the society formed at Chester for the reformation of manners deserves somewhat of minute relation. The narrative will advantageously exhibit the conduct of several excellent members of the established church. It will fully corroborate the statements of his laborious exertion as already made; and, while further evidential of his great condor, moderation, and prudence, will specially demonstrate the sincerity, the soberness, and the energy of his zeal.

The society referred to was formed in 1698 by some worthy conformists who were incited to it by a similar association in London; and as the union commenced under the immediate sanction of Dr. Stratford and Dr. Fog, the one the Lord Bishop of Chester and the other the dean: both estimable persons and eminent for their piety and learning, the prospect seemed auspicious. In aid of the benevolent design, a monthly lecture also was set up on a Friday at St. Peter's church. This, said Mr. Henry, "brings to mind the days of old." The first sermon was delivered by the worthy prelate, from Rom. 13:14. "Put ye on the Lord Jesus Christ, and make not provision for the flesh to fulfill the lusts thereof." Mr. Henry was an auditor, greatly rejoicing in the testimony thus borne against the "wickedness of the wicked."

The next discourse was preached by the dean, from Eph. 5:11. "Have no fellowship with the unfruitful works of darkness, but rather reprove them." Mr. Henry listened to it with singular delight. "It was," says he, "very much to the purpose, pressing home the necessary duty of beating down sin, and wickedness" He adds, "I bless God for this sermon; and as I have, from my heart, forgiven, so I will endeavor to forget; all that the dean has at any time said against dissenters, and against me in particular. Such preaching against sin, and such endeavors to suppress it, will contribute, as much as anything, to heal differences among those who fear God."

That the fire thus kindled in a cathedral might have a chance of burning, Mr. Henry, and his brethren likewise, acted with commendable prudence. Instead of pressing into the service with any injudicious eagerness, they studied by an attendance upon the lectures appointed by the association, to countenance and encourage the clergy.

That their hearts were set upon the work is evident from the fact that, *before* the formation of the society which has been mentioned (on the 3rd of May preceding), at one of the congregational fasts, it had been determined by them to "seek the Lord" in a very particular manner—first, for the deliverance of the protestants in France; and then, for the success and prosperity of reformation work in England; and, especially in Chester. On that occasion Mr. Henry preached from Ps. 7:9—"O let the wickedness of the wicked come to an end"—in its two great branches: persecution, and profaneness.

At the latter end of that year, on his usual lecture day, Mr. Henry directed the thoughts of his people to similar topics. He continued this course for some time. His method is worthy observation, and may be advantageously perused.

The first sermon urged the universal necessity of *personal* reformation of Jer. 25:5—"Turn ye again now everyone from his evil way, and from the evil of his doings." The next commended family-reformation from Job 22:23—"Put away iniquity from thy tabernacle." He then pressed upon those who make a more open profession of religion, the duty of first reproving and reforming one another—before the profane are interfered with His text was John 13:14—"If I then, your Lord and Master, have washed your feet, ye also ought to wash one another's feet"—not only condescend to one another, but reform one another; for Christ washed his disciples' feet, not only as a sign of his own condescension, but of their sanctification—"If I wash thee not thou hast no part in me." This was followed by a discourse from Ps. 119:52—"Horror hath taken hold of me, because of the wicked that forsake thy law," in which he showed that in our endeavors to reform sinners, we should be deeply affected with the horrid nature and consequences of sin; and afterwards, from 2 Kings 9:32—"Who is on my side?" he observed, how sad it is that there should be any siding among us but for God against Baal. A sermon from 1 Chron. 29:5—"Who then is willing to consecrate his service this day unto the Lord," intended also as a preparation for the Lord's supper, terminated the course.

About this time the nonconformist ministers in Cheshire set up a reformation lecture to be statedly observed at several places in the county. Mr. Henry preached the first sermon at Macclesfield on the sanctification of the Sabbath; Mr. Scoles the next at Knutsford, August 1, 1699, on James 5:19, 20; and Mr. James Owen, the third at Chester, on 2 Chron. 30:8.

They, nevertheless, by their presence and influence, had encouraged the lectures at St. Peter's. Mr. Henry constantly attended them, and his diary notices the good discourses he heard from Mr. Henry Newcome of Tatnal, Mr. Garenciews, Mr. Newton, Mr. Thane, Dr. Entwistle, Dr. Gipps of Bury, and divers other clergymen.

Among the members of the established church, however, many adversaries arose; and, in defiance of the exertions of the Lord Bishop and the dean, visible symptoms of decay, from time to time, presented themselves. Some openly derided. Others formed into hostile parties. At length, an army of opposition was regularly organized; and, not notwithstanding the dignitaries, whose names have been mentioned, attempted an auxiliary and counteracting association, the array became too powerful for mere partial resistance. The dean, therefore, submitted a proposal to Mr. J. Hulton, Mr. Henry's brother-in-law, that the dissenters should compose a society for the same purpose: to act in concert with the other. To this the readiest assent was given; and, on the 22nd July 1700, a meeting was convened at Mr. Henry's house and due arrangements made. Too wise to be sanguine, our author contented himself with observing—that it would turn for a testimony. Some days after he waited upon the dean, who kindly received him, and made him acquainted with the rules by which he and his coadjutors were governed, and encouraged Mr. Henry and his friends to go on.

Measures, so catholic and uniting, only increased hostility. Not a few, because members of the Church of England, seemed to fancy themselves invested with superior moral dignity, and possessed of qualities too sacred for association, even in deeds of charity, with nonconformists. The dissenters, consequently, were now publicly reflected upon; they were slandered from the pulpit, condemned as schismatics, and pronounced disqualified for the works of righteousness. Even Mr. Henry Newcome, one of the reformation lecturers and a son of that eminent nonconformist, whose name has been already mentioned, dishonored himself by becoming a railer—an office, which Archbishop Tillotson believed angelic beings have neither disposition nor talent to fill. After hearing *his* accusations and invectives, it was then that Mr. Henry, in imitation of Michael when contending with the devil, made the following solemn appeal: "The Lord be judge between us," adding with equal pertinence and correctness, "Perhaps it will be found that the body of dissenters have been the strongest bulwarks against profaneness in England."

It is pleasant to state that the moderate church party, "who were hearty in the design of reformation," expressed to the conductors of the new society their good will. They advised them to proceed and offered all possible encouragement. Indeed, the cordiality shown by the Diocesan and the dean is convincing proof, in the absence of everything else that, whatever the causes were which operated to produce such unchristian feelings, there was nothing blamable, either in the character or conduct of the dissenters.

The dean preached at length a lecture from Joshua 22:17-18— "Is the iniquity of Peor too little for us, from which we are not cleansed until this day, although there was a plague in the congregation of the Lord, but that ye must turn away this day from following the Lord? And it will be, seeing ye rebel today against the Lord, that tomorrow he will be wroth with the whole congregation of Israel." It was a sermon of which Mr. Henry often spoke in strong terms of approbation; the preacher not only reproved all, whether magistrates or ministers, who had discouraged and obstructed the work of reformation; but, he stated his belief, that if *that* opportunity were lost, God, instead of instructing them by another, would contend with them by his judgments.

That sermon had the effect of keeping on "the good design" a little longer, but it failed to infuse new life and vigor. The torrent of profaneness became impetuous, and the majority was carried away. The zeal of many waxed cold, and not a few surrendered themselves to all the malignity and exclusiveness of bigotry. The dean now addressed them once more. It was on the 5th of September, 1701. He selected as a text Heb. 12:15—"Looking diligently lest any man fail of the grace of God; lest any root of bitterness springing up trouble you, and thereby many be defiled;" and observed, in the close, after many serious warnings, that the

283

lecture had been instituted on purpose to stir up magistrates and others to be active in their places for suppressing immorality and profaneness, but that all having been said that could be said about it, it was thought convenient to adjourn it, *sine die.* "I wish it be not," said Mr. Henry, "an occasion of triumph to the profane, who have a very great antipathy to the Bishop and the dean, for their pious zeal against sin."

The dissenting ministers continued their reformation sermons both in Chester and several adjacent places, a service in which Mr. Henry was frequently employed. "But," says Mr. Tong, "they wanted power to make their endeavors effectual."

An occurrence related in the diary of Mr. Henry will explain this—"My Brother Hulton, on Lord's Day was seven-night observing the Churchwardens of St. Peter's with a strange minister and others, go to Mr. Holland's alehouse, and sit there three hours, told the Recorder of it. The Bishop came to hear of it, and Mr. Hulton desired his Lordship to admonish them. They set light by the Bishop, and challenged the magistrates to fine them; whereupon Mr. Hulton was summoned to inform against them, and did so, and they were fined; but they were very abusive to him."

The necessity for augmenting the proofs of Mr. Henry's vigilance in the work of reformation of manners is completely suspended by the "four discourses" he published "against vice and profaneness," discourses not, exceeded, perhaps either in adaptation to usefulness, solemnity, or skill by any similar addresses, either of ancient or modern date. Our author's whole strength seems to have been most vigorously put forth in them for the suppression of human depravity. And his ardor cannot, surely, be surprising, when it is considered that such evils as those be there exposed—namely drunkenness, uncleanness, Sabbath-breaking, and profane speaking—are, in an extraordinary degree, deadly; that in every age, they have served to distinguish, even in the present life, and by infallible evidence, the vile from the precious; and that they have, in not a few instances, tarnished, and in innumerable more, ruined multitudes who belonged by external profession to the heritage of God.

To zeal, indeed against *sin*, especially as combined with separation from the established church, may be fairly attributed to the severe and illiberal remarks, which have been referred to, and to which Mr. Henry, in common with his dissenting brethren, was frequently subjected from lukewarm, narrow-minded, and prejudiced professors. Whether he so viewed the matter or not is unknown, nor is it important. One thing, however, is quite certain, and it may be properly noticed in this connection—that the occurrences themselves, notwithstanding their direct tendency to such a result, were never converted by him into arguments for *disloyalty*, not even when the highest authorities were most disposed (and sometimes the disposition was distinctly evinced) to concur against nonconformists in acts of oppression and injustice. On the contrary, as a subject of the state, like his venerable father and a multitude of distinguished men, he uniformly manifested, under statutes of absolute tyranny and upon principles purely Christian, the most enlightened submission and the truest allegiance. Nor could he endure, even in common conversation, such reflections upon the rulers of the people, however artfully they were couched, as savored of insubordination and sedition. His course in reference to public affairs was invariably modest, dignified, and respectful, as free from a "discontented meddling," as "from an implicit faith and obedience," avoiding, on the one hand, unscriptural reviling, and on the other hand, the disgusting sycophancy of fawning flatterers. The counsel he gave was this:

Be not forward to arraign those whom God hath called to sit at the stern. Though everything be not just to our mind, nor consonant to our measures, we must remember that we were not cut out to be statesmen; and it is but folly to control what we do not understand. When times are bad, we must not disquiet ourselves by a repining, murmuring spirit; discontent helps to make them so. God governs the world; and is not that enough to satisfy us?

When the king (James II) visited Chester in 1687, he was waited upon at Bishop's palace by Mr. Henry and Mr. Harvey, with the heads of their respective congregations. They presented a loyal address, but studiously avoided any approbation of the illegal, dispensing power, which that monarch claimed and exercised. They restricted their expressions of gratitude to the ease and liberty enjoyed under his Majesty's protection, and only promised to lead quiet and peaceable lives.

The emotions with which Mr. Henry surveyed his country are fully expressed in his works; they are often prominent in his diary; and they uniformly evince the noblest patriotism and the most judicious moderation: moderation the more observable, because Chester then, as it has since been, was distinguished for the violence of its political agitations. "My prayer," he writes, when noticing an approaching election for the country, "is that the nations' councils may be entrusted with those who will be true to the nation's interest."

After the dissolution of the parliament in September 1710, the contest at Chester was exceedingly severe. The mob was "furious," so much so that Mr. Henry was prevented attending the interment of a friend. He "durst not," he says, "go to the funeral, not preach the funeral sermon."

On that occasion, he polled for Mr. Booth and Mr. Crew. They, however, soon afterwards retired, leaving Mr. Warburton and Mr.

Cholmondley in possession of victory. The nature of the triumph may be conceived of, when it is stated, that the picture of Dr. Sacheverell was carried before the returned members. At Northwich, too, the "candidates who lost" were "rudely insulted by one who mimicked a preacher in a tub." "It is strange," adds Mr. Henry, "how the clergy can be pleased with making a mock at preaching!"

By the vote given at that election, the political sentiments of our author may be easily inferred; but, in his record of the death of the Duke of Newcastle (an event occasioned, in July 1711, by a fall when hunting at his Grace's seat in Nottinghamshire), they appear distinctly—"The Duke was much lamented by the Whigs, for he was a faithful friend to the honest interest."

It deserves notice because to Mr. Henry's honor, that whatever views he entertained of state affairs, he wisely said little and never intruded them to the desecration of divine worship. It is his published statement, "Ministers are the unfittest persons and the pulpit the unfittest place in the world to talk of such matters." "You know," he proceeds, "it is not my practice. I am most in my element when I am preaching Jesus Christ and him crucified."

SECTION 4

His Humility, and Dependence on Divine Assistance

Mr. Henry had too accurate an acquaintance with his own heart and dependent circumstances. He perceived too clearly the spiritual extent of the unaccommodating law of God as "holy, just, and good." He thought too frequently upon the effects of pride, as displayed in the rebel angels. He had too intimate a knowledge of the Friend of sinners, in his humiliation; and had too sensibly experienced the constraining operations of redeeming love to indulge in self-exalting reflections. Such as the following characterized him, and with such his diary abounds:

> *I am come to the close of another year, but my works have not been filled up. There are many empty spaces in my time, and in my duties much amiss, little done, little gained for my soul. Though much mercy received, yet my talents have not been traded with aright. It is the blood of Christ that must set all straight between me and my God. Thee I rest my precious soul.*

On one occasion, advising others on this subject, he thus expressed his own sentiments and the dictates of Holy Scripture.

> *"Run up all the streams to the fountain. Every crown must be cast before the throne, and every song sung to that humble tune—Not unto us, O Lord, not unto us, but unto thy name give glory for thy mercy and for thy truth's sake. God plants the trees of righteousness that he may be glorified."*

"Doth it," he would say, "become us to be proud, when our Master was so humble? Read the lives of the eminent saints who are gone, and see how far you come short of their gifts and graces and performances and usefulness; and you will rather blush than be proud."

After a season of communion with the Lord at his table, his earnest desires were thus recorded: "I begged and promised with the cup of blessing—humility, humility. The Lord keep it in the imagination of the thought of my heart."

In the *Exposition* [*Commentary on the Whole Bible*]—on Job 29:14—a phrase is used with reference to the comfort afforded that upright man when deeply afflicted, on recollecting the good he had done to others, which, at first view, would seem to clash with the representations now making. Mr. Henry there speaks now, however, without prefixing a cautious modification of "holy pride." The editors of the excellent edition referred to in the present, volume, notice the observation, and "protest" very properly "against associating with pride any epithet that implies it to be in any case allowable." At the same time, it must be remarked that a perusal of the whole paragraph renders it quite obvious, that Mr. Henry did not intend either to intimate approbation of *pride*, or in the least to palliate it, but that he used the term in an ordinary acceptation (incautiously no doubt) and as synonymous with pleasure or complacency or glory.

For the movements of pride, as *such*, he made *no* allowances. He viewed haughtiness as *transgression* both against the law and the gospel. "The design of each of those," said he, "is to humble us; the former, by convincing us of sin, the latter, by making us entirely beholden to Jesus Christ for life and happiness." Instead, therefore, of tolerating it in any instance, or as is frequently done, looking upon worldly wealth as affording a plea for its indulgence, he uniformly bore his decided testimony against it. The vain conceits of the rich he confounded by such an inquiry as the following: "Why should you be puffed up because more able than others to make a figure among men, when you are less able than others to work out your own salvation?" And sometimes by that challenge, which is reported to have been put by Socrates to the boasting Alcibiades: "Show me the land you are so proud of in the way of the world."

To return to the illustration of Mr. Henry's personal humility: It was rendered particularly conspicuous by the way in which he marked, and bewailed those faults and infirmities in himself, which passed unperceived by others, not publicly to excite admiration, but in the sacredness and retirement of the closet for purposed the most devout and improving.

A few instances must suffice:

After forming a catalogue of his library, he notes:

> *I am not so much ashamed that I have so few books, and so little choice, as that I have not profited more by those I have.*

> *I have great reason to lament my slothfulness, my distractions in prayer, and the coldness of my zeal for God.*

> *O what reason have I to mourn over my dullness and deadness, and that I am not more affected myself with those things of God with which I desire to affect others.*

> *I studied for tomorrow in much weakness. I am compassed about with infirmity.*

> *A trifling world and a trifling heart are my great grievances.*

Statements like these not only evince the depth and reality and genuineness of his humility, but they read to others important lessons of instruction. If *he* deplored so many evils, and those from which, in the sight of his fellow Christians, he appeared most free, what must be the condition of the multitude, who arrogate the very excellencies themselves with no better pretensions than are furnished by their own deluded fancy, have to boast, at the utmost, of the appearance only?

Mr. Henry's *general* deportment, both at home and abroad, exhibited the same lowly and yet elevating principles; and he assiduously guarded against any encroachment upon them. He walked humbly before God *and* man, and the more so in proportion to the smiles and caresses he received. The maxim he inculcated was this: how he acted upon it is yet more fully to appear, "When the wind of applause blows fresh and strong, then steer with a steady hand."

Writing to his "dear and honored friend," Mr. Thoresby, who had addressed a letter of encouragement to him respecting the *Exposition* [*Commentary on the Whole Bible*], he says:

> *The opinion of one of your judgment, learning, and piety, as it is a temptation to pride; (against which I desire your prayers, that I may have grace always to stand upon my guard;) so it is improvable, also, as a spur to industry; and as such I desire to make use of it. I hope you will assist me in giving thanks to God for his assistance hitherto. Sure I have nothing to boast of. What have I that I have not received? I am unworthy to be thus employed. And that you will, likewise, continue your prayers for me, that I may be carried on in it in a humble dependence upon divine grace. Every page, Sir, is a child of prayer, and still must be so, or it will miscarry.*

After a journey, in which mercy had surrounded him, he writes: "I have not been exercised with the reproaches of enemies, but with a more difficult temptation from my friends—underserved respects. The Lord carry me safe through evil report and good report." And another time, under similar circumstances of respectful attention, he adds: "I am ashamed to think how unworthy I am of it."

When urged, not long after his settlement at Hackney, to undertake a catechetical lecture in London, he withheld compliance out of respect to his ministerial brethren there until he had consulted *them*. And when that consent was obtained, he declined Mr. Shower's urgencies, that the lecture might be at his meeting-house, not only because Mr. Wilcox's (Mr. Doolittle's successor) people first applied, but, he adds, "I choose it because it is a more private place."

His respectful mention of the labors of other ministers ought not to be overlooked. There was a readiness in his acknowledgment of their worth, and an expression of delight in their efforts and success, which displayed the utmost magnanimity of soul and an advancement, also, in Christian humility, not often surpassed. The frequent opportunities he took of hearing them preach, as well as his diligence and attention *in* hearing, are manifest from the very numerous manuscripts, yet extant, containing the heads of sermons delivered on such occasions.

Mr. Henry's intercourse with the great never lifted him up nor involved on his part the neglect of the poor. Instead (because of the frequency of his association with persons of rank and fortune) of treating the poor with any indifference, they were kindly considered at all times. They were often visited, and in proportion to their disclosure of moral worth, cordially esteemed.

Occasionally he referred to David's declaration that although a king, he was a "companion" of those who feared God; and he remarked upon it that "grace doth not, in such cases, love to keep state," adding, "It was written for our imitation."

Sir Henry Ashurst and his lady being on a visit at Mr. Henry's, Sir Richard Allen and his lady came also; on which he writes: "I hope I can truly say, I am not proud of an acquaintance with great people, but would rather condescend to men of low estate. The Lord clothe me with humility."

Such excerpts, written evidently without any view of disclosure, do the utmost honor to Mr. Henry's memory, and unfold his real character more accurately than the best sustained encomium.

This humbleness of mind stood in close connection, it must be remarked, with an abiding perception of his necessity of divine influence, both to help and prosper him. "I have as much need," he writes, "of the grace of God to furnish me with a heart to my work, as with a head for it; to continue my delight in it, as much as to give me ability for it."

And again:

From God is my fruit found; nor can I bring forth fruit unless I abide in Christ. Therefore, whatever opportunities I may have of doing or getting good, I depend upon his grace to enable me to improve them and to do the work of the year in the year. I depend upon that grace to enable me to go on with my present services, both in my study and in my ministerial work. And if I should be called out to any duties, or sufferings unforeseen, I depend upon the grace of God to strengthen me for them, and in everything to guide my way.

Contemplating persons whom he could not but regard as "dead in trespasses and sins," and for whose conversion he longed, he writes: "I know the great difficulty lies in the *conviction*; and Eloi, my God, is he who must do it. It is the Spirit of Truth, who must convince."

SECTION 5

His Patient Submission Under Trials

Mr. Henry's history, instead of furnishing any exception to the inspired axiom—that "many are the afflictions of the righteous"—rather supplies a further corroboration of its truth. His own trials, like those of the apostle, prepared him to "comfort such as were in any trouble, by the comfort with which he himself was comforted of God." They led him, also, as occasion served, to check, by salutary cautions, the ardor of sanguine Christians.

Some of his thoughts on the subject in its general aspect, may, in the first place, be introduced here.

"Affliction," he would remark, "is the discipline of God's school, whereby his children are trained up in the way in which they should go. And it is necessary: as needful as weeding is to a garden, as pruning to the vine, as physic to the body."

"Do not expect," he would say, "to find it all carpet on the way to heaven." He observed, nevertheless, "though the weather may be foul, and the ways dirty, home is not far off, and all is quiet and well there."

In order to induce Christians, those who fear God, to acquiesce in the divine disposals, he reminded them, "All is for good. Let that be your principle, and let it silence all repining thoughts."

Enumerating the advantages of affliction, he mentioned penitence, patience, thankfulness, a thoughtful frame of mind, watchfulness against sin, weaning from the world, activity in faith, affection in prayer, a spirit of compliance with God's word, compassion to our brethren, love to Jesus Christ, and longing for heaven. "And how," said he, "can we help loving Christ, when we find his grace working in us: his comforts delighting our souls, his blood a healing balm, a reviving cordial? And as to heaven, we have crosses in our way that we may wish for it. Stormy weather makes the harbor desirable."

He compared murmuring to squeezing wormwood into the bitter cup.

In his estimate of afflictions he took a wide range, and noticed sometimes the condition of the Psalmist, as fully descriptive of the circumstances of God's people in general. They are "plagued and chastened," not lightly touched, but plagued—with strokes sharp and heavy. And he observed that the word "chasten" had reference to offenses, to faults committed that ought, said he, to silence all complaints.

He recommended afflicted persons to search earnestly after the procuring cause—"the particular sin, the Achan that troubles the camp, the Jonah that raises the storm. See," he advised, "if the affliction have not the inscription of the crime over it, and if you cannot find out the *particular* sin, do as Herod did by the infants— destroy all. This will answer the end."

To guard, especially the poor, against improper inferences from an afflicted state, he would observe, citing Eccl. 9:1, 2—that divine love is not to be inferred from adversity any more than from prosperity. A man may live a miserable life in this world, and yet live a much more miserable one in the other. Those who have nothing *else* to show for their hope of heaven but their afflictions, deceive themselves. God needs not make any man happy in the other world to make him amends for wrong done him in this.

Afflictions are, nevertheless, he remarked, good tokens: signs that God has not left us, that his Spirit has not done striving with us, and, when *sanctified*, they are tokens of God's love.

Not a few of the trials through which he was called to pass have been already noticed, and so much at length, as to render any considerable additions here unnecessary. The record has shown an endurance both saintly and magnanimous. Mr. Henry was no stranger himself to the truth of an observation, which was once made by his revered father, when just recovering from an illness; indeed he constantly exemplified its influence: "Six things are a salve for every sore—Christ, a good conscience, the promises, patience, prayer, and heaven in foretaste."

There are many who can bear *heavy* afflictions, who yet fret and repine and become restive under those of a less pressing, but more irritating nature. With Mr. Henry, it was otherwise. Personal ills, even when apparently, or at least comparatively trivial, were borne by him patiently and as accurately observed and improved as those which were heavier. "*Every* affliction," he noticed, "has its errand. And if we are senseless under one that seems small, God will send a greater."

He remarked that great afflictions are commonly much talked of. Many, said he, do no more than talk of them. But we should hear and fear.

He viewed all afflictions as letters "of reproof and admonition;" but he had a strong aversion to hear them aggravated and continually complained of or called by harsh names—as wounds, burdens, and deaths. He would say, they are not so; they are corrections.

Following the significant advice of his own friend and his father's friend, the Rev. Edward Lawrence: "When God afflicts, put all into his hands," he made the Almighty, whatever were his circumstances of sorrow, his "refuge." He uniformly repaired to *him*, and at his throne and in his favor, he found solace and repose. It was remarked by the same good man, whose counsel has just been cited, and in immediate connection with it—that "he is a rare child who, when the rod *is* in his father's hand, runs into his arms."

At a time when Mr. Henry was seized with violent pain, which "presently grew extreme, and continued all afternoon without the least intermission or remission," he writes—and it excellently shows the habitual composure of his spirit under sorrow:

> *I bless God I had much inward comfort calling upon him, and apply the promises, and he supported me. My friends visited me and sympathized with me, for which I bless God. But the great support is that Christ bore our sicknesses, so that there is no sting in them. O that tribulation might work patience.*

It seemed to be a matter of anxiety with Mr. Henry, when afflicted to illustrate a weighty maxim, which he never failed to inculcate—that "a man may be useful to the church, by patience in suffering work, as well as by zeal in doing work."

Even before his strength failed, and when laid aside only a single day by indisposition, amidst labors in which he delighted, he penned the following striking passage: "My work stands still. I have need to redeem time when I have health, but if God takes me off from my work, his will be done.'

In sufferings of another, and oftentimes very distressing, nature, he manifested the same happy state of mind. When maligned and reproached, he aspired, with intense solicitude after meekness and patience, and, instead of rendering evil for evil, requited it with good, ever seeking to improve such occurrences for his own advancement in Christian virtue. "How pleasant is it," he would say, "to have the bird in the bosom sing sweet."

A railer once told him that he looked upon him as a deceived layman. "God give me grace," is the remark upon it, "to make this good use of the censure—to be so much the more diligent to approve myself a good minister of Jesus Christ."

Another time, recording that Alderman railed bitterly at him, and swore by his Maker three times that if the queen would give him leave, he would cut his throat, and the throats of his congregation; he meekly adds "The Lord forgive him."

After treatment unusually severe, he recorded the injury with only this observation: "He that searcheth the heart knoweth my integrity."

Mr. Henry did not, however, deem it right always so to act. "When silence," said he, "will argue guilt, we must not be silent. Ordinarily, we must deny the charge when it is false as Paul did—not in passion, for that brings neither light nor strength to a good cause, but with the meekness of wisdom. Jesus, when accused, answered, I am not a devil. Legal methods may be used for our own vindication. If a man were falsely accused, he might, under the former dispensation, confront his accuse and have justice against him. And Paul, when wronged, appealed to Caesar."

Once, when a bold attempt to destroy his reputation was made by the public slander of "a malicious person," as if Mr. Henry "was overseen in drink," he made his appeal to the magistracy. His innocence was brought forth as the light and his adversaries were confounded.

Apathy may be induced by philosophy. A constrained endurance of trials may, thereby, even assume the semblance of resignation, but the control of sensibility by an enlightened reference to the divine perfections is reserved as a triumph for Christianity. That faith and that repentance, which the Bible inculcates, will alone induce true meekness under correction. Apart from them, real contentedness of mind is impossible. And such were the springs of Mr. Henry's tranquility in sorrow.

Speaking of contentment, he remarked that, "It turns the water of affliction into the wine of consolation. It converts losses into gain." Nor was his remark upon one of the other topics less beautiful or less accurate. "If we bear the burden of sin in true repentance, we may with comfort see Christ bearing it in his satisfaction—and all our other troubles with it."

SECTION 6

His piety towards God, and Devotional Habits, as the Basis of his Character and Attainments

Mr. Henry, having been brought by divine favor to an *early* knowledge of the truth, "feared the Lord," as it is said of Obadiah, "greatly." His pursuit to alter conformity to the divine image in some degree corresponded with the magnitude of the object. It was zealous, unwearied, and persevering. He acted upon the assurance he sometimes expressed—that the work of religion requires the full stream of our affections. "We may sleep," said he, "and go to hell, but if we would go to heaven, we must wake, and watch, and run."

The rules prescribed by him for his own guidance, and the instruction of others, he called "oracles of reason," and they are well entitled to attention.

1. *We should mind that first and most that which is most needful. It is not needful that we are rich and great in the world; but it is needful that we have the favor of God, an interest in Christ, and a new nature.*

2. *We should serve, and please Him by whom we live, and without whom we cannot subsist. Of two evils, the least is to be chosen; we should, therefore, choose affliction rather than iniquity.*

3. *Great pains are well bestowed where great pains are expected. And do we not look for a kingdom, which cannot be moved? When we grow dull and slothful and indifferent, think—do I work now as one that is working for heaven? Is this running, striving, wrestling?*

4. *It is good to be sure in matters of consequence; great things should not be left at uncertainties. And when our precious souls are at stake, should we not make sure work? Build upon a rock?*

5. *We should provide most carefully for that state which is to be of longest continuance. We know, and believe we must be somewhere forever; and reason teaches us to lie up in store for the "time to come." We all profess to believe the "life everlasting," but do we indeed believe it? There is more of practical atheism, deism, infidelity, and Sadduceism, among us than we are aware of.*

6. *We should be concerned to do at the present time that which must be done sometime, or we are undone to all eternity.*

The directions he published for communion with God, showing how to begin, to spend, and to close every day, furnish, there can be no doubt, a correct clue to his own habits.

To the practice of *prayer*, Mr. Henry unceasingly addicted himself; and poetry in it loveliest form has set forth the influence of that habit upon the character.

> *When one who holds communion with the skies,*
> *Has filled his urn where these pure waters rise,*
> *And once more mingles with us meaner things,*
> *Tis e'en as if an angel shook his wings;*
> *Immortal fragrance fills the circuit wide,*
> *That tells us whence his treasures are supplied.*

Often did our author thank God for the frequent occasions he had for the exercise of this "sweet and precious duty." "I *love* prayer," said he. "It is that which buckles on all the Christian's armor. O that in it I might be inward with God. What incomes of grace, and peace, and glory; yea, and outward good things, as far as they are indeed good for us, have we by our access to God in Christ. Such have a companion ready in all their solitudes, a counselor in all their doubts, a comforter in all their sorrows, a supply in all their wants, a support under all their burdens, a shelter in all their dangers, strength for all their performances, and salvation ensured by a sweet and undeceiving earnest. What is heaven but an everlasting access to God? And present access is a pledge of it."

In Mr. Henry's case, no journey was undertaken nor any subject course of sermons entered upon, no book committed to the press or any trouble apprehended or felt without a particular application to the mercy seat for direction, assistance, and success. It was his joy that the throne of grace is always *open*. "I would not," said he—and he was in distressing circumstances when the remark was made—"I would not bring the cares of my family into the mount of communion with God to *distract* me there. Yet I have leave to bring them to present them before the Lord; and to leave them with him; and with him I have left them."

Mr. Evance, one of the most nonconformist witnesses, speaking of "prayer as the way to God," observed, that "Christ ascended from Mount Tabor—where he had often spent so much time in supplication." When preaching a funeral sermon for a Mr. Adams, Mr. Henry informed his hearers, that that good young man testified on his death-bed that *he* had "found praying hours the sweetest hours." And in one of his own letters to Mr. Thoresby, he remarked, that "If there be any comfort in this troublesome world, it is in communion with God by the Word and prayer. There we may have sweet foretastes of the pleasures of the everlasting rest."

Noticing closet prayer, Mr. Henry advised that heed be taken of indulging any vain-glorious humor. "Shut the door," said he, "lest the wind of hypocrisy blow in at it." And he gave it as his settled, and deliberate judgment, that—if secret devotion be either neglected, or negligently performed, the power of godliness will wither and decline.

In holy *meditation* he abounded, and his estimate of the influence of that duty upon the Christian life is evident from the earnestness with which he pressed Christians to its performance. "Take a walk," was his counsel, "*every* day by faith and meditation to mount Calvary. There is nothing like it." In the "Communicant's Companion," he has not only defined meditation with his usual precision, but he has also furnished a useful example for its exercise.

Adopting as an axiom the saying of his excellent father, that "all who would go to heaven when they die, must *begin* their heaven while they live," he recommended frequent contemplation upon that inconceivable state.

> *Dwell upon it (he would say) in your thoughts; set time apart to do so. Look at things which are not seen. All we do we should do with a design for heaven: pray, and hear, and talk, and walk, and live, and all for eternal life. Christians are heirs of salvation. And how doth a young heir please himself with the thoughts of his inheritance.*

Sometimes he proposed such enquiries as these:

> *When are you accustomed to think upon the heavenly happiness? What room has it in your thoughts? What walks do you take into the holy city? O get a Scripture map of the New Jerusalem, and study it well.*

Mr. Tallents says in one of his manuscripts that Mr. Calamy used to tell of a person who being asked what books he read that he lived so holily, answered, "A book of three leaves: a red, a black, and a white one. A red, of Christ's sufferings; a black, of judgment; a white, of glory. Every day I read one of these."

Much as Mr. Henry recommended to others and cultivated in them the consideration of such momentous subjects, he did not overlook himself. To the observances already mentioned, he added *self-examination*. The example, which has been given, is, of its kind, a masterpiece. And another of more general use, from which his practice may be safety inferred, occurs in the fourth chapter of the *Companion*. The fact is, he frequently attended to this duty in solitude and in the careful use of the inspired oracles. "We cannot," he remarked, "cast up our accounts in a crowd. And, the Spirit witnesseth according to the word; by an inward work of grace upon the soul, Christ in you the hope of glory." Noticing the *end* of Christians, and that, while some are "scarcely saved," others have "an abundant entrance—as a ship coming into harbor with full sail," he observed, and it is a further proof of the high station this duty occupied in his esteem, as well as a reason why it ought to do so:

> *They are such as take pains to get assurance, which cannot be obtained without diligence in prayer, reading the Scripture, self-examination, attendance upon ordinances, watchfulness against sit, and strictness in thought, word, and actions.*

To the duties which have been instanced, must be added another, as a distinguishing feature of Mr. Henry's character, and one which essentially influenced its spiritual maturity—namely, *a wise observation of the conduct of Providence*. It is his opinion that—"much of the life of religion" lies in the holy adorings of God, "which," said he, "must be excited, and cherished, and furnished with matter by our remarks upon his providence—for strengthening our faith—for our direction in prayer—for our instruction in the ordering of our conversations."

He sometimes noticed the "abundant sweetness" it imparts to "any mercy to see it growing upon the root of the promise." And he observed that "the good things" of the saints are *not* dispensed out of the basket of common providence, but out of the Ark of the Covenant."

By this habit of mind he was led, whatever were his circumstances, to cherish hope: "a duty much pressed in Scripture. It is reckoned," said he, "among a growing Christian's comforts; and it hath no less a place among a growing Christian's graces."

Hope (then, was his advice to all believers) in God. Trust him as to all your outward concerns. Live a life of dependence upon him; upon his wisdom, power, goodness, and promise. Take but the exhortations of one Psalm. It is the 37th. Be satisfied that really all is well, and shortly it will appear well which he doth. Be careful, principally, about duty. Shall I (he enquires) trust God with my soul, and shall I not trust him with everything else? Shall I trust him for a heaven here-after, and shall I not trust him for provision in the way to it?

The excellent sermon which Mr. Henry published, entitled "Hope and Fear Balanced," contains many admirable exhortations upon this subject, illustrating, at the same time, very happily, the author's personal character and temper.

Many persons of high renown in the churches, have, with great apparent reason, measured their own progress in religion, and that of others also, by the esteem they entertained for the Lord's Day: a test, if applied to Mr. Henry, which will serve to manifest with greater clearness still his spiritual advancement. He styled the Sabbath not only "a day of rest, but a day of work; the work which they do who enter into the everlasting rest." And his advice as to the performance of its social and public duties was in full correspondence.

Keep close to the God of grace. Ordinances are the golden pipes by which the oil of grace is conveyed. That holy oil keeps the lamp of hope burning; therefore David desires to dwell in the house of the Lord, all the days of his life. Let sanctuary privileges (said he) make you long to be within the veil.

Commemorating the twentieth anniversary of his second marriage, he noticed that he and Mrs. Henry had enjoyed together a thousand Sabbaths; and he testified that they were the most comfortable of their days.

He uniformly maintained that the *design* of the Sabbath is holiness; a distinction between that which is common, and that which is sacred; that it is a divine institution and not a human invention; that it is God's time and not our own; that the whole day is holy to the Lord and not church-time only; that God is jealous concerning his Sabbaths; and that care to sanctify them is a part of the character of a good Christian

He considered, too, that it is *one of the first evidences of a change wrought in the soul, to have the mind altered with reference to the Sabbath-day.*

> *Such persons (said he) dare not do as they have done, for they see it is a harvest day for their souls; time to work for eternity. (And he added) the due observation of the Sabbath will have an influence upon all the other parts of duty. It is as the hem or selvage of the cloth to keep it from reveling. Sabbaths well spent are a heaven upon earth.*

On a subject so important, the sentiments of a divine, distinguished like Mr. Henry, for calmness, judgment and devotion are at all times valuable, but peculiarly so perhaps, at the present day: the ill effects of Archdeacon Paley's efforts, not to mention others, to revive opinions which would include, among abolished ceremonies, the obligation of the fourth commandment, being in very direction, but too visible. This is not the place, however, for more than an enquiry—how such advocacy by conformists can be reconciled with the literal exposition of the Decalogue adopted in the *Book of Common Prayer?* Do not the congregations of the establishment respond to the often repeated recitals of the fourth command, in language of devout supplication—"Incline our hearts to keep this *law*!"

It cannot be amiss to introduce in this connection the "rules," which Mr. Henry suggested for observing, and sanctifying the "first day of the week." They are too judicious, as well as too intimately connected with his history and character to be omitted.

They were not intended, be it observed, as a guide for judging others, but as a comprehensive summary to furnish the means whereby each individual may be aided in the government of himself.

> *Be strict (said he) in your practice, but charitable in your censures. Let the difference, which you put between the Sabbath-day and other days be from conscience, not from custom.*

> *Have an eye to Christ. Remember it is his day. Do it as unto him. There you are in no danger of Judaizing. He came not, remember, to destroy the law. What a stress is laid upon this law. "Verily, my Sabbaths ye shall keep." Mark the promises made to its observance. "If thou turn away thy foot from the Sabbath, from doing thy pleasure on my holy day; and call the Sabbath a delight, the holy of the Lord, honorable, and shalt honor him, not doing thine own ways, nor finding thine own pleasure, nor speaking thine own words; then shalt thou delight thyself in the Lord, and I will cause thee to ride upon the high places of the earth, and feed thee with the heritage of Jacob thy father: for the mouth of the Lord hath spoken it." Observe the threatenings denounced upon transgression. "But if ye will not hearken unto me to hallow the Sabbath-day, and not to bear a burden, even entering in at the gates of Jerusalem on the Sabbath-day; then will I kindle a fire in*

the gates thereof, and it shall devour the palaces of Jerusalem, and it shall not be quenched." Cultivate acquaintance with Christ. Make him all in all.

Do your Sabbath work in dependence upon the Spirit. "I was in the Spirit," said John the divine, on the Lord's Day. Pray that the Spirit will help your infirmities, open your understandings, make intercession in you, lead you into this rest, move upon the waters, stir the pool and help you in.

Prepare for the Sabbath before it comes. Remember it. We read in the gospel of the preparation,—that is, the day before the Sabbath.

I pity those who, by Saturday's market, cannot but too often be deprived of this. Do, however, as well as you can to set the house in order, especially set the heart in order. See that nothing be done on the Lord's Day which might as well have been done the day before. God is gracious in his allowances; let not us abuse our liberty. You cannot expect things should fall as it were to be desired they should, unless you contrive them. Review the six days' work as God did. You will find all very bad. Renew repentance. I will wash my hands in innocence, so will I compass thine altar, O Lord.

Begin the day with good thoughts; wake with God; bid the Sabbath welcome; go forth to meet it; think of Christ's resurrection; think of his waking early in the morning.

Set God before you in all your Sabbath work. Do it as unto the Lord. See his eye upon you, and let your eye be *upon him. It is the Sabbath of the Lord your God; from him you are to hear; to him you are to speak; it is he with whom you have to do every day; especially this day.*

Fill up Sabbath time with duty. Be good husbands of it. Redeem it—lose no part of it—it is all precious. Instruct your families in the things of God. You would not starve their bodies, do not starve their souls. Pray with them. Let them not be doing your work when they should be doing God's, further than necessity requires. By mild and gentle reproofs restrain them as much as possible from that which is evil. Let there be a manifest difference between that day and other days in your houses. Go from one duty to another as a bee from flower to flower. Remember the nature of the work, the necessity and excellency of it. Sabbaths come but seldom; therefore be busy. Let all that is within you be at work, like all hands on a harvest day; attend to secret, family, and public ordinances. Be more mild than on other days. Show that you have laid by the world. Keep it holy by employing it in holy work, or else you keep the Sabbath no better than the brutes; for they rest. Holy work is to be done every day; but on this day it must be the work of the day.

Do common actions on that day after a godly sort. Feed the body that it may be fit to serve the soul. Take care it be not unfitted. Eat and drink as those who must pray again. Works of necessity must be done, with a Sabbath frame of heart. Pray against that which may take you off from your Sabbath work. Remember Christ allows us to do good on the Sabbath-day.

Be much in praise. Rejoice in the resurrection of Christ. Sing Psalms.

> *Carry the Sabbath with you into the week. Let it relish with all your converse. You have many thoughts of the world on Sabbath-days; have as many thoughts of God on weekdays.*
>
> *Every Sabbath-day, think much of heaven. Have it in your mind—have it in your eye. That is the general assembly. Get ready for it.*

It is no easy matter, without directly opposing the whole tenor of revelation, to elude the justice and the force of the foregoing admirable observations. A cautious thinker, indeed upon religious verities, would not wish to do so; but rather, with Mr. Henry, to look jealously upon every argument which is adverse to sanctification, and any of its bearings.

With him, too, he will readily sympathize in the remarks which follow:

> *I wonder what thoughts those have of God and their souls, and another world, who make a mock at preaching and praying, who laugh at Sabbath sanctification. Surely they, who grudge the spending of one day in a week in holy exercises, think God a master not worth serving, the soul a jewel not worth saving, and eternity a state not worth providing for. The Lord pity and awaken such out of this security.*

Nothing can be plainer than that Mr. Henry, after all, was unaccustomed to rest in the externals of worship. His devout desires could not be satisfied by a mere attendance upon even appointed institutions. That at which he so diligently aimed was the improvement of the means of grace; and the effects were visible in the whole of his demeanor. In order to quicken himself and others to this, he once remarked "a man may go from the sanctuary to hell. Judgment begins there. Nadad and Abihu died at the door of the tabernacle. Uzza by the Ark." And O "how sad it is," said he, "for men to be lighted to utter darkness by the light of the gospel; to go laden with sermons and Sabbaths, and sacraments to hell!"

Were it necessary, it would be easy to adduce and enlarge upon further evidence in proof of the fact—that piety towards God formed the basis of Mr. Henry's character. The diary, in every part of it, abounds with demonstration upon the subject, but the impressive memorials already extracted will, probably, appear to every reader sufficient—especially, since it is perfectly evident that only religion, the religion of the Bible, could have produced the effects which have been displayed.

CHAPTER 14

Same Account of His Genius, Learning, and Writings

mind combining, like Mr. Henry's, ardor and strength could not, even with moderate application, have been trained, as it was his privilege to be, in sound and classical literature without corresponding proficiency. But in quest of knowledge, his characteristic earnestness and industry displayed themselves signally. His diligence, when very young, was so unremitting and protracted as to render as we have seen, expostulation, and more than expostulation, necessary. To withdraw him from his books, even in his childhood, was no easy achievement to maternal tenderness, and to allure him into the fields, the most contriving methods were indispensable.

He not only read, but he had a taste for, and sometimes attempted, poetic composition. The elegy before noticed, and a few tributary lines on the death of the Reverend Jonathan Roberts, preserved in *the Life of Philip Henry*, however, constitute, much to the credit of his judgment, the only known instances of his efforts. He remarks, indeed, in his essay on Psalm-singing attached to a "collection of family hymns from various authors,"—"I have seen cause very often to alter and in many places to build anew."

His correspondence with "good Mr. Thoresby," as the diary sometimes styles him, discovers an interest in, and a predilection for the pursuits which distinguished that curious antiquary. Many of the existing communications which passed between them relate to manuscript and other relics. The following is a specimen:

> *I would do anything to prevent the loss of Mr. Illingworth's manuscripts, or to gain a sight of them, but know not which way to go about it, not having interest in any of his relations. I have by me many of Mr. Cook's manuscripts, but only some of them legible. Among them is a very large account of a particular reencounter between Hugh Peters and him, when Mr. Peters, without his consent, thrust into his pulpit at Ashby; and of the grievous affronts and ill language that Peters gave him. It is several sheets being (as all that Mr. Cook did was) very prolix. Your collection of autographs I could look over with abundance of satisfaction, and if I had wherewithal would contribute to, for I hate to monopolize that which may be any way serviceable. I have many letters of Mr. Steel's to my father, but cannot readily find any that may be fit to be preserved; but, meeting among my father's papers with a sheet of his in answer to Dr. Fowler's arguments for setting up rails about the communion-table, in his own hand, I sent it you enclosed; and because it may perhaps satisfy your curiosity to read a sermon in my father's own hand-writing, and in that imperfect way he used to write his notes, finding duplicates of one sermon preached near thirty years ago, I enclose it likewise.*

In one letter Mr. Henry, alluding to his expectation of "a particular account" by Mr. Thoresby, "of the antiquities of his neighborhood," says "I should be greatly well pleased it I could be any way serviceable to your noble curiosity, the pleasure of which I envy you," and another epistle represents Mr. Henry himself in the character of an autograph collector. Mentioning to

Mr. Thoresby a manuscript of Arthur Hildersham's given to him by Mr. Tallents, he adds, "He had by him many more. If you were not provided with some of that great hand I could procure on for *you*."

These eminent men must have been attracted to each other by similarity of literary taste in union with piety, for it does not appear that they ever met. Several of Mr. Henry's letters discover his desire "of a personal acquaintance," and in one he pleads for a visit from Mr. Thoresby, "Is there nothing in or about this city (Chester), this ancient city, worthy to be visited by a friend to antiquity?" In another he says, "Could I spare a week from my family and work, I would gladly spend it in your library, but I cannot foresee when that favorable juncture will happen. Perhaps we may yet see again the years of our former silence and restraint, and then we shall have time enough to visit our friends; but while our opportunity lasts, we must be doing."

Although nothing remains in proof of distinguished attainments in philology or criticism, whereby alone, according to modern opinions, education can be rendered illustrious; yet, without adverting to his printed labors, it may be observed that Mr. Henry's manuscript sermons, his diary, and his common-place book furnish abundant evidence of the most valuable acquirements; and what is even better, an application of them as edifying, as it was able and conscientious. With Latin, Greek, and Hebrew tongues he was familiar from his infancy; and to those when in London, he added, as we have seen, some knowledge of French.

Mr. Henry's reading was in early life, there can be little doubt, both varied and extensive—much more so than, after his settlement at Chester, it was practicable for it to be. But his passion for study never forsook him; time was redeemed for its prosecution; and, to the last, his mental stores were swelled by continual accessions. How well the advice he gave to others was exhibited in his own practice, the foregoing narrative has demonstrated. "Take pleasure," said he, "in your study; be in it as in your element. If it *be* weariness to the flesh, the delight of the spirit will make amends. There is much land to be conquered. Every evening ask, 'What have I learned today?'"

With energetic writings of the Puritan and nonconformist divines, he cultivated an enlightened and fond acquaintance. The practical works of Mr. Baxter, especially, occupied a very exalted place in his esteem; they are more frequently cited in his manuscripts than the productions of any other author; and he caught, in a happy measure, the holy flame by which they are animated. He did not overlook, nevertheless, or underrate the minor publications of still later days. He pointedly notices the charge of Dr. Burnet, the Reverend Prelate of Sarum, to his clergy, which appeared in 1705. He read it and "learned to be much in prayer for God's presence in his ministerial labors." He observes that it pressed "the study of the Scriptures: study with prayer." And when the private thoughts upon religion of another good Bishop, Dr. Beveridge, were published, he recorded the pleasure with which he perused them.

The harmony between the injunctions of Bishop Burnet, and Mr. Henry's own sentiments on the subject mentioned, is evinced in some degree by the special memorial which has been cited; but, in the following excellent counsel, it is yet more apparent: "Study close," said Mr. Henry (the address was made to young ministers).

> *Study close; especially make the Bible your study. There is no knowledge, which I am more desirous to increase in than that. Men get wisdom by books, but wisdom towards God is to be gotten out of God's book, and that by digging. Most people do but walk over the surface of it; they are too lazy. Read over other books to help you to understand*

that book. Fetch your prayers and sermons from thence.
The volume of inspiration is a full fountain, ever
overflowing, and hath always something new.

Mr. Henry commenced his career of authorship in the year
1689, or rather 1690, with an anonymous duodecimo of 34 pages,
entitled, *"A brief inquiry into the true nature of schism, or a*
persuasive to Christian love and charity humbly submitted to better
judgments." It was written with exemplary candor; and the
tendency, by rectifying mistakes and destroying prejudices, was
good. After proving from Scripture that schism signified "an
uncharitable distance, division, or alienation of affections among
those who are called Christians, and agree in the fundamentals of
religion, occasioned by their different apprehensions of little
things," he inferred that there may be schism where there is no
separation of communion where there is no schism.

Unexceptionable as was the spirit in which the pamphlet was
written, not to mention its Scriptural foundation, it called forth
from the pen of a writer, styling himself "T.W."—a "Citizen of
Chester" and a "sincere lover of truth," "singular and illiberal
animadversions." Mr. Henry, who neither liked "law wars, nor
sword wars, nor book wars," was silent. But Mr. Tong, at whose
instance the *Brief Enquiry* had been published, undertook the office
of a vindicator. To both of the performances it was that the
Reverend W. Turner, then Vicar of Walburton, made the following
allusion, in a letter dated May 12, 1691, and addressed to the
Reverend Phillip Henry. "Your son's book is orthodox, in my
opinion; and agreeable to my rule of faith and charity; and his
vindicator is a man of brisk brain, and a sharp-nibbled pen."

The warfare did not, however, end there. Another arm was
lifted up; and, in a letter written by Mr. Henry, April 15, 1692, to

his beloved father, the assailant and his own emotions are thus graphically delineated,

> *We were surprised the other night, with a "review" of the new notion of schism and the vindicator of it – by an unknown hand; superior to T.W. in learning and reading, and very little inferior in spleen and bitterness, and unfairness. When I speak they are for war; and who can help it? I think to hasten it to Mr. T[ong], that this may be dealt with in conjunction with T.W. I confess such reproachful language, especially in print, is sometimes a temptation to me, like that to Jeremiah (Jer. 20:8-9). "Because the word of the Lord was made a reproach to me, I said I will not make mention of him, nor speak any more in his name." And I find it not very easy to get over it. I beg your prayers for me, that I may be confirmed in the work of the Lord.*

Mr. Tong now once again wielded the weapons of defense; and, by a "brief enquiry into the nature of schism and the vindicator of it, with reflections upon a pamphlet called the review, and a brief historical account of nonconformity from the restoration," confronted and, it is believed, vanquished the champion.

Both the anonymous attackers displayed very abundantly the malignity, which everywhere in Holy Scripture is predicted, of the presumptuous and unbelieving. But the first of them, T.W., not content with epithets, actually asserted, the better to degrade the object of his hatred, that Phillip Henry's judgment of his son inclined to making him a lawyer or attorney's clerk, insinuating thereby the unfitness of our author, in the opinion of that great man, for theological pursuits. "One of the many falsehoods," says Mr. Tong, "a debauched club have contrived against a person who, upon all accounts, deserved better treatment." "Not," he adds, that he need "be ashamed to own having spent some considerable time in the Inns of Court (but with no design of making that his business); for the honorable acquaintance and respect he gained thereby have set his name far above all the little malicious calumnies of his man, or his myrmidons,"

That was not all; as if either to amuse or awe by a momentary exhibition of himself, the concealed T.W. told the world, that *he* "was put to a mercer."

Mr. Henry committed nothing more to the press until the year 1694, and then only a "collection of family hymns from various authors," to which he prefixed a brief essay on Psalmody. A second edition, "with large addition," appeared about June 1702. The hymns are omitted in the quarto edition of the *Miscellaneous Works*, *ut supra*; but in the folio edition of 1726, they are preserved.

In 1698 he published "an account of the life and death" of his venerable father Philip Henry, a volume which was so well received as to render a second edition speedily necessary; it has been frequently reprinted and often abridged, and is likely to continue a favorite book with the lovers of primitive piety in generations yet unborn. Dr. Chalmers says, it is "one of the most precious religious biographies in our language."

From the time of that publication, Mr. Henry's fame, like Joshua's after the conquest of Jericho, "was noised throughout all the country," and his services as a preacher were not only more prized, but it became needful to comply with public opinion so far as to perpetuate, by means of the press, some of those edifying labors which attracted and delighted his auditors.

The following account, in continuation of the statement already begun, will place them chronologically before the reader; and as the whole is so easily accessible, a detail more minute seems to be unnecessary.

A Discourse concerning meekness and quietness of spirit, with a Sermon appended to it, on Acts 28:22; showing that the Christian Religion is not a Sect, and yet that it is every where spoken against. 1698.

The sermon entitled "Christianity no Sect," was preached at a fast, kept at Mr. Howe's, and raised Mr. Henry high in public favor. An address by Mr. Howe, "To the Reader," was prefixed to the publication. "It was with real difficulty," says that renowned writer, "through the not easily vincible aversion of reverend author, that these discourses are now, at length, brought together into public view.

A Scripture Catechism, in the Method of the Assemblies 1702.

The answers were divided into smaller propositions; and, eventually, texts of Scripture were added in proof of each reply. The latter improvement was made in the year 1708, at the request of the Rev. Jenk Evans, who translated the whole into Welsh.

The Rev. David Some of Harborough published an excellent catechism, framed principally upon the model of Mr. Henry's, thought much abridged. A fourth edition of it appeared in 1761.

A Plain Catechism for Children; to which is added another for the instruction of those who are to be admitted to the Lord's Supper. 1703.

A Sermon concerning the right Management of Friendly Visits, preached in London at Mr. Howe's Meeting-house, April 14, 1704.

A Church in the House; a Sermon concerning Family Religion, preached in London at Mr. Shower's Meeting, April 16, 1704, and published at the request of the Congregation.

A Communicant's Companion; or Instructions and Helps for the right receiving of the Lord's Supper. 1704.

Than which volume, perhaps, none of Mr. Henry's writings have had a wider or more useful circulation. In his diary, December 31, 1705, he says:

I desire with all humility to give God praise for what acceptance my book on the sacrament has met with; the intimations I have had thereof from divers, I desire may never be the matter of my pride (the Lord mortify that in me) but ever, ever the matter of my praise.

Sir Henry Ashurst presented the *Communicant's Companion* together with the *Life of Philip Henry* to Queen Anne.

Very numerous impressions have appeared, and one lately, from the press of Messrs. Chalmers and Collins of Glasgow, with an Introductory Essay by the Rev. J. Brown.

A useful abridgment of it, entitled the *Communicant's Assistant*, was published some years ago and is sometimes to be met with. It reached a second edition in 1763, and would be again reprinted with advantage.

> *The Layman's Reasons for his joining in stated Communion with a Congregation of moderate Dissenters. 1704.*

This is assigned to the year 1704 on the authority of Dr. Calamy.

> *Four Discourses against Vice and Profaneness: vis. against: 1. Drunkenness. 2. Uncleanness. 3. Sabbath-breaking. 4. Profane speaking. 1705.*

"The four discourses against immorality I was urged to publish by some who were of the societies for reformation, when I was in London last year."

The preface to this publication, which appears in the *Miscellaneous Works*, was not written till April 30, 1713.

> *A Sermon preached at the Funeral of the Rev. Mr. James Owen, a Minister of the Gospel in Shrewsbury, April 11, 1706. duod. 1706.*

Few readers (it is hoped none) will be unwilling to peruse in this connection the enlightened improvement made by Mrs. Hunt, who was an auditor of that sermon. It is the best comment upon its excellency, and is at once so instructive and affecting, and so descriptive of Mr. Owen's ministry, as to render the insertion not justifiable merely, but desirable. Mrs. Hunt had been a hearer of Mr. Owen.

> *Thursday, April 11, 1706. I was at Mr. Owen's funeral sermon. Mr. Henry preached on Acts 20:38, and advised us to recollect our faults, which occasioned the untimely removal of so excellent a man. My conscience smote me for unprofitableness under the ministry of so good a*

teacher. I was very much affected and serious, and resolved well that night. Speaking of the account Mr. Owen would give of his hearers, and that they must give of what he taught them, when I came home I recollected the texts of the sermons I had heard him preach, and set them down in order to remember his discourses. I was affected with the thought of what account he would give of me.

If he knew my heart, what must he say but this, "Lord, I am witness to the renewing of her covenant with thee eleven times—in the sacrament of the Lord's Supper—with great seeming zeal and devotion, but this soon wears off, and given place to a contented course of lifeless duties. Religion pines and languishes in her closet; little self-examination; little mortification and self-denial; abundance of sloth, earthliness, and distraction in worship; ingratitude; unbelief; indifference for God. Security, and disregard to the motions of they grace in her, much pride and conformity to the world, little lively meditation, or fervent prayer; a visible declension from her first love, and denying the first works; and if, by thy grace, thou do not stop her, she is inclined enough to turn again into some of the most plausible paths that belong to the broad way; at least if, by thy Spirit, thou do not revive her, and work her works in her, she will fight as one that beats the air, and, after having preached unto others, will be in danger to become a cast-away. She will keep others' vineyards, and neglect her own, if thou help not; she will die in a low and weak estate of grace; lose her crown and place; and, instead of an abundant entrance into thy kingdom, which would once have been administered to her, she will be saved but so as by fire; and yet, Lord, must he say.

*I have delivered my soul. I am clear of her blood. I
have delivered thy errand, and made full proof of my
ministry, and not shunned to declare thy counsel to her. I
have told her from thee, that, except her righteousness
exceed the righteousness of the Scribes and Pharisees, she
shall not enter into thy kingdom. I have told her that, if
she would be thy disciple, she must do more than others. I
am clear of her sloth. Against her earthly-mindedness I
have told her, they that are in the flesh cannot please God;
that thy people labor, whether present or absent, to be
accepted of thee. I have informed her, that those who are
in their natural state are afar off from God; that thy people
labor, whether present or absent, to be accepted of thee. I
have informed her, that those who are in their natural state
are afar off from God; but those that are called are made
night to him; that all such have access with boldness to
this grace—as a favorite to his prince, as a wife to a
husband, as a child to a father, and as one friend to another;
this might have convinced her of her in devotion. I have
showed her that in part all the nations are blessed, and
told her that he is happy, every way happy, that hath the
God of Jacob for his God; that thou hast called, and saved
thy people with a holy calling, not according to their works,
but to thy grace. Was not this enough to have excited and
moved her to perpetual gratitude and praise? I have showed
her that thou hast appointed, whereof thou hast given
assurance unto all men, in that thou hast raised him from
the dead—this ought to have given her a lively view, by
faith, of another state. To humble her, I have told her that
unless we be converted, and become as little children, we
shall not enter into the kingdom of God. To take her off
her self-dependence, I have showed that we destroyed
ourselves, that our help is in God; that it is only Jesus who
saves his people from their sins. To quicken her to zeal, I*

have insisted on it that the kingdom of heaven suffers violence, and that the violent take it by force; that we must not walk in the broad way, and think to go to heaven. To induce her to the love of God, I have convinced her that the Word was made flesh and dwelt among us; the strongest motive to love God—and that all true Christians behold his glory, as of the only begotten of the Father, full of grace and truth. Finally, to leave her inexcusable in resisting the motions of grace, I have showed the danger of it; warned her to take heed how she heard; showed that today if we do not hear God's voice, we shall harden our hearts. I have told her that thy people long for thy coming, and say, Come, Lord Jesus, come quickly—and that all Christ's people are a willing people in the day of his power. Lord, I am free of her blood.

But surely (she proceeds) if he continues anything of that kindness he had for me on earth, in his glorified state, he wished my happiness, and desires my abundant sanctification, and return from my backsliding, and that by the abounding of iniquity my love should not wax cold. In fine, I own I have been unworthy such a minister. Lord, lay not my unprofitableness to my charge; and now at last teach me to profit by what I have heard.

A life of Mr. Owen was published in 1709, in duod. By his brother Dr. Charles Owen, of Warrington. In *Noble's Continuation of Granger*, v. ii. p. 155, it is erroneously ascribed to Mr. Henry.

Great Britain's present Joys and Hopes, opened in Two Sermons, preached in Chester. The former on the National Thanksgiving Day, December 31, 1706. The latter the day following, being New Year's Day. 1707 duod. 1707.

Prefixed to this publication appeared the following characteristic advertisement—"It was several weeks after the substance of these two sermons was preached that I was prevailed with, by the solicitations of some of my friends, to publish them; which is the reason they come abroad thus late. But, though they seem born out of due time, they are not out of their due place. For the plainness of their dress obligeth them to come in the rear of the triumph." This is dated Feb. 15, 1706-7.

A Sermon preached at the Funeral of Dr. Samuel Benion, Minister of the Gospel in Shrewsbury, who died there the 4th of March 1707-8, in the 35th year of his age; to which is added, a short Account of his Life and Death. Duod. 1708.

A Sermon preached at the Funeral of the Rev. Mr. Francis Tallents, Minister of the Gospel in Shrewsbury, who died there April 11, 1708, in the 89th year of his age, with a short account of his Life and Death. duod. 1708.

A Method for Prayer, with Scripture Expressions proper to be used under each head. October 1710.

Dr. Watts pronounced it "a judicious collection of Scriptures proper to the several parts of that duty." And Mr. Orton says, it "should be a *vademecum* with students."

A Short Account of the Life of Lieutenant Illidge, who was in the Militia of the County of Chester near fifty years, chiefly drawn out of his own papers. duod. 1710.

This publication was anonymous, but Mr. Henry's diary demonstrates that he was the author. He finished compiling it April 7, 1710.

Disputes Reviewed, in a Sermon preached at the Evening Lecture at Salter's Hal, on Lord's Day, July 23, 1710. duod. 1710.

To an edition of this Sermon, published in 1719, when the western controversy respecting the Trinity, and subscription, had reached and agitated London. Dr. Watts, prefixed "a Preface," full of eloquence, and peaceful zeal. "Surely," they are the Doctor's words, "the design to republish this useful approbation." "In my opinion," he adds, "there has not been a season these twenty years so inviting to the writers on peace and union, and so much in want of healing discourses. That great man had a most happy talent in the practical way. His easy and familiar turns of thought, and language, insinuate themselves into the conscience with so powerful and pleasing conviction, that we cannot but delight in hearing ourselves so artfully reproved, even while we blush inwardly, and own the folly that he corrects."

A Sermon concerning the Work and Success of the Ministry, preached at the Tuesday Lecture at Salter's Hall, July 25, 1710.

In the Miscellaneous works, *ut supra*, p. 550, and the folio edition, *ut supra*, p. 467, a wrong date is assigned to the delivery of this Sermon. It was *July 25*, not June 25.

Faith in Christ, inferred from Faith in God, in a Sermon preached at the Tuesday Lecture at Salter's Hall, May 29, 1711.

A Sermon Concerning the Forgiveness of Sin as a Debt, preached June 1, 1711, in London. 1711.

Hope and Fear balanced, in a Sermon preached July 24, 1711, at the Tuesday Lecture at Salter's Hall. 1711.

In the year 1711, Mr. Henry prefixed a Preface, dated March the 1st, to a small duod. volume, and now scarce, entitled *The Holy Seed*; or the *Life of Mr. Thomas Beard*, with a Funeral Sermon, by Joseph Porter. That Preface is written in his usual style of plainness and simplicity, and bears ample testimony to his earnest concern for the welfare of the young—that they may be, indeed, a seed to serve the Lord Christ. He designates the subject of the volume, "a thinking, praying, youth," and the papers themselves, considering the age of the writer, "really uncommon." duod. 1711.

A Sermon preached at Broad Oak, June 4, 1707, on occasion of the Death of Mrs. Katharine Henry, relict of Mr. Philip Henry, who fell asleep in the Lord, May 25, 1707, in the 79th year of her age.

This was appended to the third edition, of Mr. Philip Henry's Life. 1712.

A Sermon preached on Monday, June 30, 1712, to the Societies for Reformation of Manners, at Salter's Hall. 1712.

A Sermon preached at Haberdasher's Hall, July 13, 1712, on occasion of the Death of the Rev. Mr. Richard Stretton, M. A. and Minister of the Gospel, who died July 3, aged 80; to which is added, a short Account of his Life. 1712.

Mr. Henry, in his diary, says—"1712, July 7. In the evening I attended the funeral of my good old friend, Mr. Stretton, from his house in Hatton Garden, to the burying place, in Bunhill-fields.

A Sermon preached at the Funeral of Mr. Samuel Lawrence, Minister of the Gospel at Nantwich in Cheshire, who died there on April 24, 1712 in the 51st year of his age, and was buried April 28; to which is added a short Account of his Life. 1712.

Directions for Daily Communion with God, in Three Discourses; showing how to begin, how to spend, and how to close every Day with God. 1712.

Popery, a Spiritual Tyranny, showed in a Sermon, preached on the 5th of November 1712.

This Sermon was preached at Mr. Reynold's meeting-house, and afterwards at Hackney.

A neat and well printed edition, with a Preface and Notes, by "Benjamin Flower" appeared in 1779.

Sober mindedness, pressed upon Young People in a Discourse on Titus 2:6. 1713.

There is a scheme of a Sermon to young people by Mr. Henry on 2 Chron. 1:10 in the Theol. Mag. 5:3. p. 146.

A Sermon preached January 7, 1712-13, at the Ordination of Mr. Atkinson, in London. 1713.

It is probable that his Sermon was first preached at the ordination of Dr. Benyon. With the original edition was printed Mr. [Ben Andrews] Atkinson's Confession of Faith, and the Exhortation addressed by Mr. Smith.

The ordination took place, Mr. Wilson says, for convenience at Mr. Rosewell's. Mr. Smith gave the exhortation, and Dr. Oldfield prayed.

A Sermon preached upon occasion of the Funeral of the Rev. Mr. Daniel Burgess, Minister of the Gospel, who died January 26, 1712-13, in the 67th year of his age. With a short Account concerning him, 1713.

Christ's Favor to Little Children, opened and improved in a Sermon preached March 6, 1712-13 at the Public Baptizing of a Child in London. 1713.

The child referred to was Eleanor, the daughter of the Rev. Jeremiah Smith.

A Sermon Concerning the Catechizing of Youth, preached April 7, 1713, to Mr. Harris's Catechumens. 1713.

Dr. Watts has testified his approval of this excellent Sermon by some prominent notice of it in his Discourses on Instruction by Catechisms.

The Exhortation at Mr. Samuel Clark's Ordination at St. Albans: somewhat enlarged. 1713.

The Confession of Faith by Mr. Clark, with the questions proposed, and a Preface by Dr. Daniel Williams, showing the method and solemnity of Presbyterian ordinations, accompanied the first edition of *The Exhortation. The Exhortation* was delivered September 17, 1712, and as no date is attached to it in the *Miscellaneous Works*, it may be mentioned that Mr. Henry did not begin to write it for the press until April 30, 1713. "Mr. Smith being prevailed with to publish the Sermon."

Soon after Mr. Henry's settlement at Hackney, his attention was directed to a manuscript, *Closet Devotions*, in which the principle heads of divinity are meditated upon and prayed over in Scripture expressions, by "Robert Murrey, Minister of the Gospel," with which he expresses himself "wonderfully pleased." He wrote an address "to the reader," commendatory of the work and its author, whom he describes as a devout good man, whom he had long known as an intimate acquaintance, and for whom he had a great value. The volume appeared in doud. 1713.

Self-consideration necessary to Self-preservation; or, the Folly of despising our own Souls, and our own Ways; opened in Two Sermons to Young People. The former on Prov. 15:32. The latter on Prov. 19:16. 1713.

A Memorial of the Fire of the Lord, in a Sermon preached September 2, 1713, being the Day of the Commemoration of the Burning of London in 1666, at Mr. Reynolds' Meeting-house, near the Monument. 1713.

Mr. Henry returned home and preached it at Hackney.

Serious Thoughts about the Bill brought into the House of Commons against Dissenters' Schools, and Academies. 1714.

In the History of Dissenters, a full account may be seen of the Schism Bill, to which the *Serious Thoughts* refer. And the following extracts from Mr. Henry's diary furnish no uninteresting addition to that narrative.

On the 26th of May 1714, I preached the morning lecture at Mr. Manduit's, Ps. 34:2. My soul shall make her boast in the Lord. I stayed in the city, and went with Dr. Williams, and many others, to make our appearance in the Court of Requests, against this wicked bill of persecution; but no good will be done.

27. I went to London—to Wapping—to a day of prayer at Mr. Bush's. Mr. Harris, Mr. Lyde, Mr. Ridgley, Mr. Clark prayed. I preached 2 Chr. 20:12. We know not what to do. The bill this day ordered to be engrossed.

28. I wrote some thoughts about the present bill.

29. I wrote a second time; much enlarged the serious thoughts about the bill. Sent the paper to the press.

Mr. Reynolds, in his funeral sermon for Mr. Henry, noticing the pleasantness of a religious of a religious life, as then *unpublished*, adds, "He told some of us it was in the press, and it must now be the last a he will send thither."

It shortly appeared with the following attractive title:

The Pleasantness of a Religious Life opened, and proved, and recommended to the Consideration of all, particularly of Young People. duod. 1714.

The Rev. James Hervey, in his conversation with young people, usually recommended this little volume.

But the great work to which Mr. Henry's studies and pursuits had, for many years been chiefly directed—*the Exposition of the Old and New Testament*—yet remains to be noticed. It was commenced in November 1704. *[Editor's note: This is now known as* The Commentary on the Whole Bible.*]*

Mr. Henry lived to finish only the Acts of the Apostles; the residue was completed by various ministers whose names, though not originally announced, are, in the quarto edition, prefixed to each epistle.

In the letters to a young clergyman, published some years since by the late Rev. Thomas Stedman, appeared "a brief account of the progress" made by Mr. Henry when writing the *Exposition*. And as that statement was brief, but imperfect, one more at length, embracing also the list of the continuators will scarcely be regarded as uninteresting or incurious.

Those persons to whom the *Life of Philip Henry* is familiar will recollect that it was the daily practice of the eminent man to expound in his family, the Holy Scriptures in regular succession, and to require from each of his children a written report of what was said. An opportunity of acquaintance with these, and other interesting manuscripts yet preserved, warrants the conclusion, nor ought it to be regarded as derogatory to the venerated Expositor, that in the Commentary, those admirable papers were fully, but very judiciously used.

It would be easy to adduce numerous approving testimonies to the *Exposition*, were not that necessity superseded by its continued popularity. A few instances however, for Mr. Henry's greater honor, as well as the reader's satisfaction, shall be selected.

"I cannot forget," says Mrs. Savage, "what a worthy person Mr. John Hunt, of Chester, once said to me, commending the annotations on Genesis—I believe your brother was divinely inspired when he wrote them."

It is recorded of Mrs. Bury, the accomplished and very learned wife of the reverend gentleman before mentioned, and who ordinarily spent most of her mornings in her closet, that "she first lighted her lamp (as she expressed it) by reading the Holy Scriptures; for the most part, with Mr. Henry's annotations." And that "in the latter part of her life she devoted the most of her secret and leisure hours to the reading" of those "annotations which she would often say were the most plain, profitable, and pleasant she ever read; and the last books (next to her Bible) she should ever part with. She honored the author for finding so much of God in him, and for speaking the case of her own heart better than she could speak it herself."

Mr. Tong remarked that as long as the Bible continues in England, Mr. Henry's admirable *Expositions* will be prized by all serious Christians. In them his clear head, his warm heart, his life, his soul appears. While seriously perusing those excellent books, besides many others which he published, you will seem to yourselves to have Mr. Henry still with you."

Another writer says – Mr. Henry's admirable commentary on the Scriptures, which hath been blessed to the instruction and edification of hundreds of ministers and thousands of Christians for more than a century, still maintains its reputation, above most, if not all, other commentaries.

> *I could wish (said Dr. Watts) young ministers in the country might be allowed by their people to read a part of Mr. Henry's Exposition of the Bible, or repeat a sermon from some good author one part of the Lord's Day.*

Dr. Dodderidge observed that Henry is, perhaps, the only commentator so large that he deserves to be entirely and attentively read through. The remarkable passages should be marked. There is much to be learned in a speculative and still more in a practical way.

The good, but eccentric Mr. Ryland, of Northampton, was of opinion that it is impossible for a person of piety and taste to read the Exposition of Mr. Henry without wishing to be shut out from all the world to read it through without one moment's interruption.

The venerable and Rev. W. Romaine, in a prefatory recommendation to a folio edition, published in 1761, asserted that "there is no comment upon the Bible, neither ancient or modern, in all respects equal to Mr. Henry's."

"Our young preachers," said the late revered Dr. Edward Williams, "would do well to read with devotion, and care, those parts of Mr. Matthew Henry's practical, and incomparable Exposition which relate to the subject they would preach upon."

Other competent judges have observed, with equal enthusiasm and accuracy, that the "learned leisure of the universities, or the sanctioned names of dignitaries, may have produced works which rank higher in the esteem of scholars; but Matthew Henry stands without a rival as an expositor of Scripture, for the edification of the church of God."

Nor is it feeble to praise that the apostolic Whitfield whose labors and virtues inspired even the pen of Cowper, was trained as a Christian and a preacher by Mr. Henry's Commentary: that he literally studied it on his knees; read it through four times; and to the close of life spoke of its author with profound veneration: ever calling him – the great Mr. Henry.

Some years since, the Rev. William Geard, of Hilchin, published in three volumes, duod. "Beauties," selected from the Commentary.

An abridgement of it yet remains a desiratum.

Dr. Adam Clarke, advertising to the minor compilations from commentaries, which, from time to time, have appeared, notices to what a vast number of them Mr. Henry's work has given birth. Every one of which, he adds, while professing to lop off his redundancies, and supply his deficiencies, falls by semi-diameter of the immense orb of literature and religion, short of the eminence of the author himself.

At what precise time the thoughts of Mr. Henry were turned to a lengthened discussion of the subject of *baptism* is a matter of doubt. The only notice of it found among his papers is couched in the following terms:

> "*1707, August 15. I had a letter from a meeting of ministers in Buckinghamshire to urge me to publish something of the baptismal covenant: the Lord direct my studies and incline me to that in which he will own me.*"

The "Treatise," which he left, did not appear until the year 1783. It was then published by "Thomas Robbins," from the original manuscript, but in an abridged form. The abridgement was executed, to quote the opinion of the late Rev. S. Palmer, "with great judgment, so as to retain everything important, and omit only what was redundant; and thus in fact to improve the work; as," he adds, "I can testify by a comparison of the original, and the abridgment in manuscript."

The Monthly Review pronounced it "a very elaborate, methodical, and ingenious performance."

In the year 1805 was published, in 8 vol. price one shilling, by "Elizabeth Matthews, 18, Strand," *A Sermon on the Promises of*

God, preached by Mr. Henry on the 7th of May 1710. It contains a complete list of his forty-two sacramental discourses upon that interesting topic, without a devout improvement of the whole.

Mr. Henry was earnestly solicited to publish a memoir of his sister, Mrs. Hulton; and he prepared a narrative, but "having printed the well-known life of his father, he according to tradition, deemed any attempt to increase the notoriety of his family, inconsistent with modesty." The manuscript remained until the year 1819 in obscurity. It was then made public, and is now usually appended to the *Life of Mrs. Savage.*

Whether Mr. Henry be the author of any other compositions or not is uncertain. The probability is that he did contribute to an inedited manuscript, in three folio volumes, collected by the author of the "Synodicon Gallia Reformata," and now in the Redd-cross Street library. The supposition rests upon a letter addressed by Mr. Henry to his venerable father, dated 26th if June, 1694, and from which the following is an extract:

> *Last Friday, Mr. Quick, of London, Minister, author of the Synodicon, came to my house, recommended to me by Sir Henry Ashurst. He tells me he hath now under hand a book which he calls Eikones, intending an account of the lives of eminent ministers, our own and foreigners, never yet written: he casts for four volumes in folio, and obligeth me to furnish him with memoirs I can get concerning any in this country. I refer further talk of it till I can see you.*

What was lost to the world by the sudden removal of our author, cannot be ascertained. But it was stated, on unquestionable authority, that in addition to the sixth volume of his Expositions, he intended "a seventh which was to have been critical, on difficult places of scriptures; and an eighth that was to have been a body of divinity of sermons."

The best edition of the works was edited by "The Rev. G. Burder, and Joseph Hughes, M.A." in seven volumes, quarto, 1811; corrected from the "innumerable errors which had been accumulating with every edition." It contained also, the sermon entitled, "Separation without Rebellion;" and the funeral discourse preached by Mr. Tong.

It may not be improper to state here that although the valuable service just referred to was undertaken by *both* the excellent ministers (my esteemed friends), whose names have been mentioned, the public, in consequence of Mr. Burden's other and pressing engagements, is indebted to Mr. Hughes for the care, intelligence, and accuracy which distinguished the undertaking.

A stereotyped reprint if the Exposition from that corrected copy has recently appeared, with "Introductory Remarks," at once liberal and commendatory by the Rev. Edward Bickersteth, a clergyman of the Church of England.

Were it not that the representations, which have been given of Mr. Henry's humbleness of mind, were confirmed by authentic evidence, the number and variety of his publications may, singly considered, almost induce a suspicion of over-statement. But the contrary, even as to his printed works, multiplied as they were, is, in almost every instance, visible. Mr. Howe's remark on the subject has already appeared. And it is plain, from the diary, that to the urgency of others in many instances, and a sense of duty in all, and not a love of publicity, nor yet "the praise of men," must the often-repeated increase be attributed. When that good man, the Rev. Daniel Burgess, "went home," an application was made to Mr. Henry to improve the event. He "yielded" ultimately "with much fear." The time have arrived, Lord's Day, February 1, 1712-13, he went in the afternoon to Mr. Burgess' place, near Linclon's-infields, and preached his funeral sermon on 2 Cor. 4:7.

We have this treasure in earthen vessels, that the excellency of the power may be of God, and not of us," "I was even compelled to it." He adds "by opportunity, and never undertook any service with so much reluctancy; yet I do not now repent it. I wish I could have done it better."

From Mr. Henry's papers many similar records might be selected.

Without intending to frame a disquisition upon what may be called our author's creed (a reference to his confession of faith, and the full exhibition of his views of Christian truth already given, rendering that superfluous;) and, without intending to criticize or discuss any more than to condemn or defend particular terms or expressions, which now and then occur in his printed works, it is needful, perhaps, to remark that when, as is sometimes the case, he speaks of faith as a *"condition"* required in order to salvation, he plainly intends no more than "something insisted upon if we would receive benefit received, or something to be performed entirely in our own strength." "The *grace* that saves sinners," says he, "is free, underserved goodness and favor of God; and he saves them not by the works of the law, but through faith in Christ Jesus; by means of which they come to partake of the great blessings of the gospel; and both that faith and that salvation on which it has do great an influence are the gift of God." Dr. Doddridge thought the prejudice so strongly imbibed by many against the word condition, both weak and foolish; because it expresses no more than is expressed by saying, that they who *do* believe shall be, and those who do *not*, shall not be saved; which is perfectly Scriptural. It was in this sense that Mr. Henry used it.

He sometimes also speaks of the gospel as a *remedial law*, and for this, has been charged with encouraging a hope of acceptance before God by a sincere, though necessarily defective and imperfect obedience, with excluding the doctrine of justification by faith as it apprehends the righteousness of Christ, with substituting a faith self-originated, essentially meritorious, and consequently, availing.

Whether Mr. Henry felt in the long-agitated controversy upon the subject thus introduced, any interest or not, there is nothing among his papers to determine. But from his prevailing dislike to all sorts of wars, the probability is that he did *not*; especially as the contest was distressingly sharp and bitter. His printed works, however, warrant the inference that whatever course was on the occasion pursued by him, whether one of silent notice or the reverse, he was in opposition to Dr. Crisp's adherents; and must be classed, if classed at all, with those who preferred the phraseology of Dr. Daniel Williams, the avowed champion of the orthodox in the Neomanian controversy, and who was "worthy of double honor," for having, amidst excessive provocations, wielded the weapons of polemical warfare with eminent meekness, if not with consummate skill.

"The Gospel of Christ" (the language is Mr. Henry's in his "word of advice to the wanton and unclean") is a remedial law, and you hope to have a remedy by it. It is a charter of privilege and you hope to be privileged by it, but how can you expect either remedy or privilege by it, if you will not observe its precepts, nor come up to its conditions? The Gospel will never save you if it shall not rule you."

Christ (he observes elsewhere) told men in the prospect of that kingdom of God which was approaching, that they must repent and believe the gospel. They had broken the

*moral law and could not be saved by a covenant of
innocence for both Jew and Gentile are included under
guilt. They must therefore, take the benefit of a covenant
of grace, must submit to a remedial law; and this is it –
repentance toward God, and faith towards our Lord Jesus
Christ.*

But to confound Mr. Henry, on account of expressions like
these, with creeds of human construction, whether Baxterian or
Neomonian or any other, amount to positive injustice. For,
admitting that his strong attachment to the practical writings of
the heavenly-minded author, whose statements, on some
controverted points, have given rise to the one designation, did
occasion a harmless and frequent similarity, especially in diction
and earnestness. There is no proof that he either acquiesced in or
even concerned himself with, any of those excessively acute
distinctions, which confused Mr. Baxter's theology; and in which
the doctrinal peculiarities of that great man chiefly appeared. And
admitting, also, that the passages just cited give a degree of color
(and it is as faint as possible) for attributing to Mr. Henry the
views which the other term is intended to express, still, it must be
obvious to anyone acquainted with his writings, that he was not a
Baxterian; and that he was still less infected with Neonomianism.
In fact, he was no partisan; and nothing can be more unfair than
to identify him (though it is sometimes done) with a party, because
of expressions, which, how appropriate soever to the views of
that party, were never designed by him to serve the purposes of
Shibboleth.

In all Mr. Henry's writings there is the entire absence of
everything like human discipleship, or systematizing. Every
temporal head he disavowed. And, so far was he from reducing
religion to a mere system of "sounds and syllables," that he rather
viewed it, more essentially so, perhaps, than many celebrated

preachers have done, as "righteousness, and peace, and joy in the Holy Ghost."

In the reasons assigned by him for uniting with moderate dissenters (not again to allude to the sermon on Popery, or to what has appeared in the present volume) his opinions in favor of the utmost freedom of thought on religious subjects are very beautifully set forth; nor does he hesitate to say, elsewhere, with equal openness and decision—"We must not pin our faith on any man's sleeve, not the wiseth or best." Having sought by earnest prayer the "mind of the Spirit" of God upon every part of the Christian revelation, he disdained the customary trammels of prescription, as well as bigotry; and, instead of forcing divine truths into a square with any set of accredited sentiments, or abandoning suitable phrases to communicate his own impression, because other persons used the same, he studiously presented inspired announcements according to his settled convictions, and in their instructive and unrestricted latitude. As a natural consequence, he has been sometimes claimed by Calvinists; at others by Arminians; and often rejected by both.

The following remarks on the controversial subjects of freewill, and some others connected with it, which occurred in the ordinary course of Mr. Henry's ministry, and are selected from one of his unpublished manuscripts, while answering the ends of illustration, will show, at the same time, the clearness, as well as the Scriptural soundness of his views.

> *There are great disputes about freewill and how far it goes. The springs and motions of man's will are secret. But this is undoubted truth, which we are to "hold fast," that those who perish must take all the blame to themselves; and those who are saved must give all the glory to God. There is a decree that sinners shall die, but there is no*

decree that sinners shall sin. The vessels of mercy God has prepared for glory, but vessels of wrath are fitted to destruction, fitted by their own sin. It cannot be charged upon any defect in the soul, as it comes out of God's hand. Man was made upright. The soul is made capable of serving and glorifying, and enjoying God. God doth not incline the will to the sin; his hardening the hearts of sinners is but letting them alone; giving them up to their own heart's lusts; suffering all nations to walk in their own ways; and yet even then, he left not himself without witness. His grace is his own; he is not debtor to any man. If the providence of God concurs to the action that is sinful, yet it doth not at all concur to the sinfulness and obliquity of the action. If providences prove stumbling blocks, that is not God's fault. Adam was not excused by pleading, "The woman whom thou gavest to be with me, she gave me of the tree, and I did eat." It is true God made man's mouth, and in his hand our breath is; but if that mouth be "set against the heavens" and that breath be "threatening and slaughter," that is not God's work. He that speaketh a lie like his father the devil, speaketh of his own. God permits sin, that is, he doth not by his sovereign power hinder it; but he has done all to prevent it that became a good and righteous Governor. The king is not to be blamed if he promulge good and wholesome laws against treason, though he does not set a guard upon every man to keep him from committing it.

Considering the decision and publicity of Mr. Henry's writings, it is singular that so little (in fact nothing) in reprehension of his theological statements is to be found in print. At least, I have in vain endeavored to meet with a single instance of regular and adjusted criticism; or of those condemnatory reflections, which so many other authors have assailed the advocates of similar views.

It seems as though the homage so universally paid to his genius, and sanctity were such, as to have disarmed, not the enemies of truth only, but its jaundiced friends also. Even Dr. Parr, who thought it necessary, it appears, to make one awkward effort to criticize the *Exposition*, contented himself with pronouncing it— a book much esteemed by half-Methodists; a sneer, by the way, far from creditable, either to the Doctor's judgment or piety.

Mr. Henry's notes, in the commentary upon a passage in the History of Cain, indeed, have been objected to as derogatory to the truth; but as it is conceived, quite groundlessly.

The text is—"If thou doest well, shalt thou not be accepted?" Upon which he remarks:

> God is not respecter of persons, hates nothing that he has made, denies his favor to none, but those who, by sin, have forfeited it, and is an enemy to none but those who, by sin, have made him their enemy, so that if we come short of acceptance with him, we must thank ourselves. The fault is wholly our own. If we had done our duty, we had not missed of his mercy. This will justify God in the destruction of sinners, and will aggravate their ruin; there is not a damned sinner in hell, but, if he had done well, as he might have done, had been a glorified saint in heaven. Every mouth will shortly be stopped with this.

In one of his manuscripts he expatiates upon the subject, and the following sensible extract evinces not only his uncompromising, bold, and ardent spirit in maintaining what he believed to be true, but it contains also a recognition of sacred principles, which can never be unseasonable.

The promise of eternal life is offered upon reasonable terms to all men. Sometimes it is a pearl to be purchased. Sometimes a penny to be earned. Sometimes a prize to be run for. Not that there is any meritorious proportion between any things we can do, and this happiness, but it is proposed upon such and such conditions. Whoever believes in Christ shall not perish, but have everlasting life. The offer is free and general. It is true the gate is strait, and the way is narrow, but it is as true that the gate is open and the way is plain. It is true multitudes miss it and are lost forever; but it is as true that it is their own fault. In the close of the fullest description of the heavenly glory we have the invitation—"Whosoever will, let him take the water of life freely."

Being in perfect unison with those observations, one remark more shall be instanced; and the rather as it was made in express reference to himself, as well as to every Christian ambassador throughout the world. "We are ministers of Christ, and, as such, we are to invite all people to him, or else we reflect upon our commission and are sadly accessory to the ruin of souls."

A very slight acquaintance with the entire collection of our author's works will demonstrate his real orthodoxy, his superior acquirements, and the uniformity, moreover, with which all his efforts by the press, as well as by the pulpit, were directed to usefulness. "It is," said he, "the top of my ambition to assist those who are truly serious in searching the Scriptures daily."

And can the full extent of obligation which is due to him be calculated? Is it possible to conjecture in how many instances the attractions which he threw around Christianity have removed prejudice; or how many thoughtless triflers have been roused by his touching appeals; or how many wavering minds have been fixed, and irresolute spirits fortified by his cogent and pointed reasonings; or how many genuine believers have been instructed and consoled, and established by his judicious, and lively, and convincing representations? Here, however, the efficacy of divine influence must be duly recognized. How deeply Mr. Henry was affected with the thought of this we have seen; and also how he, therefore, always connected his labors with earnest prayer to God for a heavenly benediction. The knowledge of that circumstance constrained Mr. Tong to express his hope that a very signal blessing would attend them. And has not such, it may be asked, been the event—for the guidance of other writers, for a lasting commendation of prayer; and for the instruction of individual Christians and the church at large—that to God alone, from whom "every perfect gift" proceedeth, may be given the glory of the whole good manifested in the success, and by the instrumentality of his servant?

It deserves notice how entirely Mr. Henry, in all his writings, kept aloof from that specious fallacy, which pervades the works of some theologians (especially since the days of Dr. Taylor), of restricting, although discountenanced by the inspired testimony, to apostolic times, those truths and portions of holy writ, which, if not so restricted, would render indispensable a far higher style of Christianity than that which is so usually sanctioned by teachers of the class referred to. Instead of narrowing the universality of the Bible, he gave it the fullest scope, both in its application to himself and others; a circumstance to which, in a very essential degree, his great attainments in knowledge and virtue, and his usefulness in the church also, are fairly attributable. A contrary course, however it may gratify a taste of nice and unhallowed criticism will wither, perhaps unsuspectedly, the very energies of a religious life; it shakes the pillars of doctrinal truth; and, unless almost supernaturally prevented, extinguishes spirituality of mind.

The transition from those principles, when once they are fairly admitted, seems fearfully easy both to Socinianism and infidelity.

The account before given of Mr. Henry's mode of preaching and its freedom from everything trifling or disputatious or merely controversial, applies with the fullest force to his published works. The fact is that he was habitually so intent upon the great things of God's law, as to adhere closely, like that famous divine and illustrious scholar, Dr. W. Whitaker, to "sound doctrine." He had no time, any more than inclination, to frame or set forth new opinions. Hence his writings, as well as his manuscript remains, while fraught with the "wisdom which is from above," are distinguished by the absence of refined subtleties, and farfetched speculations. They are more adapted to improve the understanding, and to fill the reader with astonishment, and fear, and holy joy, than, either to gratify a vain curiosity, or to produce a caviling and contentious temper. Whenever he utters an idea or expression which seems ingenious, or strange, the slightest inspection will evince the absence of any designed eccentricity. And, generally, it will be found, either to be very harmless, or to have been employed before by men of renown in the churches. As for example, the conjecture in reference to the restoration of brutes. Several of the ancients, and that astonishing man Mr. Baxter also, understood the 21st verse of Romans 8 in like manner.

It is worthy observation that he was accustomed to lay under entire requisition, for the great purposes of his ministry, all the varied branches of knowledge with which his mind had been stored. How many of his remarks, for example, are influenced by his early study of the law? He seems to have indulged a propensity to make his acquisitions in that department of learning bear upon the illustration of biblical truth, as if to evince the value of legal science in connection with theology, or to gratify his own taste for spiritualizing ordinary things and facts, so as to furnish his instructions with increasing attractiveness. The same disposition is as distinctly visible in his manuscripts. Some of them present a continuous application of legal learning to Gospel doctrines; others to the practices of the faithful; and the allusions, and images, and maxims every where scattered, through his printed works, and his papers discover a similar origin, and the same useful tendency. Not a few, indeed, are awfully striking. "Hell," he writes, "will be hell to hypocrites. The sorest ruin is said to be their portion. As it they were the freeholders, and other sinners only inmates and undertenants." The same thought occurs in the *Exposition* on Matt. 24:51. To multiply instances would be tedious. That work is full of them.

Were it quite fair, or less invidious than it is commonly assumed to be, to institute a comparison between that part of the Exposition reaching to the end of the Acts of the Apostles, which Mr. Henry completed, and that upon the succeeding books of the received canon which was compiled and published by others, the inferiority, although the continuators were aided by his copious manuscripts, might be preeminently displayed: the task is, however, needless, because the discrepancy is, in itself, too glaring not to catch the eye of the most careless, or superficial; a result easily accounted for, since, as Mr. Orme justly remarks, they accommodated themselves to the manner of their predecessor, in which no man could excel but himself.

Viewing Mr. Henry's publications as a whole, it is rather difficult to speak of them in terms sufficiently measured. For, although they furnish much less to afford gratification, in a literary point of view, than do the works of many who are justly designated "fine writers," they possess a vigor which, without the least endeavor to attract, awakens and sustains the attention in an uncommon degree. In a single sentence, he often pours upon Scripture a flood light; and the palpableness he gives to the wonders contained in God's law occasions excitement, not unlike that which is produced by looking through a microscope. The feelings, too, which his subject had called forth in himself, he communicates admirably to others. In his whole manner—the same at nine years old as at fifty—there is freshness and vivacity, which instantly puts the spirits into free and agile motion: an effect somewhat similar to that play of intellectual sprightliness, which some minds (obviously the greatest only) have the indescribable faculty of creating, the moment other minds are brought into collision. But the crowning excellence remains; nothing is introduced in the shape of counteraction. There are no speeches, which make his sincerity questionable; no absurdities to force suspicion as to accuracy in theological knowledge or inattention to the analogy of faith; no staggering, and untoward and unmanageable inconsistencies; nothing by which "the most sacred cause can be injured;" or the highest interests of men placed in jeopardy; or which can render it imperative, exactly in proportion as the understanding is influenced, to repress or extinguish the sentiments, "in order to listen with complacency to the Lord Jesus and his apostles."

On the contrary—and it redounds to Mr. Henry's imperishable honor—his statements correspond with the loveliest uniformity, to the gospel system; all their bearings tend to promote the life of God in the soul; a "sweet savor of Christ" runs through them like a pervading principle of vitality; and so impregnates them, indeed as to communicate an impulse of devotion, perfectly sacred and sublime.

To slight such a writer merely because his style cannot be commended as a model, is just as rational as to deny nervousness to Gurnall, or wit to Andrew Marvel, or learning to Sir Thomas Browne, or genius to Pascal, because neither of them has attempted to rival those wonderful combinations of language, which have rendered some writers of antiquity the admirations of the world.

Mr. Henry's ambition, it should be remarked, never soared in the direction just noticed. To anything beyond a sound judgment and practical efficiency, whatever his prowess really was, he asserted no claims. His desire was to make things plain to ordinary capacities. He would not even "pretend to write for great ones." Instead, therefore, of wasting the invaluable moments allotted to him, like Isocrates is said to have consumed years—upon cadences and harmony—thereby seeking fame, he was bent upon "holding forth the word of life;" and in the doing of it was only anxious to interest, in order to profit his fellow men. His labor, like that of the first Christians, who took the same course, was not in vain. The reception his writings have met with is truly a large reward: with a thousand testimonies, of any other kind, to their rare and consummate excellence. And surely it does not render the high station they occupy in general favor less glorious, in that it has been gained without the aid of reviews and criticisms, or the printed lists and charges of ecclesiastical dignitaries. They have risen to their lofty height by the spontaneous and unsophisticated voice of the public. To reckon the number of households in which the Exposition has descended from father to son, with all the care of the most venerated heirloom, for more than a century, is impossible.

But the style itself of our author, notwithstanding blemishes, must not be surrendered unconditionally to the severity of censure. It has in it many real and characteristic beauties, much pathos, much persuasiveness, and, frequently, vast force. A richer or more captivating effect from the association of familiar words is seldom to be seen. Not only did it partake largely of the improvement of the times, but it triumphed over the forced conceits and deformities of many who were the predecessors and contemporaries of Mr. Henry. And, had he been so minded, indications are not wanting to show what he might have achieved very easily in a style far more conformable to the strict laws of critical taste than that which he wisely followed. Witness the peroration concluding his preface to the fourth volume of the *Exposition*; and, not to multiply references, his glowing advocacy of the cause of religion, as that which, though now spoken against and opposed, will at least infallibly prevail.

It is to the credit of the works under review, that there is in them all an entire absence of garishness and puerility; they never pander to the odious impertinence of vain, and mere curious speculators; neither are there any meretricious ornaments; instruction is never made contemptible by empty declamation. No inquisitive theologian, how rigid soever his fancy, need fear discovering in them the mawkish effusions of scholastic pedantry. He may be amused sometimes by colloquialisms approaching to undue familiarity; by associations bordering upon the ludicrous; by antitheses, too frequent and too jingling; and, occasionally perhaps, he may be surprised by typical and allegorical interpretations carried to excess. But he is in no danger of being provoked by silly airs and self-complacent tones, and, least of all, of being fatigued by monotonous stupidity. All is modest and serious, intimately connected with the conscience, and, without the slightest parade—evidential of extensive knowledge, both of books and men, of accurate and learned research, and true genius.

The very defects and peculiarities of Mr. Henry, his profuse alliterations and "little fancies," are singularly adapted for edification. Even the "quaintness," which distinguishes such a multitude of his observations, and which is somewhat repulsive to the fastidious, has upon the fancy an effect positively enchanting; it holds it, not infrequently, as if spell-bound; and the "epigrammatic turns," notwithstanding their abundance, are so unconstrained and transparent, as to sparkle very often into brilliance.

The naiveté and point referred to, and so conspicuous in the productions now under consideration, were no doubt in a great measure occasioned and certainly heightened by the wise predilection Mr. Henry cherished for "the words which the Holy Ghost teacheth;" selected, not at random or caprice, but, generally, with exquisite judgment, propriety, and beauty. Whenever practicable, they were preferred to all other phraseology; how classical or ornate soever. From the same unerring source his metaphors and allusions are perpetually deduced; and their variety and abundance, as well as their acuteness, display alike his mental taste, his laborious diligence, his unceasing vivacity, and the inexhaustible resources of his imagination. There are, perhaps, few writers whose words, to borrow a Scriptural and significant allusion, may be more aptly likened unto "goads and nails fastened by the master of assemblies."

To cherish for him the high estimate to which, as an author, he is entitled, it is by no means necessary to maintain—that he equals Dr. Owen in profound and continuous thinking, or Dr. Barrow in accuracy and elaboration, or Dr. Bates in a affluent phraseology, or Jeremy Taylor and John Howe in noble daring and seraphic elevation. Indeed to argue affirmatively as to either of those instances would betray a most ill-judged partiality. The fact is, Mr. Henry belongs to a school altogether different: one less cumbrous, less obscure, less refined, and less eloquent. It is praise sufficient to claim for him the fancy of Quarles, the affection of Flavel, the gentleness of Herbert, the good sense of Tillotson, and the terse sententiousness, and antithetical point of Bishop Hall.

In some minds there is an impression that the *Exposition* [Commentary], because not critical in its appearance and professions, is not so in reality, that it is destitute of those qualities which can render a Commentary valuable as a guide to the true import of Scripture. On examination, however, the opposite of that opinion will be found true. Not only was it Mr. Henry's leading design to "give the sense, and cause men to understand the reading;" but he made it a part of his plan to assist in doing so. He illustrates, whenever necessary, the connection of one chapter. He exhibits the thread of history, and he collects and combines disjointed parts, so as to exhibit them at one view. In a word, without any of the apparatus of criticism, he has given, and with an almost unique facility of condensation, the very pith and marrow of some of the most esteemed biblical writers—in a form so simple and unpretending as equally to suit the closet and the family. An able and acute critic well remarked—that "those parts of Scripture which seem at first sight, the least instructive, furnish, in his ingenious hands, much instruction, or at least, much opportunity of instruction."

Besides the use Mr. Henry made of the books he had read on miscellaneous subjects, for the very purpose of being the better able to understand and apply the Scriptures; and besides his access to the invaluable remarks of his renowned father upon the sacred volume, with which from a child he had been familiar, and which he, no doubt, often adopts; he drew largely (to mention no other sources) from the learned labors of Bishop Patrick, Dr. Hammond, and Dr. Whitby, the Synopsis of Pool, the Expositions of the judicious, and venerable Calvin, and the erudite researches of Dr. Lightfoot.

It is not intended by these statements to insinuate against our author a charge of plagiarism, but to evince more clearly some of his collateral claims to respect. In all things, Mr. Henry was downright honest; and what he wrote was (as strictly, perhaps, as any author's can be) his own. So far as the Commentary is concerned, the design that it should be so is distinctly avowed. He omitted many things (and the omission is a mater of regret) on purpose, not to interfere with the English Annotations of Mr. Pool.

The circumstance was accompanied in its announcement by the following profession—a profession that may be safely extended according to the reader's pleasure—"I would not, *actum agere*—do what is done; nor if I may be allowed to borrow the apostle's words, "boast of things made ready to our hand."

Upon all that bears Mr. Henry's name, the image and superscription of originality is fixed—strongly, and indelibly. His thoughts are as novel as they are natural; their celerity was indicated at a very early period by that almost unimaginable quickness of speech, which has been noticed. And their artlessness and perspicuity impart to them a charm as fascinating to the learned as it is to the illiterate.

On the historical parts of the Old Testament, and the Evangelists of the New, he is, for reasons at once obvious, unrivalled. That style and manner—the pointed, discriminating, and applicatory—(which has been represented as a capital excellency in his preaching) is seen there to special advantage. His talent lay peculiarly in the improvement of a subject; and those portions of the inspired volume, which have been just adverted to give him the fullest opportunity for its exercise. His method, unlike most other authors, but after the manner of inspiration, was, as he passed along, to dart into the reader's mind the truths he wished to convey, and in the form of concise sayings. Often they are preceded by the word—"Note"—but their appositeness their ingenuity, their shrewdness, their agreement with universal experience, and the knowledge they discover of the human heart are so striking, as seldom, if ever, to disappoint expectation, although roused so formally.

If the luster of Mr. Henry's qualifications as a minister or an author appears with more brightness in one particular than another, it is in his superlative attachment to the Bible. Nor can any one who is conversant with is numerous publications, the Commentary especially (and the remark is quite as applicable to his unpublished relics) have overlooked how constantly that engrossing interest is discovered. Had it not been stated with half its actual explicitness, it would be impossible, even on the most careless perusal of his works, not to be struck with it. There is in them all, with reference to the lively oracles, an expression of delight, "a relish, a gust," (to borrow his own words) so peculiar as to resemble in its influence, the insensible approaches of old age. The reader, before he is aware, loses sight of the author, and becomes absorbed in the subject. The display of biblical excellencies is so perpetual as to inspire a new attachment to the book of God. Even those fascinations, which before were visible, become more distinct, more vivid, and more constraining.

Nor was that all. If determined that the difference between himself and all others, whether papists or protestants who would take from mankind that "key of knowledge," or impede its circulation, should be as immense as possible, every opportunity of recommending the same superlative regard to the holy volume, was most vigilantly seized. Whether he addressed the aged or the young, whether doctrines were taught or duties urged, whether reproof was administered or "instruction in righteousness attempted," whether fears were to be awakened or consolation imparted, the topic was ever resumed, clothed with fresh attractions, and enforced by new arguments.

> *Let us acquaint ourselves (said he on one occasion) with the sweetness that is in the word of God; and let it be sweet to us. Get a new nature, spiritual senses exercised. Let the objects of faith be real. O taste that the Lord is gracious. Learn to draw sweetness from a promise.*

Let us value the written word as the Ark of the Testament. Many reckon their Bibles only according to the price they cost them; as if the Ark was worth no more than the gold with which it was overlaid. Let us lay up our Bibles as our treasure as the Israelites did the Ark in the Holy of Holies. Let us lay them up in our hearts. Wherever we go, let us take the word of God with us. The Israelites, in their march through the wilderness, acted thus with the Ark. Let it dwell in us "richly." Follow it. When ye see the Ark of the Covenant of the Lord your God, and the priests the Levites bearing it, then ye shall remove from your place and go after it. Call the Bible your glory, and dread its removal. Phinehas' wife, when the Ark was taken, named her child Ichabod—the glory is departed. Part with all rather than your Bibles. Suffer not the spiritual Philistines to rob you. Upon all occasions consult those lively oracles; and, as Moses received from over the Ark, his orders and instructions, so take your measures by the written word. Be governed by it. Covet, as David did the Ark, to have it near you.

To attempt an analysis, or a more minute account of the valuable composures already descried would be a work of supererogation. They have been, they still are, and, in all probability, they will continue to be, too widely circulated and too generally admired to render the service either necessary or expedient. It may be feared that these remarks have been already carried too far, especially when the affirmation of Dr. Watts is, as it ought to be, well considered. That enlightened and eloquent divine professed—that is was not for him to recommend the writings of a man so greatly honored of God in his ministry as Mr. Henry was and so deservedly applauded by the most popular vote of men.

CHAPTER 15

*A short account of some of his friends and neighbors,
particularly his brethren in the ministry, who died before him*

For biography Mr. Henry had a strong partiality; and he advised others to a like preference. "Read," said he, "good books: especially serious, useful history, as that of the *Lives of Holy Men*." And the use he made of his father's papers in the compilation of the beautiful memoir, which as been so often mentioned, shows abundant skill also in that department of composition.

Among his own manuscripts, numerous and interesting, and often unique sketches, well worthy of preservation, have been found. Some of them, indeed, were selected by Mr. Tong, and appeared in the former memorial, but they were so intermixed with the principle narrative as to interrupt the story, and divert the reader's attention. On the present occasion, it has been thought best to imitate the example set by Mr. Henry in the account he wrote of his father, by arranging them in chronological succession, and as a distinct chapter. The delineations of Dr. Benyon, Mr. Owen, Mr. Tallents, and Mr. Lawrence are, however, omitted— the whole respecting *them*, and more at length, appearing, and to far greater advantage, in the discourses and narratives which our author himself published.

Mr. Becket, chaplain to that great patroness of religion, and of nonconformity, the lady Sarah, daughter of the Earl of Chesterfield (widow of Sir Richard Hoghton Tower, in Lancashire, and mother of that worthy gentleman, Sir Charles Hoghton), died of a consumption, March 15, 1695, aged only twenty-five years. I often visited him. He was a very serious person and finished well. He told me he was willing to die; and, though speaking was becoming difficult to him, he called with earnestness to all about him, and bid them prepare to follow him to the glorious mansions above. His last words were – "Come, Lord Jesus. I am now going." He was buried at Wrenbury, the minister of the place preaching his funeral sermon from 2 Cor. 5:1.

Mr. John Wilson, of Warwick, my intimate and beloved friend, died of a consumption in April 1695. He was the son of the judicious and learned author of the Treatise called Nehushtan, and Judicum Discretionis, etc. nor was he inferior to his father, either in gift, or graces. His mind and temper, like his person, were remarkably elegant and comely. He was born at Chester in 1662, educated at in London by Mr. Thomas Row, and lived some time afterwards at Broad Oak with Mr. Philip Henry. He was the first minister of the Presbyterian denomination at Warwick, and his labors were singularly useful. He died early in April, 1695. He was a great loss; and I should say irreparable, did I not know that God has the residue of the spirit. He lay for some time before he died in raptures of Joy. He said he could, through grace, stand upon the brink of the world, and look into another without any amazement; that he had, indeed, had some struggles in his soul, but he had endeavored to deal roundly with himself, in renewing his repentance; and now he had boldness to enter into the holiest through the blood of Jesus.

Mr. James Newcome, grandson of the excellent Mr. Henry Newcome of Manchester, died young, May 27, 1695, deeply and universally lamented. In consequence of the decease of his father, his pious grandfather, to whom his friends delighted to observe a happy resemblance in temper, gifts, and graces, had trained him from infancy. His natural endowments were excellent; his disposition particularly sweet and unassuming. He was educated for the ministry by Mr. Timothy Jolly of Sheffield, and when only commencing his labors, was summoned to everlasting repose. His removal made a deep impression upon the spirit of his grandfather—occasioned him, it was feared, to go with sorrow to the grave.

The same year, 1695, Mr. Henry Pendlebury of Rochadale in Lancashire, a man of great learning and strict godliness and every ministerial qualification, entered upon his rest. Dr. Calamy has preserved an account of him; and Mr. Tong adds—I must be excused if I cannot pass him by without some token of esteem; he lodged in my father's house during the execution of the five-mile act, and kindly received me into his house several years after.

The week Mr. Pendlebury died (which was about the middle of June), Lancashire lost another of its worthies; the Reverend and learned Roger Baldwin of Eccles. The removal of two such men in so short a time was very affecting to Mr. Henry. He observed that breach upon breach produces sorrow upon sorrow; and prays the Lord, who has the residue of the spirit, to make it up.

Mr. Henry Newcome of Manchester died September 17, 1695, not quite half a year after the death of his beloved grandson. Mr. Henry expresses himself upon this occasion *with unusual concern; as for a very great loss to the church of God; and puts up an earnest prayer for his dear friend and brother, Mr. Chorlton, who was fellow-laborer with Mr. Newcome, that the mantle of Elijah might rest upon Elisha.*

Mr. Newcome was often styled the price of preachers and was as esteemed at Grange as Mr. Philip Henry was at Boreatton; he had his frequent times of visiting them, preaching and administering the Lord's Supper in the family; his ministry was both pleasant and profitable. He was brought, by the good providence of God, when young, into that part of England, being, it is believed, born in Northamptonshire, where that county borders upon Huntingdonshire. He married into the family of the Mainwarings of Caringham, was first minister of Goostree; then at Gosworth; from thence he was invited to Manchester to be an assistant to Mr. Heyrick, a minister of genteel extraction, and great learning. God made Mr. Newcome one of the greatest blessings to that town and the country round about, that ever came into it. I never heard of one more successful in conversion work. His person and behavior; his sweet temper; admirable sense; and unaffected piety and humility recommended him everywhere. The great men courted his acquaintance; and he was a most cordial friend to the meanest Christian.

The first Lord Delamere was his great friend, and his son the Earl of Warrington (that noble patriot) and his lady, had a sincere respect for him, but there was no house in Cheshire where he was more heartily welcome and better pleased than at Grange. The family there regarded him as their pastor; and he continued his visits to them and affection for them to the last.

Mr. Thomas Kynaston, my dear and worthy friend, younger than I, but fitter for heaven, died January 10, 1696. God do me good by this providence, that I also may watch as one that must give an account. He was the son of a very good and faithful minister, who, though he could never thoroughly conform to the Church of England, yet was satisfied to read some of the prayers, and by favor of Mr. Chetwode of Whitley (father to Sir John Chetwode), exercised his ministry at Whitley chapel without disturbance. He was an acceptable and useful preacher; his ministry was much frequented, and attended with very good success. He died in the midst of his days, and left his son very young. The father's friends did not forget their kindness to the dead or to the living. Mrs. Venables of Wincham, Mr. Greg of Chester, Mr. Bent of Warrington, and some others, were very helpful to the widow with their advice and assistance, by which means she was not only enabled to give her children a good education, but to leave them a competency when she died. Her eldest son (of whom we speak), after he had gone through his course of school learning, was sent to Natland, near Kendal, in Westmoreland, where, by the lenity of the government, the Reverend and learned Mr. Richard Frankland held a private academy for several years. After some time spent there he resided at Manchester; and under the ministry of that incomparable man, Mr. Newcome, he greatly improved in religion and in ministerial gifts. He endeavored (not to say affected) to form himself in praying and preaching upon Mr. Newcome's example, and a better he could not have chosen. He possessed a humble, meek, honest, loving disposition, which, together with his ministerial gifts, made him a very acceptable person, beloved by his people and by his brethren in the ministry. He was spoken well of by all men, but he died young, as I take it about thirty years old, not full of days, but full of faith, and of the good fruits of his ministry. A little before he died, he called some of his hearers together to tell them solemnly, and as a dying man, that he gave his hearty consent to that gospel covenant which he had made the great subject of his ministry, and in God the widow and fatherless have found mercy.

The Reverend Mr. Beresford, who was turned out of a church in Derby, by the act of uniformity, died in October, 1697. He had lived after his ejection very privately, and died at Weston near Shiffnal in Shropshire, the seat of that wise and religious lady, the Lady Wilbraham, a sincere and generous friend to all good ministers, whether conformists, or nonconformists, without any difference.

In the year 1700, June 27, died Mr. John Owen, son to that very holy, humble and laborious minister, Mr. Hugh Owen of Merionethshire, a burning and shining light in a dark, cold and barren country—one eminently self-denying and mortified to things of this world. His son John was grave and serious from his childhood; he was a student under Mr. Frankland, and after some years spent with him as his pupil, was chosen to be his assistant. Whilst he was so, his examples and endeavors were of very good use to several young men in the family. He had made great improvements in religion and learning before he left that place and entered upon the ministry with great seriousness and good acceptance, and chose to spend his time and strength in the same place where his father lived and died. He was, I think, the only dissenting minister in Merionethshire. Some occasions leading him to Salop he fell sick there at Mr. Orton's house, and in nine days' time died (being about thirty years of age) to the great grief of *all his acquaintance, and to the unspeakable loss of the church of God. Mr. Henry was sent for to his funeral, and preached on that sad occasion at Mr. Jones's meeting-house from Heb. 13:17, "They watch for your souls as they that must give account." The night before he died, Mr. James Owen, being with him, expressed his hopes and desires that God would spare him in his great usefulness in Wales, where he would be so much missed. He meekly replied, It would be a proud thought that God has need of any of us. Great lamentation was made for him, and not without reason, for there were few young men like minded.*

In July 1700 Mr. Henry was invited to attend an aged minister to his grave, the *Reverend Mr. Evans*, of Wrexham, a very serious preacher of good learning and great zeal for God. He was strictly congregational and wished all his brethren round about him had been in that respect as he was. His second wife was the widow of the famous Mr. Vavasor Powel, and though descended of an ancient family of the Gerrards, related to the Earl of Macclesfield, and of the side of the royalists, yet when very young, from convictions of conscience, was determined for the despised way of the Puritans, and chose to suffer reproach with them. She was a zealous, cheerful, and suitable companion to them in all their services and sufferings, and lived to see her only son in a station of great usefulness in the church of God. Though Mr. Evans had been for some time under a manifest decay in his memory, and so rendered unserviceable, yet a little while before he died, which was in his seventy-second year, he spoke with more apprehension than usual, rejoicing in the Lord Jesus Christ as his only rock; and when it was said to him that he was going to his Father's house, he cheerfully answered:

It will not be well with me till I am there. Some present there desired him to leave some good counsel with them; to whom he replied, —Go to God by prayer. The funeral

sermon was preached by Mr. D. Jones from Acts 21:14,
—"The will of the Lord be done." The very same ministers
who had that day three weeks laid young Mr. John Owen
in the grave now attended the funeral of good, aged Mr.
Evans.

February 12, 1701-2. –Mr. Henry preached a sermon at the
funeral of a *Mrs. Madocks*, aged about fifty-three, whom he styles
his "cousin." The text was Gen. 49-18:

> *"I have waited for thy salvation, O Lord." I have long*
> *known the deceased, he remarked, to be a humble, quite*
> *cheerful Christian, who bore with great evenness the*
> *affliction of her pilgrimage, the loss of a loving husband*
> *twenty years ago, and all the cares of a sorrowful*
> *widowhood ever since; and, at last, the fatigues of a long*
> *weakness, quieting herself with this, —God is all-sufficient*
> *for me and mine. Unless this had been her delight, she had*
> *perished in her affliction. She was one who waited for the*
> *salvation of the Lord.*

It is supposed that Mrs. Madocks was related to an excellent
person of the same name, whose memory was embalmed by P.
Henry.

> *October 10, 1702. –I hear that my worthy friend and*
> *dear brother Mr. Scoles, of Macclesfield, died last Friday.*
> *He was almost three years younger than I; a very ingenious*
> *man; a florid preacher; and very serious and affectionate*
> *in all his performances. He met with affliction in his*
> *marriage, which occasioned some unevenness in his temper,*
> *but he was a man of true piety and integrity. He died of*
> *palsy, in complication with other distempers; his afflictions*
> *had broken his spirit very much. The Lord prepare me to*

go after. His father was a learned, godly minister in Manchester.

April 16, 1703. –Mr. Henry records the death of the eminently holy minister, *Mr. Thomas Jolly*, near Clitherow, in Lancashire; an aged witness; and observes, that a little before he departed, though he was speechless, he discovered great signs of satisfaction and joy. The righteous has not only hope, but *joy* in his death.

The same year, in the month of August, died another worthy minister in Lancashire, *Mr. John Crompton*, of Cockney-chapel, a man of great worth and great humility. Mr. Thomas Jolly and Mr. John Crompton were men of the first rank, both for ministerial gifts and graces, steadfast to their principles in trying times, and an ornament to their holy profession. Their praise is in all the churches of that country.

May 18, 1705. –I hear of the death of Mr. Travers. Of Dublin, a worthy minister, aged above fifty and, on the 9th June, I received from Mr. Boyse, his funeral sermon for Mr. Travers.

My worthy friend, old Mr. Thomas Lee, of Darnal, finished his course on Friday night, May 18th. On the 22nd, I went to Darnal, and attended the funeral. He was laid in the dust at Bunbury. Mr. Edgley preached on the text he desired, Job 7:16, —"I would not live always."

Mr. Chorlton, of Manchester, my dear and worthy brother, after about a fortnight's illness of diabetes, died on Wednesday, the 16th May, 1705. He was eminent for solid judgment, great thought, and an extraordinary quickness and readiness of expression; he was a casuist, one of a thousand. He had a wonderfully clear head, and was one who did dominari in concionibus. He was of great sincerity and serious piety; has been very useful in educating youth. He was in the 40th year of his age; survived his wife by about half a year, and was my beloved friend and correspondent about sixteen years. Oh, Lord God, wilt thou make a full end? His funeral sermon was preached and published by Mr. James Coningham, his friend and fellow-laborer; and he has given him his just character. Mr. Chorlton and Mr. Scoles were born in the same town, were bred up together from their childhood, were educated together, both in languages and sciences, were very entirely knit together in affection, and have been justly accounted two of the most considerable men for good sense and learning, that the town of Manchester, or the parts adjacent, have produced.

July 31st 1705. –I heard of the death of Mr. Hammond, an aged minister in London, about eighty-five, and who could read the smallest print without spectacles.

In the same year, Mr. Henry has observed that within the compass of three months, eight nonconforming ministers died— all middle-aged, as he supposed between thirty and sixty, viz. Mr. Kentish, of Bristol; Mr. Travers, of Dublin; Mr. Chorlton, of Manchester; Mr. Anderson, of Newcastle; Mr. Milling, of Dublin; formerly Minister of the English church at Leyden; Mr. Peters, of Leeds; Mr. Hickman, of Birmingham; and Mr. Nevet, of Bridgnorth; on which he adds, –*Help, Lord, for the godly man ceaseth; for the faithful fail from among the children of men.*

Mr. Robert Holland, Minister at Bostock in Cheshire, my good friend, after nine or ten weeks of illness, finished his course on Lord's Day, December 30, 1705; and was buried in his own meeting-place the following Wednesday.

He was an honest, plain man; happily familiar with ordinary people; aged between fifty and sixty, as I suppose. He was educated to a trade, but strongly inclined to the ministry; had a good acquaintance with the Hebrew tongue, and was very useful in the times of distress.

March 4th, 1706. –I hear of the death of Mr. Thomas Bowker, of Wrexham, who had a good report of all men, and of the truth itself.

Mr. Latham, of Wem, my dear brother, died on Wednesday, March 20, 1706. He had been long under weakness, and yet kept from his work but two Lord's Days. On Tuesday, he baptized a child in his chamber, sitting on his couch; prayed thrice; and opened the covenant with affection and enlargement. After that he said little, but looked with a cheerful countenance. He was very ill when put to bed, and would get up again soon after midnight, laid him down on his couch with these words, –Now I have almost finished my course—and so departed, aged fifty-three. He was a very knowing, prudent man; a judicious and affectionate preacher. A grievous hoarseness, which was the effect of the small-pox in his youth, made speaking difficult to himself, and unpleasant to those who were not used to him; yet he went on with his work, and was in labors abundant. I first knew him at Mickledale, where he did good, but had little encouragement. He had been about ten years at Wem; he was strict dissenter, and well beloved; he was a useful man to many in their secular affairs. He left a widow and six children, the eldest about twenty, entering the ministry; the youngest, only four. On the 22nd, eight ministers attended the remains to the grave; he was buried in the church-yard at Wem.

Mr. Henry preached at the meeting-house, from Acts 20:24, – "That I might finish my course with joy."

Mr. Golborn, a schoolmaster in Chester, an excellent scholar, and a very serious, good man, after long weakness of a palsy, died April 8th, 1706, and was buried the 10th.

Mr. Lawton, a minister in Liverpool, died on Monday last, May 6, 1706, after long weakness. He is the second of the eight who were ordained at Warrington, four years ago, that are dead. He was buried at Toxteth Park Chapel last Friday, May 10; and on the 13th Mr. (Charles) Owen was at Liverpool, preaching his funeral sermon.

The Reverend *Nathaniel Long*, who, in 1705, removed from Farnham in Surrey to Wrexham, and son of the Reverend, aged Dr. Long, of Newcastle, died July 14th, 1706. The news came to Mr. Henry when he was enjoying the company of his good friends at Boreatton; "an intimation," he writes, "to be a better husband of my time." Mr. Long had been about three months declining of a consumption; he walked out the day before he died; he was about thirty years of age, a serious, good young man, and likely to have been very useful. The funeral took place at Wrexham on the 17th, and Mr. Henry preached from Cor. 4:12, –"So then death worketh in us, but life in you."

On Monday, October 21, 1706, died Mr. Pyke, of Burton-upon-Trent, in Staffordshire. He came last month to visit his son, a pupil of Dr. Benyon's, and ill of a fever; he stayed about a fortnight. On the ninth he returned, and reached home the tenth, and the next day sickened of a fever, which has proved to be mortal. He was a plain, affectionate preacher, who did a great deal of good; he was about fifty years of age. The Doctor writes that he was much edified by his company. He was as one entering heaven, and once said to the Doctor, –We are going a pace, but I intend to be at home before thee.

Monday, December 16, 1706. —I hear of the death of my good friend, Mr. Hool, of Bunbury, after long weakness. He was a serious and affectionate man, useful in his place.

Dr. Nicholas Stratford, Bishop of Chester, died at London, the 12ᵗʰ instant. On the 3ʳᵈ instant, he was one of those who voted for the perpetuating of the sacramental test. He was a very devout, charitable, good man, and moderate in his own temper; but easy and apt to say and do as those about him would have him; a great many bigoted people had his ear. He was very old, and had been near eighteen years Bishop here.

Tuesday, June 3, 1707. –At Whitchurch attended the funeral of Mr. David Jones, a mercer there. He was an active, useful, good man; aged, I suppose, about fifty.

Friday, September 19, 1707. –This evening Dr. Edmund Entwistle, Archdeacon, was buried. I suppose not much older than I am. He had long weakness; he was a very sober, devout man, and of a good character. He died at Wrexham, drinking the waters.

Mr. Samuel Weld, of Bretton, died 3ʳᵈ December, 1707; he was a silent, serious Christian. The same day I was at the funeral of Alderman Johnson, aged about seventy-one; a sober, good man, Mr. Wright, Curate of Trinity, preached, —Let me die the death of the righteous." On the 12ᵗʰ I preached the lecture, Matt. 13:43, —"Then shall the righteous shine forth;" a funeral sermon for Samuel Weld, who was an upright man, but affected obscurity. The day is coming when such shall shine forth.

Old Peter Done, of Wrexham parish, died lately; a useful man in visiting the sick. The vicar formerly checked him for it, but at his funeral praised him.

Alderman William Allen died July 3, 1708, at Eton Boat. He was a man of the best character, and most respectful to me of all the Tory Aldermen. He had a good savor of religion. I attended his funeral on the 8th, Mr. Fog preached Eccles. 12:14, —"For God shall bring every work into judgment, with every secret thing, whether it be or whether it be evil."

July 23, 1708, —I hear, with much sorrow, of the death of Cousin John Sherratt, of Wem, a useful, serious man, about thirty-two years old, as I suppose. Treading on a nail which ran into his foot, was the occasion of his death. August 23, I went to Wem, preached on occasion of his death, mindful also of Dr. Benyon's, on Amos. 8:9, —"I will cause the sun to go down at noon."

I heard by letter from Mr. Tong, Tuesday, September 7, 1708, that Mr. Spademan died last Saturday. He was not much older than I am; a man of great learning; he succeeded Mr. Howe. Help, Lord, for the standard-bearers faint; those few learned men we have, God removes. What will he do with us? I hear of the death of Mr. Morgan at Whitchurch yesterday; he sickened last Friday; both a very little older than I am; a loud call to me to get ready for death. Lord, make me ready.

On **Wednesday, January 12, 1708-9,** I *went to Tarvin to the funeral of the vicar, Mr. Joseph Gerrard; he died of an asthma aged about 56; he had been above thirty years minister there, a peaceable man, and greatly beloved by the parish. He prayed constantly in his family and repeated on the Lord's Day but one before he died; he exhorted those about him to live in peace, and to be sure to love all good people. He ordered I should be invited to his funeral. He had John Storton to pray with him, and sent to desire I would pray for him. He ordered his funeral sermon on 2 Cor. 13:11, —"Farewell: be perfect."*

Old Mr. Yates, of Danford, finished his course on Lord's Day, February 20, 1708-9. I saw him on the 10th*. He was then in the valley of the shadow of death, and took little notice, except of prayer. He was a useful, good man, aged about seventy-three, one whose mind did not rise with his condition. A man of business and ready to every good work.*

Alderman Henry Bennett was buried, February 28, 1708-9; the sixth Justice of Peace within fourteen months. He had the reputation of a devout, considerate man, and kept good orders in his family.

Mr. Samuel Low, my dear friend and brother, aged about thirty-nine, died at Knutsford, April 19, 1709, about ten o'clock of a fever on the ninth day. It is a great breach upon us; he was in the midst of his days, and seemed healthful. He was a good scholar and an excellent preacher. At the annual meeting of ministers at Knutsford, May 8, 1705, he preached an excellent sermon on Luke 14:23, "Compel them to come in," which much affected me. He was a faithful minister of whom the world was not worthy.

He had been at Knutsford about thirteen years. He was a man of eminent humility, modesty, and meekness; never known to be angry. He greatly recommended himself by a dispassionate temper of mind. He was buried in the meeting-place at Knutsford, universally lamented. Mr. Henry preached from John 12:35, —"Yet a little while is the light with you; walk while ye have the light."

Mr. Bradburn, of Chester, my cousin, died June 28, 1709. I was called up to him at four o'clock. He was then not sensible. I prayed with him, and in a few minutes, he departed. When I visited him the day before, he told me of his experience of the ways of God near forty years; and of the benefit he hoped he had got by my ministry, for which, I bless God. He was interred on Friday, July 1, at Peter's church. I preached a funeral sermon from Ps. 119-92, — "Unless thy law had been my delight, I should have perished in mine affliction."

Old Mrs. Mainwaring, of Carringham, finished her course, and went to rest, July 31[t], 1709. She was a fervent, good woman.

***August 20, 1709.** –I heard of the death of Mr. Jenkin Evans, of Oswestry, a worthy, good minister; and an excellent man.*

***On the 25,** Mr. Henry went to Oswestry, accompanied from Wrexham "by Mr. Kenrick and some others," and preached the funeral sermon on the text Mr. Evans desired, 2 Tim. 1:12, —"I know whom I have believed, and am persuaded that he is able to keep that which I have committed unto him against that day." Mr. Evans was in his 35th year; he was born in Glamorganshire, was much* beloved in Oswestry, and did good there, and in the country about.

Mr. Peter Warburton, of Bromley, my wife's uncle, died on Wednesday, October 12, 1709, and was buried on Saturday the 15*th*. He was, I think, a very good man, and very temperate; aged, as I guess, about 83 or 84.

Mrs. Hannah Amery, my children's school-mistress, died on Friday, December 2, 1709. She was an Anabaptist, but in constant communion with us. She was a very holy, good woman. She was ready in the Scriptures, and delighted in good discourse. On the 6*th*, Mr. Henry attended her funeral out of town towards Hill Cliff, the Anabaptist burying-place near Warrington, where her father was the first who was buried; and on Lord's Day the 11*th*, in the afternoon, he preached her funeral sermon, Ps. 73-24, — "Thou shalt guide me with thy counsel, and afterwards receive me to glory."

Mr. John Cheney, of Warrington, died January 22, 1709-10 or thereabouts. He was a mercer, aged about twenty-nine; married Mr. Eaton's daughter, of Manchester. He was an eminent Christian, very intelligent, obliging, and judicious. Mr. (Charles) Owen preached at his funeral, on Ps. 12:1, —"Help, Lord, for the godly man ceaseth, for the faithful fail from among the children of men." He only left one son, a month old.

Mr. Naylor, Minister of St. Helen's Chapel, Lancashire, died April 12, 1710. He left his wife pregnant with her 13*th* child. This time twelve-months died Mr. Low. This time two years Mr. Tallents and Mr. Harvey; this time four years Mr. Owen; and this time fifteen years Mr. John

Wilson. Mr. Naylor was a worthy, good man, and very useful; aged about forty-six. Somewhat younger than I.

On May 16, Mr. Henry preached to a very full congregation, though on short notice, at St. Helen's Chapel, from 2 Cor. 4:12, —"Death worketh in us."

Robert Davis, Esq., of Lanarch, died of the smallpox here in Chester, July 8, 1710, aged about 56; the 11ᵗʰ day of his distemper. He was a very learned gentleman. Studied the Scripture much; a great historian; much conversant with the apocalypse; very high for episcopacy; and rigid.

Tuesday, September 12, 1710. *–I hear of the death of Mr. Samuel Eaton, of Manchester, Minister at Stand, near Manchester; aged about 54. He was buried last Thursday. He was a man of great integrity and learning. It is time to cry, —"Help, Lord." He buried two sons and a son-in-law, Mr. Cheney (of Warrington), within two or three years last past.*

Mrs. Katharine Eddow, of Hanmer, died on Thursday, March 22, 1710-11. She was born in 1621, a widow in 1648, and ever since. She stood godmother sometime ago to her great, great grandchild. She was a very serious, good Christian, and charitable.

Friday, March 23, 1710-11. *–I studied and preached the lecture Ps. 73:26, —"My flesh and my heart fail;" a funeral sermon for Mr. Hignet, of Rowton; a quiet, serious, good man; the text he desired.*

Mr. Bagshaw, of Ford in Derbyshire, son-in-law of my brother Hardware, and grandson of Mr. Bagshaw, the

Minister of the Peak, died on Lord's Day, November 16, 1712, at night; he sickened only the Monday before. I believe he was only about twenty-four or twenty-five years of age; he married Miss Frances Hardware. He was a very sensible, serious, young man; public-spirited; active for God; a great loss. On the 20*th* I wrote a consolatory letter to my niece Bagshaw.

Tuesday, January 20*t*, 1712-13. I met with Mr. Tozer of Exeter, who tells me that worthy Mr. Tross, minister there, died aged eighty-two, on the Lord's Day. He preached with great liveliness and enlargement; was near three hours in the pulpit. As he was going home cheerfully, he fainted by the way, recovered, and walked home very well; but as soon as he came within his own door, he fainted again, and was dead in a few minutes. A great loss in city and country. He was an excellent man.

Alderman Powell, Mr. Henry's neighbor at Hackney, died about five o'clock in the evening, February 18, 1714. He was an excellent Christian, and experienced. An old disciple, aged eighty-four. He died very comfortably. I recommended Mr. Joseph Billio to Mrs. Powell for her chaplain. On the 26*th*, Mr. Henry attended his funeral to Magnus Church. Mr. Powell's sister, Mrs. Partridge, died the year before, in her hundredth year. She had been a widow near fifty years. She had eight children, but had none living descended from her, but three grandsons. She was of Mr. Caryl's congregation.

Mr. Collins, the minister and co-pastor with Mr. Brag, one of the lecturers at Pinner's Hall, died suddenly on Saturday, March 30, 1714; aged, I suppose, somewhat above forty. He preached his turn, last Tuesday at Pinner's

Hall; was here in Hackney, yesterday, with Mr. Powell, about some of his uncle's charities. He dined at Mrs. Lyde's, prayed with her, and went home in a coach between three and four o'clock. Some young men of the congregation used to meet at his house for prayer and conference. He went to his study, ordered to be called when they came. His maid went and told him, after some time, they had arrived. He said he would be with them presently. He was heard to unlock his study door, and came out. But immediately, with two groans, he fell down dead.

The Concise
Commentary
on the
Gospels

PREFACE

The one half of our undertaking upon the New Testament is now, by the assistance of divine grace, finished, and presented to the reader, who, it is hoped, the Lord working with it, may hereby be somewhat helped in understanding and improving the sacred history of Christ and his apostles, and in making it, as it certainly is, the best exposition of our creed, in which these inspired writers are summed up, as is intimated by that evangelist who calls his gospel *A Declaration of those things which are most surely believed among us* (Luke 1). And, as there is no part of Scripture in the belief of which it concerns more to be established, so there is none with which the generality of Christians are more conversant, or which they speak of more frequently. It is therefore our duty, by constant pains in meditation and prayer, to come to an intimate acquaintance with the true intent and meaning of these narratives, what our concern is in them, and what we are to build upon them and draw from them; that we may not rest in such a knowledge of them as that which we had when in our childhood we were taught to read English out of the translation and Greek out of the originals of these books. We ought to know them as the physician does his dispensatory, the lawyer his books of reports, and the sailor his chart and compass; that is, to know how to make use of them in that to which we apply ourselves as our business in this world, which is to serve God here and enjoy him hereafter, and both in Christ the Mediator.

The great designs of the Christian institutes (of which these books are the fountains and foundations) were to reduce the children of men to the fear and love of God, as the commanding active principle of their observance of him, and obedience to him, to show them the way of their reconciliation to him and acceptance with him, and to bring them under obligations to Jesus Christ as Mediator, and thereby to engage them to all instances of devotion towards God and justice and charity towards all men, in conformity to the example of Christ, in obedience to his law, and in pursuance of his great intentions. What therefore I have endeavoured here has been with this view, to make these writings serviceable to the faith, holiness, and comfort of good Christians.

Now that these writings, thus made use of to serve these great and noble designs, may have their due influence upon us, it concerns us to be well established in our belief of their divine origin. And here we have to do with two sorts of people. Some embrace the Old Testament, but set that up in opposition to the New, pleading that, if that be right, this is wrong; and these are the Jews. Others, though they live in a Christian nation, and by baptism wear the Christian name, yet, under pretence of freedom of thought, despise Christianity, and consequently reject the New Testament, and therefore the Old of course. I confess it is strange that any now who receive the Old Testament should reject the New, since, besides all the particular proofs of the divine authority of the New Testament, there is such an admirable harmony between it and the Old. It agrees with the Old in all the main intentions of it, refers to it, builds upon it, shows the accomplishment of its types and prophecies, and thereby is the perfection and crown of it. Nay, if it be not true, the Old Testament must be false, and all the glorious promises which shine so brightly in it, and the performance of which was limited within certain periods of time, must be a great delusion, which we are sure they are not, and therefore must embrace the New Testament to support the reputation of the Old.

Those things in the Old Testament which the New Testament lays aside are the peculiarity of the Jewish nation and the observances of the ceremonial law, both which certainly were of divine appointment; and yet the New Testament does not at all clash with the Old; for,

1. They were always designed to be laid aside in the fulness of time. No other is to be expected than that the morning-star should disappear when the sun rises; and the latter parts of the Old Testament often speak of the laying aside of those things, and of the calling in of the Gentiles.

2. They were very honourable laid aside, and rather exchanged for that which was more noble and excellent, more divine and heavenly. The Jewish church was swallowed up in the Christian, the mosaic ritual in evangelical institutions. So that the New Testament is no more the undoing of the Old than the sending of a youth to the university is the undoing of his education in the grammar-school.

3. Providence soon determined this controversy (which is the only thing that seemed a controversy between the Old Testament and the New) by the destruction of Jerusalem, the desolations of the temple, the dissolution of the temple-service, and the total dispersion of all the remains of the Jewish nation, with a judicial defeat of all the attempts to incorporate it again, now for above 1600 years; and this according to the express predictions of Christ, a little before his death. And, as Christ would not have the doctrine of his being the Messiah much insisted on till the great conclusive proof of it was given by his resurrection from the dead, so the repeal of the ceremonial law, as to the Jews, was not much insisted

on, but their keeping up the observation of it was connived at, till the great conclusive proof of its repeal was given by the destruction of Jerusalem, which made the observation of it for ever impracticable. And the manifest tokens of divine wrath which the Jews, considered as a people, even notwithstanding the prosperity of particular persons among them, continue under to this day, is a proof, not only of the truth of Christ's predictions concerning them, but that they lie under a greater guilt than that of idolatry (for which they lay under a desolation of 70 years), and this can be no other than crucifying Christ, and rejecting his gospel.

Thus evident it is that, in our expounding of the New Testament, we are not undoing what we did in expounding the Old; so far from it that we may appeal to the law and the prophets for the confirmation of the great truth which the gospels are written to prove – That our Lord Jesus is the Messiah promised to the fathers, who should come, and we are to look for no other. For though his appearing did not answer the expectation of the carnal Jews, who looked for a Messiah in external pomp and power, yet it exactly answered all the types, prophecies, and promises, of the Old Testament, which all had their accomplishment in him; and even his ignominious sufferings, which are the greatest stumbling-block to the Jews, were foretold concerning the Messiah; so that if he had not submitted to them we had failed in our proof; so fat it is from being weakened by them. Bishop Kidder's Demonstration of the Christian's Messiah has abundantly made out this truth, and answered the cavils (for such they are, rather than arguments) of the Jews against it, above any in our language.

But we live in an age when Christianity and the New Testament are more virulently and daringly attacked by some within their own bowels than by those upon their borders. Never were Moses and his writings so arraigned and ridiculed by any Jews, or Mahomet and his Alcoran by any Mussulmans, as Christ and his gospel by men that are baptized and called Christians; and this, not under colour of any other divine revelation, but in contempt and defiance of all divine revelation; and not by way of complaint that they meet with that which shocks their faith, and which, through their own weakness, they cannot get over, and therefore desire to be instructed in, and helped in the understanding of, and the reconciling of them to the truth which they have received, but by way of resolute opposition, as if they looked upon it as their enemy, and were resolved by all means possible to be the ruin of it, though they cannot say what evil it has done to the world or to them. If the pretence of it has transported many in the church of Rome into such corruptions of worship and cruelties of government as are indeed the scandal of human nature, yet, instead of being thereby prejudiced against pure Christianity, they should the rather appear more vigorously in defence of it, when they see so excellent an institution as this is in itself so basely abused and misrepresented. They pretend to a liberty of thought in their opposition to Christianity, and would be distinguished by the name of free-thinkers.

I will not here go about to produce the arguments which, to all that are not wilfully ignorant and prejudiced against the truth, are sufficient to prove the divine origin and authority of the doctrine of Christ. The learned find much satisfaction in reading the apologies of the ancients for the Christian religion, when it was struggling with the polytheism and idolatry of the Gentiles. Justin Martyr and Tertullian, Lactantius and Minutius Felix, wrote admirable in defence of Christianity, when it was further sealed by the blood of the martyrs. But its patrons and advocates in the present day have another sort of enemies to deal with. The antiquity of the pagan theology, its universal prevalence, the edicts of princes, and the traditions and usages of the country, are not now objected to Christianity; but I know not what imaginary freedom of thought, and an unheard-of privilege of human nature, are assumed, not to be bound by any divine revelation whatsoever.

Now it is easy to make out:

1. That those who would be thought thus to maintain a liberty of thinking as one of the privileges of human nature, and in defence of which they will take up arms against God himself, do not themselves think freely, nor give others leave to do so. In some of them a resolute indulgence of themselves in those vicious courses which they know the gospel if they admit it will make very uneasy to them, and a secret enmity to a holy heavenly mind and life, forbid them all free thought; for so strong a prejudice have their lusts and passions laid them under against the laws of Christ that they find themselves under a necessity of opposing the truths of Christ, upon which these laws are founded. Perit judicium, quando res transit in affectum – The judgment is overcome, when the decision is referred to the affections. Right or wrong, Christ's bonds must be broken, and his cords cast from them; and therefore, how evident soever the premises be, the conclusion must be denied, if it tend to fasten these bands and cords upon them; and where is the freedom of thought then?

While they promise themselves liberty, they themselves are the servants of corruption; for of whom a man is overcome of the same is he brought into bondage. In others of them, a reigning pride and affectation of singularity, and a spirit of contradiction, those lusts of the mind, which are as impetuous and imperious as any of the lusts of the flesh and of the world, forbid a freedom of thinking, and enslave the soul in all its enquiries after religion. Those can no more think freely who resolve they will think by themselves than those can who resolve to think with their neighbours. Nor will they give others liberty to think freely; for it is not by reason and argument that they go about to convince us, but by jest and banter, and exposing Christianity and its serious professors to contempt. Now, considering how natural it is to most men to be jealous for their reputation, this is as great an imposition as can possibly be; and the unthinking are as much kept from free-thinking by the fear of being ridiculed in the club of those who set up for oracles in reason as by the fear of being cursed, excommunicated, and anathematized, by the counsel of those who set up for oracles in religion. And where is the free-thinking then?

2. That those who will allow themselves a true liberty of thinking, and will think seriously, cannot but embrace all Christ's sayings, as faithful, and well worthy of all acceptation. Let the corrupt bias of the carnal heart towards the world, and the flesh, and self (the most presumptuous idol of the three) be taken away, and let the doctrine of Christ be proposed first in its true colours, as Christ and his apostles have given it to us, and in its true light, with all its proper evidence, intrinsic and extrinsic; and then let the capable soul freely use its rational powers and faculties, and by the operation of the Spirit of grace, who alone works faith in all that believe, even the high thought, when once it becomes a free thought, freed from the bondage of sin and corruption, will, by a pleasing and happy power, be captivated, and brought into obedience to Christ; and, when he thus makes it free, it will be free indeed.

Let any one who will give himself leave to think impartially, and be at the pains to think closely, read Mr. Baxter's Reasons for the Christian Religion, and he will find both that it goes to the bottom, and lays the foundation deep and firm, and also that it brings forth the top-stone in a believer's consent to God in Christ, to the satisfaction of any that are truly concerned about their souls and another world. The proofs of the truths of the gospel have been excellently well methodized, and enforced likewise, by bishop

Stillingfleet, in his Origines Sacræ; by Grotius, in his book of the Truth of the Christian Religion; by Dr. Whitby, in his General Preface to his Commentary on the New Testament; and of late by Mr. Ditton, very argumentatively, in his discourse concerning the Resurrection of Jesus Christ; and many others have herein done worthily. And I will not believe any man who rejects the New Testament and the Christian religion to have thought freely upon the subject, unless he has, with humility, seriousness, and prayer to God for direction, deliberately read these or the like books, which, it is certain, were written both with liberty and clearness of thought.

For my own part, if my thoughts were worth any one's notice, I do declare I have thought of this great concern with all the liberty that a reasonable soul can pretend to, or desire; and the result is that the more I think, and the more freely I think, the more fully I am satisfied that the Christian religion is the true religion, and that which, if I submit my soul sincerely to it, I may venture my soul confidently upon. For when I think freely,

1. I cannot but think that the God who made man a reasonable creature by his power has a right to rule him by his law, and to oblige him to keep his inferior faculties of appetite and passion, together with the capacities of thought and speech, in due subjection to the superior powers of reason and conscience. And, when I look into my own heart, I cannot but think that it was this which my Maker designed in the order and frame of my soul, and that herein he intended to support his own dominion in me.

2. I cannot but think that my happiness is bound up in the favour of God, and that his favour will, or will not, be towards me, according as I do, or do not, comply with the laws and ends of my creation, – that I am accountable to this God, and that from

him my judgment proceeds, not only for this world, but for my everlasting state.

3. I cannot but think that my nature is very unlike what the nature of man was as it came out of the Creator's hands, – that it is degenerated from its primitive purity and rectitude. I find in myself a natural aversion to my duty, and to spiritual and divine exercises, and a propensity to that which is evil, such an inclination towards the world and the flesh as amounts to a propensity to backslide from the living God.

4. I cannot but think that I am therefore, by nature, thrown out of the favour of God; for though I think he is a gracious and merciful God, yet I think he is also a just and holy God, and that I am become, by sin, both odious to his holiness and obnoxious to his justice. I should not think freely, but very partially, if I should think otherwise. I think I am guilty before God, have sinned, and come short of glorifying him, and of being glorified with him.

5. I cannot but think that, without some special discovery of God's will concerning me, and good-will to me, I cannot possibly recover his favour, be reconciled to him, or be so far restored to my primitive rectitude as to be capable of serving my Creator, and answering the ends of my creation, and becoming fit for another world; for the bounties of Providence to me, in common with the inferior creatures, cannot serve either as assurances that God is reconciled to me or means to reconcile me to God.

6. I cannot but think that the way of salvation, both from the guilt and from the power of sin, by Jesus Christ, and his mediation between God and man, as it is revealed by the New Testament, is admirable will fitted to all the exigencies of my case, to restore me both to the favour of God and to the government and enjoyment of myself. Here I see a proper method for the removing of the guilt of sin (that I may not die by the sentence of the law) by the

all-sufficient merit and righteousness of the Son of God in our nature, and for the breaking of the power of sin (that I may not die by my own disease) by the all-sufficient influence and operation of the Spirit of God upon our nature. Every malady has herein its remedy, every grievance is hereby redressed, and in such a way as advances the honour of all the divine attributes and is suited and accommodated to human nature.

7. I cannot but think that what I find in myself of natural religion does evidently bear testimony to the Christian religion; for all that truth which is discovered to me by the light of nature is confirmed, and more clearly discovered, by the gospel; the very same thing which the light of nature gives me a confused sight of (like the sight of men as trees walking) the New Testament gives me a clear and distinct sight of. All that good which is pressed upon me by the law of nature is more fully discovered to me, and I find myself much more strongly bound to it by the gospel of Christ, the engagements it lays upon me to my duty, and the encouragements and assistances it gives me in my duty. And this is further confirming to me that there, just there, where natural light leaves me at a loss, and unsatisfied – tells me that hitherto it can carry me, but no further – the gospel takes me up, helps me out, and gives me all the satisfaction I can desire, and that is especially in the great business of the satisfying of God's justice for the sin of man.

My own conscience asks, Wherewith shall I come before the Lord, and bow myself before the most high God? Will he be pleased with thousands of rams? But I am still at a loss; I cannot frame a righteousness from any thing I am, or have, in myself, or from any thing I can do for God or present to God, wherein I dare appear before him; but the gospel comes, and tells me that Jesus Christ had made his soul an offering for sin, and God has declared himself well-pleased with all believers in him; and this makes me easy.

8. I cannot but think that the proofs by which God has attested the truth of the gospel are the most proper that could be given in a case of this nature – that the power and authority of the Redeemer in the kingdom of grace should be exemplified to the world, not by the highest degree of the pomp and authority of the kings of the earth, as the Jews expected, but by the evidences of his dominion in the kingdom of nature, which is a much greater dignity and authority than any of the kings of the earth ever pretended to, and is no less than divine. And his miracles being generally wrought upon men, not only upon their bodies, as they were mostly when Christ was here upon earth, but, which is more, upon their minds, as they were mostly after the pouring out of the Spirit in the gift of tongues and other supernatural endowments, were the most proper confirmations possible of the truth of the gospel, which was designed for the making of men holy and happy.

9. I cannot but think that the methods taken for the propagation of this gospel, and the wonderful success of those methods, which are purely spiritual and heavenly, and destitute of all secular advantages and supports, plainly show that it was of God, for God was with it; and it could never have spread as it did, in the face of so much opposition, if it had not been accompanied with a power from on high. And the preservation of Christianity in the world to this day, notwithstanding the difficulties it has struggles with, is to me a standing miracle for the proof of it.

10. I cannot but think that the gospel of Christ has had some influence upon my soul, has had such a command over me, and been such a comfort to me, as is a demonstration to myself, though it cannot be so to another, that it is of God. I have tasted in it that the Lord is gracious; and the most subtle disputant cannot convince one who has tasted honey that it is not sweet.

And now I appeal to him who knows the thoughts and intents of the heart that in all this I think freely (if it be possible for a man to know that he does so), and not under the power of any bias. Whether we have reason to think that those who, without any colour of reason, not only usurp, but monopolize, the character of free-thinkers, do so, let those judge who easily observe that they do not speak sincerely, but industriously dissemble their notions; and one instance I cannot but notice of their unfair dealing with their readers – that when, for the diminishing of the authority of the New Testament, they urge the various readings of the original, and quote an acknowledgment of Mr. Gregory of Christ-church, in his preface to his Works, That no profane author whatsoever, etc., and yet suppress what immediately follows, as the sense of that learned man upon it, That this is an invincible reason for the scriptures' part, etc.

But while we are thus maintaining the divine origin and authority of the New Testament, as it has been received through all the ages of the church, we find our cause not only attacked by the enemies we speak of, but in effect betrayed by one who makes our New Testament almost double to what it really is, 2 adding to the Constitutions of the Apostles, collected by Clement, together with the Apostolical Canons, and making those to be of equal authority with the writings of the evangelists, and preferable to the Epistles. By enlarging the lines of defence thus, without either cause or precedent, he gives great advantage to the invaders. Those Constitutions of the Apostles have many things in them very good, and may be of use, as other human compositions; but to pretend that they wee composed, as they profess to be, by the twelve apostles in concert at Jerusalem, I Peter saying this, I Andrew saying that, etc., is the greatest imposition that can be practised upon the credulity of the simple.

1. It is certain there were a great many spurious writings which, in the early days of the church, went under the names of the apostles and apostolical men; so that it has always been complained of as impossible to find out any thing but the canon of scripture that could with any assurance be attributed to them. Baronius himself acknowledges it, Cum apostolorum nomine tam facta quam dicta reperiantur esse supposititia; nec sic quid de illis à veris sincerisque spriptoribus narratum sit integrum et incorruptum remanserit, in desperationem planè quandam animum dejicunt posse unquam assequi quod verum certumque subsistat – Since so many of the acts and sayings ascribed to the apostles are found to be spurious, and even the narrations of faithful writers respecting them are not free from corruption, we must despair of ever being able to arrive at any absolute certainty about them. – Ad An. Christ. 44, sect. 42, etc. There were Acts under the names of Andrew the apostle, Philip, Peter, Thomas; a Gospel under the names of Thaddeus, another of Barnabas, another of Bartholomew; a book concerning the infancy of our Saviour, another concerning his nativity, and many the like, which we all rejected as forgeries.

2. These Constitutions and Canons, among the rest, were condemned in the primitive church as apocryphal, and therefore justly rejected; because, though otherwise good, they pretended to be what really they were not, dictated by the twelve apostles themselves, as received from Christ. If Jesus Christ gave them such instructions, and they gave them in such a solemn manner to the church, as is pretended, it is unaccountable that there is not the least notice taken of any such thing done or designed in the Gospels, the Acts, or any of the Epistles.

Those who have judged the most favourable of these Canons and Constitutions have concluded that they were complied by some officious persons under the name of Clement, towards the end of the second century, above 150 years after Christ's ascension, out of the common practice of the churches; that is, that which the compilers were most acquainted with, or had respect for; when at the same time we have reason to think that the far greater number of Christian churches which by that time were planted had Constitutions of their own, which, if they had had the happiness to be transmitted to posterity, would have recommended themselves as well as these, or better. But, as the legislators of old put a reputation upon their laws by pretending to have received them from some deity or other, so church-governors studied to gain reputation to their sees by placing some apostolical man or other at the head of their catalogue of bishops (see bishop Stillingfleet's Irenicum, p. 302), and reputation to their Canons and Constitutions by fathering them upon the apostles. But how can it be imagined that the apostles should be all together at Jerusalem, to compose this book of Canons with so much solemnity, when we know that their commission was to go into all the world, and to preach the gospel to every creature? Accordingly, Eusebius tells us that Thomas went into Parthia, Andrew into Scythia, John into the lesser Asia; and we have reason to think that after their dispersion they never came together again, any more than the planters of the nations did after the Most High had separated the sons of Adam.

I think that any one who will compare these Constitutions with the writings which we are sure were given by inspiration of God will easily discern a vast difference in the style and spirit. What is the chaff to the wheat? "Where are ministers, in the style of the true apostles, called priests, high priests? Where do we find in the apostolical age, that age of suffering, of the placing of the bishop in his throne? Or of readers, singers, and porters, in the church?"

I fear the collector and compiler of those Constitutions, under the name of Clement, was conscious to himself of his honesty in it, in that he would not have them published before all, because of the mysteries contained in them; nor were they known or published till the middle of the fourth century, when the forgery could not be so well disproved. I cannot see any mysteries in them, that they should be concealed, if they had been genuine; but I am sure that Christ bids his apostles publish the mysteries of the kingdom of God upon the house-tops. And St. Paul, though there are mysteries in his epistles much more sublime than any of these Constitutions, charges that they should be read to all the holy brethren. Nay, these Constitutions are so wholly in a manner taken up either with moral precepts, or rules of practice in the church, that if they had been what they pretend they had been most fit to be published before all. And though the Apocalypse is so full of mysteries, yet a blessing is pronounced upon the readers and hearers of that prophecy. We must therefore conclude that, whenever they were written, by declining the light they owned themselves to be apocryphal, that is, hidden or concealed; that they durst not mingle themselves with what was given by divine inspiration; to allude to what is said of the ministers (Acts v. 13), Of the rest durst no man join himself to the apostles, for the people magnified them. So that even by their own confession they were not delivered to the churches with the other writings, when the New-Testament canon was solemnly sealed up with that dreadful sentence passed on those that add unto these things.

And as we have thus had attempts made of late upon the purity and sufficiency of our New Testament, by additions to it, so we have likewise had from another quarter a great contempt put upon it by the papal power. The occasion was this: – One Father Quesnel, a French papist, but a Jansenist, nearly thirty years ago, published the New Testament in French, in several small volumes, with Moral Reflections on every verse, to render the reading of it more profitable, and meditation upon it more easy. It was much esteemed in France, for the sake of the piety and devotion which appeared in it, and it had several impressions. The Jesuits were much disgusted, and solicited the pope for the condemnation of it, though the author of it was a papist, and many things in it countenanced popish superstition. After much struggling about it in the court of Rome a bull was at length obtained, at the request of the French king, from the present pope Clement 11 bearing date September 8, 1713, by which the said book, with what title or in what language soever it is printed, is prohibited and condemned; both the New Testament itself, because in many things varying from the vulgar Latin, and the Annotations, as containing divers propositions (above a hundred are enumerated) scandalous and pernicious, injurious to the church and its customs, impious, blasphemous, savouring of heresy. And the propositions are such as these – "That the grace of our Lord Jesus Christ is the effectual principle of all manner of good, is necessary for every good action; for without it nothing is done, nay nothing can be done" – "That it is a sovereign grace, and is an operation of the almighty hand of God" – "That, when God accompanies his word with the internal power of his grace, it operates in the soul the obedience which it demands" – "That faith is the first grace, and the fountain of all others" – "That it is in vain for us to call God our Father, if we do not cry to him with a spirit of love" – "That there is no God, nor religion, where there is no charity" – "That the catholic church comprehends the angels and all the elect and just men of the earth of all ages" – "That it had the Word incarnate for its head, and all the saints for its members" – "That it is profitable and necessary at all times, in all places, and for all sorts of persons, to know the holy Scriptures" – "That the holy obscurity of the word of God is no reason for the laity not reading it" – "That the Lord's day ought to be sanctified by reading books of piety, especially the holy scriptures" – And "that to forbid Christians from reading the scriptures is to prohibit the use of the light to the children of light." Many such positions as these, which the spirit of every good Christian cannot but relish as true and good, are condemned by the pope's bull as impious and blasphemous. And this bull, though strenuously opposed by a great number of the bishops in France, who were well affected to the notions of father Quesnel, was yet received and confirmed by the French king's letters patent, bearing date at Versailles, February 14, 1714, which forbid all manner of persons, upon pain of exemplary punishment, so much as to keep any of those books in their houses; and adjudge any that should hereafter write in defence of the propositions condemned by the pope as disturbers of the peace. It was registered the day following, February 15, by the Parliament of Paris, but with divers provisos and limitations.

By this is appears that popery is still the same thing that ever it was, an enemy to the knowledge of the scriptures, and to the honour of divine grace. What reason have we to bless God that we have liberty to read the scriptures, and have helps to understand and improve them, which we are concerned diligently to make a good use of, that we may not provoke God to give us up into the hands of those powers that would use us in like manner!

I am willing to hope that those to whom the reading of the Exposition of the Old Testament was pleasant will find this yet more pleasant; for this is that part of scripture which does most plainly testify of Christ, and in which that gospel grace which appears unto all men, bringing salvation, shines most clearly. This is the New-Testament milk for babes, the rest is strong meat for strong men. By these, therefore, let us be nourished and strengthened that we my be pressing on towards perfection; and that, having laid the foundation in the history of our blessed Saviour's life, death, and resurrection, and the first preaching of his gospel, we may build upon it by an acquaintance with the mysteries of godliness, to which we shall be further introduced in the Epistles.

I desire I may be read with a candid, and not a critical, eye. I pretend not to gratify the curious; the summit of my ambition is to assist those who are truly serious in searching the scriptures daily. I am sure the work is designed, and hope it is calculated, to promote piety towards God and charity towards our brethren, and that there is not only something in it which may edify, but nothing which may justly offend any good Christian.

If any receive spiritual benefit by my poor endeavours, it will be comfort to me, but let God have all the glory, and that free grace of his which has employed one that is utterly unworthy of such an honour, and enabled one thus far to go on in it who is utterly insufficient for such a service.

Having obtained help of God, I continue hitherto in it, and humbly depend upon the same good hand of my God to carry me on it that which remains, to gird my loins with needful strength and to make my way perfect; and for this I humbly desire the prayers of my friends. One volume more, I hope, will include what is yet to be done; and I will both go about it, and go on with it, as God shall enable me, with all convenient speed; but it is that part of the scripture which, of all others, requires the most care and pains in expounding it. But I trust that as the day so shall the strength be.

Matthew Henry

MATTHEW

Chapter 1

m atthew, surnamed Levi, before his conversion was a publican, or tax-gatherer under the Romans at Capernaum. He is generally allowed to have written his Gospel before any other of the evangelists. The contents of this Gospel, and the evidence of ancient writers, show that it was written primarily for the use of the Jewish nation. The fulfillment of prophecy was regarded by the Jews as strong evidence, therefore this is especially dwelt upon by St. Matthew. Here are particularly selected such parts of our Saviour's history and discourses as were best suited to awaken the Jewish nation to a sense of their sins; to remove their erroneous expectations of an earthly kingdom; to abate their pride and self-conceit; to teach them the spiritual nature and extent of the gospel; and to prepare them for the admission of the Gentiles into the church.

The genealogy of Jesus (1-17). An angel appears to Joseph (18-25).

Verses 1-17 Concerning this genealogy of our Saviour, observe the chief intention. It is not a needless genealogy. It is not a vainglorious one, as those of great men often are. It proves that our Lord Jesus is of the nation and family out of which the Messiah was to arise. The promise of the blessing was made to Abraham and his seed; of the dominion, to David and his seed. It was promised to Abraham that Christ should descend from him, Ge

12:3; 22:18; and to David that he should descend from him, 2Sa 7:12; Ps 89:3, etc.; 132:11; and, therefore, unless Jesus is a son of David, and a son of Abraham, he is not the Messiah. Now this is here proved from well-known records. When the Son of God was pleased to take our nature, he came near to us, in our fallen, wretched condition; but he was perfectly free from sin: and while we read the names in his genealogy, we should not forget how low the Lord of glory stooped to save the human race.

Verses 18-25 Let us look to the circumstances under which the Son of God entered into this lower world, till we learn to despise the vain honours of this world, when compared with piety and holiness. The mystery of Christ's becoming man is to be adored, not curiously inquired into. It was so ordered that Christ should partake of our nature, yet that he should be pure from the defilement of original sin, which has been communicated to all the race of Adam. Observe, it is the thoughtful, not the unthinking, whom God will guide. God's time to come with instruction to his people, is when they are at a loss. Divine comforts most delight the soul when under the pressure of perplexed thoughts. Joseph is told that Mary should bring forth the Saviour of the world. He was to call his name Jesus, a Saviour. Jesus is the same name with Joshua. And the reason of that name is clear, for those whom Christ saves, he saves from their sins; from the guilt of sin by the merit of his death, and from the power of sin by the Spirit of his grace. In saving them from sin, he saves them from wrath and the curse, and all misery, here and hereafter. Christ came to save his people, not in their sins, but from their sins; and so to redeem them from among men, to himself, who is separate from sinners. Joseph did as the angel of the Lord had bidden him, speedily, without delay, and cheerfully, without dispute. By applying the general rules of the written word, we should in all the steps of our lives, particularly the great turns of them, take direction from God, and we shall find this safe and comfortable.

CHAPTER 2

The wise men's search after Christ (1-8). The wise men worship Jesus (9-12). Jesus carried into Egypt (13-15). Herod causes the infants of Bethlehem to be massacred (16-18). Death of Herod, Jesus brought to Nazareth (19-23).

Verses 1-8 Those who live at the greatest distance from the means of grace often use most diligence, and learn to know the most of Christ and his salvation. But no curious arts, or mere human learning, can direct men unto him. We must learn of Christ by attending to the word of God, as a light that shineth in a dark place, and by seeking the teaching of the Holy Spirit. And those in whose hearts the day-star is risen, to give them any thing of the knowledge of Christ, make it their business to worship him. Though Herod was very old, and never had shown affection for his family, and was not himself likely to live till a new-born infant had grown up to manhood, he began to be troubled with the dread of a rival. He understood not the spiritual nature of the Messiah's kingdom. Let us beware of a dead faith. A man may be persuaded of many truths, and yet may hate them, because they interfere with his ambition, or sinful indulgences. Such a belief will make him uneasy, and the more resolved to oppose the truth and the cause of God; and he may be foolish enough to hope for success therein.

Verses 9-12 What joy these wise men felt upon this sight of the star, none know so well as those who, after a long and melancholy night of temptation and desertion, under the power of a spirit of bondage, at length receive the Spirit of adoption, witnessing with their spirits that they are the children of God. We may well think

THE CONCISE COMMENTARY ON THE GOSPELS

what a disappointment it was to them, when they found a cottage was his palace, and his own poor mother the only attendant he had. However, these wise men did not think themselves baffled; but having found the King they sought, they presented their gifts to him. The humble inquirer after Christ will not be stumbled at finding him and his disciples in obscure cottages, after having in vain sought them in palaces and populous cities. Is a soul busy, seeking after Christ? Would it worship him, and does it say, Alas! I am a foolish and poor creature, and have nothing to offer? Nothing! Hast thou not a heart, though unworthy of him, dark, hard, and foul? Give it to him as it is, and be willing that he use and dispose of it as it pleases him; he will take it, and will make it better, and thou shalt never repent having given it to him. He shall frame it to his own likeness, and will give thee himself, and be thine for ever. The gifts the wise men presented were gold, frankincense, and myrrh. Providence sent these as a seasonable relief to Joseph and Mary in their present poor condition. Thus our heavenly Father, who knows what his children need, uses some as stewards to supply the wants of others, and can provide for them, even from the ends of the earth.

Verses 13-15 Egypt had been a house of bondage to Israel, and particularly cruel to the infants of Israel; yet it is to be a place of refuge to the holy Child Jesus. God, when he pleases, can make the worst of places serve the best of purposes. This was a trial of the faith of Joseph and Mary. But their faith, being tried, was found firm. If we and our infants are at any time in trouble, let us remember the straits in which Christ was when an infant.

Verses 16-18 Herod killed all the male children, not only in Bethlehem, but in all the villages of that city. Unbridled wrath, armed with an unlawful power, often carries men to absurd cruelties. It was no unrighteous thing with God to permit this;

every life is forfeited to his justice as soon as it begins. The diseases and deaths of little children are proofs of original sin. But the murder of these infants was their martyrdom. How early did persecution against Christ and his kingdom begin! Herod now thought that he had baffled the Old Testament prophecies, and the efforts of the wise men in finding Christ; but whatever crafty, cruel devices are in men's hearts, the counsel of the Lord shall stand.

Verses 19-23 Egypt may serve to sojourn in, or take shelter in, for awhile, but not to abide in. Christ was sent to the lost sheep of the house of Israel, to them he must return. Did we but look upon the world as our Egypt, the place of our bondage and banishment, and heaven only as our Canaan, our home, our rest, we should as readily arise and depart thither, when we are called for, as Joseph did out of Egypt. The family must settle in Galilee. Nazareth was a place held in bad esteem, and Christ was crucified with this accusation, Jesus the Nazarene. Wherever Providence allots the bounds of our habitation, we must expect to share the reproach of Christ; yet we may glory in being called by his name, sure that if we suffer with him, we shall also be glorified with him.

CHAPTER 3

John the Baptist, His preaching, manner of life, and baptism. (1-6) John reproves the Pharisees and Sadducees (7-12). The baptism of Jesus (13-17).

Verses 1-6 After Malachi there was no prophet until John the Baptist came. He appeared first in the wilderness of Judea. This was not an uninhabited desert, but a part of the country not thickly peopled, nor much enclosed. No place is so remote as to shut us out from the visits of Divine grace. The doctrine he preached was repentance; "Repent ye." The word here used, implies a total alteration in the mind, a change in the judgment, disposition, and affections, another and a better bias of the soul. Consider your ways, change your minds: you have thought amiss; think again, and think aright. True penitents have other thoughts of God and Christ, sin and holiness, of this world and the other, than they had. The change of the mind produces a change of the way. That is gospel repentance, which flows from a sight of Christ, from a sense of his love, and from hopes of pardon and forgiveness through him. It is a great encouragement to us to repent; repent, for your sins shall be pardoned upon your repentance. Return to God in a way of duty, and he will, through Christ, return unto you in the way of mercy. It is still as necessary to repent and humble ourselves, to prepare the way of the Lord, as it then was. There is a great deal to be done, to make way for Christ into a soul, and nothing is more needful than the discovery of sin, and a conviction that we cannot be saved by our own righteousness. The way of sin and Satan is a crooked way; but to prepare a way for Christ, the paths must be made straight, Hebrews 12:13.

Those whose business it is to call others to mourn for sin, and to mortify it, ought themselves to live a serious life, a life of self-denial, and contempt of the world. By giving others this example, John made way for Christ. Many came to John's baptism, but few kept to the profession they made. There may be many forward hearers, where there are few true believers. Curiosity, and love for novelty and variety, may bring many to attend on good preaching, and to be affected for a while, who never are subject to the power of it. Those who received John's doctrine, testified their repentance by confessing their sins. Those only are ready to receive Jesus Christ as their righteousness, who are brought with sorrow and shame to own their guilt. The benefits of the kingdom of heaven, now at hand, were thereupon sealed to them by baptism. John washed them with water, in token that God would cleanse them from all their iniquities, thereby intimating, that by nature and practice all were polluted, and could not be admitted among the people of God, unless washed from their sins in the fountain Christ was to open, Zechariah 13:1.

Verses 7-12 To make application to the souls of the hearers, is the life of preaching; so it was of John's preaching. The Pharisees laid their chief stress on outward observances, neglecting the weightier matters of the moral law, and the spiritual meaning of their legal ceremonies. Others of them were detestable hypocrites, making their pretences to holiness a cloak for iniquity.

The Sadducees ran into the opposite extreme, denying the existence of spirits, and a future state. They were the scornful infidels of that time and country. There is a wrath to come. It is the great concern of everyone to flee from that wrath. God, who delights not in our ruin, has warned us; he warns by the written word, by ministers, by conscience. And those are not worthy of the name of penitents, or their privileges, who say they are sorry for their sins, yet persist in them. It becomes penitents to be humble and low in their own eyes, to be thankful for the least mercy, patient under the greatest affliction, to be watchful against all appearances of sin, to abound in every duty, and to be charitable in judging others.

Here is a word of caution, not to trust in outward privileges. There is a great deal which carnal hearts are apt to say within themselves, to put aside the convincing, commanding power of the word of God. Multitudes, by resting in the honours and mere advantages of their being members of an outward church, come short of heaven. Here is a word of terror to the careless and secure. Our corrupt hearts cannot be made to produce good fruit, unless the regenerating Spirit of Christ graft the good word of God upon them. And every tree, however high in gifts and honours, however green in outward professions and performances, if it bring not forth good fruit, the fruits meet for repentance, is hewn down and cast into the fire of God's wrath, the fittest place for barren trees: what else are they good for? If not fit for fruit, they are fit for fuel.

John shows the design and intention of Christ's appearing, which they were now speedily to expect. No outward forms can make us clean. No ordinances, by whomsoever administered, or after whatever mode, can supply the want of the baptism of the Holy Ghost and of fire. The purifying and cleansing power of the Holy Spirit alone can produce that purity of heart, and those holy affections, which accompany salvation. It is Christ who baptizes with the Holy Ghost. This he did in the extraordinary gifts of the Spirit sent upon the apostles, Acts 2:4. This he does in the graces and comforts of the Spirit, given to those that ask him, Luke 11:13; John 7:38,39; see Acts 11:16.

Observe here, the outward church is Christ's floor, Isaiah 21:10. True believers are as wheat, substantial, useful, and valuable;

hypocrites are as chaff, light and empty, useless and worthless, carried about with every wind; these are mixed, good and bad, in the same outward communion. There is a day coming when the wheat and chaff shall be separated. The last judgment will be the distinguishing day, when saints and sinners shall be parted forever. In heaven the saints are brought together, and no longer scattered; they are safe, and no longer exposed; separated from corrupt neighbours without, and corrupt affections within, and there is no chaff among them. Hell is the unquenchable fire, which will certainly be the portion and punishment of hypocrites and unbelievers. Here life and death, good and evil, are set before us: according as we now are in the field, we shall be then in the floor.

Verses 13-17 Christ's gracious condescensions are so surprising, that even the strongest believers at first can hardly believe them; so deep and mysterious, that even those who know his mind well, are apt to start objections against the will of Christ. And those who have much of the Spirit of God while here, see that they need to apply to Christ for more. Christ does not deny that John had need to be baptized of him, yet declares he will now be baptized of John. Christ is now in a state of humiliation. Our Lord Jesus looked upon it as well becoming him to fulfill all righteousness, to own every Divine institution, and to show his readiness to comply with all God's righteous precepts.

In and through Christ, the heavens are opened to the children of men. This descent of the Spirit upon Christ, showed that he was endued with his sacred influences without measure. The fruit of the Spirit is love, joy, peace, long-suffering, gentleness, goodness, faith, meekness, temperance. At Christ's baptism there was a manifestation of the three Persons in the sacred Trinity. The Father confirming the Son to be Mediator; the Son solemnly entering upon the work; the Holy Spirit descending on him, to be through his mediation communicated to his people. In Him our spiritual sacrifices are acceptable, for He is the altar that sanctifies every gift, 1 Peter 2:5. Out of Christ, God is a consuming fire, but in Christ, a reconciled Father. This is the sum of the gospel, which we must by faith cheerfully embrace.

CHAPTER 4

The temptation of Christ (1-11). The opening of Christ's ministry in Galilee (12-17). Call of Simon and others (18-22). Jesus teaches and works miracles (23-25).

Verses 1-11 Concerning Christ's temptation, observe, that directly after he was declared to be the Son of God, and the Saviour of the world, he was tempted; great privileges, and special tokens of Divine favour, will not secure any from being tempted. But if the Holy Spirit witness to our being adopted as children of God, that will answer all the suggestions of the evil spirit. Christ was directed to the combat. If we presume upon our own strength, and tempt the devil to tempt us, we provoke God to leave us to ourselves. Others are tempted, when drawn aside of their own lust, and enticed, James 1:14; but our Lord Jesus had no corrupt nature, therefore he was tempted only by the devil.

In the temptation of Christ it appears that our enemy is subtle, spiteful, and very daring; but he can be resisted. It is a comfort to us that Christ suffered, being tempted; for thus it appears that our temptations, if not yielded to, are not sins, they are afflictions only. Satan aimed in all his temptations, to bring Christ to sin against God.

1. He tempted him to despair of his Father's goodness, and to distrust his Father's care concerning him. It is one of the wiles of Satan to take advantage of our outward condition; and those who are brought into straits have need to double their guard. Christ answered all the temptations of Satan with, "It is written;" to set us an example, he appealed to what was written in the Scriptures. This method we must take, when at any time we are tempted to sin. Let us learn not to take any wrong courses for our supply, when our wants are ever so pressing: in some way or other the Lord will provide.

2. Satan tempted Christ to presume upon his Father's power and protection, in a point of safety. Nor are any extremes more dangerous than despair and presumption, especially in the affairs of our souls. Satan has no objection to holy places as the scene of his assaults. Let us not, in any place, be off our watch. The holy city is the place, where he does, with the greatest advantage, tempt men to pride and presumption. All high places are slippery places; advancements in the world makes a man a mark for Satan to shoot his fiery darts at.

Is Satan so well versed in Scripture as to be able to quote it readily? He is so. It is possible for a man to have his head full of Scripture notions, and his mouth full of Scripture expressions, while his heart is full of bitter enmity to God and to all goodness. Satan misquoted the words. If we go out of our way, out of the way of our duty, we forfeit the promise, and put ourselves out of God's protection. This passage, Deuteronomy 8:3, made against the tempter, therefore he left out part. This promise is firm and stands good. But shall we continue in sin, that grace may abound? No.

413

3. Satan tempted Christ to idolatry with the offer of the kingdoms of the world, and the glory of them. The glory of the world is the most charming temptation to the unthinking and unwary; by that men are most easily imposed upon. Christ was tempted to worship Satan. He rejected the proposal with abhorrence. "Get thee hence, Satan!" Some temptations are openly wicked; and they are not merely to be opposed, but rejected at once. It is good to be quick and firm in resisting temptation. If we resist the devil he will flee from us. But the soul that deliberates is almost overcome. We find but few who can decidedly reject such baits as Satan offers; yet what is a man profited if he gain the whole world, and lose his own soul?

Christ was succored after the temptation, for his encouragement to go on in his undertaking, and for our encouragement to trust in him; for as he knew, by experience, what it was to suffer, being tempted, so he knew what it was to be succored, being tempted; therefore we may expect, not only that he will feel for his tempted people, but that he will come to them with seasonable relief.

Verses 12-17 It is just with God to take the gospel and the means of grace, from those that slight them and thrust them away. Christ will not stay long where he is not welcome. Those who are without Christ, are in the dark. They were sitting in this condition, a contented posture; they chose it rather than light; they were willingly ignorant. When the gospel comes, light comes; when it comes to any place, when it comes to any soul, it makes day there. Light discovers and directs; so does the gospel. The doctrine of repentance is right gospel doctrine. Not only the austere John Baptist, but the gracious Jesus, preached repentance. There is still the same reason to do so. The kingdom of heaven was not reckoned to be fully come, till the pouring out of the Holy Spirit after Christ's ascension.

Verses 18-22 When Christ began to preach, he began to gather disciples, who should be hearers, and afterwards preachers of his doctrine, who should be witnesses of his miracles, and afterwards testify concerning them. He went not to Herod's court, not to Jerusalem, among the chief priests and the elders, but to the sea of Galilee, among the fishermen. The same power which called Peter and Andrew, could have wrought upon Annas and Caiaphas, for with God nothing is impossible. But Christ chooses the foolish things of the world to confound the wise.

Diligence in an honest calling is pleasing to Christ, and it is no hindrance to a holy life. Idle people are more open to the temptations of Satan than to the calls of God. It is a happy and hopeful thing to see children careful of their parents, and dutiful. When Christ comes, it is good to be found doing. Am I in Christ? Is a very needful question to ask ourselves; and, next to that, Am I in my calling? They had followed Christ before, as common disciples, John 1:37; now they must leave their calling. Those who would follow Christ aright, must, at his command, leave all things to follow him, must be ready to part with them. This instance of the power of the Lord Jesus encourages us to depend upon his grace. He speaks, and it is done.

Verses 23-25 Wherever Christ went, he confirmed his Divine mission by miracles, which were emblems of the healing power of his doctrine, and the influences of the Spirit which accompanied it. We do not now find the Saviour's miraculous healing power in our bodies; but if we are cured by medicine, the praise is equally his. Three general words are here used. He healed every sickness or disease; none was too bad; none too hard, for Christ to heal with a word. Three diseases are named; the palsy, which is the greatest weakness of the body; lunacy, which is the greatest malady of the mind; and possession of the devil, which is the greatest misery

415

and calamity of both; yet Christ healed all, and by thus curing bodily diseases, showed that his great errand into the world was to cure spiritual maladies. Sin is the sickness, disease, and torment of the soul: Christ came to take away sin, and so to heal the soul.

CHAPTER 5

Christ's sermon on the mount (1, 2). Who are blessed (3-12). Exhortations and warnings (13-16). Christ came to confirm the law (17-20). The sixth commandment (21-26). The seventh commandment. (27-32). The third commandment (33-37). The law of retaliation (38-42). The law of love explained (43-48).

Verses 1-2 None will find happiness in this world or the next, who do not seek it from Christ by the rule of his word. He taught them what was the evil they should abhor, and what the good they should seek and abound in.

Verses 3-12 Our Saviour here gives eight characters of blessed people, which represent to us the principal graces of a Christian.

1. The poor in spirit are happy. These bring their minds to their condition, when it is a low condition. They are humble and lowly in their own eyes. They see their want, bewail their guilt, and thirst after a Redeemer. The kingdom of grace is of such; the kingdom of glory is for them.

2. Those that mourn are happy. That godly sorrow which worketh true repentance, watchfulness, a humble mind, and continual dependence for acceptance on the mercy of God in Christ Jesus, with constant seeking the Holy Spirit, to cleanse away the remaining evil, seems here to be intended. Heaven is the joy of our Lord; a mountain of joy, to which our way is through a vale of tears. Such mourners shall be comforted by their God.

3. The meek are happy. The meek are those who quietly submit to God; who can bear insult; are silent, or return a soft answer; who, in their patience, keep possession of their own souls, when they can scarcely keep possession of anything else. These meek ones are happy, even in this world. Meekness promotes wealth, comfort, and safety, even in this world.

4. Those who hunger and thirst after righteousness are happy. Righteousness is here put for all spiritual blessings. These are purchased for us by the righteousness of Christ, confirmed by the faithfulness of God. Our desires of spiritual blessings must be earnest. Though all desires for grace are not grace, yet such a desire as this, is a desire of God's own raising, and he will not forsake the work of his own hands.

5. The merciful are happy. We must not only bear our own afflictions patiently, but we must do all we can to help those who are in misery. We must have compassion on the souls of others, and help them; pity those who are in sin, and seek to snatch them as brands out of the burning.

6. The pure in heart are happy; for they shall see God. Here holiness and happiness are fully described and put together. The heart must be purified by faith, and kept for God. Create in me such a clean

heart, O God. None but the pure are capable of seeing God, nor would heaven be happiness to the impure. As God cannot endure to look upon their iniquity, so they cannot look upon his purity.

7. The peace-makers are happy. They love, and desire, and delight in peace; and study to be quiet. They keep the peace that it be not broken, and recover it when it is broken. If the peace-makers are blessed, woe to the peace-breakers!

8. Those who are persecuted for righteousness' sake are happy. This saying is peculiar to Christianity; and it is more largely insisted upon than any of the rest. Yet there is nothing in our sufferings that can merit of God; but God will provide that those who lose for him, though life itself, shall not lose by him in the end.

Blessed Jesus! How different are thy maxims from those of men of this world! They call the proud happy, and admire the gay, the rich, the powerful, and the victorious. May we find mercy from the Lord; may we be owned as his children, and inherit his kingdom. With these enjoyments and hopes, we may cheerfully welcome low or painful circumstances.

Verses 13-16 Ye are the salt of the earth. Mankind, lying in ignorance and wickedness, were as a vast heap, ready to putrefy; but Christ sent forth his disciples, by their lives and doctrines to season it with knowledge and grace. If they are not such as they should be, they are as salt that has lost its savour. If a man can take up the profession of Christ, and yet remain graceless, no other doctrine, no other means, can make him profitable. Our light must shine, by doing such good works as men may see. What is between God and our souls, must be kept to ourselves; but that which is of itself open to the sight of men, we must study to make suitable to our profession, and praiseworthy. We must aim at the glory of God.

Verses 17-20 Let none suppose that Christ allows his people to trifle with any commands of God's holy law. No sinner partakes of Christ's justifying righteousness, till he repents of his evil deeds. The mercy revealed in the gospel leads the believer to still deeper self-abhorrence. The law is the Christian's rule of duty, and he delights therein. If a man, pretending to be Christ's disciple, encourages himself in any allowed disobedience to the holy law of God, or teaches others to do the same, whatever his station or reputation among men may be, he can be no true disciple. Christ's righteousness, imputed to us by faith alone, is needed by every one that enters the kingdom of grace or of glory; but the new creation of the heart to holiness, produces a thorough change in a man's temper and conduct.

Verses 21-26 The Jewish teachers had taught that nothing except actual murder was forbidden by the sixth commandment. Thus they explained away its spiritual meaning. Christ showed the full meaning of this commandment; according to which we must be judged hereafter, and therefore ought to be ruled now. All rash anger is heart murder. By our brother, here, we are to understand any person, though ever so much below us, for we are all made of one blood.

"Raca," is a scornful word, and comes from pride: "Thou fool," is a spiteful word, and comes from hatred. Malicious slanders and censures are poison that kills secretly and slowly. Christ told them that how light soever they made of these sins, they would certainly be called into judgment for them.

We ought carefully to preserve Christian love and peace with all our brethren; and if at any time there is a quarrel, we should confess our fault, humble ourselves to our brother, making or offering satisfaction for wrong done in word or deed: and we should do this quickly; because, till this is done, we are unfit for communion with God in holy ordinances. And when we are preparing for any religious exercises, it is good for us to make that an occasion of serious reflection and self-examination. What is here said is very applicable to our being reconciled to God through Christ. While we are alive, we are in the way to his judgment-seat; after death, it will be too late. When we consider the importance of the case, and the uncertainty of life, how needful it is to seek peace with God, without delay!

Verses 27-32 Victory over the desires of the heart, must be attended with painful exertions. But it must be done. Everything is bestowed to save us from our sins, not in them. All our senses and powers must be kept from those things which lead to transgression. Those who lead others into temptation to sin, by dress or in other ways, or leave them in it, or expose them to it, make themselves guilty of their sin, and will be accountable for it. If painful operations are submitted to, that our lives may be saved, what ought our minds to shrink from, when the salvation of our souls is concerned? There is tender mercy under all the Divine requirements, and the grace and consolations of the Spirit will enable us to attend to them.

Verses 33-37 There is no reason to consider that solemn oaths in a court of justice, or on other proper occasions, are wrong, provided they are taken with due reverence. But all oaths taken without necessity, or in common conversation, must be sinful, as well as all those expressions which are appeals to God, though persons think thereby to evade the guilt of swearing. The worse men are, the less they are bound by oaths; the better they are, the less there is need for them. Our Lord does not enjoin the precise terms wherein we are to affirm or deny, but such a constant regard to truth as would render oaths unnecessary.

Verses 38-42 The plain instruction is, "Suffer any injury that can be borne, for the sake of peace, committing your concerns to the Lord's keeping." And the sum of all is, that Christians must avoid disputing and striving. If any say, "Flesh and blood cannot pass by such an affront," let them remember that flesh and blood shall not inherit the kingdom of God; and those who act upon right principles will have most peace and comfort.

Verses 43-48 The Jewish teachers by "neighbour" understood only those who were of their own country, nation, and religion, whom they were pleased to look upon as their friends. The Lord Jesus teaches that we must do all the real kindness we can to all, especially to their souls. We must pray for them. While many will render good for good, we must render good for evil; and this will speak a nobler principle than most men act by. Others salute their brethren, and embrace those of their own party, and way, and opinion, but we must not so confine our respect. It is the duty of Christians to desire, and aim at, and press towards perfection in grace and holiness. And therein we must study to conform ourselves to the example of our heavenly Father, 1 Peter 1:15,16.

Surely more is to be expected from the followers of Christ than from others; surely more will be found in them than in others. Let us beg of God to enable us to prove ourselves his children.

CHAPTER 6

Against hypocrisy in almsgiving (1-4). Against hypocrisy in prayer (5-8). How to pray (9-15). Respecting fasting (16-18) Evil of being worldly-minded (19-24). Trust in God commended (25-34).

Verses 1-4 Our Lord next warned against hypocrisy and outward show in religious duties. What we do, must be done from an inward principle, that we may be approved of God, not that we may be praised of men. In these verses we are cautioned against hypocrisy in giving alms. Take heed of it. It is a subtle sin; and vain-glory creeps into what we do, before we are aware. But the duty is not the less necessary and excellent for being abused by hypocrites to serve their pride. The doom Christ passes, at first may seem a promise, but it is their reward; not the reward God promises to those who do good, but the reward hypocrites promise themselves, and a poor reward it is; they did it to be seen of men, and they are seen of men. When we take least notice of our good deeds ourselves, God takes most notice of them. He will reward thee; not as a master who gives his servant what he earns, and no more, but as a Father who gives abundantly to his son that serves him.

Verses 5-8 It is taken for granted that all who are disciples of Christ pray. You may as soon find a living man that does not breathe, as a living Christian that does not pray. If prayerless, then graceless.

The Scribes and Pharisees were guilty of two great faults in prayer, vain-glory and vain repetitions. "Verily they have their reward;" if in so great a matter as is between us and God, when we are at prayer, we can look to so poor a thing as the praise of men, it is just that it should be all our reward. Yet there is not a secret, sudden breathing after God, but he observes it. It is called a reward, but it is of grace, not of debt; what merit can there be in begging? If he does not give his people what they ask, it is because he knows they do not need it, and that it is not for their good. So far is God from being wrought upon by the length or words of our prayers, that the most powerful intercessions are those which are made with groanings that cannot be uttered. Let us well study what is shown of the frame of mind in which our prayers should be offered, and learn daily from Christ how to pray.

Verses 9-15 Christ saw it needful to show his disciples what must commonly be the matter and method of their prayer. Not that we are tied up to the use of this only, or of this always; yet, without doubt, it is very good to use it. It has much in a little; and it is used acceptably no further than it is used with understanding, and without being needlessly repeated.

The petitions are six; the first three relate more expressly to God and his honour, the last three to our own concerns, both temporal and spiritual. This prayer teaches us to seek first the kingdom of God and his righteousness, and that all other things shall be added. After the things of God's glory, kingdom, and will, we pray for the needful supports and comforts of this present life.

Every word here has a lesson in it. We ask for bread; that teaches us sobriety and temperance: and we ask only for bread; not for what we do not need. We ask for our bread; that teaches us honesty and industry: we do not ask for the bread of others, nor the bread of deceit, Proverbs 20:17; nor the bread of idleness, Proverbs 31:27, but the bread honestly gotten. We ask for our daily bread; which teaches us constantly to depend upon Divine Providence. We beg of God to give it us; not sell it us, nor lend it us, but give it. The greatest of men must be beholden to the mercy of God for their daily bread. We pray, "Give it to us." This teaches us a compassion for the poor. Also that we ought to pray with our families. We pray that God would give it us this day; which teaches us to renew the desires of our souls toward God, as the wants of our bodies are renewed.

As the day comes we must pray to our heavenly Father, and reckon we could as well go a day without food, as without prayer. We are taught to hate and dread sin while we hope for mercy, to distrust ourselves, to rely on the providence and grace of God to keep us from it, to be prepared to resist the tempter, and not to become tempters of others.

Here is a promise, If you forgive, your heavenly Father will also forgive. We must forgive, as we hope to be forgiven. Those who desire to find mercy with God, must show mercy to their brethren. Christ came into the world as the great Peace-maker, not only to reconcile us to God, but one to another.

Verses 16-18 Religious fasting is a duty required of the disciples of Christ, but it is not so much a duty itself, as a means to dispose us for other duties. Fasting is the humbling of the soul, Psalms 35:13; that is the inside of the duty; let that, therefore, be thy principal care, and as to the outside of it, covet not to let it be seen. God sees in secret, and will reward openly.

Verses 19-24 Worldly-mindedness is a common and fatal symptom of hypocrisy, for by no sin can Satan have a surer and faster hold of the soul, under the cloak of a profession of religion. Something the soul will have, which it looks upon as the best thing; in which it has pleasure and confidence above other things. Christ counsels to make our best things the joys and glories of the other world, those things not seen which are eternal, and to place our happiness in them.

There are treasures in heaven. It is our wisdom to give all diligence to make our title to eternal life sure through Jesus Christ, and to look on all things here below, as not worthy to be compared with it, and to be content with nothing short of it. It is happiness above and beyond the changes and chances of time, an inheritance incorruptible. The worldly man is wrong in his first principle; therefore all his reasonings and actions therefrom must be wrong. It is equally to be applied to false religion; that which is deemed light is thick darkness. This is an awful, but a common case; we should therefore carefully examine our leading principles by the word of God, with earnest prayer for the teaching of his Spirit.

A man may do some service to two masters, but he can devote himself to the service of no more than one. God requires the whole heart, and will not share it with the world. When two masters oppose each other, no man can serve both. He who holds to the world and loves it, must despise God; he who loves God, must give up the friendship of the world.

Verses 25-34 There is scarcely any sin against which our Lord Jesus more warns his disciples, than disquieting, distracting, distrustful cares about the things of this life. This often ensnares the poor as much as the love of wealth does the rich. But there is a carefulness about temporal things which is a duty, though we must not carry these lawful cares too far.

Take no thought for your life. Not about the length of it; but refer it to God to lengthen or shorten it as he pleases; our times are in his hand, and they are in a good hand. Not about the comforts of this life; but leave it to God to make it bitter or sweet as he pleases. Food and raiment God has promised, therefore we may expect them. Take no thought for the morrow, for the time to come. Be not anxious for the future, how you shall live next year, or when you are old, or what you shall leave behind you. As we must not boast of tomorrow, so we must not care for tomorrow, or the events of it.

God has given us life, and has given us the body. And what can he not do for us, who did that? If we take care about our souls and for eternity, which are more than the body and its life, we may leave it to God to provide for us food and raiment, which are less. Improve this as an encouragement to trust in God. We must reconcile ourselves to our worldly estate, as we do to our stature. We cannot alter the disposals of Providence, therefore we must submit and resign ourselves to them. Thoughtfulness for our souls is the best cure of thoughtfulness for the world. Seek first the kingdom of God, and make religion your business: say not that this is the way to starve; no, it is the way to be well provided for, even in this world.

The conclusion of the whole matter is, that it is the will and command of the Lord Jesus, that by daily prayers we may get strength to bear us up under our daily troubles, and to arm us against the temptations that attend them, and then let none of these things move us. Happy are those who take the Lord for their God, and make full proof of it by trusting themselves wholly to his wise disposal. Let thy Spirit convince us of sin in the want of this disposition, and take away the worldliness of our hearts.

CHAPTER 7

Christ reproves rash judgment (1-6). Encouragements to prayer (7-11). The broad and narrow way (12-14). Against false prophets (15-20). To be doers of the word, not hearers only (21-29).

Verses 1-6 We must judge ourselves, and judge of our own acts, but not make our word a law to everybody. We must not judge rashly, nor pass judgment upon our brother without any ground. We must not make the worst of people. Here is a just reproof to those who quarrel with their brethren for small faults, while they allow themselves in greater ones. Some sins are as motes, while others are as beams; some as a gnat, others as a camel. Not that there is any sin little; if it be a mote, or splinter, it is in the eye; if a gnat, it is in the throat; both are painful and dangerous, and we cannot be easy or well till they are got out. That which charity teaches us to call but a splinter in our brother's eye, true repentance and godly sorrow will teach us to call a beam in our own. It is as strange that a man can be in a sinful, miserable condition, and not be aware of it, as that a man should have a beam in his eye, and not consider it; but the god of this world blinds their minds. Here is a good rule for reprovers; first reform thyself.

Verses 7-11 Prayer is the appointed means for obtaining what we need. Pray; pray often; make a business of prayer, and be serious and earnest in it. Ask, as a beggar asks alms. Ask, as a traveller asks the way. Seek, as for a thing of value that we have lost; or as the merchantman that seeks goodly pearls. Knock, as he that desires to enter into the house knocks at the door. Sin has shut and barred the door against us; by prayer we knock. Whatever you pray for, according to the promise, shall be given you, if God see it fit for you, and what would you have more? This is made to apply to all that pray aright; every one that asketh receiveth, whether Jew or Gentile, young or old, rich or poor, high or low, master or servant, learned or unlearned, all are alike welcome to the throne of grace, if they come in faith. It is explained by a comparison taken from earthly parents, and their readiness to give their children what they ask. Parents are often foolishly fond, but God is all-wise; he knows what we need, what we desire, and what is fit for us. Let us never suppose our heavenly Father would bid us pray, and then refuse to hear, or give us what would be hurtful.

Verses 12-14 Christ came to teach us, not only what we are to know and believe, but what we are to do; not only toward God, but toward men; not only toward those of our party and persuasion, but toward men in general, all with whom we have to do. We must do that to our neighbour which we ourselves acknowledge to be fit and reasonable. We must, in our dealings with men, suppose ourselves in the same case and circumstances with those we have to do with, and act accordingly.

There are but two ways right and wrong, good and evil; the way to heaven and the way to hell; in the one or other of these all are walking: there is no middle place hereafter, no middle way now. All the children of men are saints or sinners, godly or ungodly. See concerning the way of sin and sinners, that the gate is wide, and stands open. You may go in at this gate with all your lusts about you; it gives no check to appetites or passions. It is a broad way; there are many paths in it; there is choice of sinful ways. There is a large company in this way. But what profit is there in being willing to go to hell with others, because they will not go to heaven with us?

The way to eternal life is narrow. We are not in heaven as soon as we are got through the strait gate. Self must be denied, the body kept under, and corruptions mortified. Daily temptations must be resisted; duties must be done. We must watch in all things, and walk with care; and we must go through much tribulation. And yet this way should invite us all; it leads to life: to present comfort in the favour of God, which is the life of the soul; to eternal bliss, the hope of which at the end of our way, should make all the difficulties of the road easy to us.

This plain declaration of Christ has been disregarded by many who have taken pains to explain it away; but in all ages the real disciple of Christ has been looked on as a singular, unfashionable character; and all that have sided with the greater number, have gone on in the broad road to destruction. If we would serve God, we must be firm in our religion. Can we often hear of the strait gate and the narrow way, and how few there are that find it, without being in pain for ourselves, or considering whether we are entered on the narrow way, and what progress we are making in it?

Verses 15-20 Nothing so much prevents men from entering the strait gate, and becoming true followers of Christ, as the carnal, soothing, flattering doctrines of those who oppose the truth. They may be known by the drift and effects of their doctrines. Some part of their temper and conduct is contrary to the mind of Christ. Those opinions come not from God that lead to sin.

Verses 21-29 Christ here shows that it will not be enough to own him for our Master, only in word and tongue. It is necessary to our happiness that we believe in Christ, that we repent of sin, that we live a holy life, that we love one another. This is his will, even our sanctification.

Let us take heed of resting in outward privileges and doings, lest we deceive ourselves, and perish eternally, as multitudes do, with a lie in our right hand. Let every one that names the name of Christ, depart from all sin. There are others, whose religion rests in bare hearing, and it goes no further; their heads are filled with empty notions.

These two sorts of hearers are represented as two builders. This parable teaches us to hear and do the sayings of the Lord Jesus: some may seem hard to flesh and blood, but they must be done. Christ is laid for a foundation, and everything besides Christ is sand. Some build their hopes upon worldly prosperity; others upon an outward profession of religion. Upon these they venture; but they are all sand, too weak to bear such a fabric as our hopes of heaven.

There is a storm coming that will try every man's work. When God takes away the soul, where is the hope of the hypocrite? The house fell in the storm, when the builder had most need of it, and expected it would be a shelter to him. It fell when it was too late to build another. May the Lord make us wise builders for eternity. Then nothing shall separate us from the love of Christ Jesus.

The multitudes were astonished at the wisdom and power of Christ's doctrine. And this sermon, ever so often read over, is always new. Every word proves its Author to be Divine. Let us be more and more decided and earnest, making some one or other of these blessednesses and Christian graces the main subject of our thoughts, even for weeks together. Let us not rest in general and confused desires after them, whereby we grasp at all, but catch nothing.

CHAPTER 8

Multitudes follow Christ (1). He heals a leper (2-4). A centurion's servant healed (5-13). Cure of Peter's wife's mother (14-17). The scribe's zealous proposal (18-22). Christ in a storm (23-27). He heals two possessed with devils (28-34).

Verse 1 This verse refers to the close of the foregoing sermon. Those to whom Christ has made himself known, desire to know more of him.

Verses 2-4 In these verses we have an account of Christ's cleansing a leper, who came and worshipped him, as one clothed with Divine power. This cleansing directs us, not only to apply to Christ, who has power over bodily diseases, for the cure of them, but it also teaches us in what manner to apply to him. When we cannot be sure of God's will, we may be sure of his wisdom and mercy. No guilt is so great, but there is that in Christ's blood which atones for it; no corruption so strong, but there is that in his grace which can subdue it. To be made clean we must commend ourselves to his pity; we cannot demand it as a debt, but we must humbly request it as a favour. Those who by faith apply to Christ for mercy and grace, may be sure that he is freely willing to give them the mercy and grace they thus seek. And those afflictions are blessed that bring us to know Christ, and cause us to seek help and salvation from him. Let those who are cleansed from their spiritual leprosy, go to Christ's ministers and open their case, that they may advise, comfort, and pray for them.

Verses 5-13 This centurion was a heathen, a Roman soldier. Though he was a soldier, yet he was a godly man. No man's calling or

431

place will be an excuse for unbelief and sin. See how he states his servant's case. We should concern ourselves for the souls of our children and servants, who are spiritually sick, who feel not spiritual evils, who know not that which is spiritually good; and we should bring them to Christ by faith and prayers.

Observe his self-abasement. Humble souls are made more humble by Christ's gracious dealings with them. Observe his great faith. The more diffident we are of ourselves, the stronger will be our confidence in Christ. Herein the centurion owns him to have Divine power, and a full command of all the creatures and powers of nature, as a master over his servants. Such servants we all should be to God; we must go and come, according to the directions of his word and the disposals of his providence. But when the Son of man comes he finds little faith, therefore he finds little fruit.

An outward profession may cause us to be called children of the kingdom; but if we rest in that, and have nothing else to show, we shall be cast out. The servant got a cure of his disease, and the master got the approval of his faith. What was said to him, is said to all, "Believe, and ye shall receive; only believe." See the power of Christ, and the power of faith. The healing of our souls is at once the effect and evidence of our interest in the blood of Christ.

Verses 14-17 Peter had a wife, yet was an apostle of Christ, who showed that he approved of the married state, by being thus kind to Peter's wife's relations. The church of Rome, which forbids ministers to marry, goes contrary to that apostle upon whom they rest so much. He had his wife's mother with him in his family, which is an example to be kind to our relations.

In spiritual healing, the Scripture speaks the word, the Spirit gives the touch, touches the heart, touches the hand. Those who recover from fevers, commonly are weak and feeble some time after; but to show that this cure was above the power of nature, the woman was at once so well as to go about the business of the house.

The miracles which Jesus did being noised abroad, many thronged to him. He healed all that were sick, though the patient was ever so mean, and the case ever so bad. Many are the diseases and calamities to which we are liable in the body; and there is more, in those words of the gospel, that Jesus Christ bore our sicknesses and carried our sorrows, to support and comfort us under them, than in all the writings of the philosophers. Let us not grudge labour, trouble, or expense in doing good to others.

Verses 18-22 One of the scribes was too hasty in promising; he proffers himself to be a close follower of Christ. He seems to be very resolute. Many resolutions for religion are produced by sudden conviction, and taken up without due consideration; these come to nothing.

When this scribe offered to follow Christ, one would think he should have been encouraged; one scribe might do more credit and service than twelve fishermen; but Christ saw his heart, and answered to its thoughts, and therein teaches all how to come to Christ. His resolve seems to have been from a worldly, covetous principle; but Christ had not a place to lay his head on, and if he follows him, he must not expect to fare better than he fared. We have reason to think this scribe went away.

Another was too slow. Delay in doing is as bad on the one hand, as hastiness in resolving is on the other. He asked leave to attend his father to his grave, and then he would be at Christ's service. This seemed reasonable, yet it was not right. He had not true zeal for the work. Burying the dead, especially a dead father, is a good work, but it is not thy work at this time. If Christ requires our service, affection even for the nearest and dearest relatives, and for things otherwise our duty, must give way. An unwilling mind never wants an excuse. Jesus said to him, Follow me; and, no doubt, power went with this word to him as to others; he did follow Christ, and cleaved to him. The scribe said, I will follow thee; to this man Christ said, Follow me; comparing them together, it shows that we are brought to Christ by the force of his call to us, Romans 9:16.

Verses 23-27 It is a comfort to those who go down to the sea in ships, and are often in perils there, to reflect that they have a Saviour to trust in and pray to, who knows what it is to be on the water, and to be in storms there. Those who are passing with Christ over the ocean of this world, must expect storms. His human nature, like to ours in everything but sin, was wearied, and he slept at this time to try the faith of his disciples. They, in their fear, came to their Master.

Thus is it in a soul; when lusts and temptations are swelling and raging, and God is, as it were, asleep to it, this brings it to the brink of despair. Then it cries for a word from his mouth, Lord Jesus, keep not silence to me, or I am undone. Many that have true faith, are weak in it. Christ's disciples are apt to be disquieted with fears in a stormy day; to torment themselves that things are bad with them, and with dismal thoughts that they will be worse.

Great storms of doubt and fear in the soul, under the power of the spirit of bondage, sometimes end in a wonderful calm, created and spoken by the Spirit of adoption. They were astonished. They never saw a storm so turned at once into a perfect calm. He that can do this, can do any thing, which encourages confidence and comfort in him, in the most stormy day, within or without, Isaiah 26:4.

Verses 28-34 The devils have nothing to do with Christ as a Saviour; they neither have, nor hope for any benefit from him. Oh the depth of this mystery of Divine love; that fallen man has so much to do with Christ, when fallen angels have nothing to do with him! Hebrews 2:16.

Surely here was torment, to be forced to own the excellence that is in Christ, and yet they had no part in him. The devils desire not to have anything to do with Christ as a Ruler. See whose language those speak, who will have nothing to do with the gospel of Christ. But it is not true that the devils have nothing to do with Christ as a Judge; for they have, and they know it, and thus it is with all the children of men. Satan and his instruments can go no further than he permits; they must quit possession when he commands. They cannot break his hedge of protection about his people; they cannot enter even a swine without his leave. They had leave.

God often, for wise and holy ends, permits the efforts of Satan's rage. Thus the devil hurries people to sin; hurries them to what they have resolved against, which they know will be shame and grief to them: miserable is the condition of those who are led captive by him at his will. There are a great many who prefer their swine before the Saviour, and so come short of Christ and salvation by him. They desire Christ to depart out of their hearts, and will not suffer his word to have place in them, because he and his word would destroy their brutish lusts, those swine which they give themselves up to feed. And justly will Christ forsake all that are weary of him; and say hereafter, "Depart, ye cursed," to those who now say to the Almighty, "Depart from us."

CHAPTER 9

Jesus returns to Capernaum, and heals a paralytic (1-8). Matthew called (9) Matthew, or Levi's feast (10-13). Objections of John's disciples (14-17). Christ raises the daughter of Jairus, He heals the issue of blood (18-26). He heals two blind men (27-31). Christ casts out a dumb spirit (32-34). He sends forth the apostles (35-38).

Verses 1-8 The faith of the friends of the paralytic in bringing him to Christ, was a strong faith; they firmly believed that Jesus Christ both could and would heal him. A strong faith regards no obstacles in pressing after Christ. It was a humble faith; they brought him to attend on Christ. It was an active faith. Sin may be pardoned, yet the sickness not be removed; the sickness may be removed, yet the sin not pardoned: but if we have the comfort of peace with God, with the comfort of recovery from sickness, this makes the healing a mercy indeed. This is no encouragement to sin. If thou bring thy sins to Jesus Christ, as thy malady and misery to be cured of, and delivered from, it is well; but to come with them, as thy darlings and delight, thinking still to retain them and receive him, is a gross mistake, a miserable delusion.

The great intention of the blessed Jesus in the redemption he wrought, is to separate our hearts from sin. Our Lord Jesus has perfect knowledge of all that we say within ourselves. There is a great deal of evil in sinful thoughts, which is very offensive to the Lord Jesus. Christ designed to show that his great errand to the world was, to save his people from their sins. He turned from disputing with the scribes, and spake healing to the sick man. Not only he had no more need to be carried upon his bed, but he had strength to carry it. God must be glorified in all the power that is given to do good.

Verse 9 Matthew was in his calling, as the rest of those whom Christ called. As Satan comes with his temptations to the idle, so Christ comes with his calls to those who are employed. We are all naturally averse from thee, O God; do thou bid us to follow thee; draw us by thy powerful word, and we shall run after thee. Speak by the word of the Spirit to our hearts, the world cannot hold us down, Satan cannot stop our way, we shall arise and follow thee.

A saving change is wrought in the soul, by Christ as the author, and his word as the means. Neither Matthew's place, nor his gains by it, could detain him, when Christ called him. He left it, and though we find the disciples, who were fishers, occasionally fishing again afterwards, we never more find Matthew at his sinful gain.

Verses 10-13 Some time after his call, Matthew sought to bring his old associates to hear Christ. He knew by experience what the grace of Christ could do, and would not despair concerning them. Those who are effectually brought to Christ, cannot but desire that others also may be brought to him.

Those who suppose their souls to be without disease will not welcome the spiritual Physician. This was the case with the Pharisees; they despised Christ, because they thought themselves whole; but the poor publicans and sinners felt that they wanted instruction and amendment. It is easy, and too common, to put the worst constructions upon the best words and actions. It may justly be suspected that those have not the grace of God themselves, who are not pleased with others' obtaining it.

Christ's conversing with sinners is here called mercy; for to promote the conversion of souls is the greatest act of mercy. The gospel call is a call to repentance; a call to us to change our minds, and to change our ways. If the children of men had not been sinners, there had been no need for Christ to come among them. Let us examine whether we have found out our sickness, and have learned to follow the directions of our great Physician.

Verses 14-17 John was at this time in prison; his circumstances, his character, and the nature of the message he was sent to deliver, led those who were peculiarly attached to him, to keep frequent fasts. Christ referred them to John's testimony of him, John 3:29. Though there is no doubt that Jesus and his disciples lived in a spare and frugal manner, it would be improper for his disciples to fast while they had the comfort of his presence. When he is with them, all is well. The presence of the sun makes day, and its absence produces night.

Our Lord further reminded them of common rules of prudence. It was not usual to take a piece of rough woolen cloth, which had never been prepared, to join to an old garment, for it would not join well with the soft, old garment, but would tear it further, and the rent would be made worse. Nor would men put new wine into old leathern bottles, which were going to decay, and would be liable to burst from the fermenting of the wine; but putting the new wine into strong, new, skin bottles, both would be preserved. Great caution and prudence are necessary, that young converts may not receive gloomy and forbidding ideas of the service of our Lord; but duties are to be urged as they are able to bear them.

Verses 18-26 The death of our relations should drive us to Christ, who is our life. And it is high honour to the greatest rulers to attend on the Lord Jesus; and those who would receive mercy from Christ, must honour him.

The variety of methods Christ took in working his miracles, perhaps was because of the different frames and tempers of mind, which those were in who came to him, and which He who searches the heart perfectly knew. A poor woman applied herself to Christ, and received mercy from him by the way. If we do but touch, as it were, the hem of Christ's garment by living faith, our worst evils will be healed; there is no other real cure, nor need we fear his knowing things which are a grief and burden to us, but which we would not tell to any earthly friend.

When Christ entered the ruler's house, he said, Give place. Sometimes, when the sorrow of the world prevails, it is difficult for Christ and his comforts to enter. The ruler's daughter was really dead, but not so to Christ. The death of the righteous is in a special manner to be looked on as only a sleep. The words and works of Christ may not at first be understood, yet they are not therefore to be despised. The people were put forth. Scorners who laugh at what they do not understand, are not proper witnesses of the wonderful works of Christ. Dead souls are not raised to spiritual life, unless Christ take them by the hand: it is done in the day of his power.

If this single instance of Christ's raising one newly dead so increased his fame, what will be his glory when all that are in their graves shall hear his voice, and come forth; those that have done good to the resurrection of life, and those that have done evil to the resurrection of damnation!

Verses 27-31 At this time the Jews expected Messiah would appear; these blind men knew and proclaimed in the streets of Capernaum that he was come, and that Jesus was he. Those who, by the providence of God, have lost their bodily sight, may, by the grace of God, have the eyes of their understanding fully enlightened. And whatever our wants and burdens are, we need no more for supply and support, than to share in the mercy of our Lord Jesus. In Christ is enough for all.

They followed him crying aloud. He would try their faith, and would teach us always to pray, and not to faint, though the answer does not come at once. They followed Christ, and followed him crying; but the great question is, "Do ye believe?"

Nature may make us earnest, but it is only grace that can work faith. Christ touched their eyes. He gives sight to blind souls by the power of his grace going with his word, and he puts the cure upon their faith. Those who apply to Jesus Christ, shall be dealt with, not according to their fancies, nor according to their profession, but according to their faith.

Christ sometimes concealed his miracles, because he would not indulge the conceit which prevailed among the Jews, that their Messiah should be a temporal prince, and so give occasion to the people to attempt tumults and seditions.

Verses 32-34 Of the two, better a dumb devil than a blaspheming one. Christ's cures strike at the root, and remove the effect by taking away the cause; they open the lips, by breaking Satan's power in the soul. Nothing can convince those who are under the power of pride. They will believe anything, however false or absurd, rather than the Holy Scriptures; thus they show the enmity of their hearts against a holy God.

Verses 35-38 Jesus visited not only the great and wealthy cities, but the poor, obscure villages; and there he preached, there he healed. The souls of the meanest in the world are as precious to Christ, and should be so to us, as the souls of those who make the greatest figure. There were priests, Levites, and scribes, all over the land; but they were idol shepherds, Zechariah 11:17; therefore Christ had compassion on the people as sheep scattered, as men perishing for lack of knowledge.

To this day vast multitudes are as sheep not having a shepherd, and we should have compassion and do all we can to help them. The multitudes desirous of spiritual instruction formed a plenteous harvest, needing many active labourers; but few deserved that character. Christ is the Lord of the harvest. Let us pray that many may be raised up and sent forth, who will labour in bringing souls to Christ. It is a sign that God is about to bestow some special mercy upon a people, when he stirs them up to pray for it. And commissions given to labourers in answer to prayer, are most likely to be successful.

CHAPTER 10

The apostles called. (1-4) The apostles instructed and sent forth. (5-15) Directions to the apostles. (16-42)

Verses 1-4 The word "apostle" signifies messenger; they were Christ's messengers, sent forth to proclaim his kingdom. Christ gave them power to heal all manner of sickness. In the grace of the gospel there is a salve for every sore, a remedy for every malady. There is no spiritual disease, but there is power in Christ for the cure of it. There names are recorded, and it is their honour; yet they had more reason to rejoice that their names were written in heaven, while the high and mighty names of the great ones of the earth are buried in the dust.

Verses 5-15 The Gentiles must not have the gospel brought them, till the Jews have refused it. This restraint on the apostles was only in their first mission. Wherever they went they must proclaim, The kingdom of heaven is at hand. They preached, to establish the faith; the kingdom, to animate the hope; of heaven, to inspire the love of heavenly things, and the contempt of earthly; which is at hand, that men may prepare for it without delay. Christ gave power to work miracles for the confirming of their doctrine. This is not necessary now that the kingdom of God is come. It showed that the intent of the doctrine they preached, was to heal sick souls, and to raise those that were dead in sin. In proclaiming the gospel of free grace for the healing and saving of men's souls, we must above all avoid the appearance of the spirit of an hireling. They are directed what to do in strange towns and cities. The servant of Christ is the ambassador of peace to whatever place he is sent. His message is even to the vilest sinners, yet it behooves him to find out the best persons in every place. It becomes us to pray heartily for all, and to conduct ourselves courteously to all. They are directed how to act as to those that refused them. The whole counsel of God must be declared, and those who will not attend to the gracious message, must be shown that their state is dangerous. This should be seriously laid to heart by all that hear the gospel, lest their privileges only serve to increase their condemnation.

Verses 16-42 Our Lord warned his disciples to prepare for persecution. They were to avoid all things which gave advantage to their enemies, all meddling with worldly or political concerns, all appearance of evil or selfishness, and all underhand measures. Christ foretold troubles, not only that the troubles might not be a surprise, but that they might confirm their faith. He tells them what they should suffer, and from whom. Thus Christ has dealt fairly and faithfully with us, in telling us the worst we can meet with in his service; and he would have us deal so with ourselves, in sitting down and counting the cost.

Persecutors are worse than beasts, in that they prey upon those of their own kind. The strongest bonds of love and duty, have often been broken through from enmity against Christ. Sufferings from friends and relations are very grievous; nothing cuts more. It appears plainly, that all who will live godly in Christ Jesus must suffer persecution; and we must expect to enter into the kingdom of God through many tribulations. With these predictions of trouble, are counsels and comforts for a time of trial. The disciples of Christ are hated and persecuted as serpents, and their ruin is sought, and they need the serpent's wisdom. Be ye harmless as doves. Not only, do nobody any hurt, but bear nobody any ill-will.

Prudent care there must be, but not an anxious, perplexing thought; let this care be cast upon God. The disciples of Christ must think more how to do well, than how to speak well. In case of great peril, the disciples of Christ may go out of the way of danger, though they must not go out of the way of duty. No sinful, unlawful means may be used to escape; for then it is not a door of God's opening. The fear of man brings a snare, a perplexing snare, that disturbs our peace; an entangling snare, by which we are drawn into sin; and, therefore, it must be striven and prayed against. Tribulation, distress, and persecution cannot take away God's love to them, or theirs to him. Fear Him, who is able to destroy both soul and body in hell. They must deliver their message publicly, for all are deeply concerned in the doctrine of the gospel. The whole counsel of God must be made known, Acts 20:27. Christ shows them why they should be of good cheer. Their sufferings witnessed against those who oppose his gospel. When God calls us to speak for him, we may depend on him to teach us what to say.

A believing prospect of the end of our troubles, will be of great use to support us under them. They may be borne to the end, because the sufferers shall be borne up under them. The strength shall be according to the day. And it is great encouragement to those who are doing Christ's work, that it is a work which shall certainly be done. See how the care of Providence extends to all creatures, even to the sparrows. This should silence all the fears of God's people; Ye are of more value than many sparrows. And the very hairs of your head are all numbered. This denotes the account God takes and keeps of his people. It is our duty, not only to believe in Christ, but to profess that faith, in suffering for him, when we are called to it, as well as in serving him. That denial of Christ only is here meant which is persisted in, and that confession only can have the blessed recompense here promised, which is the real and constant language of faith and love.

Religion is worth every thing; all who believe the truth of it, will come up to the price, and make every thing else yield to it. Christ will lead us through sufferings, to glory with him. Those are best prepared for the life to come, that sit most loose to this present life. Though the kindness done to Christ's disciples be ever so small, yet if there be occasion for it, and ability to do no more, it shall be accepted. Christ does not say that they deserve a reward; for we cannot merit any thing from the hand of God; but they shall receive a reward from the free gift of God. Let us boldly confess Christ, and show love to him in all things.

CHAPTER 11

Christ's preaching. (1) Christ's answer to John's disciples. (2-6) Christ's testimony to John the Baptist. (7-15) The perverseness of the Jews. (16-24) The gospel revealed to the simple. The heavy-laden invited. (25-30)

Verse 1 Our Divine Redeemer never was weary of his labour of love; and we should not be weary of well-doing, for in due season we shall reap, if we faint not.

Verses 2-6 Some think that John sent this inquiry for his own satisfaction. Where there is true faith, yet there may be a mixture of unbelief. The remaining unbelief of good men may sometimes, in an hour of temptation; call in question the most important truths. But we hope that John's faith did not fail in this matter, and that he only desired to have it strengthened and confirmed. Others think that John sent his disciples to Christ for their satisfaction. Christ points them to what they heard and saw. Christ's gracious condescensions and compassions to the poor, show that it was he that should bring to the world the tender mercies of our God. Those things which men see and hear, if compared with the Scriptures, direct in what way salvation is to be found. It is difficult to conquer prejudices, and dangerous not to conquer them; but those who believe in Christ, their faith will be found so much the more to praise, and honour, and glory.

Verses 7-15 What Christ said concerning John, was not only for his praise, but for the people's profit. Those who attend on the word will be called to give an account of their improvements. Do we think when the sermon is done, the care is over? No, then the greatest of the care begins. John was a self-denying man, dead to all the pomps of the world and the pleasures of sense. It becomes people, in all their appearances, to be consistent with their character and their situation. John was a great and good man, yet not perfect; therefore he came short of glorified saints. The least in heaven knows more, loves more, and does more in praising God, and receives more from him, than the greatest in this world. But by the kingdom of heaven here, is rather to be understood the kingdom of grace, the gospel dispensation in its power and purity. What reason we have to be thankful that our lot is cast in the days of the kingdom of heaven, under such advantages of light and love! Multitudes were wrought upon by the ministry of John, and became his disciples. And those strove for a place in this kingdom, that one would think had no right nor title to it, and so seemed to be intruders. It shows us what fervency and zeal are required of all. Self must be denied; the bent, the frame and temper of the mind must be altered. Those who will have an interest in the great salvation, will have it upon any terms, and not think them hard, nor quit their hold without a blessing. The things of God are of great and common concern. God requires no more from us than the right use of the faculties he has given us. People are ignorant, because they will not learn.

Verses 16-24 Christ reflects on the scribes and Pharisees, who had a proud conceit of themselves. He likens their behaviour to children's play, who being out of temper without reason, quarrel with all the attempts of their fellows to please them, or to get them to join in the plays for which they used to assemble. The cavils of worldly men are often very trifling and show great malice. Something they have to urge against every one, however excellent and holy. Christ, who was undefiled, and separate from sinners, is here represented as in league with them, and polluted by them. The most unspotted innocence will not always be a defense against reproach. Christ knew that the hearts of the Jews were more bitter and hardened against his miracles and doctrines, than those of Tyre and Sidon would have been; therefore their condemnation would be the greater. The Lord exercises his almighty power, yet he punishes none more than they deserve, and never withholds the knowledge of the truth from those who long after it.

Verses 25-30 It becomes children to be grateful. When we come to God as a Father, we must remember that he is Lord of heaven and earth, which obliges us to come to him with reverence as to the sovereign Lord of all; yet with confidence, as one able to defend us from evil, and to supply us with all good. Our blessed Lord added a remarkable declaration, that the Father had delivered into his hands all power, authority, and judgment. We are indebted to Christ for all the revelation we have of God the Father's will and love, ever since Adam sinned. Our Saviour has invited all that labour and are heavy-laden, to come unto him. In some senses all men are so. Worldly men burden themselves with fruitless cares for wealth and honours; the gay and the sensual labour in pursuit of pleasures; the slave of Satan and his own lusts, is the merest drudge on earth. Those who labour to establish their own righteousness also labour in vain. The convinced sinner is heavy-laden with guilt and terror; and the tempted and afflicted believer has labours and burdens.

Christ invites all to come to him for rest to their souls. He alone gives this invitation; men come to him, when, feeling their guilt and misery, and believing his love and power to help, they seek him in fervent prayer. Thus it is the duty and interest of weary and heavy-laden sinners, to come to Jesus Christ. This is the gospel call; Whoever will, let him come. All who thus come will receive rest as Christ's gift, and obtain peace and comfort in their hearts. But in coming to him they must take his yoke, and submit to his authority. They must learn of him all things, as to their comfort and obedience. He accepts the willing servant, however imperfect the services. Here we may find rest for our souls, and here only. Nor need we fear his yoke. His commandments are holy, just, and good. It requires self-denial, and exposes to difficulties, but this is abundantly repaid, even in this world, by inward peace and joy. It is a yoke that is lined with love. So powerful are the assistances he gives us, so suitable the encouragements, and so strong the consolations to be found in the way of duty, that we may truly say, it is a yoke of pleasantness. The way of duty is the way of rest.

The truths Christ teaches are such as we may venture our souls upon. Such is the Redeemer's mercy; and why should the labouring and burdened sinner seek for rest from any other quarter? Let us come to him daily, for deliverance from wrath and guilt, from sin and Satan, from all our cares, fears, and sorrows. But forced obedience, far from being easy and light, is a heavy burden. In vain do we draw near to Jesus with our lips, while the heart is far from him. Then come to Jesus to find rest for your souls.

CHAPTER 12

Jesus defends his disciples for plucking corn on the Sabbath day. (1-8) Jesus heals a man with a withered hand on the Sabbath. (9-13) The malice of the Pharisees. (14-21) Jesus heals a demoniac. (22-30) Blasphemy of the Pharisees. (31,32) Evil words proceed from an evil heart. (33-37) The scribes and Pharisees reproved for seeking a sign. (38-45) The disciples of Christ are his nearest relations. (46-50)

Verses 1-8 Being in the cornfields, the disciples began to pluck the ears of corn: the law of God allowed it, Deuteronomy 23:25. This was slender provision for Christ and his disciples; but they were content with it. The Pharisees did not quarrel with them for taking another man's corn, but for doing it on the Sabbath day. Christ came to free his followers, not only from the corruptions of the Pharisees, but from their unscriptural rules, and justified what they did. The greatest shall not have their lusts indulged, but the meanest shall have their wants considered. Those labours are lawful on the Sabbath day which are necessary, and Sabbath rest is to froward, not to hinder Sabbath worship. Needful provision for health and food is to be made; but when servants are kept at home, and families become a scene of hurry and confusion on the Lord's day, to furnish a feast for visitors, or for indulgence, the case is very different. Such things as these, and many others common among professors, are to be blamed. The resting on the Sabbath was ordained for man's good, Deuteronomy 5:14. No law must be understood so as to contradict its own end. And as Christ is the Lord of the Sabbath, it is fit the day and the work of it should be dedicated to him.

Verses 9-13 Christ shows that works of mercy are lawful and proper to be done on the Lord's day. There are more ways of doing well upon Sabbath days, than by the duties of worship: attending the sick, relieving the poor, helping those who need speedy relief, teaching the young to care for their souls; these are doing good: and these must be done from love and charity, with humility and self-denial, and shall be accepted, Genesis 4:7. This, like other cures which Christ wrought, had a spiritual meaning. By nature our hands are withered, and we are unable of ourselves to do any thing that is good. Christ only, by the power of his grace, cures us; he heals the withered hand by putting life into the dead soul, works in us both to will and to do: for, with the command, there is a promise of grace given by the word.

Verses 14-21 The Pharisees took counsel to find some accusation, that Jesus might be condemned to death. Aware of their design, as his time was not come, he retired from that place. Face does not more exactly answer to face in water, than the character of Christ drawn by the prophet, to his temper and conduct as described by the evangelists. Let us with cheerful confidence commit our souls to so kind and faithful a Friend. Far from breaking, he will strengthen the bruised reed; far from quenching the smoking flax, or wick nearly out, he will rather blow it up into a flame. Let us lay aside contentious and angry debates; let us receive one another as Christ receives us. And while encouraged by the gracious kindness of our Lord, we should pray that his Spirit may rest upon us, and make us able to copy his example.

Verses 22-30 A soul under Satan's power, and led captive by him, is blind in the things of God, and dumb at the throne of grace; sees nothing, and says nothing to the purpose. Satan blinds the eyes by unbelief, and seals up the lips from prayer. The more people magnified Christ, the more desirous the Pharisees were to vilify him. It was evident that if Satan aided Jesus in casting out devils, the kingdom of hell was divided against itself; how then could it stand! And if they said that Jesus cast out devils by the prince of the devils, they could not prove that their children cast them out by any other power. There are two great interests in the world; and when unclean spirits are cast out by the Holy Spirit, in the conversion of sinners to a life of faith and obedience, the kingdom of God is come unto us. All who do not aid or rejoice in such a change are against Christ.

Verses 31-32 Here is a gracious assurance of the pardon of all sin upon gospel terms. Christ herein has set an example to the sons of men, to be ready to forgive words spoken against them. But humble and conscientious believers, at times are tempted to think they have committed the unpardonable sin, while those who have come the nearest to it, seldom have any fear about it. We may be sure that those who indeed repent and believe the gospel, have not committed this sin, or any other of the same kind; for repentance and faith are the special gifts of God, which he would not bestow on any man, if he were determined never to pardon him; and those who fear they have committed this sin, give a good sign that they have not. The trembling, contrite sinner, has the witness in himself that this is not his case.

Verses 33-37 Men's language discovers what country they are of, likewise what manner of spirit they are of. The heart is the fountain, words are the streams. A troubled fountain, and a corrupt spring, must send forth muddy and unpleasant streams. Nothing but the salt of grace, cast into the spring, will heal the waters, season the speech, and purify the corrupt communication. An evil man has an evil treasure in his heart, and out of it brings forth evil things. Lusts and corruptions, dwelling and reigning in the heart, are an evil treasure, out of which the sinner brings forth bad words and actions, to dishonour God, and hurt others. Let us keep constant watch over ourselves, that we may speak words agreeable to the Christian character.

Verses 38-45 Though Christ is always ready to hear and answer holy desires and prayers, yet those who ask amiss, ask and have not. Signs were granted to those who desired them to confirm their faith, as Abraham and Gideon; but denied to those who demanded them to excuse their unbelief. The resurrection of Christ from the dead by his own power, called here the sign of the prophet Jonah, was the great proof of Christ's being the Messiah. As Jonah was three days and three nights in the whale, and then came out again alive, thus Christ would be so long in the grave, and then rise again. The Ninevites would shame the Jews for not repenting; the queen of Sheba, for not believing in Christ. And we have no such cares to hinder us, we come not to Christ upon such uncertainties. This parable represents the case of the Jewish church and nation. It is also applicable to all those who hear the word of God, and are in part reformed, but not truly converted. The unclean spirit leaves for a time, but when he returns, he finds Christ is not there to shut him out; the heart is swept by outward reformation, but garnished by preparation to comply with evil suggestions, and the man becomes a more decided enemy of the truth. Every heart is the residence of unclean spirits, except those which are temples of the Holy Ghost, by faith in Christ.

Verses 46-50 Christ's preaching was plain, easy, and familiar, and suited to his hearers. His mother and brethren stood without, desiring to speak with him, when they should have been standing within, desiring to hear him. Frequently, those who are nearest to the means of knowledge and grace are most negligent. We are apt to neglect that which we think we may have any day, forgetting that tomorrow is not ours. We often meet with hindrances in our work from friends about us, and are taken off by care for the things of this life, from the concerns of our souls. Christ was so intent on his work, that no natural or other duty took him from it. Not that, under pretence of religion, we may be disrespectful to parents, or unkind to relations; but the lesser duty must stand by, while the greater is done. Let us cease from men, and cleave to Christ; let us look upon every Christian, in whatever condition of life, as the brother, sister, or mother of the Lord of glory; let us love, respect, and be kind to them, for his sake, and after his example.

CHAPTER 13

The parable of the sower. (1-23) The parable of the tares. (24-30; 36-43) The parables of the mustard-seed and the leaven. (31-35) The parables of the hidden treasure, the pearl of great price, the net cast into the sea, and the householder. (44-52) Jesus is again rejected at Nazareth. (53-58)

Verses 1-23 Jesus entered into a boat that he might be the less pressed, and be the better heard by the people. By this he teaches us in the outward circumstances of worship not to covet that which is stately, but to make the best of the conveniences God in his providence allots to us. Christ taught in parables. Thereby the things of God were made more plain and easy to those willing to be taught, and at the same time more difficult and obscure to those who were willingly ignorant. The parable of the sower is plain. The seed sown is the word of God. The sower is our Lord Jesus Christ, by himself, or by his ministers. Preaching to a multitude is sowing the corn; we know not where it will light. Some sort of ground, though we take ever so much pains with it, brings forth no fruit to purpose, while the good soil brings forth plentifully. So it is with the hearts of men, whose different characters are here described by four sorts of ground.

Careless, trifling hearers, are an easy prey to Satan; who, as he is the great murderer of souls, so he is the great thief of sermons, and will be sure to rob us of the word, if we take not care to keep it. Hypocrites, like the stony ground, often get the start of true Christians in the shows of profession. Many are glad to hear a good sermon, who do not profit by it. They are told of free salvation, of the believer's privileges, and the happiness of heaven; and, without any change of heart, without any abiding conviction of their own depravity, their need of a Saviour, or the excellence of holiness, they soon profess an unwarranted assurance. But when some heavy trial threatens them, or some sinful advantage may be had, they give up or disguise their profession, or turn to some easier system. Worldly cares are fitly compared to thorns, for they came in with sin, and are a fruit of the curse; they are good in their place to stop a gap, but a man must be well armed that has much to do with them; they are entangling, vexing, scratching, and their end is to be burned, Hebrews 6:8.

Worldly cares are great hindrances to our profiting by the word of God. The deceitfulness of riches does the mischief; they cannot be said to deceive us unless we put our trust in them, then they choke the good seed. What distinguished the good ground was fruitfulness. By this true Christians are distinguished from hypocrites. Christ does not say that this good ground has no stones in it, or no thorns; but none that could hinder its fruitfulness. All are not alike; we should aim at the highest, to bring forth most fruit. The sense of hearing cannot be better employed than in hearing God's word; and let us look to ourselves that we may know what sort of hearers we are.

Verses 24-30, 36-43 This parable represents the present and future state of the gospel church; Christ's care of it, the devil's enmity against it, the mixture there is in it of good and bad in this world, and the separation between them in the other world. So prone is fallen man to sin, that if the enemy sow the tares, he may go his way, they will spring up, and do hurt; whereas, when good seed is sown, it must be tended, watered, and fenced. The servants complained to their master; Sir, didst thou not sow good seed in thy field? No doubt he did; whatever is amiss in the church, we are sure it is not from Christ. Though gross transgressors, and such as openly oppose the gospel, ought to be separated from the society of the faithful, yet no human skill can make an exact separation. Those who oppose must not be cut off, but instructed, and that with meekness. And though good and bad are together in this world, yet at the great day they shall be parted; then the righteous and the wicked shall be plainly known; here sometimes it is hard to distinguish between them. Let us, knowing the terrors of the Lord, not do iniquity. At death, believers shall shine forth to themselves; at the great day they shall shine forth before all the world. They shall shine by reflection, with light borrowed from the Fountain of light. Their sanctification will be made perfect, and their justification published. May we be found of that happy number.

Verses 31-35 The scope of the parable of the seed sown, is to show that the beginnings of the gospel would be small, but its latter end would greatly increase; in this way the work of grace in the heart, the kingdom of God within us, would be carried on. In the soul where grace truly is, it will grow really; though perhaps at first not to be discerned, it will at last come to great strength and usefulness. The preaching of the gospel works like leaven in the hearts of those who receive it. The leaven works certainly, so does the word, yet gradually. It works silently, and without being seen, mark 4:26-29, yet strongly; without noise, for so is the way of the Spirit, but without fail. Thus it was in the world. The apostles, by preaching the gospel, hid a handful of leaven in the great mass of mankind. It was made powerful by the Spirit of the Lord of hosts, who works, and none can hinder. Thus it is in the heart. When the gospel comes into the soul, it works a thorough change; it spreads itself into all the powers and faculties of the soul, and alters the property even of the members of the body, Romans 6:13. From these parables we are taught to expect a gradual progress; therefore let us inquire, Are we growing in grace? And in holy principles and habits?

Verses 44-52 Here are four parables.

1. That of the treasure hid in the field. Many slight the gospel, because they look only upon the surface of the field. But all who search the Scriptures, so as in them to find Christ and eternal life, John 5:39, will discover such treasure in this field as makes it unspeakably valuable; they make it their own upon any terms. Though nothing can be given as a price for this salvation, yet much must be given up for the sake of it.

2. All the children of men are busy; one would be rich, another would be honourable, another would be learned; but most are deceived, and take up with counterfeits for pearls. Jesus Christ is a Pearl of great price; in having him, we have enough to make us happy here and for ever. A man may buy gold too dear, but not this Pearl of great price. When the convinced sinner sees Christ as the gracious Saviour, all things else become worthless to his thoughts.

THE BOOK OF MATTHEW

3. The world is a vast sea, and men, in their natural state, are like the fishes. Preaching the gospel is casting a net into this sea, to catch something out of it, for His glory who has the sovereignty of this sea. Hypocrites and true Christians shall be parted: miserable is the condition of those that shall then be cast away.

4. A skilful, faithful minister of the gospel, is a scribe, well versed in the things of the gospel, and able to teach them. Christ compares him to a good householder, who brings forth fruits of last year's growth and this year's gathering, abundance and variety, to entertain his friends. Old experiences and new observations, all have their use. Our place is at Christ's feet, and we must daily learn old lessons over again, and new ones also.

Verses 53-58 Christ repeats his offer to those who have repulsed them. They upbraid him, Is not this the carpenter's son? Yes, it is true he was reputed to be so; and no disgrace to be the son of an honest tradesman; they should have respected him the more because he was one of themselves, but therefore they despised him. He did not many mighty works there, because of their unbelief. Unbelief is the great hindrance to Christ's favours. Let us keep faithful to him as the Saviour who has made our peace with God.

CHAPTER 14

Death of John the Baptist. (1-12) Five thousand people miraculously fed. (13-21) Jesus walks upon the sea. (22-33) Jesus healing the sick. (34-36)

Verses 1-12 The terror and reproach of conscience, which Herod, like other daring offenders, could not shake off, are proofs and warnings of a future judgment, and of future misery to them. But there may be the terror of convictions, where there is not the truth of conversion. When men pretend to favour the gospel, yet live in evil, we must not favour their self-delusion, but must deliver our consciences as John did. The world may call this rudeness and blind zeal. False professors, or timid Christians, may censure it as want of civility; but the most powerful enemies can go no further than the Lord sees good to permit. Herod feared that the putting of John to death might raise a rebellion among the people, which it did not; but he never feared it might stir up his own conscience against him, which it did. Men fear being hanged for what they do not fear being damned for. And times of carnal mirth and jollity are convenient times for carrying on bad designs against God's people. Herod would profusely reward a worthless dance, while imprisonment and death were the recompense of the man of God who sought the salvation of his soul. But there was real malice to John beneath his consent, or else Herod would have found ways to get clear of his promise. When the under shepherds are smitten, the sheep need not be scattered while they have the Great Shepherd to go to. And it is better to be drawn to Christ by want and loss, than not to come to him at all.

Verses 13-21 When Christ and his word withdraw, it is best for us to follow, seeking the means of grace for our souls before any worldly advantages. The presence of Christ and his gospel, makes a desert not only tolerable, but desirable. This little supply of bread was increased by Christ's creating power, till the whole multitude were satisfied. In seeking the welfare of men's souls, we should have compassion on their bodies likewise. Let us also remember always to crave a blessing on our meals, and learn to avoid all waste, as frugality is the proper source of liberality. See in this miracle an emblem of the Bread of life, which came down from heaven to sustain our perishing souls. The provisions of Christ's gospel appear mean and scanty to the world, yet they satisfy all that feed on him in their hearts by faith with thanksgiving.

Verses 22-33 Those are not Christ's followers who cannot enjoy being alone with God and their own hearts. It is good, upon special occasions, and when we find our hearts enlarged, to continue long in secret prayer, and in pouring out our hearts before the Lord. It is no new thing for Christ's disciples to meet with storms in the way of duty, but he thereby shows himself with the more grace to them and for them. He can take what way he pleases to save his people. But even appearances of deliverance sometimes occasion trouble and perplexity to God's people, from mistakes about Christ. Nothing ought to affright those that have Christ near them, and know he is theirs; not death itself. Peter walked upon the water, not for diversion or to boast of it, but to go to Jesus; and in that he was thus wonderfully borne up. Special supports are promised, and are to be expected, but only in spiritual pursuits; nor can we ever come to Jesus, unless we are upheld by his power. Christ bade Peter come, not only that he might walk upon the water, and so know his Lord's power, but that he might know his own weakness. And the Lord often lets his servants have their choice, to humble and prove them, and to show the greatness of his power and grace. When we look off from Christ, and look at the greatness of opposing difficulties, we shall begin to fall; but when we call to him, he will stretch out his arm, and save us.

Christ is the great Saviour; those who would be saved, must come to him, and cry to him, for salvation; we are never brought to this, till we find ourselves sinking: the sense of need drives us to him. He rebuked Peter. Could we but believe more, we should suffer less. The weakness of faith, and the prevailing of our doubts, displease our Lord Jesus, for there is no good reason why Christ's disciples should be of a doubtful mind. Even in a stormy day he is to them a very present help. None but the world's Creator could multiply the loaves, none but its Governor could tread upon the waters of the sea: the disciples yield to the evidence, and confess their faith. They were suitably affected, and worshipped Christ. He that comes to God, must believe; and he that believes in God, will come, Hebrews 11:6.

Verses 34-36 Whithersoever Christ went, he was doing good. They brought unto him all that were diseased. They came humbly beseeching him to help them. The experiences of others may direct and encourage us in seeking for Christ. As many as touched, were made perfectly whole. Those whom Christ heals, he heals perfectly. Were men more acquainted with Christ, and with the diseased state of their souls, they would flock to receive his healing influences. The healing virtue was not in the finger, but in their faith; or rather, it was in Christ, whom their faith took hold upon.

CHAPTER 15

Jesus discourses about human traditions. (1-9) He warns against things which really defile. (10-20) He heals the daughter of a Syrophenician woman. (21-28) Jesus heals the sick, and miraculously feeds four thousand. (29-39)

Verses 1-9 Additions to God's laws reflect upon his wisdom, as if he had left out something which was needed, and which man could supply; in one way or other they always lead men to disobey God. How thankful ought we to be for the written word of God! Never let us think that the religion of the Bible can be improved by any human addition, either in doctrine or practice. Our blessed Lord spoke of their traditions as inventions of their own, and pointed out one instance in which this was very clear, that of their transgressing the fifth commandment. When a parent's wants called for assistance, they pleaded, that they had devoted to the temple all they could spare, even though they did not part with it, and therefore their parents must expect nothing from them. This was making the command of God of no effect. The doom of hypocrites is put in a little compass; "In vain do they worship me." It will neither please God, nor profit themselves; they trust in vanity, and vanity will be their recompense.

Verses 10-20 Christ shows that the defilement they ought to fear, was not from what entered their mouths as food, but from what came out of their mouths, which showed the wickedness of their hearts. Nothing will last in the soul but the regenerating graces of the Holy Spirit; and nothing should be admitted into the church but what is from above; therefore, whoever is offended by a plain, seasonable declaration of the truth, we should not be troubled at

461

it. The disciples ask to be better taught as to this matter. Where a weak head doubts concerning any word of Christ, an upright heart and a willing mind seek for instruction. It is the heart that is desperately wicked, Jer 17:9, for there is no sin in word or deed, which was not first in the heart. They all come out of the man, and are fruits of that wickedness which is in the heart, and is wrought there. When Christ teaches, he will show men the deceitfulness and wickedness of their own hearts; he will teach them to humble themselves, and to seek to be cleansed in the Fountain opened for sin and uncleanness.

Verses 21-28 The dark corners of the country, the most remote, shall share Christ's influences; afterwards the ends of the earth shall see his salvation. The distress and trouble of her family brought a woman to Christ; and though it is need that drives us to Christ, yet we shall not therefore be driven from him. She did not limit Christ to any particular instance of mercy, but mercy, mercy is what she begged for: she pleads not merit, but depends upon mercy. It is the duty of parents to pray for their children, and to be earnest in prayer for them, especially for their souls. Have you a son, a daughter, grievously vexed with a proud devil, an unclean devil, a malicious devil, led captive by him at his will? This is a case more deplorable than that of bodily possession, and you must bring them by faith and prayer to Christ, who alone is able to heal them. Many methods of Christ's providence, especially of his grace, in dealing with his people, which are dark and perplexing, may be explained by this story, which teaches that there may be love in Christ's heart while there are frowns in his face; and it encourages us, though he seems ready to slay us, yet to trust in him.

Those whom Christ intends most to honour, he humbles to feel their own unworthiness. A proud, unhumbled heart would not have borne this; but she turned it into an argument to support her request. The state of this woman is an emblem of the state of a sinner, deeply conscious of the misery of his soul. The least of Christ is precious to a believer, even the very crumbs of the Bread of life. Of all graces, faith honours Christ most; therefore of all graces Christ honours faith most. He cured her daughter. He spake, and it was done. From hence let such as seek help from the Lord, and receive no gracious answer, learn to turn even their unworthiness and discouragements into pleas for mercy.

Verses 29-39 Whatever our case is, the only way to find ease and relief, is to lay it at Christ's feet, to submit it to him, and refer it to his disposal. Those who would have spiritual healing from Christ, must be ruled as he pleases. See what work sin has made; what various diseases human bodies are subject to. Here were such diseases as fancy could neither guess the cause nor the cure of, yet these were subject to the command of Christ. The spiritual cures that Christ works are wonderful. When blind souls are made to see by faith, the dumb to speak in prayer, the maimed and the lame to walk in holy obedience, it is to be wondered at. His power was also shown to the multitude, in the plentiful provision he made for them: the manner is much the same as before. All did eat, and were filled. Those whom Christ feeds, he fills. With Christ there is bread enough, and to spare; supplies of grace for more than seek it, and for those that seek for more. Christ sent away the people. Though he had fed them twice, they must not look for miracles to find their daily bread. Let them go home to their callings and their own tables. Lord, increase our faith, and pardon our unbelief, teaching us to live upon thy fullness and bounty, for all things pertaining to this life, and that which is to come.

CHAPTER 16

The Pharisees and Sadducees ask a sign. (1-4) Jesus cautions against the doctrine of the Pharisees. (5-12) Peter's testimony that Jesus was the Christ. (13-20) Christ foretells his sufferings, and rebukes Peter. (21-23) The necessity of self-denial. (24-28)

Verses 1-4 The Pharisees and Sadducees were opposed to each other in principles and in conduct; yet they joined against Christ. But they desired a sign of their own choosing: they despised those signs which relieved the necessity of the sick and sorrowful, and called for something else which would gratify the curiosity of the proud. It is great hypocrisy, when we slight the signs of God's ordaining, to seek for signs of our own devising.

Verses 5-12 Christ speaks of spiritual things under a similitude, and the disciples misunderstand him of carnal things. He took it ill that they should think him as thoughtful about bread as they were; that they should be so little acquainted with his way of preaching. Then understood they what he meant. Christ teaches by the Spirit of wisdom in the heart, opening the understanding to the Spirit of revelation in the word.

Verses 13-20 Peter, for himself and his brethren, said that they were assured of our Lord's being the promised Messiah, the Son of the living God. This showed that they believed Jesus to be more than man. Our Lord declared Peter to be blessed, as the teaching of God made him differ from his unbelieving countrymen. Christ added that he had named him Peter, in allusion to his stability or firmness in professing the truth. The word translated "rock," is not the same word as Peter, but is of a similar meaning. Nothing can be more wrong than to suppose that Christ meant the person of Peter was the rock. Without doubt Christ himself is the Rock, the tried foundation of the church; and woe to him that attempts to lay any other! Peter's confession is this rock as to doctrine. If Jesus be not the Christ, those that own him are not of the church, but deceivers and deceived. Our Lord next declared the authority with which Peter would be invested. He spoke in the name of his brethren, and this related to them as well as to him. They had no certain knowledge of the characters of men, and were liable to mistakes and sins in their own conduct; but they were kept from error in stating the way of acceptance and salvation, the rule of obedience, the believer's character and experience, and the final doom of unbelievers and hypocrites. In such matters their decision was right, and it was confirmed in heaven. But all pretensions of any man, either to absolve or retain men's sins, are blasphemous and absurd. None can forgive sins but God only. And this binding and loosing, in the common language of the Jews, signified to forbid and to allow, or to teach what is lawful or unlawful.

Verses 21-23 Christ reveals his mind to his people gradually. From that time, when the apostles had made the full confession of Christ, that he was the Son of God, he began to show them of his sufferings. He spake this to set right the mistakes of his disciples about the outward pomp and power of his kingdom. Those that follow Christ, must not expect great or high things in this world. Peter would have Christ to dread suffering as much as he did; but we mistake, if we measure Christ's love and patience by our own. We do not read of any thing said or done by any of his disciples, at any time, that Christ resented so much as this. Whoever takes us from that which is good, and would make us fear to do too much for God, speaks Satan's language. Whatever appears to be a temptation to sin, must be resisted with abhorrence, and not be parleyed with. Those that decline suffering for Christ, savour more of the things of man than of the things of God.

Verses 24-28 A true disciple of Christ is one that does follow him in duty, and shall follow him to glory. He is one that walks in the same way Christ walked in, is led by his Spirit, and treads in his steps, whithersoever he goes. "Let him deny himself." If self-denial be a hard lesson, it is no more than what our Master learned and Practiced, to redeem us, and to teach us. "Let him take up his cross." The cross is here put for every trouble that befalls us. We are apt to think we could bear another's cross better than our own; but that is best which is appointed us, and we ought to make the best of it. We must not by our rashness and folly pull crosses down upon our own heads, but must take them up when they are in our way. If any man will have the name and credit of a disciple, let him follow Christ in the work and duty of a disciple. If all worldly things are worthless when compared with the life of the body, how forcible the same argument with respect to the soul and its state of never-ending happiness or misery! Thousands lose their souls for the most trifling gain, or the most worthless indulgence, nay, often from mere sloth and negligence. Whatever is the object for which men forsake Christ, that is the price at which Satan buys their souls. Yet one soul is worth more than all the world. This is Christ's judgment upon the matter; he knew the price of souls, for he redeemed them; nor would he underrate the world, for he made it. The dying transgressor cannot purchase one hour's respite to seek mercy for his perishing soul. Let us then learn rightly to value our souls, and Christ as the only Saviour of them.

CHAPTER 17

The transfiguration of Christ. (1-13) Jesus casts out a dumb and deaf spirit. (14-21) He again foretells his sufferings. (22,23) He works a miracle to pay the tribute money. (24-27)

Verses 1-13 Now the disciples beheld somewhat of Christ's glory, as of the only begotten of the Father. It was intended to support their faith, when they would have to witness his crucifixion; and would give them an idea of the glory prepared for them, when changed by his power and made like him. The apostles were overcome by the glorious sight. Peter thought that it was most desirable to continue there, and to go no more down to meet the sufferings of which he was so unwilling to hear. In this he knew not what he said. We are wrong, if we look for a heaven here upon earth. Whatever tabernacles we propose to make for ourselves in this world, we must always remember to ask Christ's leave. That sacrifice was not yet offered, without which the souls of sinful men could not have been saved; and important services were to be done by Peter and his brethren. While Peter spoke, a bright cloud overshadowed them, an emblem of the Divine presence and glory. Ever since man sinned, and heard God's voice in the garden, unusual appearances of God have been terrible to man. They fell prostrate to the earth, till Jesus encouraged them; when looking round, they beheld only their Lord as they commonly saw him. We must pass through varied experiences in our way to glory; and when we return to the world after an ordinance, it must be our care to take Christ with us, and then it may be our comfort that he is with us.

Verses 14-21 The case of afflicted children should be presented to God by faithful and fervent prayer. Christ cured the child. Though the people were perverse, and Christ was provoked, yet care was taken of the child. When all other helps and succors fail, we are welcome to Christ, may trust in him, and in his power and goodness. See here an emblem of Christ's undertaking as our Redeemer. It encourages parents to bring children to Christ, whose souls are under Satan's power; he is able to heal them, and as willing as he is able. Not only bring them to Christ by prayer, but bring them to the word of Christ; to means by which Satan's strongholds in the soul are beaten down. It is good for us to distrust ourselves and our own strength; but it is displeasing to Christ when we distrust any power derived from him, or granted by him. There was also something in the malady which rendered the cure difficult. The extraordinary power of Satan must not discourage our faith, but quicken us to more earnestness in praying to God for the increase of it. Do we wonder to see Satan's bodily possession of this young man from a child, when we see his spiritual possession of every son of Adam from the fall!

Verses 22-23 Christ perfectly knew all things that should befall him, yet undertook the work of our redemption, which strongly shows his love. What outward debasement and Divine glory was the life of the Redeemer! And all his humiliation ended in his exaltation. Let us learn to endure the cross, to despise riches and worldly honours, and to be content with his will.

Verses 24-27 Peter felt sure that his Master was ready to do what was right. Christ spoke first to give him proof that no thought can be withholden from him. We must never decline our duty for fear of giving offence; but we must sometimes deny ourselves in our worldly interests, rather than give offence. However the money was lodged in the fish, He who knows all things alone could know it, and only almighty power could bring it to Peter's hook. The power and the poverty of Christ should be mentioned together. If called by providence to be poor, like our Lord, let us trust in his power, and our God shall supply all our need, according to his riches in glory by Christ Jesus. In the way of obedience, in the course, perhaps, of our usual calling, as he helped Peter, so he will help us. And if any sudden call should occur, which we are not prepared to meet, let us not apply to others, till we first seek Christ.

CHAPTER 18

The importance of humility. (1-6) Caution against offences. (7-14) The removal of offences. (15-20) Conduct towards brethren, The parable of the unmerciful servant. (21-35)

Verses 1-6 Christ spoke many words of his sufferings, but only one of his glory; yet the disciples fasten upon that, and overlook the others. Many love to hear and speak of privileges and glory, who are willing to pass by the thoughts of work and trouble. Our Lord set a little child before them, solemnly assuring them, that unless they were converted and made like little children, they could not enter his kingdom. Children, when very young, do not desire authority, do not regard outward distinctions, are free from malice, are teachable, and willingly dependent on their parents. It is true that they soon begin to show other dispositions, and other ideas are taught them at an early age; but these are marks of childhood, and render them proper emblems of the lowly minds of true Christians. Surely we need to be daily renewed in the spirit of our minds, that we may become simple and humble, as little children, and willing to be the least of all. Let us daily study this subject, and examine our own spirits.

Verses 7-14 Considering the cunning and malice of Satan, and the weakness and depravity of men's hearts, it is not possible but that there should be offences. God permits them for wise and holy ends, that those who are sincere, and those who are not, may be made known. Being told before, that there will be seducers, tempters, persecutors, and bad examples, let us stand on our guard. We must, as far as lawfully we may, part with what we cannot keep without being entangled by it in sin. The outward occasions of sin must be avoided. If we live after the flesh, we must die. If we, through the Spirit, mortify the deeds of the body, we shall live. Christ came into the world to save souls, and he will reckon severely with those who hinder the progress of others who are setting their faces heavenward. And shall any of us refuse attention to those whom the Son of God came to seek and to save? A father takes care of all his children, but is particularly tender of the little ones.

Verses 15-20 If a professed Christian is wronged by another, he ought not to complain of it to others, as is often done merely upon report, but to go to the offender privately, state the matter kindly, and show him his conduct. This would generally have all the desired effect with a true Christian, and the parties would be reconciled. The principles of these rules may be Practiced every where, and under all circumstances, though they are too much neglected by all. But how few try the method which Christ has expressly enjoined to all his disciples! In all our proceedings we should seek direction in prayer; we cannot too highly prize the promises of God. Wherever and whenever we meet in the name of Christ, we should consider him as present in the midst of us.

Verses 21-35 Though we live wholly on mercy and forgiveness, we are backward to forgive the offences of our brethren. This parable shows how much provocation God has from his family on earth, and how untoward his servants are. There are three things in the parable: 1. The master's wonderful clemency. The debt of sin is so great, that we are not able to pay it. See here what every sin deserves; this is the wages of sin, to be sold as a slave. It is the folly of many who are under strong convictions of their sins, to fancy they can make God satisfaction for the wrong they have done him. 2. The servant's unreasonable severity toward his fellow-servant, notwithstanding his lord's clemency toward him. Not that we may make light of wronging our neighbour, for that is also a sin against God; but we should not aggravate our neighbour's wronging us, nor study revenge. Let our complaints, both of the wickedness of the wicked, and of the afflictions of the afflicted, be brought to God, and left with him. 3. The master reproved his servant's cruelty.

The greatness of sin magnifies the riches of pardoning mercy; and the comfortable sense of pardoning mercy, does much to dispose our hearts to forgive our brethren. We are not to suppose that God actually forgives men, and afterwards reckons their guilt to them to condemn them; but this latter part of the parable shows the false conclusions many draw as to their sins being pardoned, though their after-conduct shows that they never entered into the spirit, or experienced the sanctifying grace of the gospel. We do not forgive our offending brother aright, if we do not forgive from the heart. Yet this is not enough; we must seek the welfare even of those who offend us. How justly will those be condemned, who, though they bear the Christian name, persist in unmerciful treatment of their brethren! The humbled sinner relies only on free, abounding mercy, through the ransom of the death of Christ. Let us seek more and more for the renewing grace of God, to teach us to forgive others as we hope for forgiveness from him.

CHAPTER 19

Jesus enters Judea. (1,2) The Pharisees' question about divorces. (3-12) Young children brought to Jesus. (13-15) The rich young man's inquiry. (16-22) The recompense of Christ's followers. (23-30)

Verses 1-2 Great multitudes followed Christ. When Christ departs, it is best for us to follow him. They found him as able and ready to help elsewhere, as he had been in Galilee; wherever the Sun of Righteousness arose, it was with healing in his wings.

Verses 3-12 The Pharisees were desirous of drawing something from Jesus which they might represent as contrary to the law of Moses. Cases about marriage have been numerous, and sometimes perplexed; made so, not by the law of God, but by the lusts and follies of men; and often people fix what they will do, before they ask for advice. Jesus replied by asking whether they had not read the account of the creation, and the first example of marriage; thus pointing out that every departure therefrom was wrong. That condition is best for us, and to be chosen and kept to accordingly, which is best for our souls, and tends most to prepare us for, and preserve us to, the kingdom of heaven. When the gospel is really embraced, it makes men kind relatives and faithful friends; it teaches them to bear the burdens, and to bear with the infirmities of those with whom they are connected, to consider their peace and happiness more than their own. As to ungodly persons, it is proper that they should be restrained by laws, from breaking the peace of society. And we learn that the married state should be entered upon with great seriousness and earnest prayer.

Verses 13-15 It is well when we come to Christ ourselves, and bring our children. Little children may be brought to Christ as needing, and being capable of receiving blessings from him, and having an interest in his intercession. We can but beg a blessing for them: Christ only can command the blessing. It is well for us, that Christ has more love and tenderness in him than the best of his disciples have. And let us learn of him not to discountenance any willing, well-meaning souls, in their seeking after Christ, though they are but weak. Those who are given to Christ, as part of his purchase, he will in no wise cast out. Therefore he takes it ill of all who forbid, and try to shut out those whom he has received. And all Christians should bring their children to the Saviour that he may bless them with spiritual blessings.

Verses 16-22 Christ knew that covetousness was the sin which most easily beset this young man; though he had got honestly what he possessed, yet he could not cheerfully part with it, and by this his want of sincerity was shown. Christ's promises make his precepts easy, and his yoke pleasant and very comfortable; yet this promise was as much a trial of the young man's faith, as the precept was of his charity and contempt of the world. It is required of us in following Christ, that we duly attend his ordinances, strictly follow his pattern, and cheerfully submit to his disposals; and this from love to him, and in dependence on him. To sell all, and give to the poor, will not serve, but we are to follow Christ. The gospel is the only remedy for lost sinners. Many abstain from gross vices who do not attend to their obligations to God. Thousands of instances of disobedience in thought, word, and deed, are marked against them in the book of God. Thus numbers forsake Christ, loving this present world: they feel convictions and desires, but they depart sorrowful, perhaps trembling. It behooves us to try ourselves in these matters, for the Lord will try us.

Verses 23-30 Though Christ spoke so strongly, few that have riches do not trust in them. How few that are poor are not tempted to envy! But men's earnestness in this matter is like their toiling to build a high wall to shut themselves and their children out of heaven. It should be satisfaction to those who are in a low condition, that they are not exposed to the temptations of a high and prosperous condition. If they live more hardly in this world than the rich, yet, if they get more easily to a better world, they have no reason to complain. Christ's words show that it is hard for a rich man to be a good Christian, and to be saved. The way to heaven is a narrow way to all, and the gate that leads into it, a strait gate; particularly so to rich people. More duties are expected from them than from others, and more sins easily beset them. It is hard not to be charmed with a smiling world. Rich people have a great account to make up for their opportunities above others. It is utterly impossible for a man that sets his heart upon his riches, to get to heaven. Christ used an expression, denoting a difficulty altogether unconquerable by the power of man. Nothing less than the almighty grace of God will enable a rich man to get over this difficulty. Who then can be saved?

If riches hinder rich people, are not pride and sinful lusts found in those not rich, and as dangerous to them? Who can be saved? Say the disciples. None, saith Christ, by any created power. The beginning, progress, and perfecting the work of salvation, depend wholly on the almighty power of God, to which all things are possible. Not that rich people can be saved in their worldliness, but that they should be saved from it. Peter said, We have forsaken all. Alas! it was but a poor all, only a few boats and nets; yet observe how Peter speaks, as if it had been some mighty thing. We are too apt to make the most of our services and sufferings, our expenses and losses, for Christ. However, Christ does not upbraid them; though it was but little that they had forsaken, yet it was their all, and as dear to them as if it had been more. Christ took it kindly that they left it to follow him; he accepts according to what a man hath. Our Lord's promise to the apostles is, that when the Son of man shall sit on the throne of his glory, he will make all things new, and they shall sit with him in judgment on those who will be judged according to their doctrine. This sets forth the honour, dignity, and authority of their office and ministry.

Our Lord added that every one who had forsaken possessions or comforts, for his sake and the gospel, would be recompensed at last. May God give us faith to rest our hope on this his promise; then we shall be ready for every service or sacrifice. Our Saviour, in the last verse, does away a mistake of some. The heavenly inheritance is not given as earthly ones are, but according to God's pleasure. Let us not trust in promising appearances or outward profession. Others may, for aught we know, become eminent in faith and holiness.

CHAPTER 20

The parable of the labourers in the vineyard. (1-16) Jesus again foretells his sufferings. (17-19) The ambition of James and John. (20-28) Jesus gives sight to two blind men near Jericho. (29-34)

Verses 1-16 The direct object of this parable seems to be, to show that though the Jews were first called into the vineyard, at length the gospel should be preached to the Gentiles, and they should be admitted to equal privileges and advantages with the Jews. The parable may also be applied more generally, and shows,

1. That God is debtor to no man.

2. That many who begin last, and promise little in religion, sometimes, by the blessing of God, arrive at a great deal of knowledge, grace, and usefulness.

3. That the recompense of reward will be given to the saints, but not according to the time of their conversion.

It describes the state of the visible church, and explains the declaration that the last shall be first, and the first last, in its various references. Till we are hired into the service of God, we are standing all the day idle: a sinful state, though a state of drudgery to Satan, may be called a state of idleness. The marketplace is the world, and from that we are called by the gospel. Come, come from this marketplace. Work for God will not admit of trifling. A man may go idle to hell, but he that will go to heaven, must be diligent.

The Roman penny was sevenpence, halfpenny in our money, wages then enough for the day's support. This does not prove that the reward of our obedience to God is of works, or of debt; when we have done all, we are unprofitable servants; but it signifies that there is a reward set before us, yet let none, upon this presumption, put off repentance till they are old. Some were sent into the vineyard at the eleventh hour; but nobody had hired them before. The Gentiles came in at the eleventh hour; the gospel had not been before preached to them. Those that have had gospel offers made them at the third or sixth hour, and have refused them, will not have to say at the eleventh hour, as these had, No man has hired us. Therefore, not to discourage any, but to awaken all, be it remembered, that now is the accepted time.

The riches of Divine grace are loudly murmured at, among proud Pharisees and nominal Christians. There is great proneness in us to think that we have too little, and others too much of the tokens of God's favour; and that we do too much, and others too little in the work of God. But if God gives grace to others, it is kindness to them, and no injustice to us. Carnal worldlings agree with God for their penny in this world; and choose their portion in this life. Obedient believers agree with God for their penny in the other world, and must remember they have so agreed. Didst not thou agree to take up with heaven as thy portion, thy all; wilt thou seek for happiness in the creature? God punishes none more than they deserve, and recompenses every service done for him; he therefore does no wrong to any, by showing extraordinary grace to some. See here the nature of envy. It is an evil eye, which is displeased at the good of others, and desires their hurt. It is a grief to ourselves, displeasing to God, and hurtful to our neighbours: it is a sin that has neither pleasure, profit, nor honour. Let us forego every proud claim, and seek for salvation as a free gift. Let us never envy or grudge, but rejoice and praise God for his mercy to others as well as to ourselves.

Verses 17-19 Christ is more particular here in foretelling his sufferings than before. And here, as before, he adds the mention of his resurrection and his glory, to that of his death and sufferings, to encourage his disciples, and comfort them. A believing view of our once crucified and now glorified Redeemer, is good to humble a proud, self-justifying disposition. When we consider the need of the humiliation and sufferings of the Son of God, in order to the salvation of perishing sinners, surely we must be aware of the freeness and richness of Divine grace in our salvation.

Verses 20-28 The sons of Zebedee abused what Christ said to comfort the disciples. Some cannot have comforts but they turn them to a wrong purpose. Pride is a sin that most easily besets us; it is sinful ambition to outdo others in pomp and grandeur. To put down the vanity and ambition of their request, Christ leads them to the thoughts of their sufferings. It is a bitter cup that is to be drunk of; a cup of trembling, but not the cup of the wicked. It is but a cup, it is but a draught, bitter perhaps, but soon emptied; it is a cup in the hand of a Father, John 18:11.

Baptism is an ordinance by which we are joined to the Lord in covenant and communion; and so is suffering for Christ, 48:10. Baptism is an outward and visible sign of an inward and spiritual grace; and so is suffering for Christ, for unto us it is given, Philippians 1:29. But they knew not what Christ's cup was, nor what his baptism. Those are commonly most confident, who are least acquainted with the cross. Nothing makes more mischief among brethren, than desire of greatness. And we never find Christ's disciples quarrelling, but something of this was at the bottom of it. That man who labours most diligently, and suffers most patiently, seeking to do good to his brethren, and to promote the salvation of souls, most resembles Christ, and will be most honoured by him to all eternity. Our Lord speaks of his death in the terms applied to the sacrifices of old. It is a sacrifice for the sins of men, and is that true and substantial sacrifice, which those of the law faintly and imperfectly represented. It was a ransom for many, enough for all, working upon many; and, if for many, then the poor trembling soul may say, Why not for me?

Verses 29-34 It is good for those under the same trial, or infirmity of body or mind, to join in prayer to God for relief, that they may quicken and encourage one another. There is mercy enough in Christ for all that ask. They were earnest in prayer. They cried out as men in earnest. Cold desires beg denials. They were humble in prayer, casting themselves upon, and referring themselves cheerfully to, the Mediator's mercy. They showed faith in prayer, by the title they gave to Christ. Surely it was by the Holy Ghost that they called Jesus, Lord. They persevered in prayer. When they were in pursuit of such mercy, it was no time for timidity or hesitation: they cried earnestly. Christ encouraged them. The wants and burdens of the body we are soon sensible of, and can readily relate. Oh that we did as feelingly complain of our spiritual maladies, especially our spiritual blindness! Many are spiritually blind, yet say they see. Jesus cured these blind men; and when they had received sight, they followed him. None follow Christ blindly. He first by his grace opens men's eyes, and so draws their hearts after him. These miracles are our call to Jesus; may we hear it, and make it our daily prayer to grow in grace and in the knowledge of the Lord and Saviour Jesus Christ.

THE CONCISE COMMENTARY ON THE GOSPELS

Christ enters Jerusalem. (1-11) He drives out those who profaned the temple. (12-17) The barren fig-tree cursed. (18-22) Jesus' discourse in the temple. (23-27) The parable of the two sons. (28-32) The parable of the wicked husbandmen. (33-46)

Verses 1-11 This coming of Christ was described by the prophet Zechariah, Zechariah 9:9. When Christ would appear in his glory, it is in his meekness, not in his majesty, in mercy to work salvation. As meekness and outward poverty were fully seen in Zion's King, and marked his triumphal entrance to Jerusalem, how wrong covetousness, ambition, and the pride of life must be in Zion's citizens! They brought the ass, but Jesus did not use it without the owner's consent. The trappings were such as came to hand. We must not think the clothes on our backs too dear to part with for the service of Christ. The chief priests and the elders afterwards joined with the multitude that abused him upon the cross; but none of them joined the multitude that did him honour.

Those that take Christ for their King, must lay their all under his feet. Hosanna signifies, Save now, we beseech thee! Blessed is he that cometh in the name of the Lord! But of how little value is the applause of the people! The changing multitude join the cry of the day, whether it be Hosanna, or Crucify him. Multitudes often seem to approve the gospel, but few become consistent disciples. When Jesus was come into Jerusalem all the city was moved; some perhaps were moved with joy, who waited for the Consolation of Israel; others, of the Pharisees, were moved with envy. So various are the motions in the minds of men upon the approach of Christ's kingdom.

Verses 12-17 Christ found some of the courts of the temple turned into a market for cattle and things used in the sacrifices, and partly occupied by the money-changers. Our Lord drove them from the place, as he had done at his entering upon his ministry, John 2:13-17. His works testified of him more than the hosannas; and his healing in the temple was the fulfilling the promise, that the glory of the latter house should be greater than the glory of the former. If Christ came now into many parts of his visible church, how many secret evils he would discover and cleanse! And how many things daily Practiced under the cloak of religion, would he show to be more suitable to a den of thieves than to a house of prayer!

Verses 18-22 This cursing of the barren fig-tree represents the state of hypocrites in general, and so teaches us that Christ looks for the power of religion in those who profess it, and the savour of it from those that have the show of it. His just expectations from flourishing professors are often disappointed; he comes to many, seeking fruit, and finds leaves only. A false profession commonly withers in this world, and it is the effect of Christ's curse. The fig-tree that had no fruit, soon lost its leaves. This represents the state of the nation and people of the Jews in particular. Our Lord Jesus found among them nothing but leaves. And after they rejected Christ, blindness and hardness grew upon them, till they were undone, and their place and nation rooted up. The Lord was righteous in it. Let us greatly fear the doom denounced on the barren fig-tree.

Verses 23-27 As our Lord now openly appeared as the Messiah, the chief priests and scribes were much offended, especially because he exposed and removed the abuses they encouraged. Our Lord asked what they thought of John's ministry and baptism. Many are more afraid of the shame of lying than of the sin, and therefore scruple not to speak what they know to be false, as to their own thoughts, affections, and intentions, or their remembering and forgetting. Our Lord refused to answer their inquiry. It is best to shun needless disputes with wicked opposers.

Verses 28-32 Parables which give reproof, speak plainly to the offenders, and judge them out of their own mouths. The parable of the two sons sent to work in the vineyard, is to show that those who knew not John's baptism to be of God, were shamed by those who knew it, and owned it. The whole human race are like children whom the Lord has brought up, but they have rebelled against him, only some are more plausible in their disobedience than others. And it often happens, that the daring rebel is brought to repentance and becomes the Lord's servant, while the formalist grows hardened in pride and enmity.

Verses 33-46 This parable plainly sets forth the sin and ruin of the Jewish nation; and what is spoken to convict them, is spoken to caution all that enjoy the privileges of the outward church. As men treat God's people, they would treat Christ himself, if he were with them. How can we, if faithful to his cause, expect a favourable reception from a wicked world, or from ungodly professors of Christianity! And let us ask ourselves, whether we who have the vineyard and all its advantages, render fruits in due season, as a people, as a family, or as separate persons. Our Saviour, in his question, declares that the Lord of the vineyard will come, and when he comes he will surely destroy the wicked. The chief priests and the elders were the builders, and they would not admit his doctrine or laws; they threw him aside as a despised stone. But he who was rejected by the Jews, was embraced by the Gentiles. Christ knows who will bring forth gospel fruits in the use of gospel means. The unbelief of sinners will be their ruin. But God has many ways of restraining the remainders of wrath, as he has of making that which breaks out redound to his praise. May Christ become more and more precious to our souls, as the firm Foundation and Cornerstone of his church. May we be willing to follow him, though despised and hated for his sake.

CHAPTER 22

The parable of the marriage feast. (1-14) The Pharisees question Jesus as to the tribute. (15-22) The question of the Sadducees as to the resurrection. (23-33) The substance of the commandments. (34-40) Jesus questions the Pharisees. (41-46)

Verses 1-14 The provision made for perishing souls in the gospel, is represented by a royal feast made by a king, with eastern liberality, on the marriage of his son. Our merciful God has not only provided food, but a royal feast, for the perishing souls of his rebellious creatures. There is enough and to spare, of every thing that can add to our present comfort and everlasting happiness, in the salvation of his Son Jesus Christ. The guests first invited were the Jews. When the prophets of the Old Testament prevailed not, nor John the Baptist, nor Christ himself, who told them the kingdom of God was at hand, the apostles and ministers of the gospel were sent, after Christ's resurrection, to tell them it was come, and to persuade them to accept the offer.

The reason why sinners come not to Christ and salvation by him, is, not because they cannot, but because they will not. Making light of Christ, and of the great salvation wrought out by him, is the damning sin of the world. They were careless. Multitudes perish for ever through mere carelessness, who show no direct aversion, but are careless as to their souls. Also the business and profit of worldly employments hinder many in closing with the Saviour. Both farmers and merchants must be diligent; but whatever we have of the world in our hands, our care must be to keep it out of our hearts, lest it come between us and Christ. The utter ruin coming upon the Jewish church and nation, is here represented. Persecution of Christ's faithful ministers fills up the measure of guilt of any people.

The offer of Christ and salvation to the Gentiles was not expected; it was such a surprise as it would be to wayfaring men, to be invited to a royal wedding-feast. The design of the gospel is to gather souls to Christ; all the children of God scattered abroad, Joh 10:16; 11:52. The case of hypocrites is represented by the guest that had not on a wedding-garment. It concerns all to prepare for the scrutiny; and those, and those only, who put on the Lord Jesus, who have a Christian temper of mind, who live by faith in Christ, and to whom he is all in all, have the wedding-garment. The imputed righteousness of Christ, and the sanctification of the Spirit, are both alike necessary. No man has the wedding-garment by nature, or can form it for himself. The day is coming, when hypocrites will be called to account for all their presumptuous intruding into gospel ordinances, and usurpation of gospel privileges. Take him away.

Those that walk unworthy of Christianity, forfeit all the happiness they presumptuously claimed. Our Saviour here passes out of the parable into that which it teaches. Hypocrites go by the light of the gospel itself down to utter darkness. Many are called to the wedding-feast, that is, to salvation, but few have the wedding-garment, the righteousness of Christ, the sanctification of the Spirit.

Then let us examine ourselves whether we are in the faith, and seek to be approved by the King.

Verses 15-22 The Pharisees sent their disciples with the Herodians, a party among the Jews, who were for full subjection to the Roman emperor. Though opposed to each other, they joined against Christ. What they said of Christ was right; whether they knew it or not, blessed be God we know it. Jesus Christ was a faithful Teacher, and a bold reprover. Christ saw their wickedness. Whatever mask the hypocrite puts on, our Lord Jesus sees through it. Christ did not interpose as a judge in matters of this nature, for his kingdom is not of this world, but he enjoins peaceable subjection to the powers that be. His adversaries were reproved, and his disciples were taught that the Christian religion is no enemy to civil government. Christ is, and will be, the wonder, not only of his friends, but of his enemies. They admire his wisdom, but will not be guided by it; his power, but will not submit to it.

Verses 23-33 The doctrines of Christ displeased the infidel Sadducees, as well as the Pharisees and Herodians. He carried the great truths of the resurrection and a future state, further than they had yet been reveled. There is no arguing from the state of things in this world, as to what will take place hereafter. Let truth be set in a clear light, and it appears in full strength. Having thus silenced them, our Lord proceeded to show the truth of the doctrine of the resurrection from the books of Moses. God declared to Moses that he was the God of the patriarchs, who had died long before; this shows that they were then in a state of being, capable of enjoying his favour, and proves that the doctrine of the resurrection is clearly taught in the Old Testament as well as in the New. But this doctrine was kept for a more full revelation, after the resurrection of Christ, who was the first-fruits of them that slept. All errors arise from not knowing the Scriptures and the power of God. In this world death takes away one after another, and so ends all earthly hopes, joys, sorrows, and connections. How wretched are those who look for nothing better beyond the grave!

Verses 34-40 An interpreter of the law asked our Lord a question, to try, not so much his knowledge, as his judgment. The love of God is the first and great commandment, and the sum of all the commands of the first table. Our love of God must be sincere, not in word and tongue only. All our love is too little to bestow upon him, therefore all the powers of the soul must be engaged for him, and carried out toward him. To love our neighbour as ourselves, is the second great commandment. There is a self-love which is corrupt, and the root of the greatest sins, and it must be put off and mortified; but there is a self-love which is the rule of the greatest duty: we must have a due concern for the welfare of our own souls and bodies. And we must love our neighbour as truly and sincerely as we love ourselves; in many cases we must deny ourselves for the good of others. By these two commandments let our hearts be formed as by a mould.

Verses 41-46 When Christ baffled his enemies, he asked what thoughts they had of the promised Messiah? How he could be the Son of David and yet his Lord? He quotes psalms 110:1. If the Christ was to be a mere man, who would not exist till many ages after David's death, how could his forefather call him Lord? The Pharisees could not answer it. Nor can any solve the difficulty except he allows the Messiah to be the Son of God, and David's Lord equally with the Father. He took upon him human nature, and so became God manifested in the flesh; in this sense he is the Son of man and the Son of David. It behooves us above all things seriously to inquire, "What think we of Christ?" Is he altogether glorious in our eyes, and precious to our hearts? May Christ be our joy, our confidence, our all. May we daily be made more like to him, and more devoted to his service.

CHAPTER 23

Jesus reproves the scribes and Pharisees. (1-12) Crimes of the Pharisees. (13-33) The guilt of Jerusalem. (34-39)

Verses 1-12 The scribes and Pharisees explained the law of Moses, and enforced obedience to it. They are charged with hypocrisy in religion. We can only judge according to outward appearance; but God searches the heart. They made phylacteries. These were scrolls of paper or parchment, wherein were written four paragraphs of the law, to be worn on their foreheads and left arms, 11:13-21. They made these phylacteries broad, that they might be thought more zealous for the law than others. God appointed the Jews to make fringes upon their garments, numbers 15:38, to remind them of their being a peculiar people; but the Pharisees made them larger than common, as if they were thereby more religious than others. Pride was the darling, reigning sin of the Pharisees, the sin that most easily beset them, and which our Lord Jesus takes all occasions to speak against. For him that is taught in the word to give respect to him that teaches, is commendable; but for him that teaches, to demand it, to be puffed up with it, is sinful. How much is all this against the spirit of Christianity! The consistent disciple of Christ is pained by being put into chief places. But who that looks around on the visible church, would think this was the spirit required? It is plain that some measure of this antichristian spirit prevails in every religious society, and in every one of our hearts.

Verses 13-33 The scribes and Pharisees were enemies to the gospel of Christ, and therefore to the salvation of the souls of men. It is bad to keep away from Christ ourselves, but worse also to keep others from him. Yet it is no new thing for the show and form of godliness to be made a cloak to the greatest enormities. But dissembled piety will be reckoned double iniquity. They were very busy to turn souls to be of their party. Not for the glory of God and the good of souls, but that they might have the credit and advantage of making converts. Gain being their godliness, by a thousand devices they made religion give way to their worldly interests. They were very strict and precise in smaller matters of the law, but careless and loose in weightier matters. It is not the scrupling a little sin that Christ here reproves; if it be a sin, though but a gnat, it must be strained out; but the doing that, and then swallowing a camel, or, committing a greater sin. While they would seem to be godly, they were neither sober nor righteous. We are really, what we are inwardly. Outward motives may keep the outside clean, while the inside is filthy; but if the heart and spirit be made new, there will be newness of life; here we must begin with ourselves. The righteousness of the scribes and Pharisees was like the ornaments of a grave, or dressing up a dead body, only for show. The deceitfulness of sinners' hearts appears in that they go down the streams of the sins of their own day, while they fancy that they should have opposed the sins of former days. We sometimes think, if we had lived when Christ was upon earth, that we should not have despised and rejected him, as men then did; yet Christ in his Spirit, in his word, in his ministers, is still no better treated. And it is just with God to give those up to their hearts' lusts, who obstinately persist in gratifying them. Christ gives men their true characters.

Verses 34-39 Our Lord declares the miseries the inhabitants of Jerusalem were about to bring upon themselves, but he does not notice the sufferings he was to undergo. A hen gathering her chickens under her wings, is an apt emblem of the Saviour's tender love to those who trust in him, and his faithful care of them. He calls sinners to take refuge under his tender protection, keeps them safe, and nourishes them to eternal life. The present dispersion and unbelief of the Jews, and their future conversion to Christ, were here foretold. Jerusalem and her children had a large share of guilt, and their punishment has been signal. But ere long, deserved vengeance will fall on every church which is Christian in name only. In the mean time the Saviour stands ready to receive all who come to him. There is nothing between sinners and eternal happiness, but their proud and unbelieving unwillingness.

CHAPTER 24

Christ foretells the destruction of the temple. (1-3) The troubles before the destruction of Jerusalem. (4-28) Christ foretells other signs and miseries, to the end of the world. (29-41) Exhortations to watchfulness. (42-51)

Verses 1-3 Christ foretells the utter ruin and destruction coming upon the temple. A believing foresight of the defacing of all worldly glory, will help to keep us from admiring it, and overvaluing it. The most beautiful body soon will be food for worms, and the most magnificent building a ruinous heap. See ye not all these things? It will do us good so to see them as to see through them, and see to the end of them. Our Lord having gone with his disciples to the Mount of Olives, he set before them the order of the times concerning the Jews, till the destruction of Jerusalem; and as to men in general till the end of the world.

Verses 4-28 The disciples had asked concerning the times, When these things should be? Christ gave them no answer to that; but they had also asked, What shall be the sign? This question he answers fully. The prophecy first respects events near at hand, the destruction of Jerusalem, the end of the Jewish church and state, the calling of the Gentiles, and the setting up of Christ's kingdom in the world; but it also looks to the general judgment; and toward the close, points more particularly to the latter. What Christ here said to his disciples, tended more to promote caution than to satisfy their curiosity; more to prepare them for the events that should happen, than to give a distinct idea of the events. This is that good understanding of the times which all should covet, thence to infer what Israel ought to do.

Our Saviour cautions his disciples to stand on their guard against false teachers. And he foretells wars and great commotions among nations. From the time that the Jews rejected Christ, and he left their house desolate, the sword never departed from them. See what comes of refusing the gospel. Those who will not hear the messengers of peace, shall be made to hear the messengers of war. But where the heart is fixed, trusting in God, it is kept in peace, and is not afraid. It is against the mind of Christ, that his people should have troubled hearts, even in troublous times. When we looked forward to the eternity of misery that is before the obstinate refusers of Christ and his gospel, we may truly say, The greatest earthly judgments are but the beginning of sorrows. It is comforting that some shall endure even to the end.

Our Lord foretells the preaching of the gospel in all the world. The end of the world shall not be till the gospel has done its work. Christ foretells the ruin coming upon the people of the Jews; and what he said here, would be of use to his disciples, for their conduct and for their comfort. If God opens a door of escape, we ought to make our escape, otherwise we do not trust God, but tempt him. It becomes Christ's disciples, in times of public trouble, to be much in prayer: that is never out of season, but in a special manner seasonable when we are distressed on every side. Though we must take what God sends, yet we may pray against sufferings; and it is very trying to a good man, to be taken by any work of necessity from the solemn service and worship of God on the Sabbath day. But here is one word of comfort, that for the elect's sake these days shall be made shorter than their enemies designed, who would have cut all off, if God, who used these foes to serve his own purpose, had not set bounds to their wrath.

Christ foretells the rapid spreading of the gospel in the world. It is plainly seen as the lightning. Christ preached his gospel openly. The Romans were like an eagle, and the ensign of their armies was an eagle. When a people, by their sin, make themselves as loathsome carcasses, nothing can be expected but that God should send enemies to destroy them. It is very applicable to the day of judgment, the coming of our Lord Jesus Christ in that day, 2 Thessalonians 2:1. Let us give diligence to make our calling and election sure; then may we know that no enemy or deceiver shall ever prevail against us.

Verses 29-41 Christ foretells his second coming. It is usual for prophets to speak of things as near and just at hand, to express the greatness and certainty of them. Concerning Christ's second coming, it is foretold that there shall be a great change, in order to the making all things new. Then they shall see the Son of man coming in the clouds. At his first coming, he was set for a sign that should be spoken against, but at his second coming, a sign that should be admired. Sooner or later, all sinners will be mourners; but repenting sinners look to Christ, and mourn after a godly sort; and those who sow in those tears shall shortly reap in joy.

Impenitent sinners shall see Him whom they have pierced, and, though they laugh now, shall mourn and weep in endless horror and despair.

The elect of God are scattered abroad; there are some in all places, and all nations; but when that great gathering day comes, there shall not one of them be missing. Distance of place shall keep none out of heaven. Our Lord declares that the Jews should never cease to be a distinct people, until all things he had been predicting were fulfilled. His prophecy reaches to the day of final judgment; therefore he here, ver. 34, foretells that Judah shall never cease to exist as a distinct people, so long as this world shall endure. Men of the world scheme and plan for generation upon generation here, but they plan not with reference to the overwhelming, approaching, and most certain event of Christ's second coming, which shall do away every human scheme, and set aside for ever all that God forbids. That will be as surprising a day, as the deluge to the old world.

Apply this, first, to temporal judgments, particularly that which was then hastening upon the nation and people of the Jews. Secondly, to the eternal judgment. Christ here shows the state of the old world when the deluge came. They were secure and careless; they knew not, until the flood came; and they believed not. Did we know aright that all earthly things must shortly pass away, we should not set our eyes and hearts so much upon them as we do. The evil day is not the further off for men's putting it far from them. What words can more strongly describe the suddenness of our Saviour's coming! Men will be at their respective businesses, and suddenly the Lord of glory will appear. Women will be in their house employments, but in that moment every other work will be laid aside, and every heart will turn inward and say, It is the Lord! Am I prepared to meet him? Can I stand before him?

And what, in fact, is the day of judgment to the whole world, but the day of death to every one?

Verses 42-51 To watch for Christ's coming, is to maintain that temper of mind which we would be willing that our Lord should find us in. We know we have but a little time to live, we cannot know that we have a long time to live; much less do we know the time fixed for the judgment. Our Lord's coming will be happy to those that shall be found ready, but very dreadful to those that are not. If a man, professing to be the servant of Christ, be an unbeliever, covetous, ambitious, or a lover of pleasure, he will be cut off. Those who choose the world for their portion in this life, will have hell for their portion in the other life. May our Lord, when he cometh, pronounce us blessed, and present us to the Father, washed in his blood, purified by his Spirit, and fit to be partakers of the inheritance of the saints in light.

CHAPTER 25

The parable of the ten virgins. (1-13) The parable of the talents. (14-30) The judgment. (31-46)

Verses 1-13 The circumstances of the parable of the ten virgins were taken from the marriage customs among the Jews, and explain the great day of Christ's coming. See the nature of Christianity. As Christians we profess to attend upon Christ, to honour him, also to be waiting for his coming. Sincere Christians are the wise virgins, and hypocrites the foolish ones. Those are the truly wise or foolish that are so in the affairs of their souls. Many have a lamp of profession in their hands, but have not, in their hearts, sound knowledge and settled resolution, which are needed to carry them through the services and trials of the present state. Their hearts are not stored with holy dispositions, by the new-creating Spirit of God.

Our light must shine before men in good works; but this is not likely to be long done, unless there is a fixed, active principle in the heart, of faith in Christ, and love to God and our brethren. They all slumbered and slept. The delay represents the space between the real or apparent conversion of these professors, and the coming of Christ, to take them away by death, or to judge the world. But though Christ tarry past our time, he will not tarry past the due time. The wise virgins kept their lamps burning, but they did not keep themselves awake.

Too many real Christians grow remiss, and one degree of carelessness makes way for another. Those that allow themselves to slumber, will scarcely keep from sleeping; therefore dread the beginning of spiritual decays. A startling summons was given. Go ye forth to meet Him, is a call to those prepared. The notice of Christ's approach, and the call to meet him, will awaken. Even those best prepared for death have work to do to get actually ready, 2 Peter 3:14. It will be a day of search and inquiry; and it concerns us to think how we shall then be found. Some wanted oil to supply their lamps when going out. Those that take up short of true grace, will certainly find the want of it one time or other. An outward profession may light a man along this world, but the damps of the valley of the shadow of death will put out such a light. Those who care not to live the life, yet would die the death of the righteous. But those that would be saved, must have grace of their own; and those that have most grace, have none to spare. The best need more from Christ. And while the poor alarmed soul addresses itself, upon a sickbed, to repentance and prayer, in awful confusion, death comes, judgment comes, the work is undone, and the poor sinner is undone for ever. This comes of having oil to buy when we should burn it, grace to get when we should use it. Those, and those only, shall go to heaven hereafter, that are made ready for heaven here. The suddenness of death and of Christ's coming to us then, will not hinder our happiness, if we have been prepared. The door was shut. Many will seek admission into heaven when it is too late. The vain confidence of hypocrites will carry them far in expectations of happiness. The unexpected summons of death may alarm the Christian; but, proceeding without delay to trim his lamp, his graces often shine more bright; while the mere professor's conduct shows that his lamp is going out. Watch therefore, attend to the business of your souls. Be in the fear of the Lord all the day long.

Verses 14-30 Christ keeps no servants to be idle: they have received their all from him, and have nothing they can call their own but sin. Our receiving from Christ is in order to our working for him. The manifestation of the Spirit is given to every man to profit withal. The day of account comes at last. We must all be reckoned with as to what good we have got to our own souls, and have done to others, by the advantages we have enjoyed. It is not meant that the improving of natural powers can entitle a man to Divine grace. It is the real Christian's liberty and privilege to be employed as his Redeemer's servant, in promoting his glory, and the good of his people: the love of Christ constrains him to live no longer to himself, but to Him that died for him, and rose again. Those who think it impossible to please God, and in vain to serve him, will do nothing to purpose in religion. They complain that He requires of them more they are capable of, and punishes them for what they cannot help. Whatever they may pretend, the fact is, they dislike the character and work of the Lord. The slothful servant is sentenced to be deprived of his talent. This may be applied to the blessings of this life; but rather to the means of grace. Those who know not the day of their visitation, shall have the things that belong to their peace hid from their eyes. His doom is, to be cast into outer darkness. It is a usual way of expressing the miseries of the damned in hell. Here, as in what was said to the faithful servants, our Saviour goes out of the parable into the thing intended by it, and this serves as a key to the whole. Let us not envy sinners, or covet any of their perishing possessions.

Verses 31-46 This is a description of the last judgment. It is as an explanation of the former parables. There is a judgment to come, in which every man shall be sentenced to a state of everlasting happiness, or misery. Christ shall come, not only in the glory of his Father, but in his own glory, as Mediator. The wicked and godly here dwell together, in the same cities, churches, families, and are not always to be known the one from the other; such are the weaknesses of saints, such the hypocrisies of sinners; and death takes both: but in that day they will be parted for ever. Jesus Christ is the great Shepherd; he will shortly distinguish between those that are his, and those that are not. All other distinctions will be done away; but the great one between saints and sinners, holy and unholy, will remain for ever. The happiness the saints shall possess is very great. It is a kingdom; the most valuable possession on earth; yet this is but a faint resemblance of the blessed state of the saints in heaven. It is a kingdom prepared. The Father provided it for them in the greatness of his wisdom and power; the Son purchased it for them; and the blessed Spirit, in preparing them for the kingdom, is preparing it for them. It is prepared for them: it is in all points adapted to the new nature of a sanctified soul. It is prepared from the foundation of the world. This happiness was for the saints, and they for it, from all eternity. They shall come and inherit it. What we inherit is not got by ourselves. It is God that makes heirs of heaven. We are not to suppose that acts of bounty will entitle to eternal happiness. Good works done for

God's sake, through Jesus Christ, are here noticed as marking the character of believers made holy by the Spirit of Christ, and as the effects of grace bestowed on those who do them. The wicked in this world were often called to come to Christ for life and rest, but they turned from his calls; and justly are those bid to depart from Christ, that would not come to him. Condemned sinners will in vain offer excuses. The punishment of the wicked will be an everlasting punishment; their state cannot be altered. Thus life and death, good and evil, the blessing and the curse, are set before us, that we may choose our way, and as our way so shall our end be.

CHAPTER 26

The rulers conspire against Christ. (1-5) Christ anointed at Bethany. (6-13) Judas bargains to betray Christ. (14-16) The Passover. (17-25) Christ institutes his holy supper. (26-30) He warns his disciples. (31-35) His agony in the garden. (36-46) He is betrayed. (47-56) Christ before Caiaphas. (57-68) Peter denies him. (69-75)

Verses 1-5 Our Lord had often told of his sufferings as at a distance, now he speaks of them as at hand. At the same time the Jewish council consulted how they might put him to death secretly. But it pleased God to defeat their intention. Jesus, the true paschal Lamb, was to be sacrificed for us at that very time, and his death and resurrection rendered public.

Verses 6-13 The pouring ointment upon the head of Christ was a token of the highest respect. Where there is true love in the heart to Jesus Christ, nothing will be thought too good to bestow upon him. The more Christ's servants and their services are caviled at, the more he manifests his acceptance. This act of faith and love was so remarkable, that it would be reported, as a memorial of Mary's faith and love, to all future ages, and in all places where the gospel should be preached. This prophecy is fulfilled.

Verses 14-16 There were but twelve called apostles, and one of them was like a devil; surely we must never expect any society to be quite pure on this side heaven. The greater profession men make of religion, the greater opportunity they have of doing mischief, if their hearts be not right with God. Observe, that Christ's own disciple, who knew so well his doctrine and manner of his life, and was false to him, could not charge him with any thing criminal, though it would have served to justify his treachery. What did Judas want? Was not he welcome wherever his Master was? Did he not fare as Christ fared? It is not the lack, but the love of money, that is the root of all evil. After he had made that wicked bargain, Judas had time to repent, and to revoke it; but when lesser acts of dishonesty have hardened the conscience men do without hesitation that which is more shameful.

Verses 17-25 Observe, the place for their eating the Passover was pointed out by Christ to the disciples. He knows those hidden ones who favour his cause, and will graciously visit all who are willing to receive him. The disciples did as Jesus had appointed. Those who would have Christ's presence in the gospel Passover, must do what he says. It well becomes the disciples of Christ always to be jealous over themselves, especially in trying times. We know not how strongly we may be tempted, nor how far God may leave us to ourselves, therefore we have reason not to be high-minded, but to fear. Heart-searching examination and fervent prayer are especially proper before the Lord's supper, that, as Christ our Passover is now sacrificed for us, we may keep this feast, renewing our repentance, our faith in his blood, and surrendering ourselves to his service.

Verses 26-30 This ordinance of the Lord's supper is to us the Passover supper, by which we commemorate a much greater deliverance than that of Israel out of Egypt. Take, eat; accept of Christ as he is offered to you; receive the atonement, approve of it, submit to his grace and his government. Meat looked upon, be the dish ever so well garnished, will not nourish; it must be fed upon: so must the doctrine of Christ. This is my body; that is, spiritually, it signifies and represents his body. We partake of the sun, not by having the sun put into our hands, but the beams of it darted down upon us; so we partake of Christ by partaking of his grace, and the blessed fruits of the breaking of his body. The blood of Christ is signified and represented by the wine. He gave thanks, to teach us to look to God in every part of the ordinance. This cup he gave to the disciples with a command, Drink ye all of it. The pardon of sin is that great blessing which is, in the Lord's supper, conferred on all true believers; it is the foundation of all other blessings. He takes leave of such communion; and assures them of a happy meeting again at last; "Until that day when I drink it new with you", may be understood of the joys and glories of the future state, which the saints shall partake with the Lord Jesus. That will be the kingdom of his Father; the wine of consolation will there be always new. While we look at the outward signs of Christ's body broken and his blood shed for the remission of our sins, let us recollect that the feast cost him as much as though he had literally given his flesh to be eaten and his blood for us to drink.

Verses 31-35 Improper self-confidence, like that of Peter, is the first step to a fall. There is a proneness in all of us to be over-confident. But those fall soonest and foulest, who are the most confident in themselves. Those are least safe, who think themselves most secure. Satan is active to lead such astray; they are most off their guard: God leaves them to themselves, to humble them.

Verses 36-46 He who made atonement for the sins of mankind, submitted himself in a garden of suffering, to the will of God, from which man had revolted in a garden of pleasure. Christ took with him into that part of the garden where he suffered his agony, only those who had witnessed his glory in his transfiguration. Those are best prepared to suffer with Christ, who have by faith beheld his glory. The words used denote the most entire dejection, amazement, anguish, and horror of mind; the state of one surrounded with sorrows, overwhelmed with miseries, and almost swallowed up with terror and dismay. He now began to be sorrowful, and never ceased to be so till he said, It is finished. He prayed that, if possible, the cup might pass from him. But he also showed his perfect readiness to bear the load of his sufferings; he was willing to submit to all for our redemption and salvation. According to this example of Christ, we must drink of the bitterest cup which God puts into our hands; though nature struggle, it must submit. It should be more our care to get troubles sanctified, and our hearts satisfied under them, than to get them taken away. It is well for us that our salvation is in the hand of One who neither slumbers nor sleeps. All are tempted, but we should be much afraid of entering into temptation. To be secured from this, we should watch and pray, and continually look unto the Lord to hold us up that we may be safe.

Doubtless our Lord had a clear and full view of the sufferings he was to endure, yet he spoke with the greatest calmness till this time. Christ was a Surety, who undertook to be answerable for our sins. Accordingly he was made sin for us, and suffered for our sins, the Just for the unjust; and Scripture ascribes his heaviest sufferings to the hand of God. He had full knowledge of the infinite evil of sin, and of the immense extent of that guilt for which he was to atone; with awful views of the Divine justice and holiness, and the punishment deserved by the sins of men, such as no tongue can express, or mind conceive. At the same time, Christ suffered being tempted; probably horrible thoughts were suggested by Satan that tended to gloom and every dreadful conclusion: these would be the more hard to bear from his perfect holiness. And did the load of imputed guilt so weigh down the soul of Him of whom it is said, He upholdeth all things by the word of his power? Into what misery then must those sink whose sins are left upon their own heads! How will those escape who neglect so great salvation?

Verses 47-56 No enemies are so much to be abhorred as those professed disciples that betray Christ with a kiss. God has no need of our services, much less of our sins, to bring about his purposes. Though Christ was crucified through weakness, it was voluntary weakness; he submitted to death. If he had not been willing to suffer, they could not conquer him. It was a great sin for those who had left all to follow Jesus; now to leave him for they knew not what. What folly, for fear of death to flee from Him, whom they knew and acknowledged to be the Fountain of life!

Verses 57-68 Jesus was hurried into Jerusalem. It looks ill, and bodes worse, when those who are willing to be Christ's disciples, are not willing to be known to be so. Here began Peter's denying him: for to follow Christ afar off, is to begin to go back from him. It is more our concern to prepare for the end, whatever it may be, than curiously to ask what the end will be. The event is God's, but the duty is ours. Now the Scriptures were fulfilled, which said,

False witnesses are risen up against me. Christ was accused, that we might not be condemned; and if at any time we suffer thus, let us remember we cannot expect to fare better than our Master. When Christ was made sin for us, he was silent, and left it to his blood to speak. Hitherto Jesus had seldom professed expressly to be the Christ, the Son of God; the tenor of his doctrine spoke it, and his miracles proved it; but now he would not omit to make an open confession of it. It would have looked like declining his sufferings. He thus confessed, as an example and encouragement to his followers, to confess him before men, whatever hazard they ran. Disdain, cruel mocking, and abhorrence, are the sure portion of the disciple as they were of the Master, from such as would buffet and deride the Lord of glory. These things were exactly foretold in the fiftieth chapter of Isaiah. Let us confess Christ's name, and bear the reproach, and he will confess us before his Father's throne.

Verses 69-75 Peter's sin is truly related, for the Scriptures deal faithfully. Bad company leads to sin: those who needlessly thrust themselves into it, may expect to be tempted and ensnared, as Peter. They scarcely can come out of such company without guilt or grief, or both. It is a great fault to be shy of Christ; and to dissemble our knowledge of him, when we are called to own him, is, in effect, to deny him. Peter's sin was aggravated; but he fell into the sin by surprise, not as Judas, with design. But conscience should be to us as the crowing of the cock, to put us in mind of the sins we had forgotten. Peter was thus left to fall, to abate his self-confidence, and render him more modest, humble, compassionate, and useful to others. The event has taught believers many things ever since, and if infidels, Pharisees, and hypocrites stumble at it or abuse it, it is at their peril. Little do we know how we should act in very difficult situations, if we were left to ourselves. Let him, therefore, that thinketh he standeth, take heed lest he fall; let us all distrust our own hearts, and rely wholly on the

Lord. Peter wept bitterly. Sorrow for sin must not be slight, but great and deep. Peter, who wept so bitterly for denying Christ, never denied him again, but confessed him often in the face of danger. True repentance for any sin will be shown by the contrary grace and duty; that is a sign of our sorrowing not only bitterly, but sincerely.

CHAPTER 27

Christ delivered to Pilate, The despair of Judas. (1-10) Christ before Pilate. (11-25) Barabbas loosed, Christ mocked. (26-30) Christ led to be crucified. (31-34) He is crucified. (35-44) The death of Christ. (45-50) Events at the crucifixion. (51-56) The burial of Christ. (57-61) The sepulchre secured. (62-66)

Verses 1-10 Wicked men see little of the consequences of their crimes when they commit them, but they must answer for them all. In the fullest manner Judas acknowledged to the chief priests that he had sinned, and betrayed an innocent person. This was full testimony to the character of Christ; but the rulers were hardened. Casting down the money, Judas departed, and went and hanged himself, not being able to bear the terror of Divine wrath, and the anguish of despair. There is little doubt but that the death of Judas was before that of our blessed Lord. But was it nothing to them that they had thirsted after this blood, and hired Judas to betray it, and had condemned it to be shed unjustly? Thus do fools make a mock at sin. Thus many make light of Christ crucified. And it is a common instance of the deceitfulness of our hearts, to make light of our own sin by dwelling upon other people's sins. But the judgment of God is according to truth. Many apply this passage of the buying the piece of ground, with the money Judas brought back, to signify the favour intended by the blood of Christ to strangers, and sinners of the Gentiles. It fulfilled a prophecy, Zechariah 11:12. Judas went far toward repentance, yet it was not to salvation. He confessed, but not to God; he did not go to him, and say, I have sinned, Father, against heaven. Let none be satisfied with such partial convictions as a man may have, and yet remain full of pride, enmity, and rebellion.

Verses 11-25 Having no malice against Jesus, Pilate urged him to clear himself, and laboured to get him discharged. The message from his wife was a warning. God has many ways of giving checks to sinners, in their sinful pursuits, and it is a great mercy to have such checks from Providence, from faithful friends, and from our own consciences. O do not this abominable thing which the Lord hates! Is what we may hear said to us, when we are entering into temptation, if we will but regard it. Being overruled by the priests, the people made choice of Barabbas. Multitudes who choose the world, rather than God, for their ruler and portion, thus choose their own delusions. The Jews were so bent upon the death of Christ, that Pilate thought it would be dangerous to refuse. And this struggle shows the power of conscience even on the worst men. Yet all was so ordered to make it evident that Christ suffered for no fault of his own, but for the sins of his people. How vain for Pilate to expect to free himself from the guilt of the innocent blood of a righteous person, whom he was by his office bound to protect! The Jews' curse upon themselves has been awfully answered in the sufferings of their nation. None could bear the sin of others, except Him that had no sin of his own to answer for. And are we not all concerned? Is not Barabbas preferred to Jesus, when sinners reject salvation that they may retain their darling sins, which rob God of his glory, and murder their souls? The blood of Christ is now upon us for good, through mercy, by the Jews' rejection of it. O let us flee to it for refuge!

Verses 26-30 Crucifixion was a death used only among the Romans; it was very terrible and miserable. A cross was laid on the ground, to which the hands and feet were nailed, it was then lifted up and fixed upright, so that the weight of the body hung on the nails, till the sufferer died in agony. Christ thus answered the type of the brazen serpent raised on a pole. Christ underwent all the misery and shame here related, that he might purchase for us everlasting life, and joy, and glory.

Verses 31-34 Christ was led as a Lamb to the slaughter, as a Sacrifice to the altar. Even the mercies of the wicked are really cruel. Taking the cross from him, they compelled one Simon to bear it. Make us ready, O Lord, to bear the cross thou hast appointed us, and daily to take it up with cheerfulness, following thee. Was ever sorrow like unto his sorrow? And when we behold what manner of death he died, let us in that behold with what manner of love he loved us. As if death, so painful a death, were not enough, they added to its bitterness and terror in several ways.

Verses 35-44 It was usual to put shame upon malefactors, by a writing to notify the crime for which they suffered. So they set up one over Christ's head. This they designed for his reproach, but God so overruled it, that even his accusation was to his honour. There were crucified with him at the same time, two robbers. He was, at his death, numbered among the transgressors, that we, at our death, might be numbered among the saints. The taunts and jeers he received are here recorded. The enemies of Christ labour to make others believe that of religion and of the people of God, which they themselves know to be false. The chief priests and scribes, and the elders, upbraid Jesus with being the King of Israel. Many people could like the King of Israel well enough, if he would but come down from the cross; if they could but have his kingdom without the tribulation through which they must enter into it. But if no cross, then no Christ, no crown. Those that would reign with him, must be willing to suffer with him. Thus our Lord Jesus, having undertaken to satisfy the justice of God, did it, by submitting to the punishment of the worst of men. And in every minute particular recorded about the sufferings of Christ, we find some prediction in the Prophets or the Psalms fulfilled.

Verses 45-50 During the three hours which the darkness continued, Jesus was in agony, wrestling with the powers of darkness, and suffering his Father's displeasure against the sin of man, for which he was now making his soul an offering. Never were there three such hours since the day God created man upon the earth, never such a dark and awful scene; it was the turning point of that great affair, man's redemption and salvation. Jesus uttered a complaint from psalms 22:1. Hereby he teaches of what use the word of God is to direct us in prayer, and recommends the use of Scripture expressions in prayer. The believer may have tasted some drops of bitterness, but he can only form a very feeble idea of the greatness of Christ's sufferings. Yet, hence he learns something of the Saviour's love to sinners; hence he gets deeper conviction of the vileness and evil of sin, and of what he owes to Christ, who delivers him from the wrath to come. His enemies wickedly ridiculed his complaint. Many of the reproaches cast upon the word of God and the people of God, arise, as here, from gross mistakes. Christ, just before he expired, spake in his full strength, to show that his life was not forced from him, but was freely delivered into his Father's hands. He had strength to bid defiance to the powers of death: and to show that by the eternal Spirit he offered himself, being the Priest as well as the Sacrifice, he cried with a loud voice.

Then he yielded up the ghost. The Son of God upon the cross, did die by the violence of the pain he was put to. His soul was separated from his body, and so his body was left really and truly dead. It was certain that Christ did die, for it was needful that he should die. He had undertaken to make himself an offering for sin, and he did it when he willingly gave up his life.

Verses 51-56 The rending of the veil signified that Christ, by his death, opened a way to God. We have an open way through Christ to the throne of grace, or mercy-seat now, and to the throne of glory hereafter. When we duly consider Christ's death, our hard and rocky hearts should be rent; the heart, and not the garments. That heart is harder than a rock that will not yield, that will not melt, where Jesus Christ is plainly set forth crucified. The graves were opened, and many bodies of saints which slept, arose. To whom they appeared, in what manner, and how they disappeared, we are not told; and we must not desire to be wise above what is written. The dreadful appearances of God in his providence, sometimes work strangely for the conviction and awakening of sinners. This was expressed in the terror that fell upon the centurion and the Roman soldiers. We may reflect with comfort on the abundant testimonies given to the character of Jesus; and, seeking to give no just cause of offence, we may leave it to the Lord to clear our characters, if we live to Him. Let us, with an eye of faith, behold Christ and him crucified, and be affected with that great love wherewith he loved us. But his friends could give no more than a look; they beheld him, but could not help him. Never were the horrid nature and effects of sin so tremendously displayed, as on that day when the beloved Son of the Father hung upon the cross, suffering for sin, the Just for the unjust, that he might bring us to God. Let us yield ourselves willingly to his service.

Verses 57-61 In the burial of Christ was nothing of pomp or solemnity. As Christ had not a house of his own, wherein to lay his head, while he lived, so he had not a grave of his own, wherein to lay his body, when he was dead. Our Lord Jesus, who had no sin of his own, had no grave of his own. The Jews designed that he should have made his grave with the wicked, should have been buried with the thieves with whom he was crucified, but God overruled it, so that he should make it with the rich in his death, Isaiah 53:9. And although to the eye of man the beholding a funeral may cause terror, yet if we remember how Christ by his burial has changed the nature of the grave to believers, it should make us rejoice. And we are ever to imitate Christ's burial in being continually occupied in the spiritual burial of our sins.

Verses 62-66 On the Jewish Sabbath, the chief priests and Pharisees, when they should have been at their devotions, were dealing with Pilate about securing the sepulchre. This was permitted that there might be certain proof of our Lord's resurrection. Pilate told them that they might secure the sepulchre as carefully as they could. They sealed the stone, and set a guard, and were satisfied that all needful care was taken. But to guard the sepulchre against the poor weak disciples was folly, because needless; while to think to guard it against the power of God, was folly, because fruitless, and to no purpose; yet they thought they dealt wisely. But the Lord took the wise in their own craftiness. Thus shall all the rage and the plans of Christ's enemies be made to promote his glory.

CHAPTER 28

Christ's resurrection. (1-8) He appears to the women. (9,10)
Confession of the soldiers. (11-15) Christ's commission to his
disciples. (16-20)

Verses 1-8 Christ rose the third day after his death; that was the
time he had often spoken of. On the first day of the first week
God commanded the light to shine out of darkness. On this day
did He who is the Light of the world, shine out of the darkness of
the grave; and this day is from henceforward often mentioned in
the New Testament, as the day which Christians religiously
observed in solemn assemblies, to the honour of Christ. Our Lord
Jesus could have rolled back the stone by his own power, but he
chose to have it done by an angel. The resurrection of Christ, as it
is the joy of his friends, so it is the terror and confusion of his
enemies. The angel encouraged the women against their fears. Let
the sinners in Zion be afraid. Fear not ye, for his resurrection will
be your consolation.

Our communion with him must be spiritual, by faith in his word.
When we are ready to make this world our home, and to say, It is
good to be here, then let us remember our Lord Jesus is not here,
he is risen; therefore let our hearts rise, and seek the things that
are above. He is risen, as he said. Let us never think that strange
which the word of Christ has told us to expect; whether the
sufferings of this present time, or the glory that is to be revealed.
It may have a good effect upon us, by faith to view the place
where the Lord lay. Go quickly. It was good to be there, but the
servants of God have other work appointed. Public usefulness must
be chosen before the pleasure of secret communion with God.

Tell the disciples, that they may be comforted under their present sorrows. Christ knows where his disciples dwell, and will visit them. Even to those at a distance from the plenty of the means of grace, he will graciously manifest himself. The fear and the joy together quickened their pace. The disciples of Christ should be forward to make known to each other their experiences of communion with their Lord; and should tell others what God has done for their souls.

Verses 9-10 God's gracious visits usually meet us in the way of duty; and to those who use what they have for others' benefit, more shall be given. This interview with Christ was unexpected; but Christ was nigh them, and still is nigh us in the word. The salutation speaks the good-will of Christ to man, even since he entered upon his state of exaltation. It is the will of Christ that his people should be a cheerful, joyful people, and his resurrection furnishes abundant matter for joy. Be not afraid. Christ rose from the dead, to silence his people's fears, and there is enough in that to silence them. The disciples had just before shamefully deserted him in his sufferings; but, to show that he could forgive, and to teach us to do so, he calls them brethren. Notwithstanding his majesty and purity, and our meanness and unworthiness, he still condescends to call believers his brethren.

Verses 11-15 What wickedness is it which men will not be brought to by the love of money! Here was large money given to the soldiers for advancing that which they knew to be a lie, yet many grudge a little money for advancing what they know to be the truth. Let us never starve a good cause, when we see bad ones so liberally supported. The priests undertook to secure them from the sword of Pilate, but could not secure these soldiers from the sword of God's justice, which hangs over the heads of those that love and make a lie. Those men promise more than they can perform, who undertake to save a man harmless in doing a willful sin. But this falsehood disproved itself. Had the soldiers been all asleep, they could not have known what passed. If any had been awake, they would have roused the others and prevented the removal; and certainly if they had been asleep, they never would have dared to confess it; while the Jewish rulers would have been the first to call for their punishment. Again, had there been any truth in the report, the rulers would have prosecuted the apostles with severity for it.

The whole shows that the story was entirely false. And we must not charge such things to the weakness of the understanding, but to the wickedness of the heart. God left them to expose their own course. The great argument to prove Christ to be the Son of God, is his resurrection; and none could have more convincing proofs of the truth of that than these soldiers; yet they took bribes to hinder others from believing. The plainest evidence will not affect men, without the work of the Holy Spirit.

Verses 16-20 This evangelist passes over other appearances of Christ, recorded by Luke and John, and hastens to the most solemn; one appointed before his death, and after his resurrection. All that see the Lord Jesus with an eye of faith, will worship him. Yet the faith of the sincere may be very weak and wavering. But Christ gave such convincing proofs of his resurrection, as made their faith to triumph over doubts. He now solemnly commissioned the apostles and his ministers to go forth among all nations. The salvation they were to preach, is a common salvation; whoever will, let him come, and take the benefit; all are welcome to Christ Jesus. Christianity is the religion of a sinner who applies for salvation from deserved wrath and from sin; he applies to the mercy of the Father, through the atonement of the incarnate Son, and by the sanctification of the Holy Spirit, and gives up himself to be the worshipper and servant of God, as the Father, Son, and Holy Ghost, three Persons but one God, in all his ordinances and commandments.

Baptism is an outward sign of that inward washing, or sanctification of the Spirit, which seals and evidences the believer's justification. Let us examine ourselves, whether we really possess the inward and spiritual grace of a death unto sin, and a new birth unto righteousness, by which those who were the children of wrath become the children of God. Believers shall have the constant presence of their Lord always; all days, every day. There is no day, no hour of the day, in which our Lord Jesus is not present with his churches and with his ministers; if there were, in that day, that hour, they would be undone. The God of Israel, the Saviour, is sometimes a God that hideth himself, but never a God at a distance. To these precious words Amen is added. Even so, Lord Jesus, be thou with us and all thy people; cause thy face to shine upon us, that thy way may be known upon earth, thy saving health among all nations.

MARK

CHAPTER 1

mark was a sister's son to Barnabas, Colossians 4:10; and Acts 12:12 shows that he was the son of Mary, a pious woman of Jerusalem, at whose house the apostles and first Christians assembled. From Peter's styling him his son, 1 Peter 5:13, the evangelist is supposed to have been converted by that apostle. Thus Mark was closely united with the followers of our Lord, if not himself one of the number. Mark wrote at Rome; some suppose that Peter dictated to him, though the general testimony is, that the apostle having preached at Rome, Mark, who was the apostle's companion, and had a clear understanding of what Peter delivered, was desired to commit the particulars to writing. And we may remark, that the great humility of Peter is very plain where any thing is said about himself. Scarcely an action or a work of Christ is mentioned, at which this apostle was not present, and the minuteness shows that the facts were related by an eye-witness. This Gospel records more of the miracles than of the discourses of our Lord, and though in many things it relates the same things as the Gospel according to St. Matthew, we may reap advantages from reviewing the same events, placed by each of the evangelists in that point of view which most affected his own mind.

The office of John the Baptist. (1-8) The baptism and temptation of Christ. (9-13) Christ preaches and calls disciples. (14-22) He casts out an unclean spirit. (23-28) He heals many diseased. (29-39) He heals a leper. (40-45)

Verses 1-8 Isaiah and Malachi each spake concerning the beginning of the gospel of Jesus Christ, in the ministry of John. From these prophets we may observe, that Christ, in his gospel, comes among us, bringing with him a treasure of grace, and a sceptre of government. Such is the corruption of the world, that there is great opposition to his progress. When God sent his Son into the world, he took care, and when he sends him into the heart, he takes care, to prepare his way before him. John thinks himself unworthy of the meanest office about Christ. The most eminent saints have always been the most humble. They feel their need of Christ's atoning blood and sanctifying Spirit, more than others. The great promise Christ makes in his gospel to those who have repented, and have had their sins forgiven them, is, they shall be baptized with the Holy Ghost; shall be purified by his graces, and refreshed by his comforts. We use the ordinances, word, and sacraments without profit and comfort, for the most part, because we have not of that Divine light within us; and we have it not because we ask it not; for we have his word that cannot fail, that our heavenly Father will give this light, his Holy Spirit, to those that ask it.

Verses 9-13 Christ's baptism was his first public appearance, after he had long lived unknown. How much hidden worth is there, which in this world is not known! But sooner or later it shall be known, as Christ was. He took upon himself the likeness of sinful flesh; and thus, for our sakes, he sanctified himself, that we also might be sanctified, and be baptized with him, John 17:19. See how honourably God owned him, when he submitted to John's baptism. He saw the Spirit descending upon him like a dove. We may see heaven opened to us, when we perceive the Spirit descending and working upon us. God's good work in us, is sure evidence of his good will towards us, and preparations for us. As to Christ's temptation, Mark notices his being in the wilderness and that he was with the wild beasts. It was an instance of his Father's care of him, which encouraged him the more that his Father would provide for him. Special protections are earnests of seasonable supplies. The serpent tempted the first Adam in the garden, the Second Adam in the wilderness; with different success indeed; and ever since he still tempts the children of both, in all places and conditions. Company and conversation have their temptations; and being alone, even in a wilderness, has its own also. No place or state exempts, no business, not lawful labouring, eating, or drinking, not even fasting and praying; often in these duties there are the most assaults, but in them is the sweetest victory. The ministration of the good angels is matter of great comfort in reference to the malignant designs of the evil angels; but much more does it comfort us, to have the indwelling of God the Holy Spirit in our hearts.

Verses 14-22 Jesus began to preach in Galilee, after that John was put in prison. If some be laid aside, others shall be raised up, to carry on the same work. Observe the great truths Christ preached. By repentance we give glory to our Creator whom we have offended; by faith we give glory to our Redeemer who came to save us from our sins. Christ has joined these two together, and let no man think to put them asunder. Christ puts honour upon those who, though mean in this world, are diligent in their business and kind to one another. Industry and unity are good and pleasant, and the Lord Jesus commands a blessing on them. Those whom Christ calls, must leave all to follow him; and by his grace he makes them willing to do so. Not that we must needs go out of the world, but we must sit loose to the world; forsake every thing that is against our duty to Christ, and that cannot be kept without hurt to our souls. Jesus strictly kept the Sabbath day, by applying himself unto, and abounding in the Sabbath work, in order to which the Sabbath rest was appointed. There is much in the doctrine of Christ that is astonishing; and the more we hear it, the more cause we see to admire it.

Verses 23-28 The devil is an unclean spirit, because he has lost all the purity of his nature, because he acts in direct opposition to the Holy Spirit of God, and by his suggestions defiles the spirits of men. There are many in our assemblies who quietly attend under merely formal teachers; but if the Lord come with faithful ministers and holy doctrine, and by his convincing Spirit, they are ready to say, like this man, What have we to do with thee, Jesus of Nazareth! No disorder could enable a man to know Jesus to be the Holy One of God. He desires to have nothing to do with Jesus, for he despairs of being saved by him, and dreads being destroyed by him. See whose language those speak, that say to the Almighty, Depart from us. This unclean spirit hated and dreaded Christ, because he knew him to be a Holy One; for the carnal mind is enmity against God, especially against his holiness. When Christ by his grace delivers souls out of the hands of Satan, it is not without tumult in the soul; for that spiteful enemy will disquiet those whom he cannot destroy. This put all who saw it upon considering, What is this new doctrine? A work as great often is wrought now, yet men treat it with contempt and neglect. If this were not so, the conversion of a notorious wicked man to a sober, righteous, and godly life, by the preaching of a crucified Saviour, would cause many to ask, What doctrine is this?

Verses 29-39 Wherever Christ comes, he comes to do good. He cures, that we may minister to him, and to others who are his, and for his sake. Those kept from public ordinances by sickness or other real hindrances, may expect the Saviour's gracious presence; he will soothe their sorrows, and abate their pains. Observe how numerous the patients were. When others speed well with Christ, it should quicken us in seeking after him. Christ departed into a solitary place. Though he was in no danger of distraction, or of temptation to vain-glory, yet he retired. Those who have the most business in public, and of the best kind, must yet sometimes be alone with God.

Verses 40-45 We have here Christ's cleansing of a leper. It teaches us to apply to the Saviour with great humility, and with full submission to his will, saying, "Lord, if thou wilt," without any doubt of Christ's readiness to help the distressed. See also what to expect from Christ; that according to our faith it shall be to us. The poor leper said, If thou wilt. Christ readily wills favours to those who readily refer themselves to his will. Christ would have nothing done that looked like seeking praise of the people. But no reasons now exist why we should hesitate to spread the praises of Christ.

CHAPTER 2

Christ heals one sick of the palsy. (1-12) Levi's call, and the entertainment given to Jesus. (13-17) Why Christ's disciples did not fast. (18-22) He justifies his disciples for plucking corn on the Sabbath. (23-28)

Verses 1-12 It was this man's misery that he needed to be so carried, and shows the suffering state of human life; it was kind of those who so carried him, and teaches the compassion that should be in men, toward their fellow-creatures in distress. True faith and strong faith may work in various ways; but it shall be accepted and approved by Jesus Christ. Sin is the cause of all our pains and sicknesses. The way to remove the effect, is to take away the cause. Pardon of sin strikes at the root of all diseases. Christ proved his power to forgive sin, by showing his power to cure the man sick of the palsy. And his curing diseases was a figure of his pardoning sin, for sin is the disease of the soul; when it is pardoned, it is healed. When we see what Christ does in healing souls, we must own that we never saw the like. Most men think themselves whole; they feel no need of a physician, therefore despise or neglect Christ and his gospel. But the convinced, humbled sinner, who despairs of all help, excepting from the Saviour, will show his faith by applying to him without delay.

Verses 13-17 Matthew was not a good character, or else, being a Jew, he would never have been a publican, that is, a tax-gatherer for the Romans. However, Christ called this publican to follow him. With God, through Christ, there is mercy to pardon the greatest sins, and grace to change the greatest sinners, and make them holy. A faithful, fair-dealing publican was rare. And because the Jews had a particular hatred to an office which proved that they were subject to the Romans, they gave these tax-gatherers an ill name. But such as these our blessed Lord did not hesitate to converse with, when he appeared in the likeness of sinful flesh. And it is no new thing for that which is both well done and well designed, to be slandered, and turned to the reproach of the wisest and best of men. Christ would not withdraw, though the Pharisees were offended. If the world had been righteous, there had been no occasion for his coming, either to preach repentance, or to purchase forgiveness. We must not keep company with ungodly men out of love to their vain conversation; but we are to show love to their souls, remembering that our good Physician had the power of healing in himself, and was in no danger of taking the disease; but it is not so with us. In trying to do good to others, let us be careful we do not get harm to ourselves.

Verses 18-22 Strict professors are apt to blame all that do not fully come up to their own views. Christ did not escape slanders; we should be willing to bear them, as well as careful not to deserve them; but should attend to every part of our duty in its proper order and season.

Verses 23-28 The Sabbath is a sacred and Divine institution; a privilege and benefit, not a task and drudgery. God never designed it to be a burden to us, therefore we must not make it so to ourselves. The Sabbath was instituted for the good of mankind, as living in society, having many wants and troubles, preparing for a state of happiness or misery. Man was not made for the Sabbath, as if his keeping it could be of service to God, nor was he commanded to keep it outward observances to his real hurt. Every observance respecting it, is to be interpreted by the rule of mercy.

CHAPTER 3

The withered hand healed. (1-5) The people resort to Christ. (6-12) The apostles called. (13-21) The blasphemy of the scribes. (22-30) Christ's relatives. (31-35)

Verses 1-5 This man's case was piteous; he had a withered hand, which disabled him from working for his living; and those that are so, are the most proper objects of charity. Let those be helped that cannot help themselves. But stubborn infidels, when they can say nothing against the truth, yet will not yield. We hear what is said amiss, and see what is done amiss; but Christ looks at the root of bitterness in the heart, the blindness and hardness of that, and is grieved. Let hard-hearted sinners tremble to think of the anger with which he will look upon them shortly, when the day of his wrath comes. The great healing day now is the Sabbath, and the healing place the house of prayer; but the healing power is of Christ. The gospel command is like that recorded here: though our hands are withered, yet, if we will not stretch them out, it is our own fault that we are not healed. But if we are healed, Christ, his power and grace, must have all the glory.

Verses 6-12 All our sicknesses and calamities spring from the anger of God against our sins. Their removal, or the making them blessings to us, was purchased to us by the blood of Christ. But the plagues and diseases of our souls, of our hearts, are chiefly to be dreaded; and He can heal them also by a word. May more and more press to Christ to be healed of these plagues, and to be delivered from the enemies of their souls.

Verses 13-21 Christ calls whom he will; for his grace is his own. He had called the apostles to separate themselves from the crowd, and they came unto him. He now gave them power to heal sicknesses, and to cast out devils. May the Lord send forth more and more of those who have been with him, and have learned of him to preach his gospel, to be instruments in his blessed work. Those whose hearts are enlarged in the work of God, can easily bear with what is inconvenient to themselves, and will rather lose a meal than an opportunity of doing good. Those who go on with zeal in the work of God, must expect hindrances, both from the hatred of enemies, and mistaken affections of friends, and need to guard against both.

Verses 22-30 It was plain that the doctrine of Christ had a direct tendency to break the devil's power; and it was as plain, that casting of him out of the bodies of people, confirmed that doctrine; therefore Satan could not support such a design. Christ gave an awful warning against speaking such dangerous words. It is true the gospel promises, because Christ has purchased, forgiveness for the greatest sins and sinners; but by this sin, they would oppose the gifts of the Holy Ghost after Christ's ascension. Such is the enmity of the heart, that unconverted men pretend believers are doing Satan's work, when sinners are brought to repentance and newness of life.

Verses 31-35 It is a great comfort to all true Christians, that they are dearer to Christ than mother, brother, or sister as such, merely as relations in the flesh would have been, even had they been holy. Blessed be God, this great and gracious privilege is ours even now; for though Christ's bodily presence cannot be enjoyed by us, his spiritual presence is not denied us.

CHAPTER 4

The parable of the sower. (1-20) Other parables. (21-34) Christ stills the tempest. (35-41)

Verses 1-20 This parable contained instruction so important, that all capable of hearing were bound to attend to it. There are many things we are concerned to know; and if we understand not the plain truths of the gospel, how shall we learn those more difficult! It will help us to value the privileges we enjoy as disciples of Christ, if we seriously consider the deplorable state of all who have not such privileges. In the great field of the church, the word of God is dispensed to all. Of the many that hear the word of the gospel, but few receive it, so as to bring forth fruit. Many are much affected with the word for the present, who yet receive no abiding benefit. The word does not leave abiding impressions upon the minds of men, because their hearts are not duly disposed to receive it. The devil is very busy about careless hearers, as the fowls of the air go about the seed that lies above ground. Many continue in a barren, false profession, and go down to hell. Impressions that are not deep, will not last. Many do not mind heart-work, without which religion is nothing. Others are hindered from profiting by the word of God, by abundance of the world. And those who have but little of the world, may yet be ruined by indulging the body.

God expects and requires fruit from those who enjoy the gospel, a temper of mind and Christian graces daily exercised, Christian duties duly performed. Let us look to the Lord, that by his new-creating grace our hearts may become good ground, and that the good seed of the word may produce in our lives those good words and works which are through Jesus Christ, to the praise and glory of God the Father.

Verses 21-34 These declarations were intended to call the attention of the disciples to the word of Christ. By his thus instructing them, they were made able to instruct others; as candles are lighted, not to be covered, but to be placed on a candlestick, that they may give light to a room. This parable of the good seed, shows the manner in which the kingdom of God makes progress in the world. Let but the word of Christ have the place it ought to have in a soul, and it will show itself in a good conversation. It grows gradually: first the blade; then the ear; after that the full corn in the ear. When it is sprung up, it will go forward. The work of grace in the soul is, at first, but the day of small things; yet it has mighty products even now, while it is in its growth; but what will there be when it is perfected in heaven!

Verses 35-41 Christ was asleep in the storm, to try the faith of his disciples, and to stir them up to pray. Their faith appeared weak, and their prayers strong. When our wicked hearts are like the troubled sea which cannot rest, when our passions are unruly, let us think we hear the law of Christ, saying, Be silent, be dumb. When without are fightings, and within are fears, and the spirits are in a tumult, if he say, "Peace, be still," there is a great calm at once. Why are ye so fearful? Though there may be cause for some fear, yet not for such fear as this. Those may suspect their faith, who can have such a thought as that Jesus careth not though his people perish. How imperfect are the best of saints! Faith and fear take their turns while we are in this world; but ere long, fear will be overcome, and faith will be lost in sight.

CHAPTER 5

The demoniac healed. (1-20) A woman healed. (21-34) The daughter of Jairus raised. (35-43)

Verses 1-20 Some openly willful sinners are like this madman. The commands of the law are as chains and fetters, to restrain sinners from their wicked courses; but they break those bands in sunder; and it is an evidence of the power of the devil in them. A legion of soldiers consisted of six thousand men, or more. What multitudes of fallen spirits there must be, and all enemies to God and man, when here was a legion in one poor wretched creature! Many there are that rise up against us. We are not a match for our spiritual enemies, in our own strength; but in the Lord, and in the power of his might, we shall be able to stand against them, though there are legions of them. When the vilest transgressor is delivered by the power of Jesus from the bondage of Satan, he will gladly sit at the feet of his Deliverer, and hear his word, who delivers the wretched slaves of Satan, and numbers them among his saints and servants. When the people found that their swine were lost, they had a dislike to Christ.

Long-suffering and mercy may be seen, even in the corrections by which men lose their property while their lives are saved, and warning given them to seek the salvation of their souls. The man joyfully proclaimed what great things Jesus had done for him. All men marveled, but few followed him. Many who cannot but wonder at the works of Christ, yet do not, as they ought, wonder after him.

Verses 21-34 A despised gospel will go where it will be better received. One of the rulers of a synagogue earnestly besought Christ for a little daughter, about twelve years old, who was dying. Another cure was wrought by the way. We should do good, not only when in the house, but when we walk by the way, De 6:7. It is common with people not to apply to Christ till they have tried in vain all other helpers, and find them, as certainly they will, physicians of no value. Some run to diversions and gay company; others plunge into business, or even into intemperance; others go about to establish their own righteousness, or torment themselves by vain superstitions. Many perish in these ways; but none will ever find rest to the soul by such devices; while those whom Christ heals of the disease of sin, find in themselves an entire change for the better. As secret acts of sin, so secret acts of faith, are known to the Lord Jesus. The woman told all the truth. It is the will of Christ that his people should be comforted, and he has power to command comfort to troubled spirits. The more simply we depend on Him, and expect great things from him, the more we shall find in ourselves that he is become our salvation. Those who, by faith, are healed of their spiritual diseases, have reason to go in peace.

Verses 35-43 We may suppose Jairus hesitating whether he should ask Christ to go on or not, when told that his daughter was dead. But have we not as much occasion for the grace of God, and the comfort of his Spirit, for the prayers of our ministers and Christian friends, when death is in the house, as when sickness is there? Faith is the only remedy against grief and fear at such a time. Believe the resurrection, then fear not. He raised the dead child to life by a word of power. Such is the gospel call to those who are by nature dead in trespasses and sins. It is by the word of Christ that spiritual life is given. All who saw it, and heard of it, admired the miracle, and Him that wrought it. Though we cannot now expect to have our dead children or relatives restored, we may hope to find comfort under our trials.

CHAPTER 6

Christ despised in his own country. (1-6) The apostles sent forth. (7-13) John the Baptist put to death. (14-29) The apostles return, Five thousand fed by a miracle. (30-44) Christ walks on the sea, He heals those that touch him. (45-56)

Verses 1-6 Our Lord's countrymen tried to prejudice the minds of people against him. Is not this the carpenter? Our Lord Jesus probably had worked in that business with his father. He thus put honour upon mechanics, and encouraged all persons who eat by the labour of their hands. It becomes the followers of Christ to content themselves with the satisfaction of doing good, although they are denied the praise of it. How much did these Nazarenes lose by obstinate prejudices against Jesus! May Divine grace deliver us from that unbelief, which renders Christ a savour of death, rather than of life to the soul. Let us, like our Master, go and teach cottages and peasants the way of salvation.

Verses 7-13 Though the apostles were conscious to themselves of great weakness, and expected no worldly advantage, yet, in obedience to their Master, and in dependence upon his strength, they went out. They did not amuse people with curious matters, but told them they must repent of their sins, and turn to God. The servants of Christ may hope to turn many from darkness unto God, and to heal souls by the power of the Holy Ghost.

Verses 14-29 Herod feared John while he lived, and feared him still more when he was dead. Herod did many of those things which John in his preaching taught him; but it is not enough to do many things, we must have respect to all the commandments.

Herod respected John, till he touched him in his Herodias. Thus many love good preaching, if it keep far away from their beloved sin. But it is better that sinners persecute ministers now for faithfulness, than curse them eternally for unfaithfulness. The ways of God are unsearchable; but we may be sure he never can be at a loss to repay his servants for what they endure or lose for his sake. Death could not come so as to surprise this holy man; and the triumph of the wicked was short.

Verses 30-44 Let not ministers do any thing or teach any thing, but what they are willing should be told to their Lord. Christ notices the frights of some, and the toils of others of his disciples, and provides rest for those that are tired, and refuge for those that are terrified. The people sought the spiritual food of Christ's word, and then he took care that they should not want bodily food. If Christ and his disciples put up with mean things, surely we may. And this miracle shows that Christ came into the world, not only to restore, but to preserve and nourish spiritual life; in him there is enough for all that come. None are sent empty away from Christ but those who come to him full of themselves. Though Christ had bread enough at command, he teaches us not to waste any of God's bounties, remembering how many are in want. We may, some time, need the fragments that we now throw away.

Verses 45-56 The church is often like a ship at sea, tossed with tempests, and not comforted: we may have Christ for us, yet wind and tide against us; but it is a comfort to Christ's disciples in a storm, that their Master is in the heavenly mount, interceding for them. And no difficulties can hinder Christ's appearance for his people, when the set time is come. He silenced their fears, by making himself known to them. Our fears are soon satisfied, if our mistakes are set right, especially our mistakes as to Christ. Let the disciples have their Master with them, and all is well. It is for want of rightly understanding Christ's former works, that we view his present works as if there never were the like before. If Christ's ministers now could cure people's bodily diseases, what multitudes would flock after them! It is sad to think how much more most care about their bodies than about their souls.

CHAPTER 7

The traditions of the elders. (1-13) What defiles the man. (14-23) The woman of Canaan's daughter cured. (24-30) Christ restores a man to hearing and speech. (31-37)

Verses 1-13 One great design of Christ's coming was, to set aside the ceremonial law; and to make way for this, he rejects the ceremonies men added to the law of God's making. Those clean hands and that pure heart which Christ bestows on his disciples, and requires of them, are very different from the outward and superstitious forms of Pharisees of every age. Jesus reproves them for rejecting the commandment of God. It is clear that it is the duty of children, if their parents are poor, to relieve them as far as they are able; and if children deserve to die that curse their parents, much more those that starve them. But if a man conformed to the traditions of the Pharisees, they found a device to free him from the claim of this duty.

Verses 14-23 Our wicked thoughts and affections, words and actions, defile us, and these only. As a corrupt fountain sends forth corrupt streams, so does a corrupt heart send forth corrupt reasonings, corrupt appetites and passions, and all the wicked words and actions that come from them. A spiritual understanding of the law of God, and a sense of the evil of sin, will cause a man to seek for the grace of the Holy Spirit, to keep down the evil thoughts and affections that work within.

Verses 24-30 Christ never put any from him that fell at his feet, which a poor trembling soul may do. As she was a good woman, so a good mother. This sent her to Christ. His saying, Let the children first be filled, shows that there was mercy for the Gentiles, and not far off. She spoke, not as making light of the mercy, but magnifying the abundance of miraculous cures among the Jews, in comparison with which a single cure was but as a crumb. Thus, while proud Pharisees are left by the blessed Saviour, he manifests his compassion to poor humbled sinners, who look to him for children's bread. He still goes about to seek and save the lost.

Verses 31-37 Here is a cure of one that was deaf and dumb. Those who brought this poor man to Christ, besought him to observe the case, and put forth his power. Our Lord used more outward actions in the doing of this cure than usual. These were only signs of Christ's power to cure the man, to encourage his faith, and theirs that brought him. Though we find great variety in the cases and manner of relief of those who applied to Christ, yet all obtained the relief they sought. Thus it still is in the great concerns of our souls.

CHAPTER 8

Four thousand fed by a miracle. (1-10) Christ cautions against the Pharisees and Herodians. (11-21) A blind man healed. (22-26) Peter's testimony to Christ. (27-33) Christ must be followed. (34-38)

Verses 1-10 Our Lord Jesus encouraged the meanest to come to him for life and grace. Christ knows and considers our frames. The bounty of Christ is always ready; to show that, he repeated this miracle. His favours are renewed, as our wants and necessities are. And those need not fear want, who have Christ to live upon by faith, and do so with thanksgiving.

Verses 11-21 Obstinate unbelief will have something to say, though ever so unreasonable. Christ refused to answer their demand. If they will not be convinced, they shall not. Alas! what cause we have to lament for those around us, who destroy themselves and others by their perverse and obstinate unbelief, and enmity to the gospel! When we forget the works of God, and distrust him, we should chide ourselves severely, as Christ here reproves his disciples. How is it that we so often mistake his meaning, disregard his warnings, and distrust his providence?

Verses 22-26 Here is a blind man brought to Christ by his friends. Therein appeared the faith of those that brought him. If those who are spiritually blind, do not pray for themselves, yet their friends and relations should pray for them, that Christ would be pleased to touch them. The cure was wrought gradually, which was not usual in our Lord's miracles. Christ showed in what method those commonly are healed by his grace, who by nature are spiritually blind. At first, their knowledge is confused; but, like the light of the morning, it shines more and more to the perfect day, and then they see all things clearly. Slighting Christ's favours is forfeiting them; and he will make those who do so know the worth of privileges by the want of them.

Verses 27-33 These things are written, that we may believe that Jesus is the Christ, the Son of God. These miracles of our Lord assure us that he was not conquered, but a Conqueror. Now the disciples are convinced that Jesus is the Christ; they may bear to hear of his sufferings, of which Christ here begins to give them notice. He sees that amiss in what we say and do, of which we ourselves are not aware, and knows what manner of spirit we are of, when we ourselves do not. The wisdom of man is folly, when it pretends to limit the Divine counsels. Peter did not rightly understand the nature of Christ's kingdom.

Verses 34-38 Frequent notice is taken of the great flocking there was to Christ for help in various cases. All are concerned to know this, if they expect him to heal their souls. They must not indulge the ease of the body. As the happiness of heaven with Christ, is enough to make up for the loss of life itself for him, so the gain of all the world in sin, will not make up for the ruin of the soul by sin. And there is a day coming, when the cause of Christ will appear as glorious, as some now think it mean and contemptible. May we think of that season, and view every earthly object as we shall do at that great day.

CHAPTER 9

The transfiguration. (1-13) An evil spirit cast out. (14-29) The apostles reproved. (30-40) Pain to be preferred to sin. (41-50)

Verses 1-13 Here is a prediction of the near approach Christ's kingdom. A glimpse of that kingdom was given in the transfiguration of Christ. It is good to be away from the world, and alone with Christ: and how good to be with Christ glorified in heaven with all the saints! But when it is well with us, we are apt not to care for others, and in the fullness of our enjoyments, we forget the many wants of our brethren. God owns Jesus, and accepts him as his beloved Son, and is ready to accept us in him. Therefore we must own and accept him as our beloved Saviour, and must give up ourselves to be ruled by him. Christ does not leave the soul, when joys and comforts leave it. Jesus explained to the disciples the prophecy about Elias. This was very suitable to the ill usage of John Baptist.

Verses 14-29 The father of the suffering youth reflected on the want of power in the disciples; but Christ will have him reckon the disappointment to the want of faith. Very much is promised to our believing. If thou canst believe, it is possible that thy hard heart may be softened, thy spiritual diseases may be cured; and, weak as thou art, thou mayest be able to hold out to the end. Those that complain of unbelief, must look up to Christ for grace to help them against it, and his grace will be sufficient for them. Whom Christ cures, he cures effectually. But Satan is unwilling to be driven from those that have been long his slaves, and, when he cannot deceive or destroy the sinner, he will cause him all the terror that he can. The disciples must not think to do their work always with the same ease; some services call for more than ordinary pains.

Verses 30-40 The time of Christ's suffering drew nigh. Had he been delivered into the hands of devils, and they had done this, it had not been so strange; but that men should thus shamefully treat the Son of man, who came to redeem and save them, is wonderful. Still observe that when Christ spake of his death, he always spake of his resurrection, which took the reproach of it from himself, and should have taken the grief of it from his disciples. Many remain ignorant because they are ashamed to inquire. Alas! that while the Saviour teaches so plainly the things which belong to his love and grace, men are so blinded that they understand not his sayings. We shall be called to account about our discourses, and to account for our disputes, especially about being greater than others. Those who are most humble and self-denying, most resemble Christ, and shall be most tenderly owned by him. This Jesus taught them by a sign; whoever shall receive one like this child, receives me. Many have been like the disciples, ready to silence men who have success in preaching to sinners repentance in Christ's name, because they follow not with them. Our Lord blamed the apostles, reminding them that he who wrought miracles in his name would not be likely to hurt his cause. If sinners are brought to repent, to believe in the Saviour, and to live sober, righteous, and godly lives, we then see that the Lord works by the preacher.

Verses 41-50 It is repeatedly said of the wicked, Their worm dieth not, as well as, The fire is never quenched. Doubtless, remorse of conscience and keen self-reflection are this never-dying worm. Surely it is beyond compare better to undergo all possible pain, hardship, and self-denial here, and to be happy for ever hereafter, than to enjoy all kinds of worldly pleasure for a season, and to be miserable for ever. Like the sacrifices, we must be salted with salt; our corrupt affections must be subdued and mortified by the Holy Spirit. Those that have the salt of grace, must show they have a living principle of grace in their hearts, which works out corrupt dispositions in the soul that would offend God, or our own consciences.

CHAPTER 10

The Pharisees' question concerning divorce. (1-12) Christ's love to little children. (13-16) Christ's discourse with the rich young man. (17-22) The hindrance of riches. (23-31) Christ foretells his sufferings. (32-45) Bartimeus healed. (46-52)

Verses 1-12 Wherever Jesus was, the people flocked after him in crowds, and he taught them. Preaching was Christ's constant practice. He here shows that the reason why Moses' law allowed divorce, was such that they ought not to use the permission; it was only for the hardness of their hearts. God himself joined man and wife together; he has fitted them to be comforts and helps for each other. The bond which God has tied, is not to be lightly untied. Let those who are for putting away their wives consider what would become of themselves, if God should deal with them in like manner.

Verses 13-16 Some parents or nurses brought little children to Christ, that he should touch them, in token of his blessing them. It does not appear that they needed bodily cures, nor were they capable of being taught: but those who had the care of them believed that Christ's blessing would do their souls good; therefore they brought them to him. Jesus ordered that they should be brought to him, and that nothing should be said or done to hinder it. Children should be directed to the Saviour as soon as they are able to understand his words. Also, we must receive the kingdom of God as little children; we must stand affected to Christ and his grace, as little children to their parents, nurses, and teachers.

Verses 17-22 This young ruler showed great earnestness. He asked what he should do now, that he might be happy for ever. Most ask for good to be had in this world; any good, psalms 4:6; he asks for good to be done in this world, in order to enjoy the greatest good in the other world. Christ encouraged this address by assisting his faith, and by directing his practice. But here is a sorrowful parting between Jesus and this young man. He asks Christ what he shall do more than he has done, to obtain eternal life; and Christ puts it to him, whether he has indeed that firm belief of, and that high value for eternal life which he seems to have. Is he willing to bear a present cross, in expectation of future crown? The young man was sorry he could not be a follower of Christ upon easier terms; that he could not lay hold on eternal life, and keep hold of his worldly possessions too. He went away grieved. See Matthew 6:24, Ye cannot serve God and mammon.

Verses 23-31 Christ took this occasion to speak to his disciples about the difficulty of the salvation of those who have abundance of this world. Those who thus eagerly seek the wealth of the world, will never rightly prize Christ and his grace. Also, as to the greatness of the salvation of those who have but little of this world, and leave it for Christ. The greatest trial of a good man's constancy is, when love to Jesus calls him to give up love to friends and relatives. Even when gainers by Christ, let them still expect to suffer for him, till they reach heaven. Let us learn contentment in a low state, and to watch against the love of riches in a high one. Let us pray to be enabled to part with all, if required, in Christ's service, and to use all we are allowed to keep in his service.

Verses 32-45 Christ's going on with his undertaking for the salvation of mankind, was, is, and will be, the wonder of all his disciples. Worldly honour is a glittering thing, with which the eyes of Christ's own disciples have many times been dazzled. Our care must be, that we may have wisdom and grace to know how to suffer with him; and we may trust him to provide what the degrees of our glory shall be. Christ shows them that dominion was generally abused in the world. If Jesus would gratify all our desires, it would soon appear that we desire fame or authority, and are unwilling to taste of his cup, or to have his baptism; and should often be ruined by having our prayers answered. But he loves us, and will only give his people what is good for them.

Verses 46-52 Bartimeus had heard of Jesus and his miracles, and learning that he was passing by, hoped to recover his eyesight. In coming to Christ for help and healing, we should look to him as the promised Messiah. The gracious calls Christ gives us to come to him, encourage our hope, that if we come to him we shall have what we come for. Those who would come to Jesus, must cast away the garment of their own sufficiency, must free themselves from every weight, and the sin that, like long garments, most easily besets them, Hebrews 12:1. He begged that his eyes might be opened. It is very desirable to be able to earn our bread; and where God has given men limbs and senses, it is a shame, by foolishness and slothfulness, to make themselves, in effect, blind and lame. His eyes were opened. Thy faith has made thee whole: faith in Christ as the Son of David, and in his pity and power; not thy repeated words, but thy faith; Christ setting thy faith to work. Let sinners be exhorted to imitate blind Bartimeus. Where the gospel is preached, or the written words of truth circulated, Jesus is passing by, and this is the opportunity. It is not enough to come to Christ for spiritual healing, but, when we are healed, we must continue to follow him; that we may honour him, and receive instruction from him. Those who have spiritual eyesight, see that beauty in Christ which will draw them to run after him.

CHAPTER 11

Christ's triumphant entry into Jerusalem. (1-11) The barren fig-tree cursed, The temple cleansed. (12-18) Prayer in faith. (19-26) The priests and elders questioned concerning John the Baptist. (27-33)

Verses 1-11 Christ's coming into Jerusalem thus remarkably, shows that he was not afraid of the power and malice of his enemies. This would encourage his disciples who were full of fear. Also, that he was not disquieted at the thoughts of his approaching sufferings. But all marked his humiliation; and these matters teach us not to mind high things, but to condescend to those of low estate. How ill it becomes Christians to take state, when Christ was so far from claiming it! They welcomed his person; Blessed is he that cometh, the "He that should come," so often promised, so long expected; he comes in the name of the Lord. Let him have our best affections; he is a blessed Saviour, and brings blessings to us, and blessed be He that sent him. Praises be to our God, who is in the highest heavens, over all, God blessed for ever.

Verses 12-18 Christ looked to find some fruit, for the time of gathering figs, though it was near, was not yet come; but he found none. He made this fig-tree an example, not to the trees, but to the men of that generation. It was a figure of the doom upon the Jewish church, to which he came seeking fruit, but found none. Christ went to the temple, and began to reform the abuses in its courts, to show that when the Redeemer came to Zion, it was to turn away ungodliness from Jacob. The scribes and the chief priests sought, not how they might make their peace with him, but how they might destroy him. A desperate attempt, which they could not but fear was fighting against God.

Verses 19-26 The disciples could not think why that fig-tree should so soon wither away; but all wither who reject Christ; it represented the state of the Jewish church. We should rest in no religion that does not make us fruitful in good works. Christ taught them from hence to pray in faith. It may be applied to that mighty faith with which all true Christians are endued, and which does wonders in spiritual things. It justifies us, and so removes mountains of guilt, never to rise up in judgment against us. It purifies the heart, and so removes mountains of corruption, and makes them plain before the grace of God. One great errand to the throne of grace is to pray for the pardon of our sins; and care about this ought to be our daily concern.

Verses 27-33 Our Saviour shows how near akin his doctrine and baptism were to those of John; they had the same design and tendency, to bring in the gospel kingdom. These elders did not deserve to be taught; for it was plain that they contended not for truth, but victory: nor did he need to tell them; for the works he did, told them plainly he had authority from God; since no man could do the miracles which he did, unless God were with him.

CHAPTER 12

The parable of the vineyard and husbandmen. (1-12) Question about tribute. (13-17) Concerning the resurrection. (18-27) The great command of the law. (28-34) Christ the Son and yet the Lord of David. (35-40) The poor widow commended. (41-44)

Verses 1-12 Christ showed in parables, that he would lay aside the Jewish church. It is sad to think what base usage God's faithful ministers have met with in all ages, from those who have enjoyed the privileges of the church, but have not brought forth fruit answerable. God at length sent his Son, his Well-beloved; and it might be expected that he whom their Master loved, they also should respect and love; but instead of honouring him because he was the Son and Heir, they therefore hated him. But the exaltation of Christ was the Lord's doing; and it is his doing to exalt him in our hearts, and to set up his throne there; and if this be done, it cannot but be marvelous in our eyes. The Scriptures, and faithful preachers, and the coming of Christ in the flesh, call on us to render due praise to God in our lives. Let sinners beware of a proud, carnal spirit; if they revile or despise the preachers of Christ, they would have done so their Master, had they lived when he was upon earth.

Verses 13-17 The enemies of Christ would be thought desirous to know their duty, when really they hoped that which soever side he took of the question, they might find occasion to accuse him. Nothing is more likely to ensnare the followers of Christ, than bringing them to meddle with disputes about worldly politics. Jesus avoided the snare, by referring to the submission they had already made as a nation; and all that heard him, marveled at the great wisdom of his answer. Many will praise the words of a sermon, who will not be commanded by the doctrines of it.

Verses 18-27 A right knowledge of the Scripture, as the fountain whence all revealed religion now flows, and the foundation on which it is built, is the best preservative against error. Christ put aside the objection of the Sadducees, who were the scoffing infidels of that day, by setting the doctrine of the future state in a true light. The relation between husband and wife, though appointed in the earthly paradise, will not be known in the heavenly one. It is no wonder if we confuse ourselves with foolish errors, when we form our ideas of the world of spirits by the affairs of this world of sense. It is absurd to think that the living God should be the portion and happiness of a man if he is for ever dead; and therefore it is certain that Abraham's soul exists and acts, though now for a time separate from the body. Those that deny the resurrection greatly err, and ought to be told so. Let us seek to pass through this dying world, with a joyful hope of eternal happiness, and of a glorious resurrection.

Verses 28-34 Those who sincerely desire to be taught their duty, Christ will guide in judgment, and teach his way. He tells the scribe that the great commandment, which indeed includes all, is, that of loving God with all our hearts. Wherever this is the ruling principle in the soul, there is a disposition to every other duty. Loving God with all our heart, will engage us to every thing by which he will be pleased. The sacrifices only represented the atonements for men's transgressions of the moral law; they were of no power except as they expressed repentance and faith in the promised Saviour, and as they led to moral obedience. And because we have not thus loved God and man, but the very reverse, therefore we are condemned sinners; we need repentance, and we need mercy. Christ approved what the scribe said, and encouraged him. He stood fair for further advance; for this knowledge of the law leads to conviction of sin, to repentance, to discovery of our need of mercy, and understanding the way of justification by Christ.

Verses 35-40 When we attend to what the Scriptures declare, as to the person and offices of Christ, we shall be led to confess him as our Lord and God; to obey him as our exalted Redeemer. If the common people hear these things gladly, while the learned and distinguished oppose, the former are happy, and the latter to be pitied. And as sin, disguised with a show of piety, is double iniquity, so its doom will be doubly heavy.

Verses 41-44 Let us not forget that Jesus still sees the treasury. He knows how much, and from what motives, men give to his cause. He looks at the heart, and what our views are, in giving alms; and whether we do it as unto the Lord, or only to be seen of men. It is so rare to find any who would not blame this widow, that we cannot expect to find many who will do like to her; and yet our Saviour commends her, therefore we are sure that she did well and wisely. The feeble efforts of the poor to honour their Saviour, will be commended in that day, when the splendid actions of unbelievers will be exposed to contempt.

CHAPTER 13

The destruction of the temple foretold. (1-4) Christ's prophetic declaration. (5-13) Christ's prophecy. (14-23) His prophetic declarations. (24-27) Watchfulness urged. (28-37)

Verses 1-4 See how little Christ values outward pomp, where there is not real purity of heart. He looks with pity upon the ruin of precious souls, and weeps over them, but we do not find him look with pity upon the ruin of a fine house. Let us then be reminded how needful it is for us to have a more lasting abode in heaven, and to be prepared for it by the influences of the Holy Spirit, sought in the earnest use of all the means of grace.

Verses 5-13 Our Lord Jesus, in reply to the disciples' question, does not so much satisfy their curiosity as direct their consciences. When many are deceived, we should thereby be awakened to look to ourselves. And the disciples of Christ, if it be not their own fault, may enjoy holy security and peace of mind, when all around is in disorder. But they must take heed that they are not drawn away from Christ and their duty to him, by the sufferings they will meet with for his sake. They shall be hated of all men: trouble enough! Yet the work they were called to should be carried on and prosper. Though they may be crushed and borne down, the gospel cannot be. The salvation promised is more than deliverance from evil, it is everlasting blessedness.

Verses 14-23 The Jews in rebelling against the Romans, and in persecuting the Christians, hastened their own ruin apace. Here we have a prediction of that ruin which came upon them within less than forty years after this. Such destruction and desolation, that the like cannot be found in any history. Promises of power to persevere, and cautions against falling away, well agree with each other. But the more we consider these things, the more we shall see abundant cause to flee without delay for refuge to Christ, and to renounce every earthly object, for the salvation of our souls.

Verses 24-27 The disciples had confounded the destruction of Jerusalem and the end of the world. This mistake Christ set right, and showed that the day of Christ's coming, and the day of judgment, shall be after that tribulation. Here he foretells the final dissolution of the present frame and fabric of the world. Also, the visible appearance of the Lord Jesus coming in the clouds, and the gathering together of all the elect to him.

Verses 28-37 We have the application of this prophetic sermon. As to the destruction of Jerusalem, expect it to come very shortly. As to the end of the world, do not inquire when it will come, for of that day and that hour knoweth no man. Christ, as God, could not be ignorant of anything; but the Divine wisdom which dwelt in our Saviour, communicated itself to his human soul according to the Divine pleasure. As to both, our duty is to watch and pray. Our Lord Jesus, when he ascended on high, left something for all his servants to do. We ought to be always upon our watch, in expectation of his return. This applies to Christ's coming to us at our death, as well as to the general judgment. We know not whether our Master will come in the days of youth, or middle age, or old age; but, as soon as we are born, we begin to die, and therefore we must expect death. Our great care must be, that, whenever our Lord comes, he may not find us secure, indulging in ease and sloth, mindless of our work and duty. He says to all, Watch, that you may be found in peace, without spot, and blameless.

CHAPTER 14

Christ anointed at Bethany. (1-11) The Passover, Jesus declares that Judas would betray him. (12-21) The Lord's supper instituted. (22-31) Christ's agony in the garden. (32-42) He is betrayed and taken. (43-52) Christ before the high priest. (53-65) Peter denies Christ. (66-72)

Verses 1-11 Did Christ pour out his soul unto death for us, and shall we think any thing too precious for him? Do we give him the precious ointment of our best affections? Let us love him with all the heart, though it is common for zeal and affection to be misunderstood and blamed; and remember that charity to the poor will not excuse any from particular acts of piety to the Lord Jesus. Christ commended this woman's pious attention to the notice of believers in all ages. Those who honour Christ he will honour. Covetousness was Judas' master lust, and that betrayed him to the sin of betraying his Master; the devil suited his temptation to that, and so conquered him. And see what wicked contrivances many have in their sinful pursuits; but what appears to forward their plans, will prove curses in the end.

Verses 12-21 Nothing could be less the result of human foresight than the events here related. But our Lord knows all things about us before they come to pass. If we admit him, he will dwell in our hearts. The Son of man goes, as it is written of him, as a lamb to the slaughter; but woe to that man by whom he is betrayed! God's permitting the sins of men, and bringing glory to himself out of them, does not oblige them to sin; nor will this be any excuse for their guilt, or lessen their punishment.

Verses 22-31 The Lord's supper is food for the soul, therefore a very little of that which is for the body, as much as will serve for a sign, is enough. It was instituted by the example and the practice of our Master, to remain in force till his second coming. It was instituted with blessing and giving of thanks, to be a memorial of Christ's death. Frequent mention is made of his precious blood, as the price of our redemption. How comfortable is this to poor repenting sinners, that the blood of Christ is shed for many! If for many, why not for me? It was a sign of the conveyance of the benefits purchased for us by his death. Apply the doctrine of Christ crucified to yourselves; let it be meat and drink to your souls, strengthening and refreshing your spiritual life. It was to be an earnest and foretaste of the happiness of heaven, and thereby to put us out of taste for the pleasures and delights of sense. Every one that has tasted spiritual delights, straightway desires eternal ones. Though the great Shepherd passed through his sufferings without one false step, yet his followers often have been scattered by the small measure of sufferings allotted to them. How very apt we are to think well of ourselves, and to trust our own hearts! It was ill done of Peter thus to answer his Master, and not with fear and trembling. Lord, give me grace to keep me from denying thee.

Verses 32-42 Christ's sufferings began with the sorest of all, those in his soul. He began to be sorely amazed; words not used in St. Matthew, but very full of meaning. The terrors of God set themselves in array against him, and he allowed him to contemplate them. Never was sorrow like unto his at this time. Now he was made a curse for us; the curses of the law were laid upon him as our Surety. He now tasted death, in all the bitterness of it. This was that fear of which the apostle speaks, the natural fear of pain and death, at which human nature startles.

Can we ever entertain favourable, or even slight thoughts of sin, when we see the painful sufferings which sin, though but reckoned to him, brought on the Lord Jesus? Shall that sit light upon our souls, which sat so heavy upon his? Was Christ in such agony for our sins, and shall we never be in agony about them? How should we look upon Him whom we have pierced, and mourn!

It becomes us to be exceedingly sorrowful for sin, because He was so, and never to mock at it. Christ, as Man, pleaded, that, if it were possible, his sufferings might pass from him. As Mediator, he submitted to the will of God, saying, Nevertheless, not what I will, but what thou wilt; I bid it welcome. See how the sinful weakness of Christ's disciples returns, and overpowers them. What heavy clogs these bodies of ours are to our souls! But when we see trouble at the door, we should get ready for it. Alas, even believers often look at the Redeemer's sufferings in a drowsy manner, and instead of being ready to die with Christ, they are not even prepared to watch with him one hour.

Verses 43-52 Because Christ appeared not as a temporal prince, but preached repentance, reformation, and a holy life, and directed men's thoughts, and affections, and aims to another world, therefore the Jewish rulers sought to destroy him. Peter wounded one of the band. It is easier to fight for Christ than to die for him. But there is a great difference between faulty disciples and hypocrites. The latter rashly and without thought call Christ Master, and express great affection for him, yet betray him to his enemies. Thus they hasten their own destruction.

Verses 53-65 We have here Christ's condemnation before the great council of the Jews. Peter followed; but the high priest's fire-side was no proper place, nor his servants proper company, for Peter:

it was an entrance into temptation. Great diligence was used to procure false witnesses against Jesus, yet their testimony was not equal to the charge of a capital crime, by the utmost stretch of their law. He was asked, Art thou the Son of the Blessed? That is, the Son of God. For the proof of his being the Son of God, he refers to his second coming. In these outrages we have proofs of man's enmity to God, and of God's free and unspeakable love to man.

Verses 66-72 Peter's denying Christ began by keeping at a distance from him. Those that are shy of godliness, are far in the way to deny Christ. Those who think it dangerous to be in company with Christ's disciples, because thence they may be drawn in to suffer for him, will find it much more dangerous to be in company with his enemies, because there they may be drawn in to sin against him. When Christ was admired and flocked after, Peter readily owned him; but will own no relation to him now he is deserted and despised. Yet observe, Peter's repentance was very speedy. Let him that thinketh he standeth take heed lest he fall; and let him that has fallen think of these things, and of his own offences, and return to the Lord with weeping and supplication, seeking forgiveness, and to be raised up by the Holy Spirit.

CHAPTER 15

Christ before Pilate. (1-14) Christ led to be crucified. (15-21) The crucifixion. (22-32) The death of Christ. (33-41) His body buried. (42-47)

Verses 1-14 They bound Christ. It is good for us often to remember the bonds of the Lord Jesus, as bound with him who was bound for us. By delivering up the King, they, in effect, delivered up the kingdom of God, which was, therefore, as by their own consent, taken from them, and given to another nation. Christ gave Pilate a direct answer, but would not answer the witnesses, because the things they alleged were known to be false, even Pilate himself was convinced they were so. Pilate thought that he might appeal from the priests to the people, and that they would deliver Jesus out of the priests' hands. But they were more and more urged by the priests, and cried, Crucify him! Crucify him! Let us judge of persons and things by their merits, and the standard of God's word, and not by common report. The thought that no one ever was so shamefully treated, as the only perfectly wise, holy, and excellent Person that ever appeared on earth, leads the serious mind to strong views of man's wickedness and enmity to God. Let us more and more abhor the evil dispositions which marked the conduct of these persecutors.

Verses 15-21 Christ met death in its greatest terror. It was the death of the vilest malefactors. Thus the cross and the shame are put together. God having been dishonoured by the sin of man, Christ made satisfaction by submitting to the greatest disgrace human nature could be loaded with. It was a cursed death; thus it was branded by the Jewish law, Deuteronomy 21:23. The Roman

548

soldiers mocked our Lord Jesus as a King; thus in the high priest's hall the servants had mocked him as a Prophet and Saviour. Shall a purple or scarlet robe be matter of pride to a Christian, which was matter of reproach and shame to Christ? He wore the crown of thorns which we deserved, that we might wear the crown of glory which he merited. We were by sin liable to everlasting shame and contempt; to deliver us, our Lord Jesus submitted to shame and contempt. He was led forth with the workers of iniquity, though he did no sin. The sufferings of the meek and holy Redeemer, are ever a source of instruction to the believer, of which, in his best hours, he cannot be weary. Did Jesus thus suffer, and shall I, a vile sinner, fret or repine? Shall I indulge anger, or utter reproaches and threats because of troubles and injuries?

Verses 22-32 The place where our Lord Jesus was crucified, was called the place of a scull; it was the common place of execution; for he was in all respects numbered with the transgressors. Whenever we look unto Christ crucified, we must remember what was written over his head; he is a King, and we must give up ourselves to be his subjects, as Israelites indeed. They crucified two thieves with him, and him in the midst; they thereby intended him great dishonour. But it was foretold that he should be numbered with the transgressors, because he was made sin for us. Even those who passed by railed at him. They told him to come down from the cross, and they would believe; but they did not believe, though he gave them a more convincing sign when he came up from the grave. With what earnestness will the man who firmly believes the truth, as made known by the sufferings of Christ, seek for salvation! With what gratitude will he receive the dawning hope of forgiveness and eternal life, as purchased for him by the sufferings and death of the Son of God! And with what godly sorrow will he mourn over the sins which crucified the Lord of glory!

Verses 33-41 There was a thick darkness over the land, from noon until three in the afternoon. The Jews were doing their utmost to extinguish the Sun of Righteousness. The darkness signified the cloud which the human soul of Christ was under, when he was making it an offering for sin. He did not complain that his disciples forsook him, but that his Father forsook him. In this especially he was made sin for us. When Paul was to be offered as a sacrifice for the service saints, he could joy and rejoice, Philippians 2:17 ; but it is another thing to be offered as a sacrifice for the sin of sinners. At the same instant that Jesus died, the veil of the temple was rent from the top to the bottom. This spake terror to the unbelieving Jews, and was a sign of the destruction of their church and nation. It speaks comfort to all believing Christians, for it signified the laying open a new and living way into the holiest by the blood of Jesus. The confidence with which Christ had openly addressed God as his Father, and committed his soul into his hands, seems greatly to have affected the centurion. Right views of Christ crucified will reconcile the believer to the thought of death; he longs to behold, love, and praise, as he ought, that Saviour who was wounded and pierced to save him from the wrath to come.

Verses 42-47 We are here attending the burial of our Lord Jesus. Oh that we may by grace be planted in the likeness of it! Joseph of Arimathea was one who waited for the kingdom of God. Those who hope for a share in its privileges, must own Christ's cause, when it seems to be crushed. This man God raised up for his service. There was a special providence, that Pilate should be so strict in his inquiry, that there might be no pretence to say Jesus was alive. Pilate gave Joseph leave to take down the body, and do what he pleased with it. Some of the women beheld where Jesus was laid, that they might come after the Sabbath to anoint the dead body, because they had not time to do it before. Special notice was taken of Christ's sepulchre, because he was to rise again. And he will not forsake those who trust in him, and call upon him. Death, deprived of its sting, will soon end the believer's sorrows, as it ended those of the Saviour.

CHAPTER 16

Christ's resurrection made known the women. (1-8) Christ appears to Mary Magdalene and other disciples. (9-13) His commission to the apostles. (14-18) Christ's ascension. (19,20)

Verses 1-8 Nicodemus brought a large quantity of spices, but these good women did not think that enough. The respect others show to Christ, should not hinder us from showing our respect. And those who are carried by holy zeal, to seek Christ diligently, will find the difficulties in their way speedily vanish. When we put ourselves to trouble and expense, from love to Christ, we shall be accepted, though our endeavours are not successful. The sight of the angel might justly have encouraged them, but they were affrighted. Thus many times that which should be matter of comfort to us, through our own mistake, proves a terror to us. He was crucified, but he is glorified. He is risen, he is not here, not dead, but alive again; hereafter you will see him, but you may here see the place where he was laid. Thus seasonable comforts will be sent to those that lament after the Lord Jesus. Peter is particularly named, Tell Peter; it will be most welcome to him, for he is in sorrow for sin. A sight of Christ will be very welcome to a true penitent, and a true penitent is very welcome to a sight of Christ. The men ran with all the haste they could to the disciples; but disquieting fears often hinder us from doing that service to

Christ and to the souls of men, which, if faith and the joy of faith were strong, we might do.

Verses 9-13 Better news cannot be brought to disciples in tears, than to tell them of Christ's resurrection. And we should study to comfort disciples that are mourners, by telling them whatever we have seen of Christ. It was a wise providence that the proofs of Christ's resurrection were given gradually, and admitted cautiously, that the assurance with which the apostles preached this doctrine afterwards might the more satisfy. Yet how slowly do we admit the consolations which the word of God holds forth! Therefore while Christ comforts his people, he often sees it needful to rebuke and correct them for hardness of heart in distrusting his promise, as well as in not obeying his holy precepts.

Verses 14-18 The evidences of the truth of the gospel are so full, that those who receive it not, may justly be upbraided with their unbelief. Our blessed Lord renewed his choice of the eleven as his apostles, and commissioned them to go into all the world, to preach his gospel to every creature. Only he that is a true Christian shall be saved through Christ. Simon Magus professed to believe, and was baptized, yet he was declared to be in the bonds of iniquity: see his history in Acts 8:13-25. Doubtless this is a solemn declaration of that true faith which receives Christ in all his characters and offices, and for all the purposes of salvation, and which produces its right effect on the heart and life; not a mere assent, which is a dead faith, and cannot profit. The commission of Christ's ministers extends to every creature throughout the world, and the declarations of the gospel contain not only truths, encouragements, and precepts, but also most awful warnings. Observe what power the apostles should be endued with, for confirming the doctrine they were to preach. These were miracles to confirm the truth of the gospel, and means of spreading the gospel among nations that had not heard it.

Verses 19-20 After the Lord had spoken he went up into heaven. Sitting is a posture of rest, he had finished his work; and a posture of rule, he took possession of his kingdom. He sat at the right hand of God, which denotes his sovereign dignity and universal power. Whatever God does concerning us, gives to us, or accepts from us, it is by his Son. Now he is glorified with the glory he had before the world. The apostles went forth, and preached every where, far and near. Though the doctrine they preached was spiritual and heavenly, and directly contrary to the spirit and temper of the world; though it met with much opposition, and was wholly destitute of all worldly supports and advantages; yet in a few years the sound went forth unto the ends of the earth. Christ's ministers do not now need to work miracles to prove their message; the Scriptures are proved to be of Divine origin, and this renders those without excuse who reject or neglect them. The effects of the gospel, when faithfully preached, and truly believed, in changing the tempers and characters of mankind, form a constant proof, a miraculous proof, that the gospel is the power of God unto salvation, of all who believe.

LUKE

CHAPTER 1

This evangelist is generally supposed to have been a physician, and a companion of the apostle Paul. The style of his writings, and his acquaintance with the Jewish rites and usages, sufficiently show that he was a Jew, while his knowledge of the Greek language and his name, speak his Gentile origin. He is first mentioned Acts 16:10,11, as with Paul at Troas, whence he attended him to Jerusalem, and was with him in his voyage, and in his imprisonment at Rome. This Gospel appears to be designed to supersede many defective and unauthentic narratives in circulation, and to give a genuine and inspired account of the life, miracles, and doctrines of our Lord, learned from those who heard and witnessed his discourses and miracles.

The Preface. (1-4) Zacharias and Elisabeth. (5-25) Christ's birth announced. (26-38) Interview of Mary and Elisabeth. (39-56) The birth of John the Baptist. (57-66) The song of Zacharias. (67-80)

Verses 1-4 Luke will not write of things about which Christians may safely differ from one another, and hesitate within themselves; but the things which are, and ought to be surely believed. The doctrine of Christ is what the wisest and best of men have ventured their souls upon with confidence and satisfaction. And the great events whereon our hopes depend, have been recorded by those who were from the beginning eye-witnesses and ministers of the word, and who were perfected in their understanding of them through Divine inspiration.

Verses 5-25 The father and mother of John the Baptist were sinners as all are, and were justified and saved in the same way as others; but they were eminent for piety and integrity. They had no children, and it could not be expected that Elisabeth should have any in her old age. While Zacharias was burning incense in the temple, the whole multitude of the people were praying without.

All the prayers we offer up to God, are acceptable and successful only by Christ's intercession in the temple of God above. We cannot expect an interest therein if we do not pray, and pray with our spirits, and are not earnest in prayer. Nor can we expect that the best of our prayers should gain acceptance, and bring an answer of peace, but through the mediation of Christ, who ever lives, making intercession. The prayers Zacharias often made, received an answer of peace. Prayers of faith are filed in heaven, and are not forgotten. Prayers made when we were young and entering into the world, may be answered when we are old and going out of the world. Mercies are doubly sweet that are given in answer to prayer.

Zacharias shall have a son in his old age, who shall be instrumental in the conversion of many souls to God, and preparing them to receive the gospel of Christ. He shall go before Him with courage, zeal, holiness, and a mind dead to earthly interests and pleasures. The disobedient and rebellious would be brought back to the wisdom of their righteous forefathers, or rather, brought to attend to the wisdom of that Just One who was coming among them. Zacharias heard all that the angel said; but his unbelief spake. In striking him dumb, God dealt justly with him, because he had objected against God's word. We may admire the patience of God towards us. God dealt kindly with him, for thus he prevented his speaking any more distrustful, unbelieving words. Thus also God confirmed his faith.

If by the rebukes we are under for our sin, we are brought to give the more credit to the word of God, we have no reason to complain. Even real believers are apt to dishonour God by unbelief; and their mouths are stopped in silence and confusion, when otherwise they would have been praising God with joy and gratitude. In God's gracious dealings with us we ought to observe his gracious regards to us. He has looked on us with compassion and favour, and therefore has thus dealt with us.

Verses 26-38 We have here an account of the mother of our Lord; though we are not to pray to her, yet we ought to praise God for her. Christ must be born miraculously. The angel's address means only, Hail, thou that art the especially chosen and favoured of the Most High, to attain the honour Jewish mothers have so long desired. This wondrous salutation and appearance troubled Mary. The angel then assured her that she had found favour with God, and would become the mother of a son whose name she should call Jesus, the Son of the Highest, one in a nature and perfection with the Lord God. JESUS! The name that refreshes the fainting spirits of humbled sinners; sweet to speak and sweet to hear, Jesus, a Saviour!

We know not his riches and our own poverty, therefore we run not to him; we perceive not that we are lost and perishing, therefore a Saviour is a word of little relish. Were we convinced of the huge mass of guilt that lies upon us, and the wrath that hangs over us for it, ready to fall upon us, it would be our continual thought, Is the Saviour mine? And that we might find him so, we should trample on all that hinders our way to him. Mary's reply to the angel was the language of faith and humble admiration, and she asked no sign for the confirming her faith. Without controversy, great was the mystery of godliness, God manifest in the flesh, 1 Timothy 3:16. Christ's human nature must be produced so, as it was fit that should be which was to be taken into union with the Divine nature. And we must, as Mary here, guide our desires by the word of God. In all conflicts, let us remember that with God nothing is impossible; and as we read and hear his promises, let us turn them into prayers, Behold the willing servant of the Lord; let it be unto me according to thy word.

Verses 39-56 It is very good for those who have the work of grace begun in their souls, to communicate one to another. On Mary's arrival, Elisabeth was conscious of the approach of her who was to be the mother of the great Redeemer. At the same time she was filled with the Holy Ghost, and under his influence declared that Mary and her expected child were most blessed and happy, as peculiarly honoured of and dear to the Most High God. Mary, animated by Elisabeth's address, and being also under the influence of the Holy Ghost, broke out into joy, admiration, and gratitude. She knew herself to be a sinner who needed a Saviour, and that she could no otherwise rejoice in God than as interested in his salvation through the promised Messiah. Those who see their need of Christ, and are desirous of righteousness and life in him, he fills with good things, with the best things; and they are abundantly satisfied with the blessings he gives. He will satisfy the desires of the poor in spirit who long for spiritual blessings, while the self-sufficient shall be sent empty away.

Verses 57-66 In these verses we have an account of the birth of John the Baptist, and the great joy among all the relations of the family. He shall be called Johanan, or "Gracious," because he shall bring in the gospel of Christ, wherein God's grace shines most bright. Zacharias recovered his speech. Unbelief closed his mouth, and believing opened it again: he believers, therefore he speaks. When God opens our lips, our mouths must show forth his praise; and better be without speech, than not use it in praising God. It is said, The hand of the Lord was working with John. God has ways of working on children in their infancy, which we cannot account for. We should observe the dealings of God, and wait the event.

Verses 67-80 Zacharias uttered a prophecy concerning the kingdom and salvation of the Messiah. The gospel brings light with it; in it the day dawns. In John the Baptist it began to break, and increased apace to the perfect day. The gospel is discovering; it shows that about which we were utterly in the dark; it is to give light to those that sit in darkness, the light of the knowledge of the glory of God in the face of Jesus Christ. It is reviving; it brings light to those that sit in the shadow of death, as condemned prisoners in the dungeon. It is directing; it is to guide our feet in the way of peace, into that way which will bring us to peace at last, Romans 3:17. John gave proofs of strong faith, vigorous and holy affections, and of being above the fear and love of the world. Thus he ripened for usefulness; but he lived a retired life, till he came forward openly as the forerunner of the Messiah. Let us follow peace with all men, as well as seek peace with God and our own consciences. And if it be the will of God that we live unknown to the world, still let us diligently seek to grow strong in the grace of Jesus Christ.

CHAPTER 2

The birth of Christ. (1-7) It is made known to the shepherds. (8-20) Christ presented in the temple. (21-24) Simeon prophesies concerning Jesus. (25-35) Anna prophesies concerning him. (36-40) Christ with the learned men in the temple. (41-52)

Verses 1-7 The fullness of time was now come, when God would send forth his Son, made of a woman, and made under the law. The circumstances of his birth were very mean. Christ was born at an inn; he came into the world to sojourn here for awhile, as at an inn, and to teach us to do likewise. We are become by sin like an outcast infant, helpless and forlorn; and such a one was Christ. He well knew how unwilling we are to be meanly lodged, clothed, or fed; how we desire to have our children decorated and indulged; how apt the poor are to envy the rich, and how prone the rich to disdain the poor. But when we by faith view the Son of God being made man and lying in a manger, our vanity, ambition, and envy are checked. We cannot, with this object rightly before us, seek great things for ourselves or our children.

Verses 8-20 Angels were heralds of the new-born Saviour, but they were only sent to some poor, humble, pious, industrious shepherds, who were in the business of their calling, keeping watch over their flock. We are not out of the way of Divine visits, when we are employed in an honest calling, and abide with God in it. Let God have the honour of this work; Glory to God in the highest. God's good-will to men, manifested in sending the Messiah, redounds to his praise. Other works of God are for his glory, but the redemption of the world is for his glory in the highest. God's goodwill in sending the Messiah, brought peace into this lower world. Peace is here put for all that good which flows to us from Christ's taking our nature upon him. This is a faithful saying, attested by an innumerable company of angels, and well worthy of all acceptation, That the good-will of God toward men, is glory to God in the highest, and peace on the earth. The shepherds lost no time, but came with haste to the place. They were satisfied, and made known abroad concerning this child, that he was the Saviour, even Christ the Lord. Mary carefully observed and thought upon all these things, which were so suited to enliven her holy affections. We should be more delivered from errors in judgment and practice, did we more fully ponder these things in our hearts. It is still proclaimed in our ears that to us is born a Saviour, Christ the Lord. These should be glad tidings to all.

Verses 21-24 Our Lord Jesus was not born in sin, and did not need that mortification of a corrupt nature, or that renewal unto holiness, which were signified by circumcision. This ordinance was, in his case, a pledge of his future perfect obedience to the whole law, in the midst of sufferings and temptations, even unto death for us. At the end of forty days, Mary went up to the temple to offer the appointed sacrifices for her purification. Joseph also presented the holy child Jesus, because, as a first-born son, he was to be presented to the Lord, and redeemed according to the law. Let us present our children to the Lord who gave them to us, beseeching him to redeem them from sin and death, and make them holy to himself.

Verses 25-35 The same Spirit that provided for the support of Simeon's hope, provided for his joy. Those who would see Christ must go to his temple. Here is a confession of his faith, that this Child in his arms was the Saviour, the salvation itself, the salvation of God's appointing. He bids farewell to this world. How poor does this world look to one that has Christ in his arms, and salvation in his view! See here, how comfortable is the death of a good man; he departs in peace with God, peace with his own conscience, in peace with death. Those that have welcomed Christ, may welcome death. Joseph and Mary marveled at the things which were spoken of this Child. Simeon shows them likewise, what reason they had to rejoice with trembling. And Jesus, his doctrine, and people, are still spoken against; his truth and holiness are still denied and blasphemed; his preached word is still the touchstone of men's characters. The secret good affections in the minds of some, will be revealed by their embracing Christ; the secret corruptions of others will be revealed by their enmity to Christ. Men will be judged by the thoughts of their hearts concerning Christ. He shall be a suffering Jesus; his mother shall suffer with him, because of the nearness of her relation and affection.

Verses 36-40 There was much evil then in the church, yet God left not himself without witness. Anna always dwelt in, or at least attended at, the temple. She was always in a praying spirit; gave herself to prayer, and in all things she served God. Those to whom Christ is made known, have great reason to thank the Lord. She taught others concerning him. Let the example of the venerable saints, Simeon and Anna, give courage to those whose hoary heads are, like theirs, a crown of glory, being found in the way of righteousness. The lips soon to be silent in the grave, should be showing forth the praises of the Redeemer. In all things it became Christ to be made like unto his brethren, therefore he passed through infancy and childhood as other children, yet without sin, and with manifest proofs of the Divine nature in him. By the Spirit of God all his faculties performed their offices in a manner not seen in any one else. Other children have foolishness bound in their hearts, which appears in what they say or do, but he was filled with wisdom, by the influence of the Holy Ghost; every thing he said and did, was wisely said and wisely done, above his years.

Other children show the corruption of their nature; nothing but the grace of God was upon him.

Verses 41-52 It is for the honour of Christ that children should attend on public worship. His parents did not return till they had stayed all the seven days of the feast. It is well to stay to the end of an ordinance, as becomes those who say, It is good to be here. Those that have lost their comforts in Christ, and the evidences of their having a part in him, must bethink themselves where, and when, and how they lost them, and must turn back again. Those that would recover their lost acquaintance with Christ, must go to the place in which he has put his name; there they may hope to meet him. They found him in some part of the temple, where the doctors of the law kept their schools; he was sitting there, hearkening to their instructions, proposing questions, and answering inquiries, with such wisdom, that those who heard were delighted with him. Young persons should seek the knowledge of Divine truth, attend the ministry of the gospel, and ask such questions of their elders and teachers as may tend to increase their knowledge.

Those who seek Christ in sorrow, shall find him with the greater joy. Know ye not that I ought to be in my Father's house; at my Father's work; I must be about my Father's business. Herein is an example; for it becomes the children of God, in conformity to Christ, to attend their heavenly Father's business, and make all other concerns give way to it. Though he was the Son of God, yet he was subject to his earthly parents; how then will the foolish and weak sons of men answer it, who are disobedient to their parents? However we may neglect men's sayings, because they are obscure, yet we must not think so of God's sayings. That which at first is dark, may afterwards become plain and easy. The greatest

563

and wisest, those most eminent, may learn of this admirable and Divine Child, that it is the truest greatness of soul to know our own place and office; to deny ourselves amusements and pleasures not consistent with our state and calling.

CHAPTER 3

John the Baptist's ministry. (1-14) John the Baptist testifies concerning Christ. (15-20) The baptism of Christ. (21,22) The genealogy of Christ. (23-38)

Verses 1-14 The scope and design of John's ministry were, to bring the people from their sins, and to their Saviour. He came preaching, not a sect, or party, but a profession; the sign or ceremony was washing with water. By the words here used John preached the necessity of repentance, in order to the remission of sins, and that the baptism of water was an outward sign of that inward cleansing and renewal of heart, which attend, or are the effects of true repentance, as well as a profession of it. Here is the fulfilling of the Scriptures, Isaiah 40:3, in the ministry of John. When way is made for the gospel into the heart, by taking down high thoughts, and bringing them into obedience to Christ, by leveling the soul, and removing all that hinders us in the way of Christ and his grace, then preparation is made to welcome the salvation of God. Here are general warnings and exhortations which John gave.

The guilty, corrupted race of mankind is become a generation of vipers; hateful to God, and hating one another. There is no way of fleeing from the wrath to come, but by repentance; and by the change of our way the change of our mind must be shown. If we are not really holy, both in heart and life, our profession of religion and relation to God and his church, will stand us in no stead at all; the sorer will our destruction be, if we do not bring forth fruits meet for repentance. John the Baptist gave instructions to several sorts of persons. Those that profess and promise repentance, must show it by reformation, according to their places and conditions. The gospel requires mercy, not sacrifice; and its design is, to engage us to do all the good we can, and to be just to all men. And the same principle which leads men to forego unjust gain, leads to restore that which is gained by wrong. John tells the soldiers their duty. Men should be cautioned against the temptations of their employments. These answers declared the present duty of the inquirers, and at once formed a test of their sincerity. As none can or will accept Christ's salvation without true repentance, so the evidence and effects of this repentance are here marked out.

Verses 15-20 John the Baptist disowned being himself the Christ, but confirmed the people in their expectations of the long-promised Messiah. He could only exhort them to repent, and assure them of forgiveness upon repentance; but he could not work repentance in them, nor confer remission on them. Thus highly does it become us to speak of Christ, and thus humbly of ourselves. John can do no more than baptize with water, in token that they ought to purify and cleanse themselves; but Christ can, and will baptize with the Holy Ghost; he can give the Spirit, to cleanse and purify the heart, not only as water washes off the dirt on the outside, but as fire clears out the dross that is within, and melts down the metal, that it may be cast into a new mould. John was an affectionate preacher; he was beseeching; he pressed things home upon his hearers. He was a practical preacher; quickening them to their duty, and directing them in it. He was a popular preacher; he addressed the people, according to their capacity. He was an evangelical preacher. In all his exhortations, he directed people to Christ. When we press duty upon people, we must direct them to Christ, both for righteousness and strength. He was a copious preacher; he shunned not to declare the whole counsel of God. But a full stop was put to John's preaching when he was in the midst of his usefulness. Herod being reproved by him for many evils, shut up John in prison. Those who injure the faithful servants of God, add still greater guilt to their other sins.

Verses 21-22 Christ did not confess sin, as others did, for he had none to confess; but he prayed, as others did, and kept up communion with his Father. Observe, all the three voices from heaven, by which the Father bare witness to the Son, were pronounced while he was praying, or soon after, Lu 9:35; Joh 12:28. The Holy Ghost descended in a bodily shape like a dove upon him, and there came a voice from heaven, from God the Father, from the excellent glory. Thus was a proof of the Holy Trinity, of the Three Persons in the Godhead, given at the baptism of Christ.

Verses 23-38 Matthew's list of the forefathers of Jesus showed that Christ was the son of Abraham, in whom all the families of the earth are blessed, and heir to the throne of David; but Luke shows that Jesus was the Seed of the woman that should break the serpent's head, and traces the line up to Adam, beginning with Eli, or Heli, the father, not of Joseph, but of Mary. The seeming differences between the two evangelists in these lists of names have been removed by learned men. But our salvation does not depend upon our being able to solve these difficulties, nor is the Divine authority of the Gospels at all weakened by them. The list of names ends thus, "Who was the son of Adam, the son of God;" that is, the offspring of God by creation. Christ was both the son of Adam and the Son of God, that he might be a proper Mediator between God and the sons of Adam, and might bring the sons of Adam to be, through him, the sons of God. All flesh, as descended from the first Adam, is as grass, and withers as the flower of the field; but he who partakes of the Holy Spirit of life from the Second Adam, has that eternal happiness, which by the gospel is preached unto us.

CHAPTER 4

The temptation of Christ. (1-13) Christ in the synagogue of Nazareth. (14-30) He casts out an unclean spirit and heals the sick. (31-44)

Verses 1-13 Christ's being led into the wilderness gave an advantage to the tempter; for there he was alone, none were with him by whose prayers and advice he might be helped in the hour of temptation. He who knew his own strength might give Satan advantage; but we may not, who know our own weakness. Being in all things made like unto his brethren, Jesus would, like the other children of God, live in dependence upon the Divine Providence and promise. The word of God is our sword, and faith in that word is our shield. God has many ways of providing for his people, and therefore is at all times to be depended upon in the way of duty.

All Satan's promises are deceitful; and if he is permitted to have any influence in disposing of the kingdoms of the world and the glory of them, he uses them as baits to ensnare men to destruction. We should reject at once and with abhorrence, every opportunity of sinful gain or advancement, as a price offered for our souls; we should seek riches, honours, and happiness in the worship and service of God only. Christ will not worship Satan; nor, when he has the kingdoms of the world delivered to him by his Father, will he suffer any remains of the worship of the devil to continue in them. Satan also tempted Jesus to be his own murderer, by unfitting confidence in his Father's protection, such as he had no warrant for.

Let not any abuse of Scripture by Satan or by men abate our esteem, or cause us to abandon its use; but let us study it still, seek to know it, and seek our defense from it in all kinds of assaults. Let this word dwell richly in us, for it is our life. Our victorious Redeemer conquered, not for himself only, but for us also. The devil ended all the temptation. Christ let him try all his force, and defeated him. Satan saw it was to no purpose to attack Christ, who had nothing in him for his fiery darts to fasten upon. And if we resist the devil, he will flee from us. Yet he departed but till the season when he was again to be let loose upon Jesus, not as a tempter, to draw him to sin, and so to strike at his head, at which he now aimed and was wholly defeated in; but as a persecutor, to bring Christ to suffer, and so to bruise his heel, which it was told him, he should have to do, and would do, though it would be the breaking of his own head, genesis 3:15. Though Satan depart for a season, we shall never be out of his reach till removed from this present evil world.

Verses 14-30 Christ taught in their synagogues, their places of public worship, where they met to read, expound, and apply the word, to pray and praise. All the gifts and graces of the Spirit were upon him and on him, without measure. By Christ, sinners may be loosed from the bonds of guilt, and by his Spirit and grace from the bondage of corruption. He came by the word of his gospel, to bring light to those that sat in the dark, and by the power of his grace, to give sight to those that were blind. And he preached the acceptable year of the Lord. Let sinners attend to the Saviour's invitation when liberty is thus proclaimed. Christ's name was Wonderful; in nothing was he more so than in the word of his grace, and the power that went along with it. We may well wonder that he should speak such words of grace to such graceless wretches as mankind. Some prejudice often furnishes an objection against the humbling doctrine of the cross; and while it is the word of God that stirs up men's enmity, they will blame the conduct or manner of the speaker. The doctrine of God's sovereignty, his right to do his will, provokes proud men. They will not seek his favour in his own way; and are angry when others have the favours they neglect. Still is Jesus rejected by multitudes who hear the same message from his words. While they crucify him afresh by their sins, may we honour him as the Son of God, the Saviour of men, and seek to show we do so by our obedience.

Verses 31-44 Christ's preaching much affected the people; and a working power went with it to the consciences of men. These miracles showed Christ to be a controller and conqueror of Satan, a healer of diseases. Where Christ gives a new life, in recovery from sickness, it should be a new life, spent more than ever in his service, to his glory. Our business should be to spread abroad Christ's fame in every place, to beseech him in behalf of those diseased in body or mind, and to use our influence in bringing sinners to him, that his hands may be laid upon them for their healing. He cast the devils out of many who were possessed. We were not sent into this world to live to ourselves only, but to glorify God, and to do good in our generation. The people sought him, and came unto him. A desert is no desert, if we are with Christ there. He will continue with us, by his word and Spirit, and extend the same blessings to other nations, till, throughout the earth, the servants and worshippers of Satan are brought to acknowledge him as the Christ, the Son of God, and to find redemption through his blood, even the forgiveness of sins.

CHAPTER 5

The miraculous draught of fishes, Peter, James, and John called. (1-11) A leper cleansed. (12-16) A paralytic cured. (17-26) Levi called, Christ's answer to the Pharisees. (27-39)

Verses 1-11 When Christ had done preaching, he told Peter to apply to the business of his calling. Time spent on week days in public exercises of religion, need be but little hindrance in time, and may be great furtherance to us in temper of mind, as to our worldly business. With what cheerfulness may we go about the duties of our calling, when we have been with God, and thus have our worldly employments sanctified to us by the word and prayer! Though they had taken nothing, yet Christ told them to let down their nets again. We must not abruptly quit our callings because we have not the success in them we desire. We are likely to speed well, when we follow the guidance of Christ's word. The draught of fishes was by a miracle. We must all, like Peter, own ourselves to be sinful men, therefore Jesus Christ might justly depart from us. But we must beseech him that he would not depart; for woe unto us if the Saviour depart from sinners! Rather let us entreat him to come and dwell in our hearts by faith, that he may transform and cleanse them. These fishermen forsook all, and followed Jesus, when their calling prospered. When riches increase, and we are tempted to set our hearts upon them, then to quit them for Christ is thankworthy.

Verses 12-16 This man is said to be full of leprosy; he had that distemper in a high degree, which represents our natural pollution by sin; we are full of that leprosy; from the crown of the head to the sole of the foot there is no soundness in us. Strong confidence and deep humility are united in the words of this leper. And if any sinner, from a deep sense of vileness, says, I know the Lord can cleanse, but will he look upon such a one as me? Will he apply his own precious blood for my cleansing and healing? Yes, he will. Speak not as doubting, but as humbly referring the matter to Christ. And being saved from the guilt and power of our sins, let us spread abroad Christ's fame, and bring others to hear him and to be healed.

Verses 17-26 How many are there in our assemblies, where the gospel is preached, who do not sit under the word, but sit by! It is to them as a tale that is told them, not as a message that is sent to them. Observe the duties taught and recommended to us by the history of the paralytic. In applying to Christ, we must be very pressing and urgent; that is an evidence of faith, and is very pleasing to Christ, and prevailing with him. Give us, Lord, the same kind of faith with respect to thy ability and willingness to heal our souls. Give us to desire the pardon of sin more than any earthly blessing, or life itself. Enable us to believe thy power to forgive sins; then will our souls cheerfully arise and go where thou pleasest.

Verses 27-39 It was a wonder of Christ's grace, that he would call a publican to be his disciple and follower. It was a wonder of his grace, that the call was made so effectual. It was a wonder of his grace, that he came to call sinners to repentance, and to assure them of pardon. It was a wonder of his grace, that he so patiently

571

bore the contradiction of sinners against himself and his disciples. It was a wonder of his grace, that he fixed the services of his disciples according to their strength and standing. The Lord trains up his people gradually for the trials allotted them; we should copy his example in dealing with the weak in faith, or the tempted believer.

CHAPTER 6

The disciples pluck corn on the Sabbath. (1-5) Works of mercy suitable to the Sabbath day. (6-11) The apostles chosen. (12-19) Blessings and woes declared. (20-26) Christ exhorts to mercy. (27-36) And to justice and sincerity. (37-49)

Verses 1-5 Christ justifies his disciples in a work of necessity for themselves on the Sabbath day, and that was plucking the ears of corn when they were hungry. But we must take heed that we mistake not this liberty for leave to commit sin. Christ will have us to know and remember that it is his day, therefore to be spent in his service, and to his honour.

Verses 6-11 Christ was neither ashamed nor afraid to own the purposes of his grace. He healed the poor man, though he knew that his enemies would take advantage against him for it. Let us not be drawn either from our duty or from our usefulness by any opposition. We may well be amazed, that the sons of men should be so wicked.

Verses 12-19 We often think one half hour a great deal to spend in meditation and secret prayer, but Christ was whole nights engaged in these duties. In serving God, our great care should be not to lose time, but to make the end of one good duty the beginning of another. The twelve apostles are here named; never were men so privileged, yet one of them had a devil, and proved a traitor. Those who have not faithful preaching near them, had better travel far than be without it. It is indeed worth while to go a great way to hear the word of Christ, and to go out of the way of other business for it. They came to be cured by him, and he healed them. There is a fullness of grace in Christ, and healing virtue in him, ready to go out from him, that is enough for all, enough for each. Men regard the diseases of the body as greater evils than those of their souls; but the Scripture teaches us differently.

Verses 20-26 Here begins a discourse of Christ, most of which is also found in 7. But some think that this was preached at another time and place. All believers that take the precepts of the gospel to themselves, and live by them, may take the promises of the gospel to themselves, and live upon them. Woes are denounced against prosperous sinners as miserable people, though the world envies them. Those are blessed indeed whom Christ blesses, but those must be dreadfully miserable who fall under his woe and curse! What a vast advantage will the saint have over the sinner in the other world! And what a wide difference will there be in their rewards, how much soever the sinner may prosper, and the saint be afflicted here!

Verses 27-36 These are hard lessons to flesh and blood. But if we are thoroughly grounded in the faith of Christ's love, this will make his commands easy to us. Every one that comes to him for washing in his blood, and knows the greatness of the mercy and the love there is in him, can say, in truth and sincerity, Lord, what wilt thou have me to do? Let us then aim to be merciful, even according to the mercy of our heavenly Father to us.

Verses 37-49 All these sayings Christ often used; it was easy to apply them. We ought to be very careful when we blame others; for we need allowance ourselves. If we are of a giving and a forgiving spirit, we shall ourselves reap the benefit. Though full and exact returns are made in another world, not in this world, yet Providence does what should encourage us in doing good. Those who follow the multitude to do evil, follow in the broad way that leads to destruction. The tree is known by its fruits; may the word of Christ be so grafted in our hearts, that we may be fruitful in every good word and work. And what the mouth commonly speaks, generally agrees with what is most in the heart. Those only make sure work for their souls and eternity, and take the course that will profit in a trying time, who think, speak, and act according to the words of Christ. Those who take pains in religion, found their hope upon Christ, who is the Rock of Ages, and other foundation can no man lay. In death and judgment they are safe, being kept by the power of Christ through faith unto salvation, and they shall never perish.

CHAPTER 7

The centurion's servant healed. (1-10) The widow's son raised. (11-18) John the Baptist's inquiry concerning Jesus. (19-35) Christ anointed in the house of the Pharisee The parable of the two debtors. (36-50)

Verses 1-10 Servants should study to endear themselves to their masters. Masters ought to take particular care of their servants when they are sick. We may still, by faithful and fervent prayer, apply to Christ, and ought to do so when sickness is in our families. The building places for religious worship is a good work, and an instance of love to God and his people. Our Lord Jesus was pleased with the centurion's faith; and he never fails to answer the expectations of that faith which honours his power and love. The cure soon wrought and perfect.

Verses 11-18 When the Lord saw the poor widow following her son to the grave, he had compassion on her. See Christ's power over death itself. The gospel call to all people, to young people particularly, is, Arise from the dead, and Christ shall give you light and life. When Christ put life into him, it appeared by the youth's sitting up. Have we grace from Christ? Let us show it. He began to speak: whenever Christ gives us spiritual life, he opens the lips in prayer and praise. When dead souls are raised to spiritual life, by Divine power going with the gospel, we must glorify God, and look upon it as a gracious visit to his people. Let us seek for such an interest in our compassionate Saviour, that we may look forward with joy to the time when the Redeemer's voice shall call forth all that are in their graves. May we be called to the resurrection of life, not to that of damnation.

Verses 19-35 To his miracles in the kingdom of nature, Christ adds this in the kingdom of grace, To the poor the gospel is preached. It clearly pointed out the spiritual nature of Christ's kingdom, that the messenger he sent before him to prepare his way, did it by preaching repentance and reformation of heart and life. We have here the just blame of those who were not wrought upon by the ministry of John Baptist or of Jesus Christ himself. They made a jest of the methods God took to do them good. This is the ruin of multitudes; they are not serious in the concerns of their souls. Let us study to prove ourselves children of Wisdom, by attending the instructions of God's word, and adoring those mysteries and glad tidings which infidels and Pharisees deride and blaspheme.

Verses 36-50 None can truly perceive how precious Christ is, and the glory of the gospel, except the broken-hearted. But while they feel they cannot enough express self-abhorrence on account of sin, and admiration of his mercy, the self-sufficient will be disgusted, because the gospel encourages such repenting sinners. The Pharisee, instead of rejoicing in the tokens of the woman's repentance, confined his thoughts to her former bad character. But without free forgiveness none of us can escape the wrath to come; this our gracious Saviour has purchased with his blood, that he may freely bestow it on every one that believes in him. Christ, by a parable, forced Simon to acknowledge that the greater sinner this woman had been, the greater love she ought to show to Him when her sins were pardoned. Learn here, that sin is a debt; and all are sinners, are debtors to Almighty God. Some sinners are greater debtors; but whether our debt be more or less, it is more than we are able to pay. God is ready to forgive; and his Son having purchased pardon for those who believe in him, his gospel promises it to them, and his Spirit seals it to repenting sinners, and gives them the comfort. Let us keep far from the proud spirit of the

Pharisee, simply depending upon and rejoicing in Christ alone, and so be prepared to obey him more zealously, and more strongly to recommend him unto all around us. The more we express our sorrow for sin, and our love to Christ, the clearer evidence we have of the forgiveness of our sins. What a wonderful change does grace make upon a sinner's heart and life, as well as upon his state before God, by the full remission of all his sins through faith in the Lord Jesus!

CHAPTER 8

The ministry of Christ. (1-3) The parable of the sower. (4-21) Christ stilleth the tempest and casteth out devils. (22-40) The daughter of Jairus restored to life. (41-56)

Verses 1-3 We are here told what Christ made the constant business of his life, it was teaching the gospel. Tidings of the kingdom of God are glad tidings, and what Christ came to bring. Certain women attended upon him who ministered to him of their substance. It showed the mean condition to which the Saviour humbled himself, that he needed their kindness, and his great humility, that he accepted it. Though rich, yet for our sakes he became poor.

Verses 4-21 There are many very needful and excellent rules and cautions for hearing the word, in the parable of the sower, and the application of it. Happy are we, and for ever indebted to free grace, if the same thing that is a parable to others, with which they are only amused, is a plain truth to us, by which we are taught and governed. We ought to take heed of the things that will hinder our profiting by the word we hear; to take heed lest we hear carelessly and slightly, lest we entertain prejudices against the word we hear; and to take heed to our spirits after we have heard the word, lest we lose what we have gained. The gifts we have, will be continued to us or not, as we use them for the glory of God, and the good of our brethren. Nor is it enough not to hold the truth in unrighteousness; we should desire to hold forth the word of life, and to shine, giving light to all around. Great encouragement is given to those who prove themselves faithful hearers of the word, by being doers of the work. Christ owns them as his relations.

Verses Those that put to sea in a calm, even at Christ's word, must yet prepare for a storm, and for great peril in that storm. There is no relief for souls under a sense of guilt, and fear of wrath, but to go to Christ, and call him Master, and say, I am undone, if thou dost not help me. When our dangers are over, it becomes us to take to ourselves the shame of our own fears, and to give Christ the glory of our deliverance. We may learn much out of this history concerning the world of infernal, malignant spirits, which though not working now exactly in the same way as then, yet all must at all times carefully guard against. And these malignant spirits are very numerous. They have enmity to man and all his comforts. Those under Christ's government are sweetly led with the bands of love; those under the devil's government are furiously driven. Oh what a comfort it is to the believer, that all the powers of darkness are under the control of the Lord Jesus! It is a miracle of mercy, if those whom Satan possesses, are not brought to destruction and eternal ruin. Christ will not stay with those who slight him; perhaps he may no more return to them, while others are waiting for him, and glad to receive him.

Verses 41-56 Let us not complain of a crowd, and a throng, and a hurry, as long as we are in the way of our duty, and doing good; but otherwise every wise man will keep himself out of it as much as he can. And many a poor soul is healed, and helped, and saved by Christ, that is hidden in a crowd, and nobody notices it. This woman came trembling, yet her faith saved her. There may be trembling, where yet there is saving faith. Observe Christ's comfortable words to Jairus, Fear not, believe only, and thy daughter shall be made whole. No less hard was it not to grieve for the loss of an only child, than not to fear the continuance of that grief. But in perfect faith there is no fear; the more we fear, the less we believe. The hand of Christ's grace goes with the calls of his word, to make them effectual. Christ commanded to give her meat. As babes new born, so those newly raised from sin, desire spiritual food, that they may grow thereby.

CHAPTER 9

The apostles sent forth. (1-9) The multitude miraculously fed. (10-17) Peter's testimony to Christ, Self-denial enjoined. (18-27) The transfiguration. (28-36) An evil spirit cast out. (37-42) Christ checks the ambition of his disciples. (43-50) He reproves their mistaken zeal. (51-56) Every thing to be given up for Christ. (57-62)

Verses 1-9 Christ sent his twelve disciples abroad, who by this time were able to teach others what they had received from the Lord. They must not be anxious to commend themselves to people's esteem by outward appearance. They must go as they were. The Lord Jesus is the fountain of power and authority, to whom all creatures must, in one way or another, be subject; and if he goes with the word of his ministers in power, to deliver sinners from Satan's bondage, they may be sure that he will care for their wants. When truth and love thus go together, and yet the message of God is rejected and despised, it leaves men without excuse, and turns to a testimony against them. Herod's guilty conscience was ready to conclude that John was risen from the dead. He desired to see Jesus; and why did he not go and see him? Probably, because he thought it below him, or because he wished not to have any more reprovers of sin. Delaying it now, his heart was hardened, and when he did see Jesus, he was as much prejudiced against him as others, Luke 23:11.

Verses 10-17 The people followed Jesus, and though they came unseasonably, yet he gave them what they came for. He spake unto them of the kingdom of God. He healed those who had need of healing. And with five loaves of bread and two fishes, Christ fed five thousand men. He will not see those that fear him, and serve him faithfully, want any good thing. When we receive creature-comforts, we must acknowledge that we receive them from God, and that we are unworthy to receive them; that we owe them all, and all the comfort we have in them, to the mediation of Christ, by whom the curse is taken away. The blessing of Christ will make a little go a great way. He fills every hungry soul, abundantly satisfies it with the goodness of his house. Here were fragments taken up: in our Father's house there is bread enough, and to spare. We are not straitened, nor stinted in Christ.

Verses 18-27 It is an unspeakable comfort that our Lord Jesus is God's Anointed; this signifies that he was both appointed to be the Messiah, and qualified for it. Jesus discourses concerning his own sufferings and death. And so far must his disciples be from thinking how to prevent his sufferings, that they must prepare for their own. We often meet with crosses in the way of duty; and though we must not pull them upon our own heads, yet, when they are laid for us, we must take them up, and carry them after Christ. It is well or ill with us, according as it is well or ill with our souls. The body cannot be happy, if the soul be miserable in the other world; but the soul may be happy, though the body is greatly afflicted and oppressed in this world. We must never be ashamed of Christ and his gospel.

Verses 28-36 Christ's transfiguration was a specimen of that glory in which he will come to judge the world; and was an encouragement to his disciples to suffer for him. Prayer is a transfiguring, transforming duty, which makes the face to shine. Our Lord Jesus, even in his transfiguration, was willing to speak concerning his death and sufferings. In our greatest glories on earth, let us remember that in this world we have no continuing city. What need we have to pray to God for quickening grace, to make us lively! Yet that the disciples might be witnesses of this sign from heaven, after awhile they became awake, so that they were able to give a full account of what passed. But those know not what they say, that talk of making tabernacles on earth for glorified saints in heaven.

Verses 37-42 How deplorable the case of this child! He was under the power of an evil spirit. Disease of that nature are more frightful than such as arise merely from natural causes. What mischief Satan does where he gets possession! But happy those that have access to Christ! He can do that for us which his disciples cannot. A word from Christ healed the child; and when our children recover from sickness, it is comfortable to receive them as healed by the hand of Christ.

Verses 43-50 This prediction of Christ's sufferings was plain enough, but the disciples would not understand it, because it agreed not with their notions. A little child is the emblem by which Christ teaches us simplicity and humility. What greater honour can any man attain to in this world, than to be received by men as a messenger of God and Christ; and to have God and Christ own themselves received and welcomed in him! If ever any society of Christians in this world, had reason to silence those not of their own communion, the twelve disciples at this time had; yet Christ warned them not to do the like again. Those may be found faithful followers of Christ, and may be accepted of him, who do not follow with us.

Verses 51-56 The disciples did not consider that the conduct of the Samaritans was rather the effect of national prejudices and bigotry, than of enmity to the word and worship of God; and through they refused to receive Christ and his disciples, they did not ill use or injure them, so that the case was widely different from that of Ahaziah and Elijah. Nor were they aware that the gospel dispensation was to be marked by miracles of mercy. But above all, they were ignorant of the prevailing motives of their own hearts, which were pride and carnal ambition. Of this our Lord warned them. It is easy for us to say, Come, see our zeal for the Lord! And to think we are very faithful in his cause, when we are seeking our own objects, and even doing harm instead of good to others.

Verses 57-62 Here is one that is forward to follow Christ, but seems to have been hasty and rash, and not to have counted the cost. If we mean to follow Christ, we must lay aside the thoughts of great things in the world. Let us not try to join the profession of Christianity, with seeking after worldly advantages. Here is another that seems resolved to follow Christ, but he begs a short delay. To this man Christ first gave the call; he said to him, Follow me. Religion teaches us to be kind and good, to show piety at home, and to requite our parents; but we must not make these an excuse for neglecting our duty to God. Here is another that is willing to follow Christ, but he must have a little time to talk with his friends about it, and to set in order his household affairs, and give directions concerning them. He seemed to have worldly concerns more upon his heart than he ought to have, and he was willing to enter into a temptation leading him from his purpose of following Christ. No one can do any business in a proper manner, if he is attending to other things. Those who begin with the work of God, must resolve to go on, or they will make nothing of it. Looking back, leads to drawing back, and drawing back is to perdition. He only that endures to the end shall be saved.

CHAPTER 10

Seventy disciples sent forth. (1-16) The blessedness of Christ's disciples. (17-24) The good Samaritan. (25-37) Jesus at the house of Martha and Mary. (38-42)

Verses 1-16 Christ sent the seventy disciples, two and two, that they might strengthen and encourage one another. The ministry of the gospel calls men to receive Christ as a Prince and a Saviour; and he will surely come in the power of his Spirit to all places whither he sends his faithful servants. But the doom of those who receive the grace of God in vain, will be very fearful Those who despise the faithful ministers of Christ, who think meanly of them, and look scornfully upon them, will be reckoned as despisers of God and Christ.

Verses 17-24 All our victories over Satan, are obtained by power derived from Jesus Christ, and he must have all the praise. But let us beware of spiritual pride, which has been the destruction of many. Our Lord rejoiced at the prospect of the salvation of many souls. It was fit that particular notice should be taken of that hour of joy; there were few such, for He was a man of sorrows: in that hour in which he saw Satan fall, and heard of the good success of his ministers, in that hour he rejoiced. He has ever resisted the proud, and given grace to the humble. The more simply dependent we are on the teaching, help, and blessing of the Son of God, the more we shall know both of the Father and of the Son; the more blessed we shall be in seeing the glory, and hearing the words of the Divine Saviour; and the more useful we shall be made in promoting his cause.

Verses 25-37 If we speak of eternal life, and the way to it, in a careless manner, we take the name of God in vain. No one will ever love God and his neighbour with any measure of pure, spiritual love, who is not made a partaker of converting grace. But the proud heart of man strives hard against these convictions. Christ gave an instance of a poor Jew in distress, relieved by a good Samaritan. This poor man fell among thieves, who left him about to die of his wounds. He was slighted by those who should have been his friends, and was cared for by a stranger, a Samaritan, of the nation which the Jews most despised and detested, and would have no dealings with. It is lamentable to observe how selfishness governs all ranks; how many excuses men will make to avoid trouble or expense in relieving others. But the true Christian has the law of love written in his heart. The Spirit of Christ dwells in him; Christ's image is renewed in his soul. The parable is a beautiful explanation of the law of loving our neighbour as ourselves, without regard to nation, party, or any other distinction. It also sets forth the kindness and love of God our Saviour toward sinful, miserable men. We were like this poor, distressed traveller. Satan, our enemy, has robbed us, and wounded us: such is the mischief sin has done us. The blessed Jesus had compassion on us. The believer considers that Jesus loved him, and gave his life for him, when an enemy and a rebel; and having shown him mercy, he bids him go and do likewise. It is the duty of us all , in our places, and according to our ability, to succor, help, and relieve all that are in distress and necessity.

Verses 38-42 A good sermon is not the worse for being preached in a house; and the visits of our friends should be so managed, as to make them turn to the good of their souls. Sitting at Christ's feet, signifies readiness to receive his word, and submission to the guidance of it. Martha was providing for the entertainment of Christ, and those that came with him. Here were respect to our Lord Jesus and right care of her household affairs. But there was something to be blamed. She was for much serving; plenty, variety, and exactness. Worldly business is a snare to us, when it hinders us from serving God, and getting good to our souls. What needless time is wasted, and expense often laid out, even in entertaining professors of the gospel! Though Martha was on this occasion faulty, yet she was a true believer, and in her general conduct did not neglect the one thing needful. The favour of God is needful to our happiness; the salvation of Christ is needful to our safety. Where this is attended to, all other things will be rightly pursued. Christ declared, Mary hath chosen the good part. For one thing is needful, this one thing that she has done, to give up herself to the guidance of Christ. The things of this life will be taken away from us, at the furthest, when we shall be taken away from them; but nothing shall separate from the love of Christ, and a part in that love. Men and devils cannot take it away from us, and God and Christ will not. Let us mind the one thing needful more diligently.

CHAPTER 11

The disciples taught to pray. (1-4) Christ encourages being earnest in prayer. (5-13) Christ casts out a devil, The blasphemy of the Pharisees. (14-26) True happiness. (27,28) Christ reproves the Jews. (29-36) He reproves the Pharisees. (37-54)

Verses 1-4 "Lord, teach us to pray," is a good prayer, and a very needful one, for Jesus Christ only can teach us, by his word and Spirit, how to pray. Lord, teach me what it is to pray; Lord, stir up and quicken me to the duty; Lord, direct me what to pray for; teach me what I should say. Christ taught them a prayer, much the same that he had given before in his sermon upon the mount. There are some differences in the words of the Lord's prayer in Matthew and in Luke, but they are of no moment. Let us in our requests, both for others and for ourselves, come to our heavenly Father, confiding in his power and goodness.

Verses 5-13 Christ encourages fervency and constancy in prayer. We must come for what we need, as a man does to his neighbour or friend, who is kind to him. We must come for bread; for that which is needful. If God does not answer our prayers speedily, yet he will in due time, if we continue to pray. Observe what to pray for; we must ask for the Holy Spirit, not only as necessary in order to our praying well, but as all spiritual blessings are included in that one. For by the influences of the Holy Spirit we are brought to know God and ourselves, to repent, believe in, and love Christ, and so are made comfortable in this world, and meet for happiness in the next. All these blessings our heavenly Father is more ready to bestow on every one that asks for them, than an indulgent parent is to give food to a hungry child. And this is the advantage of the prayer of faith, that it quiets and establishes the heart in God.

Verses 14-26 Christ's thus casting out the devils, was really the destroying of their power. The heart of every unconverted sinner is the devil's palace, where he dwells, and where he rules. There is a kind of peace in the heart of an unconverted soul, while the devil, as a strong man armed, keeps it. The sinner is secure, has no doubt concerning the goodness of his state, nor any dread of the judgment to come. But observe the wonderful change made in conversion. The conversion of a soul to God, is Christ's victory over the devil and his power in that soul, restoring the soul to its liberty, and recovering his own interest in it and power over it. All the endowments of mind of body are now employed for Christ.

Here is the condition of a hypocrite. The house is swept from common sins, by a forced confession, as Pharaoh's; by a feigned contrition, as Ahab's; or by a partial reformation, as Herod's. The house is swept, but it is not washed; the heart is not made holy. Sweeping takes off only the loose dirt, while the sin that besets the sinner, the beloved sin, is untouched. The house is garnished with common gifts and graces. It is not furnished with any true grace; it is all paint and varnish, not real nor lasting. It was never given up to Christ, nor dwelt in by the Spirit. Let us take heed of resting in that which a man may have, and yet come short of heaven. The wicked spirits enter in without any difficulty; they are welcomed, and they dwell there; there they work, there they rule. From such an awful state let all earnestly pray to be delivered.

Verses 27-28 While the scribes and Pharisees despised and blasphemed the discourses of our Lord Jesus, this good woman admired them, and the wisdom and power with which he spake. Christ led the woman to a higher consideration. Though it is a great privilege to hear the word of God, yet those only are truly blessed, that is, blessed of the Lord, that hear it, keep it in memory, and keep to it as their way and rule.

Verses 29-36 Christ promised that there should be one sign more given, even the sign of Jonah the prophet; which in Matthew is explained, as meaning the resurrection of Christ; and he warned them to improve this sign. But though Christ himself were the constant preacher in any congregation, and worked miracles daily among them, yet unless his grace humbled their hearts, they would not profit by his word. Let us not desire more evidence and fuller teaching than the Lord is pleased to afford us. We should pray without ceasing that our hearts and understandings may be opened, that we may profit by the light we enjoy. And especially take heed that the light which is in us be not darkness; for if our leading principles be wrong, our judgment and practice must become more so.

Verses 37-54 We should all look to our hearts, that they may be cleansed and new-created; and while we attend to the great things of the law and of the gospel, we must not neglect the smallest matter God has appointed. When any wait to catch something out of our mouths, that they may ensnare us, O Lord, give us thy prudence and thy patience, and disappoint their evil purposes.

Furnish us with such meekness and patience that we may glory in reproaches, for Christ's sake, and that thy Holy Spirit may rest upon us.

CHAPTER 12

Christ reproves the interpreters of the law. (1-12) A caution against covetousness The parable of the rich man. (13-21) Worldly care reproved. (22-40) Watchfulness enforced. (41-53) A warning to be reconciled to God. (54-59)

Verses 1-12 A firm belief of the doctrine of God's universal providence, and the extent of it, would satisfy us when in peril, and encourage us to trust God in the way of duty. Providence takes notice of the meanest creatures, even of the sparrows, and therefore of the smallest interests of the disciples of Christ. Those who confess Christ now, shall be owned by him in the great day, before the angels of God. To deter us from denying Christ, and deserting his truths and ways, we are here assured that those who deny Christ, though they may thus save life itself, and though they may gain a kingdom by it, will be great losers at last; for Christ will not know them, will not own them, nor show them favour. But let no trembling, penitent backslider doubt of obtaining forgiveness. This is far different from the determined enmity that is blasphemy against the Holy Ghost, which shall never be forgiven, because it will never be repented of.

Verses 13-21 Christ's kingdom is spiritual, and not of this world. Christianity does not meddle with politics; it obliges all to do justly, but worldly dominion is not founded in grace. It does not encourage expectations of worldly advantages by religion. The rewards of Christ's disciples are of another nature. Covetousness is a sin we need constantly to be warned against; for happiness and comfort do not depend on the wealth of this world. The things of the world will not satisfy the desires of a soul. Here is a parable, which shows the folly of carnal worldling while they live, and their misery when they die. The character drawn is exactly that of a prudent, worldly man, who has no grateful regard to the providence of God, nor any right thought of the uncertainty of human affairs, the worth of his soul, or the importance of eternity. How many, even among professed Christians, point out similar characters as models for imitation, and proper persons to form connections with! We mistake if we think that thoughts are hid, and thoughts are free. When he saw a great crop upon his ground, instead of thanking God for it, or rejoicing to be able to do more good, he afflicts himself. What shall I do now?

The poorest beggar in the country could not have said a more anxious word. The more men have, the more perplexity they have with it. It was folly for him to think of making no other use of his plenty, than to indulge the flesh and gratify the sensual appetites, without any thought of doing good to others. Carnal worldlings are fools; and the day is coming when God will call them by their own name, and they will call themselves so. The death of such persons is miserable in itself, and terrible to them. Thy soul shall be required. He is loathe to part with it; but God shall require it, shall require an account of it, require it as a guilty soul to be punished without delay. It is the folly of most men, to mind and pursue that which is for the body and for time only, more than that for the soul and eternity.

Verses 22-40 Christ largely insisted upon this caution not to give way to disquieting, perplexing cares, Matthew 6:25-34. The arguments here used are for our encouragement to cast our care upon God, which is the right way to get ease. As in our stature, so in our state, it is our wisdom to take it as it is. An eager, anxious pursuit of the things of this world, even necessary things, ill becomes the disciples of Christ. Fears must not prevail; when we frighten ourselves with thoughts of evil to come, and put ourselves upon needless cares how to avoid it. If we value the beauty of holiness, we shall not crave the luxuries of life. Let us then examine whether we belong to this little flock. Christ is our Master, and we are his servants; not only working servants, but waiting servants. We must be as men that wait for their lord, that sit up while he stays out late, to be ready to receive him. In this Christ alluded to his own ascension to heaven, his coming to call his people to him by death, and his return to judge the world. We are uncertain as to the time of his coming to us, we should therefore be always ready. If men thus take care of their houses, let us be thus wise for our souls. Be ye therefore ready also; as ready as the good man of the house would be, if he knew at what hour the thief would come.

Verses 41-53 All are to take to themselves what Christ says in his word, and to inquire concerning it. No one is left so ignorant as not to know many things to be wrong which he does, and many things to be right which he neglects; therefore all are without excuse in their sin. The bringing in of the gospel dispensation would occasion desolations. Not that this would be the tendency of Christ's religion, which is pure, peaceable, and loving; but the effect of its being contrary to men's pride and lusts. There was to be a wide publication of the gospel. But before that took place, Christ had a baptism to be baptized with, far different from that of water and the Holy Spirit. He must endure sufferings and death. It agreed not with his plan to preach the gospel more widely, till this baptism was completed. We should be zealous in making known the truth, for though divisions will be stirred up, and a man's own household may be his foes, yet sinners will be converted, and God will be glorified.

Verses 54-59 Christ would have the people to be as wise in the concerns of their souls as they are in outward affairs. Let them hasten to obtain peace with God before it is too late. If any man has found that God has set himself against him concerning his sins, let him apply to him as God in Christ reconciling the world to himself. While we are alive, we are in the way, and now is our time.

Chapter 13

Christ exhorts to repentance from the case of the Galileans and others. (1-5) Parable of the barren fig-tree. (6-9) The infirm woman strengthened. (10-17) The parables of the mustard seed, and leaven. (18-22) Exhortation to enter at the strait gate. (23-30) Christ's reproof to Herod, and to the people of Jerusalem. (31-35)

Verses 1-5 Mention was made to Christ of the death of some Galileans. This tragical story is briefly related here, and is not met with in any historians. In Christ's reply he spoke of another event, which, like it, gave an instance of people taken away by sudden death. Towers, that are built for safety, often prove to be men's destruction. He cautioned his hearers not to blame great sufferers, as if they were therefore to be accounted great sinners. As no place or employment can secure from the stroke of death, we should consider the sudden removals of others as warnings to ourselves. On these accounts Christ founded a call to repentance. The same Jesus that bids us repent, for the kingdom of heaven is at hand, bids us repent, for otherwise we shall perish.

Verses 6-9 This parable of the barren fig-tree is intended to enforce the warning given just before: the barren tree, except it brings forth fruit, will be cut down. This parable in the first place refers to the nation and people of the Jews. Yet it is, without doubt, for awakening all that enjoy the means of grace, and the privileges of the visible church. When God has borne long, we may hope that he will bear with us yet a little longer, but we cannot expect that he will bear always.

Verses 10-17 Our Lord Jesus attended upon public worship on the Sabbaths. Even bodily infirmities, unless very grievous, should not keep us from public worship on Sabbath days. This woman came to Christ to be taught, and to get good to her soul, and then he relieved her bodily infirmity. This cure represents the work of Christ's grace upon the soul. And when crooked souls are made straight, they will show it by glorifying God. Christ knew that this ruler had a real enmity to him and to his gospel, and that he did but cloak it with a pretended zeal for the Sabbath day; he really would not have them be healed any day; but if Jesus speaks the word, and puts forth his healing power, sinners are set free. This deliverance is often wrought on the Lord's day; and whatever labour tends to put men in the way of receiving the blessing, agrees with the design of that day.

Verses 18-22 Here is the progress of the gospel foretold in two parables, as in Matthew 13. The kingdom of the Messiah is the kingdom of God. May grace grow in our hearts; may our faith and love grow exceedingly, so as to give undoubted evidence of their reality. May the example of God's saints be blessed to those among whom they live; and may his grace flow from heart to heart, until the little one becomes a thousand.

Verses 23-30 Our Saviour came to guide men's consciences, not to gratify their curiosity. Ask not, How many shall be saved? But, Shall I be one of them? Not, What shall become of such and such? But, What shall I do, and what will become of me? Strive to enter in at the strait gate. This is directed to each of us; it is, Strive ye. All that will be saved, must enter in at the strait gate, must undergo a change of the whole man. Those that would enter in, must strive to enter. Here are awakening considerations, to enforce this exhortation. Oh that we may be all awakened by them! They answer the question, Are there few that shall be saved? But let none despond either as to themselves or others, for there are last who shall be first, and first who shall be last. If we reach heaven, we shall meet many there whom we little thought to meet, and miss many whom we expected to find.

Verses 31-35 Christ, in calling Herod a fox, gave him his true character. The greatest of men were accountable to God, therefore it became him to call this proud king by his own name; but it is not an example for us. I know, said our Lord, that I must die very shortly; when I die, I shall be perfected, I shall have completed my undertaking. It is good for us to look upon the time we have before us as but little, that we may thereby be quickened to do the work of the day in its day. The wickedness of persons and places which more than others profess religion and relation to God, especially displeases and grieves the Lord Jesus. The judgment of the great day will convince unbelievers; but let us learn thankfully to welcome, and to profit by all who come in the name of the Lord, to call us to partake of his great salvation.

CHAPTER 14

Christ heals a man on the Sabbath. (1-6) He teaches humility. (7-14) Parable of the great supper. (15-24) The necessity of consideration and self-denial. (25-35)

Verses 1-6 This Pharisee, as well as others, seems to have had an ill design in entertaining Jesus at his house. But our Lord would not be hindered from healing a man, though he knew a clamour would be raised at his doing it on the Sabbath. It requires care to understand the proper connection between piety and charity in observing the Sabbath, and the distinction between works of real necessity and habits of self-indulgence. Wisdom from above, teaches patient perseverance in well-doing.

Verses 7-14 Even in the common actions of life, Christ marks what we do, not only in our religious assemblies, but at our tables. We see in many cases, that a man's pride will bring him low, and before honour is humility. Our Saviour here teaches, that works of charity are better than works of show. But our Lord did not mean that a proud and unbelieving liberality should be rewarded, but that his precept of doing good to the poor and afflicted should be observed from love to him.

Verses 15-24 In this parable observe the free grace and mercy of God shining in the gospel of Christ, which will be food and a feast for the soul of a man that knows its own wants and miseries. All found some pretence to put off their attendance. This reproves the Jewish nation for their neglect of the offers of Christ's grace. It shows also the backwardness there is to close with the gospel call. The want of gratitude in those who slight gospel offers, and the contempt put upon the God of heaven thereby, justly provoke him. The apostles were to turn to the Gentiles, when the Jews refused the offer; and with them the church was filled. The provision made for precious souls in the gospel of Christ, has not been made in vain; for if some reject, others will thankfully accept the offer. The very poor and low in the world, shall be as welcome to Christ as the rich and great; and many times the gospel has the greatest success among those that labour under worldly disadvantages and bodily infirmities. Christ's house shall at last be filled; it will be so when the number of the elect is completed.

Verses 25-35 Though the disciples of Christ are not all crucified, yet they all bear their cross, and must bear it in the way of duty. Jesus bids them count upon it, and then consider of it. Our Saviour explains this by two similitudes; the former showing that we must consider the expenses of our religion; the latter, that we must consider the perils of it. Sit down and count the cost; consider it will cost the mortifying of sin, even the most beloved lusts. The proudest and most daring sinner cannot stand against God, for who knows the power of his anger? It is our interest to seek peace with him, and we need not send to ask conditions of peace, they are offered to us, and are highly to our advantage. In some way a disciple of Christ will be put to the trial. May we seek to be disciples indeed, and be careful not to grow slack in our profession, or afraid of the cross; that we may be the good salt of the earth, to season those around us with the savour of Christ.

CHAPTER 15

Parables of the lost sheep, and the piece of silver. (1-10) The prodigal son, his wickedness and distress. (11-16) His repentance and pardon. (17-24) The elder brother offended. (25-32)

Verses 1-10 The parable of the lost sheep is very applicable to the great work of man's redemption. The lost sheep represents the sinner as departed from God, and exposed to certain ruin if not brought back to him, yet not desirous to return. Christ is earnest in bringing sinners home. In the parable of the lost piece of silver, that which is lost, is one piece, of small value compared with the rest. Yet the woman seeks diligently till she finds it. This represents the various means and methods God makes use of to bring lost souls home to himself, and the Saviour's joy on their return to him. How careful then should we be that our repentance is unto salvation!

Verses 11-16 The parable of the prodigal son shows the nature of repentance, and the Lord's readiness to welcome and bless all who return to him. It fully sets forth the riches of gospel grace; and it has been, and will be, while the world stands, of unspeakable use to poor sinners, to direct and to encourage them in repenting and returning to God. It is bad, and the beginning of worse, when men look upon God's gifts as debts due to them. The great folly of sinners, and that which ruins them, is, being content in their life-time to receive their good things. Our first parents ruined themselves and all their race, by a foolish ambition to be independent, and this is at the bottom of sinners' persisting in their sin.

We may all discern some features of our own characters in that of the prodigal son. A sinful state is of departure and distance from God. A sinful state is a spending state: willful sinners misemploy their thoughts and the powers of their souls, misspend their time and all their opportunities. A sinful state is a wanting state. Sinners want necessaries for their souls; they have neither food nor raiment for them, nor any provision for hereafter. A sinful state is a vile, slavish state. The business of the devil's servants is to make provision for the flesh, to fulfill the lusts thereof, and that is no better than feeding swine. A sinful state is a state constant discontent. The wealth of the world and the pleasures of the senses will not even satisfy our bodies; but what are they to precious souls! A sinful state is a state which cannot look for relief from any creature. In vain do we cry to the world and to the flesh; they have that which will poison a soul, but have nothing to give which will feed and nourish it. A sinful state is a state of death. A sinner is dead in trespasses and sins, destitute of spiritual life. A sinful state is a lost state. Souls that are separated from God, if his mercy prevent not, will soon be lost for ever. The prodigal's wretched state, only faintly shadows forth the awful ruin of man by sin. Yet how few are sensible of their own state and character!

Verses 17-24 Having viewed the prodigal in his abject state of misery, we are next to consider his recovery from it. This begins by his coming to himself. That is a turning point in the sinner's conversion. The Lord opens his eyes, and convinces him of sin; then he views himself and every object, in a different light from what he did before. Thus the convinced sinner perceives that the meanest servant of God is happier than he is. To look unto God as a Father, and our Father, will be of great use in our repentance and return to him. The prodigal arose, nor stopped till he reached his home. Thus the repenting sinner resolutely quits the bondage of Satan and his lusts, and returns to God by prayer, notwithstanding fears and discouragements. The Lord meets him with unexpected tokens of his forgiving love. Again; the reception of the humbled sinner is like that of the prodigal. He is clothed in the robe of the Redeemer's righteousness, made partaker of the Spirit of adoption, prepared by peace of conscience and gospel grace to walk in the ways of holiness, and feasted with Divine consolations. Principles of grace and holiness are wrought in him, to do, as well as to will.

Verses 25-32 In the latter part of this parable we have the character of the Pharisees, though not of them alone. It sets forth the kindness of the Lord, and the proud manner in which his gracious kindness is often received. The Jews, in general, showed the same spirit towards the converted Gentiles; and numbers in every age object to the gospel and its preachers, on the same ground. What must that temper be, which stirs up a man to despise and abhor those for whom the Saviour shed his precious blood, who are objects of the Father's choice, and temples of the Holy Ghost! This springs from pride, self-preference, and ignorance of a man's own heart. The mercy and grace of our God in Christ, shine almost as bright in his tender and gentle bearing with peevish saints, as his receiving prodigal sinners upon their repentance. It is the unspeakable happiness of all the children of God, who keep close to their Father's house, that they are, and shall be ever with him. Happy will it be for those who thankfully accept Christ's invitation.

CHAPTER 16

The parable of the unjust steward. (1-12) Christ reproves the hypocrisy of the covetous Pharisees. (13-18) The rich man and Lazarus. (19-31)

Verses 1-12 Whatever we have, the property of it is God's; we have only the use of it, according to the direction of our great Lord, and for his honour. This steward wasted his lord's goods. And we are all liable to the same charge; we have not made due improvement of what God has trusted us with. The steward cannot deny it; he must make up his accounts, and be gone. This may teach us that death will come, and deprive us of the opportunities we now have. The steward will make friends of his lord's debtors or tenants, by striking off a considerable part of their debt to his lord. The lord referred to in this parable commended not the fraud, but the policy of the steward. In that respect alone is it so noticed. Worldly men, in the choice of their object, are foolish; but in their activity, and perseverance, they are often wiser than believers. The unjust steward is not set before us as an example in cheating his master, or to justify any dishonesty, but to point out the careful ways of worldly men. It would be well if the children of light would learn wisdom from the men of the world, and would as earnestly pursue their better object.

The true riches signify spiritual blessings; and if a man spends upon himself, or hoards up what God has trusted to him, as to outward things, what evidence can he have, that he is an heir of God through Christ? The riches of this world are deceitful and uncertain. Let us be convinced that those are truly rich, and very rich, who are rich in faith, and rich toward God, rich in Christ, in the promises; let us then lay up our treasure in heaven, and expect our portion from thence.

Verses 13-18 To this parable our Lord added a solemn warning. Ye cannot serve God and the world, so divided are the two interests. When our Lord spoke thus, the covetous Pharisees treated his instructions with contempt. But he warned them, that what they contended for as the law, was a wresting of its meaning: this our Lord showed in a case respecting divorce. There are many covetous sticklers for the forms of godliness, who are the bitterest enemies to its power, and try to set others against the truth.

Verses 19-31 Here the spiritual things are represented, in a description of the different state of good and bad, in this world and in the other. We are not told that the rich man got his estate by fraud, or oppression; but Christ shows, that a man may have a great deal of the wealth, pomp, and pleasure of this world, yet perish for ever under God's wrath and curse. The sin of this rich man was his providing for himself only. Here is a godly man, and one that will hereafter be happy for ever, in the depth of adversity and distress. It is often the lot of some of the dearest of God's saints and servants to be greatly afflicted in this world. We are not told that the rich man did him any harm, but we do not find that he had any care for him. Here is the different condition of this godly poor man, and this wicked rich man, at and after death. The rich man in hell lifted up his eyes, being in torment. It is not probable that there are discourses between glorified saints and damned sinners, but this dialogue shows the hopeless misery and fruitless desires, to which condemned spirits are brought. There is a day coming, when those who now hate and despise the people of God, would gladly receive kindness from them. But the damned in hell shall not have the least abatement of their torment. Sinners are now called upon to remember; but they do not, they will not, they find ways to avoid it.

As wicked people have good things only in this life, and at death are for ever separated from all good, so godly people have evil things only in this life, and at death they are for ever put from them. In this world, blessed be God, there is no gulf between a state of nature and grace, we may pass from sin to God; but if we die in our sins, there is no coming out. The rich man had five brethren, and would have them stopped in their sinful course; their coming to that place of torment, would make his misery the worse, who had helped to show them the way thither. How many would now desire to recall or to undo what they have written or done! Those who would make the rich man's praying to Abraham justify praying to saints departed, go far to seek for proofs, when the mistake of a damned sinner is all they can find for an example. And surely there is no encouragement to follow the example, when all his prayers were made in vain. A messenger from the dead could say no more than what is said in the Scriptures. The same strength of corruption that breaks through the convictions of the written word, would triumph over a witness from the dead. Let us seek to the law and to the testimony, Isaiah 8:19,20, for that is the 2 Peter Circumstances in every age show that no terrors, or arguments, can give true repentance without the special grace of God renewing the sinner's heart.

CHAPTER 17

To avoid offences, To pray for increase of faith, Humility taught.
(11-19). Ten lepers cleansed. (1-10) Christ's kingdom. (20-37)

Verses 1-10 It is no abatement of their guilt by whom an offence comes, nor will it lessen their punishment that offences will come. Faith in God's pardoning mercy, will enable us to get over the greatest difficulties in the way of forgiving our brethren. As with God nothing is impossible, so all things are possible to him that can believe. Our Lord showed his disciples their need of deep humility. The Lord has such a property in every creature, as no man can have in another; he cannot be in debt to them for their services, nor do they deserve any return from him.

Verses 11-19 A sense of our spiritual leprosy should make us very humble whenever we draw near to Christ. It is enough to refer ourselves to the compassions of Christ, for they fail not. We may look for God to meet us with mercy, when we are found in the way of obedience. Only one of those who were healed returned to give thanks. It becomes us, like him, to be very humble in thanksgivings, as well as in prayers. Christ noticed the one who thus distinguished himself, he was a Samaritan. The others only got the outward cure, he alone got the spiritual blessing.

Verses 20-37 The kingdom of God was among the Jews, or rather within some of them. It was a spiritual kingdom, set up in the heart by the power of Divine grace. Observe how it had been with sinners formerly, and in what state the judgments of God, which they had been warned of, found them. Here is shown what a dreadful surprise this destruction will be to the secure and sensual. Thus shall it be in the day when the Son of man is revealed. When Christ came to destroy the Jewish nation by the Roman armies, that nation was found in such a state of false security as is here spoken of. In like manner, when Jesus Christ shall come to judge the world, sinners will be found altogether regardless; for in like manner the sinners of every age go on securely in their evil ways, and remember not their latter end. But wherever the wicked are, who are marked for eternal ruin, they shall be found by the judgments of God.

CHAPTER 18

The parable of the importunate widow. (1-8) The Pharisee and the publican. (9-14) Children brought to Christ. (15-17) The ruler hindered by his riches. (18-30) Christ foreshows his death. (31-34) A blind man restored to sight. (35-43)

Verses 1-8 All God's people are praying people. Here earnest steadiness in prayer for spiritual mercies is taught. The widow's earnestness prevailed even with the unjust judge: she might fear lest it should set him more against her; but our earnest prayer is pleasing to our God. Even to the end there will still be ground for the same complaint of weakness of faith.

Verses 9-14 This parable was to convince some who trusted in themselves that they were righteous, and despised others. God sees with what disposition and design we come to him in holy ordinances. What the Pharisee said, shows that he trusted to himself that he was righteous. We may suppose he was free from gross and scandalous sins. All this was very well and commendable. Miserable is the condition of those who come short of the righteousness of this Pharisee, yet he was not accepted; and why not? He went up to the temple to pray, but was full of himself and his own goodness; the favour and grace of God he did not think worth asking. Let us beware of presenting proud devotions to the Lord, and of despising others. The publican's address to God was full of humility, and of repentance for sin, and desire toward God. His prayer was short, but to the purpose; God be merciful to me a sinner. Blessed be God, that we have this short prayer upon record, as an answered prayer; and that we are sure that he who prayed it, went to his house justified; for so shall we be, if we pray it, as he did, through Jesus Christ. He owned himself a sinner by nature, by practice, guilty before God. He had no dependence but upon the mercy of God; upon that alone he relied. And God's glory is to resist the proud, and give grace to the humble. Justification is of God in Christ; therefore the self-condemned, and not the self-righteous, are justified before God.

Verses 15-17 None are too little, too young, to be brought to Christ, who knows how to show kindness to those not capable of doing service to him. It is the mind of Christ, that little children should be brought to him. The promise is to us, and to our seed; therefore He will bid them welcome to him with us. And we must receive his kingdom as children, not by purchase, and must call it our Father's gift.

Verses 18-30 Many have a great deal in them very commendable, yet perish for lack of some one thing; so this ruler could not bear Christ's terms, which would part between him and his estate. Many who are loathe to leave Christ, yet do leave him. After a long struggle between their convictions and their corruptions, their corruptions carry the day. They are very sorry that they cannot serve both; but if one must be quitted, it shall be their God, not their worldly gain. Their boasted obedience will be found mere outside show; the love of the world in some form or other lies at the root. Men are apt to speak too much of what they have left and lost, of what they have done and suffered for Christ, as Peter did. But we should rather be ashamed that there has been any regret or difficulty in doing it.

Verses 31-34 The Spirit of Christ, in the Old Testament prophets, testified beforehand his sufferings, and the glory that should 1 Peter that they would not understand these things literally. They were so intent upon the prophecies which spake of Christ's glory, that they overlooked those which spake of his sufferings. People run into mistakes, because they read their Bibles by halves, and are only for the smooth things. We are as backward to learn the proper lessons from the sufferings, crucifixion, and resurrection of Christ, as the disciples were to what he told them as to those events; and for the same reason; self-love, and a desire of worldly objects, close our understandings.

Verses 35-43 This poor blind man sat by the wayside, begging. He was not only blind, but poor, the fitter emblem of the world of mankind which Christ came to heal and save. The prayer of faith, guided by Christ's encouraging promises, and grounded on them, shall not be in vain. The grace of Christ ought to be thankfully acknowledged, to the glory of God. It is for the glory of God if we follow Jesus, as those will do whose eyes are opened. We must praise God for his mercies to others, as well as for mercies to ourselves. Would we rightly understand these things, we must come to Christ, like the blind man, earnestly beseeching him to open our eyes, and to show us clearly the excellence of his precepts, and the value of his salvation.

CHAPTER 19

The conversion of Zaccheus. (1-10) The parable of the nobleman and his servants. (11-27) Christ enters Jerusalem. (28-40) Christ laments over Jerusalem. (41-48)

Verses 1-10 Those who sincerely desire a sight of Christ, like Zaccheus, will break through opposition, and take pains to see him. Christ invited himself to Zaccheus' house. Wherever Christ comes he opens the heart, and inclines it to receive him. He that has a mind to know Christ, shall be known of him. Those whom Christ calls, must humble themselves, and come down. We may well receive him joyfully, who brings all good with him. Zaccheus gave proofs publicly that he was become a true convert. He does not look to be justified by his works, as the Pharisee; but by his good works he will, through the grace of God, show the sincerity of his faith and repentance. Zaccheus is declared to be a happy man, now he is turned from sin to God. Now that he is saved from his sins, from the guilt of them, from the power of them, all the benefits of salvation are his. Christ is come to his house, and where Christ comes he brings salvation with him. He came into this lost world to seek and to save it. His design was to save, when there was no salvation in any other. He seeks those that sought him not, and asked not for him.

Verses 11-27 This parable is like that of the talents, Matthew 25. Those that are called to Christ, he furnishes with gifts needful for their business; and from those to whom he gives power, he expects service. The manifestation of the Spirit is given to 1 Corinthians 1 Peter account required, resembles that in the parable of the talents; and the punishment of the avowed enemies of Christ, as well as of false professors, is shown. The principal difference is, that the pound given to each seems to point out the gift of the gospel, which is the same to all who hear it; but the talents, distributed more or less, seem to mean that God gives different capacities and advantages to men, by which this one gift of the gospel may be differently improved.

Verses 28-40 Christ has dominion over all creatures, and may use them as he pleases. He has all men's hearts both under his eye and in his hand. Christ's triumphs, and his disciples' joyful praises, vex proud Pharisees, who are enemies to him and to his kingdom. But Christ, as he despises the contempt of the proud, so he accepts the praises of the humble. Pharisees would silence the praises of Christ, but they cannot; for as God can out of stones raise up children unto Abraham, and turn the stony heart to himself, so he can bring praise out of the mouths of children. And what will be the feelings of men when the Lord returns in glory to judge the world!

Verses 41-48 Who can behold the holy Jesus, looking forward to the miseries that awaited his murderers, weeping over the city where his precious blood was about to be shed, without seeing that the likeness of God in the believer, consists much in good-will and compassion? Surely those cannot be right who take up any doctrines of truth, so as to be hardened towards their fellow-sinners. But let every one remember, that though Jesus wept over Jerusalem, he executed awful vengeance upon it. Though he delights not in the death of a sinner, yet he will surely bring to pass his awful threatenings on those who neglect his salvation. The Son of God did not weep vain and causeless tears, nor for a light matter, nor for himself. He knows the value of souls, the weight of guilt, and how low it will press and sink mankind. May he then come and cleanse our hearts by his Spirit, from all that defiles. May sinners, on every side, become attentive to the words of truth and salvation.

CHAPTER 20

The priests and scribes question Christ's authority. (1-8) The parable of the vineyard and husbandmen. (9-19) Of giving tribute. (20-26) Concerning the resurrection. (27-38) The scribes silenced. (39-47)

Verses 1-8 Men often pretend to examine the evidences of revelation, and the truth of the gospel, when only seeking excuses for their own unbelief and disobedience. Christ answered these priests and scribes with a plain question about the baptism of John, which the common people could answer. They all knew it was from heaven, nothing in it had an earthly tendency. Those that bury the knowledge they have, are justly denied further knowledge. It was just with Christ to refuse to give account of his authority, to those who knew the baptism of John to be from heaven, yet would not believe in him, nor own their knowledge.

Verses 9-19 Christ spake this parable against those who resolved not to own his authority, though the evidence of it was so full. How many resemble the Jews who murdered the prophets and crucified Christ, in their enmity to God, and aversion to his service, desiring to live according to their lusts, without control! Let all who are favoured with God's word, look to it that they make proper use of their advantages. Awful will be the doom, both of those who reject the Son, and of those who profess to reverence Him, yet render not the fruits in due season. Though they could not but own that for such a sin, such a punishment was just, yet they could not bear to hear of it. It is the folly of sinners, that they persevere in sinful ways, though they dread the destruction at the end of those ways.

Verses 20-26 Those who are most crafty in their designs against Christ and his gospel, cannot hide them. He did not give a direct answer, but reproved them for offering to impose upon him; and they could not fasten upon any thing wherewith to stir up either the governor or the people against him. The wisdom which is from above, will direct all who teach the way of God truly, to avoid the snares laid for them by wicked men; and will teach our duty to God, to our rulers, and to all men, so clearly, that opposers will have no evil to say of us.

Verses 27-38 It is common for those who design to undermine any truth of God, to load it with difficulties. But we wrong ourselves, and wrong the truth of Christ, when we form our notions of the world of spirits by this world of sense. There are more worlds than one; a present visible world, and a future unseen world; and let every one compare this world and that world, and give the preference in his thoughts and cares to that which deserves them. Believers shall obtain the resurrection from the dead, that is the blessed resurrection. What shall be the happy state of the inhabitants of that world, we cannot express or conceive, 1 Corinthians are entirely taken up therewith; when there is perfection of holiness there will be no occasion for preservatives from sin. And when God called himself the God of these patriarchs, he meant that he was a God all-sufficient to them, genesis 17:1, their exceeding great Reward, genesis 15:1. He never did that for them in this world, which answered the full extent of his undertaking; therefore there must be another life, in which he will do that for them, which will completely fulfill the promise.

Verses 39-47 The scribes commended the reply Christ made to the Sadducees about the resurrection, but they were silenced by a question concerning the Messiah. Christ, as God, was David's Lord; but Christ, as man, was David's son. The scribes would receive the severest judgment for defrauding the poor widows, and for their abuse of religion, particularly of prayer, which they used as a pretence for carrying on worldly and wicked plans. Dissembled piety is double sin. Then let us beg of God to keep us from pride, ambition, covetousness, and every evil thing; and to teach us to seek that honour which comes from him alone.

CHAPTER 21

Christ commends a poor widow. (1-4) His prophecy. (5-28) Christ exhorts to watchfulness. (29-38)

Verses 1-4 From the offering of this poor widow, learn that what we rightly give for the relief of the poor, and the support of God's worship, is given unto God; and our Saviour sees with pleasure whatever we have in our hearts to give for the relief of his members, or for his service. Blessed Lord! The poorest of thy servants have two mites, they have a soul and a body; persuade and enable us to offer both unto thee; how happy shall we be in thine accepting of them!

Verses 5-28 With much curiosity those about Christ ask as to the time when the great desolation should be. He answers with clearness and fullness, as far as was necessary to teach them their duty; for all knowledge is desirable as far as it is in order to practice. Though spiritual judgements are the most common in gospel times, yet God makes use of temporal judgments also. Christ tells them what hard things they should suffer for his name's sake, and encourages them to bear up under their trials, and to go on in their work, notwithstanding the opposition they would meet with. God will stand by you, and own you, and assist you. This was remarkably fulfilled after the pouring out of the Spirit, by whom Christ gave his disciples wisdom and utterance. Though we may be losers for Christ, we shall not, we cannot be losers by him, in the end. It is our duty and interest at all times, especially in perilous, trying times, to secure the safety of our own souls.

It is by Christian patience we keep possession of our own souls, and keep out all those impressions which would put us out of temper. We may view the prophecy before us much as those Old Testament prophecies, which, together with their great object, embrace, or glance at some nearer object of importance to the church. Having given an idea of the times for about thirty-eight years next to come, Christ shows what all those things would end in, namely, the destruction of Jerusalem, and the utter dispersion of the Jewish nation; which would be a type and figure of Christ's second coming. The scattered Jews around us preach the truth of Christianity; and prove, that though heaven and earth shall pass away, the words of Jesus shall not pass away. They also remind us to pray for those times when neither the real, nor the spiritual Jerusalem, shall any longer be trodden down by the Gentiles, and when both Jews and Gentiles shall be turned to the Lord.

When Christ came to destroy the Jews, he came to redeem the Christians that were persecuted and oppressed by them; and then had the churches rest. When he comes to judge the world, he will redeem all that are his from their troubles. So fully did the Divine judgements come upon the Jews, that their city is set as an example before us, to show that sins will not pass unpunished; and that the terrors of the Lord, and his threatenings against impenitent sinners, will all come to pass, even as his word was true, and his wrath great upon Jerusalem.

Verses 29-38 Christ tells his disciples to observe the signs of the times, which they might judge by. He charges them to look upon the ruin of the Jewish nation as near. Yet this race and family of Abraham shall not be rooted out; it shall survive as a nation, and be found as prophesied, when the Son of man shall be revealed. He cautions them against being secure and sensual. This command is given to all Christ's disciples, Take heed to yourselves, that ye be not overpowered by temptations, nor betrayed by your own corruptions. We cannot be safe, if we are carnally secure. Our danger is, lest the day of death and of judgment should come upon us when we are not prepared. Lest, when we are called to meet our Lord, that be the furthest from our thoughts, which ought to be nearest our hearts. For so it will come upon the most of men, who dwell upon the earth, and mind earthly things only, and have no converse with heaven. It will be a terror and a destruction to them. Here see what should be our aim, that we may be accounted worthy to escape all those things; that when the judgements of God are abroad, we may not be in the common calamity, or it may not be that to us which it is to others. Do you ask how you may be found worthy to stand before Christ at that day? Those who never yet sought Christ, let them now go unto him; those who never yet were humbled for their sins, let them now begin; those who have already begun, let them go forward and be kept humbled. Watch therefore, and pray always. Watch against sin; watch in every duty, and make the most of every opportunity to do good. Pray always: those shall be accounted worthy to live a life of praise in the other world, who live a life of prayer in this world. May we begin, employ, and conclude each day attending to Christ's word, obeying his precepts, and following his example, that whenever he comes we may be found watching.

CHAPTER 22

The treachery of Judas. (1-6) The Passover. (7-18) The Lord's supper instituted. (19,20) Christ admonishes the disciples. (21-38) Christ's agony in the garden. (39-46) Christ betrayed. (47-53) The fall of Peter. (54-62) Christ confesses himself to be the Son of God. (63-71)

Verses 1-6 Christ knew all men, and had wise and holy ends in taking Judas to be a disciple. How he who knew Christ so well, came to betray him, we are here told; Satan entered into Judas. It is hard to say whether more mischief is done to Christ's kingdom, by the power of its open enemies, or by the treachery of its pretended friends; but without the latter, its enemies could not do so much evil as they do.

Verses 7-18 Christ kept the ordinances of the law, particularly that of the Passover, to teach us to observe his gospel institutions, and most of all that of the Lord's supper. Those who go upon Christ's word, need not fear disappointment. According to the orders given them, the disciples got all ready for the Passover. Jesus bids this Passover welcome. He desired it, though he knew his sufferings would follow, because it was in order to his Father's glory and man's redemption. He takes his leave of all Passovers, signifying thereby his doing away all the ordinances of the ceremonial law, of which the Passover was one of the earliest and chief. That type was laid aside, because now in the kingdom of God the substance was come.

Verses 19-20 The Lord's supper is a sign or memorial of Christ already come, who by dying delivered us; his death is in special manner set before us in that ordinance, by which we are reminded of it. The breaking of Christ's body as a sacrifice for us, is therein brought to our remembrance by the breaking of bread. Nothing can be more nourishing and satisfying to the soul, than the doctrine of Christ's making atonement for sin, and the assurance of an interest in that atonement. Therefore we do this in remembrance of what He did for us, when he died for us; and for a memorial of what we do, in joining ourselves to him in an everlasting covenant. The shedding of Christ's blood, by which the atonement was made, is represented by the wine in the cup.

Verses 21-38 How unbecoming is the worldly ambition of being the greatest, to the character of a follower of Jesus, who took upon him the form of a servant, and humbled himself to the death of the cross! In the way to eternal happiness, we must expect to be assaulted and sifted by Satan. If he cannot destroy, he will try to disgrace or distress us. Nothing more certainly forebodes a fall, in a professed follower of Christ, than self-confidence, with disregard to warnings, and contempt of danger. Unless we watch and pray always, we may be drawn in the course of the day into those sins which we were in the morning most resolved against. If believers were left to themselves, they would fall; but they are kept by the power of God, and the prayer of Christ. Our Lord gave notice of a very great change of circumstances now approaching. The disciples must not expect that their friends would be kind to them as they had been. Therefore, he that has a purse, let him take it, for he may need it. They must now expect that their enemies would be more fierce than they had been, and they would need weapons. At the time the apostles understood Christ to mean real weapons, but he spake only of the weapons of the spiritual warfare. The sword of the Spirit is the sword with which the disciples of Christ must furnish themselves.

Verses 39-46 Every description which the evangelists give of the state of mind in which our Lord entered upon this conflict, proves the tremendous nature of the assault, and the perfect foreknowledge of its terrors possessed by the meek and lowly Jesus. Here are three things not in the other evangelists. 1. When Christ was in his agony, there appeared to him an angel from heaven, strengthening him. It was a part of his humiliation that he was thus strengthened by a ministering spirit. 2. Being in agony, he prayed more earnestly. Prayer, though never out of season, is in a special manner seasonable when we are in an agony. 3. In this agony his sweat was as it were great drops of blood falling down. This showed the travail of his soul. We should pray also to be enabled to resist unto the shedding of our blood, striving against sin, if ever called to it. When next you dwell in imagination upon the delights of some favourite sin, think of its effects as you behold them here! See its fearful effects in the garden of Gethsemane, and desire, by the help of God, deeply to hate and to forsake that enemy, to ransom sinners from whom the Redeemer prayed, agonized, and bled.

Verses 47-53 Nothing can be a greater affront or grief to the Lord Jesus, than to be betrayed by those who profess to be his followers, and say that they love him. Many instances there are, of Christ's being betrayed by those who, under the form of godliness, fight against the power of it. Jesus here gave an illustrious example of his own rule of doing good to those that hate us, as afterwards he did of praying for those that despitefully use us. Corrupt nature warps our conduct to extremes; we should seek for the Lord's direction before we act in difficult circumstances. Christ was willing to wait for his triumphs till his warfare was accomplished, and we must be so too. But the hour and the power of darkness were short, and such the triumphs of the wicked always will be.

Verses 54-62 Peter's fall was his denying that he knew Christ, and was his disciple; disowning him because of distress and danger. He that has once told a lie, is strongly tempted to persist: the beginning of that sin, like strife, is as the letting forth of water. The Lord turned and looked upon Peter. 1. It was a convincing look. Jesus turned and looked upon him, as if he should say, Dost thou not know me, Peter? 2. It was a chiding look. Let us think with what a rebuking countenance Christ may justly look upon us when we have sinned. 3. It was an expostulating look. Thou who wast the most forward to confess me to be the Son of God, and didst solemnly promise thou wouldest never disown me! 4. It was a compassionate look. Peter, how art thou fallen and undone if I do not help thee! 5. It was a directing look, to go and bethink himself. 6. It was a significant look; it signified the conveying of grace to Peter's heart, to enable him to repent. The grace of God works in and by the word of God, brings that to mind, and sets that home upon the conscience, and so gives the soul the happy turn. Christ looked upon the chief priests, and made no impression upon them as he did on Peter. It was not the mere look from Christ, but the Divine grace with it, that restored Peter.

Verses 63-71 Those that condemned Jesus for a blasphemer, were the vilest blasphemers. He referred them to his second coming, for the full proof of his being the Christ, to their confusion, since they would not admit the proof of it to their conviction. He owns himself to be the Son of God, though he knew he should suffer for it. Upon this they ground his condemnation. Their eyes being blinded, they rush on. Let us meditate on this amazing transaction, and consider Him who endured such contradiction of sinners against himself.

CHAPTER 23

Christ before Pilate. (1-5) Christ before Herod. (6-12) Barabbas preferred to Christ. (13-25) Christ speaks of the destruction of Jerusalem. (26-31) The crucifixion, The repentant malefactor. (32-43) The death of Christ. (44-49) The burial of Christ. (50-56)

Verses 1-5 Pilate well understood the difference between armed forces and our Lord's followers. But instead of being softened by Pilate's declaration of his innocence, and considering whether they were not bringing the guilt of innocent blood upon themselves, the Jews were the more angry. The Lord brings his designs to a glorious end, even by means of those who follow the devices of their own hearts. Thus all parties joined, so as to prove the innocence of Jesus, who was the atoning sacrifice for our sins.

Verses 6-12 Herod had heard many things of Jesus in Galilee, and out of curiosity longed to see him. The poorest beggar that asked a miracle for the relief of his necessity, was never denied; but this proud prince, who asked for a miracle only to gratify his curiosity, is refused. He might have seen Christ and his wondrous works in Galilee, and would not, therefore it is justly said, Now he would see them, and shall not. Herod sent Christ again to Pilate: the friendships of wicked men are often formed by union in wickedness. They agree in little, except in enmity to God, and contempt of Christ.

Verses 13-25 The fear of man brings many into this snare, that they will do an unjust thing, against their consciences, rather than get into trouble. Pilate declares Jesus innocent, and has a mind to release him; yet, to please the people, he would punish him as an evil-doer. If no fault be found in him, why chastise him? Pilate yielded at length; he had not courage to go against so strong a stream. He delivered Jesus to their will, to be crucified.

Verses 26-31 We have here the blessed Jesus, the Lamb of God, led as a lamb to the slaughter, to the sacrifice. Though many reproached and reviled him, yet some pitied him. But the death of Christ was his victory and triumph over his enemies: it was our deliverance, the purchase of eternal life for us. Therefore weep not for him, but let us weep for our own sins, and the sins of our children, which caused his death; and weep for fear of the miseries we shall bring upon ourselves, if we slight his love, and reject his grace. If God delivered him up to such sufferings as these, because he was made a sacrifice for sin, what will he do with sinners themselves, who make themselves a dry tree, a corrupt and wicked generation, and good for nothing! The bitter sufferings of our Lord Jesus should make us stand in awe of the justice of God. The best saints, compared with Christ, are dry trees; if he suffer, why may not they expect to suffer? And what then shall the damnation of sinners be! Even the sufferings of Christ preach terror to obstinate transgressors.

Verses 32-43 As soon as Christ was fastened to the cross, he prayed for those who crucified him. The great thing he died to purchase and procure for us, is the forgiveness of sin. This he prays for. Jesus was crucified between two thieves; in them were shown the different effects the cross of Christ would have upon the children of men in the preaching the gospel. One malefactor was hardened to the last. No troubles of themselves will change a wicked heart. The other was softened at the last: he was snatched as a brand out of the burning, and made a monument of Divine mercy. This gives no encouragement to any to put off repentance to their death-beds, or to hope that they shall then find mercy.

It is certain that true repentance is never too late; but it is as certain that late repentance is seldom true. None can be sure they shall have time to repent at death, but every man may be sure he cannot have the advantages this penitent thief had. We shall see the case to be singular, if we observe the uncommon effects of God's grace upon this man. He reproved the other for railing on Christ. He owned that he deserved what was done to him. He believed Jesus to have suffered wrongfully. Observe his faith in this prayer. Christ was in the depth of disgrace, suffering as a deceiver, and not delivered by his Father. He made this profession before the wonders were displayed which put honour on Christ's sufferings, and startled the centurion. He believed in a life to come, and desired to be happy in that life; not like the other thief, to be only saved from the cross. Observe his humility in this prayer. All his request is, Lord, remember me; quite referring it to Jesus in what way to remember him. Thus he was humbled in true repentance, and he brought forth all the fruits for repentance his circumstances would admit.

Christ upon the cross, is gracious like Christ upon the throne. Though he was in the greatest struggle and agony, yet he had pity for a poor penitent. By this act of grace we are to understand that Jesus Christ died to open the kingdom of heaven to all penitent, obedient believers. It is a single instance in Scripture; it should teach us to despair of none, and that none should despair of themselves; but lest it should be abused, it is contrasted with the awful state of the other thief, who died hardened in unbelief, though a crucified Saviour was so near him. Be sure that in general men die as they live.

Verses 44-49 We have here the death of Christ magnified by the wonders that attended it, and his death explained by the words with which he breathed out his soul. He was willing to offer himself.

Let us seek to glorify God by true repentance and conversion; by protesting against those who crucify the Saviour; by a sober, righteous, and godly life; and by employing our talents in the service of Him who died for us and rose again.

Verses 50-56 Many, though they do not make any show in outward profession, yet, like Joseph of Arimathea, will be far more ready to do real service, when there is occasion, than others who make a greater noise. Christ was buried in haste, because the Sabbath drew on. Weeping must not hinder sowing. Though they were in tears for the death of their Lord, yet they must prepare to keep holy the Sabbath. When the Sabbath draws on, there must be preparation. Our worldly affairs must be so ordered, that they may not hinder us from our Sabbath work; and our holy affections so stirred up, that they may carry us on in it. In whatever business we engage, or however our hearts may be affected, let us never fail to get ready for, and to keep holy, the day of sacred rest, which is the Lord's day.

CHAPTER 24

The resurrection of Christ. (1-12) He appears to two disciples on the way to Emmaus. (13-27) And makes himself known to them. (28-35) Christ appears to the other disciples. (36-49) His ascension. (50-53)

Verses 1-12 See the affection and respect the women showed to Christ, after he was dead and buried. Observe their surprise when they found the stone rolled away, and the grave empty. Christians often perplex themselves about that with which they should comfort and encourage themselves. They look rather to find their Master in his grave-clothes, than angels in their shining garments. The angels assure them that he is risen from the dead; is risen by his own power. These angels from heaven bring not any new gospel, but remind the women of Christ's words, and teach them how to apply them. We may wonder that these disciples, who believed Jesus to be the Son of God and the true Messiah, who had been so often told that he must die, and rise again, and then enter into his glory, who had seen him more than once raise the dead, yet should be so backward to believe his raising himself. But all our mistakes in religion spring from ignorance or forgetfulness of the words Christ has spoken. Peter now ran to the sepulchre, who so lately ran from his Master. He was amazed. There are many things puzzling and perplexing to us, which would be plain and profitable, if we rightly understood the words of Christ.

Verses 13-27 This appearance of Jesus to the two disciples going to Emmaus, happened the same day that he rose from the dead. It well becomes the disciples of Christ to talk together of his death and resurrection; thus they may improve one another's knowledge, refresh one another's memory, and stir up each other's devout affections. And where but two together are well employed in work of that kind, he will come to them, and make a third.

Those who seek Christ, shall find him: he will manifest himself to those that inquire after him; and give knowledge to those who use the helps for knowledge which they have. No matter how it was, but so it was, they did not know him; he so ordering it, that they might the more freely discourse with him. Christ's disciples are often sad and sorrowful, even when they have reason to rejoice; but through the weakness of their faith, they cannot take the comfort offered to them. Though Christ is entered into his state of exaltation, yet he notices the sorrows of his disciples, and is afflicted in their afflictions. Those are strangers in Jerusalem, that know not of the death and sufferings of Jesus.

Those who have the knowledge of Christ crucified, should seek to spread that knowledge. Our Lord Jesus reproved them for the weakness of their faith in the Scriptures of the Old Testament. Did we know more of the Divine counsels as far as they are made known in the Scriptures, we should not be subject to the perplexities we often entangle ourselves in. He shows them that the sufferings of Christ were really the appointed way to his glory; but the cross of Christ was that to which they could not reconcile themselves. Beginning at Moses, the first inspired writer of the Old Testament, Jesus expounded to them the things concerning himself. There are many passages throughout all the Scriptures concerning Christ, which it is of great advantage to put together. We cannot go far in any part, but we meet with something that has reference to Christ, some prophecy, some promise, some prayer, some type or other.

A golden thread of gospel grace runs through the whole web of the Old Testament. Christ is the best expositor of Scripture; and even after his resurrection, he led people to know the mystery concerning himself, not by advancing new notions, but by showing how the Scripture was fulfilled, and turning them to the earnest study of it.

Verses 28-35 If we would have Christ dwell with us, we must be earnest with him. Those that have experienced the pleasure and profit of communion with him, cannot but desire more of his company. He took bread, and blessed it, and brake, and gave to them. This he did with his usual authority and affection, with the same manner, perhaps with the same words. He here teaches us to crave a blessing on every meal. See how Christ by his Spirit and grace makes himself known to the souls of his people. He opens the Scriptures to them. He meets them at his table, in the ordinance of the Lord's supper; is known to them in breaking of bread. But the work is completed by the opening of the eyes of their mind; yet it is but short views we have of Christ in this world, but when we enter heaven, we shall see him for ever. They had found the preaching powerful, even when they knew not the preacher. Those Scriptures which speak of Christ, will warm the hearts of his true disciples. That is likely to do most good, which affects us with the love of Jesus in dying for us. It is the duty of those to whom he has shown himself, to let others know what he has done for their souls. It is of great use for the disciples of Christ to compare their experiences, and tell them to each other.

Verses 36-49 Jesus appeared in a miraculous manner, assuring the disciples of his peace, though they had so lately forsaken him, and promising spiritual peace with every blessing. Many troublesome thoughts which disquiet our minds, rise from mistakes concerning Christ. All the troublesome thoughts which rise in our hearts at any time, are known to the Lord Jesus, and are displeasing to him. He spake with them on their unreasonable unbelief. Nothing had passed but what was foretold by the prophets, and necessary for the salvation of sinners. And now all men should be taught the nature and necessity of repentance, in order to the forgiveness of their sins. And these blessings were to be sought for, by faith in the name of Jesus. Christ by his Spirit works on the minds of men. Even good men need to have their understandings opened. But that we may have right thoughts of Christ, there needs no more than to be made to understand the Scriptures.

Verses 50-53 Christ ascended from Bethany, near the Mount of Olives. There was the garden in which his sufferings began; there he was in his agony. Those that would go to heaven, must ascend thither from the house of sufferings and sorrows. The disciples did not see him rise out of the grave; his resurrection could be proved by their seeing him alive afterwards: but they saw him ascend into heaven; they could not otherwise have a proof of his ascension. He lifted up his hands, and blessed them. He did not go away in displeasure, but in love, he left a blessing behind him. As he arose, so he ascended, by his own power. They worshipped him. This fresh display of Christ's glory drew from them fresh acknowledgments. They returned to Jerusalem with great joy. The glory of Christ is the joy of all true believers, even while they are here in this world. While waiting for God's promises, we must go forth to meet them with our praises. And nothing better prepares the mind for receiving the Holy Ghost. Fears are silenced, sorrows sweetened and allayed, and hopes kept up. And this is the ground of a Christian's boldness at the throne of grace; yea, the Father's throne is the throne of grace to us, because it is also the throne of our Mediator, Jesus Christ. Let us rely on his promises, and plead them. Let us attend his ordinances, praise and bless God for his mercies, set our affections on things above, and expect the Redeemer's return to complete our happiness. Amen. Even so, Lord Jesus, come quickly.

JOHN

CHAPTER 1

the apostle and evangelist, John, seems to have been the youngest of the twelve. He was especially favoured with our Lord's regard and confidence, so as to be spoken of as the disciple whom Jesus loved. He was very sincerely attached to his Master. He exercised his ministry at Jerusalem with much success, and outlived the destruction of that city, agreeably to Christ's prediction, ch. 21:22. History relates that after the death of Christ's mother, John resided chiefly at Ephesus. Towards the close of Domitian's reign he was banished to the isle of Patmos, where he wrote his Revelation. On the accession of Nerva, he was set at liberty, and returned to Ephesus, where it is thought he wrote his Gospel and Epistles, about A. D. 97, and died soon after. The design of this Gospel appears to be to convey to the Christian world, just notions of the real nature, office, and character of that Divine Teacher, who came to instruct and to redeem mankind. For this purpose, John was directed to select for his narrative, those passages of our Saviour's life, which most clearly displayed his Divine power and authority; and those of his discourses, in which he spake most plainly of his own nature, and of the power of his death, as an atonement for the sins of the world. By omitting, or only briefly mentioning, the events recorded by the other evangelists, John gave testimony that their narratives are true, and left room for the doctrinal statements already mentioned, and for particulars omitted in the other Gospels, many of which are exceedingly important.

The Divinity of Christ. (1-5) His Divine and human nature. (6-14) John the Baptist's testimony to Christ. (15-18) John's public testimony concerning Christ. (19-28) Other testimonies of John concerning Christ. (29-36) Andrew and another disciple follow Jesus. (37-42) Philip and Nathanael called. (43-51)

Verses 1-5 The plainest reason why the Son of God is called the Word, seems to be, that as our words explain our minds to others, so was the Son of God sent in order to reveal his Father's mind to the world. What the evangelist says of Christ proves that he is God. He asserts, His existence in the beginning; His coexistence with the Father. The Word was with God. All things were made by him, and not as an instrument. Without him was not any thing made that was made, from the highest angel to the meanest worm. This shows how well qualified he was for the work of our redemption and salvation. The light of reason, as well as the life of sense, is derived from him, and depends upon him. This eternal Word, this true Light shines, but the darkness comprehends it not. Let us pray without ceasing, that our eyes may be opened to behold this Light, that we may walk in it; and thus be made wise unto salvation, by faith in Jesus Christ.

Verses 6-14 John the Baptist came to bear witness concerning Jesus. Nothing more fully shows the darkness of men's minds, than that when the Light had appeared, there needed a witness to call attention to it. Christ was the true Light; that great Light which deserves to be called so. By his Spirit and grace he enlightens all that are enlightened to salvation; and those that are not enlightened by him, perish in darkness. Christ was in the world when he took our nature upon him, and dwelt among us.

The Son of the Highest was here in this lower world. He was in the world, but not of it. He came to save a lost world, because it was a world of his own making. Yet the world knew him not. When he comes as a Judge, the world shall know him. Many say that they are Christ's own, yet do not receive him, because they will not part with their sins, nor have him to reign over them. All the children of God are born again. This new birth is through the word of God as the means, 1 Peter 1:23, and by the Spirit of God as the Author. By his Divine presence Christ always was in the world. But now that the fullness of time was come, he was, after another manner, God manifested in the flesh. But observe the beams of his Divine glory, which darted through this veil of flesh. Men discover their weaknesses to those most familiar with them, but it was not so with Christ; those most intimate with him saw most of his glory. Although he was in the form of a servant, as to outward circumstances, yet, in respect of graces, his form was like the Son of God His Divine glory appeared in the holiness of his doctrine, and in his miracles. He was full of grace, fully acceptable to his Father, therefore qualified to plead for us; and full of truth, fully aware of the things he was to reveal.

Verses 15-18 As to the order of time and entrance on his work, Christ came after John, but in every other way he was before him. The expression clearly shows that Jesus had existence before he appeared on earth as man. All fullness dwells in him, from which alone fallen sinners have, and shall receive, by faith, all that renders them wise, strong, holy, useful, and happy. Our receivings by Christ are all summed up in this one word, grace; we have received "even grace," a gift so great, so rich, so invaluable; the good will of God towards us, and the good work of God in us. The law of God is holy, just, and good; and we should make the proper use of it. But we cannot derive from it pardon, righteousness, or strength. It teaches us to adorn the doctrine of God our Saviour, but it cannot supply the place of that doctrine. As no mercy comes from God to sinners but through Jesus Christ, no man can come to the Father but by him; no man can know God, except as he is made known in the only begotten and beloved Son.

Verses 19-28 John disowns himself to be the Christ, who was now expected and waited for. He came in the spirit and power of Elias, but he was not the person of Elias. John was not that Prophet whom Moses said the Lord would raise up to them of their brethren, like unto him. He was not such a prophet as they expected, who would rescue them from the Romans. He gave such an account of himself, as might excite and awaken them to hearken to him. He baptized the people with water as a profession of repentance, and as an outward sign of the spiritual blessings to be conferred on them by the Messiah, who was in the midst of them, though they knew him not, and to whom he was unworthy to render the meanest service.

Verses 29-36 John saw Jesus coming to him, and pointed him out as the Lamb of God. The paschal lamb, in the shedding and sprinkling of its blood, the roasting and eating of its flesh, and all the other circumstances of the ordinance, represented the salvation of sinners by faith in Christ. And the lambs sacrificed every morning and evening, can only refer to Christ slain as a sacrifice to redeem us to God by his blood. John came as a preacher of repentance, yet he told his followers that they were to look for the pardon of their sins to Jesus only, and to his death. It agrees with God's glory to pardon all who depend on the atoning sacrifice of Christ. He takes away the sin of the world; purchases pardon for all that repent and believe the gospel. This encourages our faith; if Christ takes away the sin of the world, then why not my sin? He bore sin for us, and so bears it from us. God could have taken away sin, by taking away the sinner, as he took away the sin of the old world; but here is a way of doing away sin, yet sparing the sinner, by making his Son sin, that is, a sin-offering, for us. See Jesus taking away sin, and let that cause hatred of sin, and resolutions against it. Let us not hold that fast, which the Lamb of God came to take away. To confirm his testimony concerning Christ, John declares the appearance at his baptism, in which God himself bore witness to him. He saw and bare record that he is the Son of God. This is the end and object of John's testimony, that Jesus was the promised Messiah. John took every opportunity that offered to lead people to Christ.

Verses 37-42 The strongest and most prevailing argument with an awakened soul to follow Christ, is, that it is he only who takes away sin. Whatever communion there is between our souls and Christ, it is he who begins the discourse. He asked, What seek ye? The question Jesus put to them, we should all put to ourselves when we begin to follow Him, What do we design and desire? In following Christ, do we seek the favour of God and eternal life? He invites them to come without delay. Now is the accepted time, 2 Corinthians 6:2. It is good for us to be where Christ is, wherever it be. We ought to labour for the spiritual welfare of those related to us, and seek to bring them to Him. Those who come to Christ, must come with a fixed resolution to be firm and constant to him, like a stone, solid and steadfast; and it is by his grace that they are so.

Verses 43-51 See the nature of true Christianity, it is following Jesus; devoting ourselves to him, and treading in his steps. Observe the objection Nathanael made. All who desire to profit by the word of God, must beware of prejudices against places, or denominations of men. They should examine for themselves, and they will sometimes find good where they looked for none. Many people are kept from the ways of religion by the unreasonable prejudices they conceive. The best way to remove false notions of religion, is to make trial of it. In Nathanael there was no guile. His profession was not hypocritical. He was not a dissembler, nor dishonest; he was a sound character, a really upright, godly man. Christ knows what men are indeed. Does He know us? Let us desire to know him. Let us seek and pray to be Israelites indeed, in whom is no guile; truly Christians, approved of Christ himself. Some things weak, imperfect, and sinful, are found in all, but hypocrisy belongs not to a believer's character. Jesus witnessed what passed when Nathanael was under the fig-tree. Probably he was then in fervent prayer, seeking direction as to the Hope and Consolation of Israel, where no human eye observed him. This showed him that our Lord knew the secrets of his heart. Through Christ we commune with, and benefit by the holy angels; and things in heaven and things on earth are reconciled and united together.

CHAPTER 2

The miracle at Cana. (1-11) Christ casts the buyers and sellers out of the temple. (12-22) Many believe in Christ. (23-25)

Verses 1-11 It is very desirable when there is a marriage, to have Christ own and bless it. Those that would have Christ with them at their marriage, must invite him by prayer, and he will come. While in this world we sometimes find ourselves in straits, even when we think ourselves in fullness. There was want at a marriage feast. Those who are come to care for the things of the world, must look for trouble, and count upon disappointment. In our addresses to Christ, we must humbly spread our case before him, and then refer ourselves to him to do as he pleases. In Christ's reply to his mother there was no disrespect. He used the same word when speaking to her with affection from the cross; yet it is a standing testimony against the idolatry of after-ages, in giving undue honours to his mother. His hour is come when we know not what to do. Delays of mercy are not denials of prayer. Those that expect Christ's favours, must observe his orders with ready obedience. The way of duty is the way to mercy; and Christ's methods must not be objected against.

The beginning of Moses' miracles was turning water into blood, Exodus 7:20 ; the beginning of Christ's miracles was turning water into wine; which may remind us of the difference between the law of Moses and the gospel of Christ. He showed that he improves creature-comforts to all true believers, and make them comforts indeed. And Christ's works are all for use. Has he turned thy water into wine, given thee knowledge and grace? It is to profit withal; therefore draw out now, and use it. It was the best wine. Christ's works commend themselves even to those who know not their Author. What was produced by miracles, always was the best in its kind. Though Christ hereby allows a right use of wine, he does not in the least do away his own caution, which is, that our hearts be not at any time overcharged with surfeiting and drunkenness, Luke 21:34. Though we need not scruple to feast with our friends on proper occasions, yet every social interview should be so conducted, that we might invite the Redeemer to join with us, if he were now on earth; and all levity, luxury, and excess offend him.

Verses 12-22 The first public work in which we find Christ engaged, was driving from the temple the traders whom the covetous priests and rulers encouraged to make a market-place of its courts. Those now make God's house a house of merchandise, whose minds are filled with cares about worldly business when attending religious exercises, or who perform Divine offices for love of gain. Christ, having thus cleansed the temple, gave a sign to those who demanded it, to prove his authority for so doing. He foretells his death by the Jews' malice, Destroy ye this temple; I will permit you to destroy it. He foretells his resurrection by his own power; In three days I will raise it up. Christ took again his own life. Men mistake by understanding that according to the letter, which the Scripture speaks by way of figure. When Jesus was risen from the dead, his disciples remembered he has said this. It helps much in understanding the Divine word, to observe the fulfilling of the Scriptures.

Verses 23-25 Our Lord knew all men, their nature, dispositions, affections, designs, so as we do not know any man, not even ourselves. He knows his crafty enemies, and all their secret projects; his false friends, and their true characters. He knows who are truly his, knows their uprightness, and knows their weaknesses. We know what is done by men; Christ knows what is in them, he tries the heart. Beware of a dead faith, or a formal profession: carnal, empty professors are not to be trusted, and however men impose on others or themselves, they cannot impose on the heart-searching God.

CHAPTER 3

Christ's discourse with Nicodemus. (1-21) The baptism of John of Christ, John's testimony. (22-36)

Verses 1-8 Nicodemus was afraid, or ashamed to be seen with Christ, therefore came in the night. When religion is out of fashion, there are many Nicodemites. But though he came by night, Jesus bid him welcome, and hereby taught us to encourage good beginnings, although weak. And though now he came by night, yet afterward he owned Christ publicly. He did not talk with Christ about state affairs, though he was a ruler, but about the concerns of his own soul and its salvation, and went at once to them.

Our Saviour spoke of the necessity and nature of regeneration or the new birth, and at once directed Nicodemus to the source of holiness of the heart. Birth is the beginning of life; to be born again, is to begin to live anew, as those who have lived much amiss, or to little purpose. We must have a new nature, new principles, new affections, new aims. By our first birth we were corrupt, shapen in sin; therefore we must be made new creatures. No stronger expression could have been chosen to signify a great and most remarkable change of state and character. We must be entirely different from what we were before, as that which begins to be at any time, is not, and cannot be the same with that which was before. This new birth is from heaven, ch. 1:13, and its tendency is to heaven. It is a great change made in the heart of a sinner, by the power of the Holy Spirit. It means that something is done in us, and for us, which we cannot do for ourselves. Something is wrong, whereby such a life begins as shall last for ever. We cannot otherwise expect any benefit by Christ; it is necessary to our happiness here and hereafter.

What Christ spoke, Nicodemus misunderstood, as if there had been no other way of regenerating and new-moulding an immortal soul, than by new-framing the body. But he acknowledged his ignorance, which shows a desire to be better informed. It is then further explained by the Lord Jesus. He shows the Author of this blessed change. It is not wrought by any wisdom or power of our own, but by the power of the blessed Spirit. We are shapen in iniquity, which makes it necessary that our nature be changed. We are not to marvel at this; for, when we consider the holiness of God, the depravity of our nature, and the happiness set before us, we shall not think it strange that so much stress is laid upon this.

The regenerating work of the Holy Spirit is compared to water. It is also probable that Christ had reference to the ordinance of baptism. Not that all those, and those only, that are baptized, are saved; but without that new birth which is wrought by the Spirit, and signified by baptism, none shall be subjects of the kingdom of heaven. The same word signifies both the wind and the Spirit. The wind bloweth where it listeth for us; God directs it. The Spirit sends his influences where, and when, on whom, and in what measure and degree, he pleases. Though the causes are hidden, the effects are plain, when the soul is brought to mourn for sin, and to breathe after Christ. Christ's stating of the doctrine and the necessity of regeneration, it should seem, made it not clearer to Nicodemus. Thus the things of the Spirit of God are foolishness to the natural man. Many think that cannot be proved, which they cannot believe. Christ's discourse of gospel truths, ver. 11-13, shows the folly of those who make these things strange unto them; and it recommends us to search them out.

Jesus Christ is every way able to reveal the will of God to us; for he came down from heaven, and yet is in heaven. We have here a notice of Christ's two distinct natures in one person, so that while he is the Son of man, yet he is in heaven. God is the "HE THAT IS," and heaven is the dwelling-place of his holiness. The knowledge of this must be from above, and can be received by faith alone. Jesus Christ came to save us by healing us, as the children of Israel, stung with fiery serpents, were cured and lived by looking up to the brazen serpent, Numbers 21:6-9. In this observe the deadly and destructive nature of sin. Ask awakened consciences, ask damned sinners, they will tell you, that how charming soever the allurements of sin may be, at the last it bites like a serpent. See the powerful remedy against this fatal malady. Christ is plainly set forth to us in the gospel. He whom we offended is our Peace, and the way of applying for a cure is by believing. If any so far slight either their disease by sin, or the method of cure by Christ, as not to receive Christ upon his own terms, their ruin is upon their own heads. He has said, Look and be saved, look and live; lift up the eyes of your faith to Christ crucified. And until we have grace to do this, we shall not be cured, but still are wounded with the stings of Satan, and in a dying state.

Jesus Christ came to save us by pardoning us, that we might not die by the sentence of the law. Here is gospel, good news indeed. Here is God's love in giving his Son for the world. God so loved the world; so really, so richly. Behold and wonder, that the great

God should love such a worthless world! Here, also, is the great gospel duty, to believe in Jesus Christ. God having given him to be our Prophet, Priest, and King, we must give up ourselves to be ruled, and taught, and saved by him. And here is the great gospel benefit, that whoever believes in Christ, shall not perish, but shall have everlasting life. God was in Christ reconciling the world to himself, and so saving it. It could not be saved, but through him; there is no salvation in any other. From all this is shown the happiness of true believers; he that believeth in Christ is not condemned. Though he has been a great sinner, yet he is not dealt with according to what his sins deserve. How great is the sin of unbelievers! God sent One to save us, that was dearest to himself; and shall he not be dearest to us?

How great is the misery of unbelievers! They are condemned already; which speaks a certain condemnation; a present condemnation. The wrath of God now fastens upon them; and their own hearts condemn them. There is also a condemnation grounded on their former guilt; they are open to the law for all their sins; because they are not by faith interested in the gospel pardon. Unbelief is a sin against the remedy. It springs from the enmity of the heart of man to God, from love of sin in some form. Read also the doom of those that would not know Christ. Sinful works are works of darkness. The wicked world keep as far from this light as they can, lest their deeds should be reproved. Christ is hated, because sin is loved. If they had not hated saving knowledge, they would not sit down contentedly in condemning ignorance. On the other hand, renewed hearts bid this light welcome. A good man acts truly and sincerely in all he does. He desires to know what the will of God is, and to do it, though against his own worldly interest. A change in his whole character and conduct has taken place. The love of God is shed abroad in his heart by the Holy Ghost, and is become the commanding principle of his actions. So long as he continues under a load of unforgiven guilt, there can be little else than slavish fear of God; but when his doubts are done away, when he sees the righteous ground whereon this forgiveness is built, he rests on it as his own, and is united to God by unfeigned love.

Our works are good when the will of God is the rule of them, and the glory of God the end of them; when they are done in his strength, and for his sake; to him, and not to men. Regeneration, or the new birth, is a subject to which the world is very averse; it is, however, the grand concern, in comparison with which every thing else is but trifling. What does it signify though we have food to eat in plenty, and variety of raiment to put on, if we are not born again? If after a few mornings and evenings spent in unthinking mirth, carnal pleasure, and riot, we die in our sins, and lie down in sorrow? What does it signify though we are well able to act our parts in life, in every other respect, if at last we hear from the Supreme Judge, "Depart from me, I know you not, ye workers of iniquity?"

Verses 22-36 John was fully satisfied with the place and work assigned him; but Jesus came on a more important work. He also knew that Jesus would increase in honour and influence, for of his government and peace there would be no end, while he himself would be less followed. John knew that Jesus came from heaven as the Son of God, while he was a sinful, mortal man, who could only speak about the more plain subjects of religion. The words of Jesus were the words of God; he had the Spirit, not by measure, as the prophets, but in all fullness. Everlasting life could only be had by faith in Him, and might be thus obtained; whereas all those, who believe not in the Son of God, cannot partake of salvation, but the wrath of God for ever rests upon them.

CHAPTER 4

Christ's departure into Galilee. (1-3) His discourse with the Samaritan woman. (4-26) The effects of Christ's conversation with the woman of Samaria. (27-42) Christ heals the nobleman's son. (43-54)

Verses 1-3 Jesus applied himself more to preaching, which was the more excellent, 1 Corinthians 1:17, than to baptism. He would put honour upon his disciples, by employing them to baptize. He teaches us that the benefit of sacraments depends not on the hand that administers them.

Verses 4-26 There was great hatred between the Samaritans and the Jews. Christ's road from Judea to Galilee lay through Samaria. We should not go into places of temptation but when we needs must; and then must not dwell in them, but hasten through them. We have here our Lord Jesus under the common fatigue of travelers. Thus we see that he was truly a man. Toil came in with sin; therefore Christ, having made himself a curse for us, submitted to it. Also, he was a poor man, and went all his journeys on foot. Being wearied, he sat thus on the well; he had no couch to rest upon. He sat thus, as people wearied with traveling sit. Surely, we ought readily to submit to be like the Son of God in such things as these.

Christ asked a woman for water. She was surprised because he did not show the anger of his own nation against the Samaritans. Moderate men of all sides are men wondered at. Christ took the occasion to teach her Divine things: he converted this woman, by showing her ignorance and sinfulness, and her need of a Saviour. By this living water is meant the Spirit. Under this comparison the blessing of the Messiah had been promised in the Old Testament. The graces of the Spirit, and his comforts, satisfy the thirsting soul, that knows its own nature and necessity. What Jesus spake figuratively, she took literally. Christ shows that the water of Jacob's well yielded a very short satisfaction. Of whatever waters of comfort we drink, we shall thirst again. But whoever partakes of the Spirit of grace, and the comforts of the gospel, shall never want that which will abundantly satisfy his soul. Carnal hearts look no higher than carnal ends. Give it me, saith she, not that I may have everlasting life, which Christ proposed, but that I come not hither to draw. The carnal mind is very ingenious in shifting off convictions, and keeping them from fastening. But how closely our Lord Jesus brings home the conviction to her conscience! He severely reproved her present state of life. The woman acknowledged Christ to be a prophet. The power of his word in searching the heart, and convincing the conscience of secret things, is a proof of Divine authority.

It should cool our contests, to think that the things we are striving about are passing away. The object of worship will continue still the same, God, as a Father; but an end shall be put to all differences about the place of worship. Reason teaches us to consult decency and convenience in the places of our worship; but religion gives no preference to one place above another, in respect of holiness and approval with God. The Jews were certainly in the right. Those who by the Scriptures have obtained some knowledge of God, know whom they worship. The word of salvation was of the Jews. It came to other nations through them. Christ justly preferred the Jewish worship before the Samaritan, yet here he speaks of the former as soon to be done away. God was about to be revealed as the Father of all believers in every nation. The spirit or the soul of man, as influenced by the Holy Spirit, must worship God, and have communion with him. Spiritual affections, as shown in fervent prayers, supplications, and thanksgivings, form the worship of an upright heart, in which God delights and is glorified. The woman was disposed to leave the matter undecided, till the coming of the Messiah. But Christ told her, I that speak to thee, am He. She was an alien and a hostile Samaritan, merely speaking to her was thought to disgrace our Lord Jesus. Yet to this woman did our Lord reveal himself more fully than as yet he had done to any of his disciples. No past sins can bar our acceptance with him, if we humble ourselves before him, believing in him as the Christ, the Saviour of the world.

Verses 27-42 The disciples wondered that Christ talked thus with a Samaritan. Yet they knew it was for some good reason, and for some good end. Thus when particular difficulties occur in the word and providence of God, it is good to satisfy ourselves that all is well that Jesus Christ says and does. Two things affected the woman. The extent of his knowledge. Christ knows all the thoughts, words, and actions, of all the children of men. And the power of his word. He told her secret sins with power. She fastened upon that part of Christ's discourse, many would think she would have been most shy of repeating; but the knowledge of Christ, into which we are led by conviction of sin, is most likely to be sound and saving. They came to him: those who would know Christ, must meet him where he records his name. Our Master has left us an example, that we may learn to do the will of God as he did; with diligence, as those that make a business of it; with delight and pleasure in it.

Christ compares his work to harvest-work. The harvest is appointed and looked for before it comes; so was the gospel. Harvest-time is busy time; all must be then at work. Harvest-time is a short time, and harvest-work must be done then, or not at all; so the time of the gospel is a season, which if once past, cannot be recalled. God sometimes uses very weak and unlikely instruments for beginning and carrying on a good work. Our Saviour, by teaching one poor woman, spread knowledge to a whole town. Blessed are those who are not offended at Christ. Those taught of God, are truly desirous to learn more. It adds much to the praise of our love to Christ and his word, if it conquers prejudices. Their faith grew. In the matter of it: they believed him to be the Saviour, not only of the Jews but of the world. In the certainty of it: we know that this is indeed the Christ. And in the ground of it, for we have heard him ourselves.

Verses 43-54 The father was a nobleman, yet the son was sick. Honours and titles are no security from sickness and death. The greatest men must go themselves to God, must become beggars. The nobleman did not stop from his request till he prevailed. But at first he discovered the weakness of his faith in the power of Christ. It is hard to persuade ourselves that distance of time and place, are no hindrance to the knowledge, mercy, and power of our Lord Jesus. Christ gave an answer of peace. Christ's saying that the soul lives, makes it alive. The father went his way, which showed the sincerity of his faith. Being satisfied, he did not hurry home that night, but returned as one easy in his own mind. His servants met him with the news of the child's recovery. Good news will meet those that hope in God's word. Diligent comparing the works of Jesus with his word, will confirm our faith. And the bringing the cure to the family brought salvation to it. Thus an experience of the power of one word of Christ, may settle the authority of Christ in the soul. The whole family believed likewise. The miracle made Jesus dear to them. The knowledge of Christ still spreads through families, and men find health and salvation to their souls.

CHAPTER 5

The cure at the pool of Bethesda. (1-9) The Jews' displeasure. (10-16) Christ reproves the Jews. (17-23) Christ's discourse. (24-47)

Verses 1-9 We are all by nature impotent folk in spiritual things, blind, halt, and withered; but full provision is made for our cure, if we attend to it. An angel went down, and troubled the water; and what disease soever it was, this water cured it, but only he that first stepped in had benefit. This teaches us to be careful, that we let not a season slip which may never return. The man had lost the use of his limbs thirty-eight years. Shall we, who perhaps for many years have scarcely known what it has been to be a day sick, complain of one wearisome night, when many others, better than we, have scarcely known what it has been to be a day well? Christ singled this one out from the rest. Those long in affliction, may comfort themselves that God keeps account how long. Observe, this man speaks of the unkindness of those about him, without any peevish reflections. As we should be thankful, so we should be patient. Our Lord Jesus cures him, though he neither asked nor thought of it. Arise, and walk. God's command, Turn and live; Make ye a new heart; no more supposes power in us without the grace of God, his distinguishing grace, than this command supposed such power in the impotent man: it was by the power of Christ, and he must have all the glory. What a joyful surprise to the poor cripple, to find himself of a sudden so easy, so strong, so able to help himself! The proof of spiritual cure, is our rising and walking. Has Christ healed our spiritual diseases, let us go wherever he sends us, and take up whatever he lays upon us; and walk before him.

Verses 10-16 Those eased of the punishment of sin, are in danger of returning to sin, when the terror and restraint are over, unless Divine grace dries up the fountain. The misery believers are made whole from, warns us to sin no more, having felt the smart of sin. This is the voice of every providence, Go, and sin no more. Christ saw it necessary to give this caution; for it is common for people, when sick, to promise much; when newly recovered, to perform only something; but after awhile to forget all. Christ spoke of the wrath to come, which is beyond compare worse than the many hours, nay, weeks and years of pain, some wicked men have to suffer in consequence of their unlawful indulgences. And if such afflictions are severe, how dreadful will be the everlasting punishment of the wicked!

Verses 17-23 The Divine power of the miracle proved Jesus to be the Son of God, and he declared that he worked with, and like unto his Father, as he saw good. These ancient enemies of Christ understood him, and became more violent, charging him not only with Sabbath-breaking, but blasphemy, in calling God his own Father, and making himself equal with God. But all things now, and at the final judgment, are committed to the Son, purposely that all men might honour the Son, as they honour the Father; and every one who does not thus honour the Son, whatever he may think or pretend, does not honour the Father who sent him.

Verses 24-29 Our Lord declared his authority and character, as the Messiah. The time was come when the dead should hear his voice, as the Son of God, and live. Our Lord first refers to his raising those who were dead in sin, to newness of life, by the power of the Spirit, and then to his raising the dead in their graves. The office of Judge of all men, can only be exercised by one who has all knowledge, and almighty power. May we believe His testimony; thus our faith and hope will be in God, and we shall not come into condemnation. And may His voice reach the hearts of those dead in sin; that they may do works meet for repentance, and prepare for the solemn day.

Verses 30-38 Our Lord returns to his declaration of the entire agreement between the Father and the Son, and declared himself the Son of God. He had higher testimony than that of John; his works bore witness to all he had said. But the Divine word had no abiding-place in their hearts, as they refused to believe in Him whom the Father had sent, according to his ancient promises. The voice of God, accompanied by the power of the Holy Ghost, thus made effectual to the conversion of sinners, still proclaims that this is the beloved Son, in whom the Father is well pleased. But when the hearts of men are full of pride, ambition, and the love of the world, there is no room for the word of God to abide in them.

Verses 39-44 The Jews considered that eternal life was revealed to them in their Scriptures, and that they had it, because they had the word of God in their hands. Jesus urged them to search those Scriptures with more diligence and attention. "Ye do search the Scriptures," and ye do well to do so. They did indeed search the Scriptures, but it was with a view to their own glory. It is possible for men to be very studious in the letter of the Scriptures, yet to be strangers to its power. Or, "Search the Scriptures," and so it was spoken to them in the nature of an appeal. Ye profess to receive and believe the Scripture, let that be the judge. It is spoken to us as advising or commanding all Christians to search the Scriptures. Not only read them, and hear them, but search them; which denotes diligence in examining and studying them. We must search the Scriptures for heaven as our great end; For in them ye think ye have eternal life.

We must search the Scriptures for Christ, as the new and living Way, that leads to this end. To this testimony Christ adds reproofs of their unbelief and wickedness; their neglect of him and his doctrine. Also he reproves their want of the love of God. But there is life with Jesus Christ for poor souls. Many who make a great profession of religion, yet show they want the love of God, by their neglect of Christ and contempt of his commandments. It is the love of God in us, the love that is a living, active principle in the heart, which God will accept. They slighted and undervalued Christ, because they admired and overvalued themselves. How can those believe, who make the praise and applause of men their idol! When Christ and his followers are men wondered at, how can those believe, the utmost of whose ambition is to make a fair show in the flesh!

Verses 45-47 Many trust in some form of doctrines or some parties, who no more enter into the real meaning of those doctrines, or the views of the persons whose names they bear, than the Jews did into those of Moses. Let us search and pray over the Scriptures, as intent on finding eternal life; let us observe how Christ is the great subject of them, and daily apply to him for the life he bestows.

CHAPTER 6

Five thousand miraculously fed. (1-14) Jesus walks on the sea. (15-21) He directs to spiritual food. (22-27) His discourse with the multitude. (28-65) Many of disciples go back. (66-71)

Verses 1-14 John relates the miracle of feeding the multitude, for its reference to the following discourse. Observe the effect this miracle had upon the people. Even the common Jews expected the Messiah to come into the world, and to be a great Prophet. The Pharisees despised them as not knowing the law; but they knew most of Him who is the end of the law. Yet men may acknowledge Christ as that Prophet, and still turn a deaf ear to him.

Verses 15-21 Here were Christ's disciples in the way of duty, and Christ was praying for them; yet they were in distress. There may be perils and afflictions of this present time, where there is an interest in Christ. Clouds and darkness often surround the children of the light and of the day. They see Jesus walking on the sea. Even the approaches of comfort and deliverance often are so mistaken, as to become the occasions of fear. Nothing is more powerful to convince sinners than that word, "I am Jesus whom thou persecutest;" nothing more powerful to comfort saints than this, "I am Jesus whom thou lovest." If we have received Christ Jesus the Lord, though the night be dark, and the wind high, yet we may comfort ourselves, we shall be at the shore before long.

Verses 22-27 Instead of answering the inquiry how he came there, Jesus blamed their asking. The utmost earnestness should be employed in seeking salvation, in the use of appointed means; yet it is to be sought only as the gift of the Son of man. Him the Father has sealed, proved to be God. He declared the Son of man to be the Son of God with power.

Verses 28-35 Constant exercise of faith in Christ, is the most important and difficult part of the obedience required from us, as sinners seeking salvation. When by his grace we are enabled to live a life of faith in the Son of God, holy tempers follow, and acceptable services may be done. God, even his Father, who gave their fathers that food from heaven to support their natural lives, now gave them the true Bread for the salvation of their souls. Coming to Jesus, and believing on him, signify the same. Christ shows that he is the true Bread; he is to the soul what bread is to the body, nourishes and supports the spiritual life. He is the Bread of God. Bread which the Father gives, which he has made to be the food of our souls. Bread nourishes only by the powers of a living body; but Christ is himself living Bread, and nourishes by his own power. The doctrine of Christ crucified is now as strengthening and comforting to a believer as ever it was. He is the Bread which came down from heaven. It denotes the Divinity of Christ's person and his authority; also, the Divine origin of all the good which flows to us through him. May we with understanding and earnestness say, Lord, evermore give us this Bread.

Verses 36-46 The discovery of their guilt, danger, and remedy, by the teaching of the Holy Spirit, makes men willing and glad to come, and to give up every thing which hinders applying to him for salvation. The Father's will is, that not one of those who were given to the Son, should be rejected or lost by him. No one will come, till Divine grace has subdued, and in part changed his heart; therefore no one who comes will ever be cast out. The gospel finds none willing to be saved in the humbling, holy manner, made known therein; but God draws with his word and the Holy Ghost; and man's duty is to hear and learn; that is to say, to receive the grace offered, and consent to the promise. None had seen the Father but his beloved Son; and the Jews must expect to be taught by his inward power upon their minds, and by his word, and the ministers whom he sent among them.

Verses 47-51 The advantage of the manna was small, it only referred to this life; but the living Bread is so excellent, that the man who feedeth on it shall never die. This bread is Christ's human nature, which he took to present to the Father, as a sacrifice for the sins of the world; to purchase all things pertaining to life and godliness, for sinners of every nation, who repent and believe in him.

Verses 52-59 The flesh and blood of the Son of man, denote the Redeemer in the nature of man; Christ and him crucified, and the redemption wrought out by him, with all the precious benefits of redemption; pardon of sin, acceptance with God, the way to the throne of grace, the promises of the covenant, and eternal life. These are called the flesh and blood of Christ, because they are purchased by the breaking his body, and the shedding of his blood. Also, because they are meat and drink to our souls. Eating this flesh and drinking this blood mean believing in Christ. We partake of Christ and his benefits by faith. The soul that rightly knows its state and wants, finds whatever can calm the conscience, and promote true holiness, in the redeemer, God manifest in the flesh. Meditating upon the cross of Christ gives life to our repentance, love, and gratitude. We live by him, as our bodies live by our food. We live by him, as the members by the head, the branches by the root: because he lives we shall live also.

Verses 60-65 The human nature of Christ had not before been in heaven, but being God and man, that wondrous Person was truly said to have come down from heaven. The Messiah's kingdom was not of this world; and they were to understand by faith, what he had said of a spiritual living upon him, and his fullness. As without the soul of man the flesh is of no value, so without the quickening Spirit of God all forms of religion are dead and worthless. He who made this provision for our souls, alone can teach us these things, and draw us unto Christ, that we may live by faith in him. Let us apply to Christ, thankful that it is declared that every one who is willing to come unto him shall be made welcome.

Verses 66-71 When we admit into our minds hard thoughts of the words and works of Jesus, we enter into temptation, which, if the Lord in mercy prevent not, will end in drawing back. The corrupt and wicked heart of man often makes that an occasion for offence, which is matter of the greatest comfort. Our Lord had, in the foregoing discourse, promised eternal life to his followers; the disciples fastened on that plain saying, and resolved to cleave to him, when others fastened on hard sayings, and forsook him. Christ's doctrine is the word of eternal life, therefore we must live and die by it. If we forsake Christ, we forsake our own mercies. They believed that this Jesus was the Messiah promised to their fathers, the Son of the living God. When we are tempted to backslide or turn away, it is good to remember first principles, and to keep to them. And let us ever remember our Lord's searching question; Shall we go away and forsake our Redeemer? To whom can we go? He alone can give salvation by the forgiveness of sins. And this alone brings confidence, comfort, and joy, and bids fear and despondency flee away. It gains the only solid happiness in this world, and opens a way to the happiness of the next.

CHAPTER 7

Christ goes to the feast of tabernacles. (1-13) His discourse at the feast. (14-39) The people dispute concerning Christ. (40-53)

Verses 1-13 The brethren or kinsmen of Jesus were disgusted, when they found there was no prospect of worldly advantages from him. Ungodly men sometimes undertake to counsel those employed in the work of God; but they only advise what appears likely to promote present advantages. The people differed about his doctrine and miracles, while those who favoured him, dared not openly to avow their sentiments. Those who count the preachers of the gospel to be deceivers, speak out, while many who favour them, fear to get reproach by avowing regard for them.

Verses 14-24 Every faithful minister may humbly adopt Christ's words. His doctrine is not his own finding out, but is from God's word, through the teaching of his Spirit. And amidst the disputes which disturb the world, if any man, of any nation, seeks to do the will of God, he shall know whether the doctrine is of God, or whether men speak of themselves. Only those who hate the truth shall be given up to errors which will be fatal. Surely it was as agreeable to the design of the Sabbath to restore health to the afflicted, as to administer an outward rite. Jesus told them to decide on his conduct according to the spiritual import of the Divine law. We must not judge concerning any by their outward appearance, but by their worth, and by the gifts and graces of God's Spirit in them.

Verses 25-30 Christ proclaimed aloud, that they were in error in their thoughts about his origin. He was sent of God, who showed himself true to his promises. This declaration, that they knew not God, with his claim to peculiar knowledge, provoked the hearers; and they sought to take him, but God can tie men's hands, though he does not turn their hearts.

Verses 31-36 The discourses of Jesus convinced many that he was the Messiah; but they had not courage to own it. It is comfort to those who are in the world, but not of it, and therefore are hated by it and weary of it, that they shall not be in it always, that they shall not be in it long. Our days being evil, it is well they are few. The days of life and of grace do not last long; and sinners, when in misery, will be glad of the help they now despise. Men dispute about such sayings, but the event will explain them.

Verses 37-39 On the last day of the feast of tabernacles, the Jews drew water and poured it out before the Lord. It is supposed that Christ alluded to this. If any man desires to be truly and for ever happy, let him apply to Christ, and be ruled by him. This thirst means strong desires after spiritual blessings, which nothing else can satisfy; so the sanctifying and comforting influences of the Holy Spirit, were intended by the waters which Jesus called on them to come to Him and drink. The comfort flows plentifully and constantly as a river; strong as a stream to bear down the opposition of doubts and fears. There is a fullness in Christ, of grace for grace. The Spirit dwelling and working in believers, is as a fountain of living, running water, out of which plentiful streams flow, cooling and cleansing as water. The miraculous gifts of the Holy Spirit we do not expect, but for his more common and more valuable influences we may apply. These streams have flowed from our glorified Redeemer, down to this age, and to the remote corners of the earth. May we be anxious to make them known to others.

Verses 40-53 The malice of Christ's enemies is always against reason, and sometimes the staying of it cannot be accounted for. Never any man spake with that wisdom, and power, and grace, that convincing clearness, and that sweetness, wherewith Christ spake. Alas, that many, who are for a time restrained, and who speak highly of the word of Jesus, speedily lose their convictions, and go on in their sins! People are foolishly swayed by outward motives in matters of eternal moment, are willing even to be damned for fashion's sake. As the wisdom of God often chooses things which men despise, so the folly of men commonly despises those whom God has chosen. The Lord brings forward his weak and timid disciples, and sometimes uses them to defeat the designs of his enemies.

CHAPTER 8

The Pharisees and the adulteress. (1-11) Christ's discourse with the Pharisees. (12-59)

Verses 1-11 Christ neither found fault with the law, nor excused the prisoner's guilt; nor did he countenance the pretended zeal of the Pharisees. Those are self-condemned who judge others, and yet do the same thing. All who are any way called to blame the faults of others, are especially concerned to look to themselves, and keep themselves pure. In this matter Christ attended to the great work about which he came into the world, that was, to bring sinners to repentance; not to destroy, but to save. He aimed to bring, not only the accused to repentance, by showing her his mercy, but the prosecutors also, by showing them their sins; they thought to ensnare him, he sought to convince and convert them. He declined to meddle with the magistrate's office. Many crimes merit far more severe punishment than they meet with; but we should not leave our own work, to take that upon ourselves to which we are not called. When Christ sent her away, it was with this caution, Go, and sin no more. Those who help to save the life of a criminal, should help to save the soul with the same caution. Those are truly happy, whom Christ does not condemn. Christ's favour to us in the forgiveness of past sins should prevail with us, Go then, and sin no more.

Verses 12-16 Christ is the Light of the world. God is light, and Christ is the image of the invisible God. One sun enlightens the whole world; so does one Christ, and there needs no more. What a dark dungeon would the world be without the sun! So would it be without Jesus, by whom light came into the world. Those who follow Christ shall not walk in darkness. They shall not be left without the truths which are necessary to keep them from destroying error, and the directions in the way of duty, necessary to keep them from condemning sin.

Verses 17-20 If we knew Christ better, we should know the Father better. Those become vain in their imaginations concerning God, who will not learn of Christ. Those who know not his glory and grace, know not the Father that sent him. The time of our departure out of the world, depends upon God. Our enemies cannot hasten it any sooner, nor can our friends delay it any longer, than the time appointed of the Father. Every true believer can look up and say with pleasure, My times are in thy hand, and better there than in my own. To all God's purposes there is a time.

Verses 21-29 Those that live in unbelief, are for ever undone, if they die in unbelief. The Jews belonged to this present evil world, but Jesus was of a heavenly and Divine nature, so that his doctrine, kingdom, and blessings, would not suit their taste. But the curse of the law is done away to all that submit to the grace of the gospel. Nothing but the doctrine of Christ's grace will be an argument powerful enough, and none but the Spirit of Christ's grace will be an agent powerful enough, to turn us from sin to God; and that Spirit is given, and that doctrine is given, to work upon those only who believe in Christ. Some say, Who is this Jesus? They allow him to have been a Prophet, an excellent Teacher, and even more than a creature; but cannot acknowledge him as over all, God blessed for evermore. Will not this suffice? Jesus here answers the question. Is this to honour him as the Father? Does this admit his being the Light of the world, and the Life of men, one with the Father? All shall know by their conversion, or in their condemnation, that he always spake and did what pleased the Father, even when he claimed the highest honours to himself.

Verses 30-36 Such power attended our Lord's words, that many were convinced, and professed to believe in him. He encouraged them to attend his teaching, rely on his promises, and obey his commands, notwithstanding all temptations to evil. Thus doing, they would be his disciples truly; and by the teaching of his word and Spirit, they would learn where their hope and strength lay. Christ spoke of spiritual liberty; but carnal hearts feel no other grievances than those that molest the body, and distress their worldly affairs. Talk to them of their liberty and property, tell them of waste committed upon their lands, or damage done to their houses, and they understand you very well; but speak of the bondage of sin, captivity to Satan, and liberty by Christ; tell of wrong done to their precious souls, and the hazard of their eternal welfare, then you bring strange things to their ears. Jesus plainly reminded them, that the man who Practiced any sin, was, in fact, a slave to that sin, which was the case with most of them. Christ in the gospel offers us freedom, he has power to do this, and those whom Christ makes free are really so. But often we see persons disputing about liberty of every kind, while they are slaves to some sinful lust.

Verses 37-40 Our Lord opposed the proud and vain confidence of these Jews, showing that their descent from Abraham could not profit those of a contrary spirit to him. Where the word of God has no place, no good is to be expected; room is left there for all wickedness. A sick person who turns from his physician, and will take neither remedies nor food, is past hope of recovery. The truth both heals and nourishes the hearts of those who receive it. The truth taught by philosophers has not this power and effect, but only the truth of God. Those who claim the privileges of Abraham, must do Abraham's works; must be strangers and sojourners in this world; keep up the worship of God in their families, and always walk before God.

Verses 41-47 Satan prompts men to excesses by which they murder themselves and others, while what he puts into the mind tends to ruin men's souls. He is the great promoter of falsehood of every kind. He is a liar, all his temptations are carried on by his calling evil good, and good evil, and promising freedom in sin. He is the author of all lies; whom liars resemble and obey, with whom all liars shall have their portion for ever. The special lusts of the devil are spiritual wickedness, the lusts of the mind, and corrupt reasonings, pride and envy, wrath and malice, enmity to good, and enticing others to evil. By the truth, here understand the revealed will of God as to the salvation of men by Jesus Christ, the truth Christ was now preaching, and which the Jews opposed.

Verses 48-53 Observe Christ's disregard of the applause of men. Those who are dead to the praises of men can bear their contempt. God will seek the honour of all who do not seek their own. In these verses we have the doctrine of the everlasting happiness of believers. We have the character of a believer; he is one that keeps the sayings of the Lord Jesus. And the privilege of a believer; he shall by no means see death for ever. Though now they cannot avoid seeing death, and tasting it also, yet they shall shortly be where it will be no more forever, Exodus 14:13.

Verses 54-59 Christ and all that are his, depend upon God for honour. Men may be able to dispute about God, yet may not know him. Such as know not God, and obey not the gospel of Christ, are put 2 Thessalonians earnestly desire to know more of him. Those who discern the dawn of the light of the Sun of Righteousness, wish to see his rising. "Before Abraham was, I AM." This speaks Abraham a creature, and our Lord the Creator; well, therefore, might he make himself greater than Abraham. I AM, is the name of God, Ex 3:14; it speaks his self-existence; he is the First and the Last, ever the same, revelation 1:8. Thus he was not only before Abraham, but before all worlds, 1:1. As Mediator, he was the appointed Messiah, long before Abraham; the Lamb slain from the foundation of the world, revelation 13:8. The Lord Jesus was made of God Wisdom, Righteousness, Sanctification, and Redemption, to Adam, and Abel, and all that lived and died by faith in him, before Abraham. The Jews were about to stone Jesus for blasphemy, but he withdrew; by his miraculous power he passed through them unhurt. Let us steadfastly profess what we know and believe concerning God; and if heirs of Abraham's faith, we shall rejoice in looking forward to that day when the Saviour shall appear in glory, to the confusion of his enemies, and to complete the salvation of all who believe in him.

CHAPTER 9

Christ give sight to one born blind. (1-7) The account given by the blind man. (8-12) The Pharisees question the man that had been blind. (13-17) They ask concerning him. (18-23) They cast him out. (24-34) Christ's words to the man that had been blind. (35-38) He reproves the Pharisees. (39-41)

Verses 1-7 Christ cured many who were blind by disease or accident; here he cured one born blind. Thus he showed his power to help in the most desperate cases, and the work of his grace upon the souls of sinners, which gives sight to those blind by nature. This poor man could not see Christ, but Christ saw him. And if we know or apprehend anything of Christ, it is because we were first known of him. Christ says of uncommon calamities, that they are not always to be looked on as special punishments of sin; sometimes they are for the glory of God, and to manifest his works. Our life is our day, in which it concerns us to do the work of the day. We must be busy, and not waste day-time; it will be time to rest when our day is done, for it is but a day. The approach of death should quicken us to improve all our opportunities of doing and getting good. What good we have an opportunity to do, we should do quickly. And he that will never do a good work till there is nothing to be objected against, will leave many a good work for ever undone, Ecclesiastes 11:4. Christ magnified his power, in making a blind man to see, doing that which one would think more likely to make a seeing man blind. Human reason cannot judge of the Lord's methods; he uses means and instruments that men despise. Those that would be healed by Christ must be ruled by him. He came back from the pool wondering and wondered at; he came seeing. This represents the benefits in attending on ordinances of Christ's appointment; souls go weak, and come away strengthened; go doubting, and come away satisfied; go mourning, and come away rejoicing; go blind, and come away seeing.

Verses 8-12 Those whose eyes are opened, and whose hearts are cleansed by grace, being known to be the same person, but widely different in character, live as monuments to the Redeemer's glory, and recommend his grace to all who desire the same precious salvation. It is good to observe the way and method of God's works, and they will appear the more wonderful. Apply this spiritually. In the work of grace wrought upon the soul we see the change, but we see not the hand that makes it: the way of the Spirit is like that of the wind, which thou hearest the sound of, but canst not tell whence it comes, nor whither it goes.

Verses 13-17 Christ not only worked miracles on the Sabbath, but in such a manner as would give offence to the Jews, for he would not seem to yield to the scribes and Pharisees. Their zeal for mere rites consumed the substantial matters of religion; therefore Christ would not give place to them. Also, works of necessity and mercy are allowed, and the Sabbath rest is to be kept, in order to the Sabbath work. How many blind eyes have been opened by the preaching of the gospel on the Lord's day! How many impotent souls cured on that day! Much unrighteous and uncharitable judging comes from men's adding their own fancies to God's appointments. How perfect in wisdom and holiness was our Redeemer, when his enemies could find nothing against him, but the oft-refuted charge of breaking the Sabbath! May we be enabled, by well-doing, to silence the ignorance of foolish men.

Verses 18-23 The Pharisees vainly hoped to disprove this notable miracle. They expected a Messiah, but could not bear to think that this Jesus should be he, because his precepts were all contrary to their traditions, and because they expected a Messiah in outward pomp and splendour. The fear of man brings a snare, proverbs 29:25, and often makes people deny and disown Christ and his truths and ways, and act against their consciences. The unlearned and poor, who are simple-hearted, readily draw proper inferences from the evidences of the light of the gospel; but those whose desires are another way, though ever learning, never come to the knowledge of the truth.

Verses 24-34 As Christ's mercies are most valued by those who have felt the want of them, that have been blind, and now see; so the most powerful and lasting affections to Christ, arise from actual knowledge of him. In the work of grace in the soul, though we cannot tell when, and how, and by what steps the blessed change was wrought, yet we may take the comfort, if we can say, through grace, Whereas I was blind, now I see. I did live a worldly, sensual life, but, thanks be to God, it is now otherwise with me, Ephesians 5:8. The unbelief of those who enjoy the means of knowledge and conviction, is indeed marvelous. All who have felt the power and grace of the Lord Jesus, wonder at the wilfullness of others who reject him. He argues strongly against them, not only that Jesus was not a sinner, but that he was of God. We may each of us know by this, whether we are of God or not. What do we? What do we for God? What do we for our souls? What do we more than others?

Verses 35-38 Christ owns those who own him and his truth and ways. There is particular notice taken of such a suffer in the cause of Christ, and for the testimony of a good conscience. Our Lord Jesus graciously reveals himself to the man. Now he was made sensible what an unspeakable mercy it was, to be cured of his blindness, that he might see the Son of God. None but God is to be worshipped; so that in worshipping Jesus, he owned him to be God. All who believe in him, will worship him.

Verses 39-41 Christ came into the world to give sight to those who were spiritually blind. Also, that those who see might be made blind; that those who have a high conceit of their own wisdom, might be sealed up in ignorance. The preaching of the cross was thought to be folly by such as by carnal wisdom knew not God. Nothing fortifies men's corrupt hearts against the convictions of the word, more than the high opinion which others have of them; as if all that gained applause with men, must obtain acceptance with God. Christ silenced them. But the sin of the self-conceited and self-confident remains; they reject the gospel of grace, therefore the guilt of their sin remains unpardoned, and the power of their sin remains unbroken.

CHAPTER 10

The parable of the good shepherd. (1-5) Christ the Door. (6-9) Christ the good Shepherd. (10-18) The Jews' opinion concerning Jesus. (19-21) His discourse at the feast of dedication. (22-30) The Jews attempt to stone Jesus. (31-38) He departs from Jerusalem. (39-42)

Verses 1-5 Here is a parable or similitude, taken from the customs of the East, in the management of sheep. Men, as creatures depending on their Creator, are called the sheep of his pasture. The church of God in the world is as a sheep-fold, exposed to deceivers and persecutors. The great Shepherd of the sheep knows all that are his, guards them by his providence, guides them by his Spirit and word, and goes before them, as the Eastern shepherds went before their sheep, to set them in the way of his steps. Ministers must serve the sheep in their spiritual concerns. The Spirit of Christ will set before them an open door. The sheep of Christ will observe their Shepherd, and be cautious and shy of strangers, who would draw them from faith in him to fancies about him.

Verses 6-9 Many who hear the word of Christ, do not understand it, because they will not. But we shall find one scripture expounding another, and the blessed Spirit making known the blessed Jesus. Christ is the Door. And what greater security has the church of God than that the Lord Jesus is between it and all its enemies? He is a door open for passage and communication. Here are plain directions how to come into the fold; we must come in by Jesus Christ as the Door. By faith in him as the great Mediator between God and man. Also, we have precious promises to those that observe this direction. Christ has all that care of his church, and every believer, which a good shepherd has of his flock; and he expects the church, and every believer, to wait on him, and to keep in his pasture.

Verses 10-18 Christ is a good Shepherd; many who were not thieves, yet were careless in their duty, and by their neglect the flock was much hurt. Bad principles are the root of bad practices. The Lord Jesus knows whom he has chosen, and is sure of them; they also know whom they have trusted, and are sure of Him. See here the grace of Christ; since none could demand his life of him, he laid it down of himself for our redemption. He offered himself to be the Saviour; Lo, I come. And the necessity of our case calling for it, he offered himself for the Sacrifice. He was both the offerer and the offering, so that his laying down his life was his offering up himself. From hence it is plain, that he died in the place and stead of men; to obtain their being set free from the punishment of sin, to obtain the pardon of their sin; and that his death should obtain that pardon. Our Lord laid not his life down for his doctrine, but for his sheep.

Verses 19-21 Satan ruins many, by putting them out of conceit with the word and ordinances. Men would not be laughed out of their necessary food, yet suffer themselves thus to be laughed out of what is far more necessary. If our zeal and earnestness in the cause of Christ, especially in the blessed work of bringing his sheep into his fold, bring upon us evil names, let us not heed it, but remember our Master was thus reproached before us.

Verses 22-30 All who have any thing to say to Christ, may find him in the temple. Christ would make us to believe; we make ourselves doubt. The Jews understood his meaning, but could not form his words into a full charge against him. He described the gracious disposition and happy state of his sheep; they heard and believed his word, followed him as his faithful disciples, and none of them should perish; for the Son and the Father were one. Thus he was able to defend his sheep against all their enemies, which proves that he claimed Divine power and perfection equally with the Father.

Verses 31-38 Christ's works of power and mercy proclaim him to be over all, God blessed for evermore, that all may know and believe He is in the Father, and the Father in Him. Whom the Father sends, he sanctifies. The holy God will reward, and therefore will employ, none but such as he makes holy. The Father was in the Son, so that by Divine power he wrought his miracles; the Son was so in the Father, that he knew the whole of His mind. This we cannot by searching find out to perfection, but we may know and believe these declarations of Christ.

Verses 39-42 No weapon formed against our Lord Jesus shall prosper. He escaped, not because he was afraid to suffer, but because his hour was not come. And He who knew how to deliver himself, knows how to deliver the godly our of their temptations, and to make a way for them to escape. Persecutors may drive Christ and his gospel our of their own city or country, but they cannot drive him or it out of the world. When we know Christ by faith in our hearts, we find all that the Scripture saith of him is true.

CHAPTER 11

The sickness of Lazarus. (1-6) Christ returns to Judea. (7-10) The death of Lazarus. (11-16) Christ arrives at Bethany. (17-32) He raises Lazarus. (33-46) The Pharisees consult against Jesus. (47-53) The Jews seek for him. (54-57)

Verses 1-6 It is no new thing for those whom Christ loves, to be sick; bodily distempers correct the corruption, and try the graces of God's people. He came not to preserve his people from these afflictions, but to save them from their sins, and from the wrath to come; however, it behooves us to apply to Him in behalf of our friends and relatives when sick and afflicted. Let this reconcile us to the darkest dealings of Providence, that they are all for the glory of God: sickness, loss, disappointment, are so; and if God be glorified, we ought to be satisfied. Jesus loved Martha, and her sister, and Lazarus. The families are greatly favoured in which love and peace abound; but those are most happy whom Jesus loves, and by whom he is beloved. Alas, that this should seldom be the case with every person, even in small families. God has gracious intentions, even when he seems to delay. When the work of deliverance, temporal or spiritual, public or personal, is delayed, it does but stay for the right time.

Verses 7-10 Christ never brings his people into any danger but he goes with them in it. We are apt to think ourselves zealous for the Lord, when really we are only zealous for our wealth, credit, ease, and safety; we have therefore need to try our principles. But our day shall be lengthened out, till our work is done, and our testimony finished. A man has comfort and satisfaction while in the way of his duty, as set forth by the word of God, and determined by the providence of God. Christ, wherever he went, walked in the day; and so shall we, if we follow his steps. If a man walks in the way of his heart, and according to the course of this world, if he consults his own carnal reasonings more than the will and glory of God, he falls into temptations and snares. He stumbles, because there is no light in him; for light in us is to our moral actions, that which light about us to our natural actions.

Verses 11-16 Since we are sure to rise again at the last, why should not the believing hope of that resurrection to eternal life, make it as easy for us to put off the body and die, as it is to put off our clothes and go to sleep? A true Christian, when he dies, does but sleep; he rests from the labours of the past day. Nay, herein death is better than sleep, that sleep is only a short rest, but death is the end of earthly cares and toils. The disciples thought that it was now needless for Christ to go to Lazarus, and expose himself and them. Thus we often hope that the good work we are called to do, will be done by some other hand, if there be peril in the doing of it. But when Christ raised Lazarus from the dead, many were brought to believe on him; and there was much done to make perfect the faith of those that believed. Let us go to him; death cannot separate from the love of Christ, nor put us out of the reach of his call. Like Thomas, in difficult times Christians should encourage one another. The dying of the Lord Jesus should make us willing to die whenever God calls us.

Verses 17-32 Here was a house where the fear of God was, and on which his blessing rested; yet it was made a house of mourning. Grace will keep sorrow from the heart, but not from the house. When God, by his grace and providence, is coming towards us in ways of mercy and comfort, we should, like Martha, go forth by faith, hope, and prayer, to meet him. When Martha went to meet Jesus, Mary sat still in the house; this temper formerly had been an advantage to her, when it put her at Christ's feet to hear his word; but in the day of affliction, the same temper disposed her to melancholy. It is our wisdom to watch against the temptations, and to make use of the advantages of our natural tempers. When we know not what in particular to ask or expect, let us refer ourselves to God; let him do as seemeth him good. To enlarge Martha's expectations, our Lord declared himself to be the Resurrection and the Life. In every sense he is the Resurrection; the source, the substance, the first-fruits, the cause of it. The redeemed soul lives after death in happiness; and after the resurrection, both body and soul are kept from all evil for ever. When we have read or heard the word of Christ, about the great things of the other world, we should put it to ourselves, Do we believe this truth? The crosses and comforts of this present time would not make such a deep impression upon us as they do, if we believed the things of eternity as we ought. When Christ our Master comes, he calls for us. He comes in his word and ordinances, and calls us to them, calls us by them, calls us to himself. Those who, in a day of peace, set themselves at Christ's feet to be taught by him, may with comfort, in a day of trouble, cast themselves at his feet, to find favour with him.

Verses 33-46 Christ's tender sympathy with these afflicted friends, appeared by the troubles of his spirit. In all the afflictions of believers he is afflicted. His concern for them was shown by his kind inquiry after the remains of his deceased friend. Being found in fashion as a man, he acts in the way and manner of the sons of men. It was shown by his tears. He was a man of sorrows, and acquainted with grief. Tears of compassion resemble those of Christ. But Christ never approved that sensibility of which many are proud, while they weep at mere tales of distress, but are hardened to real woe. He sets us an example to withdraw from scenes of giddy mirth, that we may comfort the afflicted. And we have not a High Priest who cannot be touched with a feeling of our infirmities. It is a good step toward raising a soul to spiritual life, when the stone is taken away, when prejudices are removed, and got over, and way is made for the word to enter the heart.

If we take Christ's word, and rely on his power and faithfulness, we shall see the glory of God, and be happy in the sight. Our Lord Jesus has taught us, by his own example, to call God Father, in prayer, and to draw nigh to him as children to a father, with humble reverence, yet with holy boldness. He openly made this address to God, with uplifted eyes and loud voice, that they might be convinced the Father had sent him as his beloved Son into the world. He could have raised Lazarus by the silent exertion of his power and will, and the unseen working of the Spirit of life; but he did it by a loud call. This was a figure of the gospel call, by which dead souls are brought out of the grave of sin: and of the sound of the archangel's trumpet at the last day, with which all that sleep in the dust shall be awakened, and summoned before the great tribunal. The grave of sin and this world, is no place for those whom Christ has quickened; they must come forth. Lazarus was thoroughly revived, and returned not only to life, but to health. The sinner cannot quicken his own soul, but he is to use the means of grace; the believer cannot sanctify himself, but he is to lay aside every weight and hindrance. We cannot convert our relatives and friends, but we should instruct, warn, and invite them.

Verses 47-53 There can hardly be a more clear discovery of the madness that is in man's heart, and of its desperate enmity against God, than what is here recorded. Words of prophecy in the mouth, are not clear evidence of a principle of grace in the heart. The calamity we seek to escape by sin, we take the most effectual course to bring upon our own heads; as those do who think by opposing Christ's kingdom, to advance their own worldly interest. The fear of the wicked shall come upon them. The conversion of souls is the gathering of them to Christ as their ruler and refuge; and he died to effect this. By dying he purchased them to himself, and the gift of the Holy Ghost for them: his love in dying for believers should unite them closely together.

Verses 54-57 Before our gospel Passover we must renew our repentance. Thus by a voluntary purification, and by religious exercises, many, more devout than their neighbours, spent some time before the Passover at Jerusalem. When we expect to meet God, we must solemnly prepare. No devices of man can alter the purposes of God: and while hypocrites amuse themselves with forms and disputes, and worldly men pursue their own plans, Jesus still orders all things for his own glory and the salvation of his people.

CHAPTER 12

Christ anointed by Mary. (1-11) He enters Jerusalem. (12-19) Greeks apply to see Jesus. (20-26) A voice from heaven bears testimony to Christ. (27-33) His discourse with the people. (34-36) Unbelief of the Jews. (37-43) Christ's address to them. (44-50)

Verses 1-11 Christ had formerly blamed Martha for being troubled with much serving. But she did not leave off serving, as some, who when found fault with for going too far in one way, peevishly run too far another way; she still served, but within hearing of Christ's gracious words. Mary gave a token of love to Christ, who had given real tokens of his love to her and her family. God's Anointed should be our Anointed. Has God poured on him the oil of gladness above his fellows, let us pour on him the ointment of our best affections. In Judas a foul sin is gilded over with a plausible pretence. We must not think that those do no acceptable service, who do it not in our way. The reigning love of money is heart-theft. The grace of Christ puts kind comments on pious words and actions, makes the best of what is amiss, and the most of what is good. Opportunities are to be improved; and those first and most vigorously, which are likely to be the shortest. To consult to hinder the further effect of the miracle, by putting Lazarus to death, is such wickedness, malice, and folly, as cannot be explained, except by the desperate enmity of the human heart against God. They resolved that the man should die whom the Lord had raised to life. The success of the gospel often makes wicked men so angry, that they speak and act as if they hoped to obtain a victory over the Almighty himself.

Verses 12-19 Christ's riding in triumph to Jerusalem is recorded by all the evangelists. Many excellent things, both in the word and providence of God, disciples do not understand at their first acquaintance with the things of God. The right understanding of spiritual nature of Christ's kingdom, prevents our misapplying the Scriptures which speak of it.

Verses 20-26 In attendance upon holy ordinances, particularly the gospel Passover, the great desire of our souls should be to see Jesus; to see him as ours, to keep up communion with him, and derive grace from him. The calling of the Gentiles magnified the Redeemer. A corn of wheat yields no increase unless it is cast into the ground. Thus Christ might have possessed his heavenly glory alone, without becoming man. Or, after he had taken man's nature, he might have entered heaven alone, by his own perfect righteousness, without suffering or death; but then no sinner of the human race could have been saved. The salvation of souls hitherto, and henceforward to the end of time, is owing to the dying of this Corn of wheat. Let us search whether Christ be in us the hope of glory; let us beg him to make us indifferent to the trifling concerns of this life, that we may serve the Lord Jesus with a willing mind, and follow his holy example.

Verses 27-33 The sin of our souls was the troubled of Christ's soul, when he undertook to redeem and save us, and to make his soul an offering for our sin. Christ was willing to suffer, yet prayed to be saved from suffering. Prayer against trouble may well agree with patience under it, and submission to the will of God in it. Our Lord Jesus undertook to satisfy God's injured honour, and he did it by humbling himself. The voice of the Father from heaven, which had declared him to be his beloved Son, at his baptism, and when he was transfigured, was heard proclaiming that He had both glorified his name, and would glorify it. Christ, reconciling the world to God by the merit of his death, broke the power of death, and cast out Satan as a destroyer. Christ, bringing the world to God by the doctrine of his cross, broke the power of sin, and cast out Satan as a deceiver. The soul that was at a distance from Christ, is brought to love him and trust him. Jesus was now going to heaven, and he would draw men's hearts to him thither. There is power in the death of Christ to draw souls to him. We have heard from the gospel that which exalts free grace, and we have heard also that which enjoins duty; we must from the heart embrace both, and not separate them.

Verses 34-36 The people drew false notions from the Scriptures, because they overlooked the prophecies that spoke of Christ's sufferings and death. Our Lord warned them that the light would not long continue with them, and exhorted them to walk in it, before the darkness overtook them. Those who would walk in the light must believe in it, and follow Christ's directions. But those who have not faith, cannot behold what is set forth in Jesus, lifted up on the cross, and must be strangers to its influence as made known by the Holy Spirit; they find a thousand objections to excuse their unbelief.

Verses 37-43 Observe the method of conversion implied here. Sinners are brought to see the reality of Divine things, and to have some knowledge of them. To be converted, and truly turned from sin to Christ, as their Happiness and Portion. God will heal them, will justify and sanctify them; will pardon their sins, which are as bleeding wounds, and mortify their corruptions, which are as lurking diseases. See the power of the world in smothering convictions, from regard to the applause or censure of men. Love of the praise of men, as a by-end in that which is good, will make a man a hypocrite when religion is in fashion, and credit is to be got by it; and love of the praise of men, as a base principle in that which is evil, will make a man an apostate, when religion is in disgrace, and credit is to be lost for it.

Verses 44-50 Our Lord publicly proclaimed, that every one who believed on him, as his true disciple, did not believe on him only, but on the Father who sent him. Beholding in Jesus the glory of the Father, we learn to obey, love, and trust in him. By daily looking to Him, who came a Light into the world, we are more and more freed from the darkness of ignorance, error, sin, and misery; we learn that the command of God our Saviour is everlasting life. But the same word will seal the condemnation of all who despise it, or neglect it.

CHAPTER 13

Christ washes the disciples' feet. (1-17) The treachery of Judas foretold. (18-30) Christ commands the disciples to love one another. (31-38)

Verses 1-17 Our Lord Jesus has a people in the world that are his own; he has purchased them, and paid dear for them, and he has set them apart for himself; they devote themselves to him as a peculiar people. Those whom Christ loves, he loves to the end. Nothing can separate a true believer from the love of Christ. We know not when our hour will come, therefore what we have to do in constant preparation for it, ought never to be undone. What way of access the devil has to men's hearts we cannot tell. But some sins are so exceedingly sinful, and there is so little temptation to them from the world and the flesh, that it is plain they are directly from Satan. Jesus washed his disciples' feet, that he might teach us to think nothing below us, wherein we may promote God's glory, and the good of our brethren. We must address ourselves to duty, and must lay aside every thing that would hinder us in what we have to do. Christ washed his disciples' feet, that he might signify to them the value of spiritual washing, and the cleansing of the soul from the pollutions of sin. Our Lord Jesus does many things of which even his own disciples do not for the present know the meaning, but they shall know afterward. We see in the end what was the kindness from events which seemed most cross. And it is not humility, but unbelief, to put away the offers of the gospel, as if too rich to be made to us, or too good news to be true. All those, and those only, who are spiritually washed by Christ, have a part in Christ. All whom Christ owns and saves, he justifies and sanctifies. Peter more than submits; he begs to be washed by Christ. How earnest he is for the purifying grace of the Lord Jesus, and the full effect of it, even upon his hands and head! Those who truly desire to be sanctified, desire to be sanctified throughout, to have the whole man, with all its parts and powers, made pure. The true believer is thus washed when he receives Christ for his salvation. See then what ought to be the daily care of those who through grace are in a justified state, and that is, to wash their feet; to cleanse themselves from daily guilt, and to watch against everything defiling. This should make us the more cautious. From yesterday's pardon, we should be strengthened against this day's temptation. And when hypocrites are discovered, it should be no surprise or cause of stumbling to us. Observe the lesson Christ here taught. Duties are mutual; we must both accept help from our brethren, and afford help to our brethren. When we see our Master serving, we cannot but see how ill it becomes us to domineer. And the same love which led Christ to ransom and reconcile his disciples when enemies, still influences him.

Verses 18-30 Our Lord had often spoken of his own sufferings and death, without such trouble of spirit as he now discovered when he spake of Judas. The sins of Christians are the grief of Christ. We are not to confine our attention to Judas. The prophecy of his treachery may apply to all who partake of God's mercies, and meet them with ingratitude. See the infidel, who only looks at the Scriptures with a desire to do away their authority and destroy their influence; the hypocrite, who professes to believe the Scriptures, but will not govern himself by them; and the apostate, who turns aside from Christ for a thing of naught. Thus mankind, supported by God's providence, after eating bread with Him, lift up the heel against Him! Judas went out as one weary of Jesus and his apostles. Those whose deeds are evil, love darkness rather than light.

Verses 31-35 Christ had been glorified in many miracles he wrought, yet he speaks of his being glorified now in his sufferings, as if that were more than all his other glories in his humbled state. Satisfaction was thereby made for the wrong done to God by the sin of man. We cannot now follow our Lord to his heavenly happiness, but if we truly believe in him, we shall follow him hereafter; meanwhile we must wait his time, and do his work. Before Christ left the disciples, he would give them a new commandment. They were to love each other for Christ's sake, and according to his example, seeking what might benefit others, and promoting the cause of the gospel, as one body, animated by one soul. But this commandment still appears new to many professors. Men in general notice any of Christ's words rather than these. By this it appears, that if the followers of Christ do not show love one to another, they give cause to suspect their sincerity.

Verses 36-38 What Christ had said concerning brotherly love, Peter overlooked, but spoke of that about which Christ kept them ignorant. It is common to be more eager to know about secret things, which belong to God only, than about things revealed, which belong to us and our children; to be more desirous to have our curiosity gratified, than our consciences directed; to know what is done in heaven, than what we may do to get thither. How soon discourse as to what is plain and edifying is dropped, while a doubtful dispute runs on into endless strife of words! We are apt to take it amiss to be told we cannot do this and the other, whereas, without Christ we can do nothing. Christ knows us better than we know ourselves, and has many ways of discovering those to themselves, whom he loves, and he will hide pride from them. May we endeavour to keep the unity of the Spirit in the bond of peace, to love one another with a pure heart fervently, and to walk humbly with our God.

CHAPTER 14

Christ comforts his disciples. (1-11) He further comforts his disciples. (12-17) He still further comforts his disciples. (18-31)

Verses 1-11 Here are three words, upon any of which stress may be laid. Upon the word troubled. Be not cast down and disquieted. The word heart. Let your heart be kept with full trust in God. The word your. However others are overwhelmed with the sorrows of this present time, be not you so. Christ's disciples, more than others, should keep their minds quiet, when everything else is unquiet. Here is the remedy against this trouble of mind, "Believe." By believing in Christ as the Mediator between God and man, we gain comfort. The happiness of heaven is spoken of as in a father's house. There are many mansions, for there are many sons to be brought to glory. Mansions are lasting dwellings. Christ will be the Finisher of that of which he is the Author or Beginner; if he have prepared the place for us, he will prepare us for it. Christ is the sinner's Way to the Father and to heaven, in his person as God manifest in the flesh, in his atoning sacrifice, and as our Advocate. He is the Truth, as fulfilling all the prophecies of a Saviour; believing which, sinners come by him the Way. He is the Life, by whose life-giving Spirit the dead in sin are quickened. Nor can any man draw nigh God as a Father, who is not quickened by Him as the Life, and taught by Him as the Truth, to come by Him as the Way. By Christ, as the Way, our prayers go to God, and his blessings come to us; this is the Way that leads to rest, the good old Way. He is the Resurrection and the Life. All that saw Christ by faith, saw the Father in Him. In the light of Christ's doctrine, they saw God as the Father of lights; and in Christ's miracles, they saw God as the God of power. The holiness of God shone in the spotless purity of Christ's life. We are to believe the revelation of God to man in Christ; for the works of the Redeemer show forth his own glory, and God in him.

Verses 12-17 Whatever we ask in Christ's name, that shall be for our good, and suitable to our state, he shall give it to us. To ask in Christ's name, is to plead his merit and intercession, and to depend upon that plea. The gift of the Spirit is a fruit of Christ's mediation, bought by his merit, and received by his intercession. The word used here, signifies an advocate, counselor, monitor, and comforter. He would abide with the disciples to the end of time; his gifts and graces would encourage their hearts. The expressions used here and elsewhere, plainly denote a person, and the office itself includes all the Divine perfections. The gift of the Holy Ghost is bestowed upon the disciples of Christ, and not on the world. This is the favour God bears to his chosen. As the source of holiness and happiness, the Holy Spirit will abide with every believer for ever.

Verses 18-24 Christ promises that he would continue his care of his disciples. I will not leave you orphans, or fatherless, for though I leave you, yet I leave you this comfort, I will come to you. I will come speedily to you at my resurrection. I will come daily to you in my Spirit; in the tokens of his love, and visits of his grace. I will come certainly at the end of time. Those only that see Christ with an eye of faith, shall see him for ever: the world sees him no more till his second coming; but his disciples have communion with him in his absence. These mysteries will be fully known in heaven. It is a further act of grace, that they should know it, and have the comfort of it. Having Christ's commands, we must keep them. And having them in our heads, we must keep them in our hearts and lives. The surest evidence of our love to Christ is, obedience to the laws of Christ. There are spiritual tokens of Christ and his love given to all believers. Where sincere love to Christ is in the heart, there will be obedience. Love will be a commanding, constraining principle; and where love is, duty follows from a principle of gratitude. God will not only love obedient believers, but he will take pleasure in loving them, will rest in love to them. He will be with them as his home. These privileges are confined to those whose faith worketh by love, and whose love to Jesus leads them to keep his commandments. Such are partakers of the Holy Spirit's new-creating grace.

Verses 25-27 Would we know these things for our good, we must pray for, and depend on the teaching of the Holy Ghost; thus the words of Jesus will be brought to our remembrance, and many difficulties be cleared up which are not plain to others. To all the saints, the Spirit of grace is given to be a remembrancer, and to him, by faith and prayer, we should commit the keeping of what we hear and know. Peace is put for all good, and Christ has left us all that is really and truly good, all the promised good; peace of mind from our justification before God. This Christ calls his peace, for he is himself our Peace. The peace of God widely differs from that of Pharisees or hypocrites, as is shown by its humbling and holy effects.

Verses 28-31 Christ raises the expectations of his disciples to something beyond what they thought was their greatest happiness. His time was now short, he therefore spake largely to them. When we come to be sick, and to die, we may not be capable of talking much to those about us; such good counsel as we have to give, let us give while in health. Observe the prospect Christ had of an approaching conflict, not only with men, but with the powers of darkness. Satan has something in us to perplex us with, for we have all sinned; but when he would disturb Christ, he found nothing sinful to help him. The best evidence of our love to the Father is, our doing as he has commanded us. Let us rejoice in the Saviour's victories over Satan the prince of this world. Let us copy the example of his love and obedience.

CHAPTER 15

Christ the true Vine. (1-8) His love to his disciples. (9-17) foretold. (18-25) The Comforter promised. (26, 27)

Verses 1-8 Jesus Christ is the Vine, the true Vine. The union of the human and Divine natures, and the fullness of the Spirit that is in him, resemble the root of the vine made fruitful by the moisture from a rich soil. Believers are branches of this Vine. The root is unseen, and our life is hid with Christ; the root bears the tree, diffuses sap to it, and in Christ are all supports and supplies. The branches of the vine are many, yet, meeting in the root, are all but one vine; thus all true Christians, though in place and opinion distant from each other, meet in Christ. Believers, like the branches of the vine, are weak, and unable to stand but as they are borne up. The Father is the Husbandman. Never was any husbandman so wise, so watchful, about his vineyard, as God is about his church, which therefore must prosper. We must be fruitful. From a vine we look for grapes, and from a Christian we look for a Christian temper, disposition, and life. We must honour God, and do good; this is bearing fruit. The unfruitful are taken away. And even fruitful branches need pruning; for the best have notions, passions, and humours, that require to be taken away, which Christ has promised to forward the sanctification of believers, they will be thankful, for them. The word of Christ is spoken to all believers; and there is a cleansing virtue in that word, as it works grace, and works out corruption. And the more fruit we bring forth, the more we abound in what is good, the more our Lord is glorified. In order to fruitfulness, we must abide in Christ, must have union with him by faith. It is the great concern of all Christ's disciples, constantly to keep up dependence upon Christ, and communion with him. True Christians find by experience, that any interruption in the exercise of their faith, causes holy affections to decline, their corruptions to revive, and their comforts to droop. Those who abide not in Christ, though they may flourish for awhile in outward profession, yet come to nothing. The fire is the fittest place for withered branches; they are good for nothing else. Let us seek to live more simply on the fullness of Christ, and to grow more fruitful in every good word and work, so may our joy in Him and in his salvation be full.

Verses 9-17 Those whom God loves as a Father, may despise the hatred of all the world. As the Father loved Christ, who was most worthy, so he loved his disciples, who were unworthy. All that love the Saviour should continue in their love to him, and take all occasions to show it. The joy of the hypocrite is but for a moment, but the joy of those who abide in Christ's love is a continual feast. They are to show their love to him by keeping his commandments. If the same power that first shed abroad the love of Christ's in our hearts, did not keep us in that love, we should not long abide in it. Christ's love to us should direct us to love each other. He speaks as about to give many things in charge, yet names this only; it includes many duties.

Verses 18-25 How little do many persons think, that in opposing the doctrine of Christ as our Prophet, Priest, and King, they prove themselves ignorant of the one living and true God, whom they profess to worship! The name into which Christ's disciples were baptized, is that which they will live and die by. It is a comfort to the greatest sufferers, if they suffer for Christ's name's sake. The world's ignorance is the true cause of its hatred to the disciples of Jesus. The clearer and fuller the discoveries of the grace and truth of Christ, the greater is our sin if we do not love him and believe in him.

Verses 26, 27 The blessed Spirit will maintain the cause of Christ in the world, notwithstanding the opposition it meets with. Believers taught and encouraged by his influences, would bear testimony to Christ and his salvation.

CHAPTER 16

Persecution foretold. (1-6) The promise of the Holy Spirit, and his office. (7-15) Christ's departure and return. (16-22) Encouragement to prayer. (23-27) Christ's discoveries of himself. (28-33)

Verses 1-6 Our Lord Jesus, by giving his disciples notice of trouble, designed that the terror might not be a surprise to them. It is possible for those who are real enemies to God's service, to pretend zeal for it. This does not lessen the sin of the persecutors; villainies will never be changed by putting the name of God to them. As Jesus in his sufferings, so his followers in theirs, should look to the fulfilling of Scripture. He did not tell them sooner, because he was with them to teach, guide, and comfort them; they needed not then this promise of the Holy Spirit's presence. It will silence us to ask, Whence troubles come? It will satisfy us to ask, Whither go they? For we know they work for good. It is the common fault and folly of melancholy Christians to look only on the dark side of the cloud, and to turn a deaf ear to the voice of joy and gladness. That which filled the disciples' hearts with sorrow, was too great affection for this present life. Nothing more hinders our joy in

God, than the love of the world, and the sorrow of the world which comes from it.

Verses 7-15 Christ's departure was necessary to the Comforter's coming. Sending the Spirit was to be the fruit of Christ's death, which was his going away. His bodily presence could be only in one place at one time, but his Spirit is every where, in all places, at all times, wherever two or three are gathered together in his name. See here the office of the Spirit, first to reprove, or to convince. Convincing work is the Spirit's work; he can do it effectually, and none but he. It is the method the Holy Spirit takes, first to convince, and then to comfort. The Spirit shall convince the world, of sin; not merely tell them of it. The Spirit convinces of the fact of sin; of the fault of sin; of the folly of sin; of the filth of sin, that by it we are become hateful to God; of the fountain of sin, the corrupt nature; and lastly, of the fruit of sin, that the end thereof is death.

The Holy Spirit proves that all the world is guilty before God. He convinces the world of righteousness; that Jesus of Nazareth was Christ the righteous. Also, of Christ's righteousness, imparted to us for justification and salvation. He will show them where it is to be had, and how they may be accepted as righteous in God's sight. Christ's ascension proves the ransom was accepted, and the righteousness finished, through which believers were to be justified. Of judgment, because the prince of this world is judged. All will be well, when his power is broken, who made all the mischief. As Satan is subdued by Christ, this gives us confidence, for no other power can stand before him. And of the day of judgment. The coming of the Spirit would be of unspeakable advantage to the disciples.

The Holy Spirit is our Guide, not only to show us the way, but to go with us by continued aids and influences. To be led into a truth is more than barely to know it; it is not only to have the notion of it in our heads, but the relish, and savour, and power of it in our hearts. He shall teach all truth, and keep back nothing profitable, for he will show things to come. All the gifts and graces of the Spirit, all the preaching, and all the writing of the apostles, under the influence of the Spirit, all the tongues, and miracles, were to glorify Christ. It behooves every one to ask, whether the Holy Spirit has begun a good work in his heart? Without clear discovery of our guilt and danger, we never shall understand the value of Christ's salvation; but when brought to know ourselves aright, we begin to see the value of the Redeemer. We should have fuller views of the Redeemer, and more lively affections to him, if we more prayed for, and depended on the Holy Spirit.

Verses 16-22 It is good to consider how near our seasons of grace are to an end, that we may be quickened to improve them. But the sorrows of the disciples would soon be turned into joy; as those of a mother, at the sight of her infant. The Holy Spirit would be their Comforter, and neither men nor devils, neither sufferings in life nor in death, would ever deprive them of their joy. Believers have joy or sorrow, according to their sight of Christ, and the tokens of his presence. Sorrow is coming on the ungodly, which nothing can lessen; the believer is an heir to joy which no one can take away. Where now is the joy of the murderers of our Lord, and the sorrow of his friends?

Verses 23-27 Asking of the Father shows a sense of spiritual wants, and a desire of spiritual blessings, with conviction that they are to be had from God only. Asking in Christ's name, is acknowledging our unworthiness to receive any favours from God, and shows full dependence upon Christ as the Lord our Righteousness. Our

Lord had hitherto spoken in short and weighty sentences, or in parables, the import of which the disciples did not fully understand, but after his resurrection he intended plainly to teach them such things as related to the Father and the way to him, through his intercession. And the frequency with which our Lord enforces offering up petitions in his name, shows that the great end of the mediation of Christ is to impress us with a deep sense of our sinfulness, and of the merit and power of his death, whereby we have access to God. And let us ever remember, that to address the Father in the name of Christ, or to address the Son as God dwelling in human nature, and reconciling the world to himself, are the same, as the Father and Son are one.

Verses 28-33 Here is a plain declaration of Christ's coming from the Father, and his return to him. The Redeemer, in his entrance, was God manifest in the flesh, and in his departure was received up into glory. By this saying the disciples improved in knowledge. Also in faith; "Now are we sure." Alas! they knew not their own weakness. The Divine nature did not desert the human nature, but supported it, and put comfort and value into Christ's sufferings. And while we have God's favourable presence, we are happy, and ought to be easy, though all the world forsake us. Peace in Christ is the only true peace, in him alone believers have it. Through him we have peace with God, and so in him we have peace in our own minds. We ought to be encouraged, because Christ has overcome the world before us. But while we think we stand, let us take heed lest we fall. We know not how we should act if brought into temptation; let us watch and pray without ceasing, that we may not be left to ourselves.

CHAPTER 17

Christ's prayer for himself. (1-5) His prayer for his disciples. (6-10) His prayer. (11-26)

Verses 1-5 Our Lord prayed as a man, and as the Mediator of his people; yet he spoke with majesty and authority, as one with and equal to the Father. Eternal life could not be given to believers, unless Christ, their Surety, both glorified the Father, and was glorified of him. This is the sinner's way to eternal life, and when this knowledge shall be made perfect, holiness and happiness will be fully enjoyed. The holiness and happiness of the redeemed, are especially that glory of Christ, and of his Father, which was the joy set before him, for which he endured the cross and despised the shame; this glory was the end of the sorrow of his soul, and in obtaining it he was fully satisfied. Thus we are taught that our glorifying God is needed as an evidence of our interest in Christ, through whom eternal life is God's free gift.

Verses 6-10 Christ prays for those that are his. Thou gavest them me, as sheep to the shepherd, to be kept; as a patient to the physician, to be cured; as children to a tutor, to be taught: thus he will deliver up his charge. It is a great satisfaction to us, in our reliance upon Christ, that he, all he is and has, and all he said and did, all he is doing and will do, are of God. Christ offered this prayer for his people alone as believers; not for the world at large. Yet no one who desires to come to the Father, and is conscious that he is unworthy to come in his own name, need be discouraged by the Saviour's declaration, for he is both able and willing to save to the uttermost, all that come unto God by him. Earnest convictions and desires, are hopeful tokens of a work already wrought in a man; they begin to evidence that he has been chosen unto salvation, through sanctification of the Spirit and belief of the truth. They are thine; wilt thou not provide for thine own? Wilt thou not secure them? Observe the foundation on which this plea is grounded, All mine are thine, and thine are mine. This speaks the Father and Son to be one. All mine are thine. The Son owns none for his, that are not devoted to the service of the Father.

Verses 11-16 Christ does not pray that they might be rich and great in the world, but that they might be kept from sin, strengthened for their duty, and brought safe to heaven. The prosperity of the soul is the best prosperity. He pleaded with his holy Father, that he would keep them by his power and for his glory, that they might be united in affection and labours, even according to the union of the Father and the Son. He did not pray that his disciples should be removed out of the world, that they might escape the rage of men, for they had a great work to do for the glory of God, and the benefit of mankind. But he prayed that the Father would keep them from the evil, from being corrupted by the world, the remains of sin in their hearts, and from the power and craft of Satan. So that they might pass through the world as through an enemy's country, as he had done. They are not left here to pursue the same objects as the men around them, but to glorify God, and to serve their generation. The Spirit of God in true Christians is opposed to the spirit of the world.

Verses 17-19 Christ next prayed for the disciples, that they might not only be kept from evil, but made good. It is the prayer of Jesus for all that are his, that they may be made holy. Even disciples must pray for sanctifying grace. The means of giving this grace is, "through thy truth, thy word is truth." Sanctify them, set them apart for thyself and thy service. Own them in the office; let thy hand go with them. Jesus entirely devoted himself to his undertaking, and all the parts of it, especially the offering up himself without spot unto God, by the eternal Spirit. The real holiness of all true Christians is the fruit of Christ's death, by which the gift of the Holy Ghost was purchased; he gave himself for his church, to sanctify it. If our views have not this effect on us, they are not Divine truth, or we do not receive them by a living and a working faith, but as mere notions.

Verses 20-23 Our Lord especially prayed, that all believers might be as one body under one head, animated by one soul, by their union with Christ and the Father in him, through the Holy Spirit dwelling in them. The more they dispute about lesser things, the more they throw doubts upon Christianity. Let us endeavour to keep the unity of the Spirit in the bond of peace, praying that all believers may be more and more united in one mind and one judgment. Thus shall we convince the world of the truth and excellence of our religion, and find more sweet communion with God and his saints.

Verses 24-26 Christ, as one with the Father, claimed on behalf of all that had been given to him, and should in due time believe on him, that they should be brought to heaven; and that there the whole company of the redeemed might behold his glory as their beloved Friend and Brother, and therein find happiness. He had declared and would further declare the name or character of God, by his doctrine and his Spirit, that, being one with him, the love of the Father to him might abide with them also. Thus, being joined to Him by one Spirit, they might be filled with all the fullness of God, and enjoy a blessedness of which we can form no right idea in our present state.

CHAPTER 18

Christ taken in the garden. (1-12) Christ before Annas and Caiaphas. (13-27) Christ before Pilate. (28-40)

Verses 1-12 Sin began in the garden of Eden, there the curse was pronounced, there the Redeemer was promised; and in a garden that promised Seed entered into conflict with the old serpent. Christ was buried also in a garden. Let us, when we walk in our gardens, take occasion from thence to mediate on Christ's sufferings in a garden. Our Lord Jesus, knowing all things that should come upon him, went forth and asked, Whom seek ye? When the people would have forced him to a crown, he withdrew, ch. 6:15, but when they came to force him to a cross, he offered himself; for he came into this world to suffer, and went to the other world to reign. He showed plainly what he could have done; when he struck them down he could have struck them dead, but he would not do so. It must have been the effect of Divine power, that the officers and soldiers let the disciples go away quietly, after the resistance which had been offered. Christ set us an example of meekness in sufferings, and a pattern of submission to God's will in every thing that concerns us. It is but a cup, a small matter. It is a cup that is given us; sufferings are gifts. It is given us by a Father, who has a father's authority, and does us no wrong; a father's affection, and means us no hurt. From the example of our Saviour we should learn how to receive our lighter afflictions, and to ask ourselves whether we ought to oppose our Father's will, or to distrust his love. We were bound with the cords of our iniquities, with the yoke of our transgressions. Christ, being made a sin-offering for us, to free us from those bonds, himself submitted to be bound for us. To his bonds we owe our liberty; thus the Son makes us free.

Verses 13-27 Simon Peter denied his Master. The particulars have been noticed in the remarks on the other Gospels. The beginning of sin is as the letting forth of water. The sin of lying is a fruitful sin; one lie needs another to support it, and that another. If a call to expose ourselves to danger be clear, we may hope God will enable us to honour him; if it be not, we may fear that God will leave us to shame ourselves. They said nothing concerning the miracles of Jesus, by which he had done so much good, and which proved his doctrine. Thus the enemies of Christ, whilst they quarrel with his truth, willfully shut their eyes against it. He appeals to those who heard him. The doctrine of Christ may safely appeal to all that know it, and those who judge in truth bear witness to it. Our resentment of injuries must never be passionate. He reasoned with the man that did him the injury, and so may we.

Verses 28-32 It was unjust to put one to death who had done so much good, therefore the Jews were willing to save themselves from reproach. Many fear the scandal of an ill thing, more than the sin of it. Christ had said he should be delivered to the Gentiles, and they should put him to death; hereby that saying was fulfilled. He had said that he should be crucified, lifted up. If the Jews had judged him by their law, he had been stoned; crucifying never was used among the Jews. It is determined concerning us, though not discovered to us, what death we shall die: this should free us from disquiet about that matter. Lord, what, when, and how, thou hast appointed.

Verses 33-40 Art thou the King of the Jews? That King of the Jews who has been so long expected? Messiah the Prince; art thou he? Dost thou call thyself so, and wouldest thou be thought so? Christ answered this question with another; not for evasion, but that Pilate might consider what he did. He never took upon him any earthly power, never were any traitorous principles or practices laid to him. Christ gave an account of the nature of his kingdom. Its nature is not worldly; it is a kingdom within men, set up in their hearts and consciences; its riches spiritual, its power spiritual, and it glory within. Its supports are not worldly; its weapons are spiritual; it needed not, nor used, force to maintain and advance it, nor opposed any kingdom but that of sin and Satan. Its object and design are not worldly. When Christ said, I am the Truth, he said, in effect, I am a King. He conquers by the convincing evidence of truth; he rules by the commanding power of truth. The subjects of this kingdom are those that are of the truth. Pilate put a good question, he said, What is truth? When we search the Scriptures, and attend the ministry of the word, it must be with this inquiry, What is truth? And with this prayer, Lead me in thy truth; into all truth. But many put this question, who have not patience to preserve in their search after truth; or not humility enough to receive it. By this solemn declaration of Christ's innocence, it appears, that though the Lord Jesus was treated as the worst of evil-doers, he never deserved such treatment. But it unfolds the design of his death; that he died as a Sacrifice for our sins. Pilate was willing to please all sides; and was governed more by worldly wisdom than by the rules of justice. Sin is a robber, yet is foolishly chosen by many rather than Christ, who would truly enrich us. Let us endeavour to make our accusers ashamed as Christ did; and let us beware of crucifying Christ afresh.

CHAPTER 19

Christ condemned and crucified. (1-18) Christ on the cross. (19-30) His side pierced. (31-37) The burial of Jesus. (38-42)

Verses 1-18 Little did Pilate think with what holy regard these sufferings of Christ would, in after-ages, be thought upon and spoken of by the best and greatest of men. Our Lord Jesus came forth, willing to be exposed to their scorn. It is good for every one with faith, to behold Christ Jesus in his sufferings. Behold him, and love him; be still looking unto Jesus. Did their hatred sharpen their endeavours against him? And shall not our love for him quicken our endeavours for him and his kingdom? Pilate seems to have thought that Jesus might be some person above the common order. Even natural conscience makes men afraid of being found fighting against God. As our Lord suffered for the sins both of Jews and Gentiles, it was a special part of the counsel of Divine Wisdom, that the Jews should first purpose his death, and the Gentiles carry that purpose into effect. Had not Christ been thus rejected of men, we had been for ever rejected of God. Now was the Son of man delivered into the hands of wicked and unreasonable men. He was led forth for us, that we might escape. He was nailed to the cross, as a Sacrifice bound to the altar. The Scripture was fulfilled; he did not die at the altar among the sacrifices, but among criminals sacrificed to public justice. And now let us pause, and with faith look upon Jesus. Was ever sorrow like unto his sorrow? See him bleeding, see him dying, see him and love him! Love him, and live to him!

Verses 19-30 Here are some remarkable circumstances of Jesus' death, more fully related than before. Pilate would not gratify the chief priests by allowing the writing to be altered; which was doubtless owing to a secret power of God upon his heart, that this statement of our Lord's character and authority might continue. Many things done by the Roman soldiers were fulfillments of the prophecies of the Old Testament. All things therein written shall be fulfilled. Christ tenderly provided for his mother at his death. Sometimes, when God removes one comfort from us, he raises up another for us, where we looked not for it. Christ's example teaches all men to honour their parents in life and death; to provide for their wants, and to promote their comfort by every means in their power. Especially observe the dying word wherewith Jesus breathed out his soul. It is finished; that is, the counsels of the Father concerning his sufferings were now fulfilled. It is finished; all the types and prophecies of the Old Testament, which pointed at the sufferings of the Messiah, were accomplished. It is finished; the ceremonial law is abolished; the substance is now come, and all the shadows are done away. It is finished; an end is made of transgression by bringing in an everlasting righteousness. His sufferings were now finished, both those of his soul, and those of his body. It is finished; the work of man's redemption and salvation is now completed. His life was not taken from him by force, but freely given up.

Verses 31-37 A trial was made whether Jesus was dead. He died in less time than persons crucified commonly did. It showed that he had laid down his life of himself. The spear broke up the very fountains of life; no human body could survive such a wound. But its being so solemnly attested, shows there was something peculiar in it. The blood and water that flowed out, signified those two great benefits which all believers partake of through Christ, justification and sanctification; blood for atonement, water for purification. They both flow from the pierced side of our Redeemer. To Christ crucified we owe merit for our justification, and Spirit and grace for our sanctification. Let this silence the fears of weak Christians, and encourage their hopes; there came both water and blood out of Jesus' pierced side, both to justify and sanctify them. The Scripture was fulfilled, in Pilate's not allowing his legs to be broken, Ps 34:20. There was a type of this in the paschal lamb, Ex 12:46. May we ever look to Him, whom, by our sins, we have ignorantly and heedlessly pierced, nay, sometimes against convictions and mercies; and who shed from his wounded side both water and blood, that we might be justified and sanctified in his name.

Verses 38-42 Joseph of Arimathea was a disciple of Christ in secret. Disciples should openly own themselves; yet some, who in lesser trials have been fearful, in greater have been courageous. When God has work to do, he can find out such as are proper to do it. The embalming was done by Nicodemus, a secret friend to Christ, though not his constant follower. That grace which at first is like a bruised reed, may afterward resemble a strong cedar. Hereby these two rich men showed the value they had for Christ's person and doctrine, and that it was not lessened by the reproach of the cross. We must do our duty as the present day and opportunity are, and leave it to God to fulfill his promises in his own way and his own time. The grave of Jesus was appointed with the wicked, as was the case of those who suffered as criminals; but he was with the rich in his death, as prophesied, Isaiah 53:9 ; these two circumstances it was very unlikely should ever be united in the same person. He was buried in a new sepulchre; therefore it could not be said that it was not he, but some other that rose. We also are here taught not to be particular as to the place of our burial. He was buried in the sepulchre next at hand. Here is the Sun of Righteousness set for a while, to rise again in greater glory, and then to set no more.

CHAPTER 20

*The sepulchre found to be empty. (1-10) Christ appears to Mary.
(11-18) He appears to the disciples. (19-25) The unbelief of
Thomas. (26-29) Conclusion. (30, 31)*

Verses 1-10 If Christ gave his life a ransom, and had not taken it
again, it would not have appeared that his giving it was accepted
as satisfaction. It was a great trial to Mary, that the body was
gone. Weak believers often make that the matter of complaint,
which is really just ground of hope, and matter of joy. It is well
when those more honoured than others with the privileges of
disciples, are more active than others in the duty of disciples; more
willing to take pains, and run hazards, in a good work. We must
do our best, and neither envy those who can do better, nor despise
those who do as well as they can, though they come behind. The
disciple whom Jesus loved in a special manner, and who therefore
in a special manner loved Jesus, was foremost. The love of Christ
will make us to abound in every duty more than any thing else.
He that was behind was Peter, who had denied Christ. A sense of
guilt hinders us in the service of God. As yet the disciples knew
not the Scripture; they Christ must rise again from the dead.

Verses 11-18 We are likely to seek and find, when we seek with
affection, and seek in tears. But many believers complain of the
clouds and darkness they are under, which are methods of grace
for humbling their souls, mortifying their sins, and endearing Christ
to them. A sight of angels and their smiles, will not suffice, without
a sight of Jesus, and God's smiles in him. None know, but those
who have tasted it, the sorrows of a deserted soul, which has had
comfortable evidences of the love of God in Christ, and hopes of

heaven, but has now lost them, and walks in darkness; such a wounded spirit who can bear? Christ, in manifesting himself to those that seek him, often outdoes their expectations. See how Mary's heart was in earnest to find Jesus. Christ's way of making himself known to his people is by his word; his word applied to their souls, speaking to them in particular. It might be read, Is it my Master? See with what pleasure those who love Jesus speak of his authority over them. He forbids her to expect that his bodily presence look further, than the present state of things. Observe the relation to God, from union with Christ. We, partaking of a Divine nature, Christ's Father is our Father; and he, partaking of the human nature, our God is his God. Christ's ascension into heaven, there to plead for us, is likewise an unspeakable comfort. Let them not think this earth is to be their home and rest; their eye and aim, and earnest desires, must be upon another world, and this ever upon their hearts, I ascend, therefore I must seek the things which are above. And let those who know the word of Christ, endeavour that others should get good from their knowledge.

Verses 19-25 This was the first day of the week, and this day is afterwards often mentioned by the sacred writers; for it was evidently set apart as the Christian Sabbath, in remembrance of Christ's resurrection. The disciples had shut the doors for fear of the Jews; and when they had no such expectation, Jesus himself came and stood in the midst of them, having miraculously, though silently, opened the doors. It is a comfort to Christ's disciples, when their assemblies can only be held in private, that no doors can shut out Christ's presence. When He manifests his love to believers by the comforts of his Spirit, he assures them that because he lives, they shall live also. A sight of Christ will gladden the heart of a disciple at any time; and the more we see of Jesus, the more we shall rejoice. He said, Receive ye the Holy Ghost, thus showing that their spiritual life, as well as all their ability for their work, would be derived from him, and depended upon him.

Every word of Christ which is received in the heart by faith, comes accompanied by this Divine breathing; and without this there is neither light nor life. Nothing is seen, known, discerned, or felt of God, but through this. After this, Christ directed the apostles to declare the only method by which sin would be forgiven. This power did not exist at all in the apostles as a power to give judgment, but only as a power to declare the character of those whom God would accept or reject in the day of judgment. They have clearly laid down the marks whereby a child of God may be discerned and be distinguished from a false professor; and according to what they have declared shall every case be decided in the day of judgment.

When we assemble in Christ's name, especially on his holy day, he will meet with us, and speak peace to us. The disciples of Christ should endeavour to build up one another in their most holy faith, both by repeating what they have heard to those that were absent, and by making known what they have experienced. Thomas limited the Holy One of Israel, when he would be convinced by his own method or not at all. He might justly have been left in his unbelief, after rejecting such abundant proofs. The fears and sorrows of the disciples are often lengthened, to punish their negligence.

Verses 26-29 That one day in seven should be religiously observed, was an appointment from the beginning. And that, in the kingdom of the Messiah, the first day of the week should be that solemn day, was pointed out, in that Christ on that day once and again met his disciples in a religious assembly. The religious observance of that day has come down to us through every age of the church.

There is not an unbelieving word in our tongues, nor thought in our minds, but it is known to the Lord Jesus; and he was pleased to accommodate himself even to Thomas, rather than leave him in his unbelief. We ought thus to bear with the weak, Romans 15:1, 2. This warning is given to all. If we are faithless, we are Christless and graceless, hopeless and joyless. Thomas was ashamed of his unbelief, and cried out, My Lord and my God. He spoke with affection, as one that took hold of Christ with all his might; "My Lord and my God." Sound and sincere believers, though slow and weak, shall be graciously accepted of the Lord Jesus. It is the duty of those who read and hear the gospel, to believe, to embrace the doctrine of Christ, and that 1 John

Verses 30-31 There were other signs and proofs of our Lord's resurrection, but these were committed to writing, that all might believe that Jesus was the promised Messiah, the Saviour of sinners, and the Son of God; that, by this faith, they might obtain eternal life, by his mercy, truth, and power. May we believe that Jesus is the Christ, and believing may we have life through his name.

CHAPTER 21

Christ appears to his disciples. (1-14) His discourse with Peter. (15-19) Christ's declaration concerning John. (20-24) The conclusion. (25)

Verses 1-14 Christ makes himself known to his people, usually in his ordinances; but sometimes by his Spirit he visits them when employed in their business. It is good for the disciples of Christ to be together in common conversation, and common business. The hour for their entering upon action was not come. They would help to maintain themselves, and not be burdensome to any. Christ's time of making himself known to his people, is when they are most at a loss. He knows the temporal wants of his people, and has promised them not only grace sufficient, but food convenient. Divine Providence extends itself to things most minute, and those are happy who acknowledge God in all their ways. Those who are humble, diligent, and patient, though their labours may be crossed, shall be crowned; they sometimes live to see their affairs take a happy turn, after many struggles. And there is nothing lost by observing Christ's orders; it is casting the net on the right side of the ship. Jesus manifests himself to his people by doing that for them which none else can do, and things which they looked not for. He would take care that those who left all for him, should not want any good thing. And latter favours are to bring to mind former favours, that eaten bread may not be forgotten.

He whom Jesus loved was the first that said, It is the Lord. John had cleaved most closely to his Master in his sufferings, and knew him soonest. Peter was the most zealous, and reached Christ the first. How variously God dispenses his gifts, and what difference there may be between some believers and others in the way of their honouring Christ, yet they all may be accepted of him! Others continue in the ship, drag the net, and bring the fish to shore, and such persons ought not to be blamed as worldly; for they, in their places, are as truly serving Christ as the others. The Lord Jesus had provision ready for them. We need not be curious in inquiring whence this came; but we may be comforted at Christ's care for his disciples. Although there were so many, and such great fishes, yet they lost none, nor damaged their net. The net of the gospel has enclosed multitudes, yet it is as strong as ever to bring souls to God.

Verses 15-19 Our Lord addressed Peter by his original name, as if he had forfeited that of Peter through his denying him. He now answered, Thou knowest that I love thee; but without professing to love Jesus more than others. We must not be surprised to have our sincerity called into question, when we ourselves have done that which makes it doubtful. Every remembrance of past sins, even pardoned sins, renews the sorrow of a true penitent. Conscious of integrity, Peter solemnly appealed to Christ, as knowing all things, even the secrets of his heart. It is well when our falls and mistakes make us more humble and watchful. The sincerity of our love to God must be brought to the test; and it behooves us to inquire with earnest, preserving prayer to the heart-searching God, to examine and prove us, whether we are able to stand this test. No one can be qualified to feed the sheep and lambs of Christ, who does not love the good Shepherd more than any earthly advantage or object. It is the great concern of every good man, whatever death he dies, to glorify God in it; for what is our chief end but this, to die to the Lord, at the word of the Lord?

Verses 20-24 Sufferings, pains, and death, will appear formidable even to the experienced Christian; but in the hope to glorify God, to leave a sinful world, and to be present with his Lord, he becomes ready to obey the Redeemer's call, and to follow Him through death to glory. It is the will of Christ that his disciples should mind their own duty, and not be curious about future events, either as to themselves or others. Many things we are apt to be anxious about, which are nothing to us. Other people's affairs are nothing to us, to intermeddle in; we must quietly work, and mind our own business. Many curious questions are put about the counsels of God, and the state of the unseen world, as to which we may say, What is this to us? And if we attend to the duty of following Christ, we shall find neither heart nor time to meddle with that which does not belong to us. How little are any unwritten traditions to be relied upon! Let the Scripture be its own interpreter, and explain itself; as it is, in a great measure, its own evidence, and proves itself, for it is light. See the easy setting right such mistakes by the word of Christ. Scripture language is the safest channel for Scripture truth; the words which the Holy Ghost teaches, 1Co 2:13. Those who cannot agree in the same terms of art, and the application of them, may yet agree in the same Scripture terms, and to love one another.

Verse 25 Only a small part of the actions of Jesus had been written. But let us bless God for all that is in the Scriptures, and be thankful that there is so much in so small a space. Enough is recorded to direct our faith, and regulate our practice; more would have been unnecessary. Much of what is written is overlooked, much forgotten, and much made the matter of doubtful disputes. We may, however, look forward to the joy we shall receive in heaven, from a more complete knowledge of all Jesus did and said, as well as of the conduct of his providence and grace in his dealings with each of us. May this be our happiness. These are written that ye might believe that Jesus is the Christ, the Son of God; and that believing ye might have life through his name, ch. 20:31.